SECOND EDITION

Child Welfare
Connecting Research, Policy, and Practice

Kathleen Kufeldt and Brad McKenzie, editors

WILFRID LAURIER
UNIVERSITY PRESS

Wilfrid Laurier University Press acknowledges the financial support of the Government of Canada through the Canada Book Fund for our publishing activities.

Library and Archives Canada Cataloguing in Publication

Child welfare : connecting research, policy, and practice / Kathleen Kufeldt and Brad McKenzie, editors. — 2nd ed.

Includes bibliographical references.
Issued also in electronic format.
ISBN 978-1-55458-330-0

1. Child welfare—Canada. 2. Child welfare—Research—Canada. I. Kufeldt, Kathleen II. McKenzie, B. D. (Bradley Douglas)

HV745.A6C545 2011   362.7'0971   C2011-902266-4

Electronic formats.
ISBN 978-1-55458-368-3 (PDF), ISBN 978-1-55458-349-2 (EPUB)

1. Child welfare—Canada. 2. Child welfare—Research—Canada. I. Kufeldt, Kathleen II. McKenzie, B. D. (Bradley Douglas))

HV745.A6C545 2011a   362.7'0971   C2011-902267-2

Cover design by Blakeley Words+Pictures. Cover photo by Stuart Murray Imaging / iStockphoto. Text design by Catharine Bonas-Taylor.

© 2011 Wilfrid Laurier University Press
Waterloo, Ontario, Canada
www.wlupress.wlu.ca

This book is printed on FSC recycled paper and is certified Ecologo. It is made from 100% post-consumer fibre, processed chlorine free, and manufactured using biogas energy.

Printed in Canada

RECYCLED
Paper made from recycled material
FSC
www.fsc.org   FSC® C103567

CONTENTS

Foreword xi
Evariste Thériault

Preface xiii
Kathleen Kufeldt and Brad McKenzie

Acknowledgements xv

Setting the Context: Child Welfare Law in Canada 1
Nicholas Bala

I Insights from the *Canadian Incidence Study of Reported Abuse and Neglect*

1 *Canadian Incidence Study of Reported Child Abuse and Neglect*:
Changing Patterns of Reported Maltreatment, 1998 and 2003 23
Nico Trocmé, Barbara Fallon, and Bruce MacLaurin

2 The Response of the Ontario Child Welfare System to Neglect:
1993 to 2003 37
Kate Schumaker, Barbara Fallon, and Nico Trocmé

3 Factors Associated with the Decision to Provide Ongoing Services:
Are Worker Characteristics and Organizational Location
Important? 57
Barbara Fallon and Nico Trocmé

4 Canadian Child Welfare Worker Qualifications: Examining a
Changing National Profile 75
*Barbara Fallon, Bruce MacLaurin, Nico Trocmé, Jordan Gail,
and Carolyn Golden*

5 *Canadian Incidence Study of Reported Child Abuse and Neglect*:
Themes and Implications 89
Brad McKenzie and Kathleen Kufeldt

II The Continuum of Care

Early Intervention and Support

6 Differential Response in Child Welfare: A New Early Intervention Model? 101
   Brad McKenzie

7 Doing the Work: Child Protection Jobs in Centralized and Accessible Service Delivery Models 117
   Gary Cameron, Nancy Freymond, and Lirondel Cheyne-Hazineh

8 Child Welfare Interventions That Make Sense to Mothers 131
   Nancy Freymond and Gary Cameron

9 Projet Famille: A Family Therapy Project for Neglectful Families 145
   Michèle Brousseau, Madeleine Beaudry, Marie Simard, and Cécile Charbonneau

Out-of-Home Care

10 Foster Care: An Essential Part of the Continuum of Care 157
   Kathleen Kufeldt

11 Finding the Best Home: A Comparative Analysis of Kinship and Foster Care Placements 173
   Katharine Dill

12 A Bicultural Response to Children in Need of Care and Protection in New Zealand 187
   Jill Worrall

13 Experiences of Foster Carers' Children: An Overview of the Research 201
   Tracy Swan and Robert Twigg

14 Making Group Home Care a Positive Alternative, Not the Last Resort 215
   James Anglin

15 The Changing Face of Adoption 229
   Kathleen Kufeldt

Youth Transitions

16 Factors Associated with Family Reunification among Adolescents in Residential Care: A Quebec Perspective 245
   Marie-Claude Simard and Marie-Andrée Poirier

17 Aging Out of Care and the Transition to Adulthood: Implications
for Intervention 259
Varda Mann-Feder

18 Knock, Knock, Who's There … for Youth? The Experience of Support
When Aging Out of Foster Care 267
Deborah Rutman and Carol Hubberstey

19 Providing a Seamless Continuum of Care: Themes and
Implications 281
Kathleen Kufeldt and Brad McKenzie

III Indigenous Issues in Child Welfare

20 Disproportionate Representation of Indigenous Children in Child
Welfare Systems: International Comparisons 293
Clare Tilbury and June Thoburn

21 Understanding the Overrepresentation of First Nations Children in
Canada's Child Welfare System 307
*Vandna Sinha, Nico Trocmé, Cindy Blackstock, Bruce MacLaurin,
and Barbara Fallon*

22 From Child Protection to Community Caring in First Nations
Child and Family Services 323
Brad McKenzie and Corbin Shangreaux

23 Wrap a Star Blanket around Each One: Learning from the
Educational Experiences of Indigenous Former Children
in Care on Coast Salish Territory 339
Shelly Johnson (Mukwa Musayett)

24 Indigenous Issues in Child Welfare: Themes and Implications 353
Brad McKenzie and Kathleen Kufeldt

IV Selected Practice Issues

25 Risk Assessment in Child Welfare: Use and Misuse 369
Jan Christianson-Wood

26 Engaging with Fathers in Child Welfare 385
*Christopher Walmsley, Leslie Brown, Marilyn Callahan,
Lena Dominelli, and Susan Strega*

27 Critical Issues of Practice and Protection in Relation to Families
and Fetal Alcohol Spectrum Disorder 399
Dorothy Badry

28 Children with Disabilities in Care in Manitoba 411
   Don Fuchs

29 Child Welfare Challenges for Developing Nations 423
   Myrna McNitt

30 Selected Practice Issues: Themes and Implications 437
   Kathleen Kufeldt and Brad McKenzie

V The Search for Best Practice

31 Family-Centred Child Welfare Practice 445
   Alexandra Wright and Diane Hiebert-Murphy

32 Using *Looking After Children* Data to Link Research to Policy and
   Practice in Out-of-Home Care 459
   Sarah Wise and Ruth Champion

33 The *Looking After Children* Approach in Quebec: An Evaluation of
   the Experiences of Youth, Caseworkers, and Foster Parents 473
   Marie-Andrée Poirier, Marie-Claude Simard, Véronique Noel,
   and Béatrice Decaluwe

34 Guided Practice in Australia: Research, Implementation, and Child
   and Family Perspectives on *Looking After Children* and the
   Assessment Framework 487
   Deirdre Cheers, Elizabeth Fernandez, Jude Morwitzer, and Sue Tregeagle

35 Resiliency: Embracing a Strength-Based Model of Evaluation
   and Care Provision 501
   Tyrone Donnon and Wayne Hammond

36 The National Child Welfare Outcomes Indicator Matrix (NOM) and
   Its Application in a Child Welfare Agency 515
   Nico Trocmé, Tonino Esposito, Meghan Mulcahy, Lorry Coughlin,
   Barbara Fallon, Bruce MacLaurin, and Aron Shlonsky

37 Implementing the Integrated Children's System in the United
   Kingdom: A Summary of the Main Findings 531
   Jane Scott

38 The Search for Best Practice: Themes and Implications 545
   Kathleen Kufeldt and Brad McKenzie

VI The Future of Child Welfare

39 Critical Issues in Current Practice 553
  Kathleen Kufeldt and Brad McKenzie

40 The Policy, Practice, and Research Connection:
  Are We There Yet? 569
  Kathleen Kufeldt and Brad McKenzie

  References 589
  List of Contributors 673

FOREWORD

The second edition of *Child welfare: Connecting research, policy, and practice* evolved from an event 17 years ago. In 1994, the first Canadian Child Welfare Research and Policy Symposium, sponsored by the former National Welfare Grants Program of Human Resources Development Canada, took place in Kananaskis, Alberta. The proceedings, edited by Joe Hudson and Burt Galaway, were published in 1995 as *Child welfare in Canada: Research and policy implications*. A second symposium took place in 2000 in Cornwall, Ontario, co-sponsored by the Bell Canada Research Centre, the Muriel McQueen Fergusson Centre for Family Violence Research at the University of New Brunswick, and the Child Welfare League of Canada. The Social Development Partnerships Program of Human Resources Development Canada was the main financial contributor. From this second symposium, Kathleen Kufeldt and Brad McKenzie edited the proceedings, published in 2003, as the first edition of *Child welfare: Connecting research, policy, and practice.*

This first edition was a success and reached its intended audience. Now there is a need to draw on current research and update the information; there is still scope for work in pursuing the challenge of the child welfare research agenda enunciated at the 1994 symposium and described in the book by Hudson and Galaway. Seventeen years have elapsed since the first symposium, and the field of child welfare has evolved during that period.

As I indicated in the introduction of the first edition, the aim of the 1994 symposium was to determine the status of child welfare research in Canada and identify policy implications. The second symposium added practice to this aim, and now the second edition can reflect on at least 17 years of activities in research and practice, as well as changing policy imperatives.

Child welfare is a complex domain, and each Canadian province and territory enacts its own legislation. It is noteworthy that the second edition is introduced by a discussion of the application of child welfare law in Canada. The body of the book includes updates from the first edition and presents new longitudinal, historical, and international perspectives. This adds significantly to the breadth and currency of the book.

My participation in the child welfare field has been indirect from a practice perspective, but very direct from a research and development angle. For over three decades I was a proud federal public servant involved with the development and funding of social welfare research capacity (institutions and human resources) in the social welfare/social development fields in general and in child welfare in particular. In the mid-'90s I was instrumental in the development of a child welfare research agenda, which led to a significant presence of Canadian child welfare researchers at the international level. The second edition includes many chapters resulting from this agenda.

Examining the contents for the second edition was a source of great satisfaction, and reinforced my view that it takes time to develop child welfare researchers and the capacity to sustain them. It is gratifying to realize that the researchers whose careers were launched around the time of the 1994 symposium have evolved into experienced child welfare researchers who now act as mentors to young researchers and who are trailblazers in the field. An example is that of the editors. I have witnessed their evolution and development in becoming experienced researchers in their own right.

I am thankful for their dedication to child welfare issues and their abilities to edit this second edition into a comprehensive whole. They have obtained new material from both Canadian and international contributors. The inclusion of child welfare research issues pertaining to Indigenous peoples in Canada and abroad adds significantly to the scope and depth of this edition.

The book is broad in scope and deals at length with issues identified in the research agenda. As such, it should be of interest to a large audience of professionals and others interested or involved with the child welfare field. Readers will appreciate the dedication of the editors and the perseverance of the contributors in working towards service improvements in child welfare for children and families in need. My final thanks go to the contributors, whether new or seasoned researchers, for work well done.

Evariste Thériault
Retired Research Consultant
Social Development Partnerships Program
Human Resources Development Canada

PREFACE

Kathleen Kufeldt
Brad McKenzie

Strengthening the connection between research, policy, and practice is imperative if we wish to improve life chances for children in care. The number of children in care is significant, and growing. In the first edition of this book, Thériault (2003) reported that there were over 60,000 Canadian children in care in 2000, and that this constituted an increase of about 30% in the previous three years (Human Resources Development Canada, 2000). Farris-Manning and Zandstra (2003) estimated that there were 76,000 children in care in Canada by 2002, and this number has grown since that time.

In an introductory chapter, Bala provides an overview of child welfare legislation in Canada, and this establishes a general context for the issues raised throughout the remaining sections of the book. Part I of this book suggests that the number of children needing care and protection increased quite dramatically between 1998 and 2003. Protecting children is not an easy task, and several authors highlight the tension between the rights of children and parents, and the care and control aspects of state intervention into family life. The challenge is to connect our growing knowledge about child welfare to policy development and evidence-based practice in order to achieve good outcomes for children growing up in care.

In 1994 the editors were privileged to participate in the first Canadian Child Welfare Research and Policy Symposium funded by Health and Welfare Canada. Its aim was to determine the status of child welfare research in Canada and identify policy implications. The symposium developed an eight-point research agenda (Galaway & Hudson, 1995). In 2000, a follow-up symposium was held in Cornwall, Ontario, that enlarged the scope to include practice. Particularly encouraging was the decision in 2000 to include foster parents and to increase participation from youth in care, First Nations, and service providers. Their voices added more authenticity to the discussions that took place.

Much of the research presented in 2000 reflected issues that were similar to those identified in the eight-point research agenda by Galaway and Hudson (1995) at the first symposium. Accordingly, when asked to organize the research and proceedings as a book, the editors used those eight points as an organizing device in considering the implications of new research presented at this symposium (Kufeldt & McKenzie, 2003b). We return to this agenda again in the final chapter as we consider developments in research, policy, and practice during the past 15 years.

In this second edition we examine research trends over the past several years. These trends help in highlighting major developments that have taken place in the child welfare field, whether they have resulted in improvements to practice, and how these inform recommendations for the future. In order to do this we depart from the usual practice in producing second editions. Rather than updating earlier chapters we have asked our contributors to present new material. A separate section on Indigenous issues in child welfare has been included to highlight the systemic issues affecting these children, their parents, and their communities. We continue to include contributions from international colleagues. Doing so allows us the opportunity to learn from their successes; it also helps illustrate the endemic nature of challenges in the field of child welfare and child protection. We have also identified and solicited work from new scholars: they are building on prior work and will be the torchbearers in the continuing efforts to achieve the objective of providing good parenting to those children who are unable to receive it within their family of origin. Recommendations for improved practice, policy, and research are included within recommendations in Chapters 39 and 40, but we also revisit a number of key issues and include a number of general recommendations.

The children associated with our child welfare system are the most vulnerable group in our society, yet are expected to achieve success in life without the resources available to their more privileged peers. Our contributors provide useful suggestions for promoting best practice and enhancing resilience. The challenge to our readers is to translate good research into policy and practice to enhance life chances for those children who need our care and protection.

ACKNOWLEDGEMENTS

As noted in the preface, the second edition of *Child Welfare* contains entirely new material. Every effort has been made to include coverage of the key issues and contemporary research findings that might illuminate this complex and challenging field of practice. To do this, we surveyed the work of Canadian scholars and consulted with international colleagues. Having identified significant areas to be covered, we engaged with potential contributors to assist us in our task. In doing so, we paid particular attention to the identification of new scholars. We wish to thank our contributors for their willingness to rise to the challenge and their patience with us as the project unfolded. We also owe a special debt of thanks to the growing numbers of those on the receiving end— children, youths, and families who are willing to cooperate with researchers in order to improve services for those who follow.

A special thank-you is extended to Claudette Cormier of the Faculty of Social Work at the University of Manitoba. As in the first edition, she worked patiently and tirelessly with us through the drafting and revision stages of this edited collection.

We also express appreciation to Brian Henderson and his helpful and talented staff at Wilfrid Laurier University Press. Their assistance and the collaborative approach they followed with us helped to bring this project to its successful conclusion.

Setting the Context: Child Welfare Law in Canada

Nicholas Bala

Child welfare is a unique and challenging context for social workers, in large part because the provision of many of the services to children and families takes place through the legal process. The child welfare worker is motivated by a desire to help children who may be abused or neglected, preferably by helping parents to provide better care. However, parents are also aware of the enormous legal powers of the worker, who has the potential to remove children from their care and to put their lives under scrutiny in the court process. Children, despite abuse or neglect, may also fear the intrusion of the worker in their lives, and the worker has to manage the delicate interplay between care and control (Martin, 2003). At the same time, the awareness of parents and children of the role and power of the worker may colour even the warmest of relationships, and can result in strained or even hostile exchanges.

Because child welfare is social work practised in a legal context, it is essential for child welfare workers and those with an interest in policy issues in this area to understand the legal process, and to recognize that it affects virtually all aspects of child welfare work. This chapter[1] discusses the principles of child welfare law in Canada, offering a context for the rest of the book. However, readers are cautioned that this is a complex area of law, with significant variation between provinces, and this chapter provides only an overview of key legal issues in this field. Those who practise in the field of child welfare will need more detailed knowledge than can be provided here. A much fuller discussion of the legal issues that arise in child welfare proceedings is provided in *Canadian Child Welfare Law* (Bala, Zapf, Williams, Vogl, & Hornick, 2004).

A Brief History of Child Protection

It is a general premise of our society that government interference in family life should be kept to a minimum. However, there are some situations in which the care parents provide is considered so inadequate that direct interference by the state is justified to protect children. These are situations in which parental care has fallen below the minimum standards our society will tolerate. However, state interference in the family and removal of a child is not legally justified because the child might have greater opportunities elsewhere. Rather, removal from parental care will only be justified if it can be demonstrated that remaining in parental care poses significant risk to the child.

It has not always been accepted that the state has a duty to protect children. The legal system of ancient Rome gave a father absolute authority over his children, including the lawful authority to sell them into slavery or even put them to death (DeMause, 1976). English common law recognized a parental right of "reasonable chastisement," which in practice gave parents the authority to subject their children to harsh discipline, and the right to sell them into apprenticeship. Through the Middle Ages there was little social recognition of the concept of childhood as a time of special needs, and there was a tendency to treat children as young as seven years of age as miniature adults. Gradually provision was made to care for orphans, first by religious bodies and later by municipal institutions; however, little was done to protect children from abuse or neglect if they were in the care of a parent or guardian. Although criminal law made it an offence to kill or maim a child, the laws were sporadically enforced, and children were regularly beaten by parents, subjected to sexual exploitation, and often forced to work long hours under terrible conditions. Prompted by the work of such social critics as Charles Dickens, whose *Oliver Twist* described the fate of children in institutions, the nineteenth century was a period of social reform in much of the industrialized world. Many developments in this era improved the lot of children, and the latter part of the century witnessed the establishment of a compulsory, publicly-funded school system, as well as special courts and corrections facilities to deal with juvenile offenders.

Children's aid societies were established in various Canadian municipalities in the last decade of the nineteenth century, with the objective of helping orphaned, abandoned, and neglected children. In 1893, reformers persuaded the Ontario legislature to grant these privately controlled agencies broad legal powers, including the right to remove neglected or abused children from their homes and to become legal guardians for such children. By the early twentieth century, agencies had been established throughout Canada, and child welfare legislation enacted in each province. However, the enormous growth and legalization of the field occurred only in the last half-century. Until the early 1960s, child welfare agencies dealt largely with the most obvious cases of abuse, and with children deemed "out of control" or delinquent; this was a period before there was adequate social assistance, and many children from impoverished families came into agency care. The agencies also had responsibility for the placement and adoption of children orphaned or born to single mothers.

While the courts exercised a supervisory function over the removal of children from their homes and adoption, in practice the system operated informally. Historically, most of the judges who sat in the family courts and dealt with this type of case lacked legal training, and lawyers rarely appeared at these proceedings. Many of the parents whose children were removed from their care were poor or socially marginalized; large numbers of Aboriginal children came into care, also with little or no judicial scrutiny. Parents involved in the protection process often lacked the sophistication and resources to challenge the actions of the agencies, and there was little thought to notions of children's rights in this era.

Enormous changes have occurred in the last 50 years. An important influence was the identification of battered child syndrome in the early 1960s (Helfer & Kempe, 1968; Kempe, Silverman, Steele, Droegemueller, & Silver, 1962). This raised awareness of the fact that parents might lie about abusing their children, describing injuries they inflicted as the result of "accidents," and that children were often too frightened or loyal to parents to disclose the truth to investigators. Increased understanding led to changes in legislation to require professionals and members of the public to report suspected cases of child abuse or neglect.

Beginning in the 1960s, the numbers of Aboriginal children in care began to increase significantly, and Aboriginal children in care are now vastly over-represented relative to their proportion within the general Canadian population (see Chapters 20 and 21). The early 1980s were marked by growing awareness of child sexual abuse, similar to the earlier recognition of physical abuse. Researchers learned that children were often too intimidated, ill-informed, or traumatized by feelings of guilt to report their victimization, and that parents and professionals often ignored disclosures or symptoms of sexual abuse. Changes in public and professional awareness resulted in increases in reported cases of child sexual abuse; as well, children and adult survivors of abuse from previous decades came forward to disclose. There were also fundamental changes in how child witnesses were treated in the Canadian criminal justice system, resulting in many more prosecutions of abusers (Bala, 1999).

3

While child welfare agencies are now dealing with more reports of child maltreatment than in previous decades, their involvement in other areas has declined. Illegitimacy no longer carries a great stigma. This fact, and the availability of effective birth control, have dramatically reduced the numbers of infants surrendered for adoption. The direct involvement of child welfare agencies with young offenders largely ceased with the repeal of the federal *Juvenile Delinquents Act* in 1984. In most provinces, the child welfare and juvenile justice systems are now separate, though it is not uncommon for adolescents in the care of child welfare agencies to be charged with offences, and there are concerns that child welfare youth with behavioural problems are being "dumped" into the youth justice system.

The Legal Revolution

Related to some of the fundamental changes in child welfare, there has been a veritable revolution in the role of law and the courts in Canadian society. Until about 1980, the law was primarily concerned with the regulation of economic, commercial, and property affairs, and with the control of deviant personal behaviour by means of the criminal law. Over the past three decades, however, the role of law in Canadian society has changed dramatically. Law has become an important social policy tool, affecting virtually every aspect of Canadian public policy and many aspects of life. Both reflecting and reinforcing the importance of law in defining society was the enactment of the *Canadian Charter of Rights and Freedoms*[2] in 1982. The *Charter* has had a profound effect on Canadian society. Initially it had only limited impact on child welfare law. However, a 1999 decision of the Supreme Court of Canada, *New Brunswick (Minister of Health and Community Services) v. G. (J.)* (reported at [1999] 3 S.C.R. 46), sent a strong message that parents have a vital interest in their relationship with their children, an interest that is entitled to protection under section 7 of the *Charter* as an aspect of "security of the person." Both Bala (2001) and Thomas (2003) provide a full discussion of this case, but, in brief, Chief Justice Antonio Lamer ruled as follows: that the state may only remove custody from a parent when it is necessary to protect the best interests of the child; that both the parent's and the child's rights to security of the person, as outlined in the *Charter*, are at stake in such proceedings; and that because of the need for a fair process in determining custody, an indigent parent is entitled to legal aid counsel in such proceedings.

The *Charter* has been used to ensure that the child protection process be procedurally fair, and has also been used by the courts to eliminate unjustified discrimination—for example, to ensure that biological fathers have greater rights in the adoption process. However, *Charter* rights are not absolute; rather, they are subject to "reasonable limits," and the courts are continually struggling to balance concerns about the protection of the rights of parents and children with the need to ensure that children are not endangered by the recognition of these legal rights. The result is a much more legally oriented child protection process.

This increased emphasis on due process is not without costs. The increased legalization of the child protection system has given rise to an expanded legal aid system, to ensure representation for parents, and, in some Canadian jurisdictions, for children. Child protection proceedings have become more complex and hence more costly, not only for legal aid plans, but for child protection agencies and for the court system. More serious than the financial costs of due process are the human costs. Due process takes time. Delays due to the court process are very stressful for children and families, though sometimes parents can take advantage of delays to improve their parenting skills and relationships with their children.

While due process may ensure fairness and considered decision-making, it can make the job of social workers and other child welfare professionals seem more difficult. Over time, the child protection process has become more adversarial, and child welfare professionals have their opinions and decisions challenged in the sometimes hostile environment of the courtroom by lawyers, who may seem insensitive to the constraints that they face. It must be appreciated that parents and children separated from one another by the child welfare system often feel a level of hostility toward agency workers. While there are disadvantages with this system, the increased focus on due process gives parents and children an opportunity to challenge the child welfare decisions that profoundly affect their lives. Although due process considerations are important, more recently the human and financial costs associated with a process that places too much emphasis on adversarial proceedings have been recognized. To counter these costs, there is growing emphasis on the use of negotiation, mediation, settlement conferences, and other methods to try to resolve child welfare cases without a trial (Crush, 2006).

The Child Welfare Dilemma: Balancing Parental Rights and Protection Concerns

One of the most significant developments in the child welfare field in Canada in the late 1990s was a growing concern about the difficulties in protecting children from abusive or neglectful home situations, and providing them with permanent, safe homes. It arose, in part, because of concern that efforts in the 1980s and early 1990s directed toward "family preservation" and protection of parental rights impacted negatively on the protection of children. These concerns were heightened by some highly publicized, tragic cases involving children who died in the care of their parents, even though child welfare workers were aware of some problems in the home. There was also growing awareness of the potentially negative effects on child well-being from emotional neglect and abuse that might, for example, result from poor attachment to parent figures in a child's early years or from witnessing spousal abuse. While there were important differences in the approaches to child welfare reform in different North American jurisdictions during this period, the theme of developing more effective measures to remove children from the care of parents who were perceived to be inadequate, and to having "permanent decisions" about children's futures made more quickly once children were in care, was common across jurisdictions.

The concern that agencies were not doing enough to protect children resulted in investigations and inquiries in a number of provinces in the late 1990s and early years of the new millennium. Two of these were the Gove Inquiry in British Columbia (Gove, 1995) and the Turner Review in Newfoundland (Markesteyn & Day, 2006). In Ontario, a series of coroners' inquests into child abuse deaths resulted in significant legislative amendments in 2000 which both facilitated earlier intervention in cases of physical abuse or neglect, and broadened the grounds for intervention in cases of emotional abuse or neglect (Bala, 1999–2000).

In addition to the legislative changes that occurred in some Canadian provinces, most jurisdictions have developed more standardized approaches to the assessment of current safety and future risk of abuse or neglect. These tools are intended to promote a consistent, structured approach to the investigation of cases, and to assist decision-making about the type of intervention required in cases where abuse or neglect has been substantiated (see Chapter 25 on risk assessment). Although information used in the risk assessment process is admissible in court, a judge is not obliged to accept the assessment of agency workers based on these instruments.

The changes described above were intended to better protect children, but combined with cuts to support services and social assistance for families and a greater focus on professional responsibility for the failure to protect children, there have been significant increases in the numbers of children coming into care. In the last several years more attention has been directed to the need for "differential response" where cases involving lower risk of future maltreatment are referred for voluntary family support services rather than services that focus on more intrusive investigation and protection services. Differential response services are explored later in the book.

Legal Contexts for the Protection of Children

There are two legal contexts in which issues related to child protection can arise: criminal law and civil law (family court processes). While the factual issues may be similar, the legal outcome that is being sought varies considerably, and there are important procedural differences.

Application of Criminal Law

Criminal law has an important role in responding to child abuse and serious neglect. For example, it is a criminal offence to sexually abuse or physically assault a child, though parents charged with physical assault may invoke the defence of s. 43 of the *Criminal Code*—that is, that they were using "reasonable force" for the purpose of "correction."[3]

It is also an offence for a parent or guardian to fail to provide a child with the "necessaries of life," or to abandon a child under the age of 10. While the *Criminal Code* can be used to prosecute those who harm children, it is a blunt tool that is often difficult to employ. There is an onus upon the state to prove guilt according to the highest legal standard, "proof beyond a reasonable doubt." Abuse cases can be especially difficult to prove because they often rely heavily on the evidence of the child who was the victim of abuse.

The traditional rules of evidence and procedure governing criminal cases made it difficult for children to testify, and the courts could discount their evidence. In the late 1980s, legal reforms made it easier for children to testify, resulting in a significant increase in the number of child abuse prosecutions in Canada, especially for sexual abuse (Bala, 1999). However, it can still be difficult to prove in a criminal proceeding that a particular person has been guilty of abuse "beyond all reasonable doubt."

Criminal investigations are handled by the police, and the presentation of the case in criminal court is the responsibility of the Crown attorney. Thus there may be simultaneous investigations by police and child protection workers. Ambivalence with respect to the effect on a child of prosecuting a parent, and the strength of available evidence, can affect whether or not criminal charges should be laid. Accordingly, there have been efforts to improve liaison and coordination between child protection agencies and those responsible for criminal prosecutions, and it is now common for local police and child welfare agencies to have a "protocol" or joint policy to guide joint investigations. Although improved coordination has resulted in more support for children in the prosecution of cases in the criminal justice system, criminal prosecutions for cases involving neglect or abuse are generally confined to cases involving serious injury or death.

Family Court Proceedings

Allegations of parental abuse and neglect are most commonly dealt with in family court proceedings. These are civil proceedings in which the child welfare agency seeks to intervene in the family, either by making the child the subject of court-ordered supervision, or by having the child removed from parental care. It is easier to establish abuse or neglect in a civil child protection proceeding than in a criminal proceeding, even if exactly the same conduct is at issue in both cases. The rules about what types of evidence a court may consider are less restrictive in a civil trial, and the standard of proof is lower, requiring only proof "on the balance of probabilities." While the *Charter of Rights and Freedoms* is applicable, the types of rights granted to parents alleged to have abused or neglected their children in these civil proceedings are much narrower than the rights afforded to them if they are accused of the same acts in the criminal justice process. For example, the right to remain silent in criminal proceedings does not apply: failure to answer questions adequately can be used as evidence against parents in child welfare proceedings.

The Legal Mandate of the Child Welfare Agency

In every Canadian jurisdiction there is an agency which has legal responsibility for investigating reports that a child may be in need of protection. The agency may provide services to the child and parents in their home, or remove the child from the home on a temporary or permanent wardship basis. The child welfare agency may provide services on either a voluntary or an involuntary basis, making use of the legal system to require children and parents to receive services. Child welfare agencies are also responsible for arranging adoptions, although increasingly private adoption agencies are becoming involved in this type of work. In some localities child welfare agencies assume other responsibilities related to their principal mandates, such as providing programs for improving parenting and preventing child abuse.

Child welfare agencies have significant powers under legislation to search for children who may be in need of protection and, if necessary, to force parents to surrender custody. These agencies receive all or most of their funding from the state; thus, from a conceptual perspective, child welfare agencies are agents of the state, and may exercise the coercive power of the state.

In most Canadian jurisdictions, child welfare services are provided by provincial employees. In Manitoba, Nova Scotia, and Ontario there are local child welfare agencies, called children's aid societies or child and family service agencies. These non-profit agencies normally serve a particular geographical area. In Ontario, a few children's aid societies are denominational, serving only Catholic or Jewish families and children in their region. Over the past three decades a growing number of child welfare agencies have been established to serve Aboriginal children and families. Regardless of the type of provision, ultimate statutory and financial responsibility rests with the provincial government, and the employees of these agencies exercise important government-mandated functions.

The structure of agencies and local offices may vary, but they do share central features. Agencies have two basic functions: child protection (or family services), and care of children removed from their homes. In some agencies, workers have both child protection and child care responsibilities, whereas other agencies employ workers who have more specialized functions.

Child protection workers are responsible for investigating suspected cases of abuse or neglect, and working with children and parents in their homes. Some agencies have intake departments, with a special mandate to deal with initial investigations and crisis situations; if ongoing service is required, the cases are usually transferred to a family service worker. Child care workers have responsibility for children who have been taken into care on either a temporary or permanent basis. Typically, children are actually cared for in foster or group homes, and child care workers have a liaison function with foster parents and group home staff. In some agencies, adoption work is done as part of the child care function, while in others it is the responsibility of a separate department.

Child welfare agencies are involved with the court system and must have access to adequate legal services. In some localities staff lawyers may work exclusively for agencies on child protection cases. In other places, child welfare agencies hire lawyers in private practice to provide representation in individual cases. In larger agencies, court workers who are familiar with the court system may also be hired as agency staff.

Working for a child welfare agency can be a difficult, stressful job. High staff turnover rates are common at these agencies, especially at those working with parents. While most child welfare workers are relatively well educated, usually having a social work degree, they may be relatively young and inexperienced.

Not infrequently, young social workers start their careers at child welfare agencies, and, after gaining some experience, move to other types of work elsewhere in the helping professions.

Much of the stress in the child protection field relates to both the nature of the cases and the nature of the work. There is an inevitable degree of tension, as the role of child protection workers has both supportive and investigative functions. Child protection workers usually try to be supportive to parents and to provide services on an informal, voluntary basis. Indeed, most families involved with child welfare agencies do not end up in court, and in these "voluntary" cases the role of the protection worker can be regarded as similar to that of a counsellor or an educator in parenting skills. However, the role of a child protection worker can also be viewed as similar to that of a police officer in that protection workers have a legal responsibility to investigate allegations of abuse or neglect. Even if a worker's involvement with a family is initially voluntary, anything a parent or child has told a worker may be relevant and admissible, in the event of later difficulties, at a subsequent protection hearing.

Through education and disposition, most child protection workers want to have a therapeutic role, and provide help to children and parents. Nevertheless, they may be viewed with hostility and distrust by parents because of their investigative role. This often makes the job frustrating, and can contribute to the high staff turnover rate. Some would argue that legal constraints make child protection work even more demanding. The law sometimes makes it difficult for child protection staff to take effective measures to protect a child. It is not enough for a worker to feel or believe that a child is at risk and should be removed from parental care. Involuntary removal of a child from parental care can only occur if legal requirements are satisfied and the need is documented in court. However, if a child is inappropriately left in parental care and suffers further abuse, the worker will inevitably feel a sense of guilt and moral responsibility.

A worker also faces the stress of accountability for taking inappropriate actions. If a worker is too aggressive in removing a child, a family court may decide that removal was unjustified and return the child to parental care. If the child is left in the care of parents and further abused or even killed, there will be an investigation of the worker's decision, and potentially a public inquiry. Although the likelihood of legal liability is relatively low, even the threat of this can add to a worker's stress level.

Child Welfare Legislation

Every Canadian jurisdiction has legislation to regulate the child welfare field. While there are variations in philosophy and approach, all of the legislative regimes deal with the same fundamental issues, and have similar basic features.

Declaration of Principles and the "Best Interests of the Child"

Almost all child welfare statutes in Canada have a statement of principles that are intended to guide the courts and child welfare agencies in the implementation of the law, as well as a definition of "best interests" of the child that requires consideration of a number of listed factors when making a decision about a child. These are to be considered in any decision that a court is to make if a child is found to be in need of protection. There is a significant core of common ideas across different jurisdictions provided by these principles and the definition of "best interests." The central themes are identified below.

- *Respect for family autonomy and support of families.* This principle reinforces the parents' primary responsibility for the well-being of their children.
- *Continuity of care.* This principle emphasizes the importance of permanence for children, a preference for children continuing to remain with their own family, and, if removal is necessary, the need for a stable foster or adoptive family.
- *Consideration of the views of children.* Although decision-makers are to consider the views and wishes of children, these are not necessarily determining factors in the final decisions that are made.
- *Respect for cultural heritage, especially for Aboriginal children.* Particular emphasis is given to the need to respect Aboriginal cultural heritage.
- *The paramount objective is the protection of children from harm.*

These statements of principle and definitions provide guidance to judges and social workers in making decisions under the legislation. Most of these declarations and definitions, however, do not clearly prioritize how different considerations are to be weighed in individual cases. Hence, significant discretion rests with individual decision-makers. In practice, child protection workers are more likely to be influenced by government and agency policies, while courts receive more direction from specific provisions of the legislation and from leading judicial precedents that may have interpreted certain principles in legislation or in the *Charter of Rights and Freedoms.*

The Child in Need of Protection

Each child welfare statute has a definition of a "child in need of protection" or an "endangered child." This is a key legal concept, as only children within this definition are subject to involuntary state intervention. While there is some variation in the definitions, there is a common core of situations that involve physical abuse, sexual abuse, and parental neglect, including failure to provide needed medical treatment and abandonment. Further, in all jurisdictions, a child may brought into agency care with the consent of the parents, and there are provisions for finding a child in need of protection in cases of emotional maltreatment or if a child is having serious behavioural problems. In some jurisdictions (e.g., New Brunswick), the fact that a child resides in a home where spousal abuse has occurred is in itself a basis for finding a child in need of protection, while in other provinces (e.g., Ontario), spousal abuse is not a specific ground for establishing that a child is in need of protection, but could be a contributing factor in determining that a child is at risk of suffering "emotional harm" or physical injury.

One significant variation between provinces is the maximum age for children to receive child welfare services (i.e., from 16 to 19). In all jurisdictions, financial assistance may be given to young adults who were in permanent care. However, assistance for youth who "age out of care" is not provided to everyone, and conditions are attached to the provision of such support. Youth who age out of care face particular challenges, especially if they want to pursue post-secondary education, and in most provinces there is no support after a young adult reaches the age of 21.

Voluntary Involvement

A child welfare agency may also be involved with a family on a voluntary basis. In some cases, the parents may only be "consenting" to agency involvement because of the potential threat of involuntary child protection proceedings. In other cases, however, the parents may genuinely wish for and appreciate the help and support that the agency and its staff can provide. It is not uncommon for parents to contact agencies and ask them to take their "out of control" adolescent children into care.

In several provinces there are legislative provisions governing situations in which a parent voluntarily agrees to place a child in care for a temporary period. In all jurisdictions there are statutory provisions that allow for a child to be permanently taken into care with the consent of the parents, as might for example occur if a single unmarried mother wanted a child welfare agency to place her newborn child for adoption.

Reporting, Apprehension, and Interim Care

Child welfare legislation governs the reporting of child abuse, and every Canadian jurisdiction imposes an obligation on individuals who become aware of possible situations of abuse or neglect to report the situation to their local child welfare agency or the police so that an investigation can be carried out. If a child protection worker has reasonable grounds to be believe that a child may be at risk, legislation allows the worker to "apprehend" the child—that is, to immediately take the child into the care of the agency. Apprehensions may occur without prior court approval, but there must be a court hearing within a specified time frame to determine whether the child will remain in care.

The Child Protection Hearing

When a child protection proceeding has been initiated, either by apprehension of a child or by filing an application with the court, it will usually take several weeks or more, typically months, before a full hearing can take place. During this period, arrangements will be made for the parents, and in some provinces the children, to have legal representation. Most parents involved in the child protection process are unable to afford a lawyer, but will be eligible for legal aid. In preparation for a trial, counsel for parents will have the opportunity to have disclosure of documents and records that the agency has acquired during the course of its investigation. The agency will contact third parties, like a family doctor or relatives, to prepare for the trial, and will develop a "plan of care" that will be put before the court. Outside experts may also be retained to assess the child or the "parenting capacity" of the parents, and ultimately to provide testimony in court.

A child protection trial is held in private, though legislation generally allows for the publication of non-identifying information about child protection proceedings in the relatively rare cases that attract media attention. The judges who decide child protection cases generally have a special expertise in family and children's law, and these cases never involve a jury. While the strict laws of evidence that govern criminal cases do not apply in child protection cases, there are rules of evidence that may result in the exclusion of certain types of evidence in child protection cases or may restrict what witnesses can say when testifying.

Most cases are resolved without trial. Parents, or lawyers acting on their behalf, may negotiate an acceptable resolution or agree to the order that the agency wants. In these circumstances parents may recognize that the agency action was justified or may feel that the outcome of court proceedings is inevitable, or lack the emotional or financial resources to challenge the agency in court. Negotiated agreements often include provisions for visitations or access if the child remains in care, and an outline of conditions to be met by the parents if a case plan is established under which the child is to be returned to the parents.

The Onus in a Protection Case

If a child protection trial is held, there is a legal onus on the agency to clearly establish the need for intervention. The nature of this burden was discussed by Judge Stortini in *Re Brown* (1975):

> In attempting to establish what is best for the children, I must accept the realities and accidents of life and refrain from judging the needs of the children and the parents' ability to satisfy them on an unfair or unrealistic basis … In other words, the community ought not to interfere merely because our institutions may be able to offer a greater opportunity to the children to achieve their potential. Society's interference in the natural family is only justified when the level of care of the children falls below that which no child in this country should be subjected to. (9 o.r. (2d) 185 at 189 (Ont. Co. Ct.))

At least part of the rationale for placing an onus on child welfare agencies to justify their intervention is based on fundamental values of our society. In *Re Chrysler* (1978), Judge Karswick frankly recognized the potential risk of placing the burden on the children's aid society (C.A.S.) to prove its case:

> … the potential for real and immediate abuse must be clear before the state should be permitted to intervene by removing the child from her parents. If it were otherwise, it would allow a C.A.S. to be the final arbitrator in a so-called child abuse case and would leave the parents and the child with no real recourse to a really independent and impartial court. In adopting this principle, I realize that there is always the danger that some real and even irreparable harm may be inflicted upon the child if the parents are really potential child abusers, but the C.A.S. has not been able to prove that fact because of the unavailability of witnesses who can testify to the alleged abuse and therefore has not been able to meet the standard of proof required by the court…. this risk must still give way to the greater risk of the irreparable harm that can be inflicted upon a child and the danger to society of the serious undermining of the parents and the family if a C.A.S. is permitted to act in an arbitrary way, even though its intentions are motivated by the highest ideals and concerns. (5 r.f.l. (2d) 50 at 58 (Ont. Prov. Ct. – Fam. Div.))

While placing an onus on child welfare agencies to prove their case creates the risk that in some cases the courts may fail to take appropriate steps to protect children, inappropriate intervention also creates risks for children. Removal of children from their homes is always disruptive and often emotionally traumatic for children, even if the parents were neglectful or abusive. Assessing what will be best for a child is often very difficult. Children who are placed in agency care often experience emotionally damaging moves from one placement to another. Placements that are intended to be temporary and short-term often turn out to be long-term, sometimes extending indefinitely.

Types of Orders

At a child protection hearing, the court may determine that a child is not in need of protection, and dismiss the agency application. Most commonly, however, the agency has legitimate cause for concern, and the court will find that the child is in need of protection. If a child is found to be in need of protection, the judge then makes a decision in accordance with the "best interests" of the child. There are three basic types of orders that can be made: supervision, temporary wardship (or guardianship), or permanent wardship. These same types of orders can also be agreed to in advance of a child welfare hearing or trial, and in these cases the agreement will be referred to a judge, who will in turn make a "consent order."

Under a supervision order, the child remains at home under parental care, but the agency staff will conduct supervisory visits at the child's home, and the parents may be subject to other conditions, such as a requirement that they attend a parenting effectiveness course. Temporary wards are placed in the care of the protection agency, usually in a foster or group home; increasingly efforts are being made by agencies to place children with relatives under some form of "kinship care." Reunification with parents is generally contemplated when a child is made a temporary ward, and parents typically have the right to visit with children who are temporary wards. Children who are made permanent (or Crown) wards usually remain wards of the agency until they reach adulthood. Parental access to a child who is a permanent ward may be terminated, especially if the child is young, and the child is considered eligible for adoption. If the child is older when made a permanent ward, it is likely that the child will remain in a foster home or group home, and the parents are more likely to be given a continuing right to see their child. With the growing acceptance of open adoption, it is likely that policies terminating parental access may change.

Child protection legislation provides for court review of prior orders, and may result in the termination, extension, or alteration of a prior order. If a permanent ward is placed for adoption, the parents lose the right to seek a review. In some cases a child who is a permanent ward and is not adopted may be returned to parental care; in those cases wardship is normally terminated.

Who Speaks for the Child?

A fundamental question in the child welfare field is: "Who speaks for the child?" It is a question which defies an easy answer. Some would argue that the child welfare agency, with its mandate to protect children and promote their welfare, is advocating for the child. Others would point out that child welfare agencies often have financial, institutional, and professional constraints which prevent them from truly advocating what is best for the child. There may, for example, be disagreement between the agency and foster parents, or among agency staff, about how a particular case should be handled. While the agency will have an administrative mechanism for establishing how such disagreements will be resolved, there may still be controversy over what is truly best for the child.

Children in care are a particularly vulnerable population. To protect the rights of children in care and to give them access to advocates, several provinces have established a Child Youth Advocate's office with responsibility to offer service for children involved in the protection process or in the legal care of a protection agency. These offices are not intended to provide legal representation for children in court, but rather to act as advocates for them within the context of the child protection system. Their establishment reflects a concern that the bureaucratic nature of child welfare agencies may result in situations in which the agencies are not acting in the best interests of children. In some provinces, child youth advocates have powers that extend beyond the child welfare system, and in these cases issues which adversely affect the well-being of other groups of children may be addressed, often through research and public disclosure of their needs and rights.

Parents involved in protection cases also typically believe that they know and care for their children more than any of the professionals. Thus parents may claim that they speak for their children.

The children who are the subject of a protection case may also have their own views about what they want to have happen. Some children are too young to express their views, and older children are sometimes reluctant or ambivalent about expressing their views. However, many children involved in the protection process have definite ideas about their futures. In some jurisdictions children involved in child protection proceedings can have lawyers who represent them in court, and older children sometimes come to court and speak on their own behalf.

The judges who make decisions on child protection matters also have a role in acting on behalf of children. Although judges have a responsibility for balancing the rights of the litigants and acting in accordance with the legislation, they have ultimate responsibility for the protection of children before the court, and the promotion of their welfare.

Child Welfare Law in a Social Context

Child abuse and neglect are not restricted to a particular region, economic or cultural group, or race. The Canadian public has learned that even trusted and respected community members such as coaches, doctors, teachers, and priests can be guilty of sexual abuse. Despite the widespread nature of child abuse and neglect, child welfare agencies are more likely to be involved with families from disadvantaged economic, social, and cultural groups. Although the profile of child welfare workers is changing, child protection workers are still predominantly middle-class and well educated, whereas their clients are generally disadvantaged and socially marginalized.

Little has changed since 1979, when the National Council of Welfare observed that the clients of the child welfare system are "overwhelmingly drawn from the ranks of Canada's poor." In some cases, the personal or emotional problems that result in a life of poverty may also make it difficult to parent adequately. As the Council explained:

> There are two major reasons why poor families are more likely than those with higher incomes to use children's social services. First, low-income parents run a greater risk of encountering problems that reduce their capacity to provide adequate care for their children. Second, poor families are largely dependent upon a single, overburdened source of help—the child welfare system—in coping with their problems, whereas more affluent families enjoy access to a broader and superior range of supportive resources. (pp. 2–3)

The Council further observed:

> Despite what most would consider a more enlightened and compassionate attitude than in the past, our society still stands in judgment on parents who are unable to care for their children.... What is often forgotten, however, is that the term "unable or unwilling to provide care" is nothing more than a convenient administrative label lumping together a wide variety of family problems, many of which stem from inadequate income, unemployment and other factors that cannot fairly be blamed on their victims. (p. 11)

Most judges dealing with child protection cases are aware of the need to be sensitive to the realities of poverty in Canada. Indeed, all those who work in the child welfare system must be sensitive to problems of poverty. They must also be sensitive to the social, cultural, and racial differences that often exist between them and their clients. A number of racial minorities and immigrant groups are overrepresented in Canada's child welfare system, but this is particularly apparent in the case of Aboriginal children. In response, policies and practices to transfer increased levels of jurisdictional responsibility for these services to Aboriginal agencies and authorities have been developed. These issues are explored more fully in several chapters included in this book.

The role of the child protection worker has become a complex and highly demanding one, requiring a unique blend of knowledge, skill, sensitivity, and dedication. In the context of child protection cases that are resolved through the judicial process, agency staff and parents are often engaged in an adversarial relationship. In this context it is often easy to forget that the majority of parents, even those involved with the child welfare system, have a genuine love for their children and want what is best for them. Recognizing the important role of parents and the many challenges they face, while taking required steps to ensure the protection of children and their long-term well-being, continues to be the core challenge for both policy-makers and practitioners in child welfare.

Notes

1 This is a revised version of N. Bala (2004), Child welfare law in Canada: An introduction. In N. Bala, M. K. Zapf, R. J. Williams, R. Vogl, & J. P. Hornick (Eds.), *Canadian child welfare law: Children, families and the state* (2nd ed.) (pp. 1–25). Toronto: Thompson Educational Publishing. Reproduced with permission from the publisher.

2 The *Charter of Rights and Freedoms* comprises Part I of the *Constitution Act, 1982*, being Schedule B to the *Canada Act 1982* (U.K.), 1982, c. 11.

3 For a discussion of the constitutionality and scope of s. 43 of the *Criminal Code*, see *Canadian Foundation for Children, Youth and the Law v. Canada*, SCC 4, published at [2004] 1 S.C.R. 76.

Insights from the *Canadian Incidence Study of Reported Child Abuse and Neglect*

Introduction

P art I provides information from the *Canadian Incidence Study* about the child welfare landscape in Canada. The first province-wide incidence study of abuse and neglect in Canada was completed in Ontario in 1993, and the *Canadian Incidence Study* (CIS) in 1998 was the first national study to document the incidence of reported maltreatment in Canada. A second cycle was completed in 2003. This research describes the characteristics of children reported to child welfare agencies across Canada, as well as characteristics of workers serving them. Data derived from this research focus provide opportunities to study trends which have emerged from existing policies and which have implications for the development of future policies and practices in child welfare. The CIS–1998 collected data on the incidence and characteristics of child maltreatment from 51 child welfare sites across Canada, with a final sample of 7,672 child maltreatment investigations pertaining to children under the age of 16. The CIS–2003 obtained data from 63 sites, with a final sample of 14,200 child maltreatment investigations. Data collection for the third cycle of the study, the CIS–2008, has been completed, and major findings from this cycle were released in October 2010 (Public Health Agency of Canada, 2010). The original study was an important milestone in Canadian child welfare, and now, with planned repetitions at five-year intervals, these studies are invaluable sources of information collected about child protection in this country.

In addition to examining trends and the related consequences of various policy choices, the data has other important uses. First, it provides national information that can be compared with similar studies in other countries, notably the United States. Second, it provides important baseline information on the Canadian child welfare field, including data on staff characteristics. Finally, it provides a database that permits continuing analysis of the complex nature of child protection services.

One major limitation of the CIS is the sampling methodology, which is described in Chapter 1. The CIS–1998 also acknowledged a serious limitation with respect to its ability to report on services provided by First Nations child and family service agencies, as its sample included only three mandated First Nations child welfare sites. Special efforts were made in 2003 to address this limitation. The CIS–2003 sample included Aboriginal children served by the random sample of provincial/territorial agencies, but also those investigated by a convenience sample of eight First Nations agencies. Aboriginal children comprised 15% of the CIS-2003 sample; 12% were First Nations children (status or non-status) and 3% were Métis or Inuit. However, this does not yet reflect population estimates of Aboriginal children and families served by child welfare agencies. Since Aboriginal children were estimated to represent between 30% and 40% of all children in care in 2002 (Chapter 22), one would assume that the percentage of Aboriginal children being investigated in 2003 would be significantly greater than 15%. Findings from CIS-2003 with respect to First Nations children are presented in chapter 21 of this book.

The first four chapters in Part I provide very important snapshots of patterns in reported cases of neglect and abuse in 1998 and 2003. Chapter 1 provides a summary of the study's methodology and major findings, including major differences between 1998 and 2003. Chapter 2 focuses on neglect in Ontario, the type of maltreatment behind referrals to child welfare agencies for the majority of children who come under the aegis of provincial and territorial child welfare services. This is timely, as research over the years has demonstrated that chronic neglect can be as damaging to children's development as the more serious forms of abuse. The focus on this one province is deliberate, as it allows for discussion of the characteristics of the children and families, and the provincial response, over a 10-year period. Chapter 3 summarizes results from an analysis of the degree to which agency and worker characteristics may affect decision- making. In Chapter 4, Fallon and her research team examine the qualifications of child protection workers, how their profile is changing, and some of the general effects on service delivery. Together, these chapters provide a useful analysis of incidence, service response, and the characteristics not only of children and families, but also of workers and the agencies involved in the provision of child welfare services in Canada. Chapter 5 identifies and discusses key themes and implications emerging from the first four chapters.

Canadian Incidence Study of Reported Child Abuse and Neglect: Changing Patterns of Reported Maltreatment, 1998 and 2003

Nico Trocmé
Barbara Fallon
Bruce MacLaurin

Over the past 25 years, clinical research involving abused and neglected children has shifted the focus from battered and sexually abused children to understanding the emotional, social, and cognitive effects of a range of forms of maltreatment, including neglect, emotional maltreatment, and exposure to intimate partner violence. In response, a number of provinces and territories have amended their statutes, and professionals working with children have become far more aware of the risks associated with these forms of maltreatment. By describing the characteristics of children reported to child welfare authorities across Canada, the *Canadian Incidence Study of Reported Child Abuse and Neglect* (CIS) provides an important perspective on these policy and service changes. Two national cycles of the CIS were completed in 1998 and 2003, in addition to the first province-wide incidence study completed in Ontario in 1993. This chapter describes the methodology of the CIS, and compares the results from the 1998 and 2003 cycles of the study. Findings in this chapter, including the tables, are based on results and tables published in the CIS–2003 *Major Findings* report published by the Public Health Agency of Canada (see Trocmé et al., 2005). Chapters 2, 3, and 4 discuss in more detail the characteristics of neglected children, the influence of location on service patterns, and the changing professional profile of staff conducting child welfare investigations. Chapter 21 includes information from the CIS–2003 on the characteristics of Aboriginal children referred to child welfare agencies.

CIS Methodology

Information on children and families who receive child welfare services across Canada is generally not available at a national level. Some provinces have fairly elaborate province-wide information systems, while in other provinces most service information is available only at a local level. Variations in provincial and territorial statutes and service delivery models further complicate the task of producing national child welfare statistics. The CIS was developed to overcome these limitations by directly surveying child welfare staff responsible for intake investigations.

The CIS is conducted every five years with core funding from the Public Health Agency of Canada and oversampling funding from a number of provinces, territories, and various granting agencies. The following section provides an overview of the sampling, measurement, and weighting procedures used. For more detailed descriptions of the methodologies used, readers are referred to the CIS–1998 and CIS–2003 study reports, available at no cost from the Public Health Agency of Canada (Trocmé et al., 2001; Trocmé et al., 2005).

Sampling

The CIS uses a stratified cluster sampling design that in the first stage selects a nationally representative sample of child welfare offices. In large offices with a large volume of investigations (over 100 a month), a second sampling stage was used to select a subsample of cases. The office level sampling varied in accordance to the structure of the office: in some instances, case selection moved from one team to the next with each team participating for two or three weeks; in others, a random or systematic sample was drawn. In two instances, team or worker participation was limited to a non-systematic group of volunteer workers.

The CIS–2003 tracked a sample of 14,200 child maltreatment investigations conducted during the fall of 2003 in 63 out of 400 child welfare sites across Canada. Due to the large amount of missing data in the Quebec portion of the study, most of the analyses presented in the following chapters examine a smaller sample of 11,562 investigations conducted in 55 sites outside of Quebec and involving children up to 15 years of age. The CIS–1998 examined a sample of 7,672 child maltreatment investigations conducted in 51 out of 327 child welfare sites.

Measurement

The CIS collects information directly from investigating workers using a three-page data collection form describing the alleged maltreatment, in addition to other child, family, and investigation-related information that includes: (a) child age, sex, Aboriginal status, and a child functioning checklist; (b) family size, structure, and housing conditions; (c) caregiver age, education, ethnicity, income, and a caregiver risk factor checklist; and (d) source of report, caregiver response to investigation, ongoing service status, service referrals, out-of-home placement, and child welfare court application, as well as police and criminal court involvement.

A significant challenge for the study is to overcome the variations in definitions of maltreatment used by different jurisdictions. The CIS uses a common classification system across all jurisdictions based on five primary categories of maltreatment: physical abuse, sexual abuse, neglect, emotional maltreatment, and exposure to domestic violence. The CIS maltreatment classification reflects a fairly broad definition of child maltreatment, and includes several forms of maltreatment that are not specifically included in some provincial and territorial child welfare statutes (e.g., educational neglect and exposure to domestic violence). All CIS maltreatment definitions also use a harm or substantial risk of harm standard that includes situations in which children have been harmed, as well as situations in which children have not yet been harmed but are considered to have been at substantial risk of harm. The inclusion of substantial risk of harm reflects the clinical and legislative definitions used in most Canadian jurisdictions.

To ensure that cases involving multiple forms of maltreatment are tracked, every investigation can be classified as having up to three forms of maltreatment. For each form of maltreatment the study tracks information on substantiation, duration, perpetrator, physical harm, and use of punishment. A case is considered "substantiated" if the balance of evidence indicates that abuse or neglect has occurred. If there is not enough evidence to substantiate maltreatment, but there remains a suspicion that maltreatment has occurred, a case is classified as "suspected." A case is classified as "unsubstantiated" if there is sufficient evidence to conclude that the child has not been maltreated.

All participating workers receive a half-day training session covering key definitions and study procedures. Site researchers conduct follow-up visits in order to verify adherence to the sampling protocol and the data collected on the CIS forms.

Weighting and Analysis

In order to derive national annual estimates, the data collected over three months in the sampled agencies must be weighted. The annualization weights are the ratio of cases opened by each site in the calendar year to cases sampled. To account for the non-proportional sampling design, regional weights were applied to reflect the size of each site relative to the child population in the region that the site was sampled from. National incidence estimates were calculated by dividing the weighted estimates by the child population (0 to 15-year-olds).

The analysis for this chapter was completed by comparing the CIS–2003 and CIS–1998 in terms of changes in case characteristics that best explained the changes in incidence rates. Because of incomplete data in the Quebec portion of the 2003 study, analyses focus on changes across Canada, excluding Quebec. Since the pattern of change varied significantly by primary category of maltreatment, we conducted separate analyses for cases of physical abuse and neglect, cases of sexual abuse, and cases of emotional maltreatment and exposure to domestic violence.

Variance estimates that take into consideration the stratified cluster sampling design were calculated using the replicate weights method with the WesVar PC jackknife (JKn) procedure (Efron, 1982; Lehtonen & Pahkinen, 1995). Chi-square analyses were used to test for significance in comparing characteristics associated with different forms of maltreatment. The WesVar RS2 adjusted chi-square statistic was used to take into account variance estimates (Brick & Morganstein, 1996). To avoid inflating chi-square statistics, all analyses were conducted using a weighted sample equivalent to the original sample size rather than the population estimates.

Limitations

In interpreting CIS findings, several limitations to the design should be noted. The data collected are limited to information that workers gather during their standard investigation; no additional instruments are used to collect information from children or families. The study examines only cases that are open for investigation by a child welfare authority, and do not track screened-out reports or internal reports on already open cases. To avoid double-counting children, subsequent reports are removed if children are reported more than once during the sampling period. However, the weights used to develop annual estimates reflect an unknown proportion of duplicate reports that are included in the sites' annual case volume statistics; thus the unit of analysis of the study is the child maltreatment investigation. Finally, the study tracks only case activity that occurs during the initial investigation period, in most cases within the first two months of contact.

Major Findings

Increase in Substantiated Maltreatment

Table 1 describes the increase in child maltreatment investigations from 1998 to 2003 across all of Canada, and in Canada excluding Quebec. Across the whole country, the estimated rate of investigations increased 78% from a rate of 21.5 per 1000 children to 38.3 per 1000. During the same period, the estimated number of investigations increased from 135,573 to 235,315. Excluding Quebec, the increase has been even more pronounced, with the incidence of investigations growing by 86% from 24.6 to 45.7 per 1000 children.

The rate of substantiated maltreatment in the core CIS sample for Canada, excluding Quebec, increased 125%, from 9.6 substantiated cases per 1000 children in 1998 to 21.7 in 2003. Subsequent tables examine changes in the core CIS sample in Canada, excluding Quebec.

Table 1 *Child Maltreatment Investigations by Level of Substantiation in Canada, 1998 and 2003*

| | Child Maltreatment Investigations | | | | | |
| | 1998[a] | | | 2003[b] | | |
Level of Substantiation	Number of Investigations	Rate per 1000 Children	Substantiation Rate	Number of Investigations	Rate per 1000 Children	Substantiation Rate
Canada, including Quebec						
Substantiated	58,201	9.24	43%	114,607	18.67	49%
Suspected	30,334	4.81	22%	28,053	4.57	12%
Unsubstantiated	47,039	7.46	35%	90,869	14.80	38%
Missing	0	0	0%	1,786	.29	1%
Total	**135,573**	**21.52**	**100%**	**233,315**	**38.33**	**100%**
Canada, excluding Quebec (Core CIS Sample)						
Substantiated	46,574	9.64	39%	103,298	21.71	47%
Suspected	28,718	5.95	24%	28,053	5.90	13%
Unsubstantiated	43,260	8.96	36%	85,969	18.07	40%
Total	**118,552**	**24.55**	**100%**	**217,320**	**45.68**	**100%**

Source: *Canadian incidence study of reported child abuse and neglect, 2003: Major findings* (Trocmé et al., 2005), Table 9.1.

[a]Based on a sample of 7,672 and 5,359 child maltreatment investigations.

[b]Based on a sample of 14,200 and 11,562 child maltreatment investigations.

Part of the increase in substantiated cases appears to reflect a shift in the way investigating workers classify cases, with a much smaller proportion of cases being classified as suspected (13% in 2003 compared to 24% in 1998 in Canada, excluding Quebec). It is difficult to determine the extent to which these changes are due to changes in child welfare policies and practices or changes in the types of cases being referred.

More Children Investigated in Each Family

Table 2 shows the relationship between the number of investigated families and the number of investigated children in 1998 and 2003 in Canada, excluding Quebec. Between 1998 and 2003 the number of families investigated increased 56% from an estimated 83,976 to 130,594. During the same period, the number of investigated children increased 83% from an estimated 118,552 investigated children to 217,320.

Like most public health statistics, the CIS is designed to track incidence of investigated maltreatment by child, not by family. Many jurisdictions, however, process investigations at the family level. The dramatic increase in the rate of investigated and substantiated children appears in part to be due to a shift in investigation practices. As shown in Table 2, the average number of investigated children per family has increased from 1.41 to 1.66. This increase may reflect a greater understanding of the impact of maltreatment, as well as changes in the types of maltreatment investigated, and possibly, in some jurisdictions, changes in administrative procedures.

Table 2 *Investigated Families Compared to Investigated Children in Canada, Excluding Quebec, in 1998 and 2003*

Source of Investigation	1998 Number of Investigations	2003 Number of Investigations	% Increase
Investigated families	83,976	130,594	56%
Investigated children	118,552	217,320	83%
Average number of investigated children per family	**1.41**	**1.66**	

Source: *Canadian incidence study of reported child abuse and neglect 2003: Major findings* (Trocmé et al., 2005).

Note: This table does not include the incidence rate of investigations per 1000 families with children, as the CIS–2003 was not designed to track incidence rates at this level.

Variations by Category of Maltreatment

Table 3 provides further indication of some of the factors underlying the increase in the rate of substantiated maltreatment. With the exception of sexual abuse, all categories of maltreatment had much higher incidence rates of substantiation in 2003 when compared with 1998. The increase is driven primarily by two categories of maltreatment: exposure to domestic violence and emotional maltreatment. The rate of reported exposure to domestic violence increased 259% from 1.7 substantiated cases per 1000 to 6.2, and the rate of reported emotional maltreatment increased 276% from 0.9 substantiated cases per 1000 to 3.2. In 1998, these two forms of maltreatment accounted for 27% of substantiated cases; by 2003 they accounted for 43% of cases. These differences reflect a shift in awareness, and in some cases in legislation, with respect to the impact of emotional maltreatment and exposure to domestic violence.

During the same period, rates of physical abuse and neglect also increased significantly, although at a slower pace than exposure to domestic violence. Substantiated physical abuse increased 107% from 2.6 cases per 1000 to 5.3, and neglect increased 78% from 3.6 to 6.4. In sharp contrast to all other forms of maltreatment, cases of substantiated sexual abuse decreased by nearly a third (30%), dropping from 0.9 substantiated victims per 1000 children to 0.6. While this decrease was not statistically significant, it is consistent with decreasing rates of reported sexual abuse noted across the United States (Finkelhor & Jones, 2006; United States Department of Health and Human Services, 2006).

Table 3 *Substantiated Child Maltreatment Investigations by Primary Category in Canada, Excluding Quebec, in 1998 and 2003*

| | Child Maltreatment Investigations | | | | | |
| | 1998[a] | | | 2003[b] | | |
Maltreatment Type	Number of Investigations	Rate per 1000 Children	% of Substantiated Investigations	Number of Investigations	Rate per 1000 Children	% of Substantiated Investigations
Physical abuse	12,353	2.56	27%	25,257	5.31	25%
Sexual abuse	4,322	0.89	9%	2,935	0.62	3%
Neglect	17,292	3.58	37%	30,366	6.38	29%
Emotional maltreatment	4,137	0.86	9%	15,369	3.23	15%
Exposure to domestic violence	8,284	1.72	18%	29,370	6.17	28%
Total	**46,388**	**9.60**	**100%**	**103,297**	**21.71**	**100%**

Source: *Canadian incidence study of reported child abuse and neglect 2003: Major findings* (Trocmé et al., 2005).
[a]Based on a sample of 2,046 substantiated investigations with information on maltreatment category.
[b]Based on a sample of 5,660 substantiated investigations.

Lower Proportion of Cases Involving Harm

Table 4 compares rates of physical harm, emotional harm, and duration of maltreatment in 1998 and 2003. While there was an increase in the incidence of physical harm from 1.8 harmed victims per 1000 children in 1998 to 2.1 in 2003, this increase is not statistically significant. There is, however, a significant difference in the incidence of emotional harm, which increased from 3.0 emotionally harmed victims per 1000 children in 1998 to 4.4 in 2003. These represent increases in the order of 22% and 45% respectively, far less than the overall 125% increase in substantiated cases of maltreatment. Between 1998 and 2003, the proportion of victims of maltreatment who displayed signs of harm decreased from 18% to 10% for physical harm and from 32% to 20% for emotional harm. In other words, the increase in maltreatment rates documented by the CIS appears to be driven primarily by cases in which children have not been visibly harmed.

Changes in the distribution of cases relative to the duration of maltreatment indicate that the increase in maltreatment rates is driven most strongly by single incident cases. Single incident cases have increased at the fastest rate, a 153% increase from 2.7 substantiated single incident cases per 1000 children to 6.9. Multiple incidents over the short and longer term have also increased significantly, from 127% and 103% respectively. Although single incident cases have

Table 4 *Case Characteristics of Substantiated Child Maltreatment Investigations in Canada, Excluding Quebec, in 1998 and 2003*

Type of Harm and Duration	1998[a]			2003[b]		
	Number of Child Investigations	Rate per 1000 Children	% of Substantiated Investigations	Number of Child Investigations	Rate per 1000 Children	% of Substantiated Investigations
Any physical harm	8,519	1.76	18%	10,195	2.14	10%
Any emotional harm	14,704	3.04	32%	20,959	4.41	20%
Duration of maltreatment						
Single incident	13,154	2.72	28%	32,673	6.87	32%
Multiple incidents < 6 months	7,950	1.65	17%	17,793	3.74	17%
Multiple incidents > 6 months	18,210	3.77	39%	36,328	7.64	35%
Duration unknown	6,965	1.44	15%	15,413	3.24	15%
Total substantiated maltreatment	**46,574**	**9.64**	**NA**	**103,093**	**21.67**	**NA**

Source: *Canadian incidence study of reported child abuse and neglect 2003: Major findings* (Trocmé et al., 2005).
[a]Based on a sample of 2,050 substantiated investigations.
[b]Based on a sample of 5,660 substantiated investigations.

Note: Columns add up to more than 100% since variable categories are not mutually exclusive.

increased at the fastest rate, multiple incident cases occurring over more than six months continue to account for the largest proportion of cases (35%).

Child Welfare Interventions

Comparisons between rates of previous openings, ongoing service provision, out-of-home placement, and child welfare court applications in 1998 and 2003 in Canada, excluding Quebec, are presented in Table 5. The number of substantiated investigations involving children who had previously received child welfare services more than doubled, from 23,470 to 54,001.

The decision to provide ongoing child welfare service was made in 24,906 substantiated child maltreatment investigations, a rate of 5.2 per 1000 children in 1998. In 2003, ongoing child welfare services were provided to nearly twice as many children, with 45,885 substantiated maltreatment investigations receiving ongoing services, a rate of 9.6 per 1000 children. However, since the increase in the total number of substantiated cases was even greater, the proportion of substantiated cases being kept open for ongoing services dropped from 53% in 1998 to 44% in 2003.

In contrast, the number of children who had been previously investigated kept pace with the overall increase in substantiated maltreatment. From 1998

Table 5 *Child Welfare Interventions in Substantiated Child Maltreatment Investigations in Canada, Excluding Quebec, in 1998 and 2003*

Child Welfare Interventions	1998[a]			2003[b]		
	Number of Child Investigations	Rate per 1000 Children	% of Substantiated Investigations	Number of Child Investigations	Rate per 1000 Children	% of Substantiated Investigations
Child previously investigated	23,470	4.86	50%	54,001	11.35	52%
Open for ongoing services	24,906	5.16	53%	45,885	9.64	44%
Child welfare placement	5,307	1.10	11%	8,263	1.74	8%
Child welfare court application	4,399	0.91	9%	7,261	1.53	7%
Total Substantiated Investigations	**46,574**	**9.64**	**NA**	**103,298**	**21.71**	**NA**

Source: *Canadian incidence study of reported child abuse and neglect 2003: Major findings* (Trocmé et al., 2005).
[a]Based on a sample of 2,050 substantiated investigations.
[b]Based on a sample of 5,660 substantiated investigations.

Note: Columns add up to more than 100% since more than one intervention may apply to the same child.

to 2003, the incidence of substantiated maltreatment involving previously investigated children increased 134% from 4.9 per 1000 children to 11.4 per 1000 children.

In 1998, 5,307 substantiated investigations (1.1 per 1000 children) resulted in a child welfare placement. In 2003, 8,263 substantiated investigations (1.7 per 1000 children) involved a child welfare placement. However, the rate of increase in placements was less pronounced than the overall increase in substantiated cases, and this change was not statistically significant. As a result, the proportion of maltreated children who experienced some type of placement during the investigation decreased from 11% in 1998 to 8% in 2003.

A similar development is apparent with the use of child welfare courts. The number of investigations involving child welfare court applications increased from 4,399 in 1998 to 7,261 in 2003, an increase that was not statistically significant. The proportion of substantiated cases being brought to court decreased from 9% to 7% between these two time periods.

More Reports from Professionals

Table 6 details the increase in the number of substantiated cases reported by professionals. Substantiated cases referred by professionals increased by 170% from 29,089 substantiated cases (6.0 per 1000 children) in 1998 to 77,199 substantiated cases (16.2 per 1000 children) in 2003. The proportion of substantiated

Table 6 *Referral Sources in Substantiated Child Maltreatment Investigations in Canada, Excluding Quebec, in 1998 and 2003*

Referral Source	1998[a]			2003[b]		
	Number of Child Investigations	Rate per 1000 Children	% of Substantiated Investigations	Number of Child Investigations	Rate per 1000 Children	% of Substantiated Investigations
Any non-professional referral source	16,042	3.32	34%	21,214	4.46	2%
Any professional referral source	29,089	6.02	62%	77,199	16.23	75%
Any anonymous source	3,788	0.78	8%	3,061	0.64	3%
Missing	0	NA	0%	1,824	NA	2%
Total Substantiated Investigations	**46,574**	**9.64**	**NA**	**103,298**	**21.71**	**NA**

Source: *Canadian incidence study of reported child abuse and neglect 2003: Major findings* (Trocmé et al., 2005).
[a]Based on a sample of 2,050 substantiated investigations.
[b]Based on a sample of 5,660 substantiated investigations.

Note: Columns add up to more than 100% because referrals can be made from more than one source. Some data on referral sources in 2003 was missing.

cases referred by professionals increased from 62% to 75%. During the same time period there was an increase in the rate of referrals from non-professionals and a decrease in the rate of referrals from anonymous or other sources, although these changes are not statistically significant. Referrals from professionals accounted for 85% of the total increase in reports of maltreatment between these two time periods.

Implications for Policy and Practice

Child welfare services in Canada have been undergoing a significant expansion in focus. Emotional maltreatment and exposure to interpersonal violence accounted for 27% of substantiated cases of maltreatment in 1998. By 2003, these two forms of maltreatment accounted for 43% of cases. During the same period, sexual abuse cases dropped from 9% to 3% of investigations, and the proportion of cases of maltreatment involving some type of physical harm dropped from 18% to 10%. While there are no national statistics available prior to the CIS–1998, the 1993 Ontario Incidence Study provides a helpful point of comparison (Trocmé, McPhee, Tam, & Hay, 1994). In 1993, less than 10% of investigations were substantiated because of emotional maltreatment or exposure to interpersonal violence. In contrast, sexual abuse accounted for 23% of substantiated investigations; physical abuse for 40%, and 28% of substantiated cases involved some type of documented harm. By 2003, exposure to domestic violence accounted for 32% of substantiated cases, sexual abuse 3%, physical abuse 24%, and 8% involved some type of documented harm (Fallon et al., 2005, p. 160).

A significant shift is also evident in the way in which child welfare services are delivered. At the front end, it is interesting to note that the increase in reports is primarily driven by reports from professionals as opposed to reports from neighbours, relatives, and victims. Three-quarters of substantiated investigations were reported by professionals in 2003 compared to 62% in 1998. In 1993 in Ontario, professionals accounted for only half of all referrals (Trocmé et al., 1994).

As noted in the introduction, this expansion is consistent with the growing amount of evidence that the emotional dimensions of maltreatment are as harmful, and in the long term more harmful, than the physical dimensions (Gibb, Chelminski, & Zimmerman, 2007; Iwaniec, Larkin, & Higgins, 2006; Maughan & Cicchetti, 2002). The policy and service implications from this expanded understanding of child maltreatment must, however, be carefully considered. Situations requiring urgent intervention to assess immediate safety concerns—sexual abuse, physical abuse involving serious injuries, and neglect of very young children—represent fewer than 15% of substantiated cases. For the other 85% of substantiated cases, the primary concern is that children are at high risk of developing severe socio-emotional and cognitive problems if they continue to be exposed to a combination of disorganized, neglectful, or harsh parenting in environments that are marked by deprivation and violence (Cicchetti & Lynch, 1993; Dubowitz, 1999; Erickson, Egeland, & Pianta, 1989; Maughan & Cicchetti, 2002).

Although the effects of neglect and emotional maltreatment can severely compromise children's development, it is important to distinguish between different types of situations. For example, an urgent forensic investigation may be required in some cases to determine whether or not a specific incident of maltreatment has occurred (e.g., Is the broken arm from a playground accident or an inflicted injury? Or is a child's sexualized behaviour a result of abuse?). These types of situations differ from cases where assessments of parenting capacity and available support networks are required to determine the long-term capacity of parents to adequately meet their children's needs. Both types of situations fall under the jurisdiction of child welfare authorities; indeed, the child welfare statutes in all provinces and territories make specific reference to child protection *and* well-being as the primary concern of mandated child welfare agencies. For example, Manitoba's *Child and Family Services Act* states, in its Declaration of Principles (section 1), that "[t]he safety, security and well-being of children and their best interests are fundamental responsibilities," while Quebec's *Youth Protection Act* states in section 2 that the Act "applies to any child whose security or development is or may be considered to be in danger."

As the mandate for child welfare intervention broadens across Canada, it is therefore important to differentiate between situations requiring urgent intervention and the equally serious but less urgent situations in which families, professionals, and the extended community can be engaged in better planned assessment and decision-making processes. Failing to differentiate between these two types of cases could in the long term seriously hamper our ability to respond effectively. With urgent cases representing an increasingly small proportion of reports, there is a risk that investigating social workers will not have the training and experience needed to intervene in some of the cases of child sexual abuse or child battery (Gove, 1995). In contrast, the less urgent but chronic cases of maltreatment require a very different set of practices, including alternative response models (Waldfogel, 2001), more extensive family assessments, and case planning methods such as family group conferences that engage the child's extended family and community (Chandler & Giovannucci, 2004).

Acknowledgements

Funding for this research was provided by the Public Health Agency of Canada and the Canadian Institutes of Health Research.

2

The Response of the Ontario Child Welfare System to Neglect: 1993 to 2003

Kate Schumaker
Barbara Fallon
Nico Trocmé

Canada's first child protection legislation, Ontario's *Children's Protection Act* (1893), was originally conceived to respond to the plight of abandoned and neglected children (Swift, 1995a). However, by the 1960s, with elevated concerns about "battered child syndrome" (Kempe, Silverman, Steele, Droege-mueller, & Silver, 1962), attention shifted to the issue of severe abuse and child neglect, and "the original impetus behind child protection legislation ... moved to the far background" (Swift, 2003, p. 2).

More recently, evidence indicates that outcomes for neglected children are poorer than those for children who have been abused (Erickson & Egeland, 1996; Gauthier, Stollak, Messe, & Arnoff, 1996; Kaplan, Pelcovitz, & Labruna, 1999; Garbarino & Collins, 1999). In their review of developmental outcomes for neglected children, Hildyard and Wolfe (2002) conclude that neglect has a "pervasive, negative impact on children's early competence across major developmental dimensions" (p. 685), with neglected children suffering from more severe cognitive and academic deficits, social withdrawal and limited peer acceptance, and internalizing problems than children who are physically abused. In general, children who experience neglect are at risk for a host of troubling short- and long-term outcomes, including anxiety, depression, social and behavioural problems, poor educational progress, and parenting diffi-culties (English, Upadhyaya et al., 2005; Springer, Sheridan, Kuo, & Carnes, 2007). And yet, despite the seriousness of the issue, child welfare profession-als are often uncertain about when and how to intervene with families where neglect is a concern because of the multiple problems often faced by these families and the complicated underlying causes of this maltreatment.

Child neglect has long been considered the "poor cousin" of abuse in child welfare research and policy. There is a fairly robust body of literature regarding the correlates and outcomes of neglect; however, in what has previously been dubbed the "neglect of neglect" (Wolock & Horowitz, 1989), there has been limited documentation of the child welfare system's response to these families, and evaluation to determine effective interventions with this population is in its infancy (DePanfilis & Dubowitz, 2005).

In Ontario's child protection legislation, neglect has been less of a priority for many years than the more emotionally charged issue of child abuse (Swift, 2003), and was only recently referred to explicitly in Ontario's *Child and Family Services Act* through amendments made in 2000. Despite this lower profile in both research and policy, cases where neglect is the primary reason for investigation account for the largest proportion of all maltreatment investigations in the province, indicating that a substantial share of front-end resources are going toward investigating this phenomenon (Trocmé, Fallon, MacLaurin, Daciuk, et al., 2005).

The *Ontario Incidence Study of Reported Child Abuse and Neglect* (OIS) was first conducted in 1993; prior to this, there were no reliable provincial data on the reported incidence of child abuse and neglect in Ontario. The OIS was repeated in 1998 and 2003 as part of the larger national study—*the Canadian Incidence Study of Reported Child Abuse and Neglect* (CIS)—with the primary purpose of providing reliable estimates of the scope and characteristics of investigated maltreatment in Ontario. Using data from the three available cycles of the OIS (1993, 1998, and 2003), the objectives of the current study are twofold. The first is to examine and compare the child welfare system's response to cases of primary neglect over these three cycles, a time period during which significant policy and legislative changes highlighting the seriousness of neglect took place. The second objective is to use the most recent available OIS data (OIS–2003) to compare the characteristics of children and families in cases where neglect is the primary problem to cases of other maltreatment, and to identify any differences in how the system currently responds to these families and children. Thus, results are presented as two sections: the first section presents the results of analyses examining neglect in Ontario between 1993 and 2003, and the second reviews findings comparing cases of neglect to cases of other maltreatment based on the 2003 data.

Previous Research

Existing research suggests that cases of neglect receive less priority for service than cases of other maltreatment, particularly physical and sexual abuse (Browne & Lynch, 1998; Dubowitz, 1999). Wilson and Horner (2005) state that the amount of attention neglect receives by child welfare agencies, as measured by hours of specialized training and numbers of specialized units, is "in inverse relation to frequency … sexual abuse receives the most specialized attention, followed by physical abuse and then neglect" (p. 471). Buckley (2005), summarizing research conducted in the United Kingdom, Ireland, the United States, and Australia, concludes that the majority of referrals for neglect are "filtered out, often without a service, at an early stage" (p. 116).

In a 1998 study, English, Marshall, Brummel, Novicky, and Coghlan conducted telephone and mail-out surveys with 223 child protection workers in Washington State about substantiation practices; workers indicated they were less likely to substantiate cases of neglect, particularly failure-to-supervise allegations, than other types of maltreatment. Studies have also demonstrated that cases of neglect are less likely to be opened for ongoing protection services than cases of abuse, and may receive fewer referrals for supportive services than do cases of other maltreatment (DePanfilis & Zuravin, 2001; Gaudin, 1999).

English, Thompson, Graham, and Briggs (2005) note that for cases opened for service in the United States, those involving neglect are more likely to result in child placement than other types of maltreatment. Canadian data paint a similar picture, with 14% of cases where neglect is the primary reason for substantiation resulting in a formal child welfare placement, a rate higher than any other maltreatment typology (Trocmé et al., 2005). Somewhat counterintuitively, given these documented high rates of placement, DePanfilis (2006) asserts that court involvement is less likely to occur in cases of neglect than in cases of either physical or sexual abuse.

This review of existing research suggests that the response of the child welfare system to cases of neglect may be an ambivalent one. On the one hand, cases of neglect may receive fewer supportive post-investigatory services either through child protection or through community referrals, while, on the other hand, children in cases of neglect are more likely to be placed than children in other cases. Horwath (2007) elaborates on this incongruity, stating that child protection workers may be both *under-* and *over*whelmed by child neglect; alternatively, workers may view neglect as not particularly serious due to the lack of immediately observable harm, and at other times experience a sense of hopelessness related to the chronicity, intractability, and pervasiveness of the problems experienced by these families.

There is a particularly high need for further exploration of effective child welfare responses to neglect, as research has demonstrated that cases of neglect, whether substantiated or not, are more likely to be referred again to child protection services (CPS) than any other type of maltreatment, suggesting that despite identification and/or intervention, children in these cases continue to grow up in environments that do not meet their basic needs (Jonson-Reid, Drake, Chung, & Way, 2003). Additionally, subsequent referrals to CPS are more likely to be for reasons of neglect regardless of the original reason for referral (Jonson-Reid et al., 2003), indicating that neglect is likely to be part of the picture for many chronic cases of child maltreatment, regardless of their original reason for identification. Experts are practically unanimous that intervention for neglect requires a long-term, multi-service approach by an interdisciplinary team (see Gaudin, 1993; DePanfilis, 2006; Dubowitz, 1999; Stevenson, 2007; Horwath, 2007), and it is generally accepted that the child protection system plays a central role in assessment, service plan development, and the brokering and coordination of services.

Methods

Data Collection

All three cycles of the OIS utilized a multi-stage sampling design to select a representative sample of child welfare agencies across Ontario, and obtained data on child maltreatment investigations conducted by these agencies during the identified case selection period. All data were collected directly from the investigating worker—and represent the worker's judgment at the time of the investigation—using a similar data collection instrument for each cycle. All three cycles of the OIS exclude cases that were not reported to a children's aid society, reported cases that were screened out before an investigation was initiated, new reports on open child protection cases, and cases reported only to the police.

The data collection instrument for each cycle was designed to capture standardized information about child maltreatment investigations that workers would normally gather during the course of an investigation, such as type of abuse/neglect investigated; level of substantiation; physical and/or emotional harm to the child; child functioning concerns; caregiver risk factors; source of income; housing issues; and short-term service disposition of the case. The resulting sample for each cycle was as follows: 2,477 child maltreatment investigations in 1993; 3,050 in 1998; and 7,172 in 2003. Provincial estimates were generated by applying annualization and regionalization weights to these data.

The final weighted estimates for each cycle were 44,900 child maltreatment investigations in 1993; 64,658 in 1998; and 128,108 in 2003. Chapter 1 provides additional information on the CIS methodology.

Analytic Strategy

For the analyses reported in this chapter, only those investigations where neglect was the primary reason for investigation (called "primary neglect" throughout the chapter) were included in the "neglect" group. Additionally, only substantiated primary neglect investigations were included in the "substantiated neglect" group. In the first section, comparisons of the number and incidence of neglect investigations included all investigations of primary neglect in each OIS cycle ($Ns = 667$ in 1993, 1,081 in 1998, and 2,204 in 2003). Primary neglect cases were 27% of all maltreatment investigations in 1993, 36% in 1998, and 32% in 2003; across all three cycles the average was 31%. The comparisons of child welfare service response between 1993 and 2003 presented in this section included all substantiated primary neglect investigations in each OIS cycle ($Ns = 197, 334,$ and 833 for 1993, 1998, and 2003, respectively). Substantiated primary neglect was 30% of investigated primary neglect cases in 1993, and 31% in 1998. However, the rate of substantiation in 2003 was 38%. In the second section, analyses of the profile of children and families, and of the child welfare service response to cases of primary neglect in 2003, includes all substantiated primary neglect investigations in the OIS–2003 data set ($N = 833$). As well, substantiated cases of primary neglect are compared to "other maltreatment" in 2003, which includes physical abuse, sexual abuse, or emotional maltreatment, but excludes substantiated exposure to domestic violence investigations ($N = 1,290$). It has been demonstrated elsewhere (see Black, Trocmé, Fallon, & MacLaurin, 2008) that the substantiation rate for exposure to domestic violence cases is much higher than the rates of substantiations for other types of maltreatment.

The raw sample data were weighted to show the estimated numbers for the population of Ontario. The final weighted estimates for primary neglect investigations used in the first section were as follows: 12,278 in 1993; 23,444 in 1998; and 41,424 in 2003. Weighted estimates for substantiated primary neglect investigations used in this section were: 3,597 in 1993; 8,054 in 1998; and 15,660 in 2003, and the 2003 weighted estimate was also used for analyses in the second section. The weighted estimate for substantiated investigations of "other maltreatment" in 2003 was 24,247. In the first section, t-tests were performed to assess whether or not there were statistically significant differences between 1998 and 2003 data. In the second section, Pearson's chi-square tests were calculated to see if there were statistically significant differences in the 2003 data between cases of primary neglect and other maltreatment. Both chi-square analyses and t-tests were conducted using the sampling weight. The sampling weight maintains the influence of the final OIS population estimates, while reducing the number of cases analyzed to the original sample size. In this way, use of the sampling weight prevents inflation of the statistical significance of results that would occur as a result of the large number of cases in the final OIS estimates.

Results: Child Neglect in Ontario: 1993 to 2003

Investigations

Comparisons between the 1993, 1998, and 2003 cycles of the OIS are presented in Tables 1 and 2. The data in Table 1 demonstrate that significant increases took place between 1993 and 2003 with respect to both the estimated number and the incidence of primary neglect investigation. This increase in neglect investigations took place within the context of marked increases in the number and incidence of all investigations conducted by the province's children's aid societies during this time period: from 44,900 (or 20.5 investigated children per 1000) in 1993 to 128,108 (or 53.6 investigated children per 1000) in 2003, an increase of 185% over 10 years. The increase in primary neglect investigations accounted for 56% of the overall increase in all maltreatment investigations between 1993 and 1998, and 29% of this increase between 1998 and 2003. Analysis of the average number of children investigated per household suggests that the rise in the number and incidence of neglect investigations between 1998 and 2003 is, in part, accounted for by new child protection standards implemented in the late 1980s that required workers to investigate siblings of referred children. For example, the average number of children investigated per household in 1998 and 2003 was 1.9 and 2.3 respectively.

Substantiation

Data presented in Table 1 also indicate that the estimated number of substantiated primary neglect investigations and the incidence of substantiated primary neglect increased significantly across the 10-year period examined by this study. The proportion (rate) of primary neglect investigations that were substantiated also increased over these three time periods, from 29% of all primary neglect investigations in 1993 to 34% in 1998, and finally to 38% in 2003, an increase of 31% between 1993 and 2003.

Table 1 *Primary Neglect in Ontario: 1993 to 2003*

Year	1993[a]		1998[b]		2003[c]		t-test
Primary neglect investigations	12,278	27%	23,444	36%	41,424	32%	3.16*
Incidence per 1000 children	5.60		9.90		17.33		
Substantiated neglect investigations	3,597	8%	8,054	12%	15,660	12%	3.47**
Incidence per 1000 children	2.00		3.41		6.55		

Note: All percentages calculated as a per cent of the estimated total investigations conducted in the year:
1993, $N = 44,900$; 1998, $N = 64,658$; 2003, $N = 128,108$.
[a]Based on a sample of 2,477 child maltreatment investigations in 1993
[b]Based on a sample of 3,050 child maltreatment investigations in 1998.
[c]Based on a sample of 7,172 child maltreatment investigations in 2003.
*$p < .01$
**$p < .001$

Neglect Subtypes: Substantiated Primary Neglect

An overview of substantiated primary neglect investigations, by subtype, is presented in Table 2. In each of the OIS cycles, the most commonly substantiated form of neglect was "Failure-to-supervise: physical harm" followed by "Physical neglect." Together these two subtypes comprise the majority of substantiated neglect investigations in all three cycles of the OIS (77% in 1993; 65% in 1998; and 70% in 2003). The significant increase in neglect investigations between 1993 and 2003 is driven primarily by increases in substantiated investigations for "Failure-to-supervise: physical harm" and "Physical neglect."

Table 2 *Substantiated Neglect by Subtype: 1993 to 2003*

Year	1993[a]		1998[b]		2003[c]	
Failure-to-supervise: physical harm	1,605	44%	4,013	50%	6,759	43%
Failure-to-supervise: sexual harm	51	1%	305	4%	1,022	7%
Permitting criminal behaviour	62	2%	527	7%	204	1%
Physical neglect	1,203	33%	1,257	16%	4,208	27%
Medical neglect	126	4%	713	9%	887	6%
Failure to provide psych. treatment	0	–	153	2%	313	2%
Abandonment	496	14%	750	9%	1,758	11%
Educational neglect	54	2%	336	4%	509	3%
Total	3,597	100%	8,054	100%	15,660	100%

Note: All percentages calculated as a per cent of total investigations for the year, as shown in Total line.
[a]Based on a sample of 2,477 child maltreatment investigations in 1993.
[b]Based on a sample of 3,050 child maltreatment investigations in 1998.
[c]Based on a sample of 7,172 child maltreatment investigations in 2003.

Service Response to Primary Neglect: 1993 to 2003

Table 3 presents data comparing the child welfare system's response to substantiated cases of primary neglect between the three cycles of the OIS, including use of court applications, formal child welfare placement, transfer to ongoing child protection services, and any referrals for supportive services. While the number and incidence of cases with court applications increased with each cycle of the OIS, this increase was not statistically significant when controlling for increases in Ontario's child population. However, data indicate a substantial decrease in the rate (proportion) of primary neglect investigations resulting in an application to child welfare court—from 23% of cases in 1993 to 11% of cases in 2003, a decrease of 51% over the 10-year period.

Similarly, while the number of children placed increased with each cycle of the OIS, this increase in child placements was not statistically significant when controlling for the increases in Ontario's child population. However, as a system response to primary neglect, the rate of child welfare placement for children in substantiated cases of primary neglect decreased substantially over the 10-year period: from 21% of children in substantiated primary neglect investigations in 1993 to 11% of children in substantiated primary neglect investigations in 2003 (a decrease of 47%). This notably lower rate of placement can be attributed to the significant increase in the total number of substantiated

Table 3 *Service Response: Substantiated Cases of Primary Neglect in Ontario, 1993 to 2003*

Year	1993[a]		1998[b]		2003[c]		t-test
Application to child welfare court	814	23%	1,044	13%	1,726	11%	ns
Incidence per 1,000			0.44		0.72		
Child welfare placement	760	21%	1,455	18%	1,747	11%	ns
Incidence per 1,000			0.62		0.73		
Transferred to ongoing child protection services	1,568	44%	4,181	52%	8,360	53%	3.37*
Incidence per 1,000			1.77		3.50		
At least one referral: child or family	565	16%	4,412	55%	7,930	51%	3.21*
Incidence per 1,000			1.87		3.23		

Note: All percentages calculated as a per cent of total substantiated primary neglect investigations for the year: 1993, N = 3,597; 1998, N = 8,054; 2003, N = 15,660.
[a]Based on a sample of 197 substantiated primary neglect investigations in 1993.
[b]Based on a sample of 334 substantiated primary neglect investigations in 1998.
[c]Based on a sample of 833 substantiated investigations in 2003.
*p < .01

primary neglect investigations, the majority of which did not result in a child being placed. Whether these cases driving the increase were, on average, less serious than cases substantiated in prior years remains an area for further study.

Data in Table 3 indicate that both the number and percentage of cases transferred for ongoing services increased significantly between 1993 and 2003. The rate of transfer for ongoing services increased between the OIS–1993 and the OIS–1998 (44% of investigations resulted in a transfer for ongoing services in 1993, compared to 52% in 1998). Although the number and incidence rate for cases transferred for ongoing protection services more than doubled between 1998 and 2003, the percentage of substantiated cases transferred for ongoing services in 2003 (53%) was not substantially different from 1998.

Finally, the number of cases with at least one referral to supportive services increased significantly between 1993 and 2003. Data also illustrate the increased rate of referrals for cases of primary neglect, with only 16% of investigations in 1993 receiving at least one referral, compared to 51% of investigations in 2003. The notably low rate of referral(s) in 1993 should be viewed within the context of the low rate of referral(s) across other maltreatment typologies in the OIS–1993 cycle (a rate of 15% for physical abuse and 12% for sexual abuse). The one exception during this cycle was emotional maltreatment, for which 49% of cases had at least one referral to supportive services outside the child welfare system; it is important to recognize, however, that in 1993, exposure to domestic violence was subsumed under the category of emotional maltreatment. Variations in the data collection instrument for questions related to supportive service referrals between the 1993 and 1998 cycles may account for at least some of the differences noted between 1993 and 1998.

Results: Child Neglect versus Other Maltreatment in the OIS–2003

The following section presents a detailed profile of cases of substantiated primary neglect in 2003, including household characteristics, child functioning concerns, maltreatment characteristics, caregiver risk factors, and the service system's response to these cases, compared to cases of other maltreatment.

Household Characteristics

As indicated in Table 4, workers assessed the housing as "unsafe" significantly more frequently in primary neglect investigations (16%) compared to investigations of other maltreatment (2%). Further, workers identified that a significantly

Table 4 *Household Characteristics, Substantiated Investigations in Ontario in 2003*

Type of Maltreatment	Neglect[a]		Other Maltreatment[b]		Chi-Square
Unsafe housing					
Yes	2,473	16%	594	2%	126.98*
No	12,258	78%	22,047	91%	
Unknown	929	6%	1,606	7%	
Total	15,660	100%	24,247	100%	
Overcrowded housing					
Yes	1,560	10%	1,294	5%	17.42*
No	13,506	86%	22,202	92%	
Unknown	594	4%	751	3%	
Total	15,660	100%	24,247	100%	
Housing status					
Own home	3,750	24%	9,980	41%	104.54*
Rental	7,809	50%	8,570	35%	
Public housing	2,477	16%	1,992	8%	
Shelter	125	1%	345	1%	
Other	392	3%	762	3%	
Unknown	1,107	7%	2,598	11%	
Total	15,660	100%	24,247	100%	
Household structure					
Two biological parents	4,600	29%	8,275	34%	ns
Two-parent blended / step	2,312	15%	3,712	15%	
Biological parent & other	673	4%	965	4%	
Lone mother	6,600	42%	8,786	36%	
Lone father	639	4%	1,187	5%	
Other	836	5%	1,322	5%	
Total	15,660	100%	24,247	100%	
Number of children in household under 20 years					
One	3,626	23%	5,653	23%	28.63*
Two	5,545	35%	9,395	39%	
Three	3,174	20%	5,953	25%	
Four or more	3,315	21%	3,246	13%	
Total	15,660	100%	24,247	100%	

[a]Based on a sample of 833 substantiated primary neglect investigations.
[b]Based on a sample of 1,290 substantiated investigations of "other maltreatment" (excludes exposure to domestic violence).
*$p < .001$

greater percentage of children who were the subjects of substantiated primary neglect investigations lived in "overcrowded" housing (10%) compared to children in cases where another form of maltreatment was the primary reason for substantiation (5%).

Significantly fewer primary neglect investigations involved families living in homes that they owned (24%) compared to investigations where another form of maltreatment was predominant (41%). Additionally, significantly more investigations of primary neglect involved families living in public housing (16%) compared to investigations of other maltreatment (8%).

Analysis of the six different household structures outlined in Table 4 revealed no significant differences between cases of primary neglect and other maltreatment. However, when household structure is collapsed into a dichotomous category ("lone mother," yes/no), there is significantly higher proportion of investigations of primary neglect involving children living in single, female-led households (42%) compared to investigations of other maltreatment (36%).

A significantly higher number of children in cases of primary neglect are living in households with four or more children (21%) compared to children in cases where another form of maltreatment in the predominant reason for substantiation (13%). Additionally, the average number of children in households where neglect is the primary reason for substantiation is higher than the average number of children living in households where another form of maltreatment is primary ($M = 2.45$ vs 2.34). Of note, households where neglect is a concern also have, on average, significantly more children in residence compared to the Ontario average of 1.2 children per household (Statistics Canada, 2006a).

Child Functioning Concerns

The OIS–2003 collected data on several child functioning concerns, and these are listed in Table 5. As this table illustrates, workers noted a significantly higher rate of concerns regarding alcohol and drug/solvent abuse, *Youth Criminal Justice Act* involvement, inappropriate sexual behaviour, physical disabilities, running, and other health conditions, for neglected children compared to children who experienced another primary form of maltreatment.

For children in cases of primary neglect, workers also noted functioning concerns that impact education and learning (i.e., learning disabilities, the need for special education services, irregular school attendance, and developmental delay) at a significantly higher rate compared to children where another form of maltreatment was the primary reason for substantiation. Overall, analysis reveals that in each functioning domain covered by the OIS, workers noted concerns for neglected children at a rate equal to or greater than that for children in cases of other maltreatment; notable exceptions were depression/anxiety and other behavioural/emotional concerns, where the rate of concerns noted by workers was significantly higher for cases of other maltreatment.

Table 5 *Child Functioning Concerns, Substantiated Investigations in Ontario in 2003*

Maltreatment Type	Neglect[a]		Maltreatment[b]		Chi-Square
Depression / anxiety	2,136	14%	5,313	22%	22.79***
ADD / ADHD	2,255	14%	3,486	14%	ns
Negative peer involvement	2,752	18%	4,090	17%	ns
Alcohol abuse	749	5%	734	3%	4.47*
Drug / solvent abuse	961	6%	892	4%	7.07**
Self-harming behaviour	723	5%	1,103	5%	ns
Violence towards others	2,037	13%	3,312	14%	ns
Inappropriate sexual behaviour	1,060	7%	1,013	4%	6.63*
Other behavioural / emotional difficulties	3,829	24%	7,566	31%	11.3**
Learning disability	3,204	20%	3,998	16%	5.2*
Special education services	2,554	16%	2,970	12%	7.06*
Irregular school attendance	2,895	18%	2,118	9%	43.56
Developmental delay	1,940	12%	1,892	8%	11.99**
Physical disability	454	3%	151	1%	17.42***
Substance-abuse-related birth defects	209	1%	197	1%	ns
Positive toxicology at birth	145	1%	0	–	–
Other health conditions	1,336	9%	807	3%	26.83***
Psychiatric disorder	728	5%	954	4%	ns
YCJA involvement	588	4%	439	2%	7.67**
Running (one and multiple incidents)	1,394	9%	1,515	6%	5.07*

Note: All perentages calculated as a per cent of total substantiated investigations in 2003, $N = 15,660$.
[a]Based on a sample of 833 substantiated primary neglect investigations.
[b]Based on a sample of 1,290 substantiated investigations of "other maltreatment" (excludes exposure to domestic violence).
*$p < .05$
**$p < .01$
***$p < .001$

Maltreatment and Case Characteristics

Table 6 presents the maltreatment and case characteristics for substantiated cases of primary neglect compared to cases where another maltreatment typology was predominant, including measures of severity (physical harm and emotional harm), duration, and chronicity (number of previous openings) for the maltreatment. Workers noted a significantly lower rate of emotional harm for cases of primary neglect compared to cases where another form of maltreatment was the primary reason for substantiation (17% of neglect cases compared to 22% of other maltreatment cases). Further, workers were also significantly less likely to assess the emotional harm as serious enough to require therapeutic treatment in cases of neglect (16% of cases of neglect cases compared to 21% of cases of other maltreatment).

Table 6 *Maltreatment and Case Characteristics, Substantiated Investigations in Ontario in 2003*

Type of Maltreatment	Neglect		Other Maltreatment		Chi-Square
Harm					
Signs of emotional harm[a]	2,653	17%	5,379	22%	8.82**
Requiring therapy/treatment	2,531	16%	5,002	21%	8.99*
Physical harm[b]	1,214	8%	3,607	15%	23.94***
Requiring medical treatment	787	5%	544	2%	12.2***
Duration of maltreatment[c]					
< 6 months	7,617	49%	12,653	53%	15.29***
> 6 months	4,715	30%	8,073	34%	
Unknown	3,127	20%	3,314	14%	
Total	15,458	100%	24,040	100%	
Previous openings[d]					
Never	4,875	31%	10,299	43%	49.97***
1 time	2,850	18%	4,853	20%	
2–3 times	3,529	23%	4,802	20%	
> 3 times	4,235	27%	3,906	16%	
Unknown	171	1%	352	1%	
Total	15,660	100%	24,212	100%	

[a]Based on a sample of 2,122 substantiated child maltreatment investigations with information about emotional harm and treatment.
[b]Based on a sample of 2,122 substantiated child maltreatment investigations with information about physical harm and treatment.
[c]Based on a sample of 2,101 substantiated child maltreatment investigations with information about duration.
[d]Based on a sample of 2,121 substantiated child maltreatment investigations with information about previous family openings.
*p <.05
**p < .01
***p < .001

Findings are different for physical harm. Although the rate of noted physical harm is significantly lower for cases of primary neglect (8%) compared to cases of other maltreatment, the proportion of cases that require medical treatment is substantially higher for cases of primary neglect (5% of all neglect cases, or 65% of neglect cases in which physical harm was noted) compared to cases of other maltreatment (2% of all other maltreatment cases, or 15% of the other maltreatment cases in which physical harm was noted).

Workers were somewhat more likely to indicate that, in their assessment, the maltreatment had been occurring for less than six months in investigations of primary neglect (49%) compared to investigations for other maltreatment (53%). However, cases of neglect had a significantly higher number of previous openings than investigations for other types of maltreatment, with over one-quarter (27%) of neglect cases having been referred more than three times prior to the current investigation, compared to 16% of cases where another form of maltreatment was predominant.

Caregiver Risk Factors

Table 7 presents the rate of caregiver risk factors at the household level (i.e., one or more caregivers in the household present with the specific risk factor) for cases of neglect compared to other maltreatment. Investigations for primary neglect had significantly higher rates of caregiver alcohol abuse, drug/solvent abuse, cognitive impairment, and/or physical health problems, compared to investigations in which another form of maltreatment was predominant. Further, neglectful households were substantially more likely to have at least one caregiver assessed as having "few social supports" compared to households where another form of maltreatment was the primary reason for substantiation.

Table 7 *Caregiver Risk Factors at the Household Level, Substantiated Investigations in Ontario in 2003*

Maltreatment Type	Neglect[a]		Other Maltreatment[b]		Chi-Square
Alcohol problem	3,485	22%	4,211	17%	7.64**
Drug / solvent problem	3,196	20%	2,513	10%	41.43***
Criminal activity	1,838	12%	2,294	9%	ns
Cognitive impairment	2,058	13%	1,254	5%	42.39***
Mental health issues	4,601	29%	6,828	28%	ns
Physical health issues	2,619	17%	2,442	10%	19.98***
Few social supports	7,487	48%	7,966	33%	47.43***
Maltreated as child	4,274	27%	5,956	25%	ns
Victim of domestic violence	4,347	28%	8,452	35%	11.89**
Perpetrator of domestic violence	1,424	9%	4,653	19%	39.94***

Note: All percentages calculated as a per cent of total substantiated investigations in 2003, $N = 15,660$.
[a]Based on a sample of 833 substantiated primary neglect investigations.
[b]Based on a sample of 1,290 substantiated investigations of "other maltreatment" (excludes exposure to domestic violence).
*$p < .05$
**$p < .01$
***$p < .001$

Service Response

Table 8 presents the response of the child welfare system to cases of substantiated primary neglect compared to cases of other maltreatment. Examination of service decisions and short-term service outcomes reveals several statistically significant differences between these two categories of cases. First, workers are more likely to make an application to child welfare court in cases of primary neglect (11% of cases) compared to cases of other maltreatment (5% of cases). Second, placement rates for children in cases of neglect are also significantly higher (11%) compared to children in cases of other maltreatment (5%). Third, cases of neglect are significantly more likely to remain open for ongoing child protection services (53% of cases) compared to cases of other maltreatment (35% of cases). Finally, while just over half (51%) of all cases involving primary neglect are provided with at least one referral to supportive services outside child welfare, 57% of other maltreatment cases receive at least one referral by the conclusion of the investigation.

Table 8 *Service Response, Substantiated Investigations in Ontario in 2003*

Maltreatment Type	Neglect[a]		Other Maltreatment[b]		Chi-Square
Application to child welfare court	1,726	11%	1,243	5%	25.36**
Incidence per 1,000	0.72		0.53		
Placement	1,747	11%	1,283	5%	24.92**
Incidence per 1,000	0.73		0.53		
Transferred to ongoing child protection services	8,360	53%	8,606	35%	66.9**
Incidence per 1,000	3.50		3.60		
At least one referral: child or family	7,930	51%	13,913	57%	9.18*
Incidence per 1,000	3.23		4.32		

Note: All percentages calculated as a per cent of total substantiated investigations in 2003, N = 15,660.
[a]Based on a sample of 833 substantiated primary neglect investigations.
[b]Based on a sample of 1,290 substantiated "other maltreatment" investigations (excludes exposure to domestic violence).
*$p < .01$
**$p < .001$

Discussion and Conclusion

Limitations to the data that pertain to cases not included in the OIS data sets (i.e., screened-out cases, non-referred cases, new investigations on open cases, and investigations conducted only by the police) were earlier noted. There are also additional cautions. First, the data collection form is completed at the conclusion of the investigation, and the data usually reflects the worker's knowledge and assessment of a case approximately 30 days following the initial referral. As a result, certain child and caregiver functioning issues, risk factors, or household characteristics may not be known at the time of completion of the data collection instrument. In addition, a comprehensive service plan may not be complete, resulting in an underestimation of services offered to cases. Finally, as the OIS does not follow cases throughout their involvement with child protection services and beyond, longer term child welfare decision-making and child and family outcomes are not known. Nevertheless, the extent of comparative data collected on neglect at three different time periods permits a number of important observations.

A particularly important limitation of the current study also bears mentioning. Previous research has clearly demonstrated the strong correlation between poverty and neglect (Lindsey, 1994; Pelton, 1989; Wolock & Horowitz, 1979), with Wolock and Horowitz's 1979 study showing that neglect occurs most often among the "poorest of the poor" (p. 186). Although many writers have pointed out that not all poor parents neglect or maltreat their children, there is general consensus that poverty has a deleterious effect on families, making neglect more likely. While the OIS does collect data regarding household income, the high number of cases with missing data for this variable made its inclusion in the current study inappropriate. Results regarding home ownership, number of children in the family, and single female-led households may be proxy indicators of the relationship between poverty and neglect. The importance of gathering complete and accurate data regarding variables such as income cannot be overstated. Such information can serve as a powerful tool to highlight the shared experience of poverty that exists for an overwhelming number of child welfare service recipients, and can help to flesh out our understanding of root causes of neglect that go beyond individual parental risk factors.

Previous research into the child welfare system's response to cases of child neglect has raised concerns about the relatively low priority attached to this particularly harmful maltreatment typology. These prior findings, combined with the large body of literature that documents the negative outcomes for neglected children, even when compared to other maltreated children, is of particular concern. Moreover, the relative dearth of evidence-based practice research into effective interventions for neglect makes the plight of neglected children particularly troubling, and the job of child protection workers working with families where neglect is a concern especially difficult.

In 2000, the government of Ontario took a significant step toward reinforcing an emphasis on neglect in provincial child protection legislation. The documented increase in the number of neglect investigations that took place between 1998 and 2003 was an intended consequence of the changes made to the *Child and Family Services Act* that explicitly referenced a pattern of neglect as grounds for intervention. However, it should be noted that the more significant increase in both investigated and substantiated neglect took place between the 1993 and 1998 cycles even before these changes were enacted, suggesting that prior to the passing of the new legislation, public and professional behaviour had already changed. Elsewhere, Trocmé, Fallon, MacLaurin, and Neves (2005) have attributed this increased awareness, in part, to the series of high-profile inquests into the deaths of children known to Ontario children's aid societies in the mid-1990s, in which neglect was deemed a factor. They also note the influence of the field's adoption of the *Eligibility Spectrum*, a tool designed to standardize decision-making regarding eligibility for service, which included an entire section dedicated to neglect. Finally, changes to child protection standards in the province, requiring workers to investigate all children in families referred to the province's children's aid societies regardless of whether the child was the subject of the referral, accounts for some of the increase in neglect investigations between 1998 and 2003.

In and of itself, an increase in referrals and substantiated investigations does not translate into children receiving more or better service. This study has demonstrated that the way in which the child protection system responded to cases of neglect between 1993 and 2003 shifted over the course of 10 years: the rate of applications to child welfare court and the proportion of neglect investigations resulting in child placement decreased substantially, suggesting a less intrusive approach to the vast majority of neglect investigations by 2003. At the same time, the percentage of cases remaining open for ongoing service, and in receipt of referrals for supportive services outside child welfare, increased, suggesting a longer-term commitment to these families involving a more multi-sectoral response. This approach is supported by several writers who argue that, due to the often chronic nature of neglect, and the multiple problems usually faced by these families, caregivers and children of neglectful families require a sustained intervention with a wide range of services (Gaudin, 1993; Mayer, Lavergne, Tourigny, & Wright, 2007; DePanfilis, 2006). The extent to which this more sustained, interdisciplinary approach might have resulted in a reduction in the proportion of investigations with multiple prior referrals remains an area for further study.

Although the data demonstrates that between 1993 and 2003, the *response* of Ontario's child welfare system to primary neglect investigations became less intrusive, analysis of the most recent data (2003) suggests that cases of neglect at that time were receiving a *service response* that was both more intrusive (evidenced by significantly higher rates of court applications and child placement) and longer term (evidenced by the significantly higher rate of transfer to ongoing protection services) when compared to investigations in which another form of maltreatment was predominant. The finding that neglect investigations result in a higher rate of placement than other forms of maltreatment is consistent with previous research (English, Thompson, et al., 2005), and this more intrusive approach may be in response to the significantly higher rates of poor housing conditions, child functioning concerns, and caregiver risk factors such as alcohol and drug use, cognitive impairment, and physical health problems compared to cases of abuse. These factors, coupled with the greater likelihood of harm requiring medical treatment in cases of neglect, paint a picture of a particularly high risk group of children and caregivers—a client group that, based on the high rate of multiple previous openings for these families, presents particular service challenges for the child welfare system.

Findings from the current study have also highlighted the fact that neglected children experience functioning concerns that impact education and learning (e.g., irregular school attendance, learning disabilities, the need for special educational services, developmental delay, and ADD/ADHD) at higher rates than other maltreated children. As a result, it is especially important for child welfare workers, where appropriate, to engage school personnel in assessment and treatment planning for children known to child protection services for reasons of neglect, whether these children are in care or living at home.

In addition to engaging the school system, results of the current study indicate that almost half of neglected families have few social supports, a significantly higher proportion than families in which another form of maltreatment has occurred. This finding points to the need to engage families within their neighbourhoods and communities, and to develop and implement interventions that not only address individual parental deficits in caregiving, but also strengthen community supports, both formal and informal, in high-risk neighbourhoods.

One finding from this study that merits further investigation is the rate of referrals for supportive services outside of the child welfare system. Despite the multi-problem nature of many neglectful families, and the almost unanimous assertion in the practice literature that child protection services alone cannot address the multiple needs of these families, almost half of substantiated cases do not receive any referrals for supportive services at the conclusion of the investigation (compared to just over one-third of other maltreatment cases). This may simply be a limitation of the OIS data in that it reflects short-term service outcomes only, and, as such, may underestimate the extent to which these cases are ultimately referred for supportive services once a comprehensive assessment and service plan has been developed. On the other hand, it may reflect a lack of appropriate community services for these families, or an insufficiency of worker training and knowledge about intervention for neglectful families. This remains a question for further research and focus.

3

Factors Associated with the Decision to Provide Ongoing Services: Are Worker Characteristics and Organizational Location Important?

Barbara Fallon
Nico Trocmé

October, 1998—Concerned neighbours refer two children to two child protection agencies in Canada for reported neglect. One child is referred to a large child protection agency in a metropolitan area, the other to a small rural agency. The characteristics of the cases are remarkably similar. Both involve a six-year-old child left by herself for the afternoon by a mother on social assistance. No physical harm is noted for either child, but the workers suspect that this is not the first time the child has been left alone, and worry that there has been emotional harm caused by the mother's behaviour. Both mothers are isolated from their communities, abuse alcohol, and are suspected to have mental health problems. Although the clinical concerns for the cases are comparable, the investigating workers possess different traits. The worker in the rural agency has a master's degree in social work, but has practised in child welfare for only six months. This worker has both intake responsibilities and open family service files, and her caseload can be as high as 10 files. The worker in the metropolitan site has only intake responsibilities, conducting investigations about alleged or suspected maltreatment made to her agency about children in the community. Her caseload can reach upwards of 30 open files. She has been employed as a child protection worker for 10 years and has a community college degree in social services. She has been the recipient of many trainings specializing in different aspects and typologies of child maltreatment. The rural agency recently experienced a very high-profile case that received intense media coverage, critiquing the agency's practice, and it has contributed to low agency morale. The metropolitan agency has not experienced any media coverage or high-profile cases, and maintaining its good morale is one of the focuses of monthly management meetings. Both agencies have difficulty recruiting qualified workers.

One would expect the decisions made concerning the two children in question should be similar given the clinical concerns presented. However, both the theoretical organizational literature and the child welfare literature make assumptions that services clients receive from child welfare organizations can vary, not because of the severity of the case, but because of the characteristics of the organization, the worker involved, and the availability of resources.

The purpose of this study is to examine the relative importance of clinical factors, worker characteristics, and organizational location to the decision to provide ongoing services at the conclusion of a child maltreatment investigation. Any child welfare service worker, administrator, or policy analyst would argue that despite the differing characteristics of workers and agencies responsible for child maltreatment assessments, the decision to provide child welfare services should be driven by the clinical concerns of the case. However, many critics of the child welfare system—and less explicitly many researchers—assume that decisions are inordinately driven by organizational and worker characteristics rather than clinical concerns. This study challenges that assumption.

Literature Review

The literature describes a number of biases that may influence both which families and children are reported to a child welfare service, and the decisions made after a maltreatment investigation has taken place. Several studies have noted that child welfare clients are overrepresented in the system by women, the poor, and ethnic and racial minorities (Besharov & Laumann, 1997; Pecora, 1991; Pelton, 1989; Sedlak, 1991; Trocmé et al., 2001). Most of the documented cases of substantiated neglect involve lone-mother households (Sedlak, 1991; Trocmé et al., 2001). Drake and Zuravin (1998), in a review of the empirical literature concerning the relationship between poverty and child maltreatment, found that there was little basis to conclude that the overrepresentation of the poor was the result of bias. The exact nature of the reason for the overrepresentation of families who live in poverty and visible minorities in the child welfare system is difficult to dissect. Income is rarely controlled for in any analyses of child welfare decisions. Hence, whether there are systematic biases at work, or whether these groups actually are more likely to experience conditions that result in a referral to a child welfare system, is still the subject of debate.

Other factors may also be considered as potential causes of bias in the delivery of child welfare services. Organizations and workers which deliver child welfare services possess diverse characteristics. Although it is assumed that characteristics of organizations and workers influence service decisions, there is little if any evidence in the literature that the structure of an organization and its human resources can be manipulated to produce a desired change in a client. An important question remains unaddressed in the field of child welfare: To what extent do the characteristics of child welfare organizations and their workers impact the decision to provide services?

Child protection workers are a major focus in the child welfare literature. There is, however, limited evidence that workers with different experience levels, education, training, and ethnicity make disparate service decisions. There are several common measurement issues related to the child welfare worker literature reviewed. First, the few studies that have addressed the success and failure of child welfare interventions have not succeeded in evaluating and isolating which specific worker variables have contributed to those outcomes (Grasso & Epstein, 1988; Hoagwood, 1997; Yoo, 2002). Second, the child welfare literature generally does not include organizational variables as independent measures, although there is a substantial body of literature that addresses the importance of organizational characteristics in child welfare services as an outcome or dependent variable. The characteristics of a worker and/or organization are conceptualized in the literature as an end in themselves (e.g., worker burnout or stress) without considering their relationship to services or client outcomes. Finally, the child welfare organizational literature is characterized by a lack of theoretical delineation and therefore clarity (Drasgow & Schmitt, 2002). There is a fundamental failure to explain why certain variables are considered important enough to be the focus of the research.

Several studies examine the presumed influence of worker ethnicity and related variables to the service outcomes experienced by clients. Worker ethnicity and education (Ryan, Garnier, Zyphur, & Zhai, 2006), ethnicity and gender (Woldeguiorguis, 2003), ethnicity and political ideology (Jayaratne, Faller, Ortega, & Vandervort, 2008), and age and ethnicity (Surbeck, 2003) are theorized as influential to the services received by a family in the child welfare system. In one of the few multivariate analyses examining client outcomes that included worker characteristics, Ryan and colleagues (Ryan et al., 2006) examined the role of worker turnover, racial match between worker and client, and a graduate degree on family reunification and the length of stay in care. While controlling for the clinical concerns of the case, the study found that White workers with an MSW degree were more likely to achieve family reunification for Hispanic children than African-American caseworkers. Jayaratne et al. (2008) found African-American caseworkers more likely than White workers to consider race in both general and placement decisions, and agreed more often with placing children in single parent families.

There is some evidence that education type can influence worker decisions. Britner and Mossler (2002) found that workers from various professions placed different levels of importance on information in cases of physical abuse when deciding whether a child should remain in the home or be placed in foster care. Kominkiewicz (2004) found that workers with a degree in psychology were more likely to identify siblings of the identified child as victims of maltreatment than social workers.

The decision to provide ongoing services after a child maltreatment investigation has serious resource implications. In a fiscally constrained child welfare service environment, decisions regarding which families and children receive scarce services needs to be understood. Studies that have examined decisions to provide ongoing services have overlooked some key clinical factors associated with maltreatment; in particular, the failure to account for the severity of physical and emotional harm to the child (Inkelas & Halfon, 1997; Zuravin, Orme, & Hegar, 1995). Generally, substantiation is highly correlated with the decision to provide ongoing services (DePanfilis & Zuravin, 1999; Freeman, Levine, & Doueck, 1996; Winefield & Bradley, 1992). However, DePanfilis and Zuravin (2001) found that families with a previous substantiated report were 22 per cent less likely to receive ongoing services than families with no previous substantiated maltreatment. This finding indicates that workers may pay attention to factors other than relevant clinical ones.

Referrals made by a professional and prior case opening were a predictor of case opening (Rossi, Schuerman, & Budde, 1999; Zuravin et al., 1995). Non-compliance or a lack of co-operation from the caregivers was associated more with the decision to open the case than to close it (Wolock, 1982). Other predictor variables which have been found to be associated with the decision to provide ongoing services include: type and severity of maltreatment; childhood history of abuse or neglect by a parent; mother's age; the number of children in the home; caregiver impairments; and level of social support (DePanfilis & Zuravin, 2001; English, Marshall, Brummel, & Orme, 1999).

There is evidence in the literature that suggests that intervention standards vary by neighbourhood (Giovannoni & Becerra, 1979; Johnson & L'Esperance, 1984; Wolock, 1982). Social workers rating a vignette were significantly more likely to make a decision to refer a case for ongoing services with limited information in high- and low-risk areas than in medium-risk areas (Craft & Bettin,

1991). Agencies located in high-risk areas were less likely to open an investigation with the same clinical issues than agencies in lower risk areas (Giovannoni & Becerra, 1979).

Few studies are able to empirically account for organizational factors, even when examining service decisions (Hoagwood, 1997; Grasso & Epstein, 1988; Yoo, 2002). Organizations serve diverse populations, but studies that examine differences in worker and organizational characteristics have not controlled for differences in the population served. Relevant clinical factors are rarely taken into consideration. Dissimilarities in clinical factors may explain divergent case dispositions for different groups. The following study will explore the influence of organizational location and worker characteristics to the decision to provide ongoing services by controlling for clinical severity.

Methodology

Data Collection

This study is based on a secondary analysis of data collected in the *Canadian Incidence Study of Reported Child Abuse and Neglect, 1998* (CIS–1998) (Trocmé et al., 2001). Data were collected directly from child protection workers about child welfare investigations, using a three-page data collection instrument and spanning a three-month case selection period from October 1, 1998, to December 31, 1998. The CIS–1998 study collected information about the participating child welfare workers using a Worker Information Form. Workers were asked their age, caseload size, position, educational degree, and years of experience in social services and child protection. They were also asked what additional training they had received in the course of their child protection experience. Information about organizational size and location was collected for the 55 participating sites. Forty sites completed an organizational questionnaire that included questions about the structure of the organization, organizational morale, staffing vacancies, and whether the organization had recently experienced a death or high-profile case. For more information on the CIS methodology, please see Chapter 1.

Study Sample

Since one of the objectives of this study was to examine the contribution of worker characteristics to the decision to provide ongoing services, only those child maltreatment investigations from the CIS–1998 sample in which the worker had completed a Worker Information Form were selected. In Quebec,

Table 1 *Agency Characteristics (N = 47) and Number of Investigations (N = 4,787)*

Characteristic	Agencies		Investigations	
	N	%	N	%
Metropolitan	10	21	2,023	42
Urban–rural mix	15	32	1,869	39
Rural	22	47	895	19
Total	47	100	4,787	100

the CIS–1998 design and survey instrument was modified to address a broader set of research questions. Workers were not asked to complete a Worker Information Form. In the rest of Canada, 574 workers were asked to complete a Worker Information Form, and 496 responded. These 496 investigating workers yielded a final sample of 4,787 child maltreatment investigations and 47 child welfare agencies. Workers indicated whether the family would receive ongoing child welfare services at the conclusion of the investigation. Thirty-three per cent of investigations (n=1,549) received ongoing services.

The 47 agencies with information about the characteristics of the investigating workers were divided into metropolitan, mixed urban–rural, and rural agencies. Forty-two per cent of investigations were from metropolitan agencies, 39% of investigations were from mixed urban–rural agencies, and 19% of investigations were from rural agencies (see Table 1). Other organizational variables that could potentially explain some of the variance in short-term service dispositions, such as resource availability, were not measured in this data set.

Analytic Strategy

The selected analysis developed separate logistic regression models for the agency location variable because it had a significant interaction with predictor variables. Although entering agency level variables into the models directly would have produced fewer models and a more streamlined analysis, the decision to develop separate models depending on the agency's location was a result of a thorough exploration of the appropriate statistical technique for analysis of the CIS–1998 data set.

First, bivariate analyses were conducted between agency location and the decision to provide ongoing services in order to test the assumption that the decision to provide ongoing services varies by agency location. Tests of significance reveal associations between location of agency (χ^2=97.30, p<.001). Based on these findings, bivariate analyses were conducted between the dependent variable (opened / not opened for ongoing services), clinically relevant variables (chosen because they represent the factors most understood in the literature to be related to child maltreatment or risk of child maltreatment), and variables that might influence the disposition but were deemed to be extraneous to the clinical assessment of a child maltreatment investigation: referral source, ethnicity, and worker level variables. The results determined the variables that were entered into the main effects logistic regression model.

In order to assess whether the decision to provide ongoing services varies because different types of agencies are serving varied families and children, agency location was tested for its interaction with all other variables in the model to determine whether associations between the dependent variable and the predictor variables were moderated by the agency's location. Models were constructed taking statistically significant moderators into account.

Variables were entered into the regression in theoretically related blocks. Statistically significant clinical variables were included in the multivariate models in order to determine the relative contribution of clinical variables and variables that, in principle, should be extraneous to the case disposition—specifically, worker and organizational variables. The first block of clinical variables entered into the models were: type of maltreatment, whether or not the child had been physically or emotionally harmed, and the number of child functioning concerns noted for the child during the investigation. The second block of clinical variables was related to the family: how many times the family had moved in the past year; income source; the number of caregiver functioning concerns noted for the caregiver(s); and level of co-operation with the investigation. Referral source and ethnicity were chosen because of their importance in the case disposition literature. In theory, these variables should be extraneous to the clinical dispositions of the worker. Worker and organizational variables were chosen to reflect those variables that had been theorized in literature as having an influence on services provided to children and families by child welfare agencies. After each block of variables was entered, the change in Nagelkerke's R-square was noted in order to assess the amount of variance explained by the clinical concerns of the cases versus the amount explained by worker variables. Nagelkerke's R-square is a measure of the strength of association to the dependent variable.

Results

Bivariate Analyses

The decision to provide ongoing services varied by the agency's location. Metropolitan agencies provided ongoing services to the lowest proportion of cases

(27%), mixed urban-rural agencies provided ongoing services in 33% of cases, and rural agencies provided ongoing services in 45% of cases.

Provision of ongoing child welfare services varied depending on the primary maltreatment investigated. Emotional maltreatment had the highest rate of opening of the four typologies of maltreatment (39% of investigations). Children who were physically harmed had a significantly higher rate of opening (47%) than children who were not physically harmed (31%). Children who were emotionally harmed had the highest rate of opening of any noted clinical concern. Fifty-nine per cent of investigations that documented emotional harm were opened for ongoing service provision. Investigations that noted a previous child welfare opening for the child had a higher rate of ongoing service provision (39%) than those with no previous opening (27%).

Cases where household income was obtained from part-time employment or income benefits had a considerably higher rate of opening (45% and 36%) than households where at least one parent was fully employed (24%). Half of the investigations with families who had experienced two or more moves received ongoing child welfare services. The more caregiver concerns that were noted for the household at the conclusion of the investigation, the higher the rate of ongoing service provision. Just under half of the investigations with caregivers who were deemed unco-operative (47%) were opened for ongoing service provision, versus 32% of investigations with co-operative caregivers. Investigations with at least one Aboriginal caregiver in the household had an ongoing service provision rate of 47%. There was no difference in ongoing service provision between those investigations that were referred by a professional and those that were referred by a relative, neighbour, or friend.

As indicated in Table 2, investigations involving workers who had a generic caseload designation had a significantly higher rate of provision of ongoing services (46%) than investigations conducted by workers with only intake responsibilities (29%). Investigations by workers with either a BSW or MSW had a lower rate of ongoing service provision (31%) than those investigations conducted by workers who were not social workers (38%), and this difference was statistically significant. As shown in Table 3, there was a statistically significant difference in the mean caseload of workers conducting investigations that were not opened for ongoing child welfare services (M=19.8) compared to caseloads for workers conducting investigations opened for ongoing service provision (M=22.0).

Table 2 *Worker Characteristics of Investigations (%) by Provision of Ongoing Services*

Worker Characteristics	Ongoing Services	χ^2
Worker position		188.56***
Intake caseload (N = 3,124)	29	
Generic caseload (N = 1,625)	46	
Degree		
No social work degree (N = 1,177)	38	20.52***
Social work degree (N = 3,574)	31	

***p < .001

Table 3 *Differences between Worker Characteristics of Investigations Opened and Not Opened for Ongoing Services Provision*

	Not Opened		Opened			
Worker Characteristics	M	SD	M	SD	df	t
Caseload size	19.83	10.71	21.99	11.32	2742.711	−6.023***
Years of experience	5.71	5.67	5.38	5.38	4647	1.879
Worker training	5.94	2.73	6.00	2.78	4756	−0.727

***p < .001

Multivariate Analysis

Previous openings and social work degree were not related to ongoing service provision in the main effect model and were therefore excluded from the interaction model. One interaction was statistically significant for agency location: child functioning concerns and rural agencies (β=2.15, SE=.65, OR=8.55, p<.001). Based on a conservative alpha level of <.001, investigations from rural agencies were different in the number of child functioning concerns noted from investigations in metropolitan or mixed urban agencies.

Agency Location and Provision of Ongoing Services

Predictors of the decision to provide ongoing services varied depending on the location of the investigating agency. Child level and family level concerns described all of the explained variance (27%) in the decision to provide ongoing services for investigations from metropolitan sites (Nagelkerke R^2=.27) (see Appendix A). Ethnicity and the characteristics of the worker conducting the investigation were not significant in the overall model.

In contrast, caseload size and worker position described an additional six per cent of the explained variance for investigations from mixed urban-rural agencies (see Appendix B). As the caseload size of workers increases in mixed urban-rural agencies, workers are slightly more likely to open a case. Intake workers are less likely to open a case for ongoing services than generalist workers. Thirty-eight per cent of the variance in the decision to provide ongoing services is explained by child level and family level variables in mixed urban-rural sites, compared to 27% in metropolitan sites and 24% in rural agencies. In rural agencies, worker position explained an additional two per cent of the variance in the decision to provide ongoing service (see Appendix C). Caseload size was a significant predictor.

The clinical concerns of the investigation are the most significant predictors of the decision to provide ongoing services. In each of the three models, the presence of emotional harm meant that a case was more than twice as likely to be transferred for ongoing service as an investigation where there was no emotional harm. Similarly, the presence of physical harm also resulted in an increased likelihood of a transfer to ongoing services. The child's overall level of functioning was also related to the opening decision: for example, in rural agencies, a worker noting two or more functioning concerns for the child was two times more likely to open the case for ongoing services than an investigation which identified no child functioning concerns (see Appendix C). The number of caregiver functioning concerns noted for the investigation was positively and significantly associated with cases opened for ongoing services. In metropolitan agencies, the families who had moved two or more times in the past year were more likely to be the recipients of ongoing services (see Appendix A).

Discussion

The importance of clinical factors to the decision to provide ongoing services is encouraging to the child welfare field, given the assumptions in the literature and in child welfare practice settings that there are strong biases unrelated to clinical concerns associated with maltreatment, influencing which families and children receive child welfare services. Workers are considering the dynamics of child maltreatment, the overall functioning of the child, the influence of caregiver risk factors, and the stability of the household. In each of the models presented, overwhelmingly, the clinical factors associated with the investigation are explaining the decision to provide ongoing services. The analysis does indicate, however, that both the characteristics of the worker and the location of the agency do impact the decision to provide services.

Importance of Clinical Characteristics

Families and children who are highly symptomatic are more likely to be provided with child welfare services. Whether the child has been physically and/or emotionally harmed as a result of the investigated maltreatment is an important consideration in the decision to provide ongoing services. Physical and/or emotional harm can result in high levels of emotional distress, causing delays in development, emotional problems, and behavioural problems in children. Further, the greater number of functioning concerns that the investigating worker noted for the child, the more likely it is that there would be provision of services. Child functioning concerns included behavioural, cognitive, physical and/or emotional problems suspected or confirmed by the investigating worker. The clinical literature has clearly documented that as the number of functioning issues increases, so too does the risk for child maltreatment (Malamuth, Sockloskie, Koss, & Tanaka, 1991). These clinical factors that are associated with the child and the harmful sequelae of child maltreatment consistently explain approximately one-half of the total explained variance in each model examining the decision to provide ongoing services.

Clinical concerns associated with the family are important predictors for the decision to provide ongoing services. Caregivers with multiple functioning concerns are more likely to receive services from the child welfare system. In mixed urban-rural agencies, caregivers with three or more functioning concerns are 11 times more likely to be provided with ongoing services. Again, the relationship between caregiver functioning and maltreatment has been consistently documented in the clinical literature (Belsky, 1984; Culbertson & Schellenbach, 1992). The presence of alcohol, drugs, social isolation, mental health problems, criminal activity, previous caregiver history of maltreatment, and violence between caregivers increases the likelihood for child maltreatment (Belsky, 1984). Multiple functioning concerns also increase the likelihood that families would receive services from the child welfare system. Furthermore, the judgments of child protection workers result in a triage process in which the most symptomatic families and children investigated by the child welfare system are prioritized for services.

Influence of Extraneous Case Variables

Although factors unrelated to the clinical concerns of the investigation were not highly influential to the decision to provide ongoing services, there were instances where they played a statistically significant role in the decision. Households with at least one Aboriginal caregiver that were investigated by rural agencies were overrepresented in the provision of ongoing services (four times more likely to be provided with ongoing services than White caregivers). Although this finding is not the focus of the study, it is nonetheless an important one.

Two explanations are possible. The first is that there are systematic biases at work. Aboriginal households are identified in a prejudicial way by child welfare services. The second possible explanation is that the predictor variables in the model do not explain the reasons why Aboriginal households were overrepresented in the decision to provide ongoing services in rural agencies. For example, rural agencies may have differential access to service resources, or the child welfare agency may be the only alternative to not providing services for high-risk Aboriginal families. An analysis that includes constructs that address the environmental context of the organization would further illuminate this issue.

Intake Specialists versus Generalists

Although caseload size was statistically significant in some models, workers with a larger caseload size were only slightly more likely to open a case for ongoing services. By far the most important worker characteristic identified in the decision to provide ongoing services is the worker's specialization. Investigations conducted by intake workers were less likely to be kept open for ongoing services than investigations conducted by generalists. There is little empirical research about the differences between a specialist model of practice and a generalist model of practice. In a study of occupational therapists and social workers in a mental health setting (n=304) using a self-report measure of work activities, occupational therapists reported more complex clinical activities than did social workers (Lloyd, King, & McKenna, 2004). The authors assume that the outcome of more clinically specialized work is a positive outcome for clients, although this assumption is not measured or tested. The methodology used for the study may, however, be of use in efforts to study whether differences in the decision to provide ongoing child welfare services varies between positions. Are there differences in activities between intake workers and generic workers, despite the highly prescribed risk assessment approach to the investigation of child maltreatment used in most provinces and territories?

Agency Location

In metropolitan agencies, neither years of experience, caseload size, nor level of specialization remained significantly associated with service disposition once child and family characteristics were controlled for. In mixed urban–rural agencies and rural agencies, worker characteristics explain some of the variance in the decision to provide ongoing services. The potential differences in child welfare services depending on the geographic location of the agency are not addressed in the child welfare literature. Location is likely a proxy measure for a number of underlying organizational constructs such as differential access to resources, historical connections between social services, and geographical positioning. Metropolitan agencies may have greater access to services, but these services may be subject to greater demand. The relationship between child welfare and the use of other social service sectors is not a focus of this study, but the greater influence of worker characteristics depending on geographic location requires further investigation.

Limitations

The primary objective of the CIS was to develop reliable estimates of reported child abuse and neglect in Canada in 1998. Although organizational information was collected about the participating child welfare organizations, this was not a primary focus of the study. Therefore, the quality and number of organizational variables associated with this data set are limited. The study's analytical approach of using a series of logistic regression models does not allow for the relative influence of organizational factors to be determined. For example, the likelihood of a child receiving services from a rural agency versus a metropolitan agency with the same clinical concern is not controlled for, as the location of the agency was not directly entered into the model. The analysis is therefore limited to noting differences between organizations concerning the provision of ongoing services based on their characteristics. The models are unable to control for differences in resource availability.

The main methodological limitation of this study is that it can only identify *differences* in the decision to provide ongoing services between intake workers and generalist workers. Which position is making more clinically relevant decisions is an area that should be further explored in future research. Are intake workers more skilled at identifying the clinical concerns of families and children identified to the child welfare system than generalist workers, and are they therefore assigning resources to only the most symptomatic families? Do intake workers and generalist workers perceive the role of the child welfare system differently? What is the role of organizational culture and values in selecting one or the other model of service delivery?

Conclusion

The needs of families and children are the most important considerations in the provision of ongoing services. Clinical characteristics account for most of the explanation concerning the provision of ongoing services. Although few factors extraneous to the clinical concerns of the case influence the decision to provide ongoing services, there is evidence that the characteristics of the worker, namely worker position, can influence the decision to provide ongoing services depending on the geographic location of the agency. Although the statistical models presented in this analysis explain a large degree of the variance in the decision to provide child welfare services, over half of the variance remains unexplained. How much of the influence on the decision to provide an ongoing service is explained by organizational factors should continue to be addressed in the evaluation of child welfare organizational research. Ongoing development of the theoretical, substantive, and methodological literature for child welfare organizations will help to ensure accountability for the families and children served by the child welfare system.

Acknowledgements

Data used in this publication are from the *Canadian Incidence Study of Reported Child Abuse and Neglect*, and are used with the permission of the Public Health Agency of Canada. The study was funded by the federal, provincial, and territorial governments of Canada, and the Bell Canada Child Welfare Research Unit of the University of Toronto.

Appendix A *Logistic Regression Predicting Provision of Ongoing Services from Metropolitan Agencies (N = 1312)*

Predictor	B	SE	Adjusted Odds Ratio
Block 1			
Physical abuse			
Sexual abuse	−0.36	0.3	0.7
Neglect	0.17	0.18	1.18
Emotional maltreatment	0.04	0.2	1.04
Emotional harm	1.09***	0.2	2.97
Physical harm	0.84***	0.22	2.32
No child functioning concerns			
One child functioning concern	0.28	0.19	1.33
Two or more child functioning concerns	0.56**	0.18	1.75
Block 2			
No moves			
One move	0.37*	0.17	1.44
Two or more moves	0.78***	0.24	2.18
Full-time employment			
Part-time employment	0.55*	0.24	1.74
Benefits	0.01	0.16	1.01
No caregiver functioning concerns			
One caregiver functioning concern	0.61**	0.2	1.84
Two caregiver functioning concerns	1.13***	0.21	3.09
Three or more caregiver functioning concerns	1.65***	0.21	5.2
Co-operation with investigation	−0.45*	0.23	0.64
Block 3			
White			
Aboriginal	−0.23	0.24	0.79
Visible minority	0.24	0.17	1.27
Block 4			
Caseload size	0.01	0.01	1.01
Worker position	−0.04	0.37	0.96

	Block 1	Block 2	Block 3	Block 4
-2LL (Constant)-2LL Model	1591.57-1441.49	1591.57-1320.44	1591.57-1317.22	1591.57-1314.45
Model X²	150.08***	271.13***	274.35	277.12
Df	7	15	17	19
Nagelkerke R²	0.15	0.27	0.27	0.27
Correct Classification Rate				73%

*p <.05, **p < .01, ***p < .001

Appendix B *Logistic Regression Predicting Provision of Ongoing Service Provision from Mixed Urban–Rural Agencies (N = 1049)*

Predictor	β	SE	Adjusted Odds Ratio
Block 1			
Physical abuse			
Sexual abuse	−0.19	0.3	0.83
Neglect	0.3	0.21	1.34
Emotional maltreatment	0.67*	0.26	1.95
Emotional harm	1.53***	0.22	4.6
Physical harm	0.84**	0.27	2.32
No child functioning concerns			
One child functioning concern	−0.17	0.23	0.85
Two or more child functioning concerns	0.64**	0.21	1.89
Block 2			
No moves			
One move	0.42**	0.2	1.52
Two or more moves	0	0.3	1
Full-time employment			
Part-time employment	0.69*	0.3	1.99
Benefits	0.52**	0.2	1.69
No caregiver functioning concerns			
One caregiver functioning concern	0.89***	0.26	2.43
Two caregiver functioning concerns	1.62***	0.28	5.04
Three or more caregiver functioning concerns	2.40***	0.27	11.02
Co-operation with investigation	−0.38*	0.29	0.69
Block 3			
White			
Aboriginal	0.24	0.21	1.27
Visible minority	−0.71	0.75	0.49
Block 4			
Caseload size	0.03***	0.01	1.03
Worker position	−1.13***	0.18	0.32

	Block 1	Block 2	Block 3	Block 4
-2LL (Constant)-2LL Model	1333.08-1155.70	1333.08-1000.28	1333.08-993.45	1333.08-929.33
Model X²	177.38***	332.80***	339.63***	403.76***
Df	7	15	17	19
Nagelkerke R²	0.22	0.38	0.38	0.44
Correct Classification Rate				78%

*p < .05, **p < .01, ***p < .001

Appendix C *Logistic Regression Predicting Provision of Ongoing Service Provision from Mixed Urban–Rural Agencies (N = 1049)*

Predictor	β	SE	Adjusted Odds Ratio
Block 1			
Physical abuse			
Sexual abuse	−0.08	0.368	0.92
Neglect	−0.75**	0.252	0.47
Emotional maltreatment	0.22	0.284	1.25
Emotional harm	0.75**	0.254	2.13
Physical harm	0.25	0.327	1.28
No child functioning concerns			
One child functioning concern	0.83**	0.276	2.29
Two or more child functioning concerns	0.70**	0.258	2.01
Block 2			
No moves			
One move	−0.31	0.246	0.73
Two or more moves	0.09	0.347	1.09
Full-time employment			
Part-time employment	0.87**	0.344	2.38
Benefits	0.50*	0.23	1.65
No caregiver functioning concerns			
One caregiver functioning concern	0.91***	0.277	2.49
Two caregiver functioning concerns	0.97**	0.312	2.64
Three or more caregiver functioning concerns	1.20***	0.271	3.31
Co-operation with investigation	−0.25*	0.327	0.78
Block 3			
White			
Aboriginal	1.36***	0.272	3.91
Visible minority	0.37	0.509	1.45
Block 4			
Caseload size	0.01	0.009	1.01
Worker position	−0.72***	0.218	0.49

	Block 1	Block 2	Block 3	Block 4
-2LL (Constant)-2LL Model	826.24-766.23	826.24-709.23	826.235-676.46	826.23-662.40
Model X²	60.00***	117.01***	149.78'***	163.78***
Df	7	15	17	19
Nagelkerke R²	0.13	0.24	0.3	0.32
Correct Classification Rate				69%

*$p < .05$, **$p < .01$, ***$p < .001$

4

Canadian Child Welfare Worker Qualifications
Examining a Changing National Profile

Barbara Fallon
Bruce MacLaurin
Nico Trocmé
Jordan Gail
Carolyn Golden

The dramatic increase in reports of child abuse and neglect to Canadian child welfare authorities between 1998 and 2003 has been well documented by analyses comparing data from two cycles of the *Canadian Incidence Study of Reported Child Abuse and Neglect* (CIS–1998 and CIS–2003) (Trocmé et al., 2001; Trocmé et al., 2005). Reports of alleged maltreatment received by a child welfare agency are investigated by professionals trained to identify child maltreatment and make assessments about appropriate services for children and families. The optimal qualifications, education, and experience of child protection workers have been the subjects of much debate given the increase in service volume, which has also resulted in a high demand for child protection workers. Over the past 20 years of child welfare practice, there is growing concern that child welfare agencies are having difficulty both in attracting qualified staff and retaining experienced child protection workers. Front-line child protection workers are reporting high degrees of stress caused in the performance of their job responsibilities. Burgeoning caseloads, a scarcity of treatment resources, and increased pressure from the tragic outcomes of high-profile cases have created a difficult environment for child protection workers, and much of the focus in the empirical literature (worker stress, worker burnout, lack of available treatment resources) reflects this reality.

The CIS–1998 was the first study in Canada to estimate the incidence of child abuse and neglect reported to and investigated by the Canadian welfare system; in 2003 it was repeated, and the Public Health Agency of Canada is committed to continuing a five-year cycle of data collection. The sampling design for the study was summarized in Chapter 1. The primary focus of the Canadian Incidence Studies is to collect information from child welfare workers about investigated children and their families as they come into contact with child welfare authorities. The CIS also collects information about the workers who conduct child protection investigations. There are no other national sources of information about child welfare workers in Canada. Whereas Chapter 3 examined the influence of location and worker characteristics on short-term service decisions based on data from CIS–1998, this chapter compares the educational credentials, years of experience, age, gender, ethnicity, and average caseload size of workers who participated in the CIS–1998 and in the CIS–2003. The present chapter begins with a brief review of the literature, highlighting some of the emerging findings about the importance of workers as a human resource prior to presenting the profiles of workers participating in the CIS–1998 and the CIS–2003. It also examines the distribution of social work qualifications and child protection experience based on the population density of the child welfare service area across Canada. Potential implications for child welfare services and opportunities for further research are discussed.

Literature Review

Enhanced training is often proposed as a solution to many demands facing public child welfare, although the relationship between training and implementation in practice is unclear (Collins, Amodeo, & Clay, 2007; Curry, McCarragher, & Dellmann-Jenkins, 2005). A few studies have shown that a readiness to learn, managerial support, and knowledge gain are predictive of transfer of training knowledge and skills to practice (Antle, Barbee, & van Zyl, 2008). Similarly, organizational context (motivation, skills, caseloads, supervision, and support) and culture have also been found to influence the training knowledge transfer (Luongo, 2007). While supervisory support may be related to the retention of less experienced workers (Curry et al., 2005), the provision of continual training opportunities has been found to be an important factor in keeping experienced and inexperienced workers at the agency. The existing literature consistently points to the need for a more encompassing and broader view of training that facilitates ongoing development at both the individual and organizational level (Collins et al., 2007; Luongo, 2007).

The size of worker caseloads is hypothesized to be related to worker satisfaction, retention, and turnover. In some studies, caseload size is positively associated with staff retention. One explanation for this finding is the disproportionately higher number of cases assigned to more experienced workers in order to decrease the burden on less experienced workers who are at higher risk of leaving (Curry et al., 2005). While agencies may have little control over caseload size, characteristics such as supervisor support and availability of resources have a direct impact on workload management (Juby & Scannapieco, 2007).

Rural and small offices are described by child welfare workers as considerably more agreeable workplaces than their urban and larger counterparts. Practitioners report remaining in their positions longer, having greater autonomy and decision-making authority, and experiencing greater agency support, fairness, and opportunities for professional growth than practitioners in urban and larger agencies (Landsman, 2002). Landsman also found that workers experienced less demanding workloads and higher job satisfaction, and planned to remain at the agency for longer periods of time. Similar results were documented by Strolin-Goltzman, Auerbach, McGowan, and McCarthy (2008). The authors found that suburban workers were less likely to report an intention to leave the agency than workers in urban and rural agencies.

Several studies address staff retention in child welfare services. The ability to maintain an adequate staffing complement is viewed as a major factor in providing effective and efficient delivery of services (Bednar, 2003; Powell & York, 1992). A study conducted in 43 U.S. states estimated that child protection agencies have an average vacancy rate of 10% and that vacant positions require five to seven weeks to fill (Child Welfare League of America, 2001). By calculating costs related to separation, replacement, and training, Graef and Hill (2000) approximated the financial cost of rapid staff turnover for a child protection agency in a Midwestern state as $10,000 per staff vacancy in 1995. The retention of staff is linked to multiple constructs, including organizational climate, a positive working environment, workplace morale, and occupational commitment (Alwon & Reitz, 2000; Dickinson & Perry, 2002; Landsman, 2001; Mancuso, 1998; Okamura & Jones, 2000; Pecora, Briar, & Zlotnik, 1989).

In a naturalistic study of 18 child welfare workers, Reagh (1994) found that workers were more likely to stay in an environment where they felt rewarded and valued. In a volunteer survey of workers examining the issue of staff retention in the Maine child protection system, four factors were identified as key for retaining staff: clarity of mission, goodness of fit between workers and organization, quality of supervision, and investment in staff (Rycraft, 1994). Confidence in abilities and support of colleagues are also predictors of whether a worker remains at a child welfare organization (Fryer, Miyoshi, & Thomas, 1989; Okamura & Jones, 2000; Samantrai, 1992). Landsman (2001) conducted a survey of a random sample of 990 child protection workers, examining their commitment to their child welfare organizations. He concluded that job stressors, the structural features of the organization, and job satisfaction were highly correlated with the workers' commitment to the organization.

Methodology

The purpose of the CIS was not to provide data about the characteristics of workers across Canada. Nonetheless, the study does provide a unique opportunity to examine a profile of workers who conduct child protection investigations from a nationally representative sample of agencies. Workers who performed child maltreatment investigations at CIS sites from October 1 to December 31, 2003, were eligible for inclusion in the study. For a detailed description of the project's methodology, please see Chapter 1.

Workers participating in the study completed a data collection instrument for each investigation eligible for inclusion in the CIS sample. A Worker Information Form was used to collect information about the worker completing the child maltreatment investigation. The one-page form included information about the worker's role and position, training, and education. Forms were usually completed during the preliminary CIS worker training, prior to the start of the case selection period. If a worker did not complete a Worker Information Form at the training session, the Site Researcher would ask for it to be completed during a subsequent visit to the agency. In both cycles of the CIS, workers who conducted investigations in Quebec did not complete CIS Worker Information Forms. The response rate in regions where the Worker Information Form was used was 85% in 1998 and 87% in 2003. The CIS data set includes the geographic location of the agency in which the investigation originated (rural, mixed urban–rural, or large metropolitan) and the size of agency in which the investigation originated (large, medium, or small).

In order to provide an estimate of the number of workers conducting investigations in the year of the study cycle for Table 1, regional weights were applied to the sample of workers to reflect the relative sizes of the selected sites. Each study site was assigned a weight reflecting the proportion of the child population of the site relative to the region that the site represented. The data presented in Tables 2 to 8 in the chapter are based on (1) a sample of 490 workers who completed child maltreatment assessments and who completed Worker Information Forms in 1998, and (2) 819 workers who completed Worker Information Forms and child maltreatment assessments in 2003.

The mean number of Maltreatment Assessment Forms completed by workers during the CIS–1998 was nine. In the CIS–2003, the mean number of

Figure 1 *Canadian Incidence Study of Reported Child Abuse and Neglect (1998, 2003): Worker Samples*

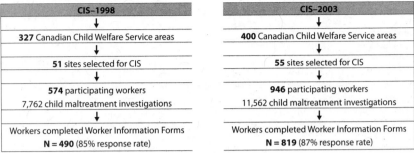

instruments completed by a participating worker was 13. The number of investigations conducted by workers was dependent on the size of the worker caseload, the agency/office caseload, the number of children investigated in one family investigation, and the level of intake activity at the time of the study. Tests of significance were not conducted, as there is no way to control for changes in the number of workers eligible to conduct investigations.

Results

Worker Position

Table 1 presents the number of estimated child maltreatment investigations for which worker information was obtained, including the estimated number of workers who participated in the CIS cycles and their position. The CIS found that outside Quebec, 193,087 child maltreatment investigations were conducted in 2003 by an estimated 2,314 child protection workers. In 1998, 100,740 child maltreatment investigations were conducted by an estimated 2,125 child protection workers.

In 1998, investigations in the CIS were almost evenly divided between intake workers (53% of investigations) and the combined total of generalist workers conducting investigations as well as providing ongoing services and other workers (44% and 3% of investigations, respectively). In 2003, workers with an investigation specialist designation completed 79% of investigations in the CIS, reflecting the widespread adoption by participating agencies of an investigation specialist model. In 1998, workers who participated in the CIS were evenly divided between investigation specialists and generalists or other. In 2003, more workers (57%) with an intake specialist designation participated.

Table 1 *Estimated Number of Investigations by Position of Investigating Worker in Canada, excluding Quebec*

	Investigations[a]				Investigators[b]			
	2003		1998		2003		1998	
Job Position	N	%	N	%	N	%	N	%
Investigation specialists	152,311	79%	53,098	53%	1263	57%	829	52%
Generalist	33,709	18%	43,934	44%	891	32%	1139	40%
Other	7,067	3%	3,708	3%	161	11%	157	8%
Total	**193,087**	**100%**	**100,740**	**100%**	**2,314**	**100%**	**2,125**	**100%**

[a]Weighted estimates of the number of investigations are based on a sample of 7,762 child maltreatment investigations in 1998 and 11,562 child maltreatment investigations in 2003.
[b]Weighted estimates of the number of workers are based on a sample of 490 workers in 1998 and 819 workers in 2003.

Table 2 *Age, Gender, Language, and Ethnicity of Investigating Workers: CIS–1998 and CIS–2003*

Age	1998 Per cent (N = 461)	2003 Per cent (N = 780)
25 years or less	12	8
26 to 34 years	41	48
35 to 44 years	31	26
45 to 54 years	13	14
55 years or more	3	5
Total	**100**	**100**

Gender	1998 Per cent (N = 486)	2003 Per cent (N = 819)
Female	80	82
Male	20	18
Total	**100**	**100**

Primary Language	1998 Per cent (N = 490)	2003 Per cent (N = 802)
English	95	97
French	3	1
Other	2	2
Total	**100**	**100**

Ethnicity	1998 Per cent (N = 485)	2003 Per cent (N = 804)
White	89	81
Aboriginal	4	7
Black	1	4
Chinese	1	1
South Asian	2	3
Other	3	4
Total	**100**	**100**

Table 2 shows that the age, gender, primary language, and ethnicity of workers participating in the two cycles of the CIS were very similar. Slightly more workers in the 26-to-34-year age category participated in the CIS–2003 than the CIS–1998 (48% versus 41%). In 2003, fewer workers (81%) described themselves as white than in 1998 (89%), as more Aboriginal and Black workers participated in the 2003 study than in 1998.

Caseload Size and Training

Workers were asked to describe the average size of their caseload in both the CIS–1998 and the CIS–2003. There were dramatic differences in the caseload size reported in the two study cycles. The mean caseload size in 1998 was 21.1 cases (SD 11.2). In 2003, the mean caseload size of workers participating in the study was 13.60 (SD 9.3). As indicated in Table 3, in 2003, 85% of workers reported an average caseload of 20 cases or fewer, compared to 53% of workers in the 1998 cycle reporting 20 cases or fewer. Sixteen per cent of the workers in 1998 had caseloads of 31 cases or higher compared to 5% of workers in the 2003 study. Among intake workers, the largest shift in caseload size was the 21–30 range: in 1998, 22% of workers reported their caseload at this size compared to only 8% of intake workers in 2003. Almost half of the intake workers in 2003 reported caseloads of 10 or less. While caseload sizes were slightly higher for generalists, only 5% of participating workers had a caseload size of 31 or higher compared to 20% of generalist workers in the CIS–1998.

Workers were asked to select all categories that described the specific child protection/child welfare training they had received. Workers endorsed as many categories as were applicable to their training experience. The length and description of the training was not specified on the one-page worker

Table 3 *Caseload at Time of Study by Job Position*

			Job Position (%)					
	All Positions (%)		Intake Specialist		Generalist		Other	
Case Distribution	1998 (*N* = 4410)	2003 (*N* = 756)	1998 (*N* = 234)	2003 (*N* = 434)	1998 (*N* = 184)	2003 (*N* = 249)	1998 (*N* = 23)	2003 (*N* = 73)
0–10 cases	19	43	26	48	7	29	52	53
11–20 cases	34	42	39	39	29	47	17	37
21–30 cases	31	12	22	8	45	19	22	7
31–40 cases	9	3	9	2	10	4	9	1
Over 40 cases	7	1	5	2	10	1	0	1
Total	100	100	100	100	100	100	100	100

instrument. For all but one category of training (risk assessment), workers participating in the CIS–2003 reported more training opportunities than workers participating in the CIS–1998 (see Table 4). Ninety-two per cent of workers in the 2003 study had received some type of general training on child abuse, compared to 85% in 1998. Sixty-six per cent of workers participating in the 2003 study had received cultural sensitivity training, compared to 48% of workers in 1998. More workers in the CIS–2003 had received crisis intervention training (76%) than workers participating in the CIS–1998 (57%), and 80% of workers in the 2003 cycle had received child development training compared to 64% in the 1998 cycle.

In both cycles of the CIS, approximately 60% of participating workers had four or fewer years of child protection experience (see Table 5). The mean number of years of child protection experience for workers participating in the CIS–2003 was 2.4 (SD 1.2), compared to 5.5 (SD 5.8) in the CIS–1998. There was a lower rate of workers participating in the CIS–2003 with less than one year of child protection experience (4%) compared to the CIS–1998 (26%); however, a smaller number of workers with social work degrees participated in the CIS–2003 than in the CIS–1998. Seventy-three per cent of workers participating in the CIS–1998 had either an MSW degree (17%) or a BSW degree (56%). Ten per cent of participating workers had an MSW degree in the 2003 study, and 50% of participating workers had a BSW degree. There was a 6% increase in workers participating in the CIS–2003 with a bachelor's degree other than social work, and a 6% increase in workers participating with a certificate or diploma.

Table 4 *Type of Training of Investigating Workers: CIS–1998 and CIS–2003*

Type of Training	1998 Per cent (N = 490)	2003 Per cent (N = 819)
General information on child abuse	85	92
Risk assessment ·	94	87
Child development	64	80
Sexual abuse assessment and intervention	69	78
Solution-focused interventions	45	52
Family preservation interventions	27	36
Physical abuse assessment and intervention	66	76
Neglect assessment	44	65
Cultural sensitivity training	48	66
Crisis intervention	57	76
Other	25	21

Table 6 examines the distribution of years of child protection experience by education level: social work education (either an MSW or a BSW) versus other types of education. In the CIS–2003, participating social workers and workers with other types of education are relatively evenly distributed in their years of child protection experience. In the CIS–1998, 52% of workers with another type of education had more than six years of experience. In the CIS–2003, the number of workers with another type of education and six years or more of child protection experience had declined by 25%. For both social workers and workers

Table 5 *Years of Child Protection Experience and Highest Degree Completed of Investigating Workers*

Child Protection Experience	1998 per cent (N = 477)	2003 per cent (N = 782)
Less than 1 year	26	4
1 year to 2 years	12	24
3 years to 4 years	19	31
5 years to 6 years	13	15
Over 6 years	32	26
Highest Degree Completed	**(N = 486)**	**(N = 802)**
MSW	17	10
BSW	56	50
Other graduate degree	1	3
Other bachelor's degree	18	24
Certificate or diploma	7	13
Partial degree	2	—
Total	**100**	**100**

Table 6 *Years of Child Protection Experience by Social Work versus Non-Social Work Education (N in 1998 = 473; N in 2003 = 770)*

	Social Work Education (per cent)		Education in a Discipline Other Than Social Work (per cent)	
Child Protection Experience	1998 (N = 344)	2003 (N = 469)	1998 (N = 129)	2003 (N = 301)
< 1 year	28	2	18	6
1 to 2 years	14	25	6	22
3 to 4 years	22	30	12	22
5 to 6 years	12	16	12	13
> 6 years	25	26	52	27
Total	**100**	**100**	**100**	**100**

with another type of degree, there were fewer workers with less than one year of child protection experience in the 2003 cycle. However, the percentage of social workers participating in the CIS–2003 study with less than two years of child protection experience declined by 15%, whereas there was little difference in the percentage of workers with other type of education and less than two years of experience (28% in the CIS–2003 versus 24% in the CIS–1998).

Distribution of Workers by Location of Agency

The CIS sites were categorized into three service classifications reflecting their population density:

- Large Metropolitan Service Area: providing child welfare services to densely populated urban settings, including suburban sites within a metropolitan site;
- Mixed Urban/Rural Service Area: providing child welfare services to sites with a wide population density range; and
- Primarily Rural Service Area: providing child welfare services primarily to sparsely populated areas.

Traditionally it has been more difficult for rural child protection agencies/offices to attract social workers because the population base is smaller. The CIS worker database provides an opportunity to examine whether worker qualifications and experience varied depending on the location of the agency while comparing the distribution or worker qualifications at two points in time.

As shown in Table 7, in the CIS–2003 participating workers with less than one year of experience were evenly distributed between metropolitan, mixed urban/rural, and rural geographic areas. In the CIS–1998, 30% of workers with less than one year of experience were located in metropolitan areas, compared to 20% in mixed urban/rural and 25% in rural areas. Thirty-six per cent of participating workers in rural agencies had more than six years of child protection experience in the CIS–2003, compared to 26% of workers from mixed urban/rural areas and 25% of workers from metropolitan areas.

The decline in workers with a social work degree participating in the CIS is unevenly distributed between the geographic areas. Metropolitan areas had the highest proportion of participating workers with a social work degree in the CIS–2003 (69% versus 49% in mixed urban/rural areas and 47% in rural areas). However, in the CIS–1998, 91% of participating workers from metropolitan areas had a social work degree. This suggests there had been a 22% decrease in the number of workers with a social work degree in metropolitan

Table 7 *Years of Child Protection Experience by Service Area*
(N in 1998 = 477; N in 2003 = 782)

	Service Areas (per cent)					
	Metropolitan		Urban/Rural Mix		Rural	
Child Protection	1998	2003	1998	2003	1998	2003
Experience	(*N* = 191)	(*N* = 481)	(*N* = 162)	(*N* = 256)	(*N* = 124)	(*N* = 45)
Less than 1 year	30	4	20	4	25	4
1 year to 2 years	10	26	13	21	14	18
3 years to 4 years	19	32	20	32	17	24
5 years to 6 years	9	14	14	17	12	18
Over 6 years	31	25	33	26	32	36
Total	**100**	**100**	**100**	**100**	**100**	**100**

Table 8 *Educational Background of Child Protection Workers by Geographic Service Area*

	Service Area (per cent)					
	Metropolitan		Urban/Rural Mix		Rural	
	1998	2003	1998	2003	1998	2003
Educational Background	(*N* = 195)	(*N* = 494)	(*N* = 163)	(*N* = 263)	(*N* = 128)	(*N* = 45)
Social work education	91	69	62	49	58	47
Other educational discipline	9	31	38	51	42	53
Total	**100**	**100**	**100**	**100**	**100**	**100**

areas. Similarly, mixed/urban areas and rural areas also experienced a decline in participating workers with a social work degree during this time period. Mixed urban/rural areas had 62% of workers with a social work degree in 1998 and 49% in 2003, while 58% of participating workers in rural areas had a social work degree in 1998 and less than half of workers (47%) in rural areas had a social work degree in 2003.

Discussion

The profile of child welfare workers participating in the two CIS cycles should be interpreted with caution, given that the study was not designed to provide nationally representative estimates of child protection workers; thus, one cannot use the data to estimate a profile of all child welfare workers in Canada. For example, the increase in Aboriginal child protection workers participating in the CIS from 1998 to 2003 is more than likely a direct result of an increased participation in the study from Aboriginal agencies. Nonetheless, given the lack of any other source of data, the study does provide a valuable picture of the child protection workforce in a large Canadian sample.

There were a number of differences in the qualifications of workers participating in the two cycles of the CIS. In the late 1990s, partially as a result of the restraints on funding and partially as a response to criticism of the system, child welfare services redefined themselves by focusing on a timely response to the initial report (Pecora, 1989; Schene, 1998). Many provinces and territories adopted some type of standardized risk assessment, designed to assess the risk of harm to children during an investigation and at various points in a case. The CIS–1998 was conducted during the beginning of the shift toward a risk assessment approach. Five years later, specialized teams were clearly doing the investigatory work of child welfare agencies—a worker with an intake designation conducted 79% of investigations in the CIS–2003. Investigation specialists, by definition, conduct more investigations than workers who both conduct investigations *and* provide ongoing services to children and families. Further, there was a significant increase in the number of children investigated in the family in the CIS–2003. In the CIS–1998, 1.4 children in the family were the subject of the investigation; in 2003, the number of children in the family investigated had risen to 1.7. Interestingly, the caseload size of workers participating in the two study cycles was dramatically different. Workers participating in the CIS–2003 reported much lower average caseloads than workers participating in the CIS–1998. How the staggering increase in investigations was accommodated by child welfare organizations while lowering the average size of a caseload is a topic that requires further inquiry.

There is little empirical research about the differences between a specialist model of practice and a generalist model of practice. In a study of occupational therapists and social workers in a mental health setting (n = 304), using a self-report measure of work activities, occupational therapists reported more complex clinical activities than did social workers (Lloyd, King, & McKenna, 2004). The authors assume that the outcome of more clinically specialized work is a positive outcome for clients, although this assumption was neither measured nor tested.

The distinction between intake workers and generalist workers represents how the work of the identification and verification of child maltreatment is organized within the agency. Further, the model chosen by the organization to investigate allegations of maltreatment may be a reflection of the organization's culture. Are there differences in activities between intake workers and generic workers despite the highly prescribed risk assessment approach to the investigation of child maltreatment used in most provinces and territories? Given the adoption of a specialist designation by most agencies participating in the CIS–2003, it seems clear that answering this question is fundamental to understanding the impact of organizing the work of the agency through a specialist model.

The minimum educational credentials for child protection workers set by policy vary between, and within, provinces and territories. There were far fewer workers with a social work degree participating in the CIS–2003 than in the CIS–1998. Seven per cent fewer workers with a master's degree in social work participated in the CIS–2003 than in the CIS–1998, and 6% fewer workers with a bachelor's degree of social work participated in the CIS–2003 than in the CIS–1998. Unlike many other social work settings, individuals who do not hold a social work degree or diploma but would still like to practise in a social work setting can be employed by child welfare agencies. Metropolitan agencies had the sharpest decline in social workers participating in the CIS, and while mixed urban-rural and rural agencies also had fewer social workers participating in the CIS–2003, the decrease was not as dramatic. The explanation for the shift in educational credentials requires further inquiry. Are social workers less attracted to child protection work? Does the increased service volume result in a demand for workers that can no longer be primarily filled by social workers?

Perhaps not unrelated to the issue of changing educational credentials is the increase in the training workers have received. With the exception of risk assessment training, workers reported more training opportunities in the CIS–2003. Is the reporting of additional training opportunities reflective of the need to compensate for fewer social workers? If this is the case, does increased training result in similar clinical decisions by workers who do not have a social work degree? Only two-thirds of respondents in the CIS–2003 cycle reported receiving training in neglect assessment, although neglect remains the most investigated and substantiated type of child maltreatment. There was, however, an increase in the number of workers reporting additional neglect training from 1998 to 2003.

The ability to retain experienced staff is identified by most child protection agencies as an organizational goal. The differences in child protection years of experience reported by workers in the CIS–1998 cycle and the CIS–2003 cycles raises some interesting questions about the relationship between education and child protection experience. It should be noted that the overall estimate of the number of workers conducting investigations in the study year does not fully account for worker turnover during the year, since estimates are based on a three-month sampling period. In the CIS–1998, 52% of workers with educational credentials other than social work had more than six years of child protection experience. Only 27% of workers who were not social workers had more than six years of experience in the CIS–2003—reflecting a change in the distribution of child protection years of experience among workers other than social workers. The distribution of child protection experience among social workers was similar between cycles, with the exception of the one-to-two-years-of-experience category. Although the question cannot be answered by analysis of the CIS worker data, understanding whether workers who are not social workers but are experienced workers are leaving child welfare at a disproportionate rate to social workers, as well as any resulting impact on services, requires further research. Part of the explanation may be the shift from a generalist model to a specialist model of service delivery in the agencies participating in the cycles of the CIS. Experienced workers who are not social workers may no longer be conducting child maltreatment investigations.

Conclusion

The worker information collected by two cycles of the CIS provides a partial profile of Canadian child welfare workers and critical data about changes in experience, training, and work environment between cycles of the CIS. Canadian child welfare workers are the first point of contact for arguably the most high-risk children and families in Canada. While providing a unique opportunity to examine the characteristics of workers from a nationally representative sample of agencies, there is a need for more systematic research regarding child protection workers in Canada. There were differences in the characteristics of workers who participated in the CIS–1998 and the CIS–2003; whether these variations impact the services delivered to children and families is a question that is fundamental to the child welfare system.

Canadian Incidence Study of Reported Child Abuse and Neglect
Themes and Implications

Brad McKenzie
Kathleen Kufeldt

M any advocates of child welfare reform will point to the inherent limitations of the child protection paradigm of practice, where primary attention and most resources are devoted to the investigation of referrals alleging child abuse or neglect. More resources, it is argued, ought to be devoted to prevention, early intervention, and family support. Why, then, begin a review of research, policy, and practice in child welfare with a section that documents the nature and scope of child maltreatment? Aside from the legislative requirements outlined by Bala in the Introduction, which mandate child protection as the primary function of the child welfare system, we suggest that the goal of promoting the well-being of children cannot be separated from the goal of ensuring that children are safe and protected from harm. We need more comprehensive information on the reported incidence of child maltreatment, and the responses to allegations of abuse and neglect, in order to understand the interface between these two goals. The *Canadian Incidence Study* (CIS) and the plan to continue gathering comparative information on child maltreatment at five-year intervals provide important information on service and policy trends. Analysis of this information can assist us in understanding how we can promote family and child well-being, and at the same time ensure the protection of children from harm. It will also serve to meet the more general need to support evidence-based decision-making.

Tonmyr[1] summarizes the Public Health Agency of Canada's interest in surveys like the CIS. She suggests that the purpose of such surveys is the collection and analysis of information for dissemination to decision-makers so that they can identify emerging trends and set priorities for programs and policies. In the case of the CIS, a follow-up study of senior child welfare decision-makers in Ontario was conducted to assess the utilization of these findings in agencies across Ontario (Jack et al., 2007). Most respondents interviewed were aware of the CIS, and had access to results through the Internet. Though seldom used in direct fashion to create policy, CIS analyses had been used to guide policy development at the Ministry level. At the agency level, CIS data had been used predominantly in two ways: (1) to build the agency's knowledge base and provide background information about child maltreatment characteristics; and (2) to validate local experiences and professional knowledge about child maltreatment trends in their communities. The information about changes in child maltreatment estimates has also been used at times to influence or justify resource allocation. Several suggestions for improving the utilization of CIS data were made, including the linking of CIS findings to practical interventions and disseminating the findings through face-to-face meetings and interactive technology (Tonmyr, Jack, Brooks, Kennedy, & Dudding, 2008).

The first two chapters in Part I provide important data on changing trends in the nature and scope of child maltreatment in Canada, particularly between two national iterations of the Canadian Incidence Study (CIS–1998 and CIS–2003). Chapters 3 and 4 provide a perspective on decision-making in child welfare, with particular attention to data on child welfare worker characteristics. In the final part of our discussion on themes and implications, we will briefly highlight the ongoing debate about the mandate for child welfare services.

Themes and Implications

The Nature and Scope of Child Maltreatment

The most important finding from the comparative analysis of data in the 1998 and 2003 versions of the *Canadian Incidence Study* is the growth in the estimated number of children investigated in these two different years. Although incomplete data from Quebec in 2003 prevent detailed comparisons on some variables, the incidence of investigation per 1000 children increased by 86% in the rest of Canada, and substantiation rates were up by 125%. Recently released findings from the CIS–2008 indicate that the number of maltreatment investigations in 2008 was quite similar to the 2003 number (235,842 and 235,315 respectively) (Public Health Agency of Canada, 2010). However, the dramatic changes between 1998 and 2003 have placed increasing pressures on resources within the child welfare field, including staff time, to respond appropriately to these demands.

What are the drivers of these increases, and what are the implications for policy and practice? There are significant variations between 1998 and 2003 with respect to the type of maltreatment, and these are summarized briefly below.

- *Physical abuse:* Chapter 1 identified a significant increase (107%) in the incidence of substantiated physical abuse. Cases involving physical abuse constituted 24% of all substantiated investigations in 2003.
- *Neglect:* The incidence of substantiated neglect between 1998 and 2003 also increased (78%) and, as outlined in Chapter 2 with respect to Ontario, this reflects a steady increase which occurred over a 10-year period of time since 1993. In the CIS–2003, neglect was the primary form of maltreatment in 29% of substantiated investigations.
- *Sexual abuse:* There was a decline in the incidence of substantiated sexual abuse investigations over this same time period. In 2003, sexual abuse cases made up only 3% of substantiated investigations, compared to 9% in 1998.
- *Emotional maltreatment and exposure to domestic violence:* The more significant drivers of the increase in substantiated investigations were the areas of emotional maltreatment and exposure to domestic violence (i.e., the incidence rate increases from .86 in 1998 to 3.23 per 1000 children in 2003 for emotional maltreatment, and from 1.72 in 1998 to 6.17 in 2003 for exposure to domestic violence). In 2003, emotional maltreatment comprised 15% of substantiated investigations, and exposure to domestic violence accounted for 28% of substantiated investigations.

Two other drivers of the general increase in investigations and substantiations are noted in Chapter 1. First, with respect to investigations, the tendency in 2003 was to investigate more children within each family (mean of 1.41 in 1998 and 1.66 in 2003). Second, with respect to substantiations, a lower proportion of cases were classified as suspected in 2003 (24% in 1998 and only 13% in 2003), while the proportion of cases identified as unsubstantiated increased only marginally (36% in 1998 versus 40% in 2003).

A major reason for the rise in investigations and substantiations is the increased sensitivity to the potential for harm from chronic neglect, emotional maltreatment, and exposure to domestic violence. This has broadened the interpretation of child maltreatment, and in several jurisdictions this has been reinforced by legislative and policy changes which encourage or require investigation of referrals where these issues are identified. This raises the question of harm. As documented in Chapter 1, the incidence rates of emotional and physical harm identified by workers were somewhat higher in 2003. However, the percent of substantiated cases where physical harm was identified declined from

18% of cases in 1998 to 10% in 2003, and the percent of substantiated cases where emotional harm was noted declined from 32% of cases in 1998 to 20% in 2003. Thus, the proportion of substantiated cases identified as being harmed was relatively low in both years, and declined significantly between 1998 and 2003. Black, Trocmé, Fallon, and MacLaurin (2008) elaborate on these findings with respect to exposure to domestic violence from the CIS–2003 in noting that children with substantiated investigations of exposure to domestic violence along with another form of substantiated maltreatment were four times more likely to be placed than investigations of cases involving exposure to domestic violence only. The authors note that the child welfare system is substantiating such cases at a higher rate, but is concluding that these families do not require child protection placement services. In a more general sense, the increase in the maltreatment rate between 1998 and 2003 is driven primarily by cases where children have not been significantly harmed.

The nature and scope of services that are or can be provided is also somewhat controversial. Although there was a higher incidence rate of cases open for ongoing services in 2003 when compared with 1998, less than half of the cases in 2003 continued to remain open for such services. At the same time, more than half of all substantiated investigations in 2003 had been previously investigated. This raises the question of whether more extended service might be in the children's best interests in the long term. Neglect is a particularly persistent form of child maltreatment. As noted in Chapter 2, neglect is associated with adverse short- and long-term outcomes for children, and cases involving neglect are more likely to be re-reported than other forms of maltreatment. Neglect cases are more likely to receive ongoing services; as well, placement is more likely in these cases than in other types of cases. General findings pertaining to neglect, emotional maltreatment, and exposure to domestic violence beg the question about whether the right services are being provided.

In the case of exposure to domestic violence, intrusive investigations often fail to engage the non-offending parent (usually the mother), as the mother is reluctant to trust the child welfare worker because of the fear that her children will be removed. Although services remain underdeveloped for this type of maltreatment, one response has been a more collaborative approach to service provision. In this response, community service providers are engaged along with child welfare workers to ensure that both the adult victim and the child receive needed services (Banks, Hazen, Coben, Wang, & Griffith, 2009; Kohl, Barth, Hazen, & Landsverk, 2005; Moles, 2008). Friend, Shlonsky, and Lambert (2008) propose an approach that includes harm reduction, evidence-based practice, and access to low threshold alternatives to investigation and treatment. This approach is consistent with the evolution of differential response in child welfare discussed in Chapter 6.

A somewhat contrasting perspective emerges from Nixon, Tutty, Weaver-Dunlop, and Walsh (2007), who reviewed changes to legislation and policies affecting intimate partner violence in child welfare. These authors note that there is no consensus about the extent to which exposure to domestic violence constitutes child maltreatment, and that broad inclusion of these types of cases risks opening the floodgates to a system that is already overburdened. In addition, this solution may tend to further victimize the abused woman and her children. A narrower approach focusing on harm or increased risk of harm is advocated, along with clear guidelines and standards for practice.

In considering neglect, it is important to recognize the distinction between neglect emerging from parental omission and structural neglect, where the root causes, including unemployment, poverty, and poor housing, may be the result of circumstances outside of the individual's ability to control. Chapter 2 notes the strong relationship between poverty and neglect, and the overrepresentation of Aboriginal children in the child welfare system appears, in part, to be explained by higher rates of neglect (see Chapter 21). These connections, and the implications for policy and practice, are explored in more detail in Chapters 24 and 39.

One of the questions pertaining to evidence about the correlation between poverty and child maltreatment is whether the overrepresentation of the poor in the child welfare system reflects a class bias in reporting because the poor are scrutinized more closely than other groups. Jonson-Reid, Drake, and Kohl (2009) explore this question by examining data from California. When compared to non-poor children and non-reported poor children, poor reported children presented with much higher risk profiles, more severe forms of maltreatment, and higher rates of recidivism. In essence, poor families appeared to display higher levels of problems before child welfare services became involved. These findings suggest that overreporting is not the major problem, and reinforce other evidence that multi-faceted forms of intervention, including poverty reduction strategies, are required in dealing with neglect in poor families.

The types of services to be provided by the child welfare system in cases involving neglect and exposure to domestic violence remain somewhat unclear. However, two general principles are important. First, the nature of intervention must be expanded beyond the level of the individual, and address multiple ecological contexts, including the child, family, community, and society. This principle, articulated by Peirson, Nelson, and Prilleltensky (2003) in relation to child and family welfare in general, is particularly important in circumstances involving neglect and exposure to domestic violence. Better parenting out-comes as an attribute of well-being are more likely if services include a well-coor-dinated range of community services coupled with supportive interventions by the child welfare system. Second, the provision of concrete services, such as assistance in meeting basic needs and locating adequate housing, is critical to many families. This is not new in that it has been previously identified as an important element in the success of family-based services (Pecora, 1995). Although it is beyond the capacity of the child welfare system to address the structural factors that contribute to neglect and family violence, the next chap-ter demonstrates that an expanded toolbox, including the ability to provide financial resources to families, can make a positive difference.

Decision-Making and Human Resources

In Chapter 3, the CIS–1998 data were analyzed to better understand some of the organizational and worker characteristics associated with decision-making in child welfare. A number of individual studies were examined in the literature review. Although these studies demonstrate that certain factors appear to have some influence, there is little evidence of a consensus about a common set of factors that affect decision-making. Instead, decision-making appears to be heavily influenced by contextual factors such as referral sources and the type of neighbourhood or community being served. The CIS data analyzed in Chap-ter 3 indicate that agency location (i.e., rural, metropolitan, and mixed urban–rural) has some influence on the decision to provide ongoing services, but clinical issues, including the presence of emotional and physical harm, and child and parent functioning concerns, were the most influential factors. The importance attributed to clinical factors is encouraging, although more focused research on decision-making variables, including organizational characteris-tics and service philosophy, is required.

Human resource issues affect both the quality and effectiveness of child welfare services, and several dimensions need to be considered. One factor is the question about whether there are enough resources. High caseloads are often reported, and these are an impediment to enhanced services. In addition, the field of child welfare has become more and more focused on regulation and accountability, and this has been accompanied by excessive amounts of paper-work. Such demands limit the time available for providing direct services to children and families. Another factor is the quality of staff, including manage-ment, supervisors, and front-line staff. Arguably one needs the most experi-enced, well-trained staff on the front line, yet this is often a training ground for new workers who move on to other fields of practice after a few short years in the field of child welfare. Training and support can help to mitigate these shortcomings to some extent, but both organizational and systemic factors are also influential. Child welfare work involves significant stress and changes to the work environment, including reasonable caseloads and opportunities to develop practice methods that can enhance the provision or services to children and families, help to empower front-line staff, and limit the extent of job burnout and alienation.

Staff recruitment and retention was the subject of a special issue of *Child Welfare* in 2009 (Volume 88, Number 5), and Zlotnik, Strand, and Anderson (2009) summarize some of the key findings from research on recruitment and retention in the United States. As they note, much of the research has focused on individual factors; organizational factors, including leadership, supervision, and workload, have been considered only on an issue-by-issue basis. New evidence suggests the importance of addressing problems from both an individual and organizational perspective simultaneously. Leadership is critical in supporting staff in a cultural change process so that cultural competence, family support, and strength-based work underlie child welfare work. Good supervision that provides support but respects worker autonomy and competency is also important. Professional development opportunities for both supervisors and workers are critical, but it is also important that organizations ensure reasonable workloads and promote a shared commitment to agency goals and initiatives. Some research suggests that education, especially a social work degree and a specialized child welfare focus, can support worker retention and enhance service provision. In Canada, there have been efforts to develop a specialization in child welfare within some Schools of Social Work, notably in British Columbia; however, there has been limited research on the impact of this change.

Chapter 4 provides information on the workers participating in the 1998 and 2003 cycles of the *Canadian Incidence Study*. Although these staff are not necessarily representative of all child welfare staff in Canada, the numbers included in these samples (477 in 1998 and 782 in 2003) provide important snapshots of workers engaged in the investigative functions within the child welfare field. Between 1998 and 2003 there was little change in the experience profile of investigating workers; in both cycles approximately 60% of participating workers had less than four years' experience in child protection work. However, there was a significant shift in the educational background of these workers over the two time periods; in 1998, 73% of participating workers had a social work degree, and five years later this was the case for only 60%. In general, a higher proportion of workers in 2003 had received specialized training in topics relevant to assessment and intervention in child welfare. When compared with 1998, there was somewhat more diversity in the 2003 sample of workers; there was also a greater tendency to utilize specialized intake workers rather than generalists as investigating workers in 2003. Average caseload numbers were lower in 2003. Although this may be partly explained by the increased use of specialized intake staff, those with generic child welfare responsibilities in 2003 also reported smaller caseloads. Although these data highlight some of the differences in the profile of child welfare workers between 1998 and 2003, what is not clear is whether these had any effect on the quality of services delivered to children and families.

The Child Welfare Mandate

The growth in the numbers and incidence rates of both referrals for maltreatment and substantiated investigations underscores the debate about the child protection paradigm in North America. Many families are coming to the attention of child welfare agencies without receiving an intervention. While reporters seem to recognize that these families need some kind of help, this help is apparently not within the purview of child welfare services. Yet more than half of the substantiated investigations in the CIS–2003 had been previously investigated. This pattern is not unusual, and U.S. data suggests that there are only modest differences in re-referral rates among substantiated and unsubstantiated cases (Drake, Jonson-Reid, Way, & Chung, 2003; Wolock, Sherman, Feldman, & Metzger, 2001). Many (see Conley, 2007; Waldfogel, 1998) argue that this reinforces the need for interventions for families and children that promote well-being rather than limiting services to a "search and rescue" response. These reform advocates focus on the problems of under-inclusion and service delivery, and argue for a broader child welfare mandate. Two service needs are recognized: high-risk families who are unreported, and low-risk families who are dismissed without the offer of early intervention and support services. Too many screened-out families, it is argued, are re-reported again later after problems have become more serious. Service delivery issues are also identified as problematic; families have multiple problems, yet services are fragmented rather than responsive to needs in a more holistic fashion.

In contrast, an alternative strategy is proposed by Besharov and Laumann (1996). They argue that the high volume of unsubstantiated cases represents an unnecessary intrusion into the lives of families and a waste of resources that prevents more serious cases of maltreatment from getting the attention they need. This is not helped by an alternating emphasis on child rescue and family preservation which overshadows a more individualized approach that focuses on harm to the child (Lowry, 1998). These advocates believe that reform should focus on addressing problems of overinclusion and system capacity by narrowing the child welfare mandate to more serious cases involving harm or potential harm.

As data from the *Canadian Incidence Study* suggest, there is little evidence that Canadian policy-makers are prepared to narrow the mandate for child protection services, at least in the near term. Instead, the emerging policy position, based on precedents established in Australia and the United States, is to adopt a system of differential response. Models of differential response are proposed to address the critique of the child protection services by narrowing the focus of investigative services to high-risk cases, and simultaneously expanding the nature and scope of services to families at lower levels of risk. Families assessed at lower levels of risk can voluntarily elect services designed to respond to needs without having to reach an arbitrary threshold of risk for ongoing services. Differential response systems are discussed in more depth in the next chapter, but it is important to note that even in a differential response system, a significant number of families are screened out from receiving agency services. This has important implications for community partnerships and the early intervention and prevention programs that must accompany reforms associated with differential response.

Nowhere is this gap more important than in addressing the problem of child neglect. Although neglect is often influenced by factors related to poverty and inadequate housing, the responses of the child welfare system are largely restricted to addressing the symptoms displayed by individuals. Focusing on private troubles rather than public issues is an insufficient response, yet the resources available to the child welfare system limit the ability to address these public issues. Although the child welfare system has an important role to play, measures to address the underlying causes of neglect require more systemic and coordinated responses. At the same time there is little doubt that reducing referrals pertaining to neglect, and enhancing the likelihood of reunification for children in care due to neglect, is dependent on exactly these types of actions.

Note

1   We are grateful to Lil Tonmyr, senior researcher with the Injury and Child Maltreatment Section, Health Surveillance and Epidemiology Division, Public Health Agency of Canada, for providing information on the utilization of the CIS data in Ontario.

The Continuum of Care

Introduction

Part II consists of three sections. The first, early intervention and support, focuses on research aimed at services that can assist families and avoid the need to take children into care. The second section is concerned with the various options available when a child is in need of alternative care, including adoption. The third section covers the transition from care. We have brought these three aspects of child welfare work under the umbrella of the "continuum of care" to emphasize that the various phases of the work in serving children's welfare should not be conceived of as discrete entities. The present fragmented approach to protection of children does not serve them or their families well. What is required is a seamless continuum of care that addresses the particular needs of individual children, in the context of their families and communities.

The three different sections reflect different overlapping points on the continuum. The real beginning is in the child's family of origin. Families are interdependent with the community in which they live. Thus Chapter 6 discusses the growing interest in differential responses that place a priority on the particular needs of families referred for service, and not simply those who cross some arbitrary threshold of risk. Chapters 7 and 8 address the issue of accessibility, not only in terms of location, but also with respect to reducing barriers imposed by power imbalance and a consequent failure of the system to draw parents into a co-operative working alliance for the sake of the children.

The final chapter in this section presents the results of a project designed to reduce neglect in the home and to avoid removal of children.

Similarly, as we move into consideration of the various approaches to substitute care, we must also be aware that we do work along a service continuum. The chapter on foster care has a central theme of promoting connection and continuity between child, family, and foster carers. It also suggests how the role of foster carers can be expanded in ways in which they can contribute to the seamlessness of the continuum. Chapters 11 and 12 address the growing use of kinship care, an approach to substitute care that maintains children within their extended families. Chapter 13 draws attention to forgotten members of the care system, foster carers' own children, who can, and should be, included as important partners in the provision of alternate care. In Chapter 14, Anglin points out that many children received into care experience such overwhelming pain that they may require the security and structure of a professionally staffed group home. The last chapter in this section identifies the changes that have occurred in the field of adoption over the past several decades.

The third and final section, youth transitions, is an essential reminder of the abrupt and premature launching into adulthood of the graduates of care. In current society this transition has become more prolonged, often with young adults experiencing episodes of returning home before achieving full independence. This has given rise to the recognition that between adolescence and adulthood there is a stage of *emerging adulthood*. This stage is not yet well recognized in child welfare policy and practice. The experiences before and during their care career affect young persons' readiness to face adult life, and those who are the least prepared receive the least help and support. When the state takes on parental responsibilities its duty of care should extend, as does that of the responsible parent, to support in successfully negotiating the tasks of "emerging adulthood."

6

Differential Response in Child Welfare
A New Early Intervention Model?

Brad McKenzie

This chapter reviews the development of differential response systems in child welfare since the late 1990s, with particular attention to Australia, the United States, and Canada. It describes the nature and scope of differential response systems, reviews some of the findings from early efforts to evaluate results, and discusses implications for research, policy, and practice.

Over the past two decades child and family welfare systems in North America and other English-speaking countries have faced continuing challenges in responding to the needs of both children and families. Problems include significant growth in the number of referrals for child protection investigations, more children in care, related increases in costs, and growing concerns about the effectiveness of the current child protection model. With respect to increases in referrals for child maltreatment, in Australia both notifications of suspected child abuse and neglect and costs doubled between 1999 and 2005 (Australian Institute of Health and Welfare, 2005; Steering Committee for the Review of Commonwealth/State Service Provision, 2006). In Canada, the rate of investigated children increased by 78% between 1998 and 2003; excluding Quebec, the rate of substantiated maltreatment cases increased by 125% (Chapter 1). As indicated in Chapter 1, the rate of children in care increased by 58% over this five-year period. As to effectiveness, there are persistent concerns about the mixed outcomes for children in care, and whether or not children from families referred for services are being adequately protected from harm. For example, large numbers of children are referred for investigations, but only a minority receives ongoing services. Yet a significant number of children are re-referred later. In the Australian state of Queensland in 2003–4, 15% of children where a finding of maltreatment was unsubstantiated and 25% of all children where maltreatment was substantiated were harmed again within 12 months (Australian Institute of Health and Welfare, 2006). Similar trends have been observed in the United States (Shusterman, Hollinshead, Fluke, & Yuan, 2005) and New Zealand (Waldegrave & Coy, 2005). In Canada, 52% of substantiated child maltreatment investigations in 2003 had been previously investigated (Chapter 1). Faced with increased referrals for service, and families with multiple, complex problems, child protection services have become more bureaucratic, standardized, and legalistic (Farrow, 1997).

These trends are consistent with some criticisms of the child protection system raised by Waldfogel (1998):

- *overinclusion* – some families are unnecessarily referred to child protection services;
- *capacity* – the number of families referred exceeds the system's capacity to respond appropriately;
- *underinclusion* – some families who should receive services do not;
- *service delivery* – some families are referred appropriately and receive services, but not necessarily the right types of services; and
- *service orientation* – the authoritative approach of child protection services is not appropriate for many families who are referred.

Defining Differential Response

Differential response (DR) systems, also labelled as "alternative response" (AR), allow for more than one service path or method of response to reports of child abuse and neglect (Child Welfare Information Gateway, 2008). Definitions and approaches vary significantly across jurisdictions, but two service pathways are normally established:

- an investigation track which assesses safety and risk to determine whether neglect or abuse is substantiated, and then whether placement and/or other types of intervention are required; and
- an assessment track or approach which focuses more deliberately on an assessment of family strengths and needs and the offer of voluntary family support services.

In general, the alternative response of assessment and family support services occurs in cases where risk is assessed as low or moderate. Although substantiation of child maltreatment may occur in some cases, the level of need is the primary criterion for opening a case. Normally, an AR response is not used when more serious allegations of maltreatment, such as sexual abuse or serious harm, are received (Child Welfare Information Gateway, 2008). Although it is more common for child welfare agencies to remain involved with AR cases, in some U.S. jurisdictions these services are provided solely by community agencies.

The intervention hypothesis in differential response is that both families who require investigation services and families who need more voluntary support-oriented services will benefit. Families not requiring investigation services will be referred quickly to an AR stream where more appropriate services may prevent repeated referrals, and investigation services will be more clearly targeted where necessary with related benefits for the children. DR services also encourage more collaborative engagements with other community service providers, particularly where families require support services that cannot be directly provided by the child welfare agency.

There is an argument that differential response is not really "new," and that it simply reflects good child welfare practice which incorporates interventions based on family-centred practice, increased use of community-based resources, and an earlier form of intervention for some families. This observation has some validity, and there are a number of examples in Canada of community-based early intervention responses (e.g., resource centres, prevention workers) that date back to the 1980s. However, these service initiatives tended to be agency-specific rather than system-wide reforms. The value of DR is its clearly defined alternative response track, including relevant assessment tools, service protocols, and staff with appropriate skills and training. The effort to incorporate this type of response as a broad reach program in child welfare also sets it apart from the more selective provision of voluntary, family-based services normally provided after an investigation has occurred.

Differential response systems are more developed in Australia and the United States (U.S.) than in Canada. In Australia, several states have initiated some form of alternative response to the one-size-fits-all investigation approach. DR systems in the U.S. were first developed in Florida and Missouri, and more than two dozen states have now implemented some form of differential response system (Child Welfare Information Gateway, 2008). A form of differential response has also been developed in New Zealand. In Canada, DR systems have been established or are in the process of being developed in several provinces, including Ontario, Alberta, Quebec, Manitoba, and British Columbia.

There are similarities between differential response and traditional child protection services. For example, both focus on the safety and well-being of the child, promote permanency within the family wherever possible, and recognize the authority of the agency to make decisions about placement in out-of-home care when necessary. Differences include a clearly identified service track with less adversarial assessment responses, an increased focus on providing services to fit families' strengths, needs, and resources, greater emphasis on engaging parents and other family members in service planning and providing support, the offer of voluntary services, and the more extensive use of community resources in partnership with agency services (Child Welfare Information Gateway, 2008).

Implementing Differential Response

Implementation Processes

Assessing the most appropriate service track requires clearly identified procedures and standards as well as necessary tools for assessments. Assessment protocols include a safety assessment tool designed to assess immediate safety concerns at the intake stage, a short form actuarial risk assessment instrument, and a family needs and strengths assessment tool. A variety of child-outcome measures and supplementary tools (e.g., assessment for domestic violence issues) may also be used. The Structured Decision Making (SDM) model developed by the Children's Research Center (CRC, 2008) in Madison, Wisconsin, which incorporates specific safety, risk, and family assessment tools, is used in jurisdictions in Australia, the U.S. and Canada (e.g., Ontario and Manitoba). Typically, the appropriate service track is determined at the intake stage, although there are options to refer cases to different tracks later in the process. A formal finding of maltreatment is not required to trigger services from the assessment response (AR) track. In many jurisdictions, an assessment of future risk of maltreatment occurs for referrals to both tracks; however, the use of a formal risk assessment tool for AR referrals is not universal.

Initially DR systems reflected only two tracks; however, multiple tracks have evolved in some jurisdictions. For example, some states in the U.S. include a prevention track for cases with no clear allegation of abuse or neglect, but where identified risk factors suggest a need for service (Child Welfare Information Gateway, 2008), and a domestic violence service response system has been developed in Olmsted County, Minnesota (Sawyer & Lohrbach, 2005b). The enhancement of family and kinship involvement is a common focus in the AR service stream.

Relationships with community agencies, including service contracts, case management conferences, and referrals are a feature of traditional child protection activities. However, in DR, relationships with community agencies are expanded to include an increased emphasis on partnerships, more emphasis on communication, and a shared responsibility to ensure that community-based agencies have the necessary resources to provide enhanced family support services that cannot be provided by the child welfare agency on its own.

Staff training is critical. Most DR systems utilize different staff for each service track to facilitate the development of specialized skills for the respective functions within these service pathways. However, the overall service model in both tracks often emphasizes a family-centred approach to practice; thus training for both staff and supervisors is regarded as a key element for successful implementation (Sawyer, personal communication; Schene, 2001a).

DR systems include a special emphasis on evaluation and accountability (Schene, 2001a). Evaluation of different pilot models prior to a decision to revise and roll out a full-scale model has enabled important adjustments in service delivery. In addition, evaluation is important to monitor outcomes, especially whether child safety is affected by the use of a differential response system.

A Differential Response Model

One example of a differential response model is that developed in Olmsted County in Minnesota (Sawyer & Lohrbach, 2005a). All reports detailing community concerns about children are screened by experienced social workers, and if the presenting information meets a statutory threshold for intervention, the report is referred to a review, evaluate, and direct (RED) team, composed of representatives from service teams in the agency, for disposition. This team meets each morning to review and assign cases, and team membership rotates every six months. The screening process includes an assessment for child safety, and if child safety is a concern, an actuarial risk assessment will be completed. Later on, an assessment of family needs and strengths will be completed. An evaluation form for assessing child outcomes following service provision is also utilized. Reports of serious harm or imminent danger require an immediate response, but are then brought to the RED team for review. Concerns not accepted for assessment may be referred to community-based services. The RED team will determine whether agency intervention of some kind is required, and if so, assign the case to one of two pathways: the traditional investigation stream or the alternative response (AR) or assessment stream. Each year approximately 38% of accepted reports are assigned to the investigation stream and 62% are assigned to the AR stream.

A specific response stream has also been developed for cases where there is a presenting report of child exposure to domestic violence, and cases may be referred to this stream from either the traditional investigation or the AR stream. A tool for assessing family violence issues is used in helping to determine service-related responses in this stream.

Service teams in the agency are organized by function (e.g., intake, traditional child protection, alternative response, domestic violence). If the case is assigned to a family assessment worker, that worker will continue to provide service until termination. In the investigation stream, initial assessment and short-term service is provided by an intake worker, and if ongoing service is required, the case will be transferred to a worker in the child protection stream.

The agency's special emphasis on a service model designed to enhance family involvement and attention to staff training were identified by Sawyer (personal communication) as key elements in the success of the Olmsted County model. The focus on family-centred practice in the agency has not been restricted to the AR service stream in that significant efforts have been made to engage parents and kinship networks in cases referred to the investigation stream. The agency-wide use of a family-focused model of practice was associated with a decline in the number of children admitted to care and improved satisfaction with agency services by both family members and other community service providers. In this agency, the number of children served over a 12-year period of time tripled, and the number of children taken into care and the number of families contesting agency decisions concerning their children were reduced by 50%.

Sawyer and Lohrbach (2005b) also provide a summary of the work of the domestic violence response team, which includes staff from the child welfare agency and a local family service agency. The domestic violence service model is based on partnership not only between these two agencies, but also with other key stakeholders, including law enforcement and women's advocacy organizations. By sharing responsibility, the safety concerns of both child and adult victims (most often the mother) are addressed. In 2003 this team worked with 260 children exposed to intimate partner abuse, and only nine children were placed outside of the family home. Eight of these children were placed in care voluntarily, with no court involvement, and all of these children were reunited with family members after short periods of time in care. The remaining young person was placed in another resource due to young offender issues.

Results from Early Research on Differential Response

Early research on differential response systems has been primarily limited to descriptive studies, although some data has been compared across service pathways and with baseline information to permit some tentative observations about effects. One of the most comprehensive evaluations was completed in Minnesota, where multiple methods were employed, including analysis of cost data and an experimental design where outcomes for families assigned to the investigation and alternative response streams were reported over a follow-up time period (Loman & Siegel, 2004a).

Descriptive information on differential response systems in the U.S. is available from the *National Study of Child Protective Services Systems and Reform Efforts*, which included a nationally representative sample of 300 county child protective agencies (U.S. Department of Health and Human Services, 2003). Based on 2002 data, 64% of these agencies employed some form of AR practices, in addition to a traditional investigation response. Using this data set, Shusterman et al. (2005) completed a study of almost 14,000 reported children from six states where both alternative response and traditional investigation services were provided. There was significant variation among states in the proportion of reported children referred for alternative response services (between 20% and 71%). Cases involving sexual abuse, particularly to younger children, were not normally referred for AR. Reports involving older children were more likely to receive an alternative response, and cases involving prior victimization were more likely to be referred for an investigation response. Reports from non-professionals and school sources were more likely to be referred to the AR stream than reports from social workers, medical personnel, legal services, or criminal justice services. In-home services were provided more often to families in the AR stream. Over a six-month follow-up period, the rate of re-reporting did not vary significantly for families assigned to either response stream.

Child Safety and Rates of Re-Reporting

Child safety has been a focus of research, and this is generally assessed by comparing the rates of referrals for neglect or abuse during the early stage of service, in that a higher rate of referrals from AR families might indicate that child safety concerns were not being adequately considered at case assignment. In early research on the AR system in the state of Washington, English, Wingard, Marshall, Orme, and Orme (2000) found that the rates of re-referrals were similar for families who did and did not engage with AR services offered by the agency, and were highest for families where domestic violence was present.

Although it was concluded that child safety was not jeopardized in this AR system, the risk level and severity of some referrals to AR were inappropriately high.

Ortez, Shusterman, and Fluke (2008) conducted an analysis of children referred for neglect in the 2004 and 2005 data set of the *National Child Abuse and Neglect Data System* (NCANDS) because neglect cases are more likely to be re-reported. Based on their assessment of risk factors and the rates of reporting, it was concluded that children in the AR stream were kept as safe as children receiving traditional investigations. Although re-reporting rates were not significantly different between streams, these authors note that re-reporting in the AR stream may have a different meaning than those in the investigation track in that more of these referrals may have been voluntary, and more likely to reflect the willingness of families to re-engage with services in the face of new or recurring needs.

Other research has drawn similar conclusions about child safety, and single state studies have found that when compared with children in the investigation track, children in the AR track were somewhat less likely to experience a subsequent report (Shusterman et al., 2005; Virginia Department of Social Services, 2008).

In Western Australia, a differential response model with three pathways to service was established in 1995. In addition to investigation and assessment tracks, a third classification of *Child Concern Report* was introduced for referrals where there was no indication of maltreatment but concerns about a child's well-being that required further assessment. If further assessment identified a need for services, these were offered on a voluntary basis. Results reported by Parton and Mathews (2001) suggested that the new model reduced the number of child maltreatment allegations and improved services to those at higher risk.

It may be argued that lower re-referral rates among AR families is partly explained by the fact that most children in the alternative response track have already been identified as lower risk. However, there is some evidence that families with substantiated and unsubstantiated allegations of maltreatment experience similar rates of recurrence and contact with the child welfare system (Drake, Jonson-Reid, Way, & Chung, 2003; Wolock, Sherman, Feldman, & Metzger, 2001), and that if the same services were provided to families assigned to the investigation and alternative service tracks, this same pattern would hold. Support for differences in re-reporting rates as a result of AR services comes from the experimental study conducted in Minnesota, where families were randomly assigned to investigation and assessment tracks, and the assessment track cases were still less likely to be reported (27% vs. 30%). In addition, child safety factors, as rated by workers, improved more for assessment track families (Loman & Siegel, 2005).

Family Engagement and Satisfaction

In a review of very early findings in Canada, Crain and Tonmyr (2007) reported an increase in services for families in the Outaouais region of Quebec under DR, increased use of community resources and lower use of child protection services following receipt of family enhancement services in Alberta, and some indications from families that they were treated better in a DR response system.

In the Minnesota study, families in the AR stream were seen more often (e.g., average number of meetings with assessment and investigated families were 5.4 and 2.9, respectively) (Loman & Siegel, 2005). In addition, 54% of families in the assessment track received services other than case management compared to 36% of families in the investigation track (Loman & Siegel, 2004a). The number of services received by families and the type of support services provided to families related to basic financial needs were greater in the assessment track; as well, counselling and therapeutic services were offered more frequently to these families. Similar findings were also reported in Missouri (Loman & Siegel, 2004b) and Virginia (Virginia Department of Social Services, 2008).

Families have reported satisfaction with differential response in several states (Child Welfare Information Gateway, 2008), and this was true for families in Minnesota. For example, 48% of AR families said they received the kind of service they needed compared to 33% of investigation track families one year after case closure. As well, 44% of AR track families said they received enough services to really help them compared to 27% of investigation track families. AR families were also more likely to report being treated fairly by workers, feeling connected to other community resources, and feeling hopeful and encouraged (Loman & Siegel, 2005).

Research indicates that AR families felt more involved in decision-making (Child Welfare Information Gateway, 2008); for example, in Minnesota 68% of families in the assessment track said they were involved "a great deal" in decisions about their families and children, and this was the case for only 45% of investigated families (Loman & Siegel, 2005). Family engagement is a key to success in family-centred practice, and in the Minnesota study workers rated the primary caregiver as unco-operative in less than 2% of assessment families compared to 44% of investigated families.

Placement Rates and Costs

The impact of services on placement rates in a DR system is difficult to determine because service models and evaluation methods vary significantly across jurisdictions. As earlier noted, Olmsted County reported a significant reduction in placement rates (Sawyer & Lohrbach, 2005a), and in the multiple agency experiential study conducted by Loman and Siegel (2004a) in Minnesota, follow-up placement rates were lower for children from the AR stream. What is important here is that the reduction in reoccurrence of maltreatment and placement rates was attributed to the new approach (Loman & Siegel, 2005). In Missouri, however, cases referred to the assessment track were slightly more likely to be placed during a five-year follow-up period (28% vs. 25%) (Loman & Siegel, 2004b). Further analysis in the Missouri study revealed that families more likely to experience out-of-home placements were those with no prior history of placement, and whose families were composed only of teenage children at the time of the original report.

Follow-up referrals for investigation and placement rates have cost implications, and a cost effectiveness study was included in the Minnesota study (Loman & Siegel, 2005). Consistent with findings related to increased services, costs were higher in the early period of providing alternative response services. However, in the follow-up period after service contact had ended, costs were much less for the experimental group (AR families) because these families had fewer re-reports during this time period and fewer children placed in care. Although the average overall costs for families in the experimental group were lower than the control group over the two time periods, a longer term follow-up study of costs was recommended.

Service Capacity

Staff have reported satisfaction with the service model in differential response in Minnesota (Loman & Siegel, 2005), Missouri (Loman & Siegel, 2004b), and North Carolina (Center for Child and Family Policy, 2006). At the same time, large caseloads can be an obstacle to effectiveness. In the evaluation of Missouri's program, it was concluded that the impact of differential response was mitigated by large caseloads and limited resources. Similar findings were reported in North Carolina, where it was recommended that caseloads be reduced or a team service model be adopted.

Ambivalent findings related to community engagement are also reported. In the Minnesota study, Loman and Siegel (2005) found greater use of community resources in a DR system, and this finding was replicated in Missouri

(2004b). However, in another study conducted in Washington (Washington State Department of Social and Health Services, 2005), community agencies were not always able to make contact with families, or see them within the time frames anticipated by the child protection agency. These findings underscore the issue of agency and community capacity. If a key underlying problem is the number of child maltreatment allegations being referred, there must be enough capacity within the agency (e.g., staff, manageable caseloads, and skills) to pro-vide both child protection services to those children at risk and family support services to the children and families in need. In addition, community service providers who are expected to work in partnership with the child welfare agency in this new enhanced service model must have enough resources to play their part. In the absence of these resources, the restructuring of services under DR may not achieve intended results.

Although many of the effects reported from differential response have been positive, many differences, including those in the Minnesota study, have been modest in size. As well, the Minnesota study found no significant differences in ratings of child well-being or parent–child relationships between the two groups one year after case closure (Loman & Siegel, 2005).

Discussion and Implications

Research on differential response systems, conducted primarily in the U.S., sug-gests changes are not revolutionary. However, evaluations have demonstrated that there are positive outcomes from intervening with families in a less adver-sarial way without any adverse effects on child safety. Benefits associated with this shift to a more family-friendly approach include more co-operative work-ing relationships with families, an increase in the number of families served, a broader range of services based on the needs of families, and some evidence that future referrals for maltreatment and/or out-of-home placement may be reduced.

To what extent these results can be generalized to other jurisdictions, includ-ing Canada, is yet to be determined. Nevertheless, there are some lessons emerg-ing from research findings that need to be considered. They include:

- the need for clear procedures and tools for assessing child safety, risk, and the underlying needs and conditions that affect the well-being of children and families;
- well-designed training for staff, supervisors, and administrators on how to engage with families and kinship networks in ways that focus on needs and strengths;

- the need for adequate resources within the agency, including reasonable workloads for staff, and access to appropriate community resources; and
- evaluation procedures to help guide service modifications, and assess child and family outcomes.

The importance of training is illustrated by the inconsistencies in screening, notably between sites, and the variations between the rates of families referred to the alternative response stream. For example, in Minnesota, referrals to the assessment track varied from 27% to 61% across 20 demonstration sites (Loman & Siegel, 2005). Given the generally positive effects of AR across all sites, these differences may indicate that many families are being unnecessarily restricted from accessing AR services.

The need for adequate infrastructure to support DR services cannot be underestimated, as several findings suggest that the full benefits of DR were not being realized because of the pressure of large caseloads (Child Welfare Information Gateway, 2008). How infrastructure needs, such as reasonable staff caseloads and other needed resources, are to be addressed, particularly as demonstration projects are rolled out across the system, is a significant challenge.

One of the more important aspects of DR is the increased focus on family engagement or involvement, and this is illustrated in practice examples from the Olmsted County experience (Lohrbach et al., 2005). A key element in this transition is a practice model which builds trust and a commitment to engagement among families. However, the family-focused approach to practice developed by this agency has not been limited to the AR stream. Family involvement strategies, including the use of family group conferences, case planning conferences, and rapid response case planning (i.e., engagement of key stakeholders, including relevant family members at the point of a crisis), are used across all agency programs in an attempt to capture the wisdom of parents and kinship networks in decision-making and intervention (Christenson, Curran, DeCook, Maloney, & Merkel-Holguin, 2008). Added value comes from the infusion of this way of working in all agency services, including the investigation track in DR systems. Although the goals and specific applications of family involvement strategies may vary based on the service pathway and characteristics of the case, the shift from a more professionally driven service model to family-centred processes can make a significant difference to the way child welfare services are perceived by families.

The title of this chapter invites consideration of the extent to which differential response models address early intervention and prevention goals in child and family welfare. The answer is not straightforward. Based on findings from Minnesota, Loman and Siegel (2005) conclude that the alternative response system did shift services in the direction of secondary and tertiary prevention in some modest ways: the number of families receiving assistance increased, there was increased attention to low-risk families, and family support services directed toward basic, financially-related needs increased. The focus on the provision of basic needs, including attention to financial needs, was important to families, and the amounts spent on these services were not insignificant. At the same time, child welfare agencies are not primarily income support agencies, and do not have the capacity to fully address these needs. Enhanced resources for early intervention and prevention programs are required to enable a more comprehensive response to the needs of families and children.

Increased engagement with community-based agencies can enhance early intervention goals, and this is encouraged in DR. However, the needs of families that may be screened out, even under a DR system, as well as additional outreach to families who may be in need of services but have not yet been referred, will not be adequately addressed without increased attention to these partnerships. For example, approximately 60% of referrals in Minnesota were screened out in 2006 (the national U.S. rate was 38% in 2005) (Thompson, Siegel, & Loman, 2008, p. 23). In an effort to respond to the needs of these families, a parent support program was initiated in 2005, and several pilot project sites initially targeted families with at least one child less than five years old (the age criterion has now been changed to 10 years). A wide range of services have been provided under the program, including funded services from the program designed to support families and referrals to other community service providers. All services are voluntary, but a needs and strengths assessment is completed prior to service provision. Based on feedback from families, 88% received some type of funded services and 72% received referrals to various community resources. In addition, 50% of the families reported receiving some type of assistance directly from social workers, and 47% said they had become aware of resources in their communities that they had not known about before (Thompson et al., 2008).

Research data from families referred to investigation and assessment tracks in differential response systems indicate that family needs and profiles are quite similar across all groups, even if there is variation in immediate safety concerns and risk levels. This underscores the importance of early intervention and prevention programs, but also raises questions about how such services should be delivered and by whom. One approach is to integrate needs- and strengths-based assessment processes with family-centred practices across both investigation and AR service tracks, and to respond in a more comprehensive fashion to all families. To some extent this response was illustrated by the service model in Olmsted County. Yuan (2005) outlines another approach in which the primary focus of maltreatment investigations is restricted to cases involving past or likely harm to the child, with all other cases routed to the needs-focused assessment track. This approach effectively narrows the definition of maltreatment in a way that seems to contrast sharply with recent trends which have broadened the concept of maltreatment (e.g., emotional maltreatment and exposure to incidents of domestic violence) in ways that have contributed to net-widening effects on referrals for investigation.

Three other issues that may affect policy and practice in DR require further study. First is the assumption that the assignment to specific service streams can be made at the intake stage (Yuan, 2005). Factors that influence assignment, such as whether all intake workers have the required skills or training, or whether there is adequate information to make a decision at this stage, require closer examination.

Second are the relatively modest differences between investigation and assessment track families in many DR programs in the U.S. Based on these data, outcomes and family satisfaction with assessment track services are better, yet there is still a significant proportion of families in both service tracks who are dissatisfied with services or did not receive the help they wanted. Although child safety must remain a primary objective under either response, it is important to assess whether service responses provided by child welfare agencies can be enhanced for these families, or whether these unmet needs reflect responses that must come from other government or community service providers.

Third is the question of the disproportionality (i.e., overrepresentation) of children in care. In the U.S. there is a disproportionate number of African-American children in care; in Canada, New Zealand, and Australia there are disproportionate numbers of Indigenous children in care (Chapter 20). There are a number of possible explanations for this pattern, but Richardson (2008) suggests that differential response could help to address some of the service gaps, including immediate financial needs that contribute to these differences. This potential has not yet been fully explored, but more attention to enhanced financial supports and other types of direct services where neglect is a precipitating cause of maltreatment might make a difference. In addition, disadvantaged communities and neighbourhoods often lack adequate community support services for families, and improved access to these types of resources may also help.

Differential response is not a replacement for other types of early intervention and prevention programs that must be available for children and families, but it has the potential to shift the focus of practice to a more family-centred approach and provide more services to an increased number of families. As differential response systems are in a relatively early stage of development in Canada, research and evaluation efforts should initially focus on implementation issues, including a number of the policy and practice concerns raised in this chapter. In addition, outcomes must be carefully considered in helping to determine whether the new approach makes a difference to the well-being of children and families.

7

Doing the Work: Child Protection Jobs in Centralized and Accessible Service Delivery Models

Gary Cameron
Nancy Freymond
Lirondel Cheyne-Hazineh

The purpose of this chapter is to explore the effects of service delivery location on child protection services. In particular, it examines whether locating child protection services in settings that are more accessible to clientele makes a difference in how front-line child protection employment is understood and appreciated by service providers. The evidence about child protection employment presented in this chapter comes from front-line child protection workers at 11 service delivery sites in southern Ontario. This research is part of a larger study that also documents parents' experiences as well as service outcomes across the 11 sites. More information about the broader program of research is available at <http://www.wlu.ca/pcfproject>.

Background

The Canadian experience in child welfare is illustrative of the challenges facing child protection systems in most English-speaking countries. Common concerns include the rapid expansion of the numbers of families investigated, greatly increasing costs, minimal levels of assistance provided to children or parents, frequent adversarial service relationships, increasing reliance on formal court authority, rising numbers of children in out-of-home care, few service partnerships, excessive stress on service providers, and high staff turnover (Differential Response Sub-Committee of Ontario Children's Aid Society Directors of Service, 2004; Freymond & Cameron, 2006; Kufeldt & McKenzie, 2003b).

Consequently, there is growing interest in the creation of more flexible response child protection systems in some Canadian provinces—maintaining procedure-driven risk emphases in "core" investigatory child protection services, while encouraging a more collaborative service response to less "dangerous" family situations. This shift follows earlier differential response reforms in the United States, England, and Australia (Freymond & Cameron, 2006). The province of Ontario in Canada has recently initiated its *Transformation Agenda*, which includes *greater* emphases on differential response, increasing local communities' capacities to support families and to protect children, and sharing more of the child welfare mandate with formal service partners (Child Welfare Secretariat, 2005, 2006).

There is agreement in the literature about the complex challenges of creating productive differential response systems. In particular, system effectiveness has been linked to having access to supportive resources for families, creating partnerships and co-locating with services and community associations, being accessible to families, providing service provider training, and child welfare organizations demonstrating leadership in the development processes (Child Welfare Secretariat, 2005, 2006; Hornberger & Briar-Lawson, 2005; Howell, Kelly, Palmer, & Mangum, 2004; Schene, 2001a, 2001b, 2006). While the research is sparse, there is some evidence of more encouraging results from enriched differential response demonstration projects, those with greater access to service and community partnerships in local communities benefiting from greater implementation support (Chahine, van Straaten, & Williams-Isom, 2005; Differential Response Sub-Committee of Ontario Children's Aid Society Directors of Service, 2004; Schene, 2006).

As part of the Partnerships for Children and Families Project's program of research (see <http://www.wlu.ca/pcfproject>), an exploratory study of three community- and school-based models of child welfare service delivery in Ontario was completed (Frensch, Cameron, & Hazineh, 2005). The study produced evidence that these community and school settings led to more assistance being available to children and families, as well as more co-operative helping relationships. These findings led to a larger study (2006–9) of front-line child protection practice in 11 service delivery settings. These settings varied on dimensions theoretically important to differential response models of child welfare: (1) physical accessibility to clients, (2) service and community partnerships, and (3) co-location with other services.

Method and Research Questions

This chapter focuses on how front-line service providers perceived their jobs in centrally located and more accessible school and community service delivery models.[1] It is based on individual and group qualitative interviews with about 150 front-line child protection service providers and supervisors at 11 research sites. These were located in six partner agencies in southern Ontario. Four agency delivery sites were included, three sites were located in schools, three others were located at decentralized sites in the community, and one site was in an integrated children's service centre. The agency sites provided services from a central location, and this was the most common child welfare service delivery model in Ontario. School sites involved the placement of individual service providers in schools with the intention of being more accessible to children and parents as well as school personnel. Community sites were located in the neighbourhoods they served. Sometimes they co-located with service and community partners. They also tended to be more accessible to clients. Both school and community models placed a high priority on establishing more co-operative helping relationships with children and parents. The integrated services site joined child welfare and children's mental health services under a single administration. The overarching goal was to realize service delivery efficiencies and to have more resources available to clients. These integrated services were situated at a single central location.

The broader program of research utilized qualitative methods and a quasi-experimental outcome design. It gathered data from child protection service providers and parents about their service involvement experiences. It assessed child, parent, and family functioning as well as selected system indicators (e.g., child placements) over a 12-month period from case opening.

Results reported in this chapter focus on comparison between how front-line service providers perceived their jobs in the two types of service delivery models, those centrally located and the more accessible school- and community-based sites. More specifically, this investigation was guided by the following questions:

- Are front-line child protection service providers more satisfied with their jobs within some service delivery models than others?
- Do the sources of job satisfaction and dissatisfaction differ across these service delivery models?
- Do service providers believe that they are able to do their jobs better within some models than others?
- Are service providers more likely to want to continue their child protection employment within certain approaches?

Results: Job Sustaining Narratives

It is normal for colleagues sharing a workplace to elaborate a shared story about what makes their work worthwhile and what is hard to accept. This chapter presents two contrasting general narratives about employment realities in agency-based and accessible service delivery settings. These are entitled: (1) Pride and Endurance, and (2) Belief and Integration. The first narrative was more common in centralized agency-based sites, whereas the second narrative was more characteristic of accessible community-based sites. A third narrative, entitled "It can't be done," was elaborated at all 11 service delivery sites. It focused on how the expectations of the formal child protection often made their jobs unsustainable, and greatly circumscribed their abilities to do good work with children and families. The chapter concludes with a discussion of the service delivery implications of these three narratives.

Pride and Endurance

This narrative reflected a pride in being able to do a very difficult and important job that many others could not do. As noted above, this type of response was more common to agency-based workers at the more centrally located service delivery sites. Related to this were feelings that this difficult work was not understood or appreciated by families and outsiders. Agency-based workers also were much more likely than service providers at more accessible sites to talk about adversarial relations with parents, and to feel misunderstood by service providers and others in their community. The following quotations illustrate this pride in being able to do a difficult job, and how it's not a job for everyone:

> P1: I think, for me, it's a very, very difficult job that I don't think a lot of people could do. I don't know certainly not every social worker could do it.... I find it rewarding to do a job that a lot of people couldn't do... so it's a sense of giving something back something, of doing some service ... Again, someone has to do it ...

> P2: ... someone says, "So what do you do?" And I say, "Well, I'm a child protection worker," and they're like, "Whoa, I could not do that job, oh my goodness; you guys should get a medal." That is kind of rewarding when that happens. (Agency-Based Site 1: Front-line Workers)

> P2: They say it's a calling.

> P6: Yes, well, I would rather get called to the nunnery right now, because I'd get a rest. [laughter] (Agency-Based Site 2: Front-line Workers)

Oh, my God. How did I get into this job? We ask ourselves that a lot. [laughs] … people find out fairly quickly, child welfare generally is not a good job for me … (Agency-Based Site 4: Front-line Worker)

Agency-based child protection service providers described a more insular world of work than their more accessible model counterparts. They were more likely to focus on the obstacles to connecting with families and, with the exception of those at the integrated service site, to perceive their work as misunderstood and unappreciated by other service providers. These service providers focused more within their own teams for support and a sense of employment identity than did school- or community-based service providers. From our perspective, this distinction between perceptions of relatively insular and connected worlds of work was one of the most important distinctions between agency-based and accessible service delivery models in this research. The following illustrate feelings expressed of being misunderstood by other service providers and frustrations at being unable to connect with families:

… we work really hard to do that but we can only do what we can do and sometimes it's just not possible, but it seems like the common misconception is that we're just trying to tear families apart, but we work extremely hard to try to do the opposite, but sometimes it can't be done. (Agency-Based Site 3: Front-line Worker)

But you get a couple of cases where you get countless different people calling you from the community, you know, from different realms, and just sort of "You guys aren't doing anything or …" And it's just—it's very frustrating because then you're the one who's got to go back and talk to the family and you're trying to build a relationship with them, and, you know, not think about all the other stuff that's coming in a negative way. And at the same time you're like, "Why did you mess up your kid so much?" (Integrated Services Site: Front-line Worker)

We're not often that direct service delivery person. We rarely would ever get opportunity to do, you know, a counselling session and all those … it's always, you know, trying to connect them with others and so, you know, it's the frustration of not having as big a role in it sometimes … (Agency-Based Site 2: Front-line Worker)

While concerns with heavy documentation demands were voiced at every research site, and service providers everywhere were cognizant of personal liability risks in their work, agency service providers talked more explicitly about these liability fears:

P3: Yes, the liability is huge. I don't worry about that as much as I worry about other things, but it's always in the back of your head.

P4: It's with you every day. You can never turn it off. You just have to learn how to live with it. (Agency-Based Site 2: Front-line Workers)

There was agreement that access to the support of other child welfare service providers in their service team was highly appreciated and important to being able to cope with the pressures of their job. Closely connected was the importance placed on having accessible support from a supervisor. This was an aspect of their employment that agency-based workers overall found more satisfactory than front-line service providers at the more accessible sites. Agency-based service providers sometimes presented loss of team support and personal safety concerns as main objections to working within more accessible service delivery models.

Some service providers expressed strong commitment to and appreciation of their child welfare jobs at several agency-based sites. The most common appreciations expressed were when good helping relationships with children and families were established and when workers were a part of facilitating positive changes in families. These are illustrated below; however, as noted earlier, agency-based service providers generally described greater barriers to establishing co-operative helping relationships with parents than service providers at school- or community-based service delivery sites:

… I've been an ongoing worker for three years, and for me the most meaningful part is connecting with the families and providing meaningful help to them, any kind of meaningful connection …

…

It would have to be working with the kids, especially some of the older ones, making that connection, helping them, assisting them in making some decisions that can change where they're going to end up for the future … (Agency-Based Site 3: Front-line Workers)

There were several dominant themes in these agency child protection service providers' narratives about their employment. There was a belief that the work they were doing was important and necessary. And for some, there was a commitment to continuing to do this type of work. There was a pride expressed in "having what it takes" to carry out this stressful and personally demanding work. On the other hand, they talked about the personal costs for themselves and their families.

Access to team, colleague, and supervisor support were seen as integral to doing their jobs. They also portrayed a fairly insular everyday world of work, with their main referents being within the formal child protection system. There was a sense that "outsiders" would not understand their challenges or necessarily be supportive.

They said that the work was "never boring." It was characterized as fast-paced, with lots of variety. While they did talk about obstacles to establishing co-operative relationships with families, they also drew succour from instances when they were able to establish good helping relationships with parents or children, and when they were able to perceive positive benefits for kids or families from their efforts.

Belief and Integration

There was an enthusiasm among front-line workers and their supervisors about their school- and community-based service delivery approaches that was not evident in the agency-based employment narratives. There was satisfaction expressed with specific aspects of these approaches, and also belief in the value of the accessible service delivery models. Positive statements about these service delivery approaches were common:

> It's nice when you run into clients that maybe you're not working with, or that you are working with, and you know, they just stop and say hello. They're not intimidated to come up to you in public and speak with you; that it's more than just a relationship with an authoritative figure. (Community-Based Site 1: Front-line Worker)

> I think every school, anywhere, not in just this community or any community, every school should have a social worker in it, because that's where a lot of our problems are identified, and I just don't understand schools that wouldn't want to have a social worker in it. (School-Based Site 2: Supervisor)

> You're a part of that whole family and the teachers like to know who they're dealing with as well.... it's a huge piece. It's wonderful, I think. (School-Based Site 3: Front-line Worker)

From our perspective, these front-line service providers provided a relatively integrated conception of their service jobs. They talked about their protection and prevention responsibilities with little evidence of tension between these undertakings. They described being accessible and being able to engage co-operatively with many families. Partnerships with other types of service providers were normal parts of everyday work. They talked positively of "doing more than child protection." These aspects were considered to be rewarding aspects of their jobs. For the most part, as illustrated below, they felt there was a "good fit" between how they wanted to relate to clients and partners and the intentions of their local service delivery model.

> ... It's fun, because, y'know, I tell the kids, y'know, the principal's office and y'know, bring a book, bring some spelling sheets, I'm doing paperwork, so you could read to me, did you do spelling while I'm typing ... type on the cube for all I care. I love it. (School-Based Site 2: Front-line Worker)

> ... New Year's Eve day I was working and saw a client that morning. A newborn baby, like a week old, and the baby wasn't nursing well. Mom's milk hadn't come in, or so she thought. Anyhow, I was worried, you know, very vulnerable baby. So I come back here to the office and I just, you know, zipped down to the next door, to Public Health. They sent a public health nurse over right away with a scale, weighed the baby, did some nursing instruction. About an hour later the public health nurse comes to my office and says, "Here's a prescription for Mom." I just went to the community health clinic. "Here's a prescription for Mom, can you fill it and get it to her?" (Community-Based Site 2: Front-line Worker)

> I think it's enhanced me as a person, too, because I've met such wonderful people in the community, whether it's partnerships or community members. And, um, they all bring something to the table, they all bring something to us ... I'm just really quite thrilled to be part of the community. I love that whole aspect. So that's really rewarding. (School-Based Site 3: Front-line Worker)

One of the frustrations of being a front-line service provider in some of the accessible service delivery sites was coping with periodic isolation from other child protection service providers. Because they were often dispersed across different school or community settings, a common lament was not having quick access to a colleague for support or assistance when making decisions. Coping with this relative isolation was seen as one of the major employment challenges in the more accessible service models.

Front-line service providers valued their accessibility to clients and to service partners. Nonetheless, this openness also contributed to their sense of working in a fishbowl. They described frequent interruptions to their everyday work routines. Overall, most of these service providers believed in the merit of their accessible service models, but the price was some unique employment frustrations:

> Well, it can be quite disruptive to—and I hate to say this as a downside, because it's a plus side, but it can be quite disruptive to your day when you have these walk-ins all the time ... they're ex-clients ... but they drop in all the time just to say hi, and the kids want to give me a picture or invite me to their school play and

just to say how they're doing. I love that ... oh, there are times when the recep-
tionist calls me and says, oh, you know, "Your favourite client's here," and I just
go, "Not today"—like, I don't have 20 minutes to sit with her. I mean, that's a very
minor downside, right? (Community-Based Site 2: Front-line Worker)

This perception was supported by a school-based supervisor, who said of the
staff:

They're on all the time, they don't—they're never—they can never come back and
kick their feet up, they are visible all the time. (School-Based Site 3: Supervisor)

School-based and community-based service providers enjoyed when they
were able to establish welcoming, helping relationships with parents and children. They believed that they were able to establish co-operative relationships
with a larger proportion of families they served than agency-based service
providers. Accessible site service providers recounted with pride instances when
kids and parents appeared to benefit from their interventions.

Workers believed that these service delivery models allowed them to be flexible and to do more things to be helpful to children and parents. They also felt
that these approaches provided them with earlier and more complete information about what was going on in the lives of children and families. For example, they described sometimes being able to respond to requests for assistance
or to perceptions of danger to children more rapidly because of their informal
contacts and networks. They talked about being more accessible to service partners and, in some instances, being able to access resources for kids and parents
faster.

On the other hand, they had to manage the unique challenges of working
in "fish bowl environments," and to having less access to the support of child
protection colleagues, teams, or supervisors. A few thought that they might
be less safe from angry clients by working in less physically secure premises.
Nonetheless, overall, there was a clear impression from these service providers
that the benefits of working in these accessible service models outweighed
the costs.

It Can't Be Done

The central theme of the narrative about the formal provincial child protection
system was that the job expectations were very excessive. This theme was not
only pervasive but expressed with emotion. Front-line service providers were
expected to do far too much. The job was never done. It was not possible to meet

all expectations or to remain up to date with their responsibilities. There were always trade-offs and choices about what could wait. They felt there was a serious disconnection between what the formal system demanded of them and the realities of front-line work. There were many vivid descriptions of the inordinate pressures these expectations placed on front-line service providers, sometimes with significant negative personal and professional consequences. This feeling of being overloaded was expressed at every central and accessible research site. For example, as noted by one agency-based front-line service provider:

> … that's when I'll have my anxiety attacks, my panic attacks. I'll get sick. I always get sick on vacation because it's like my body is like, staying well, staying well, okay, I'm on vacation, whoosh. … And then two days before you come back, sleepless nights again, thinking, "What's going to hit me when I come back, what's it going to be?" (Agency-Based Site 1: Front-line Worker)

A front-line service provider at a school-based site agreed:

> … the job's never done, you could work overtime forever, you know, but you just can't do it, otherwise you sacrifice your own physical, mental health and it's not worth it—but yet if we don't get all our stuff done, then that's just stress. (School-Based Site 2: Front-line Worker)

One of the biggest demands on front-line service providers' time was completing the formal documentation requirements of their jobs. At all sites, front-line service providers talked about spending 60% to 70% of their time on documentation. Service providers thought that compliance with the accountability requirements of their work outweighed any other priorities in their jobs. They perceived that this emphasis reflected a self-protection device for the Ministry and child welfare agencies. Also, being compliant with these documentation requirements was seen as a way for these service providers to protect themselves.

One of the original intentions of the child protection *Transformation Agenda* in Ontario was to reduce documentation time to free up more service time for children and families. With the caution that these data were gathered early in the process of implementing the *Transformation Agenda*, these service providers thought that, overall, documentation requirements for their jobs might have increased under these reforms. They linked this increase to additional documentation required by new mandated procedures (e.g., arranging for kinship care, mediation services, or family group conferencing) and by the new expectation that *all* contacts relevant to a case be recorded in computerized case notes.

Front-line service providers understood that the reason for these case notes was to have credible evidence if involvement with the court was necessary:

> And we're measured by our paperwork. Not by our social work, we're measured by our paperwork, and that is so frustrating … (School-Based Site 1: Front-line Worker)

> … it's mostly about the recording, and that's because for the last 10 years, it's been hammered into our heads … (Agency-Based Site 1: Manager)

> Paperwork is crazy; frustration, you're never ahead of the game, and when you get ahead of the game … (Integrated Services Site: Front-line Worker)

> … Everything is done in a legal context, it's about us being accountable for what we're doing with our families, and it's 70% of our job, to report, it's a huge, huge component … (Agency-Based Site 3: Front-line Worker)

Many of the service providers at these research sites implied or stated explicitly that it was very hard and perhaps impossible to do good work with children or their parents under these conditions:

> I think when you talk about limits, we're talking about workload and not being able to do good social work in the amount of time that we have to do it. (School-Based Site 1: Front-line Worker)

> I mean, how much can you accomplish when you only are able to visit a family once a month, or once, and you miss that month and it's two months—what's really being done—not much other than the file is just continuing … (Integrated Services Site: Front-line Worker)

> … that's right, you do band-aids… you don't have the time to give them actual help, all you do is hang around and wait for the next crisis. (Agency-Based Site 2: Front-line Worker)

A second negative consequence of these formal system expectations was the high turnover rate among front-line service providers. The impression from these narratives was that agency-based front-line child protection service providers simply wear down, and that many left their jobs. Despite providing a more enthusiastic local employment narrative, in the words of one respondent, community- and school-based front-line child protection service providers "speak well [of the program] and leave":

> One of the things that I find very frustrating would have to be along the same lines as the client's is—the worker turnover, you know, I have a hard time dealing with all the different workers and the turnover … (Integrated Services Site: Front-line Worker)

And that takes years to learn, as a worker, and people are burning out in their third, fourth year—like it's just that learning curve over and over and over again, you know, you never get to that point where you recognize, as a worker, you know, what you can actually do for families. (Agency-Based Site 2: Front-line Worker)

… people are simply leaving … the individuals' experiences are not reflective of what they're being told … (Community-Based Site 2: Front-line Worker)

Conclusion

When interpreting these findings, it is important to keep in mind that in all instances the service providers were providing mandated front-line child protection services. There was no infusion of supplementary funds or any relaxation of the formal child protection system expectations at any of these research sites. Thus, the prime mandate at each of these sites was to protect children from specific types of maltreatment, and each site had to satisfy the same provincially stipulated service delivery timelines and documentation requirements.

However, there were important differences in intentions across these service delivery models. The school and community sites tried to establish more frequent and co-operative relationships with parents. They wished to be visible and approachable to children and parents in local schools and neighbourhoods. Although less clearly articulated, most of these sites wanted to engage other service providers in helping children and parents. One neighbourhood site explicitly tried to engage community residents in protecting children and supporting parents.

These intentions were much less prevalent among service providers at the more centralized service delivery sites. However, the integrated children's services site was created in part to facilitate service coordination, and its service providers described greater service co-operation and access capacities than service providers at the agency-based sites. More information on service philosophies and service partnerships is available at <http://www.wlu.ca/pcfproject>.

This research demonstrates that changes in service philosophy, locating front-line service providers in settings that are more accessible to children and parents, and sharing settings with other services can make significant differences to how child protection service providers understand and appreciate their jobs. Other research has shown that such changes can also affect how children and parents engage with these services (Frensch, Cameron, & Hazineh, 2005). On the other hand, formal child protection system expectations challenged the feasibility and sustainability of employment in every service delivery approach examined in this study.

Suppose we were looking at an organization other than a child welfare agency. And assume we knew little about what a certain category of employees did. To find out, we asked these workers to describe how they spent their time at work. Would it not be reasonable to assume that the tasks that they spent most of their time doing illustrated the primary contributions of their work?

Let's ask this question about the employment profile provided by front-line child protection service providers in this research. Should we not conclude that their core task was to provide formal documentation for the child protection system? Why would we not think the primary purposes served were accountability, system and professional protection, and preparation for court proceedings? It is striking that no front-line service provider at any of the research sites linked these accountability procedures to better protection of children or to providing needed assistance to families. They were much more likely to believe that these accountability procedures represented obstacles to providing useful help.

Is it not clear that the service provision and accountability expectations of this formal child protection system are seriously unbalanced? These service providers felt that this imbalance made the challenges of protecting children and helping families more difficult. As well, they thought that the very high work demands, combined with excessive accountability requirements, made too many of their jobs unsustainable.

When efforts have been made to improve this child protection model, they have focused on increasing funding and hiring more service providers. Emphases have shifted back and forth from investigation to assessment, from more child apprehensions to increased diversity of service responses, and from court orders to voluntary service agreements. Local jurisdictions have tried innovative service delivery and programming strategies. Yet the core employment realities for front-line child protection service providers seem to have been only marginally affected by such shifts.

Is it feasible to examine the nature and consequences of the formal centralized bureaucratic organization of child protection services? If our analyses are correct, this bureaucratic organization will transform any service innovations to conform to its culture—that is, standardization, control, and the avoidance of risk. This observation is not new. Schorr (1997), in describing how even demonstration projects with excellent outcomes became ineffective when absorbed by established bureaucracies, laments regulatory realities that, in order to avoid anything going wrong, make it impossible to do anything right.

From our perspective, several elements should be part of modifying this culture. There is a need to broaden our service intentions. A narrow conception of protecting children is not sufficient to guide interventions for children or parents. While tough choices about how to intervene are inevitable in this work, overall, there are close connections between child welfare and family welfare. These need to be reflected in our intentions.

We need to become less risk adverse. Improving our group decision-making capacity when it is not clear how to intervene could help (Hetherington & Nurse, 2006). Formal risk assessments could inform these decisions; however, formal procedures are not substitutes for service relationships. Rich relationships with children, parents, communities, and service partners are central to service providers having good information about families and a reasonable capacity to protect children and support parents. Accountability procedures are essential. But these procedures should not overshadow the need for sufficient investments into creating and sustaining service relationships.

Clearly, front-line service providers have to spend much less time in front of their computers. This would require a deep systemic disengagement from the courts. Service providers cannot properly protect children or support parents if their attention is focused on producing evidence suitable for a trial. Court involvement procedures are needed that do not dominate front-line child protection services. Changing this systemic context for child protection services is daunting. However, without doing so, our ability to protect children and help families is unlikely to get much better.

Note

1 The need for brevity in this chapter allowed us to include relatively few illustrations of the points made. For access to more supporting data, readers are referred to longer discussions at <http://www.wlu.ca/pcfproject>.

8

Child Welfare Interventions That Make Sense to Mothers

Nancy Freymond
Gary Cameron

C hild welfare interventions focus heavily on the evaluation and rehabilita-tion of mothering practices (Davies & Krane, 1996; Miller, 1991; Scour-field, 2001; Swift, 1995b; Turney, 2000; Risley-Curtiss & Heffernan, 2003). For mothers, involvement with systems of child welfare, particularly child placement, evokes intense emotions. This chapter presents the findings from a study that examined the child placement experiences of 31 mothers in Ontario, Canada. It explores reasons for the marginalization of these mothers, and how this process may diminish possibilities for creating positive responses for children and parents in these circumstances.

The Importance of Mothers' Experiences

The past two decades have witnessed a growing body of literature focused on mothers and mothering in child welfare in Canada (see, for example, Callahan, 1993; Davies, Collings, & Krane, 2003; Davies & Krane, 1996; Krane & Davies, 2000; Swift, 1995b, 1998), with recent scholarship emphasizing child welfare, domestic violence, and mothers (see, for example, Damant et al., 2010; Davies & Krane, 2006; Lapierre, 2008). Despite the profound impact of out-of-home placement in mothers' lives and substantial Canadian child welfare involve-ments in removing children from their family homes, representations of moth-ers' placement experiences either in child welfare practice or scholarship are limited. Some examples include McCallum (1995), who focused on the expe-riences of ten Canadian parents, including six mothers of children placed in out-of-home care as a result of a child sexual abuse investigation. Although her research does not centre on the experience of placement, it does include the voices of mothers speaking about placement experiences. Anderson (1998) studied the views of six Native mothers, four of whom had experienced the apprehension of a child by a Children's Aid Society. Dumbrill and Maiter (2003) reported on the views of eight parents who had experienced the placement of a child in out-of-home care about how to improve child protection services. This study does not indicate the gender of participating parents, although references to mothers are made repeatedly, with only one reference to a father. Callahan et al. (2003) focused on young mothers in substitute care and their experience of mothering. Collectively, these scholars draw attention to the challenges of child placement for mothers, and the intense, often negative feelings associated with this event.

The representation of mothers' experience in child welfare has been eclipsed by a pervasive discourse that presents an unsympathetic characterization of these women. Within this discourse, mothers are assessed in part based on the criterion of a dominant mothering ideology (Kline, 1995). Mothering profiles inconsistent with this ideology are described using deviancy discourses (Arendell, 1999; Gergen, 1999; Gustafson, 2005): mothers of children placed in out-of-home care are constructed as bad mothers (Swift, 1995b). Their mothering is portrayed as deficient and potentially abusive. They are separated conceptually and morally from socially acceptable mothers.

Canadian child welfare policy and practice are dominated by a strongly child-centred discourse, with child protection as the foremost concern (Greaves et al., 2002). In this discourse, mothers of children in out-of-home placements "have failed" to provide for the care and safety of their children. From this perspective, impacts on mothers' lives of child placements are inconsequential in making "child safety" decisions. Why would we listen to them? What would be gained from understanding their experiences?

Children are entitled to physical and emotional protection, and measures should be taken to protect their safety. Sometimes it is essential to remove children from potentially unsafe environments. Yet it remains true that decisions about child placement, and about the possibility of children's reunification with parents, are among the most complex facing child welfare service providers. The best course of action is often not clear. Knowing more about mothers' lives and service experiences has the potential to contribute to practice and policy options that are more congruent with family realities.

More importantly, the lives of children and mothers are intrinsically connected. Most children involved with child welfare will either continue to live at home or return home. Also, maintaining involvement with parents, the inclusive care approach, is beneficial for many children in care (Kufeldt, 1995; Kufeldt, Armstrong, & Dorosh, 1996; Palmer, 1995). Improving family and child well-being in most instances are interconnected processes.

In addition, recipients of helping services do not make changes in their lives based simply on professional recommendations. Services must make sense in the context of their lives; otherwise, offers of help will provoke frustration and resistance. Knowledge of mothers' experience can contribute to creating interventions that are more likely to be welcomed by mothers and their children.

Methodology

Life story research was the preferred approach for this study. Oral traditions are distinguished by their capacity to illuminate the experiences and perspectives of non-authoritative, marginalized groups (Biddle, 1996; Perks & Thomson, 1998). Life story research also aids in understanding the social contexts in which people live (Goodson & Sikes, 2001; McAdams, 1993). The stories used in this analysis were collected for the Partnerships for Children and Families Project, a multi-year research project focused on improving child protection and children's mental health services. This purposive sample is comprised of a subset of 31 mothers who had experienced child welfare child placement. Eighteen of the mothers had their children apprehended by child welfare against their wishes, and thirteen mothers had requested child welfare involvement, usually to assist with difficult child behaviour.

Twenty-six life histories were collected using a single comprehensive semi-structured interview. Specific questions were asked about mothers' living circumstances, their initial contacts with child welfare service providers, and about the nature of their relationships with these service providers over time. The participants were also asked about the types of help offered to their families, and about the impact of that help.

Five life histories were collected using an oral story approach (Plummer, 2001; Reinharz, 1992). The oral story is an interviewing strategy that offers minimal structure. Each mother was invited simply to recount her life, speaking about any issue she wished. Data were typically gathered over the course of three interviews, each ranging from 90 minutes to two hours in length.

Life story analysis is concerned with everyday language and how people construct and make sense of their own reality (McAdams, 1993; Plummer, 2001). In this analysis, recurring idea clusters were identified across the stories to organize and inform the interpretation of these experiences. The data were coded using three integrating meta-themes: everyday realities, life challenges, and child placement experience. The data for this paper focused on mothers' child placement experiences. This meta-theme was further refined, and a number of subthemes were identified. Particular attention was paid to the mothers' level of resistance or compliance with child welfare service plans. QSR NUD*IST Vivo (NVivo), a computer program designed specifically for research projects that require qualitative data analysis, was used. Each of the themes was organized in the node system.

Results

Rethinking First Encounters

Mothers' daily living realities coloured the first impressions that child welfare workers created. Most mothers who receive child welfare services face relentless challenges in daily living (see Cameron & Hoy, 2003; Freymond & Cameron, 2007). Many live with poverty. Some deal with extreme behaviours of a child (de Boer, Cameron, & Frensch, 2007). Often, their struggle is compounded by adversities such as violence, substance abuse, and mental health issues. The mothers in this study consistently described how the arrival of child welfare services in their lives coincided with periods of crisis, and they spoke passionately about first encounters with investigating workers. If the adage that first impressions are lasting impressions is true, these mothers' stories suggest that child welfare systems need different strategies for entering mothers' lives.

Mothers are aware that child welfare has the authority to remove their children, so initial engagements with child welfare workers are particularly frightening. Repeatedly, these mothers spoke about knowing someone whose child had been removed; some remembered their own experience of apprehension as a child. On receiving a hospital visit from a child welfare worker, Tanya (all names used in this chapter are fictitious) thought, "Oh, my God, they're going to take my kid." This response sums up the initial reaction of most mothers in this study.

This fear is intensified by the nature of child abuse investigations, which often come suddenly, catching the mother unprepared and not knowing what to expect. Geraldine described her first encounters with investigating workers:

> It all happened so fast … They questioned me, they brought a detective in, they questioned me, asked me all these questions about [her son] having marks on the sides of his fingers. "Well, he said, 'Daddy put my body in hot water.'" I said if Daddy put his hands in boiling water he wouldn't be able to touch a pencil. He

would be crying. But their minds were already made up. It didn't matter what I said, they weren't listening to me. Then they asked me about spanking the kids; I said we're no longer spanking the kids. And they kept saying, "Your husband is." I said, "No, he's not." And then they start with the sexual abuse bit. I lost it. That was it. There was nothing I could say ... They weren't going to believe me. I didn't know what to expect, and then when they told me this ... I was dumb-founded. I didn't know what to do.

Repeatedly, these mothers described how their explanations were dismissed or misunderstood. It must be difficult to respond to demanding and intrusive questions, to explain your life, to defend against allegations of child abuse, and to speak reassuringly about your mothering abilities while feeling extreme fear.

Of the 31 mothers in this study, only Wanda described a positive first encounter. I highlight her words because she emphasized the importance of workers who take time to listen:

That was the night I called, I was crying pretty hard on the phone and I told them I didn't wanna give her up, I just wanted help.

Q. What happened then?

Well, they ... I'm not sure if I know exactly. I do remember two really wonderful ladies. They sent them out to the house. They talked to me, and ... I think I talked to them for about two hours ... I remember I was crying pretty hard ... I was telling them I just really needed some help.

Notice that she could not remember exactly what happened, but was aware that the "wonderful" workers took time to talk with her. First encounters are difficult, emotional, and memorable even when intervention is requested. The meeting establishes the climate in which the working relationship will unfold. This mother, whose first impressions were favourable, described enjoyable subsequent visits from the worker, and constructive assistance that allowed her to have a positive experience of reunification with her daughter.

Earlier Intervention

In contrast with Wanda's words, the majority of the mothers who wanted intervention pleaded repeatedly with child welfare workers to become involved with their family before they received an offer of help.

I had phoned up Children's Aid and I said, "Lookit ... things are getting worse between her and I. She's in my face yelling at me. She's very rude to me. She's doing everything to push my buttons." And I said, "I don't know how much more of this I can take. Can you please give me some relief here? Take her out of my home. I can't take it anymore. If you don't, something's gonna become violent between her and I, and I don't want that to happen."

These mothers were not aware of the words that trigger a child protection investigation. They experienced as exasperating the reluctance of child welfare workers to respond. Kathy described the consequences:

They should have been here long before anything ever happened. They waited for an assault to happen in the family before they even came to my doorstep … They couldn't help him in my family and then they take him into care, like that will cure him, or something.

In a similar vein, Gillian said:

They didn't help me, is what I'm trying to say. I was crying out to them. I was saying, "I've got a drug problem, help me"… but they weren't even giving me no research, nothing, to get help for my drug problem. Nothing … I didn't understand.

Ironically, the mothers who had requested services, with the exception of Wanda, were as dissatisfied and distressed by the child welfare response as those who were surprised by the arrival of a worker.

Investigative processes that are triggered in narrowly prescribed circumstances and proceed on rapid timelines do not create space for a reasoned and comprehensive exploration of issues. A consistent theme in these mothers' stories was that their family situation was not properly understood or appreciated: "They never listened and didn't care … other than screwing up your life, that's all they do … I felt like my privacy was being totally invaded. Like you can't say nothing and I want someone to talk to." The mothers in this study wanted to talk about their lives and to feel understood. In sum, careful interaction from the first contact is crucial to gathering information that will lead to helpful interventions and positive, more open relationships between mothers and service providers.

Ongoing Support

These mothers' stories emphasized the importance of timely and engaging first encounters. They also pointed to the need for increased intervention options. And they suggested the usefulness of negotiated service plans that made more sense in the context of the everyday realities of these children's and families' lives. Across these stories, child placement was typically the only alternative presented to these mothers. Christine, a mother of five young children, said:

> … nothing was ever offered. I'm the one that's applied for Habitat for Humanity … all I ask for is some help to get out of where we weren't doing well, with the bad water, which was a concern. They [child welfare workers] were asking me about that. Like, well, you know if you wanna call the public health unit, call the public health unit. You're not gonna listen to me. If they woulda just said, "How about some respite for the summer while you guys work on this House for Habitat," we would have been fine …

Although child placement made sense to this mother, she also needed to hear how it fit into a broader plan that made sense to her given her housing conditions.

More Respite Care

On several occasions, these mothers talked about needing time and space to respond to adversity in their lives. Many mothers felt alone with the work of parenting, even in situations where male partners were present. Often family members or friends were not able or willing to provide parenting relief. This was particularly prevalent in the stories where children exhibited behavioural problems. For these mothers, there was little, if any, time away from child care routines and parenting responsibilities. The resources to initiate a planned break generally did not exist.

Potentially, access to respite care could create many positive benefits for service providers, children, parents, and families. For service providers, respite care can alleviate safety concerns and create opportunities to build positive relationships. For children, respite care may provide a safe, supportive environment. If respite care is well presented and used periodically, children may develop ongoing relationships with a supportive family without the threat of losing contact with their families. For mothers, respite care may provide an opportunity to rest and renew energy for parenting and to manage adversity without the stigma associated with the loss of parental rights.

More In-home Supports

For many mothers, particularly when their children were apprehended without their agreement, child placement was devastating. Some mothers suggested more in-home supports and willingness for ongoing surveillance of their homes as alternatives to child placement. For example, Tanya said:

> They could have worked with us from our home. I didn't care if they had to come every day. Why couldn't they keep us as a family? I didn't care if they came every day, ten times a day. They could have just worked with us as a family, but they didn't. They tore us apart, and that was that.

Child placement was not a neutral event in these stories. Perhaps it resolved specific short-term safety concerns of the service provider. But did the benefits outweigh the costs, even for the children involved? Since most of the placed children returned to their homes in these stories, the benefits of greater access to service options that keep children safe yet are agreeable to parents as well as children, and minimize the need to sever connections between children and their families, are self-evident.

The importance of adequate in-home supports was again highlighted when the mothers described the return of children to their care. Michelle's child was apprehended because of concerns about her mental stability. She talked about her relationship with child welfare services at the point of reunification:

> So I got a new worker. It was okay, I guess … they're so worried about you and what you do, and they put a supervision order on you. And for that whole six months they only checked on me once. What if I was suicidal? What if I was gonna kill somebody? They don't even bother you. What's the whole point of that order, if they're not gonna check on you? That's the part I didn't understand.

Mothers often described child welfare exiting from their lives abruptly. This was confusing, particularly when the involvement was short-term and the intervention was as disruptive to family life as child removal. Child welfare entered the lives of mothers who were facing many adversities. The pervasive daily living challenges that faced these families would not be substantially altered over a brief period of time. Mothers understood this. Even the mothers who were most resistant to child welfare involvement in their lives were baffled by the abruptness of service withdrawal.

More Concrete Supports

Many of these mothers spoke of the need for practical assistance. In this study, 30 of the 31 mothers talked about the negative effects of insufficient access to daily living resources. They needed more supports such as money, transportation, reliable babysitting, daycare services, suitable housing, or home management assistance. They were frustrated and confused by service providers who refused to provide practical support. Gillian presented a picture of how this shortfall affected her life:

> Like, we would ask her [the worker] if we can get a voucher for extra food because we have the kids Wednesdays, Saturdays, and Sundays … She says, "Well, our agency isn't out for doing that. Like, we can't give it to you all the time." And we're like, "Why not? You're supposed to be there to help, and we don't get no money or extra stuff for the kids." … That's what I mean about helping out. And then one time, my car broke down and I couldn't get the kids. And I asked if she could get a cab or … somehow, they can drive him over here. But she was working, so she couldn't do it.

Gillian, like many others in this study, felt an incongruity between what she believed she needed and the assistance offered. Rarely were concrete supports such as food, transportation, or babysitting offered to these mothers. However, the mothers who received practical assistance welcomed this type of help and found it useful.

More Appreciation

The mothers in this study were offended by intruding workers who did not acknowledge their efforts under adversity. Cheryl described the feeling of being judged:

> You come into my home and treat me like I'm this awful, nasty mother. I said, "Forget it … I cook. I work." I said, "I spend time with my children. My children are well provided for." So don't make me out to be this nasty mother. It's not going to wash.

These mothers wanted recognition that they were doing the best they could for their families. They were highly sensitive to the implication that child welfare involvement meant they were bad mothers.

There is a perception that the relationship between parents and child protection workers must be adversarial. However, even under such trying conditions, it was important to mothers that their parenting efforts and challenging circumstances be acknowledged. Laura described the person who apprehended her children:

> … she was very understanding; this was the intake worker. She was more on our side as well … But the only thing she had to be bound on was the sexual abuse. So that's what they had to go on that one. Then she kept telling me about her

son; she had trouble with her son and this and that. So she was more or less on both sides. She'd take the agency's side for the sexual bit and our side for the other bit. She was very understanding.

These mothers resisted service involvements that made them feel judged, or failed to appreciate their efforts or what they had done well. Moreover, they resisted services that felt imposed rather than negotiated. Notably missing from these mothers' stories were descriptions of front-line service providers spending time to develop an appreciation for their unique circumstances, and being open to negotiating service packages that met family as well as agency concerns. In these circumstances, most mothers demonstrated compliance, but never commitment to imposed service plans.

When Child Placement Is Necessary

The distress of placing a child was intensified when mothers did not have information about their child's well-being and whereabouts. Angie said: "They weren't letting me see him. And I didn't know if he was fine, or not, or where he was, nothing … What am I supposed to do? How do you think it is up here in my head?"

Mothers described intense grief after their child was placed, even when they had requested the placement. They talked about profound sadness and much crying; some experienced suicidal thoughts. It was important to these mothers to have basic information about the placement and how their child was doing. Service provider empathy with their loss was highly valued. From our perspective, such empathy helps mothers to make the emotional adjustment necessary to resist hopelessness and to encourage them to make the changes necessary to secure the return of their children. Almost all of these mothers were powerfully motivated to get their children back home. Knowing someone cared meant they didn't need to feel alone in these efforts.

Empathy from service providers may also motivate mothers to engage in making useful changes rather than in "playing the game." These mothers believed that they had to do everything child welfare told them to do if they wanted to get their children back. They felt they had no choice. Sometimes they did things that made no sense to them. They were cautious about sharing information with the child welfare service providers. Appearing compliant and not being forthcoming about their lives made sense.

More Contact with Substitute Care Providers

Some of these mothers expressed gratitude toward the substitute care providers for their children. Initially, Laura was afraid and worried because she did not know where or how her children were. Later, she felt intimidated by the middle-class lifestyle and possessions that the substitute parents could provide for her children. She worried that her children might not want to return to her care. Over time, she was able to meet with the foster parents, who modelled some strategies for helping her children to complete their homework. Her fears subsided, and she was relieved that her children were with kind and caring people.

It has been common practice to keep foster parents and biological parents separated. In this study, there was a pronounced absence of contact between mothers and foster parents. The few mothers, like Laura, who were able to meet substitute care providers, were relieved. Most of these mothers worried because they did not know where their children were, who was caring for them, or how they were doing. They felt disrespected when significant decisions about their children transpired without their knowledge or input.

Expanding relationships between foster care providers and mothers could yield many opportunities for mothers and children. It could assist in maintaining family connections for children. Such collaborations could increase the support network for biological mothers and create opportunities for foster care providers to model sound parenting skills. For young mothers, the example of an experienced mother who models appropriate parenting and offers encouragement and support may be invaluable.

Implications and Conclusion

These mothers' stories are about struggles under difficult circumstances. They are about individual and family successes as well as breakdowns. These women had much to say about the adversities in their lives, and they had ideas about the interventions that would be welcome for them and their children. Many hoped for positive relationships with service providers in which their circumstances could be understood and their mothering supported. They wanted opportunities to share their concerns and negotiate interventions that were congruent with their lived realities. When child placement was necessary, they desired ties to their children to be respected by sharing information and creating linkages with substitute care providers.

Although this is a small sample study, which limits the extent to which one can generalize to the larger child welfare population of mothers, these stories challenge us to hear that these are mothers concerned about the safety and well-being of their children. These are stories about mothers making sacrifices for their children and persisting in their efforts to bring their children home. These stories also require us to see the strengths and victories in these women's lives (Freymond & Cameron, 2007). On the other hand, all of these women acknowledged limitations in caring for their children. In many instances, it is not hard to understand why child welfare service providers had misgivings about their children's welfare. Nonetheless, there remains a need to create helping responses grounded in a more balanced representation of these women and their family lives.

Some of these women's children may not return to their care in the near future or at all; however, most of the children either had been returned during the project or would eventually return to their care. It matters whether life at home has improved in the interim, and it is important that these mothers and their children feel safe enough to ask for assistance in the future. It is not sufficient to keep children safe for a while but have little to offer most of them over the longer term.

In spite of the magnitude of the public investment in child welfare, the system has surprisingly little to offer children or their parents. There is no real effort to share family responsibilities and to create capacities to provide ongoing resources to children or families. Cameron, Freymond, and Cheyne-Hazineh (see Chapter 7) locate some of the child welfare system's inefficiency in its excessive preoccupation with risk avoidance through service regulation and documentation. They argue that this aversion to risk, coupled with a focus on producing evidence suitable for court, make it very hard to have service involvements different from those described by these mothers.

There is an acknowledgement of these limitations, and an interest in exploring alternative child welfare service models, among an increasing number of Canadian child welfare service providers and policy-makers. Inevitably, child welfare service providers will confront family situations where the safety of children in their own homes is a concern. How they respond to such circumstances will be shaped both by systemic service values and the service options available to them.

If the child welfare system has a variety of placement options available (e.g., treatment homes, inclusive family foster care, kinship care, respite care, and placement options for mothers and children together), then service providers will be more nuanced in selecting placements. If more alternatives exist to maintain children safely at home (e.g., daily monitoring, in-home supports, access to daycare and afterschool programs for children, and connections with contact families), service providers would be able to construct more satisfying service packages. There also has to be a system-wide commitment to negotiate mutually acceptable service packages with most families involved with child welfare. And there has to be a new willingness to share the risks involved in delivering more congruent services for children and families, especially when it is not clear if children need to come into state care (Freymond & Cameron, 2006).

Even with access to these intervention options and with supportive system intentions, child welfare service providers will need to invest more of their time in services for children and families. They need to spend much less time in front of their computers documenting what they have done, and what they need to feel it is safe for them to do. Without service providers having more time to help, all of the above changes will not matter much.

In addition, child welfare service providers need more complete images of the children, parents, families, and neighbourhoods with which they are engaged. For example, child welfare service providers in community settings talk of the value of seeing a client volunteering in a breakfast program or speaking at a community meeting. School-based child welfare service providers value seeing children they serve every day, and being able to chat informally with parents. Not only do they learn more, but they begin to think about children and parents differently (Frensch, Cameron, & Hazineh, 2005).

This chapter began with a criticism of child welfare's excessive focus on assessing mothers. While the intent is different, this discussion runs a similar risk. Others are relevant to the care of children and willing to contribute—fathers, extended family, friends, and neighbours. In this regard, child welfare service providers need support in identifying how to engage more of these partners in keeping children safe and families well.

Acknowledgement

The life histories used in this chapter were collected as part of the *Partnerships for Children and Families Project* at the Faculty of Social Work, Wilfrid Laurier University. The program of research was funded by the Social Sciences and Humanities Research Council of Canada (Ref: 833-2002-2002).

9

Projet Famille: A Family Therapy Project for Neglectful Families

Michèle Brousseau
Madeleine Beaudry
Marie Simard
Cécile Charbonneau

Experienced researchers and social workers in the field of youth protection in Quebec wanted to examine a key intervention related to the following question: Does ecosystemic family intervention aiming to improve family functioning help neglectful or at-risk families respond more adequately to their children's needs? They recognized the complexity of the issue of neglect, and the conceptual and methodological difficulties in intervention evaluation. To answer the question, they pooled their expertise in an action research project aiming to develop and test a structured family intervention model adapted to the problem of neglect. The action research study was entitled *Projet famille*.

Families were recruited for the project from the *Centres Locaux de Services Communautaires* (CLSCs) and the *Centres Jeunesse*. The CLSCs offer front-line services to children and to families. When the project began, these centres had not yet been reconfigured as Health and Social Service Centres (CSSSs). Since the name CLSC is still used within the community health and social services network, and since the available research data is on this clinical population, the name CLSC will be used throughout the chapter. The *Centres Jeunesse* offer youth protection and other services to children and their families.

This chapter describes the project, and each of its five stages: (1) examining the theoretical foundations and reviewing existing intervention programs; (2) identifying the intervention model for *Projet famille*; (3) verifying the applicability of the chosen model; (4) testing the model; and (5) assessing the families' progress and the changes observed. The chapter concludes with a discussion of the implications of the project's results for practice and research.

Research Problem and Objectives

Families displaying neglectful behaviour (deficiencies in physical, emotional, and educational care necessary for children's development) represent a major challenge to youth protection services and front-line family services. Indeed, neglect is the problem most frequently substantiated by youth protection services in Quebec, with a rate of 7.1 per 1000 (Turcotte et al., 2007) compared to 6.4 per 1000 in the rest of Canada (Trocmé et al., 2005). In the CLSCs, service providers are confronted with high-risk situations of neglect (Éthier, Couture, Lacharité, & Gagnier, 2000) and parents who are overwhelmed by their children's behavioural problems, the principal reason for seeking help (Beaudoin et al., 2006). Several risk factors are associated with these problems: poverty, single parenthood, low educational and socio-economic status, isolation, childhood history of violence, neglect or removal from the family of origin, conjugal or family violence, mental illness, and substance abuse (Beaudoin et al., 2006; Pauzé et al., 2004).

Alhough these families present multi-dimensional problems that require diverse health and social services, their functioning has been the subject of few studies. Only recently have studies shown that family dysfunction can compromise children's security and development (Brousseau, 2000; Brousseau & Simard, 2000; Gaudin & Dubowitz, 1997). Moderately successful results have been reported from intervention evaluations in experimental programs involving neglectful families that included intensive intervention, multi-dimensional programs, the development of the parent–child relationship, and the expansion of the family's social support network (Berry, Charlson, & Dawson, 2003; DePanfilis, 1999; Dufour & Chamberland, 2004; Dufour, Chamberland, & Trocmé, 2003). These results encourage the exploration of alternative approaches to intervention. Other researchers report that family therapy and consultation seem particularly effective in modifying the values, attitudes, and practices that perpetuate maltreatment behaviours (Daro, 1988; Daro & McCurdy, 1994; Gaudin & Dubowitz, 1997), and neglect in particular (DePanfilis, 1999). However, interventions in cases of neglect are the least likely to be evaluated (Dufour & Chamberland, 2004; Dufour et al., 2003). Thus, it is pertinent, even urgent, to carry out better intervention evaluation "to find out what works and what does not, with whom, and in what situations" (Dufour et al., 2003, p. 2).

Convinced of the importance of close collaboration between researchers and social practitioners in the progress of practice among neglectful families, three researchers and four social workers undertook this action research project. The objectives were twofold: (1) to develop a structured family intervention strategy based on solid empirical and theoretical foundations, directed toward the analysis and the modification of family functioning in families presenting problems of neglect; and (2) to evaluate the relevance and feasibility of this strategy in psychosocial intervention in both an authority-imposed setting (*Centres Jeunesse*) and a voluntary setting (CLSC).

Theoretical Foundations

In family functioning theories, neglect is viewed as the incapacity of the family system to fulfill its essential functions of protecting and socializing children, an incapacity that affects the children's development (Brousseau, 2000; Brousseau & Simard, 2000; Gaudin & Dubowitz, 1997). When these functions are accomplished adequately, children's physical, emotional, and educational needs are considered to have been met. When these are not adequately accomplished, children become victims of one or more forms of physical, emotional, or educational neglect. Thus, to reduce neglectful behaviours, it is necessary to act upon the overall family system and promote the active collaboration of the family members in the problem-solving process.

The survey of the literature was as exhaustive as possible, with the aim of pinpointing the characteristics of the most effective interventions carried out among neglectful families and of programs that focus on the family, and to identify those that specifically aim to improve family functioning. Briefly, the review brought out the fact that several intervention programs or models that defined themselves as *family* interventions often only dealt with one or more family members separately or in groups, and that only a few programs approached the family as a system. These were mainly developed for families with adolescents presenting problem behaviours, and were not always clearly defined; for this reason, it was difficult to replicate them (see, among others, Berry et al., 2003; Daro, 1988; DePanfilis & Dubowitz, 2005; DePanfilis, Glazer-Semmel, Farr, & Meek, 1999; Dufour & Chamberland, 2004; Éthier et al., 2000; Nelson, Laurendeau, Chamberland, & Peirson, 2001). Moreover, the results obtained to date have not been particularly promising, whether they were from experimental programs (intensive interventions, multi-dimensional programs, development of the parent-child relationship and the family social support network, etc.), or regular intervention services. In our review, the McMaster family therapy model (Epstein, Ryan, Bishop, Miller, & Keitner, 2003; Ryan, Epstein, Keitner, Miller, & Bishop, 2005) seemed the most appropriate framework for the objectives associated with this study on neglectful families.

The Ecosystemic Family Intervention Model Selected for this Project

The family intervention approach developed in *Projet famille* was based on ecosystemic, behavioural, and cognitive theories of family functioning found in the McMaster Model of Family Functioning. Intervention dealing with the family as a system can include, when needed, services that focus on parents at the personal or parental level, on the children, as well as on developing the family's social network and improving its material conditions, while remaining centred on family functioning.

The McMaster model considers six aspects of family functioning: problem-solving, communication, roles, affective responsiveness, affective involvement, and behaviour control. It is an integrated system that includes evaluation tools, an articulated intervention model, and intervention strategies. These characteristics are essential for the research. The model comprises four macro stages: assessment, contracting, treatment, and closure; each of these includes sub-stages accompanied by appropriate strategies. Task accomplishment is an important part of the treatment stage.

The model proposes an intervention approach that its authors have summarized in the following basic principles: (1) the active collaboration of the family; (2) an emphasis on macro treatment stages; (3) open and direct communication with the family; (4) a focus on the family's responsibility to effect change; (5) an emphasis on assessment (full assessment may be delayed in crisis situations); (6) inclusion of the entire family, including fathers (or mothers' partners) and the children, the aim being to act upon the family system; (7) an emphasis on current problems; (8) a focus on the family's strengths, not just its difficulties; (9) a focus on behavioural change, and (10) the limited length of treatment (between 10 and 15 sessions, of which two or three are for assessment) (Epstein et al., 2003; Miller et al., 2000; Ryan et al., 2005).

Finally, the McMaster model is compatible with a multi-dimensional approach that considers the family environment (in particular, school, daycare, and the extended family) and responsiveness to the individual needs of the parents and the children, as well as the progress of the family over time, according to its development stages. Its basic principles correspond to several of the characteristics of effective programs on neglect, particularly the emphasis on the family's strengths, intervention which is directed at the family system, and the attention given to evaluation which is shared with the family as a strategy in empowering the family.

Verification of the Model

The purpose of this stage was to ensure that the proposed intervention program was applicable to practice in the *Centres Jeunesse* (the authority-imposed context) and the CLSCs (voluntary context), since the implementation of a new approach might imply major challenges within the agencies. This verification process was done using the focus group method (Krueger, 1988; Morgan, 1988, 1993; Simard, 1989; Stewart & Shamdasani, 1990) with social workers who were experienced in the field of child neglect and who represented the two targeted intervention establishments. They had already agreed to participate in the study, and had received training in neglect and in family functioning theory.

The social workers were consulted during four meetings in which the models surveyed were presented and discussed from the points of view of relevance and feasibility, family recruitment criteria, and intervention objectives. Briefly, this consultation confirmed the relevance of applying the McMaster model in an ecosystemic perspective; it helped to establish the family recruitment criteria, taking the practice milieu into account, and raised issues related to the definition of the family.

Testing the Model

During this stage, the longest by far, several activities were carried out simultaneously (e.g., recruitment of the families, continuing caseworker training, clinical supervision of the intervention, and implementation follow-up). There were meetings every two weeks with researchers, practitioners, research professionals, and students when needed. A logbook for each family was filled out by the social workers, and a scale was created to measure the application of the basic principles of the intervention model, allowing the researchers to gauge the degree to which the model was implemented in each case.

The intervention model was implemented with 13 families, each with at least one child between the ages of 5 and 13. Seven families had been referred to youth protection for neglect, and six families who had sought help at the CLSC were at risk of neglect. Among them, there were three intact two-parent families, five single-parent families of whom four were headed by the mother, and five reconstituted families of whom three were formed around the mother and two around the father. Twenty parents (and their partners) participated in the research interviews. The families had 27 children in all between the ages of 5 and 13. Families presented a per-family average of seven risk factors associated with child neglect, such as low income, early motherhood, single parenthood, poverty, youth protection histories in the case of a parent or a child, physical or mental health problems, substance abuse, and the absence of social support.

The assessment of the families' current situations was based on two sources: the parents within these families and the caseworkers. Several aspects were measured, including neglect, family functioning, social support, depression, and psychological distress. Particular attention was paid to the family functioning assessment. This was carried out by the social workers using the McMaster Clinical Rating Scale (Miller et al., 1994; Ryan et al., 2005), translated into French for the purposes of this study, and by the parents who used the Family Assessment Device (FAD) (Kabacoff, Miller, Bishop, Epstein, & Keitner, 1990; Miller, Epstein, Bishop, & Keitner, 1985; Ryan et al., 2005). The FAD used was a French-language version (Brousseau, 2000). Whenever possible, these measurements were carried out before and after participation in the program. Besides the comparison of before-and-after measurements to identify changes in the families' situations, team meetings were held to review the implementation of the model among the families, and involved the social workers in the analysis of the results.

Assessing Family Progress

As outlined below, the intervention model was not applied equally to all families because of difficulties in engaging all members of the families. Of interest is the fact that there was a relationship between the progress of the families and implementation indicators that included the degree to which the intervention model was applied, the extent to which the basic principles of the model were implemented, and the percentage of meetings that included all the significant family members.

In the first group of five families, all the stages of the model were applied to each family, and the assessment covered all the family functioning dimensions. The basic principles of the model were applied to a high degree in the caseworkers' opinion, and there were a high number of family meetings with all relevant family members. Data collection indicated good family participation and active involvement by its members. Most of the intervention objectives were achieved and, with one exception, the families' problems were resolved. In one case, ongoing long-term regular support was required. Three of these families presented a low number of risk factors for child neglect. Based on the opinions of both parents and caseworkers, however, these families improved their levels of family functioning. Although the parents did not report any significant problems at the outset, the caseworkers evaluated family functioning more critically than the parents themselves. In general, however, the situations of the families in this group seemed less serious than many others, and there were lower levels of neglect and children's behavioural problems. These problems improved with intervention; in addition, both parents and caseworkers assessed the family's motivation to participate in a family intervention process positively, and parents reported a high degree of satisfaction with the intervention. The involvement of the members of the family and its structural stability, more than the type of family structure, appeared to facilitate the application of the model and the improvement in family functioning.

In a second group of five families, based on feedback from caseworkers, the basic principles of the family intervention model were only applied to a moderate degree. The percentage of family interviews that included all the significant family members was lower than in the first group; thus there was a higher number of interviews with individuals. Some families did not engage in the therapy in spite of their initial commitment to do so, and the caseworkers said it was more difficult to apply a new model that they hadn't yet completely mastered under those circumstances. In these cases, the objectives were not reached for four families by the time the study ended. In one family, the objectives were reached by means of individual interviews with certain family members. Intervention continued with the other four families beyond the study period. Three of the families in this group presented a low number of risk factors for child neglect. The parents in this group had reported a healthy family functioning level before the intervention, and an improved level when the second assessment was carried out. However, the caseworkers said that certain problems requiring clinical intervention were still present at the time of the second assessment. When compared with the first group, there was a larger gap between the evaluations of the parents and those of the caseworkers in this group. The situations of these families could also be described as more serious with respect to the degree of child neglect. Problems, including the children's behavioural problems, persisted after intervention among the families who continued to receive services from the *Centre Jeunesse*.

A third group consisted of three families. In this group as well, the intervention model was only partially applied, and the evaluation stage carried out with these three families was limited to those members who had participated in meetings. The basic principles of the model were applied to a lesser degree, according to the caseworkers, and the proportion of family interviews remained low, with intervention being carried out mainly in individual interviews. Two families from this group presented a high number of risk factors for child neglect. In two cases, the parents acknowledged the problems identified, but were reluctant to make the necessary changes or to continue the intervention process. These families were followed by the CLSC on a voluntary basis. In one case, a little girl returning to her reconstituted family formed around the father had to be placed in foster care again. The assessment made it possible to identify the low level of affective involvement on the father's part, as well as other functional problems in the reconstituted family, and this was an essential contribution to the revisions in the girl's care plan toward an alternative permanency option.

To summarize, *Projet famille* demonstrated the value of the selected intervention model among neglectful and at-risk families known to the *Centre Jeunesse* or the CLSC. The improvements in family functioning and the decrease in child neglect among families where the intervention process was more fully applied suggest that the chosen model is promising. Questions were raised by the persistence of problems, in the caseworkers' judgment, in families where the model was only partially applied, and by the gap shown between the caseworkers' opinions and those of parents who did not identify any family functioning problems. Of importance also were the degree of recognition of problems, the motivation to change, and the conditions for applying the intervention model in these situations. In some cases, for example, the initiation of the change process may take more time.

Implications for Practice and Research

The results from this pilot project suggest a number of conclusions for practice and future research.

An Intervention Strategy in Cases of Neglect

Family intervention should be considered as a specific intervention strategy within a broader ecosystemic approach. Rather than being seen as a panacea, it should be part of a caseworker's set of tools to be applied according to the differentiated needs of families. At the clinical level, however, using family intervention rather than individual intervention presents a challenge. Maintaining the "family" orientation in the context of a protection mandate, with the need to respond to multiple requests for services, deal with crises, and cope with the difficulties of bringing all family members together for meetings, is a significant challenge and requires a significant shift in practice. For example, the family caseworker must involve fathers (even current and former partners) in the intervention, whereas current front-line youth protection services are primarily addressed to mothers (Brousseau & Morel, 2006; Callahan, 1993; Swift, 1995b; Trocmé, 1996). The proposed model also implies shifting from problem-oriented practice intervention to practice based on a more structured analysis, that of the family strengths. The value of a shift to ecosystemic family intervention is the support that can be provided to families in child neglect situations, which in turn can contribute to keeping children with their families. In addition, the in-depth assessment of the family situation, which accompanies the model, is valuable in determining the best option for the child: to stay with family or to be placed in foster care.

Standardized Assessment Measurements

An important issue is the standardized measures, which give prominence to the assessment of families, in the McMaster model of family intervention. Carrying out the assessment with the French-language version of the McMaster Clinical Rating Scale (Miller et al., 1994; Ryan et al., 2005) contributed to the development of the caseworkers' clinical judgment. In addition, the use of these tools encourages systematic feedback to the families regarding their functioning, helping them to recognize and name both their strengths and their problems. The comparison of the results from the Family Assessment Device, which is filled out by the parents, and results from the McMaster Clinical Rating Scale, which is filled out by the caseworkers, brought different perceptions of family functioning to the surface. The question remains whether these differences were real or whether they were artifacts of the assessment tools. Until this gap between the caseworkers' and the families' perceptions is better understood, caseworkers must be careful to make sure that the evaluation of the situation is shared with the family before proceeding to the intervention stages.

Testing the Model in Practice

The close collaboration between the researchers and the social service practitioners in testing the model in the field helped in determining the feasibility of applying the model in practice, clarifying the eligibility criteria for families, and identifying organizational challenges for eventual implementation on a wider scale. This process was essential to the elaboration of a clearly-defined intervention model, sufficiently developed to be evaluated empirically, and adapted to the two practice milieux associated with this project. Although consultation with the caseworkers by the focus group method confirmed the relevance and feasibility of the project, it failed to anticipate or solve all implementation problems, even though these social workers had lengthy and relevant experience.

Training and Supervision

Intervening with the families requires in-depth training that should include the theoretical bases of the model, practical exercises, and good supervision, particularly when faced with the difficulties, including resistance from families. For caseworkers familiar with the individual approach, this change in practice requires a more systemic view of the problems, a modification of the usual intervention methods, and the clinical space for adapting the new model. Training and supervision for work with families is particularly important in that youth protection and child welfare caseworkers typically work with one family member, usually the mother. They need support to be able to achieve what represents a paradigm shift in the focus of intervention.

Eligibility of the Families and their Contribution to Change

The implementation of this family-focused model also helped clarify the definition of the family unit (the subject of the intervention), and the inclusion criteria initially established. The diversity of the families followed in the project (single-parent, intact two-parent, and reconstituted) raised a number of questions. How and to whom should the intervention model be applied? Who is part of the family, particularly when the child is the subject of a youth protection report or referral, and the biological parents are not living together? The research team opted for an inclusive definition of all the significant family members. For example, in the case of an at-risk teenage girl living in a single-parent home headed by her mother, the father and his new partner were invited to participate in the family meetings during the intervention. It was decided that the "family unit" should involve all the persons who played a parental role with respect to the adolescent, irrespective of biological relationship, as the quality of the interactions among all the members contribute to change in the family. With the growing diversity of family forms in our society, it is important to consider three aspects as consensual guidelines for defining the family: the members who constitute the family; co-residence; and the biological, affective, or legal bonds that unite its members (Partenariat familles en mouvance et dynamique intergénérationnelles, 2005). The challenge is to define family composition according to each unique situation.

Impact on Practice

Although this was not one of the project's objectives, participation in the development of the approach had an impact on the caseworkers themselves. They identified a growth in professional skills during the project, and an increased attention to some of the basic values of social work. *Projet famille* enabled growth in knowledge and the identification of links between theory and practice. The model also helped give the families a clear idea of the social workers' roles and mandates, instilling a sense of responsibility and respect. Group support helped maintain the motivation to refine and re-examine practice, fostered a better understanding of the role of partners, and led to reflection on the values and ethical dilemmas associated with family intervention.

Limitations of the Project

The promising results observed in the families to which the intervention model was more fully applied should be evaluated in the light of the project's limitations; more specifically, its application to a small number of families whose problems and structural composition differed. This context, and the fact that the social workers applied the model to the families while they were still learning to use it, may also have influenced the results, particularly when families displayed resistance. A greater mastery of the model, for example, may be required in dealing with resistant families. The design of this study was exploratory and not experimental, and the results need to be considered in light of its exploratory nature. As indicated, the results presented here are based on observations during the implementation phase of *Projet famille*, and from the analysis of measures used to assess and understand the progress of the participating families.

Conclusion

This research project achieved its goal of elaborating a structured family intervention with well-defined content, objectives, and strategies. It permitted the identification of the necessary conditions for its implementation. These stages proved essential for the evaluation of the implementation stage of the intervention and of its effects on a broader scale. In addition, the project contributed to the development of a training program in ecosystemic family intervention by enriching the initial theoretical content with teaching exercises adapted to the context of youth protection and front-line services to children and families. In spite of the promising results of this study, broader application of the model, supported by a more experimental research design, is required in order to better understand the relevance and usefulness of the family systems approach to the field of child and youth protection. A broader study, carried out by social workers who have received training in family intervention and have mastered the intervention model, will contribute to a better understanding of "what works and what does not, with whom, and in what situations" (Dufour et al., 2003, p. 2).

10

Foster Care: An Essential Part of the Continuum of Care

Kathleen Kufeldt

This chapter's focus is on fostering by unrelated families. Chapters 11 and 12 consider kinship care. Traditional foster care is practised within the social and cultural norms of a society and its particular construct of child welfare. In some countries identity is very much tied into family, and taking in a "stranger" does not fit easily within the culture. Thus, in some countries, for example Japan and Jordan, elimination of institutional care through promotion of foster care can be problematic. In the Western world generally, "family" is seen as the ideal setting for child-rearing, and so foster care is well entrenched as the placement of choice for children needing substitute care. Nevertheless, this positive acceptance of foster care has to be considered in the context of the prevailing social constructs. Child welfare, and particularly child protection, is practised within cultural imperatives which include the privacy of the family and the importance of family preservation. These in turn result in legislative dictates which restrict child welfare workers through policies of *least intrusion*—that is, the protection of children should be ensured with the least intrusion possible into family affairs. In this context, taking children into care is seen as a last resort measure. Documentation in the literature suggests that this approach serves neither children nor families well. Children have to be hurt, too often seriously, before they can be helped. Once significant abuse has been established, then the provision of substitute care becomes necessary. Within the prevailing cultural and value system, such intervention creates a paradox for workers: the need to protect the child may run counter to the protection of family privacy and autonomy. The antidote, in current policy, is the achievement of family reunification as soon as possible. Success in child protection is measured in terms of return rates; success in foster care tends to be measured in terms of stability of placement. What is too often overlooked is the inherent contradiction in these two measures of success. Nor does either measure tell us much about the impact on the child's well-being.

This chapter will examine these contradictions and paradoxes, unintended consequences, and remedial approaches. The examination is primarily based on the findings of a series of research projects, ranging from interviews with key stakeholders, including the children, demonstration of best practice, focus groups, and a survey of adults who grew up in foster care. These findings and those of other researchers in this field will be used to identify key concepts, understanding of which can contribute to improved practice and the well-being of the children in foster care. What did become apparent within this series of projects is that properly trained foster carers have special skills that can contribute to permanency for children who are unable to reside with their own families. Descriptions and recommendations for expanded use of such skills are included. The chapter includes a theoretical framework developed for foster care practice, and concludes with recommendations for policy, research, and practice.

Background

Early experience of working in a children's residential setting, albeit organized in "family" groupings of 12 children, sensitized the author to the too frequent failure of state care to provide the quality of nurturing provided by the average responsible parent. Subsequent experience in the field of child protection provided confirmation of these early reactions, and in particular the difficulty of providing for each child the secure base that total commitment of at least one adult can provide (Bowlby, 1988; Bronfenbrenner, 1979). The provision of that secure base was, and still is, rendered more difficult by the fragmentation of services and lack of permanency. Temporary care and reunifications that are not always enduring leave too many children in limbo for much of their childhood. Maluccio and his colleagues have addressed the issue repeatedly, and their definition of permanency is worth repeating here, as it continues to be a concept that is not well understood:

> Permanency planning is the systematic process of carrying out within a brief time-limited period, a set of goal-directed activities designed to help children live in families that offer continuity of relationships with nurturing parents or caretakers and the opportunity to establish life-time relationships. (Maluccio & Fein, 1983, p. 197)

Implicit in their definition is that permanence can be established in foster care and kinship care as well as through reunification that is permanent, or through adoption. More contemporary research supports their contention. Sinclair, Wilson, and Gibbs called for permanence after studying a large sample of foster children (n=596) on two occasions, 14 months apart: "These findings suggest that the care system needs to provide long term stability. This however rarely seemed on offer" (2005, p. 234). The study included 150 questionnaires filled out by children over 5 years old. Two-thirds wanted to stay with their foster carers until they were 18 or older.

The findings of a United Kingdom National Children's Bureau Working Party (Parker, 1980) affirmed observations derived from field experience. A search for clearer understanding and possible solutions to the challenges posed by child neglect and abuse began.

Summary Description of Projects and Key Findings

How Well Is Foster Care Serving the Needs of Children?

The search began with a review of current literature and small-scale survey of the key stakeholders, children, parents, foster parents, and social workers. The survey was later replicated with larger samples (Kufeldt, 1979, 1982; Kufeldt, Armstrong, & Dorosh, 1995, 1996). As a result of the findings, later research used participatory action methodology and subsequently included a demonstration and evaluation of inclusive foster care (Kufeldt, 1993, 1995), as well as piloting and implementation in Canada of the United Kingdom's *Looking After Children* (LAC) methodology as a best practice approach (Parker, Ward, Jackson, Aldgate, & Wedge, 1991; Ward, 1995). This latter methodology enabled comparison of developmental achievements of children in foster care to that of children in the general population (Kufeldt, Simard, Vachon, Baker, & Andrews, 2000; Kufeldt, Simard, & Vachon, 2002, 2003; Kufeldt, Simard, Thomas, & Vachon, 2005). The comparison group was obtained from Statistics Canada's National Longitudinal Survey of Children and Youth (NLSCY, information about which is available at <http://www.statcan.gc.ca/>). Additional studies included a survey of three cohorts of adults who had grown up in the care system (Kufeldt, 2003) and a cross-national comparison of children in Canada and Australia (Cheers, Kufeldt, Klein, & Rideout, 2007; Kufeldt, Cheers, Klein, & Rideout, 2007).

Full details of the methods and findings of this ongoing search for knowledge can be found in the citations listed. For the purposes of this chapter a brief summary of lessons learned is presented here. It was clear from the start that the theoretical basis for foster care was not well defined, apart from the assumption, based on child development and attachment theory, that family-based care would be the best option for children who needed to be removed from their own homes. Additionally, there did not appear to be a proactive policy formulation. Rather, foster care was the default option when protection of children warranted removal.

In the initial search for theory, three key themes emerged. These were the significance of the separation experience, the place of the natural parents, and the need for role clarification. These themes, together with Holman's earlier conceptualization of inclusive versus exclusive foster care (Holman, 1975) and Kirk's identification of the role handicap in adoption (Kirk, 1981, 1984, 1988) assisted in the development of a theoretical basis for foster care practice, (Kufeldt, 1991) and in the design of an inclusive care project.

The proposed theory (see Figure 1) begins with the premise that attachment forms the basis of healthy child development. This in turn is dependent on a reciprocal parent-child relationship and on what Marris (1987) refers to as a sense of manageable continuity in life. If the child welfare intervention required is removal and placement of a child in substitute (foster) care, there is disruption both of family relationships and the sense of continuity. Implementation of Holman's inclusive care mitigates these disruptions. When fully understood and practised, then the third theme, that of the need for role clarification, is also attended to. Inclusive care necessitates sharing of information, including clarity regarding the reason and purpose of placement. It also calls for a clear differentiation of roles and assignment of tasks leading to greater congruence of perceptions and actions of the various members of the role set.

Findings from the inclusive care project demonstrated both the feasibility and the value of inclusive care. The definition of inclusive care prepared for the project is "Substitute family care for children that respects the existence of the child's family of origin and from the point of entry into care maintains contact between the child and the family and *to the degree possible* provides for a continuing role for the child's own parents" (Kufeldt & Armstrong, 1993, p. 7).

Tangible and measurable outcomes were an increase in:

- the number of visits taking place;
- visits in the children's own parents' homes;
- children's parents suggesting and deciding the location of visits;
- joint decision-making and planning by both sets of parents;
- numbers of foster parents who think visits should take place more often; and
- satisfaction of children and their parents.

Figure 1 *Schematic Presentation of Theoretical Framework*

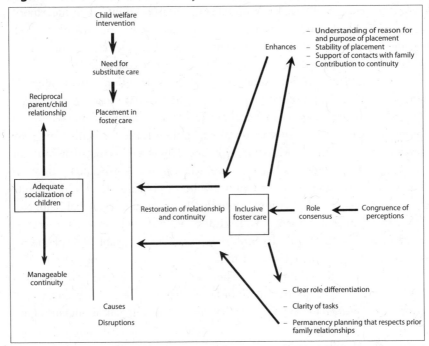

A more recent study in Sweden (Höjer, 2008) reported similarly that sharing the care resulted in positive effects.

The projects using the LAC Assessment and Action Records (AARs) produced a complex and rich data set, including comparison of results at the beginning and end of the project. These records, as noted in other chapters in this book, measure and monitor age-related developmental outcomes with respect to health, education, emotional and behavioural development, identity, family and social relations, self-presentation, and self-care skills. They are used conversationally with children and their caregivers and include action plans where deficiencies are identified. Their use allowed us to compare the progress of foster children with the general population using data from the NLSCY. However, encapsulating the key findings is not a simple task. There were high points (e.g., improved monthly contact with mothers) and low points (e.g., indications of possible continued abuse), areas where the youth in care did well in comparison to their peers (e.g., health), and areas where they did poorly (e.g., education). While the data showed general improvements over time, the improvements tended to be small. Realistically, these small changes are a positive sign. Given that the participating youth were all over 10 years of age, their pre-care and in-care experiences had time to become firmly entrenched into their life experiences. As the youth so often reminded us, "You should start doing this earlier." Small changes over a nine-month period are optimistic signs. They could doubtless be enhanced if workers were helped in the task of formulating action plans.

A general summary of overall results follows. Health care was generally good, as was social presentation. In fact, we found that most aspects of care over which foster parents had control were very well done. The most negative outcome related to educational progress. Young people fell behind in grade level, with continuing deterioration over time. This was exacerbated by constant moves, and use of various addictive substances was closely associated with number of changes of school. Learning difficulties were assessed at a higher rate than in the general population, but with a lower level of remedial help. Not surprisingly, there were identity issues. Information about birth families was relatively poor, and there was discomfort expressed in being able to explain why they were in care. Knowledge of birth family is related to findings with respect to family and social relationships. There was confirmation of other research findings with respect to disruption of family ties. On the positive side, young people were pleased to have a vehicle that enabled them to talk about family and to strategize with their worker ways to re-establish contact with family (including extended family members). Outcomes with respect to emotional and behavioural development were similar to other research findings; the incidence was high, with boys tending to deal with issues through externalized behaviour and girls through symptoms of internalization. Though all teenagers tend to worry, we found that while the general population of teens has worries regarding the future, those in care have to deal with more immediate problems, particularly about where they will live after care. The AARs gave them the opportunity to voice some of these concerns. Finally, the AARs measured self-care skills, particularly practical skills that are appropriate at different ages.

> The most problematic aspect ... was post-care planning (e.g., finances, living arrangements, etc.). Generally, there was a low level of knowledge held by the youth in care in relation to these topics. While skills increased between the two applications, the gains need to be larger. (Kufeldt et al., 2000, p. 219)

Also disturbing was the lack of congruence between youths' and social workers' perceptions of what the long-term plans were.

However, the return four years later to an agency that had consistently used the AARs and was committed to the philosophy of LAC showed promising results (Kufeldt, McGilligan, Klein, & Rideout, 2004). In the *health* dimension there was considerable improvement in the completion rate of medical recommendations and immunizations, and greater identification of ongoing health conditions. It was heartening to see the advances made in paying attention to *education*. There were fewer school changes, and the degree to which school performance matched ability had risen from 36% in 2000 to 70% in 2004. This was in part due to provision of extra tutoring when required. In addition, young people of school leaving age were now being encouraged and supported in higher education. *Family and social relationships* also showed improvement. There were far fewer placement changes and workers ensured that any changes that become necessary were well planned. Positive contact with family had risen from 31% to 60%. With respect to *emotional and behavioural development*, there was a reduction in those who were prone to fight with other children and also a decrease in feeling sad. *Self-care*, interestingly, showed a lower level of competence, but the explanation given by the supervisor was that, as a result of using LAC, the standards had been raised with respect to the desired level of competence, particularly when leaving care (hence lower ratings). The social workers in this agency liked LAC's proactive quality and thus its ability to avoid negative outcomes.

The cross-national comparison with Australia (Cheers et al., 2007; Kufeldt et al., 2007) confirmed earlier findings, and although there were some small measurable differences, the overall conclusion was that problems within foster care tend to be endemic. The good news was that these problems are not irremediable, but affected by quality of practice. We did perceive consistent application of the AARs as an example of best practice, with the potential to promote resilience. This is similar to the findings and conclusions of the series of studies conducted by Flynn and his team in Ontario (Flynn, Ghazal, Legault, Vandermeulen, & Petrick, 2004; Legault et al., 2004).

How Well Are Young Adults Functioning Who Were Formerly in Permanent Care?

The survey of three cohorts of adults who had grown up in the care system (Kufeldt, 2003) had three objectives:

- To identify how well these young adults were functioning;
- To determine which aspects of service were most helpful and, conversely, which inhibited healthy development; and
- To determine what potential changes in practice might improve the health and social functioning of youth in care.

The results reported here are based on 87 surveys (response rate 53%) that highlighted both negative and positive aspects of growing up in care. The surveys were designed to document the degree to which the normal developmental tasks of young adulthood were achieved. These tasks are commonly considered to be: (1) educational achievement; (2) establishment of some form of family status independent of family of origin; (3) a meaningful occupation; and (4) financial independence.

Though difficult to quantify, it is reasonable to say that roughly half of those who responded had achieved an overall positive outcome. Nevertheless, as a group, they functioned less well than their peers on the above criteria. They were disadvantaged financially compared to the general population, and less likely to have achieved a meaningful occupation. Lag in educational achievement at time of leaving care was most serious for the youngest cohort. Members of this cohort entered care when they were older. Despite their shorter overall time in care, they experienced greater discontinuity in placements and schooling. The indications were that the philosophy of least intrusion and the family preservation movement, in the long term, had not been in the best interests of these particular young people. Indeed, some said that they should have been taken into care earlier. Marital and family status was also a tenuous goal for a sizeable proportion. More than one-fifth lived in isolation, with apparently little hope of achieving a satisfactory family life. Thirteen per cent of those with children were not living with them. Some had experienced child welfare intervention with respect to their children. For many, the lack of family connections was not mitigated by a strong friendship network. One-fifth had no close friends; a little over one-third had only one or two close friends. Seven said they had no friends at all.

Which Aspects of Service were Most Helpful and Which Inhibited Healthy Development?

If one were to conceptualize the purpose of child welfare services narrowly as protection, then by and large this was achieved initially. Long-term results were more equivocal, as some suffered further abuse and most experienced discontinuity and disruption within care. And if one enlarges the role of the state to ensure that the child's best interests and well-being are protected, then results are not promising. Coming into care provides risks as well as opportunities.

Several comments about helpful aspects of the in-care experience were received. The provision of good substitute family life emerged as the most positive aspect of service, followed by good social work that enhanced life chances. The majority received reasonably good health care. Worthy of note was the fact that many had maintained contact with former foster carers. Some used the opportunity the research provided to send thanks to a particularly good social worker. There were indications that, where abuse had occurred in the foster home, those making a disclosure were listened to.

Despite a pervasive aura of sadness and disconnectedness, the majority expressed themselves as reasonably content with their lives. Those who were surveyed impressed us with their resilience, their continuing optimism that life would get better, and the considerable efforts that they put into daily living.

Negative aspects tended to be the reverse side of the good. Frequent changes in placement, and consequent changes in schools, intensified damage inflicted by early experiences in family of origin. These changes affected attachment problems and interfered with education and social relationships. Particular aspects of normal healthy development became sacrificed to a crisis orientation. This interfered with attention to education, health, and skills required for successful transition into adulthood. Despite knowledge gained from research, it seemed that little social work attention was given to the importance of family contact (let alone former friends). It may be that contact is inhibited by assumptions and value considerations. For instance, one young woman described how she was able to renegotiate a positive relationship in adulthood with a formerly incestuous uncle. She described the healing that this brought about for both of them. The social work response would most likely be complete separation of victim from perpetrator (an example of a short-term rather than long-term perspective).

The abrupt transition from care provided yet another stumbling block to successful adulthood. Clearly, the lack of continuity was an overwhelming negative aspect. Its effect was exacerbated by the assumption that, on the young person's attainment of the age of majority, child welfare responsibility ceased.

Some of the changes suggested by the respondents included earlier intervention, earlier permanency planning, improved educational opportunity, collaboration with school personnel, enhancement of social work skills, recognition and respect for the importance of the foster family role, as well as opportunities for children and youth to have direct and private access to social workers, and to be treated as individuals. Further, there was clearly a need to improve the transition out of care and to continue to provide help and support after care.

Strengths and Weakness of Current Practice

The results from this survey of adults who had grown up in care are indicative of both strengths and weaknesses in the provision of foster care. As well as protection from imminent harm, a major strength is its potential to provide a nurturing home in a normative setting. The *Looking After Children* studies also indicated that foster carers provide a good standard of physical care and attention to children's education. Where foster carers are provided with a greater degree of autonomy, as in the inclusive care project, they demonstrate an ability to develop contacts and work with the children's own parents.

The weaknesses had more to do with system problems than with any inherent negative aspect of foster care itself. The systemic problem in child welfare and child protection can be encapsulated in its description as a reactive, crisis-driven service. Children are usually at high risk for harm before protective services will intervene. Foster homes are too often selected on the basis of availability rather than on purposeful matching. When problems occur in foster care, the reactive response is to move the child rather than to work with the family. Foster parents and children identify insufficient monitoring of placements. Workers feel under siege because of a shortage of homes, and foster carers complain of insufficient support and respite. The end result is too many moves with disastrous effects on schooling, family, and social relationships, and on children's emotional well-being.

Success and Failure in Foster Care

Family preservation and family reunification are primary goals in current child welfare practice. These are very much influenced by negative outcomes documented in studies of foster care. This raises the question of what exactly is the place of foster care in the care continuum. Is it merely a temporary stopgap or default option, or does it have an essential role? A clear answer to these questions is needed in order to determine policy options and also to define just what is success and failure. Where family preservation or reunification is the ultimate goal, then continued stay in, or return to, foster care will be seen as failure. If one considers promotion of child well-being and safety as the aims of child welfare and child protection, then the important indicators are the developmental outcomes, the children's own perceptions and their success as adults. The conclusion drawn from the series of studies outlined in this chapter is that family reunification is a worthwhile goal, and, if achievable, is usually reached fairly early in the child's care career. However, there are many children who should not, or may not want to, return home. For some, return home may expose them to further abuse and neglect, and may even have lethal consequences, as high profile deaths of children testify. For others, while family ties may continue to be important, their best life chances lie elsewhere than return home. Young people themselves testified to this in Canada and elsewhere: "The great majority of children who answered our questionnaires said they were happy with their placement ... Social workers judged that around seven out of ten placements were going or had gone very well (Sinclair, Wilson & Gibbs, 2005, p. 232). Sinclair and his associates reported that others had similar findings (Rowe, Hundleby, & Garnett, 1989; Cliffe & Berridge, 1992). To determine the best option for each child, early permanency planning is warranted. In such a scenario, foster care is an essential service. Indeed, it is not only essential, but is capable of an expanded role to assist in family preservation and reunification. The inclusive care projects demonstrated the effectiveness of foster carers in work with and supporting the children's parents. Instead of a narrow definition of foster care as a temporary home for children, the role of foster care can be expanded to include the tasks outlined below.

Foster Care as Prevention

Successful families are characterized by openness, access to support networks, and connection to services that can help in time of emergency. Troubled families lack these qualities. Foster families helping families can fill the gap by providing support and encouragement to parents and children (Kufeldt & Allison, 1990; Seaberg, 1981). With careful assessment and matching, such a service can provide role modelling, mentoring, child care, and acceptance. These are factors identified by Benzies and Mychasiuk (2009) as major contributors to family resilience. If preventive measures are insufficient, then the children can move into a foster home that is already known to them.

Foster Care and Family Preservation

Suggesting foster care as a family preservation measure is based on the findings of the inclusive care project, summarized earlier. It is clear that inclusive care, properly practised, does preserve the child's sense of family and belonging to that family. It promotes and maintains the connection and continuity that is part of the theoretical framework. Family preservation in this model is conceptualized not necessarily by co-domicile, but by continuation of the family relationships. It is happening increasingly in families separated by divorce and separation. It can also happen in families separated because of protection issues.

Foster Care and Family Reunification

Just as foster parents can maintain children's family connections, so too can they assist in family reunification. If trained and encouraged in inclusive care, foster parents are in a good position to assess families' readiness to be united. They can also aid in a more gradual process of reunification and provide ongoing support and after care. Pine, Warsh, and Maluccio (1993) provide useful coverage of roads to family reunification. One of the chapters in their book presents a model program that includes assessment and treatment but also stresses the need for after care:

> At first services began to decrease shortly after the family was reunified, but it soon became apparent that this was a critical mistake. The first three months after a family is reunified are often fraught with difficulties and stress of learning to be together again ... (Boutilier & Rehm, in Pine et al., p. 60)

Bullock, Little, and Millham (1993) reported similar findings. Folaron (1993) provides a comprehensive description of the many ways in which foster parents can assist in re-entry. Odell (2008), in arguing for recognition of foster parents' strengths, provided a case study of foster parents preparing a child for moving into an adoptive home. The same set of skills can apply to family reunification.

Barth and Berry (1987) assessed permanency planning outcomes involving reunification, adoption, guardianship, and long-term foster care. The indicators they used were abuse, placement stability, developmental outcomes, and children's satisfaction with their placement. They found that the children reunified were the most poorly served, and needed increased and longer lasting services. The use of foster families in reunification would undoubtedly improve outcomes and ensure the children's continuing safety.

Foster Care and Permanency Planning

Finally, there is a legitimate role for foster families as permanent homes for children, rather than as a temporary refuge. Where children are well settled, attached, and thriving, particularly those older children for whom adoption may not be an option, it would make sense to support establishing a permanent guardianship arrangement.

Treatment Foster Care

Since the 1980s, an addition to the continuum of care provisions is that of treatment foster care (TFC). Multidimensional Treatment Foster Care (MTFC) is an even more recent development, originating in Oregon. Though not specifically targeted in the projects outlined above, some youth participants who had experienced treatment foster care did have comments to make. Their comments clustered around two themes. One was that they would prefer that the costs for treatment be re-diverted to allow them to have more time with their social worker. The other was their perception that such placements labelled them as the problem instead of the events that brought them into care. Empirical foundation for such relabelling occurred in a Newfoundland study. Using a systematic random sample, this study followed all children received into care in a 10-year period. As in other studies, children experienced considerable discontinuity. One-third of the sample currently in care had been returned home at least twice. Reasons for coming into care the first time were cross-tabulated with reasons for care at last entry. One-fifth of those who had been physically abused were later labelled as "out of control." Nearly one-third of those who had been sexually abused were similarly labelled at last entry (Kufeldt & Klein, 1998).

Youth respondents, it seems, had a good case to make. Nevertheless, TFC and MTFC do have a role to play in the current continuum of services. Initially, TFC was developed as an alternative to institutional care (Hazel, 1981). Foster carers received adequate recompense in return for nurturing adolescents and preparing them for independence. TFC continues to be an option for more difficult children and youth, is task-oriented, and provides higher recompense to the foster carers. MTFC was developed also as an alternative to institutional care, primarily targeted to young offenders. Two-year follow-up studies have indicated lower pregnancy rates and reduced rates in delinquency compared to control groups in institutional care (Chamberlain & Moore, 1998; Chamberlain & Reid, 1998; Eddy, Bridges Whaley, & Chamberlain, 2004; Fisher & Chamberlain, 2000; Kerr, Leve, & Chamberlain, 2009).

The Oregon program has been imported to England with the aim of promoting permanency through family rehabilitation, adoption, or long-term foster care. The 2008 project report indicated that 56 of the 100 young people who have left completed the program successfully and moved to family or foster family placements or independent living. Thirty-three left prematurely and eleven moved to non-family-based placements, such as residential children's homes (Department for Children, Schools, and Families, 2008). The roughly 50/50 successful completion rate in this project echoes findings reported elsewhere with respect to specialist foster care (Kelly, 2002). Sinclair (2005) also reported mixed results, with 5 out of 20 participants achieving success. The U.K. study indicated that all those admitted had high levels of complex needs. They had experienced multiple placements, exhibited serious behavioural problems, and most had experienced neglect and/or abuse. Girls were significantly more likely to have a history of sexual abuse than boys, and boys were significantly more likely to have a history of physical abuse than girls.

Clearly there is a place for specialized or treatment foster care for young people with severe difficulties. The downside is that TFC and MTFC are costly and time-limited, thus imposing another move for those who have already experienced too much discontinuity in their lives. In studying costs and consequences of placement, Ward and her colleagues had this to say:

> So far the data appear to show an inverse relationship between the costs and conditions under which adequate attachments might form, so that children and young people who follow the least costly care pathways have the best opportunities for developing and sustaining secure relationships with adults and peers and vice versa. (Ward, Holmes, & Soper, 2008, p. 168)

Selection factors are clearly related to this finding. TFC and MTFC may well be a useful adjunct to current services. However, the need for such placements could arguably be reduced through preventive measures such as properly resourced foster homes, including respite care, preservation of attachments with family of origin, promotion of attachments with foster carers, earlier permanency planning, and reduction in the discontinuity that sadly complicates the lives of too many young recipients of care. These types of investments might in the long run prove to be more beneficial to the children, and more cost-effective than widespread expansion of treatment foster care.

Implications for Policy and Practice

Clearly, the use of foster care and any expansion of its tasks should be well grounded in theoretical knowledge, primarily of the implications of separation and loss, of recovery from trauma, and of promotion of healthy development and resilience in children who have suffered neglect and abuse. An important component of such knowledge is the fact that attachment issues are compounded by the need to adjust to a new family, and most often a change of school and loss of peer relationships. This calls for well-trained and well-qualified social workers and foster carers. In addition, if children are to be well served, then child welfare and child protection must be proactive. A focus on the child's needs and interests rather than on an arbitrary threshold of harm would constitute a major step in this direction. Rather than "least intrusion," a fair degree of intrusion is necessary in order to adequately assess what those needs and interests are. Further, it is essential to understand that foster care and family preservation are not incompatible when inclusive care is practised.

It is also clear that good foster care is an absolutely essential part of child protection provisions. Early permanency planning has at times been viewed as a panacea for what ails the service, and foster care thereby seen as a temporary option. As noted above, the currently preferred goal of family reunification, while admirable, may have unintended negative consequences. Early permanency planning is essential and more readily attained where the options can be a permanent foster home or open adoption. Family preservation is possible if measured by a continuing set of relationships, rather than cohabitation. This is certainly recognized in family law. Permanent placement can be practised on a continuum between acknowledgement of family of origin through to shared care, or what Forsythe (1989) would call a family connectedness hierarchy. As Thoburn (1994) stated: "A sense of identity can best be achieved by continued contact with parents and other members of the natural family and with other people who have cared for—or about—a youngster in the past" (p. 39). Clearly the parents and other family members of children placed in foster care have a continuing role to play in their children's lives, and they should be encouraged to do so to the degree that it is helpful to the children.

The current tendency to ignore fathers also needs to be reversed. The *Looking After Children in Canada* study (Kufeldt et al., 2000) was instrumental, in some cases, in establishing connections to fathers. In addition, children want and need contact and continuity with the extended family. The young people interviewed in the series of studies cited identified the need to reconnect with families. Nevertheless, some were clear that they did not want to, and should not, return home. In saying so, they were not rejecting their families, but were being realistic about their best life chances. We need to view family preservation not in terms of residence or custody, but rather as a continuing set of relationships.

Recommendations

Changing the approach to service from being crisis-driven to having a child development orientation is a challenge, but achievable, particularly given the availability of good models of guided practice. The ideal would be to recognize that practice in child welfare is one of the most complex and demanding fields of practice of social work, and would be best served by well-trained, experienced workers. Since such a utopian goal is not readily achievable, then guided practice is essential to ensure that children's needs are met.

The findings of various studies have affirmed the value of one such model, *Looking After Children*. It has the potential to achieve the changes that proactive practice requires. Its values are multiple, but can be summarized as:

- focusing social work attention on the full spectrum of developmental needs;
- acknowledging the fact of *corporate parenting*: taking care of children in guardianship is shared by a number of people;
- recognizing that shared parenting requires free flow of communication between all parties, including educational and health personnel;
- ensuring that children are given a voice; and
- enabling a proactive, action-oriented approach to caring for children.

Above all, it gives children and young people themselves a voice, and respects the contribution made by foster carers. The major challenge to its implementation is that *Looking After Children* demands a cultural shift, or radical reorientation, in the way in which child welfare services conduct their business. It will be difficult, but not impossible. The series of projects referred to in this chapter provided a forum whereby the voice of children, young people, and adults who have graduated from the system could be heard. Their voice, if heard, can be a catalyst, and a powerful force for change.

11

Finding the Best Home: A Comparative Analysis of Kinship and Foster Care Placements

Katharine Dill

Being a child protection worker in today's changing social context can be a very daunting position. One of the most critical decisions that front-line workers and supervisors face is whether to remove children from the care of their parents, and if so, where to place these children. Often, the decision to remove children from the care of their parents is by necessity made swiftly, and there is little time to consider where the children should be placed. Should they be moved to a kinship home, foster home, or group care? Frequently, this decision is based on the reality of the day—where there is a placement available at the time. However, front-line workers and supervisors in the field want to make the best possible decision for the children. They recognize the magnitude of a decision which will have far-reaching implications, enduring long after the decision of that day to apprehend and place the children in substitute care.

The goal of this chapter is to explore the similarities and differences between kinship and foster care placement options through a review of the literature. This is designed to assist child welfare professionals in making key decisions with respect to the placement of children in substitute care. The review focuses on the following subject areas: placement stability, child well-being, financial remuneration, maltreatment episodes in out-of-home care, and diversity issues. It also includes a discussion of participants' perspectives. The chapter concludes with a section on policy and practice implications.

About Kinship

Kinship care has been defined as "the full-time nurturing and protection of children by relatives, members of their tribes or clans, godparents, stepparents, or other adults who have a kinship bond with the child" (Child Welfare League of America, 2000, p. 1). Testa (2008) defined the word "bond" as commonly deriving from a relationship by blood or marriage to one of the child's parents or from any number of "fictive kin" relationships, such as godparent, family friend, or tribal (or community) member. Kinship homes include: (1) private kinship placements that receive no support from or intervention by child welfare agencies; (2) kinship foster care, whereby the family may receive full financial and support services from child welfare organizations; and (3) kinship guardianship and adoption (Testa, 2008).

Emerging Use of Kinship Placements

Over the past decade, child welfare practitioners have expressed increased interest in the growing use of kinship placements for children and youth in need of protection (Albert, Iaci, & Catlin, 2004; Berrick, 1997; Leschied, MacKay, Raghunandan, Sharpe, & Sookoor, 2007). Attention to kinship placements has expanded because many child welfare practitioners consider family-based care a better arrangement for children or youth than foster homes or group care (Albert et al., 2004; Barber & Delfabbro, 2004). This is rooted in the belief that kinship placements offer children a greater opportunity for continuity and stability than foster homes (Geen, 2003a, 2003b, 2003c; Gleeson & Hairston, 1999; Scannapieco & Hegar, 1999). In essence, there are three deeply entrenched assumptions about the benefits of kinship placements: (1) kinship placements have greater longevity than foster care situations; (2) kinship homes are more likely to accept sibling groups and sustain those relationships; and (3) most children and parents would prefer that children live with family members or friends rather than with strangers (Barth, Guo, Green, & McCrae, 2007).

An additional, more pragmatic influence is the limited availability of homes. In the province of Ontario, as in much of Canada, the child welfare system has experienced significant changes and growth that have resulted in fewer available foster homes and an increased need for extended-family placements. Since the mid-1990s, there has been a substantial increase in the number of children entering the child welfare system (Leschied et al., 2007). This surge in the rate of children coming into care has resulted in an increased utilization of both in-care (with the same funding as foster placements) and voluntary kinship placements (Ontario Association of Children's Aid Societies, 2008).

Controversy and Challenge

Nevertheless, this shift is not without controversy in relation to the safety and well-being of the children involved. Concerns surfaced in an Ontario case of a young boy, Jeffrey Baldwin, who died of starvation while in the care of his maternal grandparents, despite supervision by the Toronto Catholic Children's Aid Society (Appleby, 2006; Lewis, 2005; Pron, 2006). The case highlighted the need to understand complex issues related to kinship caregiving. It also exemplified the need for child welfare authorities to ensure the protection of children by having a structure and screening system in place for kinship placements.

Placement Stability

In a seminal publication on permanency and foster care, Australian researchers Barber and Delfabbro (2006) articulated the sometimes tragic consequences of a child's entrance into the foster care system. Their study employed a diverse, mixed-methods design (N=235 children in foster care over 12 months), exploring the quantitative and qualitative perspectives relating to these children. One of the key findings was that children who experienced a placement breakdown within the first four months of foster care went on to become members of what the authors termed the "serially evicted" cohort of children—children who were likely to face a significant number of placement moves or disruptions.

The research related to placement stability for children placed in kinship homes appears positive. Webster, Barth, and Needell (2000) conducted a large (N=15,517 children), eight-year longitudinal study that highlighted the permanency outcomes for children in kinship care. The research found that children placed in kinship homes were less likely to experience placement disruption than those in foster placements. More recent research from Illinois found that 82% of children in kinship homes remained in their placement after one year compared to 65% of children in foster care (Rolock & Testa, 2007). Unfortunately, the statistics provided by Rolock and Testa do not identify whether the lower placement stability rates in foster homes are attributed to children returning to their respective birth homes. This could be a causative factor, as other studies (Geen, 2003a, 2003c; Rubin, Downes, O'Reilly, Mekonnen, Luan, & Localio, 2008; Scannapieco & Hegar, 1999) suggest that children in kinship care are less likely to return home. In a study on kinship care in the United Kingdom, Farmer and Moyers (2008) determined that the average duration of a kinship placement is four years and nine months, as compared to three years and eleven months for foster placements. The emerging evidence does therefore suggest that children in kinship placements are likely to attain greater placement sta-bility than those living in foster care.

Terling-Watt (2001) explored the barriers to permanency in kinship homes. The mixed-methods study design employed a sample population of 2,515 fam-ily reunification cases in Texas. It included a qualitative analysis of interviews with 26 child welfare professionals to ascertain the factors that had contributed to placement disruption in kinship homes. Barriers identified were: (1) bio-logical parents interfering with the kinship placements; (2) caregivers strug-gling with multi-dimensional issues that included lack of social support, and age and health limitations; and (3) the requirements of special-needs children extending beyond the capacity of their aging kinship caregivers.

Child Well-Being

A fundamental question is whether the well-being of children placed in kinship homes is equivalent to, or surpasses, that of children in foster care. Research findings suggest that all children in substitute care tend to enter the child wel-fare system with many developmental delays and challenges (Leslie et al., 2000). The well-being of children in care covers a wide range of issues, including emo-tional, physical, and mental health, as well as placement stability.

Educational and Behavioural Outcomes

Canadian child welfare systems are making great strides in understanding the issues related to outcomes for children in care. *Looking After Children* is a tool that examines children's overall well-being from the perspective of seven dimen-sions: health, education, identity, family and social relationships, social presen-tation skills, emotional and behavioural development, and self-care skills. Using information from this outcome measurement tool, Kufeldt, Simard, Tite, and Vachon (2003) examined outcomes for children and youth in child welfare placements. One of their striking findings was that those in care did signifi-cantly less well on educational outcomes compared to the general population. This study did not examine specific outcomes related to children in kinship placements, but an Ontario study (Leschied et al., 2007) compared behavioural outcomes for children placed in kinship and foster care (Leschied et al., 2007). Children in kinship homes showed greater improvement on various different behavioural measures, including physical and verbal aggression, fire-setting, and hyperactivity. This study was conducted in one mid-size agency, and requires replication.

Timmer, Sedler, and Urquiza (2004) performed a quantitative analysis of 102 kinship and 157 non-kinship foster parents. They determined that foster parents' ratings of the severity of the behavioural problems of the children in their care were much higher and more negative than those of kinship caregivers. In addition, kinship caregivers tended to follow through more consistently with mental health treatment for children and youth compared to their foster parent counterparts.

Farmer and Moyers (2008) determined that compared to children placed in unrelated foster homes, children in kinship placements had spent less time in care before being placed in the kinship home, were less likely to show emotional distress before placement, and were less apt to have multiple health difficulties. A sample of 270 children was included in the cross-sectional design of this study; as well, other methods such as file reviews, and qualitative interviews with carers, children, parents, and biological parents were incorporated. A limitation to this research and other similar studies is the possibility that other extraneous factors such as previous abuse, and the overall physical and emotional well-being of the children prior to placement, may have influenced these findings.

A more recent study by Rubin et al. (2008) compared kinship to foster care placements. The data were drawn from the U.S. National Survey of Child and Adolescent Well-Being (NSCAW) between October 1999 and March 2004. Using a sample of 1,309 children in care (N=710 in foster care and N=599 in kinship homes), this study determined that children who moved to kinship care, after a length of time in foster care, were more likely to demonstrate behavioural challenges than children who started out their placement experiences in kin homes. The study did not elaborate on whether the children who began their placement journey in foster care, and then transitioned to kinship homes, demonstrated a reduction in behavioural challenges after this transition. If data on this issue had been examined, it might have helped in determining whether kinship placements had had a moderating influence on the behavioural outcomes of children in care. Future research should examine this issue in more detail.

Health Outcomes

In a rare study that examined health outcomes of children in kinship homes, Dubowitz et al. (1992) found significant health problems among children placed in kinship homes, including poor visual acuity, hearing, and growth, obesity, and dental problems. More research is needed to assess health issues in both kinship and foster homes, as another study had contrasting findings. Engaging a retrospective study design, Carpenter and Clyman (2004) conducted a quantitative study of 8,760 subjects using secondary data from the National Survey of Family Growth in the United States, and compared this population to a sample of 471 adult women who were placed in kinship care in their childhood years. The findings suggested that women who were placed in kinship care as children were likely to have better physical outcomes—but worse emotional outcomes—than those who grew up in foster care. This information is important, but its clinical implications are unclear.

Maintaining Sibling Connections

There is clearly a need for studies on sibling placements from the perspective of child well-being and Canadian child welfare placements. In a qualitative study, Shlonsky (2008) conducted two focus groups with 23 youth at one child welfare agency in southwestern Ontario. Many of the youth articulated a profound sense of loss at being separated from a sibling when entering care, and said that busy child welfare professionals often found it challenging to maintain access between siblings.

In research undertaken by Webster et al. (2000), there was a larger proportion of sibling placements in kinship homes as compared to foster or group care settings. In contrast, Farmer and Moyers (2008) found no significant difference in the rate of sibling placements between kinship and foster care. Emerging research suggests that sibling placements create a protective "layer" for children entering care that results in a reduced likelihood of placement disruption. In a review of research on sibling relationships, Hegar (2005) provided important insights into the role of siblings in the context of child welfare practice. This meta-analysis determined that some studies reported fewer placement disruptions for children who were placed together with their siblings (Boer & Spiering, 1991; Drapeau, Simard, Beaudry, & Charbonneau, 2000; Thorpe & Swart, 1992). Evidence regarding the role of sibling placements in the context of placement stability for children is still lacking, particularly within the context of kinship homes. However, the preponderance of research on child welfare placements in general suggests that siblings who are placed together stay together (Hegar, 2005). It is clear that sibling relationships are a foundational issue when discussing child welfare placements.

Assessing Kin Care Providers

Through a critical analysis of the literature, Shlonsky and Berrick (2001) built a framework for assessing kin care providers that extends beyond the physical safety of the home environment. They posited that assessments of kinship homes must include an analysis of the family in the context of its larger environment. Based on their review, the authors concluded that children in kinship care typically reside in homes with significant poverty (Geen, 2003a, 2003c; Wyatt, Simms, & Horwitz, 1997). They also provided child welfare practitioners with the "blueprint" for a kinship assessment tool that is linked to the complexities of such placements. The authors provided a unique perspective on how to assess kinship homes that does not borrow from the "cookie-cutter" approach of traditional foster care placement-assessment frameworks. This differentiation between the assessment of kinship and foster care homes recognizes the distinctly different clinical issues that do exist in kinship placements, and that may be overlooked if a foster family assessment framework is utilized.

Ehrle and Geen (2002) examined foster care (147 children), in-care kinship placements (148 children), and voluntary kinship placements (167 children). They determined that the vast majority of children residing in voluntary kinship placements were living in relative poverty, with little or no social supports. The authors challenged policy-makers to consider the potentially dire conditions of these voluntary placements, as well as the need for a social policy framework and adequate financial compensation to support and encourage them. This study again highlights the unique economic circumstances related to kinship placements that cannot be overlooked, and which require special analysis by child welfare practitioners and policy-makers.

Financial Remuneration

As noted above, many children in kinship placements, particularly those residing in voluntary kinship placements, live in situations of relative poverty. Because of how financial remuneration is structured, foster parents are automatically given greater economic support than their kinship counterparts. Some Canadian jurisdictions provide financial remuneration to kinship carers, although not always at the same rate as for other foster parents. A fact sheet published by the Centre of Excellence for Child Welfare in Canada (Gough, 2006) examined variations in funding frameworks for kin caregivers across Alberta, British Columbia, the Northwest Territories, Ontario, and Saskatchewan. This publication emphasized the need for a national examination of the funding framework related to kinship and foster placements. In some Canadian jurisdictions, kin caregivers must apply for welfare in order to receive compensation for the children placed in their care (CANGRANDS, 2008). In contrast, foster parents are provided with financial support directly from the child welfare agency.

The issue of financial remuneration has been examined in the United Kingdom (U.K.) by Farmer and Moyers (2008) and Hunt (2009), who have concluded that the issue of financial remuneration is complex and that, more often than not, kin caregivers receive substantially less funding than their foster parent counterparts. In the Farmer and Moyers (2008) study, the researchers found evidence of financial difficulty in 75% of kinship placements. Hunt (2009) outlined a number of concrete ways of assisting kin caregivers, including monthly stipends, reimbursements for recreation and child care costs, and assistance with court-related costs.

The tragic death of a 19-month-old First Nations girl, Heshook-ish Tsawalk, in kinship care in Port Alberni, British Columbia, caused the B.C. government to initiate a report addressing the systemic factors related to the child's death. The report by the Child and Youth Officer for British Columbia (2006c) outlined policy recommendations, including a more comprehensive funding support system for kin caregivers, designed to benefit the children they are caring for.

Maltreatment Episodes in Out-of-Home Care

One of the most salient issues to be addressed relates to the safety of children in kinship and foster care placements. Are children more at risk in substitute care in general? If so, are children more or less safe in foster versus kinship homes? This issue is always raised following the tragic death of any child who has been placed in care. Most evidence suggests that children in kinship homes are at less risk of further abuse than those in foster placements.

Winokur, Crawford, Longobardi, and Valentine (2008) also contrasted kinship and foster placements by examining critical elements of care, including permanency, safety, and stability outcomes. A key finding from their study was the strikingly different reported rates of maltreatment between the two placements: 18% of foster children were reported to have been maltreated in their care home compared to 2.2% of children in kinship homes. These numbers indicate that children are nearly eight times more likely to report being maltreated in a foster home than in a kinship placement. However, these authors caution that foster homes may have higher reported rates of maltreatment because they are subject to greater scrutiny than kinship placements. In a review of the literature, Hunt (2009) found that the risk of abuse in kinship placements was relatively low (between 2% and 10% of all kinship placements). These rates were identified as no higher than in foster care, although the rates of reported abuse in foster care were not specified.

It is still not clear why some studies show that kinship homes appear to be a protective factor against future maltreatment. One hypothesis is that the extended family relationship protects children from future harm, that kin caregivers are simply more invested in terms of ensuring the overall safety and well-being of the children. The bond and attachment that exists between kin caregivers and children may be the protective layer that protects these children from higher rates of reported maltreatment. This hypothesis requires further study, but the above-noted studies dispel the myth that children in extended-family placements are at high risk for future maltreatment.

Aboriginal and First Nations Children and Families

The *Canadian Incidence Study of Reported Child Abuse and Neglect* (Trocmé et al., 2005) determined that Aboriginal children are four to six times more likely to be taken into care than the general population. A pioneering study by Fuller-Thomson (2006) highlighted some important findings about Canadian Aboriginal grandparents caring for grandchildren. Using census data, the study concluded that, compared with the general population, these caregivers are more likely to be female (64% vs. 58% in the general population) and less likely to be employed (29% vs. 40% in the general population). In addition, 42% of First Nations caregiver grandparents had an income of less than $15,000 per annum. These findings correlate with similar research of American Indian grandparents by Minkler and Fuller-Thomson (2005). Both studies are striking in their parallel findings of kin grandparents caring for children in relative poverty.

A report by Wright, Hiebert-Murphy, Mirwaldt, and Muswaggon (2008) examined a kinship care program located on a Cree reserve in northern Manitoba. Using a mixed-methods design, the research team interviewed children and youth (n=18), staff members (n=22), kinship foster parents (n=15), and a community stakeholder. The researchers determined that 75% of children remained in their kinship homes four years after initial placement. This study demonstrates the resilience of kin families and the capacity of extended-family networks to provide stability for children requiring out-of-home placements.

Family Group Conferencing

Family group conferencing (FGC) is a mechanism that can be used to bring together the extended family network (Hill, 2005; Holland & O'Neill, 2006; Schmid & Goranson, 2002; Schmid, Tansony, Goranson, & Sykes, 2004; Sundell & Vinnerljung, 2004; Waites, Macgowan, Pennell, Carlton-LaNey, & Weil, 2004). Guidelines for conducting family group conferences in child welfare have been developed by the American Humane Association and Family Group Decision Making Committee (2010) in the U.S. The concept is seen as culturally relevant because of the way it preserves relationships within the extended family network (Hill, 2005). Some view the concept of FGC as being culturally sensitive—embracing a strengths-based approach that is sometimes lacking in the child welfare arena (Waites et al., 2004). The mechanism of conferencing can promote the connection of family members and the recruitment of other extended family caregivers. By working within the context of the family system, FGC is by its very nature attuned to the complex and diverse needs of the families serviced by child welfare organizations (Schmid et al., 2004).

Participants' Perspectives

Child Welfare Professionals

Studies have examined child welfare professionals' perspectives on kinship care. In an American study, Peters (2005) surveyed child welfare professionals' values and beliefs about kinship care using a content-analysis qualitative study with a sample size of 63 front-line child protection workers. On the positive side, workers indicated that kinship care helped to reduce the stigma for children entering care, and kept them from being labelled "foster children." These same professionals reported that the "fruit doesn't fall far from the tree," indicating a presumption on behalf of the workers that extended family networks will demonstrate the same types of maltreating behaviours that were demonstrated by the biological parents. In another U.S. study, Beeman and Boisen (1999) used quantitative measures in engaging a robust sample population of 261 child protection workers from both urban and rural settings. The findings were intriguing; the authors determined that most child protection workers felt that kinship care was adequate, but a "second-class" option to the more desirable foster home placement. In addition, 42% of respondents felt that kinship care placements were more difficult to supervise. This highlights the need to educate child welfare professionals about the complexities, but overall success rates, of kinship placements.

Children's Perceptions

Children's perceptions are equally important. Chapman, Wall, and Barth (2004) employed quantitative methods to elicit information about the differences between the two distinct placement options of kinship and foster care. This exploratory American study was based on a sample population of 727 children who had been in an out-of-home placement for one year at the time of the research. Children in kinship placements reported feeling closer to their caregivers than children placed in group care. In addition, children in kinship homes felt that their (kin) caregivers cared for them more compared with children in foster placements. This study was unusual in the researchers' capacity to analyze the unique perspectives of children and youth residing in out-of-home care.

A U.K. study by Broad, Hayes, and Rushforth (2001) interviewed 50 youth residing in kinship homes. The positive themes that emerged included feeling safe, maintaining links with family and siblings, feeling settled and well cared for, and maintaining their cultural/racial heritage. An interesting negative theme emerged from some youth who had brothers or sisters residing in parallel foster care placements. There was a perception that these siblings had more access to material possessions because of their placement in foster care. The youth in kinship homes perceived foster care to be better subsidized than kinship homes. This study did not compare the perceptions of youth residing in kinship homes with those residing in foster homes. However, it does provide valuable insights into the unique attributes of these extended-family placements.

Conclusions and Implications

Summary of Research Findings

Emerging evidence suggests the following:

(1) children in kinship homes experience fewer placement disruptions when compared to children in foster care (Farmer & Moyers, 2008; Webster et al., 2000);

(2) select studies suggest that behavioural and emotional outcomes for children in kinship homes are better than for those in foster care (Farmer & Moyers, 2008; Leischied et al., 2007; Timmer et al., 2004), but overall physical well-being outcomes are unclear (Carpenter & Clyman, 2004; Dubowitz et al., 1992);

(3) maltreatment rates seem to be the same or lower in kinship homes as compared to foster care; however, future research is required to closely examine

other potential confounding issues, such as higher levels of surveillance in foster homes, child behaviour, and the training and support provided to caregivers, as these factors may affect maltreatment reports in both types of placements (Hunt, 2009; Winokur et al., 2008);

(4) child protection workers believe that kinship homes reduce stigma for children, while potentially increasing the level of risk to the child placed in the home (Peters, 2005); and

(5) children report a greater sense of overall well-being when placed in kinship homes (Broad et al., 2001; Messing, 2006). Much more research is required on well-being, as the two studies cited here reported only very tentative findings.

Overall, the preponderance of evidence suggests positive outcomes for children placed in kinship homes. In a meta-analysis completed by Winokur, Holtan, and Valentine (2009), the authors echo these sentiments about positive outcomes related to kinship placements, but caution that many of the studies that explore such placements contain significant methodological design flaws; thus the interpretation of results to date must be treated with caution, and much more research on kinship care outcomes is required.

Practice, Policy, and Research Implications

There are significant policy and practice implications related to the provision of services to both foster and kinship placements.

Practice Implications

This literature review demonstrates the complexity of clinical issues and unique challenges inherent to kinship and foster placements. Emerging themes from this author's doctoral dissertation (Dill, 2009) highlight the need for specialized kinship programs in child welfare agencies. The benefit of such kinship-focused programs is the potential to develop more unique clinical expertise with respect to the recruitment, assessment, and retention of kin families. When specializations do not exist in agencies, the capacity of caseworkers to identify and manage the complexity of clinical issues is diminished. In contrast, workers who specialize in the area of kinship placements articulate significant knowledge with respect to the underlying clinical issues inherent in kinship placements, such as divided loyalties, social isolation, and financial and resource challenges.

Another emergent finding from the research highlights the need for specialized kin training and support programs. Kin caregivers report feeling alienated in training sessions: these focus exclusively on the needs of foster parents (Dill,

2009). The child welfare system must recognize that the training needs of kin families are unique and require specialized clinical knowledge and application. Kin caregivers also report feeling isolated from the traditional foster parent support network. A new paradigm of support and training for kin caregivers is required if we are to adequately support these unique family systems.

Policy Implications

In his book *Kinship Care: Making the Most of a Valuable Resource*, Geen (2003c) highlighted the practical reality that most kinship placements exist in large urban settings where child protection caseloads are at their highest. High caseloads and decreasing funding sources are accompanied by the desire to move toward what are perceived to be less expensive placement options for children and youth. The challenge is to embrace kinship care in the fundamental belief that these types of placements can and do make a difference in the lives of children. With the increased use of kin families, we must ensure that standards and policies are in place to ensure the safety of children in these homes. However, as Shlonsky and Berrick (2001) highlighted, kinship homes must be assessed within the context of a larger social environment that often includes high rates of poverty, social isolation, and lower rates of education for kin caregivers. Unique policies must be developed for kinship placements that are separate and apart from those of the traditional structure, and not simply an add-on to the current foster care system.

Research Implications

The current state of knowledge on this subject suggests that more research is required on outcomes for children and youth in kinship and foster placements, including research on physical well-being in each placement setting. Emerging research must integrate the voices of children in order to ascertain the subjective and lived experiences of children and youth residing in kinship and foster placements (Messing, 2006; Nixon, 2007). Canadian research is required that explores the cultural context of kinship and foster placements, as well as the challenges of financial remuneration and social supports. Participatory action research that engages caregivers, children, and youth in the design, implementation, and dissemination of research findings would ensure that the complexities of both kinship and foster placements are explored and examined (Nixon, 2007).

12

A Bicultural Response to Children in Need of Care and Protection in New Zealand

Jill Worrall

New Zealand (*Aotearoa*) is a South Pacific island nation of 4.17 million people, whose population is 15% indigenous Maori, 68% European (*Pakeha*) descent, 6% Pacific Island, and 9% Asian (Statistics New Zealand, 2007). Ethnic diversity is increasing: immigration policies have resulted in communities being enriched by Middle Eastern, Latin American, and African peoples. The need for culturally sensitive foster care practice is therefore a constant challenge.

New Zealand was a leader in international child welfare legislation reform with the passing of the *Children, Young Persons, and their Families Act* (1989). This Act mandated the extended family as the preferred placement for children in need of care and protection, respecting traditional Maori concepts of family responsibility and decision-making. It is questionable, however, whether the Maori model of collective responsibility translates to European families. This chapter examines traditional Maori child welfare practice, kinship care, and placement permanence, with reference to New Zealand research. It concludes with discussion of the implications for social work practice and policy of the dilemmas related to cross-cultural placements and the search for better outcomes for children in need of care and protection.

The History of Child Protection Law in New Zealand

In 1840, New Zealand's colonizing forefathers signed the Treaty of Waitangi with the indigenous Maori tribes to prescribe equitable relationships between

Maori and Pakeha, and continuing respect for Maori values and customs. Within this Treaty, children are recognized as *"taonga,"* or treasures of Maori society. However, colonization has taken a terrible toll on the country's Indigenous peoples, and Maori children are disproportionately represented in child welfare statistics. In early New Zealand both Maori and Pakeha children in need of care were most often consigned to institutional care, and, in later decades, to stranger foster care. The Maori people were never involved in the establishment of the child welfare system; their cultural values and social needs were ignored, and systems and institutions integral to the structure of Maori society went unrecognized. A critical report to the government had this to say:

> ... the central State's chosen administrators supplant traditional leaders; the State's agents impose new structures; legal-judicial processes replace the traditional tribal law; and most significantly, permanent government forces enforce the new rules ... Weaving a fine bureaucratic net about traditional society, they impose regulations, restrictions and obligations upon the people ... For the Maori, political modernisation resulted in a systematic and unrelenting assault on their traditional society. (Ministerial Advisory Committee on a Maori Perspective for the Department of Social Welfare, 1986, pp. 7–8)

Traditional Maori society was based on the organic solidarity of kinship and tribal autonomy. The extended family (*whanau*) was the most basic of kinship levels, and was responsible for the support, education, and rearing of its members. A child was seen not as the child of his or her biological parents, but as a child of the whanau, which had communal responsibility for all of its members. Jackson (1988) described the strength of the whanau system:

> The kinship ties of the large family unit implied a sharing of support, discipline and comfort for all members of the whanau. Its structure provided young people with their feeling of well-being, their security and their sense of a group good greater than their own. It provided them with a sense of their place in the scheme of things and ensured rules of behaviour and cultural transmission were maintained. (Jackson, 1988, p. 76)

When parents were under stress, children were cared for within the extended family, to the mutual advantage of all concerned. Contact with parents was usually assured, and placements seen as a temporary arrangement. The Ministerial Advisory Committee claimed that "Maori children knew many homes but still one whanau" (1986, p. 23).

Walker (1990), in her historical review of kinship care in New Zealand, found no evidence of any policy to place Maori children in need of care and protection within their whanau. Early departmental letters illustrated racist practice and little understanding of whanau systems. Although she found evidence of policy that Maori children should be placed with Maori foster parents, it was rarely adhered to, and when it was, a lower board rate was paid. The evidence was that Maori children were taken into care and placed with Pakeha foster families from the beginning of state intervention, and were disenfranchised from all that was familiar to them.

Child protection law was therefore perceived as part of an assimilation process (Ministerial Advisory Committee, 1986). Research undertaken in 1980 showed that 53% of children in care were Maori, although they represented 12% of children under 16 years. Most were placed in Pakeha foster homes. The research also revealed that children in state care were subject to "foster care drift," with many children unable to establish continuity of carer relationships (Worrall, 1996). In the past, judgmental attitudes toward all families of children requiring care stood in the way of placement with kin, irrespective of race (Walker, 1990). Ryburn made the point that very often the professional view of the family was a deficit one, based on contact with its "most problematic members" (1993, pp. 2–3). This view ignored strengths that might have existed in the wider family, and also the fact that what might have been lacking were resources.

Current Child Welfare Practice

Child Welfare practice in New Zealand is now prescribed by the *Children, Young Persons, and their Families Act* (CYPFA) (1989). This Act clearly states that any intervention into family life should be the minimum necessary to ensure a child or young person's safety. The first response must be to provide, where practicable, the necessary assistance and support to enable that child to remain within its own family/whanau. A child should only be removed where there is serious risk of harm, and all efforts made to reunite the family, after ensuring the environment is safe. If the child's immediate family/whanau cannot offer care, attempts must be made to place the child on a short-term basis in a culturally matched family, either with people unrelated but known to the child, or in stranger foster care outside the family and preferably in the same locality so that family links can be maintained (CYPFA, 1989, s.13). If return to parents is unlikely within a reasonable time frame, attempts are then made to seek permanent placement within the wider extended family/whanau or tribe/*iwi*. Stranger foster care is seen only as a short-term arrangement.

This Act has been described as the first serious attempt by a New Zealand government to take into account the cultural values and perspectives of Maori and Pacific Island peoples in dealing with issues of care and protection. It represents a shift from British models of legislative authority to intervene in the lives of families (contained in the *Child Welfare Act 1925* and the *Children and Young Persons Act 1974*), to giving families/whanau the chance to reclaim and nurture their own children. The tool of the Act is the Family Group Conference— an Indigenous cultural construct of family decision-making which seeks to find family solutions to family problems (Cockburn, 1994; Mason, Kirby, and Wray, 1992). This family decision-making model has since been emulated by many international child welfare jurisdictions. The concept of "family continuity" and the sustaining of family links and identity for children unable to live with their biological parents is recognized as good child welfare practice with exponential growth in the social phenomenon of kin, particularly grandparents, of all cultures assuming custody for their grandchildren (Worrall, 2007; see also Chapter 11).

At the time the 1989 Act was passed, social workers were divided into two camps. Some held a rosy view that stranger foster care would become a thing of the past and that kin would stand up and be counted when needed, keeping their children safe. Others voiced some skepticism that the practice held inherent risks that might be difficult to navigate. It would be naive to think that these risks are not present, but how they are managed is the key issue.

Although there are no comparable data over time, current government statistics show an increasing trend toward placing children with kin. However, the chances of being placed with whanau/extended family differ across cultures. At the end of June 2008, a total of 4,470 children were under the jurisdiction of the national child protection agency, Child, Youth and Family (CYF). Of these, 2,166 were Maori; 1,888 were New Zealand Pakeha; 278 were of Pacific Island ethnicity; 100 were recorded as other; and 35 were recorded as being European. The ethnicity of three children was not recorded. Pacific Island children were those most likely to be placed with kin (59%), followed by Maori children (53%), compared to only 31% of Pakeha children (see Table 1).

While the first idealistic notions of stranger foster care becoming redundant have not materialized, many families are now caring for their kin/whanau children. However, the data raise the question of why Pakeha children are less likely to be with kin and whether it is an issue of nuclear family constructs, or extended family willingness or ability to care. The concerted effort to employ Maori and Pacific Island social workers may be a critical contributing factor, as they work in an appropriate way with their own people to identify the child's extended family links and ensure that the child is placed appropriately. Pakeha social workers may not be so diligent. Both Australian and New Zealand

Table 1 *Numbers of Children in Care Placements by Care Type and Ethnicity*

		Number			Proportion		
Fiscal Year	Ethnic Group	Non-Kin	Kin	Total	Non-Kin	Kin	Total
At June 2007	NZ Maori	1,143	1,234	2,377	48%	52%	100%
	NZ Pakeha	1,512	633	2,145	70%	30%	100%
	Pacific Islands	136	175	311	44%	56%	100%
	European	12	11	23	52%	48%	100%
	Others	81	42	123	66%	34%	100%
	Not recorded	49	21	70	70%	30%	100%
	Total	2,933	2,116	5,049	58%	42%	100%
At June 2008	NZ Maori	1,008	1,158	2,166	47%	53%	100%
	NZ Pakeha	1,306	582	1,888	69%	31%	100%
	Pacific Islands	113	165	278	41%	59%	100%
	European	22	13	35	63%	37%	100%
	Others	81	19	100	81%	19%	100%
	Not recorded	2	1	3	67%	33%	100%
	Total	2,532	1,938	4,470	57%	43%	100%

Source: Worrall, 2008.

Indigenous children have a greater chance of being placed with kin than those of the dominant ethnic group (Butcher, 2004; Worrall, 2005). Current data cannot tell us whether children are placed with aunts, uncles, or grandparents, but it would appear that many grandparents are putting up their hands: the Aotearoa/New Zealand Grandparents Raising Grandchildren Trust has almost 4,000 families listed as members, the majority of whom are grandparents. The emergence of such organizations throughout the Western world gives testimony to the need for advocacy and support for this group of people.

How closely the state should monitor a child who has been previously neglected or abused, when placed with family, is still open to debate. Unless clearly stated in the care plan, extended family placements are not monitored as of right, in the belief that extended families will keep their own children safe. In the past, both Maori and Pakeha extended family/whanau structures were considerably more intimate than they are today. In Polynesian cultures the whanau lived, to all intents and purposes, under the same roof, and therefore exerted a measure of authority and control over its members. This is now less likely as both Maori and Pakeha families/whanau move away from former family supports in order to find work.

A review of the literature (see Chapter 11) provides no definitive answers regarding the costs and benefits of kin taking custody of children who have suffered abuse and/or neglect. There is positive evidence to show that children placed with relatives are more likely to experience placement stability, a key factor in attaining good outcomes for children living away from their biological parents. They are also more likely to have contact with their parents, to remain with siblings, and to sustain schooling, as they tend to remain in the same neighbourhood (Connolly, 2003; Rubin, Downes, O'Reilly, Mekonnen, Luan, & Localio, 2008). They are able to retain their identity and be surrounded by their family group. While this is encouraging, the research also indicates that issues exist across the personal and socio-political milieu that could place both carers and the children in their custody "at risk."

Experiences of Kin Care in Aotearoa / New Zealand

A critical analysis of the 1989 CYPFA places it within a wider context of government fiscal policies at the time; they placed a greater onus on families to be financially responsible for the education, health, and welfare of their members. It is a continuing indictment that in spite of passing child welfare legislation that was both controversial and groundbreaking, there has been no substantial research undertaken since then on outcomes for children who have been the subject of a care and protection investigation. There has been no tracking of children, and no comparative outcome data for children placed with kin and those placed outside of families in foster care. In the absence of such information, the Grandparents Raising Grandchildren Trust commissioned a research study on this topic, and this study is summarized below.

Methods

The study involved a large postal survey of the membership of the Trust (N=700) in which demographic and experiential data were collected from 323 kin caregiving families representing 526 caregivers, 492 children, and their biological parents (Worrall, 2005). The survey had a return rate of 46% and yielded an underrepresentation of Maori and Pacific Island respondents. Postal surveys are not suited to Maori or Pacific Island communities, whose research protocols about ownership and methodology are critically different from the dominant group—namely, oral methods of data gathering and the sharing of information only with honoured and validated members of their own culture. Additionally, at that time, the membership was 75% Pakeha, although since then there has been a substantial increase in Maori members. While the sample may not be representative of the total New Zealand kin carer population, the results are very similar to international research outcomes. Data were collected with respect to age, marital status, ethnicity, biological children, employment, health status, social activities, and household income. Additionally, information was collected about the children and their relationship to the primary carer, age distribution, physical and psychological health status, duration of care, legal status, educational progress, and other agency involvement. The carers' involvement with the legal system and any social and financial support they did or did not receive was also recorded.

The survey respondents were predominantly grandparents, reflecting the data source of the organization. Other kin carers have affiliated to the Trust, however, in the absence of any other kin carer organization. Government statistics have not captured relationship data, although anecdotal reports would suggest that grandparents are most likely to take custodial responsibility.

Results

The Carers: Ethnicity, Age, and Marital Status

Goodman and Silverstein (2002) found in their study on caregiver well-being that the cultural lens through which intergenerational relationships are viewed has a marked impact on the adaptation to custodial caregiving. In this study 72% of respondents identified themselves as New Zealand European, 21% as Maori, 3% as Pacific Island, and 4% as other (Dutch, English, South African, and Australian). The higher Pakeha/New Zealand European response to the survey is representative of sample bias. Maori children aged 0–16 years actually comprised 24% of that age group (see Melville, 2003) and 48% of children in the care of CYF as at June 2004. More recent statistics indicate that this overrepresentation continues (see Table 1).

Indicative of the data source, 81% of the caregivers were over 50 years of age, the largest representation being the 50–59 cohort, followed by those aged 60–69. Seven caregivers were great-grandparents. The effect of age on energy levels and physical fitness was commented on by the participant grandparents. One participant noted:

> As grandparents, we are unable to meet the physical demands the child needs, or play sport with him.... Sometimes I feel so very weary, it is my age, I suppose, but it could be the stress of it all.

Single carers accounted for 37% of the participants. Several persons in the study stated that they had separated since taking custody of the children.

Income Distribution

The average annual household income in 2005 in New Zealand was $65,520 (Statistics New Zealand, June 2005). Not including any benefits received for the children, total family income for 37% of the participants (the largest grouping) was under NZ $20,000 per annum; 19% between NZ $20,000–29,000; and 10% between NZ $30,000–39,000. Seventy-one of the 323 respondents were supported by a benefit of some type, including sickness and invalids' benefits, but excluding universal superannuation. While the low mean income level of the participants could be reflective of the age distribution of the carers and the high number of beneficiaries, Frengley (2007) found an even lower income level in her recent study of 33 kin carers, 50% of whom had incomes of under $20,000, the median being just above $15,000. Family income levels for Maori are considerably lower than for those of European ethnicity, and when age is factored into the analysis, the difference is even greater (Statistics New Zealand, 2007). Well over half (58%) of the study respondents were employed full- or part-time. Many retirees commented on the difficulty of managing financially, and that they now had to work part-time as casual labourers to have enough money to keep the family:

> My husband had retired, he is 72. Now he works at the gas station pumping gas three days a week and also mows lawns to make ends meet.

Of those who were employed, 53% made changes to their occupation in order to provide care. Women were most affected, many stating that they had been forced to retire from their employment because of the caregiving demands, or had to move from full- to part-time work:

> Since taking the children I have gone from working 42 hours a week and earning $650.00 weekly for just myself, to $200.00 per week to keep three of us.

Across the broad spectrum of kinship care, kin carers have suffered discrimination financially by virtue of relationship, though the trauma of abuse and neglect results in the same challenging behavioural and physical problems. Recent policies have gone some way to lessening this inconsistency for those whanau/kin who cared for children previously under legal custody of CYF. They now receive the same basic board payments, but there the similarity stops. Unrelated carers receive clothing, medical, educational, and recreational expenses that are not afforded to kin carers. In situations of informal custody, some carers feared that the parent might take the child back if they received financial aid:

To allow our daughter's benefit to go towards her cost of living, we have never been able to claim any financial assistance, and our pensions have been sorely eroded.

The low socio-economic status of many ethnic minority families practically ensures financial stress. Financial support is necessary if the placement is to continue, and the best interests of the child maintained.

Contributing Factors to the Need for Care

Respondents were asked to name all major contributing factors that resulted in the need for care. Neglect, cited in 46% of cases, was associated with most other variables, although, in some instances, it was cited as a sole reason. Excluding neglect, drug abuse was identified as the major contributing factor, cited by 40% of respondents, followed by alcohol abuse (29%), child abuse (28%), mental illness (27%), and domestic violence (27%). Abandonment (22%) was frequently abandonment at birth, although some respondents described how the children were taken for a short agreed period of time and the parents absconded. Death of a parent accounted for 7%, and this was described variously as due to drug abuse, domestic violence, suicide, illness, or intellectual disability of the parent. Eight per cent were imprisoned.

The reasons for care affected the grandparents emotionally. Grief, anger, shame, and remorse were described. However, the task of caring took precedence, and the grandparents stated that they had no opportunity to resolve these feelings:

> I stopped work to take the children who were abandoned because both parents are drug addicts. My daughter is now dead of an overdose and the children's father is in prison for 10 years for making drugs. The children have fetal alcohol syndrome, add, conduct disorder, are aggressive and constantly absconding from school and here. The children only have contact with their father if I take them to the prison. The children are angry, and to tell you the truth, so am I, and sad!

Physical and Emotional Well-being of the Children

Most children had experienced some form of physical illness or disability either currently or in the past, some severe and ongoing, such as blindness, fetal alcohol syndrome, severe multiple disabilities, and Down's syndrome, as well as soiling, wetting, and severe asthma. Forty per cent of respondents stated that the children in their care exhibited severe aggressive and/or destructive behaviour.

Autism, conduct disorder, attention deficit disorder (ADD), and attention deficit hyperactivity disorder (ADHD) were some of the other conditions listed. The majority of respondents stated that they had not been given financial aid to pay for professional assistance, and had to meet the costs themselves.

Attachment research literature confirms that relational security is central to ensuring positive outcomes for children (Whitelaw Downs, Moore, McFadden, & Costin, 2004). Almost one-quarter of the caregivers had cared for the children since birth. Some caregivers described being called to the hospital to collect a child they had not known existed until that point. Drug abuse, mental illness, abandonment, and parental incapacity or incapability were cited in these cases. The mean length of time that children had been placed with their kin carers was 5.4 years. Comparatively, Saunders (2005) identified that some children in the New Zealand foster care system at the time had experienced 15 or more placements (Saunders, 2005).

Attachment to siblings is often overlooked by child welfare professionals, yet for the neglected child may be a primary attachment. While the majority of respondents (63%) were caring for just one child, 79 caregivers had two siblings; 22 caregivers had three; 11 had four; three families had five, and one solo grandmother was caring for six grandchildren from two different families. There were 12 sets of twins. Sixty-three respondents (20%) stated that children had left their care, and the majority of these were still caring for other siblings or other kin children. Ten children had moved to CYF care, two to institutional care; 21 had gained independence.

Legal Issues

Most international commentators note that the establishment of legal status for kinship caregivers is complex and problematic, particularly for Indigenous families. Commitment of family members to care for their own should be honoured, and not forced to fit within narrow legal definitions established by the white dominant culture (Council on the Aging, 2003; Minkler & Roe, 1993). While gaining legal status may be inappropriate for Maori, who see the issue as one of community ownership, the legal costs of gaining this are often prohibitive for families of any culture. However, set against these arguments is a need to secure safety, stability, and permanency for the children and their caregivers, particularly when challenged by capricious biological parents. Many respondents in the study expressed their need for legal protection, but commented on the fact that they found the legal system frustrating, confusing, and unaffordable. More than one-fifth of the caregivers (21%) had no formal legal status. Some families who began care with an informal family agreement later assumed formal legal status to achieve custody. Those who maintained informal agreements stated a variety of reasons. Some felt that the children were safer this way and that if formal custody were sought, the parents might contest it, thereby endangering the placement. One-fifth (20%) had assumed care through a formal family/whanau agreement obtained through CYF, preventing the need for court involvement. The remainder took care by means of a formal Family Group Conference under the CYPFA, or a court order to establish custody and/or guardianship.

When grandparents take custody, there are issues of impending morbidity and mortality that are rarely discussed. Nevertheless, these are serious issues for the family to consider when making decisions relating to the ongoing care of a child. It is important that practitioners help families to explore them and to consider the appointment of a testamentary guardian for the child, who can ensure that the child's best interests are preserved in the event of the grandparents being no longer able to care.

Cross-Cultural Foster Care Placements

With such a strong emphasis on keeping children within their family/whanau and culture in the New Zealand legislation, it is unfortunately still a matter of fact that children are placed cross-culturally with stranger carers, placements made on the basis of availability rather than suitability. The reasons for this are manifold. Firstly, as in other countries, New Zealand is experiencing serious difficulties in the recruitment and retention of a viable foster care workforce (Tapsfield & Collier, 2005; Worrall, 2005). Contributing factors are economic stressors, leading to a need for two-family incomes and a subsequent increase of women in the workforce; changes in family structures, with a higher proportion of families headed by single parents; increasing behavioural and physical problems exhibited by the children; media attention to allegations of abuse by carers; and the low status given to foster caring by society at large (Schwartz, 2002; Triseliotis, Borland, & Hill, 2000; Worrall, 2005).

There is a paucity of international literature around particular issues of culture and how this might affect practice models. However, internationally, there is an ethnic imbalance between minority children needing care and availability of culturally matched carers (Worrall, 2005; see also Part III with respect to Canadian First Nations). When a child is placed cross-culturally, it is important for the carer to be well acquainted with the child's culture and family practices. In particular, carers should be well versed in Maori *tikanga* (cultural practices).

Law dictates that Family Group Conferences must be held regularly for children in care, and caregivers are entitled by right to attend the information sharing part of such meetings, which for Maori families are based on Maori traditions of *karanga* (greeting calls), *karakia* (prayer), and *whakapapa* (the making of genealogical links). Taking the child to his or her own *marae* (tribal village), if Maori, is a most rewarding experience for all concerned. Meeting the tribal and whanau elders who will take the child to visit whanau burial grounds and tell the tribal and whanau history will give that child a sense of identity that is badly needed. The place of cultural identity and family gathering for Pacific Island families is often the church, and carers of any culture should endeavour to take the child to this place, which he or she may know and where he or she may be known.

Training

In 2002, CYF, in partnership with the New Zealand Family and Foster Care Federation, established a national foster care training program. A compulsory induction program is followed by eight non-compulsory core workshops. A Certificate and Diploma in Foster Care have been instituted requiring papers based on the eight core modules. *Noho Marae* (Maori village protocol) and Treaty of Waitangi papers must also be gained, as well as a first aid certificate. The Diploma program is an extensive course of study, and includes six social work papers. The attainment of competency standards is a step toward the professionalization of foster care and recognition of the vulnerability of both children in care and their caregivers. However, there is no mandatory requirement to participate. It is a troubling fact that carers, both kin and foster carers, have suffered the consequences of having an allegation of abuse laid against them. Even if unsubstantiated, carers and their families suffer extreme stress (Worrall, 2001). The provision of training is seen as a preventive move to enhance safe caring practice. However, sadly, kin/whanau carers are not required to undertake any training, leaving them at further risk.

Issues for Social Work Practice and Policy

There is a wide difference of approach, in both social work practice and policy, to the foster care and kinship care populations with regard to assessment, ongoing financial and social work support, and training, yet both groups are caring for children who have suffered the trauma of neglect and abuse. The philosophy in the CYPFA of family self-determination, and the respect paid to that by social workers, has meant that many families struggle without the support they need to keep the children safe and the placement maintained.

The issues are complex, however, and any social work with kinship families necessitates the skills to negotiate a maelstrom of family dynamics that does not exist in non-family foster care placements. While the Family Group Conference process is seen as empowering, it must also be recognized that such family meetings are charged with high emotion: feelings of shame, guilt, grief, and anger are evident. Fraught family relationships over decades are often the backdrop to the decision-making process. Once the decision is made about who will provide care, many families are reluctant to have ongoing "interference" by state social workers.

Kinship research illustrates, nevertheless, the pressure of responsibility that many carers experience in caring for their kin/whanau children. The stresses of child behavioural issues, the pressure this exerts on family relationships, and the additional financial burden can all weigh heavily on the carer. Recent Australian research exploring the psychological health of custodial grandparents found that they scored significantly higher on anxiety and stress level measures than a control group of non-custodial grandparents, identifying a need for increased levels of psychological support for both the grandparents and their grandchildren (Dunne & Kettler, 2008).

Ensuring that carers receive all that they are entitled to is clearly important with respect to both financial support and social support such as respite care. Responding sensitively to carers in ways that acknowledge the turmoil of kin/whanau experience is an important aspect of social work in the context of supporting kinship placements. The debate about allowing kin/whanau placements to be outside the proven good foster care practice standards of assessment and training should be about child safety and well-being. Kin/whanau carers are not immune from allegations of abuse, and providing respectful and culturally responsive induction training for carers will surely help them provide a strong and safe care environment for the children. Although kinship care has its frustrations and is undoubtedly demanding for many carers, it is also clear that it can have significant rewards:

> This isn't the life I would have chosen or the road I would have wished to travel. It's not the dream I had but I am amazed to see where I have come, where I am going, where I am from! My grandchild makes life so worth waking up for. So we walk this journey together and dream new dreams together. Together life will be different.

The crisis in recruitment and retention of foster carers is a key issue for child welfare in New Zealand. The need for two incomes in families is a key factor. The increasingly demanding nature of the fostering role has given rise to serious consideration of whether foster care can, or even should, continue to be a voluntary undertaking, or should assume professional status with a prescribed role and educational requirement. Critics of this model argue that it is fundamentally inconsistent with the idea of family, and that professional concerns will interfere with the spontaneity of the parent/child relationship (Christian, 2002). The introduction of a model that will acknowledge foster carers' qualifications and skill remuneratively and allow carers to choose the level of caring they wish to undertake may go some way to alleviating the problem. The issue is complicated, however, by the legal mandating of whanau/kinship care and the particular difficulties encountered by those carers.

The way forward is to ensure that:

- social workers are given specific training in regard to understanding, managing, and supporting the complexities of whanau/kinship care;
- kin/whanau carers are equally rewarded and involved in devising models of preparation, training, and support that are culturally acceptable and particular to their specific needs;
- foster care models of practice are regularly audited and revised to ensure systems are in place that can accommodate children with high needs;
- all carers are recognized financially in terms of their skill and experience, and care is seen as an employment option for families; and
- research is undertaken to identify the reasons for the disparity between the fewer number of Pakeha children placed with kin compared to Maori and Pacific Island children, who have a greater likelihood of remaining in their whanau/extended family systems.

New Zealand has led the way in innovative legislation, and is now considering ways to implement professional and respectful practice principles for both social workers and carers. We are still on a journey.

13

Experiences of Foster Carers' Children
An Overview of the Research

Tracy Swan
Robert Twigg

Although research about foster carers' children has existed for 37 years, a systematic body of research only began to emerge after 1993. This chapter is based on research findings from thirteen studies and two projects conducted between 1993 and 2007 that, taken together, capture the voices of approximately 1,230 foster carers' children. The words of the young people are used to illustrate experiences and themes found in the majority of these studies. Their voices present the richly woven tapestry of the lives of carers' children, many of whom continue to be "unknown soldiers of foster care" (Twigg, 1994) in many foster care organizations. Policy and practice implications of the findings will be considered within the context of the current Canadian foster care field.

The Child Welfare Context

Foster family care did not become the preferred form of care for children in need until the 1950s (McKenzie, 1993). Based on the premise that family life can make an integral contribution to a child's healthy growth and development, foster family care currently includes kinship care, regular foster care, and all forms of treatment foster family care, each designed to address the challenges faced by specific populations of children and youth (Crosson-Tower, 2006; Downs, Moore, McFadden, Michaud, & Costin, 2004; Steinhauer, 1991). British researchers reported that in 1997 approximately 60% of children placed in out-of-home care facilities resided in foster care (Wilson, Sinclair, & Gibbs, 2000; Gibbs & Wildfire, 2007). Published data confirming the percentage of Canadian children in foster care is more difficult to obtain. Farris-Manning and Zandstra (2003) estimate that between 2000 and 2002, there were 76,000 Canadian children in care. Employing 1998–99 provincial and territorial statistics which excluded data from Ontario, Quebec, Nunavut, and the Yukon, they also indicate that the percentage of children in different forms of family-based care (foster care, adoption, and kinship care) ranged from 59% to 93%, with an average percentage of 88% or 6,707 children. Because it is generally assumed that two-thirds of the total population of the children in care are placed with foster families, it is estimated that the number of children in foster care during the 2000–2 period was approximately 50,616, and constituted the greatest percentage of children in family-based care. This number is likely higher now, as Twigg (2009) reports a significant rise in the number of children in foster care since 2005.

Over the years the foster care system, foster caregivers, and the children placed in foster family care have undergone considerable scrutiny (Cautley, 1980; Fanshel, Finch, & Grundy, 1990; Kufeldt, Armstrong, & Dorosh, 1995). This scrutiny was primarily driven by concerns about foster care drift and the treatment children receive in foster care. In the last decade, an increased emphasis on inclusive foster care (Kufeldt, 1995; Palmer, 1996, 1992) and the developing focus on attachment theory (Bowlby, 1971; Steinhauer, 1991) contributed to a reshaping of foster care. Until very recently, carers' own children have not received the same level of attention (Nuske, 2006; Twigg & Swan, 2007; Watson & Jones, 2002).

While the contributions foster families make to the well-being of foster children is recognized, the demand for viable foster homes continues to outstrip the capacity of agencies to recruit and retain them. Factors such as inadequate financial compensation, limited support and training, poor communication with agency representatives, and the challenges of children entering care not only contribute to persistent difficulties with recruitment and retention, but also place serious demands on all foster family members, including the caregivers' children (Sinclair, Gibbs & Wilson, 2004; Twigg, 2009). Additionally, concern about their own children is the reason many foster caregivers give for leaving fostering, and that newly recruited foster caregivers give for not pursuing it. It is also the most frequently cited reason for requesting a foster child's replacement (Twigg & Swan, 2007). For these reasons, the continued failure to meaningfully acknowledge the needs of caregivers' children is perplexing.

Research on Caregivers' Children

The first research directly involving carers' children was published in 1972 (Ellis, 1972). Subsequent research on caregivers' children was conducted sporadically, and at different intervals a gap of a decade existed between studies. Consequently, a more comprehensive picture of the world of caregivers' children has been slow to emerge. In an effort to address this gap, the chapter will present the findings of 13 research studies conducted between 1993 and 2007. These are listed and described in the Appendix. Two projects that creatively capture the voices of caregivers' children from the United Kingdom have also been included in this review. The first resulted in a groundbreaking video, *Children Who Foster*, developed by the Natural Children's Support Group (Martin, 1993; Martin & Stanford, 1990); the second entailed a conference established for the purpose of understanding fostering from the perspective of carers' children (Pat Doorbar & Associates, 1996). Taken together, the material reviewed reflects the experiences of 1,230 caregivers' children, and includes studies from Canada, the United Kingdom, the United States, Australia, and Sweden.

Ten of the studies listed in the Appendix entailed individual interviews or a combination of individual and group interviews with caregivers' children. In three others, parents and/or other family members were also interviewed. Two studies conducted surveys in addition to individual and/or group interviews. Three administered only surveys.

Research Limitations

All studies were qualitative and exploratory in nature. All but three were based on small sample sizes. The particular focus of the research also varied. For example, Twigg (1993) focused on the impact of fostering on the caregivers' child's psychological development, and Heidbuurt (1995) studied foster family dynamics.

Some researchers chose to include children who were latency age and older, while others, employing methods such as art, drama, and short sentence completion questions geared to younger children, involved children as young as five. The length of time families fostered, the number of children they cared for, the nature of the foster care provided, and other relevant variables, were not specified and could affect findings. Although almost all the studies quote from Twigg's (1993) seminal research, his work has not been replicated. In spite of these limitations, the research has produced consistent findings that convey a story of caregivers' children characterized by ambivalence, or what Nuske (2006) describes as "living within a contradictory experience" (p. 256).

The Research Findings

The research suggests that three interconnected and seemingly contradictory themes permeate the lives of the young people. Caring, concern, and responsibility are juxtaposed against feelings of rejection, hurt, frustration, and anger. Although many caregivers' children identify the benefits of fostering and genuinely care for the young people placed with their families, this caring often develops despite negative experiences, which include being the target of aggression. For many carers' children, love, respect, and concern for parents are experienced alongside feelings of displacement and loss associated with the need to compete for parental attention. Additionally, concern for the well-being of their parents is juxtaposed against feelings of resentment that pertain to the caring roles foster carers' children are often expected to assume. As carers' children attempt to maintain a place in their family structure and develop their sense of identity, they struggle with these contradictory feelings and endeavour to make meaning of experiences that generate considerable inner conflict and stress. This struggle occurs while foster care agencies and agency workers fail to recognize them as important family members and individuals in their own right, and significant members of the fostering team.

Are There Benefits for Foster Carers' Own Children?

Almost all caregivers' children identified both positive and negative aspects to living in a foster caregiving family. Eighty per cent of the young people surveyed by Part (1993) indicated that they liked fostering, and Nuske (2006) noted that even young people who were quite negative maintained that they would not have forgone the experience. The majority of participants cited benefits that included having companionship, gaining self-confidence, developing communication and listening skills, and contributing to the well-being of children. When asked about the best aspects of fostering, 86% of the respondents in the Watson and Jones (2002) survey demonstrated altruism—for example, "meeting new people and befriending them," "helping those who need it," "seeing a child smile and be happy," and "providing love" (pp. 52–3). Others spoke to personal qualities acquired as a result of being part of a caregiving family, qualities such as becoming more understanding, socially aware, empathic, caring, and responsible. For example, one participant stated, "You learn how to care for other people and what is going on [in] the world ... if anyone has any problems at school they always come to me because I know how to deal with it, I just talk to them and help them" (Fox, 2000, p. 37). Reed (1994) found that older children took pride in the achievements of the children living with their families.

Three studies (Nuske, 2006; Spears & Cross, 2003; Swan, 2000) reported that some caregivers' children go on to foster and/or enter caring professions.

While acknowledging benefits, carers' children also describe many stressors, some of which relate to caring responsibilities they assume for children, experiences of loss, and experiences of aggression perpetrated by the children placed in their home.

Assuming a Caregiving Role: A Conundrum

Watson and Jones (2002) found that 83 of the 114 participants in their study assumed some responsibility for the foster children. Some believed they had an important role to play as mediators between the children and their parents (Fox, 2000; Spears & Cross, 2003), while others felt a need to nurture, to provide practical assistance, and to be positive role models (Höjer, 2004; Nuske, 2006; Swan, 2000; Younes & Harp, 2007). Some latency age children entertained the foster children. Younger teens provided babysitting, and older teens and young adults provided babysitting and respite care. Young adults involved in caring professions often functioned as consultants for their parents.

Two studies (Reed, 1994; Younes & Harp, 2007) reported that caregivers' children, who derived gratification from assuming a caring role, appeared to do so when expectations were congruent with what they perceived would take place in a "normal" family, and/or in situations where expectations did not challenge their confidence or comfort level. These studies, and results reported by Nuske (2006) and Swan (2000), indicated that they may also perceive their involvement as a support to their parents, especially for their mothers, whom they recognized not only assumed most of the caring work but also were particularly stressed by the multiple demands of being the primary caregiver in the family. A respondent's concern for her mother was reflected in the following comment: "Sometimes I worry about her because she's running around all day and she just gets really cranky and you just feel bad for her because you know what she is going through … So if you help her out it gets better" (Swan, 2000, pp. 24–5).

In addition to providing concrete support, many caregivers' children strive to be "good kids" to avoid adding to their mother's stress. However, as one young man indicated, this can contribute to the young person's own stress and to feelings of resentment: "I guess it was difficult … I always felt like I couldn't act up, like … I had to be there to help, to take care of things and be a support to my parents" (Swan, 2000, p. 29). Other participants took a stronger view. For example, a participant in the Spears and Cross study stated: "I don't want to be good all the time. It's a big responsibility" (2003, p. 42). This was echoed by a participant in the Younes and Harp study: "I don't like to have to be good and don't want to be good sometimes" (2007, p. 34).

Results from some of these studies (namely Nuske, 2006; Twigg, 1993; Watson & Jones, 2002) underscore the fact that many carers' children are conflicted about providing care. While experiencing the positive aspects of fostering, they found parental expectations that they assume a caring role to be a heavy burden they longed to escape. A number of young people struggled to understand and make meaning of the experiences they had with their parents and the children in their home, experiences that were simultaneously gratifying and challenging. What, then, is the nature of these different experiences, and how do caregiving children perceive them?

Experiencing Loss and Aggression

Caregivers' children commonly identify two areas in which living with foster children negatively impact them: experiences of loss and of aggression. Here, too, feelings of care and distress coexist.

Many participants who cared about the children placed with their family found it quite difficult to cope with loss when children moved on. A number of younger respondents indicated: "[They] are like your brothers and sisters and then they're just gone" (Norrington, 2002, p. 34). Another young man expressed a deeply felt sense of loss and an inability to share his grief, an experience common to many carers' children.

> … they were gone and there wasn't going to be that daily contact, there wasn't going to be any contact at all … I cried when they left … there was a void and there wasn't any space or anywhere for me to express my feelings about the fact that kids aren't here … a decision is made and you have no say in that decision. (Swan, 2000, p. 16)

Although caring about the foster children, carers' children also struggled with feelings associated with many negative experiences, such as theft and/or destruction of their possessions, overt and covert threats of physical violence, and overt acts of physical aggression. A latency age child indicated that younger foster children "took all her stuff and broke it" (Norrington, 2002, p. 36). As the following example demonstrates, siblings, friends, other foster children, and their parents were also targets of aggression.

> We had this boy … and he was nice when he came and he never touched me, or anything. … they put him on … Ritalin and one time he threatened my Mum, to

stab her when she was asleep and he was going to stab me as well. I never went to sleep. One time he got really psycho and started throwing sticks and stuff at Dad and Dad got this really big cut there. Me and my friends were in the house and thought he was going to come back. We had to lock every door in the house and we were really scared. (Nuske, 2006, pp. 197–8)

Caregivers' children were often wrongly accused and blamed by the foster children. Younger participants often found "story telling," stealing, and destruction of their belongings more difficult to understand than older carers' children, who had learned to be more understanding, but all respondents generally perceived these experiences as a betrayal of trust.

Whether caregivers' children experienced aggression personally or witnessed aggressive acts against family members, they found aggressive behaviour difficult to understand and accept. A young adult, who witnessed her mother being attacked by an adolescent boy in her home, captured the emotional conflict that results from experiencing or witnessing aggression, while struggling to understand:

> … it is hard to put up with a lot of stuff that they put you through and still be OK about it. Genuinely OK about it … and it's hard for the trust issue … And it is hard to understand why you can't trust them, and why they steal from you and why they lie, and stuff like that … but we can't really look at me because I'm fine with everything, my life has been fine … and these people are coming into our house so we could help them, not so they can be fair to us … You have to [understand] because if you don't it's not fair to them … You have to put them before us because that is why they are there. (Swan, 2000, p. 32)

How the carers' children responded to these different experiences was significantly influenced by how parents reacted to conflicts between their children and children in care; by parents' expectations that their children act responsibly; and by the caregivers' children's felt need to "protect" their mothers from any negative feelings they had about fostering.

Caring for Parents, Loss of Family Role, and Parental Attention

Positive aspects of fostering identified by many carers' children were countered by the experience described by almost all caregivers' children, of a sense of loss regarding their place and role in the family. This loss appears to be experienced as displacement and a loss of a secure sense of belonging, experiences that relate to what the young people perceive as loss of parental attention. A young woman, looking back at the time when her family began fostering, described her sense of displacement with these words:

[T]here are these kids coming into your home, and this your home … it is like your little nest, and then it's sort of like disrupted … strangers com[e] into your home. It is hard … because you don't know who they are or what to expect … [or] how is your life going to be changed this time? (Swan, 2000, p. 14)

One of the authors was requested to speak to a caregiver's daughter to reassure her that she would not be removed from her parents' care if she misbehaved. She had seen a series of foster "brothers" replaced for that reason and believed the same thing could happen to her, in spite of her parents' consistent reassurance to the contrary.

Looking back, older participants mourned what they perceived as a lost childhood (Swan, 2000; Twigg, 1994). One young man stated: "Like I always think what would it be like to grow up without foster kids? Always, forever I'll think that, and that is what the parents have to accept that they're taking away a normal childhood" (Swan, 2000, p. 20).

Many caregivers' children perceived that their needs were not as important as those of the "more needy" foster children. One young man estimated that his parents spent 90% of their time with children living with his family and 10% with him and his brother (Twigg, 1994, p. 307). Another participant stated:

Sometimes if you want to go out you can't go … well you can never go with your mum and dad together because one of them has always got to be there … it's just times like Christmas and holidays that are worst … you just want to be with your own parents and with your own family … you think they're "my" mum and dad. (Fox, 2000, p. 33)

For some, the need to vie for parental attention and the disruptions in their relationship with parents contributed to feelings of anger, resentment, and jealousy. However, fearing they would either add to their mothers' stress or disappoint her, and/or fearing they might not be heard if they did complain, many caregivers' children hesitated to directly express their concerns about fostering and the foster children. A young man, commenting on his feelings of responsibility and the destruction of his belongings, shared the reason for his silence.

That's the thing [that feeling of responsibility] … you are young, you are 12 years old, what are you really going to do? You kind of carry losses and move on … some things that were really expensive were compensated for … And what fear you have … because it is your mum's job you can't say "mum stop working, stop making money, stop putting food on the table", 'cause someone broke your Transformer. (Nuske, 2004, p. 9)

Caregivers' children also did not voice their complaints because they struggled with guilt for wanting more time with their parents. Guilt is captured in the following words:

> ... I thought that this [fostering] was the wrong thing, I wished it was just us again ... I felt very guilty for feeling that way and I never voiced it to anyone ... there were times I would say "you know mom let's ... just spend some time together ... and feeling guilty about wanting to do that as well. (Swan, 2000, p. 22)

In addition to remaining silent, many older participants coped with these conflicts by creating different space for themselves in the family. Some older participants in Heidbuurt's (1995) research developed a stance the author identified as "partial seclusion," whereby they remained in the family, but separated from fostering. One participant, who felt "crowded," attempted to break the tension by sneaking out and climbing a tree "just to be alone" (Younes & Harp, 2007, p. 32), while others indicated they spent considerable time in their rooms or outside the home (Heidbuurt, 1995; Nuske, 2006).

Agency Workers, the Agency, and Caregivers' Children

Child welfare agencies and their workers significantly influence caregiving families. Caregivers' children are not immune to their influences, which the findings indicate can be both positive and negative (see for example Höjer, 2004, and Watson & Jones, 2002). Some caregivers' children who reported having a positive relationship with an agency worker maintained that the workers recognized the stresses they experienced and their positive contribution to the care of children in their home (Norrington, 2002; Swan, 2000). However, most research findings indicate that caregivers' children have either no direct contact with workers, or minimal contact that tends to be negative. Nuske (2006), for example, found that 18 of the 23 participants had never been in contact with a social worker. One child commented, "I don't see why we have to keep out of the way when they have meetings, it's really annoying" (Fox, 2000, p. 26). Others stated: "They [the social workers] never talk to us" ... "They never talk to me, only to my parents" (Norrington, 2002, pp. 38–9).

Many caregivers' children found that when they did have contact and raised concerns about experiences with a child, and/or asked questions about different aspects of fostering, questions were often ignored and/or their concerns dismissed or minimized. Dickenson (2008) described her initial interview, at age seven, with the foster home assessment worker.

I can remember a social worker visiting on a regular basis ... to [do] the foster-ing assessment with my parents. I also remember the single visit when she asked to speak to me alone, I had a mental list of all the questions I wanted to ask ... would they be older or younger, what if they didn't like me, and how long would they be staying? [She] asked me whether I was happy to share my bedroom [and] as soon as she ascertained that I was, [she] left. (Dickenson, 2008, p. 5)

Interactions of this nature reinforced the message that the needs of the car-ers' children were secondary, and, for some, negatively impacted their already tenuous sense of belonging in their family. The following quotation conveys experiences common to many participants:

A lot of the workers don't bother to talk to children in the family. They talk to the parents, they talk with the foster children ... biological children are often over-looked ... they push them aside as if they don't have needs. They are not foster children [and] they are not parents. They are just there. (Swan, 2000, p. 37)

Some older carers' children expressed frustration because they were not involved in case planning processes or training, even though they often assumed responsibility for younger children placed with their families and knew a great deal about them (Fox, 2000; Nuske, 2006; Watson & Jones, 2002). Others reported that they were either not consulted about many important questions, including the initial decision to foster and the decision to terminate a placement (Swan, 2000; Twigg, 1993; Younes & Harp, 2007). A participant suggested this was like "Playing the role of Cinderella ... expected to do all the work but not invited to the ball" (Doorbar, 1999, as cited in Dickenson, 2008, p. 12). As these words suggest, many caregivers' children long to have their contributions to the care of children recognized.

In addition to these experiences with workers, caregivers' children were very conscious of the power the agency had over their family's life, particularly the power to refuse to place children (Twigg & Swan, 2007). The power of the agency in their family appears to reinforce the children's propensity to strive to be good and responsible (see, for example, Norrington, 2002, and Younes & Harp, 2007). The children were aware that their family was open to scrutiny, that "workers look at you too," and that "things had to be perfect" (Swan, 2000, p. 30). By contributing to the perception that they had to be good, agencies also contributed to their reluctance to behave in a way that would create any additional stress for a mother and potentially jeopardize her career. This in turn reinforced the children's tendencies to keep their feel-ings and worries to themselves.

Implications for Policy and Practice

The findings of the studies on carers' children highlight both positive and negative aspects of being a member of a caregiving family. While the words of many of the young people capture their caring and commitment to the well-being of children placed with their families, they also demonstrate the conflicted feelings resulting from the more negative aspects of fostering. Their words capture the complexity of making meaning of different experiences—experiences which generate feelings of rejection, hurt, and anger alongside experiences that foster their caring, compassion, and desire to act responsibly. At different junctures, their words express resiliency, pride, and positive self-esteem. At other times the participants convey a sense of futility and powerlessness about the potential to effect any change in their lives. What, then, can others who have power to make changes do to address the issues and concerns the children raise? What policy, program, and practice changes are needed to enhance the well-being of all caregivers' children, those whose voices are captured here and those who remain silent?

Two broad program and practice recommendations highlighted in the research literature are the need for support and training for caregivers' children. These recommendations build on two other interrelated recommendations: the need to develop policy and procedures that address the children's desire for meaningful inclusion in all aspects of fostering, and the recognition of the significant contribution they make to the well-being of children in care.

While we support and add our voice to those who call for such changes, we also recognize that without conscientious attention to broader concerns about the place of foster care in the child welfare field, few of the children's issues will be meaningfully addressed. Major policy and program changes are needed to address many of the issues which contribute to the crisis of recruitment and retention that has plagued the foster care system for decades—issues many believe stem from the continued failure to recognize foster parents as equal partners on the foster care team (Kadushin & Martin, 1988; McFadden, 1985; McKenzie, 1993; Steinhauer, 1991). Being an equal partner means having equal power and voice in decision-making and receiving adequate financial compensation, support, and training that reflect the important responsibility caring for children demands. These kinds of changes not only "allow [caregivers] to see themselves as part of a professional team" (Sinclair, Gibbs, & Wilson, 2004, p. 17), they contribute to others seeing them in the same way. Over the years, the need for such changes has been raised by others, including national and provincial foster family associations (Diane Molloy, personal communication, November 3, 2008). Significant provincial policy changes are required to realize these objectives. Such changes must begin with the foster care system receiving the same level of attention and financial investment historically received by investigative and protection services.

With greater emphasis on, and financial investment in, the foster care system, policy changes, programs, and strategies that meaningfully address the needs and concerns identified by caregivers' children have a greater potential to become standard features of a foster care support system. Agency workers are more likely to receive much-needed training on the impact of fostering on carers' children and the valuable contribution they make to the provision of foster care (Twigg & Swan, 2007; The Fostering Network, 2003; Watson & Jones, 2002). With this training, all workers should be better equipped to respond to the children's desire and need to be heard, and to provide the support they need. Specifically designated workers might assume new positions whereby they have primary responsibility to meet the needs of carers' children (The Fostering Network, 2003). In such a position, workers would be better situated to advocate and/or create opportunities for the child's involvement in aspects of fostering that impact her/his life. Children would automatically receive relevant information about the fostering experience, and training that pertains to the caring responsibilities they might assume. Support groups for carers' children would then become an integral aspect of a foster care support system.

Beyond these initiatives, the caregivers' children have the right to be recognized and included in the development of policy and programs that affect them. Article 12 of the United Nations (UN) *Convention on the Rights of the Child* speaks to the child's "overall right to be heard in any judicial and administrative procedures" (United Nations Office of the High Commissioner for Human Rights, 1989). As Watson and Jones (2002) note, specific provisions of Article 12 state that in "all matters of foster family care, the prospective foster parents and as appropriate the child and his or her own parents should be properly involved" (Appendix 2 of the UN *Convention on the Rights of the Child*). Further, Kufeldt, Este, McKenzie, and Wharf (2003) address the importance of children in care and their parents having involvement in any and all research, policy, and practice partnerships. We add our voice to those who encourage the extension of these rights to foster caregivers' children, and call for their active participation in policy and program development, and any future research that impacts their lives.

Appendix *Caregivers' Children Research Summary*

Author	Methodology	Number of Participants	Age Range of Participants	Gender	Total Caregivers' Children
Part, 1993	Survey/questionnaire	75	3–24	Not specified	75
Poland & Groze, 1993	Survey/questionnaire for: (a) 8–13 years (b) 14+ years (c) parents	51 children 52 parents	8–32	Not specified	51
Twigg, 1993	Individual interviews with children and family interviews	9 children 8 families	15–28	5 female 4 male	9
Martin, 1993	Small-group video discussion	7 core members	10–15	Not specified	7
Reed, 1994	Individual interviews	23	8–20	8 male 14 female	23
Heidbuurt, 1995	Individual interviews with children and two focus groups with parents	9 children 5 parents	7–16	4 male 5 female	9
Swan, 2000	Individual interviews with young adults and three focus groups with adolescents	12 young adults 19 adolescents	Young adults 19–30 (mean 26) Adolescents 12–18 (mean 15)	6 male 6 female 12 female 7 male	31
Norrington, 2002	Focus groups	17	7–12	9 male 8 female	17
Watson & Jones, 2002	Survey/questionnaire	114	7 years +	Not specified	114
Höjer & Nordenfors, 2003	Three focus groups, three surveys, discussion groups, and individual interviews	Focus groups: 17	9–12, 13–17, 18–25		17[a]
		Surveys: 684	Not specified		684
		Discussion groups: 16	11–14, 15–17, 18–25		16
		Interviews: 8	12–28	4 female 4 male	8
Doorbar, 1996	Individual interviews, sentence picture completion, questionnaires, drama workshops, and art workshops	145	5–16	65 male 80 female	145
Spears & Cross, 2003	Interviews	20	8–18	4 male 16 female	20
Fox, 2000	Interviews	8	8–23	2 male 6 female	8
Nuske, 2006	Interviews	22	10–30	8 male 14 female	8 male
Younes & Harp, 2007	Individual interviews and parent interviews	16 children 10 families	8 +	Not specified	16

[a]A few of these children participated in two different forms of data collection, but the exact number was not specified.

14

Making Group Home Care a Positive Alternative, Not the Last Resort

James Anglin

R esidential care for young people has been challenged in recent decades in terms of its suitability as a form of extrafamilial care for children and youth. Based upon the findings of a research study of 10 residential programs in British Columbia, this chapter presents a theoretical framework for understanding the key elements and dynamics of a well-functioning group home, and offers several examples of how this framework is influencing group care training and practice initiatives internationally. In addition, the place of group homes relative to foster homes in the child welfare system of care is discussed and assessed.

Background

A review of the British and North American literature on residential care for children and youth over the past 35 years reveals the impressive resilience of this form of service. Despite many rather scathing critiques (Rae-Grant & Moffat, 1971; Rubin, 1972; Steinhauer, 1991; Vail, 1966), revelations of institutional abuse (Bloom, 1992; Collins & Colorado, 1988; Levy & Kahan, 1991), and attempts to eliminate residential programs altogether (Cliffe & Berridge, 1992; Coates, Miller, & Ohlin, 1978), residential care continues to play a significant role in virtually all child and family service systems. Further, while the number of children in residential programs has decreased significantly since the 1970s, it appears that most jurisdictions have accepted the inevitability of preserving at least a minimal number of residential care programs in perpetuity. While treatment foster homes which offer a blend of familial and specialized care have been developed, staffed group care residences, generally with between two and eight young people, have become the preferred form of residential care in many Western countries, and one preferred to large institutions. It would seem that, in relation to the social service system as a whole, residential care is something like tip of the iceberg that protrudes out of the water; if you try to remove it, the iceberg moves upward to maintain its overall balance.

In recent decades, a number of political forces and ideological movements have placed considerable pressure on residential care programs. These have included deinstitutionalization, recessionary economic conditions, increased demand for accountability and quality assurance, the mandating of permanency planning, and the assertion of children's rights, among others.

As well, there has been a strong movement in favour of "homebuilder" and "family preservation" programs in North America and internationally. These programs seek to provide brief interventions into the lives of client families in order to defuse a problem, or resolve a crisis, without having to remove children from their own homes. In the minds of some, traditional residential care has come to be seen as passé, misguided, overly intrusive, ineffective, and exorbitantly expensive. In fact, it has become a commonplace belief that residential care for young people is to be avoided at almost all costs. Brown and Hill (1996) say, in reference to a wraparound service, that the goals of the program include "preventing admission to residential care" (p. 38).

Such challenges to the provision of residential care as a positive service have created a need to take a careful, in-depth look at the nature of residential care as a modality of child welfare, and to understand what makes a well-functioning residential home. The findings reported here resulted from a study of staffed group homes designed to assess whether group home care could be a positive service for young people, and if so, to identify the characteristics and dynamics of a well-functioning home and to understand better the place of residential care in the overall child welfare system.

Creating a Framework for Understanding "Well-Functioning" Residential Care

The author undertook a research study involving in-depth involvement with 10 group care residences in British Columbia over a 14-month period. The purpose of this study was to construct a theoretical framework that would offer an understanding of what makes a well-functioning group home for young people. The research approach selected as most appropriate to this task was the grounded theory method, as articulated in a variety of texts by the co-founders of the method, Glaser and Strauss (Glaser, 1978, 1992; Glaser & Strauss, 1967; Strauss, 1987; Strauss & Corbin, 1990).

The basic aim of grounded theory is to generate theory from social data derived inductively from research in social settings (Strauss & Corbin, 1990, p. 23). Such data gathering techniques as participant observation, semi-structured interviews, informal conversations, and document analysis are typical of a grounded theory inquiry (Chenitz & Swanson, 1986), and were utilized in this study. The basic elements of the theoretical framework resulting from the application of the grounded theory method in this study are presented in summary form. A more complete presentation of this research study and resulting framework can be found in Anglin (2002).

The Core Theme

The core theme that was found to permeate the data across all of the homes, and which encompassed the other major categories, was *congruence in service of the children's best interests.* This core variable provides both a theoretical and practical touchstone for understanding and assessing virtually all other group home elements, their significance, and their patterns of interrelation within group home life and work.

A group home may demonstrate congruence or incongruence to varying degrees across its elements, processes, and overall operation, and it may do so with a variety of *congruence orientations.* For example, there may be an orientation toward operational efficiency, to the preferences of the staff, or to reducing the budget. In actuality, there are always competing interests and intentions within an organization as complex as a group home, and *full congruence* throughout an organization can best be understood as an ideal state never actually achieved in reality.

This study found that each home was engaged in what could be termed a *struggle for congruence,* and what was discovered to be at the centre of most of the struggles was the intention to serve "the children's best interests." Related and virtually synonymous terms such as "child-centred" and "child-oriented" were also used by research participants to express this notion, but *the children's best interests* wording seemed most precise and evocative of the ideal being sought in practice. At the same time, while most of the homes in this study gave at least some evidence of holding this goal as an ideal, some of the homes clearly were not being guided in their work by such a focus. Further, no home was fully consistent in making all decisions on this basis (nor could one expect them to be), given both the competing interests that form the reality of group home operation and the natural variability of staff in their understandings and abilities to achieve congruence in their actions.

The concept of *children's best interests* has become a widely accepted notion in international instruments such as the United Nations *Convention on the Rights of the Child* (United Nations Office of the High Commissioner for Human Rights, 1989) as well as in the child welfare and child protection literatures in North America and the United Kingdom (Alston, 1994; Goldstein, Freud, & Solnit, 1973, 1979). It is interesting to note that even the first book on residential child and youth care published in North America by Aichhorn (1935) includes the notion of acting "in the child's interest" (p. 194) as a touchstone for child and youth care practice. Therefore, it should not be too surprising that this long-standing and currently dominant concept was echoed in the words of some of the supervisors and managers of homes and agencies within the research sample. A full discussion of the notion of "best interests," and its variety of interpretations, is beyond the scope of this chapter. It is important to note, however, that homes that sincerely struggled to identify and define what was in their resident children's best interests were consistently functioning more effectively than those where this struggle was not evident.

Other major competing interests observed within the homes, and present in all homes to varying degrees and in various manifestations, included cost containment, worker preferences, and maintaining control. For example, in one home, *maintaining control of the youth* was a dominant theme, whereas in another the focus was on a *manager's efforts to maintain control* of the staff and the mode of operation of the home. In both instances, these efforts to *maintain control* were seen to be competing in multiple ways with serving *the best interests* of the residents, resulting in a strong sense of incongruence within the culture of these two homes.

In summary, the core challenge for the group homes studied was to achieve *congruence in service of the children's best interests.* The specific processes and interactions found to be most significant in creating such congruence will now be outlined.

Basic Psychosocial Processes

In grounded theory, the terms *basic social process* (BSP) and *basic social psychological process* (BSPP) are used to designate those processes that have considerable explanatory power in relation to the phenomenon being studied (Chenitz & Swanson, 1986, p. 134; Glaser, 1978, p. 102). The more common and compact term "psychosocial" will be used here in lieu of "social psychological" to refer to processes that combine in an integral manner both individual and collective elements. The ongoing comparative analysis of the data generated in this study revealed three dominant and pervasive psychosocial processes related to the central problematic of the *struggle for congruence in service of the children's best interests*. These are described in the next three sections. While each process is subsidiary to the main theme, each could also be viewed as a core category in its own right in relation to a sub-problem within group home life and work.

Creating an Extrafamilial Living Environment

The most general, or pervasive, psychosocial process identified pertains to the overall development and ongoing operation of a group home, namely, *creating an extrafamilial living environment*. The notion of an extrafamilial living environment, or "extrafamilial home," captures a fundamental tension inherent in this form of setting and helps to clarify the group home's unique nature in juxtaposition to foster care and institutional care on the continuum of residential services. As its name implies, a group home strives to offer a home-like environment not attainable within an institutional setting, while removing the intimacy and intensity of a family environment. Much of the ongoing confusion and disagreement concerning the need for group homes can be attributed to a lack of appreciation of the importance of the "extrafamilial home" dimension. Group home managers and staff members themselves frequently do not grasp the significance of this defining aspect of group home life, and they often feel the need to proclaim the "family-like" nature of their settings.

Responding to Pain

At the level of the carework staff, the primary challenge was found to be *responding to pain and pain-based behaviour*. While the residential child and youth care literature frequently mentions the "troubled and troubling" nature of the youth in care (for example, Hobbs, 1982), and acknowledges their traumatic backgrounds, there is a tendency to "gloss over" the deep-seated and often long-standing pain carried by these youth. The term "pain-based behaviour" has been used in this framework to remind us that so-called "acting-out" behaviour and internalizing processes such as "depression" are very frequently the result of a triggering of this internalized pain. A more extensive discussion of this concept can be found in Anglin (2002), and its manifestations are well documented in the literature written by youth themselves (e.g., Raychaba, 1993). Perhaps more than any other dimension of the carework task, the ongoing challenge of dealing with such primary pain without unnecessarily inflicting secondary pain experiences on the residents through punitive or controlling reactions can be seen to be the central problematic for the carework staff. One of the observed characteristics of a well-functioning home is an awareness of the need to respond effectively and sensitively to both the youth residents' behaviour and their own personal anxieties. At the same time, few managers, supervisors, and staff in this study demonstrated an understanding of the underlying pain in the residents and within themselves. This intensive psychosocial process, and its frequent repression, makes acting in the best interests of the residents very difficult, and represents perhaps the greatest potential barrier to achieving a high level of congruence within the home in service of the children's best interests.

Developing a Sense of Normality

A third basic psychosocial process was identified as *developing a sense of normality*. This psychosocial process not only captures the central task, or goal, to be accomplished by the residents, it also serves to define a key element of what constitutes the resident *children's best interests*. There is an apparent paradox at the heart of this process that can be confusing and worrisome to critics of group home care. How can an "abnormal" (or "artificial") living environment such as a staffed group home foster the development of normality? Won't the residents simply become institutionalized in such an extrafamilial context? This study suggests that what a well-functioning group home can offer residents is *a sense of* normality, thus providing a bridging experience in terms of the residents' readiness to engage successfully in more normative environments.

Of course, each of these three psychosocial processes is closely interrelated with the others, and in reality they exist as three interwoven threads or interrelated facets of the overall struggle for congruence within a home. To illustrate this point, a significant factor in residents' experience of developing a sense of normality will be the manner in which staff respond to their pain and pain-based behaviour in the course of creating and shaping the extrafamilial living environment. Further, these pervasive psychosocial processes are made up of many moment-by-moment interactions between individuals, and some of the most pervasive and pivotal of these interactional dynamics will be outlined next. These interactional dynamics provide an important means for understanding and assessing the degree of congruence throughout a group home organization and its functioning.

Interactional Dynamics

The category of *interactional dynamics* identifies the most significant modes of relation between persons within and connected to the group home. On the basis of a comparative analysis of the interpersonal interactions occurring within the homes, as noted during the on-site visits and discussed in interviews, 11 dynamics emerged as most pervasive and influential in relation to positive change. These interactional dynamics can be understood as the key relational ingredients of group home life and work and as elements of the larger psychosocial processes already identified. Briefly stated, the dynamics include the following:

1. listening and responding with respect;
2. communicating a framework for understanding;
3. building rapport and relationship;
4. establishing structure, routine, and expectations;
5. inspiring commitment;
6. offering emotional and developmental support;
7. challenging thinking and action;
8. sharing power and decision-making;
9. respecting personal space and time;
10. discovering and uncovering potential; and
11. providing resources.

Each of these can come together with various others in a single moment or episode, much in the same way as various ingredients combine in the preparation of different culinary preparations. The creation of a *residents' best interests* environment can be seen to be largely a matter of combining these interactional ingredients in a highly congruent manner, while sensitively addressing the three major and intertwined psychosocial processes of *creating the extrafamilial living environment, responding to pain and pain-based behaviour,* and *developing a sense of normality.*

Finally, one additional category was also found to be important in completing the framework for understanding group home functioning: namely, the *levels of group home operation.*

Levels of Group Home Operation

Organizations such as group homes are not simply assemblages of people, paper, procedures, and premises. As the term "organization" suggests, these elements must be brought together in an organized fashion. As with most such

Figure 1 *Framework Matrix for Understanding Group Home Life and Work*

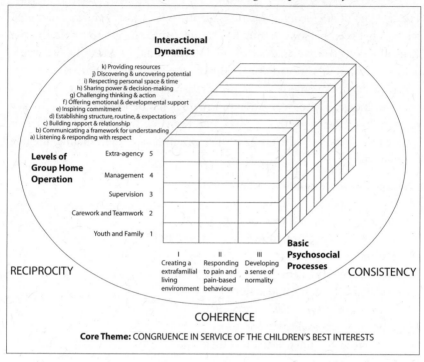

settings, group homes consist of a hierarchy of operating levels, or domains, each with its defined set of roles and responsibilities. In this study, five such levels were clearly evident, as reflected in participants' ongoing thinking and action within the homes:

1. Extra-agency level (contracting, funding, liaison, etc.);
2. Management level (administration, budgeting, resource allocation, personnel management, etc.);
3. Supervision level (overseeing careworkers, team development, programming, resident care, etc.);
4. Carework and Teamwork level (working individually and collectively with youth and family members, completing reports, linking with community agencies, etc.); and
5. Youth Resident and Family level (daily living, visiting, etc.).

The word "levels" rather than "domains" is used to reflect more explicitly the hierarchical nature of these operational dimensions. The notion of a *flow of congruence* from the higher levels of the group care organization to the lower levels was also identified as an important aspect of the core category of *congruence in service of the children's best interests,* and how it comes to be realized (or not) in actual practice.

Figure 1 graphically illustrates the various elements of the theoretical model, and suggests, with its rectangular cube and sub-cubes, encompassed within an oval design, the degree of their key linkages and inter-relations.

Utilizing the Framework to Improve Residential Care

This theoretical framework can assist not only in determining the degree to which a group home is well-functioning or poorly functioning, but also in identifying areas of specific strength and weakness. Thus, it offers a theoretical tool grounded in the realities of group home life and work to assist in enhancing practice, drafting sensitive policies, targeting standards, ensuring the relevance of education and training, focusing research, and guiding evaluation.

Several international training and program development initiatives have been initiated utilizing this framework. The Residential Child Care Project based at Cornell University in Ithaca, New York, has been working with the South Carolina Association of Children's Homes and Family Services for several years to develop a new training curriculum to improve the congruence of agencies in the best interests of the children, and to strengthen careworker training. It is hoped that an evaluation of this initiative, inspired and informed by this theoretical framework, will offer insight into the advantages and possible limitations of implementing such an approach.

In addition, beginning in 2007, service systems in three Australian states have been drawing on this framework in their policy development and program design to rethink the role and functioning of residential care for young people within their child welfare systems. Several state-wide conferences with keynote presentations delivered by the author have helped to introduce the findings of this research to hundreds of policy-makers, managers, supervisors, and careworkers across dozens of residential care agencies and government departments. A number of initiatives at different levels of the system have already been implemented to operationalize the framework.

Finally, several recent books and manuals have drawn upon the notion of pain-based behaviour, articulated for the first time in this study, to more clearly identify the needs of children in care and provide more trauma-sensitive and responsive care (Brendtro & du Toit, 2005; Bath, Atkin, & Boswell, 2008).

A System of Care

The notion of a "system of care" has emerged in recent years, and this way of thinking has advantages in counteracting a tendency to view residential care as "end of the line" or "last resort." Thinking about residential care as a last resort can only have unfortunate consequences.

First, residential care is understood by placing workers as a service to be used only after all else has failed. One consequence is that of young people being bounced from foster home to foster home in the belief that "every child needs to be living in a family" and that a residential placement "is never the best option for any child" (Boone, 1999).

Second, the existing pain and sense of unworthiness and failure of the affected children are compounded, and this situation is then often summarized as "child shows serious problems with attachment." In the author's own research, there were several instances of young people who had been placed in over 20 foster homes, and one who had been through 32 foster homes over a six-year period. When asked about this experience, the young woman said: "When I was placed in a foster home, the first thing I tried to do was break it down." For a young person not considered successful in traditional terms, she was certainly highly successful according to her own criteria. In such instances as this, one is faced with the question: who is the slow learner here? Do the placing workers and agencies need to think differently about what is in the best interests of this child—not to mention the third unfortunate consequence, namely, the unfortunate experience of the foster families whose efforts have now been labelled as another "foster care breakdown"? A well-functioning (or at least "well-enough" functioning) system of care would not be so insensitive to the demonstrated needs of such young people, nor so careless with valuable and all-too-scarce placement resources (that is, willing and capable foster families). Such a misuse and squandering of both foster family and placement agency time, energy, and resources is a fourth unfortunate consequence of faulty thinking about the place and appropriate use of residential group care.

The Place of Residential Group Care in a System of Care

There appears to be quite widespread confusion in many social services departments and agencies about when and how to determine if a child needs a residential placement rather than a foster care placement. A previous publication (Anglin, 2002) drew from the experiences of young people who were current or former youth in care to explore this issue from the child's perspective. Residents and former residents in this study who believed that their experiences in group homes had been largely beneficial identified a number of common pre-ferred characteristics, and in several instances explicitly contrasted these to some of their negative experiences in foster homes. It is important to recognize that a number of the youth respondents also had very positive foster home experiences. What this section is exploring are aspects of the group homes in this sample that were experienced by some residents to be positive and pre-ferred in their experience, at a particular stage in their life and "career in care" (Brown, Bullock, Hobson, & Little, 1998, p. 3). Also reflected in this discussion are some of the perceptions and observations of careworkers and supervisory staff members that speak to the benefits and advantages of group homes for addressing certain needs of youth.

Seven characteristics of group home environments emerged over the course of the study, and each characteristic will now be briefly presented. Once again, it is important to keep in mind that this analysis is not implying that foster homes are not suitable placements for many young people in care. Quite to the contrary, it would appear that a foster family is a preferred placement for many young people, even the majority of young people in care. However, it is equally evident that for some young people, at certain times in their lives, a group home can be the preferred setting.

Staff–Youth Relationships

The findings of this study strongly challenge the notion that group homes should strive to be surrogate families. Sometimes, when foster placements are not acceptable or helpful for a youth, it is because they experience a sense of betrayal when they are faced with the expectation to "treat strangers as family." The reality can be, as one girl said: "I feel I'm just some intruder in someone's house." Another young group home resident said: "I don't need a family; I already have a family!"

Several young people expressed the feeling that they had to "behave them-selves" when in foster care to the degree that they did not feel they could really be themselves, and begin to address the issues that led them to be put there in the first place.

Family Home versus Agency Home

Whereas a group home is usually owned by an agency, or in some cases the gov-ernment, a foster home is rented or owned by the foster parents. The furnish-ings, personal belongings, and the house itself represent a significant emotional as well as financial investment for the parents and other family members. To damage or treat with disrespect someone's valued and sentimental belongings is to inflict, to a greater or lesser degree, both an emotional hurt and a financial burden upon their owner. As the manager of an agency observed: "Parents cannot accept a young person doing damage to their home; it's beyond the limits they can tolerate."

There is also an issue of safety for both the parents and youth and any children or other relatives living in the foster home. Some of the youth in this study who enjoyed living in foster care when things were going well knew at the same time that there were occasions when they were unable to control their outbursts of anger and rage, and realized themselves on these occasions that they were unable to deal with their psychological and emotional problems adequately within a family home setting.

In a well-functioning group home, a young person knows that the staff will be able to accept more challenging behaviour, and can offer a safer environment while he or she can, in the words of another former group home resident, "work out a lot of my problems."

Number of People in the Household

While many young people want and need the intimacy of a foster home in lieu of their own family context, some young people are only too ready to trade what they experience as a stifling level of intimacy in a foster home for the variety of possible relationships and role models that they can experience in a group home setting. As one youth commented:

> I never had a favourite staff. Overall they were pretty neat people. One lady, she was a leading horse trainer in Canada, and [another staff] climbed Canada's highest mountain, and stuff. They were pretty interesting people to me.

While foster parents can also offer impressive life experiences and serve as powerful role models, there are only one or two of them, and there is more pressure on these relationships to "click" than with a range of full-time, part-time, and relief staff found in a group home situation. While adult relationships are often experienced as very important for youth in care, the young people in this study—who were going through intense personal struggles and were at their least likeable—sometimes expressed appreciation for caring relationships that came without the expectation of close or ongoing intimacy.

Time Element

While it was evident in this study that the longer staff shifts (e.g., three or four days straight) were often preferred by the youth to the eight- or twelve-hour shifts, the residents also realized that the staff needed a break to refresh themselves if they were going to be able to work effectively with them. Staff were typically very clear about the advantages of regular and frequent breaks, given the demanding needs and behaviours of some of the residents, but so were some of the resident youth. One resident eloquently acknowledged the demands that he knew his behaviour placed on residential staff: "I knew the staff got changed every four days, and that would be enough time for them to have a break, and calm down, and come back to work and deal with me."

For foster parents, respite tends to be quite brief and infrequent, when it happens at all, and the youth noticed and could speak to the difference it made for the atmosphere that they experienced. The image of a foster home setting as an "emotional hothouse" would be an apt characterization of some youths' experiences. In a group home, to continue the image, the air may get quite heavy and steamy, but the walls are not made with so much glass and there are many more gardeners to call upon when needed.

Style of Care

While the intimate and familial aspects of foster care can be an important source of nurturing and offer a sense of belonging for many young people, for those who are suffering through the deep-seated effects of trauma and who have difficulty controlling their "acting-out" or "pain-based behaviour," the less intimate and more youth-centred attention of staff members may make the difference between an experience of personal change and yet another failure experience (i.e., a foster home breakdown). As one young group home resident observed: "In a foster home I am expected to fit in; here, they work to fit in with me."

One of the staff members in a home observed:

> Having two full-time staff on plus a supervisor allows you to stay on top of things … There is just so much more support here, and that's what we're structured to do. There are no other things we need to look after. We don't need to look after our private life, because it's not here!

Intensity of Care/Treatment

The well-functioning group homes in this study were continually seeking to provide therapeutic care and a consistency of structure and expectations with an intensity that is virtually impossible to maintain in a family or foster family setting.

Supervision of Carers

In a foster home setting, the parents are on their own except for occasional consultations and perhaps a few visits per year from a Ministry resource worker. Even the current standard (not often met in practice) that calls for monthly visits allows for monitoring and occasional support, rather than close supervision. Typically, in a well-functioning group home situation, there is quite close and direct supervision, and what can be termed "co-vision" by a co-worker working on the same shift. In the homes studied, most of the supervisors were more seasoned staff whose role it was to ensure that their colleagues were functioning appropriately, both in the moment and over time. Attentive and competent supervision emerged as one of the core and essential elements contributing to a well-functioning group home.

In summary, what a well-functioning group home can offer is an intense, supervised, staffed, structured, less emotionally charged, and more consistently responsive environment for promoting the personal growth and development of youth who require such intensive care and support. If a service is to be utilized, then we need to know how, when, and for whom it can best be used, and value it as *a positive choice* in these circumstances. A service that is not valued, or that is considered always to be an unsatisfactory or second-rate option, will inevitably deteriorate, and will ultimately reflect these self-fulfilling expectations. The findings of this study suggest that group homes need to be appreciated for their strengths as extrafamilial developmental and therapeutic environments, and ought not to be denigrated for not being made up of "natural" or "real" families.

Conclusion

The creation of a true system of care is seen as necessary in order for residential group care to be appropriately utilized within a community. Understanding the differing characteristics of foster care and group care, and the different impacts on the potential residents, is also important. Finally, having a clearly articulated framework for creating and assessing individual residential programs can facilitate program development and the provision of program support, thus ensuring the high quality of residential care that many of our young people need and deserve.

15

The Changing Face of Adoption

Kathleen Kufeldt

At one time adoption was a means of finding families for babies, usually surrendered by the birth mother for reasons of poverty or the stigma of single parenthood. By the end of the twentieth century, there were far fewer babies being placed for adoption. More efficient birth control methods and the availability of abortion reduced the number of unplanned pregnancies. Single parenthood was less stigmatized; social security support enabled more mothers to keep their babies. Adoption is now considerably different.

There is extensive literature pertaining to adoption. The purpose of this chapter is to draw from that literature to illustrate the changes in adoption and the issues they raise. It looks in turn at theory, the changing paths to adoption, and the views of the different players. The chapter finishes with the implications and recommendations for policy, practice, and research.

Theoretical Issues

Searching for Theory

Adoption lacks coherent theory. The best we have to date, though over forty years old, is that of Kirk, a sociologist and adoptive father of four children. His hypothesis is that adoptive parents are affected by a role handicap that is reinforced by the attitudes of others. The two common coping mechanisms are either acknowledgement or rejection of difference. In his own words:

Adopters, along with other parents, seek to have families of stability and permanence ... Stability requires rules of conduct. Families that are not regulated by tradition must depend on the interpersonal skills of their members for their internal order. In the situation of adoption, these skills imply empathic and ideational communication with the child about his background ...

... Adoptive parental coping activities of the type of "acknowledgment of difference" are conducive to good communication and thus to order and dynamic stability in adoptive families. (Kirk, 1964, pp. 98–9)

More than thirty years later, Webber echoes Kirk when she describes adoption as "culturally unscripted, complex kinship" (1998, p. 84).

Today there is growing acceptance of a variety of family forms, including traditional two-parent families, single parenthood, common law partnerships, divorced but co-parenting couples, blended families, gay couples, adoptive families, and grandparents raising grandchildren. The "different-ness" should theoretically no longer constitute role handicap, yet there still is, on the part of some, the desire to resort to "rejection of difference," and Kirk's theory continues to be relevant because adoptive parenthood *is* different; being an adopted child is different. Acknowledgement of that difference is crucial if we are to honour the rights of the children. It would allow them to have knowledge of their origins and biological heritage, and, unless contrary to their best interests, contact with extended family members.

Adoption Outcomes

Studies of adoption cited here are presented with the caveat that the outcomes apply only to the particular cohort accessed. Tizard (1977) studied children who had been placed in an institution before the age of four months and did not leave until at least two years of age. Some were later restored to their families (n=15); some were adopted (n=25). Tizard found that the adopted children, by age eight, "were in a more stable situation, had fewer emotional problems, and were intellectually and academically superior to the fostered, institutional and restored children" (1977, p. 232). Of interest, and relevant to current family reunification policy, is the fact that "[t]he blood tie by no means implied a love tie: few of the natural mothers expressed the warmth and affection which most of the adoptive mothers did," and "adoptive fathers appeared to be as deeply committed" (p. 233).

Raynor (1980) interviewed 83 sets of adoptive parents who had begun as foster families and 77 who adopted directly, as well as 105 adoptees (56 originally fostered and 49 adopted). She found very little difference between the two groups, though the previously fostered were more likely to experience some insecurity. Parental satisfaction was associated with a sense that the child was like them in some way. Problems tended to be attributed to genetics. Seventy per cent of the adoptees were rated as well adjusted by the interviewer. The problems of some of the less well adjusted could be traced to life circumstances, such as death of the adoptive mother or parental rejection. What was apparent in reading this study was the pervasiveness of secrecy at the time these adoptions took place, in an era of closed adoptions. Adoptees were interviewed only where parental consent was given. In some cases it was refused because the young person was unaware of the adoption. It would be interesting to know the degree to which any of the less successful life histories were related to "rejection of difference."

In contrast, 10 years later, Silber and Dorner (1990) presented the advantages of open adoption. Silber's adoption agency pioneered open adoption. Dorner is an adoptive mother and worker in the field. Their book provides rich anecdotal information obtained from interviews and questionnaires. Many of the anecdotes were from those involved from the start with open adoption, some from later reunions. Consistent themes emerged from those reunited. The children wished to know "whom do I look like" and "why was I given up." Birth parents were keen to know whether the child was all right, and declared, "I never did forget." The negatives that emerged appeared to be of a minor nature, such as timing and frequency of visits, or value differences. The authors reflect an issue that is problematic in studying adoption:

> One criticism of open adoption is that there is not enough data to know the long-term effects on the child. However, the problems associated with traditional adoption have been well documented. We must recognize that there is no "perfect adoption" just as there are no perfect biological families. (1990, p. 17)

An evaluation of adoption of older children was conducted by the International Social Services/International Rights of Children (ISS/IRC) by canvassing experts and reviewing publications. The conclusion was that "the adoption of older children succeeds, on average, no less well than the adoption of babies, on the condition that these children and their adoptive family are prepared." These children experience slower integration and bonding and behavioural difficulties, but it was noted that "very often, these shortcomings disappear once the child has fully been integrated" (ISS/IRC, 2008b, p. 7).

What is missing in the study of outcomes is knowledge of the alternative: what would be the life course of a child if not adopted, of the birth parents, or of an adoptive family if achieving parenthood were not possible?

Developmental Theory

Also of relevance is developmental theory. The preference of the majority of adopters for a newborn or very young child reflects actual or intuitive knowledge of bonding and attachment. It may reflect concern regarding negative effects of early experience. Nevertheless, there is ample evidence that attachment can develop at later ages, and, of particular concern to prospective adopters, that effects of early adverse experience can be overcome (Clarke & Clarke, 1976, 2000, 2003; Howe, 1995, 1997).

Rosenberg (1992) proposes that different issues arise for all three members of the adoption triad—adoptees, adoptive parents, and birth parents—at every stage of life. This is echoed by Silber and Dorner (1990), who provide children's reactions at different ages. The chapter on the teenage years, for instance, relates to the search for identity. This may exacerbate acting out, a need to search, or, conversely, denial of grief and loss related to the birth parent. Open communication and open adoption bring positive contributions to resolution of developmental issues at each stage. Argent (2002) provides helpful information on managing contact. She includes an appendix which gives a useful synopsis of research related to open adoption (Sales in Argent, 2002, pp. 226–35).

Parkes and his colleagues have expanded the study of attachment to the world of social relationships and ideology. Pertinent to the study of adoption is their assertion that "[i]n their attempt to achieve security for themselves and for those who are attached to them, the more powerful members of society constantly seek to control the uncertainty in the behaviour of others" (Parkes, Stevenson-Hinde, & Marris, 1991, pp. 2–3). This could explain the old world of sealed adoption, with its "rejection of difference" regarding the newly formed family. Marris (1996) adds that a balanced reciprocity is necessary to achieve successful social relationships. Open adoption does allow reciprocity for, and provides the child with, that connection and manageable continuity in life that we all strive for (Marris, 1974). It can also provide for the family a "constructed world of predictable relationships" (Marris, 1996, p. 3).

International Adoption

As the numbers of babies available for adoption in North America dwindled, interest in adopting infants from overseas increased. To an extent this coincided with historical events that raised the profile and acceptability of adopting a child of a different race or culture. The Canadian Paediatric Society provides historical background:

After World War II, many Canadian and American soldiers and their families adopted children from the war-ravaged countries of Asia. Nearly 3000 Japanese children and 840 Chinese children were adopted mostly by white American families between 1948 and 1962 (Weil, 1984). The Korean War (1950 to 1953) renewed interest in transracial adoption … There was also an increase in Asian adoptions as a result of the Vietnam War. Since the 1950s, the US has experienced a gradual increase in adopted children from Central and South America, with approximately 1000 adoptees annually. (2006, p. 1)

There has been a similar increase in Canada, with an average of almost 2,000 international adoptions per year during the years 1995 to 2004 (Adoption Council of Canada, 2005). Yet there are more than 22,000 children lingering in foster care in Canada, and about 126,000 in the United States available for adoption since parental rights have been terminated (Adoption Council of Canada, 2005, 2009). The average age of the American children is 8 years. Though the majority of children adopted from overseas by Canadians are under the age of 4, in 2004 4.5% were between the ages of 5 and 9, and nearly 4% were 10–14 years old.

International adoption is not trouble-free. Register (1991) draws on her experience as the mother of two Korean-born daughters, as well as interviews with other adoptive families, to illustrate the special challenges multicultural families face in the United States. She is often asked, "Are these kids yours?" She also addresses global issues related to "supply," such as the ethics of uprooting children from their heritage, racism encountered by these children, and the rights (or lack thereof) of birth parents.

Intrusion on parental rights is highlighted by Kligman (1998) and Chai (2005), who discuss discrimination against Romani people in Romania:

> Coercion of Romanian mothers happened in various ways. By law, a mother had fifteen days in which to change her mind about consenting to the adoption of her child.… When a mother had a change of heart (or conscience), her decision was not necessarily accepted graciously by the adoptive parents or their negotiators, regardless of the law. One Romanian woman was told by the translator that she would be responsible for the costs accrued during the stay of the American adoptive parents. (Kligman, 1998, p. 249)

More subtle coercion is the suggestion that the child will have a better life than the birth mother can provide. This is mirrored by the altruistic motives of many overseas adopters. However, international organizations concerned with the rights of children and families have raised concerns about the removal of children from their home countries, and the financial profiteering of some private adoption agents. ISS/IRC (2008a) has refuted many of the myths concerning adoptable babies and children, and calls for precision in the definition of who are truly orphans. The response of the International Foster Care Organization (IFCO) is to offer consultancy and training in the development of within country foster care and adoption. Browne estimates that only 4% of children in European institutions are actual orphans, and that "at least eight countries require the urgent development of foster care and rehabilitation services" (2005, p. 31). Chou and Browne (2008) suggest that international adoption may actually encourage or contribute to placement of young children in institutional care.

Some countries have since placed a moratorium on international adoption. In a response to critics of their work, Browne and Chou point out that following its moratorium, international adoptions from Romania fell from 2,017 in 1998 to 251 in 2004, and "children living in domestic substitute families (kinship and foster care) increased by two-thirds" (2008, p. 72). However, they note that they "are not opposed to international adoption when it is in the best interests of the child ... following Article 21 of UNCRC" (2008, p. 73).

Transracial Adoption

Up until the 1950s, adoption agencies made efforts to "match" children to prospective adoptive parents. In the latter half of the twentieth century, increasing numbers of international adoptions influenced a cultural shift such that transracial adoption was no longer considered unusual. White families in the United States began to adopt black children; First Nations children in Canada were placed for adoption with non-Native families, some with families in the United States. This practice has generated serious counter-reactions as formerly oppressed groups have found their voice; for example, several First Nations agencies have been successful in promoting the rights of bands to approve adoption placements of their children. In the U.S., the National Association of Black Social Workers has become a powerful advocacy group for preservation of family and culture among African-Americans. They emphasize that "trans-racial adoption of an African American child should only be considered after documented evidence of unsuccessful same race placements has been reviewed and supported by appropriate representatives of the African American community" (National Association of Black Social Workers, 2003, p. 1).

Canadian First Nations and African-Americans are not alone in grieving the loss of their children. Australian Aboriginals speak of the "Stolen Generation." Following an Australian government edict in 1931, black Aboriginal children and children of mixed marriages were gathered up and taken to government-run settlements to be assimilated. Pilkington (2002) brought this sad history to an international audience in telling the story of her mother, one of three young girls uprooted from their community and taken to the Moore River Native Settlement. There, the children were forbidden to speak their native language, forced to abandon their Aboriginal heritage, and taught to be culturally white (Pilkington, 2002). The story of their escape reached a wider audience through the 2002 film *Rabbit-Proof Fence*. These children and their peers were not placed for adoption, but their plight is relevant to any discussion of transracial placements in that it illustrates not only a compelling need to connect with family and culture, but the impact on the bereaved parents and family left behind. A sad corollary is that Pilkington's younger sister was taken from her mother and raised to believe she was white. She has absorbed racial prejudice, does not want contact with her birth family, and refuses to acknowledge her heritage (Pendreigh, 2002). Australia, like Canada and the U.S., now has provisions to ensure that Aboriginal communities are consulted regarding the placement of their children.

An interesting take on transracial adoption is presented by Pertman (2000). As a journalist, he was nominated for a Pulitzer Prize for his articles on adoption. He has two adopted children himself, and now directs a policy and education think tank. He believes that adoptive families have benefited from increased acceptance of racial diversity, and that adoption itself has helped to instigate social change: adoption as an institution provides a model for formation of non-traditional families.

Special Needs Adoption

At one time certain children in permanent care were considered unadoptable, or at best "hard to place." These were children with various handicapping conditions, those in sibling groups, and older children. As the applicants for adoption began to exceed infants available for adoption, child welfare agencies took a second look and began more vigorous efforts to find adoptive homes for these children.

Studies indicate that the age of the child is not necessarily a barrier to finding an adoptive home. The Oregon Permanency Planning Project discovered that the major barrier to permanence was worker attitudes: if a worker believed a child to be unadoptable, then adoption did not happen (Emlen, Lahti, Downs, McKay, & Downs, 1979).

Foster carers have expressed willingness to adopt their foster children with special needs, but have at times been deterred because of the potential costs involved. Barth (1993) argued that human service programs should be funded in ways that support effective practice, and that adoption assistance payments should support the objective of helping children get adopted and stay adopted. Efforts to permanently place through adoption those foster children who are not returning to their birth families is now supported in the United States by the federal Adoption Assistance Program. The findings of a demonstration project supported the value of a subsidized guardianship permanency option in establishing legal permanency (Lehman, Liang, O'Dell, & Duryea, 2003; Lehman, Liang, & O'Dell, 2005). Hansen and Hansen (2005) also found that subsidies were positively correlated with adoptions from foster care.

A Canadian study (Scully, 1986), though written two decades ago, is still relevant today. It was carried out in a decade when there was expanding inter-ʾst in adoption of older children and those with special needs, and child welfare agencies were seriously addressing the issue of permanency planning for children in their care. With the co-operation of provincial authorities in Alberta, Scully was able to survey the universe of those who adopted special needs children in that province between 1980 and 1985 (n=510). The return rate was an impressive 81%. However, 17% of respondents were excluded from the final analysis since they did not perceive their child to have special needs (in some cases because earlier problems had been outgrown). Worthy of note is the finding that there was not a significant shortage of approved homes, but the process of placement was slow, with some prospective parents waiting years, and children lingering in care longer than might have been necessary. The findings also indicated the need for pre- and post-placement support. A potentially significant observation was the fact that the emotional fall out of abuse, neglect, and foster home placement changes presented often as a greater challenge than the identified "special need." Eight years later, Whitford-Numan (1994) reported similar findings, and again emphasized the need for post-adoption supports. Some of her respondents were unable to continue to adopt because of lack of support. Since that time, Alberta and the Adoption Council of Canada have increased their outreach efforts, including a photo gallery to increase and expedite adoptive placements.

Babies as Commodities

Perhaps it was inevitable that, as the search by would-be adopters for a baby outstripped the number of babies available, there would be unscrupulous opportunists emerging. A pioneer in the "business," until 1950, was Georgia Tann, who founded the Tennessee Children's Home Society to further her activities of taking, even stealing, babies and selling them to adopters. She quickly discovered that with private adoption to wealthy clients (including Joan Crawford), she could charge up to $5,000 per child for her services. The full story has since been documented by Raymond (2007).

The fact that babies continue to be a trading commodity is highlighted by two articles in the *Calgary Herald* in January of 2009. The first refers to the selling of babies for illegal adoption via a private Egyptian hospital. The eleven accused included doctors, nurses, a tour guide, and two American women. They were charged with trading children for up to $4,500 for a girl and $5,600 for a boy (Egypt charges 11, 2009). The second article highlights the growing use of the Internet for such purposes. In this case a surrogate mother in Belgium reneged on her arrangement with an infertile couple. Instead, she sold the baby to a Dutch couple through an Internet auction (Internet baby's new parents, 2009).

Pertman (2000) also deplores the negative effect of this "industry." He provided an example of one woman who tried to sell her baby on eBay; the highest bid was $109,100. Spar (2006) explores the commercial exploitation of the full gamut of means of obtaining a baby, reproductive technology, surrogacy, and adoption.

Sadly, the current interest in international adoption has enabled exploitation of those desperate to be parents and of mothers living in poverty. Webber calls it adoption skullduggery, and documents what she terms "hustlers and horror stories" in many countries (1998, pp. 191–5).

Voices from the Adoption Triad

The term "triad" is convenient shorthand for the fact that there are three sides to each adoption: child, birth family, and adoptive family. This may translate into more than three stories as mothers and fathers experience the event differently. Some birth fathers may not be included, or even told. And there are grandparents and extended family in birth and adoptive families whose views are rarely sought or expressed. A common theme is management of disappointments and loss, but each voice is a reflection of personal history and prevailing philosophies at the time the child was born.

Birth Parents

Jones (1993) surveyed 72 American mothers who gave their babies up for adoption when, for the most part, records were sealed. Almost all had regrets, and the majority experienced troubled marriages. Most troubled were those who were teenagers at the time of birth, and felt they had no choice or were stigmatized. These themes are repeated by Fessler (2006), who documents the tremendous family and social pressures of that era. She herself is an adoptee who was later reunited with her birth mother. Robinson (2003), whose early life was in Scotland, describes similar experiences and enormous grief. She writes with passion about her early life, the lack of choices, her failed marriage, single parenthood, and reunion with her first-born. In her book and her public speaking she expresses continuing anger, and would like legislation to make adoption a thing of the past.

As indicated earlier, birth mothers involved in open adoption have a very different experience:

> Birth parents who experience open adoption are much more at peace with their adoption decision and are better able to process their feelings of grief. We must recognize that there is always a grief experience for birth parents as they grieve for the loss of the parenting role. (Silber & Dorner, 1990, p. 15)

It is clear from the literature that the grief is more profound than the loss of the parenting role alone. There is also the wrenching separation from the newborn infant at a time when, developmentally, there is the yearning to bond and nurture. Nevertheless, there is peace of mind for those unready or unable to take on the parenting role, and pleasure in seeing the child flourish:

> I think that openness has had a wonderful effect on my daughter, her family, and me. My decision for adoption was of course emotionally difficult, but I felt, and feel that it was the most practical and logical decision I have ever made. (Silber & Dorner, 1990, p. 179)

Mewshaw (2006) provides some insight into the loss experienced by a birth father. As a 21-year-old student, he had no choice when his girlfriend placed their child for adoption. Thirty years later, his daughter contacted him; his book documents the impact of that call, and the opportunity to review his own life. There are hints in his book that he carries anger against the child's mother, but the reunion provided him with opportunity to resolve questions in his own life.

Those Who Adopt

Adopters have their own grief experiences. Hansen (2008) describes the sense of loss of those unable to conceive: for four years he and his wife endured the trials and pitfalls of reproductive technology in her attempts to get pregnant. They then spent two years trying to adopt, culminating in overseas adoption. Webber (1998) presents a somewhat different experience. An unplanned, untimely pregnancy nevertheless produced euphoria, but the child was born dead. Her grief, though understated, is palpable: it takes two years to contemplate another pregnancy. Like the Hansens, she experienced the roller coaster of medical interventions before turning to adoption:

> The bottom line for me was I could love anyone's child, so why become a guinea pig when what I really wanted to become was a mother? Once I got over the hurdle of deciding whether or not to have a family, deciding to adopt was a breeze. (1998, pp. 2–3)

She portrays the trials and tribulations of trying to adopt in graphic and engaging fashion. Ironically, as American couples are searching overseas, Webber's baby was from the U.S., a transracial adoption. Her experience sparked the research that forms the basis of her book. It is unique in the adoption literature in that its focus is fairly and squarely on the interests of children.

The end of a search and finding a child to adopt is not always the end to heartache and grief, but may be the beginning of new hurts and losses. Foli and Thompson (2004), professionals and adoptive parents, wrote about "post-adoption blues." Keck and Kupecky, discussing the modern world of adoption, caution that many children "bring into their new families the remnants of problems that began with the birth families" (1995, p. 13). Buxton describes this graphically:

> We are all interconnected—our lives profoundly influenced by small events that may have happened years ago, involving people we may never know. Back in April of 1979, a woman addicted to alcohol, whom I have never met, became pregnant with her third child, continued to drink throughout her pregnancy—and whirled my life into an unending orbit of love, grief, despair and hope. (2004, p. 1)

Some adopters are aware that their child has been diagnosed with special needs. Others enter what Webber describes as "the heartbreak world of hidden disabilities" (personal communication, May 2009). The beautiful baby handed to her by his mother and birth mother later exhibited a variety of learning disabilities. Problems that may emerge over time include attachment disorders, fetal alcohol syndrome, and other injuries engendered by a toxic intrauterine environment or by early neglect or abuse. Some adoptive parents enter this world with eyes wide open, accepting a "special needs child." Others seeking a child overseas or directly from a birth mother may enter the heartbreak world unwittingly. Attachment may be problematic, the unanticipated needs and problems may overwhelm, and residual grief may be exacerbated, particularly if no help or support is available. Some don't make it. Euphemistically termed disruption or dissolution, this is family breakdown, and ultimate heartbreak and rejection for the child (Barth & Berry, 1988; Scully, 1986; Whitford-Numan, 1994).

The Adopted

In the era of closed adoption and "denial of difference," little thought was given to allowing for connection to, or knowledge of, the child's family of origin. Relevant to the thesis of Parkes and his associates, closed adoption and sealed records would certainly allow the state to establish some order and certainty with respect to this family form, but "the power to control uncertainty is very unequally distributed" (Marris, 1996, p. 1). Birth parents relinquish control, and thus power over events, though not necessarily willingly (Robinson, 2003). The one with the least power is the child. In earlier times there was an assumption that this did not matter, but it is now clear that many adoptees want knowledge of their origins, continuity with their past, and connection with an expanded kinship. Mewshaw's daughter assured him that all she wanted was to know about her biological family and its medical history. Nevertheless, a bond grew between them as they examined the past. Robinson's son, unknown to her, had been searching for her as she searched for him. At their reunion, commenting on his own likeness to her next eldest son, he said, "It's the first time in my life that I've seen someone with my face" (Robinson, 2003, p. 93). Most people take family likenesses for granted. One of Webber's interviewees expresses being different even more strongly: "I love my mother very much, and I know how much she loves me. But there are certain things about being black in America that a white mother just can't teach a black child" (1998, p. 143).

Eldridge is an adoptee who took control, and overcame the power imbalance by writing and public speaking. She has interviewed many adoptees and adoptive families, and has written books both for adoptees (1999, 2003) and for adoptive parents (2009). Her own adoption took place in an era of "rejection of difference," but she is clearly in favour of acknowledgement of difference and openness.

Summary

There are now fierce debates about the pros and cons of adoption. Issues of relevance include family preservation, identity, and children's rights and needs. Two books in particular (Espejo, 2002; Harnack, 1995) clearly portray the lack of consensus and strong emotions that colour these debates. Robinson (2002), against adoption in any form, reflects on a study by Armstrong and Slaytor (2001) that portrays the struggle of older international adoptees to obtain a sense of their own identity and belonging. She raises the question of whether there will be a backlash to international adoptions similar to those triggered by First Nations communities, African-Americans, and Australian Aboriginals:

> But what of the children ... who are now being brought to Australia from countries in Asia, South America and Africa?... Sadly, we seem to be creating a new *Stolen Generation* of displaced persons ... (Robinson, 2002, p. 2)

There are no simple answers. Results of studies are very much influenced by prevailing philosophy and culture at the time of the adoption, as well as by individual experiences. Birth parents and would-be parents suffer grief and loss. Nevertheless, the evidence leans toward adoption as a positive option for the majority of children who grow up in adoptive homes. It also refutes old ideas that certain children are unadoptable.

Conclusions and Recommendations

Adoption is an important part of the continuum of care. As earlier chapters show, that continuum begins with supporting families, includes foster care, and should be characterized by early permanency planning and decision-making so that children can settle into a loving home with the security of knowing that this family is theirs for the rest of their childhood—and beyond. When parents wish to have their child placed for adoption, or when removal from family is necessary, inclusive care in foster care and open adoption serve the best interests of all concerned.

Transracial and international adoption can be considered where it is clearly the only option available for a particular child. Families involved may require assistance in enabling the child to maintain links with his or her own country and culture. However, international organizations such as UNICEF and IFCO should continue efforts to assist countries to develop their internal systems of child care and protection, and in-country adoption.

Current family support and advice programs tend to be offered only where there is a question of abuse or neglect. If available to all, regardless of circumstance, they might help to prevent adoptive family breakdown. Teachers and other professionals are in need of education and training in the diagnosis and treatment of the array of hidden disabilities that affect a growing number of adopted children. Kirk (1964) and Atkinson (1988) suggest a preparation process for infertile couples prior to adoption. The ability to process the grief involved may allow some to decide that adoption is not the answer. Those who do adopt would thereby have "a reality-based orientation toward the challenges that lie ahead" (Atkinson, 1988, p. 90). Further implications for policy, practice, and research are summarized in the following recommendations.

Policy

Children deserve the security of a permanent home as early as possible. Child welfare policy should be committed to early permanency planning, and thereby place limits on the number of attempts at family reunification. This should not be dependent on complete severance of family ties, but allow, where feasible, for continued family contact, including extended family members. Policy initiatives should also:

- provide guidelines and training in early permanency planning;
- develop strategies to create awareness of the need for permanency for children in foster care limbo, and their adoptability;
- establish ongoing support for foster care adoption and special needs adoption;
- promote and support open adoption; and, above all else,
- prohibit trading in children.

Practice

Child welfare and child protection constitute the most challenging of social work tasks: greater emphasis is needed on training and readiness regarding all aspects, including adoption. Specific recommendations are that practitioners:

- engage in a partnership with families to determine the best long-term option for the child from the moment of entry into care;
- encourage ongoing contact with families;
- identify as early as possible those children who are eligible for adoption and make every effort to raise awareness and recruit permanent families;

- consider that there is a potential family for each child rather than having a hierarchy of desirability;
- expand the repertoire of permanent families for children (see Webber, 1998, pp. 33–64, for her description of "family new-sorts"); and
- encourage a balanced reciprocity in adoption (Parkes et al., 1991) by ensuring that all voices are heard, including that of the older child.

Research

Much of the available research is based on outcomes of practices that for the most part have been abandoned. Too little is known about the effects of newer forms of adoption and of international adoption. In Canada there is opportunity for Statistics Canada to partner with child welfare authorities in order to include samples of fostered and adopted children in the National Longitudinal Survey of Children and Youth. This would provide data for social researchers to determine not only outcomes, but also determinants of outcomes, in order to provide children with the best possible life chances.

"As if Kids Mattered" is the challenging title of Webber's book (1998). Indeed they do matter, and should be the primary concern not only in the troubled and complex task of child protection, but within the adoption triad.

16

Factors Associated with Family Reunification among Adolescents in Residential Care
A Quebec Perspective

Marie-Claude Simard
Marie-Andrée Poirier

Placement in substitute care, generally viewed as a temporary measure, too often becomes long-term. Studies have shown that children risk being adrift in the substitute care system (Bullock, Gooch, & Little, 1998; Johnson, 1998; Millham, Bullock, Hosie, & Haak, 1986; Proch & Howard, 1986; Vachon, 1997). In the meantime, both children and families continue to evolve and change during the separation. The result may be that there is no longer a place for the child within the family. When family reunification takes place, it is not simply a question of the child re-entering the niche he or she has left empty. The family situation may no longer correspond to the image the child has retained of it, and since the child has also changed, expectations of one another have altered (Bullock, Little, & Millham, 1993). To offset this, contact should be maintained, and planning for family reunification, when appropriate, should begin as soon as the child enters the care system (Pine, Warsh, & Maluccio, 1993; Thomlison, Maluccio, & Abramczyk, 1996; Simard, 2007).

This chapter presents the results of a Quebec study (Simard, 2007) that focused on the factors associated with the family reunification of adolescents placed in residential care and group homes. We identify and discuss the principal factors that emerged in the context of relevant literature. Following our discussion of results, directions for future research are suggested.

Family Reunification

On March 31, 2008, of the 11,914 youths in out-of-home care in the province of Quebec, 3,101 were living in residential care (Association des Centres Jeunesse du Québec, 2008). Figure 1 shows the distribution among all youths in care by different types of substitute care.

Of the total, 5,090 were under youth protection custody until the age of 18 by virtue of court orders, and 2,684 of these were between 13 and 17 years old. These youths will remain away from their families of origin for a period of several months, if not years. Their destinies after leaving care are unknown at the moment, as no study on this subject has been done recently in Quebec.

Research findings suggest that most of these young people will return to their families of origin at the end of the placement. Many authors maintain that family reunification is the most likely and often the favoured outcome for youths in placement (Frame, Berrick, & Brodowski, 2000; Wulczyn, 2004). However, family reunification is more difficult to achieve for older children (Greenwald, 1998; Harris & Courtney, 2003; Landsverk, Davis, Ganger, Newton, & Johnson, 1996; Thomlison, Maluccio, & Wright, 1996; Thompson, Safyer, & Pollio, 2001; Wells & Guo, 2004). Adolescence is a stage of differentiation and independence with respect to the family. The search for identity and the need for independence weaken the attachment to the family, particularly for adolescents in the youth protection system whose family ties may have been severed. Moreover, problems in the relationships between adolescents and their parents, which are frequently the reason for placement (Teare, Peterson, Authier, Schroeder, & Daly, 1998), can persist beyond the placement and hinder the

Figure 1 *Distribution by Type of Substitute Care*

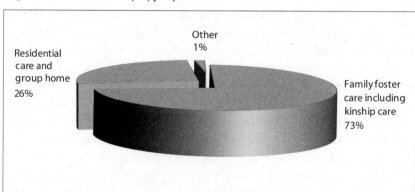

smooth achievement of family reunification. Consequently, family reunification is a major challenge for all concerned.

One of the principal objectives of this study was to identify the factors associated with family reunification of adolescents placed in residential care. The study examines five main categories of variables. They are those that relate to the adolescent, the parents, family and environment, interventions, and the history and conditions of the placement. For the purposes of this chapter, the results of the second and third categories (parents and family) are presented together. The intent of the study is to build a portrait of those youths who have a better chance of reuniting with their families when their placement ends.

Methodology

In order to determine factors associated with family reunification, the study compared two equal-sized groups of care leavers: 51 who were returned to their own home (R) and 51 who left care but did not go home (NR). The survey used for collecting data contained five main sections: preliminary information; the adolescent's socio-demographic characteristics and his/her placement history; the adolescent's family; the maintenance of links with the parent(s) and their engagement; and the last section, describing the characteristics of the adolescent's final placement as well as the intervention carried out during the placement.

Sampling

The population sampled consisted of adolescents, 12 years and older, placed with the Centre Jeunesse de Montréal in the years 1995–2002, either in need of protection or as young offenders. These young people were placed in foster care, in group care, or in institutions. A first random sample of 250 did not provide the desired number of "not reunited" (NR) youth. Accordingly, another 250 were randomly drawn. Excluded were those in care less than three months and those whose files contained insufficient information. The final count consisted of 180 who returned home and 56 who left care without reunification. Random selection of those in the "reunited" (R) group occurred at this stage to ensure equal numbers in each group. Of the 102 youths in the sample, 78% were boys and 22% girls. Thirty-six young people in the sample were of immigrant background, mostly from Haiti, and 14 of those 36 were second-generation immigrants. The average age of the adolescents in the sample was 15.6 years old.

The study had three specific objectives: to provide a snapshot of the adolescents; to explore and identify variables associated with family reunification; and to elaborate a model to predict family reunification. For the purposes of this chapter, only significant results are presented and discussed (the level of significance was set at $p < .05$). Bivariate analysis (chi-square and T-test) was conducted to determine which of the factors studied were significantly associated with family reunification.

Results

In this section, the statistically significant variables associated with family reunification are presented and discussed.

Personal Factors

As shown in Table 1, variables related to the adolescents are essentially socio-demographic, such as gender, age, and ethnocultural origin. The study also considered behavioural problems and education during placement.

Table 1 *Characteristics of Adolescents Associated with Reunification*

	Reunited (R)		Non-Reunited (NR)		Total		
Variable	**N**	**%**	**N**	**%**	**N**	**%**	**p value[a]**
Gender (N = 102)							
1. Boys (N = 80)	36	45.0	44	55.0	80	100	
2. Girls (N = 22)	15	68.2	7	31.8	22	100	0.091
Age at Beginning of the Last Placement (N = 102)							
1. Under 12 (N = 5)	0	0	5	100	5	100	
2. 12–14 (N = 24)	17	70.8	7	29.2	24	100	
3. 15 or over (N = 73)	34	46.6	39	53.4	73	100	
Average (SD)	15.7 (1.5)		15.5 (3.1)		15.6 (2.4)		0.639
Immigrant origin (N = 102)							
1. No (N = 66)	26	39.4	40	60.6	66	100	
2. Yes (N = 36)	25	69.4	11	30.6	36	100	0.007
School Attendance							
1. Yes (N = 36)	30	83.3	6	16.7	36	100	
2. No (N = 52)	16	30.8	36	69.2	52	100	0.000
School Dropout							
1. Yes (N = 34)	9	26.5	25	73.5	34	100	
2. No (N = 57)	39	68.4	18	31.6	57	100	0.000
Number of Problems							
1. 2 to 7 problems (N = 52)	32	61.5	20	38.5	52	51.0	
2. 8 to 13 problems (N = 50)	19	38.0	31	62.0	50	49.0	0.029

[a]The *p* value is that of chi-square for the category variables, based on the distribution of the exact *p* and of the Student T-test for the numerical variables.

The average age of both groups was similar. However, none of the adolescents who were reunited with their families had been placed in out-of-home care before the age of 12, whereas five of the youths who were not reunited had been in care before that age. Analysis of the data also showed a statistically significant link between ethnocultural origin and family reunification: the adolescents of immigrant background were more likely to return home to their families after placement than those of non-immigrant origin. The reunited adolescents were more likely to have been attending school, and less likely to become school dropouts during placement, than were the non-reunited group.

With respect to problems presented by the youth, externalized behavioural problems (learning or other problems related to school, oppositional behavior, aggression and/or violence, delinquent activity, family relationship problems, drug and/or alcohol consumption, and running away) were the most common (i.e., presentation in more than half of the subjects). However, it is important to note that what differentiated the reunited adolescents from the non-reunited ones was the cumulative aspect of their problems—that is, the non-reunited adolescents had more problems, on average, than their peers in the reunited group.

Parental and Family Factors

Since the focus of our study is family reunification when exiting care, it is essential to consider the characteristics of the adolescents' parent(s) and family. The mothers and fathers who were reunited with their adolescents were older on average than the parents whose adolescents did not return to live with them. Fewer parents in the reunited group had multiple problems; however, this particular difference between the two groups was not statistically significant.

There were limitations with respect to the information on file. Within those limits, none of the family characteristics except for the father's termination of parental rights were statistically associated with family reunification. Families in both the reunited and the non-reunited groups presented similar profiles.

Intervention Processes

The focus of intervention is a central element in the study of family reunification. Several aspects characterizing the intervention process were considered in order to better understand what does or does not influence the family reunification process. The principal characteristics of the casework trajectories of the young people and of the intervention carried out during the placement appear in Table 2.

Table 2 *Intervention Characteristics among Adolescents and Their Families Associated with Reunification*

	Reunited (R)		Non Reunited (NR)		Total		
	N	%	N	%	N	%	p value[a]
Types of Legal Casework of							
Adolescents (N = 102)							
1. Consecutive or concurrent							
YPA and YOA (N = 72)	27	37.5	45	62.5	72	100	
2. YPA only (N = 12)	11	91.7	1	8.3	12	100	
3. YOA only (N = 18)	13	72.2	5	27.8	18	100	0.000
Intervention by Principal							
Caseworker (N = 100)[b]							
1. Individual parent(s) (N = 4)	2	50.0	2	50.0	4	100	1.000
2. Family of the adolescent							
and his/her parent(s) (N = 37)	29	78.4	8	21.6	37	100	0.000
3. Family, including other							
members (N = 4)	3	75.0	1	25.0	4	100	0.618
4. Adolescent group (N = 3)	0	0	3	100	3	100	0.114
5. Parent groups (N = 2)	2	100	0	0	2		0.495
6. No intervention process (N = 57)	19	33.3	38	66.7	57	100	0.000
Family Reunification							
Activities (N = 95)							
1. Yes (N = 50)	41	82.0	9	18.0	50	100	
2. No (N = 45)	8	17.8	37	82.2	45	100	0.000
Number of Respondents							
Ambivalent toward Family							
Reunification[b]							
1. Father (N = 11)	1	9.1	10	90.9	11	100	0.000
2. Mother (N = 21)	2	9.5	19	90.5	21	100	0.000
3. Adolescent (N = 16)	0	0	16	100	16	100	0.000

[a]The p value is that of chi-square for the category variables, based on the distribution of the exact p and of the Student T-test for the numerical variables.
[b]The categories of these variables are not mutually exclusive.

This analysis revealed that the majority of the adolescents in the study were followed concurrently under Quebec's *Youth Protection Act* (YPA) and the federal *Young Offenders Act* (YOA). Almost all adolescents in the non-reunited group had a YOA file, and many also had a YPA file. Slightly more than half of the adolescents of the reunited group were followed both by YPA and YOA. Having a protection file only was significantly associated with family reunification. Eleven of the twelve adolescents who had never had a YOA file were reunited.

Results revealed that the reunited group was more likely to be discharged from care due to improvements in their situations, while more than half of their peers in the non-reunited group were discharged when they reached the age of majority. Thus, many adolescents who do not return to their families appear to remain within the continuum of youth protection services until age 18.

As for the intervention process carried out by the principal caseworker, over half of the adolescents in the study received no intervention beyond the regular individual meetings with their caseworkers. However, there was a significant difference between the two groups. The lack of additional casework was more frequent among the non-reunited group (78% versus 37%). When an additional intervention activity was indicated in the adolescents' files, intervention with the family and the parents was the predominant form.

Results indicate that the majority of those who received preparation for their eventual return to the family were from the reunited group. These activities consisted mainly of meetings with the adolescent to discuss the return and the intensification of contacts with the family, including visits to the family. Very few of the adolescents benefited from follow-up activities designed to support family reunification.

Activities that measure the degree of parental involvement during the placement of the adolescents in the sample were analyzed. Following the adolescent's progress at school is an example of parental involvement that was documented in the majority of case files. A significant difference was observed between the frequency of school follow-up carried out by the parents of the adolescents in the reunited group (98%) compared to the parents of the adolescents in the non-reunited group (53%). Parental concern with respect to their adolescents' progress at school was much greater in the reunited group.

The parents' participation in drawing up the adolescents' plan of care and the regularity of their contacts with caseworkers were two other aspects of parental involvement analyzed. Similar to the variable measuring concern with the adolescents' school progress, both of these examples of parental engagement were associated with family reunification. The parents of the reunited group had a much higher degree of involvement in all of the aspects of parental engagement analyzed in this study. Results also showed more ambivalence on the part of the parents and the adolescents regarding family reunification in the non-reunited group. There is no doubt that this ambivalence is an obstacle to family reunification.

Placement Factors

The final category analyzed included factors linked to the adolescents' placement history and conditions related to the last placement before leaving care. Results indicate that the total number of months spent in care, the number of placements, and the type of resource in which the adolescent was placed were significantly associated with family reunification. The adolescents reunited with their families had spent less time in care overall (an average of 17.5 months compared to 41 months for the non-reunited group); a higher proportion of them were placed only once (63% versus 45%); and they were more frequently placed in one substitute care setting (75% compared to 43%).

Analysis of the factors related to the maintenance of contacts between the adolescents and their families showed some interesting results. Some of the young people in our sample were not able to spend time in their family. Permission might be refused because of a tendency to run away, or because of the seriousness of the acts of delinquency committed. The results showed that a significantly higher number of adolescents in the reunited group were free to leave their placement facilities in order to visit with their families.

In spite of some missing data, the analysis revealed a strong association between parental visits and family reunification. A higher proportion of the young people in the reunited group were visited by their parents while in care (97% compared to 40%). These observations would indicate that the parents of the adolescents in the reunited group tended to remain present in their children's lives when the latter were placed in care.

Discussion

In our sample, a higher proportion of girls than boys reunited with their families at the end of their placement. This non-significant but worrying result is in concordance with the findings of Harris and Courtney (2003). In view of these results, it is legitimate to ask why boys are less likely than girls to achieve family reunification when they leave their placement situations. Is it because of the nature of their behavioural problems?

Several researchers have studied the relationship between behavioural problems and family reunification. However, since these studies do not share a common definition of behavioural problems, it is difficult to compare results. Some of the studies considered problems such as delinquency and drug addiction (Bullock et al., 1998; Jones, 1998); others focused on functioning problems or specific handicaps such as mental deficiency and physical health problems (Courtney, 1994, 1995; Courtney, McMurtry, & Zinn, 2004; Landsverk et al., 1996; McMurtry & Lie, 1992; Wells & Guo, 1999); and certain studies have examined the relationship between multiple behavioural problems and family reunification (Teare, Becker-Wilson, & Larzelere, 2001; Thompson et al., 2001).

The results of this study show a clear association between the existence of multiple problems in adolescents and the reduced likelihood of family reunification. We can conclude that the number of problems manifested by the adolescent influences the family reunification process. It is also important to note that there was a high rate of externalized behavioural problems in our sample group as a whole. In this respect, researchers have reported that the problems of adolescents in foster care have become more serious in the last few years (Charles & Nelson, 2000; Le Blanc, 1995; Gaudet & Chagnon, 2003; Pauzé & al., 2004). It appears that, in general, adolescents in foster care are more likely to have multiple, complex problems.

A surprising finding was the significant number of the adolescents who did not benefit from any specific intervention process from caseworkers. An even more worrying finding is that most of the young people who did not receive specific services belonged to the non-reunited group. When a paucity of support is provided to the adolescents in care and their families, it is as if the adolescents no longer have a family, and that they alone are responsible for being in out-of-home care. Worse still, if no intervention is carried out with the family, there is a strong probability that family reunification will fail.

Similarly, the analysis of the activities put in place to prepare for the eventual reunification of the adolescent with his or her family showed that the non-reunited group did not benefit as often from activities such as meetings to discuss and plan for the return to the family or the intensification of contacts with the family, including visits to the family. The fact that the adolescents in the reunited group benefited more from these activities is not surprising, and the presence of other factors in the reunited group may well have contributed to this result. Nonetheless, considering that the objective in the majority of placements is family reunification, it would be better to extend these activities to all the young people in care, insofar as their individual circumstances allow.

The limited number of reunification activities for the adolescents in the non-reunited group may be due to the abandonment, or at least the diminishing prospect, of family reunification. The absence of parental involvement during the placement, for example, may indicate that such activities are superfluous.

In the same way, when we examine the results closely, we notice that parental visits have a significant association with other forms of parental involvement. As parental visits are one indicator of parental involvement, they should be strongly encouraged when family reunification is the goal. Parental visiting is a factor around which there is considerable consensus in the literature. All the studies reviewed have shown that parental visits are associated with an increased

likelihood of family reunification and/or a reduction in the length of the placement (Bullock et al., 1998; Davis et al., 1996; Fanshel & Shinn, 1978; Farmer,
1996; Gillespie, Byrne, & Workman, 1995; Lawder, Poulin, & Andrews, 1986;
Leathers, 2002; Loar, 1998; McMurtry & Lie, 1992; Millham et al., 1986; Proch &
Howard, 1986). However, a study by Barber and Delfabbro (2004) found that
parental visiting increased the probability of family reunification in the first
four months of the placement, but that this association was no longer apparent when the placement lasted for one or two years.

Parents' problems represent a factor that must be taken into account to
better understand the complicated issues of the family reunification process.
Certain problems may be detrimental to parental involvement during placement, to the maintenance of contact with the adolescent, to the level of participation in the therapeutic intervention process, and to the actual return of
the adolescent to the family. However, the analysis of an array of parental problems did not yield significant results. The fact that a portion of the data was
unavailable, particularly in the case of the fathers, made the analysis of these
problems difficult. Two of the mothers' problems showed a significant association with family reunification: drug and/or alcohol abuse and domestic violence. Several studies have concluded that substance abuse by parents reduces
the likelihood of family reunification, or causes it to fail (Blanchard, 1999;
Frame & al., 2000; Hoffman & Rosenheck, 2001; Smith, 1999; Smith, 2003;
Terling, 1999).

It is essential that closer attention be paid to the reasons for the end of placement, particularly in light of the reality of the non-reunited adolescents. These
adolescents, who appear to be the most troubled, with no other options and no
clear plans for the future, are obliged to leave care because they are no longer
covered by the YPA at age 18. They are forced to leave care whether they are ready
for this transition or not, or, more to the point, whether they have been prepared
for the transition or not. For these adolescents to become responsible citizens,
to integrate into society and into a particular community, it is essential to prepare them for exiting care and to do so before their eighteenth birthday. Rigorous and systematic planning is needed that takes into account the particular
reality of all adolescents and the options available to them at discharge. If started
at the beginning of the placement, it is more likely to improve their future life
chances. This would not only contribute to preparation for family reunification,
but might also prevent some adolescents from being abruptly abandoned as
soon as they leave foster care.

Implications for Future Research

Future research should be carried out on a longitudinal basis using the method of event-history analysis. Event-history analysis, like logistic regression, makes it possible to verify the effects of several variables on the probability of family reunification, and unlike logistic regression, it allows us to consider the probabilities of family reunification as a continuous function in time (Delfabbro, Barber, & Cooper, 2003). Future studies in Quebec cannot overlook the effect of time in the process of family reunification; thus it is important to refine our research methodology and undertake longitudinal studies with larger samples, using event-history analysis.

Moreover, further research should approach family reunification not as a single event, but as part of a continuum, as has been proposed by Pine, Warsh, and Maluccio (1993) in their definition:

> Family reunification is the planned process of reconnecting children in out-of-home care with their families by means of a variety of services and supports to the children, their families, and their foster parents or other service providers. It aims to help each child and family to achieve and maintain, at any given time, their optimal level of reconnection, from full re-entry of the child into the family system to other forms of contact and visiting that affirm the child's membership in the family. (p. 6)

At the Fourth International *Looking After Children* Conference Project at Oxford University in 1999, Maluccio and Pine presented this same definition, adding the phrase "… and to contact with family even after the termination of parental rights and responsibilities." One presumes they were referring to open adoption as well as permanent care. For Maluccio and his colleagues (1994), family reunification refers to the quality of relationships, not necessarily the place where the child is living. Taking cultural diversity and the changing definition of "family" into account, a wider concept of family reunification is needed (Thomlison, Maluccio, & Wright, 1996). In this broader view, family reunification allows the child to form different levels of reconnection, not only with the family of origin (Jackson, 1996) but also with the community, if he or she has been placed outside of it (Petr & Entriken, 1995).

In addition to viewing family reunification as part of a continuum, future studies should take into account the concept of family reunification elaborated by Delfabbro and his colleagues (2003). These researchers suggest that reunification should be understood as either a passive or an active process: passive when family reunification occurs without intervention, due to changes in the situation of the young person in care, such as an improvement in the health of a parent or the release of a parent from prison; or active when it occurs follow-ing intervention by caseworkers, such as parenting skills training and conflict resolution. In these two cases, the family reunification process is experienced dif-ferently, and therefore it is likely that different results will be obtained.

Finally, to contribute to the body of knowledge on family reunification, we must carry out studies that identify the most effective services (Goerge, 1990; Teare, Furst, Peterson, & Authier, 1992). These types of studies can lead to improvements in practice among adolescents and their families when they are in the process of reunification, and also to the development of programs that encourage this process. When we look at the many programs of this kind devel-oped in the United States, it is hard to imagine that we can achieve best prac-tice without them.

Conclusion

The results of our study provide greater awareness of the factors that influence family reunification outcomes for adolescents placed in residential settings. The factors identified help to establish targets for action in establishing more effective practice and better service planning for the adolescent. According to Cordero (2004), this type of research contributes to the development of a best practice model.

The limitations of our study, particularly the lack of details concerning each adolescent's individual case, may hinder our full understanding of the effects of certain factors. In general, however, it is apparent that the situations of the adolescents in the non-reunited group are more complex than those of the ado-lescents who reunited with their families.

The results regarding the association between the length of placement and family reunification speak in favor of starting family reunification planning as soon as youth enter out-of-home care. The entry can be a key moment with respect to the process of returning home (Bullock, Little, & Millham, 1993). By preparing for and planning the exit from the very beginning of placement, the adolescent immediately becomes involved in the trajectory of a life project, whether it is family reunification or an alternative plan. This would also make possible the early identification of those who are likely to achieve family reuni-fication and those for whom that probability is low. With adequate planning for the end of placement, the adolescents and families aiming for reunification will be more likely to achieve it, and those adolescents obliged to look at other alter-natives, including independent living, will also benefit from a better prepara-tion for that crucial transition.

In conclusion, we argue that it is important to change the way adolescents in substitute care are viewed and treated. These vulnerable young people are not a priority for policy-makers, even if some will find themselves literally in the street at age 18. Once they are placed, they and their families need enhanced support services to allow them to develop in a positive manner.

17

Aging Out of Care and the Transition to Adulthood: Implications for Intervention

Varda Mann-Feder

The purpose of this chapter is to highlight critical areas for intervention with Canadian young people who are exiting care to live on their own as young adults. The chapter is based on a review of literature documenting the clinical and developmental issues that arise in this population. It draws on recent outcome research, findings regarding normative transitions in developing countries, writings on termination processes in residential treatment, and the results of the author's own program of qualitative research.

Outcomes for Youth Leaving Care

As many as 6,000 youth in Canada leave government care (foster homes, group homes, and residential treatment) every year because they have reached the legal age of majority and must move out on their own when services end (Flynn, 2003). Despite the fact that most of these young people are compromised developmentally, many as victims of abuse, neglect, and abandonment (Mann-Feder, 2007), they have no choice but to live independently at an earlier age than other Canadians (Rutman, Barlow, Alusik, Hubberstey, & Brown, 2003). This is commonly referred to as "aging out" of care (Courtney & Heuring, 2005).

A growing body of outcome research indicates that young people do not adjust well once leaving care, and many suffer from social exclusion, material disadvantage, and marginalization (Stein, 2006). A recent review by Tweddle (2007) states: "(in) looking at recent Canadian, American and International research on what happened to youth who age out of the child welfare system …

the findings show a consistently disturbing pattern of poor outcomes" (p. 15). These poor outcomes were documented as early as the 1980s (Meston, 1988; Raychaba, 1993), and despite numerous efforts at program development since that time (Collins, 2001) there are few indications that our interventions are any more successful now.

Studies continue to demonstrate that youth who age out of care do not function well as adults. They are more likely than other young people to be: undereducated; underemployed or unemployed; living below the poverty line; and incarcerated, homeless, or dependent on social assistance (Courtney & Heuring, 2005; Osgood, Foster, Flanagan, & Ruth, 2005; Rutman, Hubberstey, & Feduniw, 2007; Tweddle, 2007). They are at high risk for early parenthood, substance abuse, and mental health problems (Rutman et al., 2007). To make matters worse, recent research suggests that adjustment problems in the transition to adulthood have far-reaching effects that can compromise development throughout life (Osgood et al., 2005). The costs to society of the failure to successfully launch young people who are leaving care are considerable.

Data on Normative Development

While legislation in most Canadian provinces terminates substitute care at age 18 or 19, and even earlier in some cases, there is significant evidence that young people all over the industrialized world are taking longer than ever to move out on their own (Arnett, 2007). The average age for home leaving in North America and Northern Europe is now between 25 and 30, and up to 40% of home leavers return at least once before moving out permanently (Arnett, 2006). Young people in many countries are also marrying and having children later (Molgat, 2007). This has prompted developmental psychologists to propose a new life stage between adolescence and early adulthood, which begins at age 18 and lasts until at least the mid-twenties. This stage has been dubbed "Emerging Adulthood" (Arnett, 2007), and inherent in its formulation is the view that the attainment of an autonomous adult lifestyle is a gradual and incremental process which is not complete until the late 20s or early 30s.

Economic realities have played a major role in the lengthening of the transition to adulthood, as securing permanent employment is a longer and more complex process than ever. The consequence of this delay in the attainment of financial independence is that the degree of parental assistance required post-adolescence has increased significantly. Emotional and financial support provided by parents facilitates an extended period of semi-autonomy for young people (Osgood et al., 2005), which in turn exacerbates and lengthens the process of identity development (Coté, 2006). Erik Erikson's (1968) original concept of a moratorium is relevant to discussions of Emerging Adulthood (Côté, 2006). In his theory of psychosocial development, adolescents require an extended period of freedom from responsibility so that they can experiment with different roles in order to develop a healthy sense of adult identity. The theory of Emerging Adulthood acknowledges that while identity exploration may begin in adolescence, identity consolidation is supported by a moratorium that continues beyond the teen years.

During the moratorium in Emerging Adulthood, young people can undertake progressive attempts at autonomy, beginning with the freedom to make small everyday decisions and extending over time to include control over the rhythm of their own comings and goings. At the same time, they renegotiate their relationships with the adults who care for them, resulting in "a shift in power, agency, responsibility and dependency between Emerging Adults and their social contexts" (Tanner, 2006, p. 27). Optimally, young people also experiment with longer absences from home and eventual attempts at moving out. Practising with independence in larger doses over time facilitates a shift from external to self-regulation (Tanner, 2006). Healthy development requires that significant adults will stand by while a young person experiments with independence, but remain ready to step in and take over if they falter and fail. The safety net in Emerging Adulthood is similar to the psychodynamic concept of refuelling in toddlerhood, when a child's repeated experiences of moving away from a safe haven, usually an attachment figure, are best balanced with the ongoing provision of a secure base (Kroger, 1996). In Emerging Adulthood, young persons without a safety net experience insecurity, which (as in toddlerhood) will further compromise their ability to explore and develop a healthy sense of adult identity.

Research does confirm that young people today do seek a period of freedom and experimentation after adolescence, and are reluctant to embrace commitment in their 20s (Arnett, 2007). However, Emerging Adulthood is qualitatively different from adolescence or early adulthood, and findings from cross-cultural research have identified five unique features of this phase: residential, occupational, and relational instability; active engagement in identity explorations; reported feelings of being in-between; a focus on self; and, lastly, a strong sense of future possibilities (Arnett, 2000). While Emerging Adulthood is experienced as a turbulent time, research also suggests that life satisfaction and feelings of well-being increase over the course of this stage. Even many disadvantaged young people experience Emerging Adulthood as a time when change is possible, and express strong optimism that they are going to get where they want to be in life (Arnett, 2006). However, the outcomes of this stage are heavily dependent on an individual's personal resources, the availability of support, and access to appropriate opportunities for exploration.

Comparing Youth Leaving Care to Their Age Cohorts

The contrast between the findings of researchers focusing on normative development and the literature on youth leaving care is striking. Youth in care are more marginalized than ever, as the gap between their experiences and those of their age cohorts who live at home is continuously widening (Munro, Stein, & Ward, 2005). As these researchers noted, youth in care are expected to live autonomously at a much earlier age than other young people; they have fewer internal resources and less support on all levels. Most came into care with a history of early trauma and problematic attachment. Relatively few youth leaving care can rely on family members or the system they have left to provide financial help or even consistent involvement (Stein, 2006). As stated by Arnett (2007), "the lack of family connection and support experienced by Emerging Adults who have been in care does not bestow on them a freedom that allows them to be self-focused in their pursuit of self development" (p. 115).

Youth leaving care express less hope about the future than other Emerging Adults, and do not necessarily look forward to being on their own (Stein, 2006). They lack peer support (Mann-Feder & White, 2004), which is a critically important resource in normative development. As these authors note, there are even indications that youth leaving care do not anticipate the same age-related pleasures as other young people when thinking about the benefits of moving out on their own. Compounding all this is the fact that youth leaving care struggle with even greater ambivalence about growing up than other young people. They are faced with the need to develop an adult sense of self without a safety net while coping with the emotional impact of terminating a period in substitute care.

How Being in Care Compromises Development in Emerging Adulthood

Like other Emerging Adults, youth leaving care face the necessity for identity explorations that will help them to achieve some measure of independence. Yet, they rarely have access to critical ingredients required for the successful development of autonomy. This author undertook a qualitative study, in partnership with a scholar in organizational development, which looked at how agency structure and policy impact on youth transitions. Front-line staff and managers were engaged in a method of organizational analysis (Guérard, 2008) with a focus on the mandate of launching clients at the age of majority. Results suggested that our organizations may not be geared to facilitate healthy development in Emerging Adulthood (Mann-Feder & Guérard, 2008). Most substitute care environments are not flexible enough to tolerate much experimentation. At the same time, the apparent need to contain and maintain control over youth in care may limit the degree to which young people can experience any degree of self-regulation prior to leaving (Mann-Feder & Guérard, 2008). Organizational requirements that residential beds be used at close to 100% capacity precludes ease of movement in and out for Emerging Adults in care. The youth often are not even active participants as decision-makers in their own discharge process. This deprives them of an opportunity to practise critical decision-making skills, despite indications that involving them is growth-promoting and can even result in improved care plans (Crowe, 2007). Certainly our findings indicated that the timing of a move from care can be more reflective of administrative considerations than any true assessment of young persons' readiness or even desire to move out on their own (Mann-Feder & Guérard, 2008).

The provision of a safety net is often beyond the capacity of most substitute care facilities (Reid, 2007). Youth may not have even had the opportunity for consistent relationships with adults given high turnover rates of staff, especially in group care facilities (Courtney & Heuring, 2005). This deprives them of relational safe havens and lasting involvement with reliable role models. The rigidity of agency and governmental requirements usually precludes any option for returning to care if needed (Stein, 2006).

The net result of these deficits in our systems of care is additional trauma: that of being pushed into instant adulthood (Stein, 2006). The emotional impact of leaving care adds to the challenges associated with the transition to adulthood.

The Impact of Leaving Care

For most young people, leaving care represents both an achievement and a loss. In many cases, it means leaving the only safe place a young person has ever known (Mann-Feder & Garfat, 2006). At the same time, it forces these young people to revisit the conditions of their original placement, resurfacing issues of separation and loss in relation to family. The transition from care evokes re-mourning (Gordy-Levine, 1990), especially because in most youth-serving agencies moving out on one's own is a default option, after multiple attempts to reintegrate into the family have failed (Mann-Feder & White, 2004).

Young people who age out are in the position of having to face what they do not have (family) at precisely a time in their lives when they need a supportive social network the most. While it has been documented that a significant percentage of youth who age out of care do return home eventually (Bullock, 1995), few can rely on active support during their transition out of care (Courtney & Heuring, 2005). In addition, research suggests that when they do return home later, they tend to have serious family difficulties to contend with, suggesting that these young people "must often weigh the benefits of ongoing family contact against risk" (Courtney & Heuring, 2005, p. 43).

The pain associated with family relations in youth who have been placed is compounded by a natural tendency for all adolescents to focus on childhood trauma as part of their identity explorations. At best, this is an opportunity to re-experience the injury and master it psychologically (Kroger, 1996). However, this can also lead to regression, and a recurrence of behavioural problems that have long seemed to be resolved (Gordy-Levine, 1990; Mann-Feder & Garfat, 2006). Some young people become so enraged and non-compliant, or depressed and apathetic, that they cannot engage constructively in programs designed to prepare them for leaving care. They may be so caught up in their feelings that they resist the transition. "Agencies and foster homes are not always able to tolerate this regression, and sometimes, the result, ironically, is an abrupt discharge from care" (Mann-Feder, 2007, p. 6). Thus, a period of transition from care, if it exists at all, may be aborted for those young people who may need it most, resulting in their being "discharged and displaced" (Rutman et al., 2007, p. 46). At best, the transition is "compressed and accelerated" (Stein, 2006, p. 197), and "akin to an 'expulsion'" that leaves the youth "adrift and alone" (Rutman et al., 2007, pp. 3, 45), at a time when they are vulnerable and emotionally volatile. These sudden departures deprive youth leaving care of a critical period of emotional healing (Reid, 2007), which should be a cornerstone of any discharge from care (Mann-Feder & Garfat, 2006).

Implications

There is ample evidence that policies and practices in relation to youth exiting care in Canada must change. There is also a great deal of consistency in the results of outcome research. These results are also remarkably compatible with new data on the nature of the transition to adulthood.

The process of leaving care to live on one's own is a complex one, which encompasses both the developmental tasks of Emerging Adulthood and termination processes that bring forward unresolved issues from the past. In many child welfare contexts, this process may be hastily attempted and poorly planned. As suggested by findings from the author's own research with youth, staff, and agency managers, a transition to living on one's own is often treated as a default option which emphasizes the failure of all attempts by professionals at successful family reunification (Mann-Feder & Guérard, 2008; Mann-Feder & White, 2004). Sufficient time and flexibility must be built into the transition process, and there must be a continuity of relationships with reliable adult mentors who can both address emotional issues and allow for adequate experimentation in the development of the capacity for autonomy. A common tendency of workers is to adopt a future focus with youth who are moving out on their own. However, each young person should first have the opportunity to re-examine feelings associated with the past (Bullock, 1995), lest these inhibit future development (Reid, 1997).

Optimally, the transition from care to independent living should take place in the context of a permissive approach that accepts behavioural regression and supports healthy experimentation over time. The encouragement of successive attempts at autonomy, beginning first with instrumental independence (tasks of daily living) and then extending to executive independence (decision-making), is optimal. The ambivalence and upheaval many youth experience in this transition should be normalized, and administrative requirements relaxed to allow for refuelling and frequent comings and goings, even beyond age of majority and well into their 20s. Our policies in Canada need to change to reflect the reality that now, more than ever, reaching the age of majority does not imply that young people are ready to function as autonomous adults.

Best practices documented from other countries suggest that strong youth participation, both in terms of individual discharge plans and policy formulation, promotes engagement and a sense of agency in youth exiting care (Crowe, 2007). "Planfulness" has been identified as an important factor in the development of late-blooming resilience (Masten, Obradovic, & Burt, 2006), and this can assist youth in turning their lives around. Involving youth in care as decision-makers makes use of natural opportunities to develop much-needed competencies for Emerging Adulthood.

There is a current example in Quebec of an attempt to develop developmentally appropriate programming for youth aging out of care. A recent province-wide initiative, *Projet des Qualifications des Jeunes,* stresses the provision of a stable long-term relationship with one adult for the highest risk youth who are exiting care (Association des Centres Jeunesse du Québec, 2008). Each young person in the program has a youth worker assigned prior to discharge who stays involved until one year after discharge. The overall goal of the program is to assist young people in developing a sense of autonomy through active involvement in the development of a life plan that takes into account their functional level of autonomy (Goyette, 2007). This plan includes both a larger vision of career and steps to establish healthy interdependence in the context of an appropriate social network. There is recognition along the way that the program needs to provide "room for youth experimentation, with a full appreciation that the process leading to independent living is full of obstacles and setbacks" (Goyette, 2007, p. 101). The program began as a pilot project in 2002, and based on the positive outcomes to date that have been documented through program evaluation, it has been implemented currently for a number of youth in each region of the province (Goyette, 2007).

While the challenges that the literature on Emerging Adulthood pose to our systems of care are considerable, the potential benefits of striving for developmentally appropriate policies and practices may be considerable as well. Researchers have consistently stressed that Emerging Adulthood is a time of tremendous flexibility and opportunity for positive change (Arnett, 2007). Our research efforts to date have focused on outcomes for youth exiting care. We need now to shift our attention to normative processes, with a view toward developing interventions and programs that facilitate healthy identity development for all youth in care.

18

Knock, Knock, Who's There … for Youth?
The Experience of Support When Aging Out of Foster Care

Deborah Rutman
Carol Hubberstey

This chapter provides a summary of selected results from a longitudinal study designed to examine what happens to youth following their exit from government care in British Columbia. The overall goal was to better understand the supports and resources that make a positive difference to youth and that help lead to successful transitions from care. The study was unique in Canada in that it was prospective. A full discussion of the study's findings can be found in the project's final report: *When youth age out of care—Where to from there?* (Rutman, Hubberstey, & Feduniw, 2007).

In this chapter, we discuss findings from the study related to the experience of support, including young people's sources of practical and emotional support, who supported them during their transition from government care, who or what was most helpful to them, and what they would have needed at the time they aged out of care. These findings are based on responses from interviews with youth one to two years after aging out of the child welfare system.

Summary of Relevant Literature

The transition from adolescence to adulthood is a time of rapid change and multiple transformations in social relations (Canadian Mothercraft Society, n.d.; Osgood, Foster, Flanagan, & Ruth, 2004). At the same time, the ways in which this transition take place have changed markedly over the past two decades, becoming more gradual, progressive, and dependent on the emotional, financial, and practical support of family (Arnett, 2007; Jones, 2002; Kufeldt & Stein, 2005). Between 1981 and 1996, the percentage of young people living at home until their early 30s increased markedly (Boyd & Norris, 1999; Myles, 2005), and census data from 2006 showed that 44% of young adults in British Columbia between the ages of 20 and 29 were living at home with their families (Statistics Canada, 2006b). For the majority of Canadian young people, leaving home—a symbol of adulthood—is often not completed until they are in their mid- to late 20s. In addition, this may involve several episodes of leaving home and moving back again before leaving permanently.

In contrast to this trend for the normative population of young people, the government's role and status as substitute parent for young people in care typically ends with finality when the person reaches an arbitrary age of majority. For these young people, leaving state care involves a transition from living with substitute caregivers, with access to a social worker, to living on their own. In addition, the leave-taking process is depersonalized in that it is based on chronological age, irrespective of developmental readiness or maturity. Unlike most mainstream youth, youth in care do not have the option of returning home in times of need. For many youth leaving the government care system, the irrevocability of this transition means that they are left at a much earlier age without the level of personal, emotional, and financial support that their mainstream counterparts can rely on (Courtney & Dworsky, 2005; Mendes & Moslehuddin, 2003; Osborn & Bromfield, 2007; Osgood, Foster, Flanagan, & Ruth, 2004).

The presence of supportive and caring relationships with adults is considered very important in facilitating young people's passage into adulthood (Canadian Mothercraft Society, n.d.; Maunders, Liddell, Liddell, & Green, 1999); as well, it is a protective factor that can help improve outcomes for vulnerable children and youth (Child and Youth Officer for British Columbia, 2006a; Kufeldt & Stein, 2005; McCreary Centre Society, 2006). Indeed, having access to some combination of formal and informal support networks has been found to be one of the factors that can make a positive difference for those aging out of care (Collins, 2001; Courtney & Dworsky, 2005; Kufeldt & Stein, 2005; Schibler & McEwan-Morris, 2006). For example, a longitudinal study in Australia found that the presence of and continuity in social supports, such as those provided by family members, partners, mentors, foster parents, social workers, and community organizations, were significant contributors to positive outcomes for young adults several years after exiting the care system (Cashmore & Paxman, 2006a; Osborn & Bromfield, 2007).

Literature from the United States, the United Kingdom, and Australia points out that youth from foster care also rely on case managers, foster parents, and social workers for support during their transition (Cashmore & Paxman, 2006; Children's Action Alliance, 2005; Courtney & Dworsky, 2005). Nevertheless, research in the United Kingdom found that support from social workers was episodic and "reactive," particularly in relation to helping youth work through residual family issues and/or helping to facilitate family connections (Dixon, Wade, Byford, Weatherly, & Lee, 2006).

Although most jurisdictions in Canada have policies relating to preparing youth in care for the transition to independence, little has been written about the extent to which youth are being actively connected with supportive networks prior to leaving care, or whom youth rely upon after leaving the care system (Schibler & McEwan-Morris, 2006). Moreover, support has tended to be described in very broad terms. This has not provided a complete picture about whom youth turn to upon leaving care, and whether the chosen support person(s) vary according to whether the youth is seeking practical, financial, or emotional assistance. In Canada, longitudinal research on outcomes for Canadian youth from care is essentially non-existent, and has been recognized as a major knowledge gap by researchers, practitioners, and policy-makers alike (Craig, 2001; Schibler & McEwan-Morris, 2006; Tweddle, 2005).

In order to begin addressing this knowledge gap, the authors undertook the *Promoting Positive Outcomes for Youth from Care* project. As a secondary aspect of the research, the project explored whether and how the provision of "peer support" made a difference to youth following their exit from care. As reported in both our Interim and Final reports, our findings suggest that the social support networks for many youth during and following their exit from care are quite fragile (Rutman, Hubberstey, Barlow, & Brown, 2005; Rutman et al., 2007). Some of these results are discussed in this chapter.

Methodology

The study employed a longitudinal research design and followed a cohort of youth in transition from care over a 2.5-year period. The research plan called for youth from care to take part in a total of four interviews, scheduled six to nine months apart. In keeping with research exploring people's lived experiences, the project was informed by qualitative methodologies; as well, the research was informed by participatory methods whereby those who have direct experience with the focal issues are centrally involved in the research process (Barnsley & Ellis, 1992). The project team was composed of two researchers with experience undertaking academic and community-based research, and two former "youth in care" experienced in providing peer support.

A volunteer sample of 37 youth, living in two communities in British Columbia (a metropolitan centre and a small city), participated in the study at Time 1. To be eligible, youth who were in care had to be 19 years of age in 2003 or be turning 19 in 2004. Over three-quarters of the study cohort were female (78%; n=29). At Time 1, 46% were under the age of majority (i.e., under 19) and 54% had already aged out of care. Our sample of 37 youth represented 27% of the total population of youth (n=135) who would be aging out in 2003 or 2004 and who lived in the study's catchments areas (Russell, 2004).

Given that this was a prospective study involving a disadvantaged and transient participant group, we anticipated that participant attrition would likely be an issue. Indeed, as youth "aged out" of care, a number of participants were lost due to attrition. At Time 2, four youth were lost; at Time 3, an additional seven were lost; and by Time 4 five more dropped out. Thus, there were 21 participants who remained in the study at Time 4. Table 1 shows participation in the study over time by gender.

All participants were lost because the research team could not locate them, and not because participants refused to be interviewed; regardless of the reasons, participant attrition represents a limitation in interpreting results.

Semi-structured interviews involving both fixed-choice and open-ended questions were carried out as guided conversations about participants' experiences. Interviews took about 60 minutes and were carried out in a private location of the participant's choice. An informed consent process was adhered to prior to commencing interviews.

Our interview guide was developed following a review of the literature and consultations with other researchers in this field. Interviews covered young people's experiences in relation to a wide range of life domains. With regard to social support, the interviews explored young people's sense of connectedness with family, practical and emotional supports, and community involvement. In

Table 1 *Participants by Gender at Different Time Intervals*

Time	Gender		Total
	Female	Male	
Time 1	29	8	37
Time 2	27	6	33
Time 3	20	6	26
Time 4	17	4	21

the Time 4 interview, additional questions were included that focused on social support needs during and following their departure from care.

The interviews were not audiotaped; however, detailed notes were made by interviewers at the time of the interview, with every effort made to record participants' comments in their own words and terminology. In keeping with established qualitative data analysis techniques, the interview data and emerging themes were reviewed and discussed multiple times by all team members as a means of researcher triangulation.

Results

Case Stories

We begin with two brief case stories which illustrate the highly varied nature and level of social support experienced by those participants when leaving care.

Shawna

Shawna entered government care as a young teen. According to Shawna, her mother was depressed and unable to care for her, and they were not getting along. Shawna subsequently went to live with her father. That did not work out, and she became homeless for a period of time. When this was reported to authorities, Shawna ended up in care, first in a receiving home, followed by a foster home.

Shawna did not complete Grade 9, and at the time of leaving care had just quit her part-time minimum wage retail job. She reported smoking cigarettes daily, drinking daily, and using marijuana several times a week.

Despite the circumstances that led to her entering foster care, Shawna had a strong family support network, comprised of her grandparents, boyfriend, mother, and father. Shawna said she felt closest to her mother, whom she spoke to daily, and she was satisfied with the level of emotional support she experienced.

At the time of our first interview, Shawna was about to turn 19 and was anxious to leave the care system. She said she "wanted to be independent" and was looking forward to "a new job, moving, and figuring things out with her boyfriend."

At the time of the final interview, Shawna was living with her boyfriend and his parents and continued to report having a very strong social support network, including her grandparents who "were there to help [her] with whatever [she] needed and no matter what the circumstances were." Her support network included her parents, boyfriend, and friends, and connections with these individuals were also listed as the most important relationships in her life.

Although she still had not completed high school and continued to work at part-time, low-wage retail jobs, Shawna reported that she had quit smoking and using marijuana. She also reported a noticeable drop in her consumption of alcohol. Of these changes, Shawna said, "When I left care I was drinking and doing a lot of drugs. Then I completely stopped after I left." Shawna attributed this change in lifestyle and behaviours to the presence of her boyfriend, and "wanting to have kids and not screw myself up."

Susan

Susan's mother had bipolar disorder and was physically and emotionally abusive. As a result, Susan came to the attention of the child welfare authorities at age 10 and entered foster care at the age of 14.

Susan reported few natural supports in her life. At each of the four interviews, Susan said she had limited contact with all of her family members, and there was no one in her family with whom she felt connected. Two former workers—a social worker and a youth worker—were her primary and only consistent sources of practical and emotional support. As well, Susan reported experiencing post-traumatic stress disorder and seeking psychiatric help for this.

Susan became pregnant one month after leaving care. She approached her social worker and asked to be taken back into care, but was told this was not possible. Susan stayed with her mother for a brief time before accessing community-based pregnancy-related supports.

Susan's pregnancy gave her access to a number of community resources, such as housing and support for pregnant teens, Best Babies, and an alternative high school for girls that included child care. These became Susan's primary sources of support during this transitional period. In addition, Susan was committed to completing high school and continuing her education.

At the final interview, Susan was living in low-income supportive housing. Although the Ministry had taken her daughter into foster care twice over the preceding two years, Susan had custody at the time and was confident that her life was now stable and that she would be able to continue to care for her daughter. While Susan said she had only one close and trustworthy friend, living in the housing complex gave her access to a women's support group, which she cited as a primary source of support. Having access to support for psychiatric issues was important in promoting Susan's increasing stability over time and her ability to manage her level of stress.

When asked if she would have wanted access to supports/resources beyond the age of 19, Susan stated: "Yes, I wanted to have more transitional supports; I felt forced to leave [care] and was totally unprepared." She elaborated that she was lacking "emotional and financial support, a safe place to live, someone to listen to me, and someone to care about what I was concerned about."

Summarized Responses to Research Questions

Family Relations and Social Support During the "Aging Out" Period

Based on analyses of our four waves of interviews, more participants said they felt connected to their sibling(s) than to parents or extended family members (Rutman et al., 2007), and these feelings of connectedness to family did not change markedly over the study period. Similarly, the frequency of contact with family did not change substantially following participants' exit from care. Overall, about half of the participants felt connected to their mother, while the majority said they felt disconnected from their father.

In terms of social support, over the four waves of interviews, participants' sources of support decreased slightly. By the end of our study, the number of participants naming a parent as a support person had decreased. Similarly, over the course of the study, there were more participants who said they did not have close and trustworthy friends.

Who Helped or Provided Support When First Leaving Care?

Participants were asked who helped or supported them when they first left care. All but one young person named at least one person who provided support when they first left care; however, many of these participants named only a single person. The most frequently named category of support person was the youth's (former) social worker: "The social worker stayed in touch. She would call and she would point me in the right direction."

For the majority of participants, at least one of the support person(s) named was a "natural" (i.e., unpaid) support person such as a family member, boyfriend/partner, or partner's family. Nevertheless, several youth only named people who, at the time, would have been a paid worker or caregiver—for all of these youth, the person named was either a social worker or a caregiver. Among these youth, three suggested that their social worker or foster parent remained involved as a support person after they had reached the age of majority. For another two, it was unclear whether the support person remained in the young person's life after the individual was no longer involved as a paid worker.

Roughly half of participants named a family member (i.e., a parent or a member of the extended family) as the person(s) who provided them with support. At the same time, only one youth named two different members of the family as support people. In some cases, responses were qualified in some way, e.g.: "parents assisted *with money*"; "a teacher at the school provided emotional support"; and "Mom provided support *at the time*" (emphasis added).

Three participants named their partner/boyfriend as being someone who provided support to them during the transition from care. As well, two young women named their partner's family as supports; for one of these participants, the boyfriend's family was named as support people even though the boyfriend himself was not.

People Counted on for Practical and Emotional Support Two Years Post-Care

The majority of respondents at Time 4 said they had someone that they could turn to for day-to-day practical support. Nevertheless, a number of participants reported that they had no one they could call for this type of support, and about one-third of participants named only one person. In terms of emotional support, all but one participant at Time 4 reported that they currently had a source of emotional support. However, as with practical support, a considerable number of study participants named one support person only.

Moreover, closer examination of the data showed that many participants had a very limited circle of people they felt they could rely on for practical support. Family members—that is, parents, siblings, and grandparents—were named as a source of practical support by about half of the participants. However, very few participants named more than one family member, and most participants were very specific in terms of the family member whom they named, i.e., they named a sister or their mother, but rarely did they name a combination of family members. In terms of emotional support, a theme emerging in the data was that youth were more likely to name siblings and various extended family members than parents.

Partners (i.e., boyfriend, girlfriend, common-law spouse, or ex-boyfriend) were frequently named by participants as people who provided practical and emotional support. Among female respondents who named only one source of support, their boyfriend was most frequently named. For example, Shawna described the positive effect her boyfriend had on her substance use. A few participants also spoke of their boyfriend's parents (or in one case, ex-boyfriend's parent) as a key source of support.

Only a few current and/or former service providers (i.e., paid support people) were named as people whom youth relied upon for either practical or emotional support. As discussed in our final report, it is also interesting to note that the frequency with which service providers and caregivers were named as support people by participants steadily diminished over the course of the study (Rutman et al., 2007). This likely reflects the fact that by the final interview all participants were over the age of majority, which also meant that they had limited access to youth-oriented community-based services and fewer opportunities to be involved with paid support people such as child and youth care workers. That said, and as Susan's situation illustrated, pregnancy could result in increased access to community resources, and former social workers were sometimes an important source of support. One person named a former social worker as the sole source of practical support, and two youth named service providers only (e.g., a youth worker, the peer support worker available through our research project, and professional counsellors who facilitated a support group) as their key sources of support for emotional concerns.

Who Provided Unconditional Acceptance?

Participants were also asked who cared about them and accepted them unconditionally. Again, the majority named someone. However, several participants included their infant son or daughter on the list, and of these participants, all but one named only one other person in addition to their son or daughter. Most often, the other person named was a boyfriend. One participant named only her son. For these participants, being totally accepted was in large measure tied to their role as parent and being in a relationship.

Presence of a Support Network

At Time 4, participants were asked: "Do you currently feel like you have a support network?" Approximately two-thirds said "yes." Those named included the participant's boyfriend or girlfriend and the partner's family, friends, current counsellors, former social worker and/or youth worker, individual family members, and their children's social workers. In contrast with the seven youth who named their partner (or partner's family) as members of their support network, only two youth included their mother and/or father as part of their network.

At the same time, about one-third of these participants stated that they either did not have a support network or that they were not sure they had one. Several expressed doubt that they had anyone to whom they could go in a crisis. As one youth stated, "I'm not sure. Sometimes, but [the network] isn't always there when I need it."

Another youth wondered about the true depth of her network and/or the reliability of her support people, as indicated in her response: "Not really. [I have] no one to fall back upon or who is reliable."

Similarly, two stated that they felt as though they were on their own, although one of these participants indicated that, relative to when she first left care, "was pregnant, had no transportation, was missing her youth worker, and had $175 to prepare for the baby," she felt the need for a support network less acutely at this point in time.

Who or What Has Been Most Helpful In or Since Leaving Care?

Another question asked about who or what was most helpful in or since leaving care. Consistent with the responses to a number of other questions, the most frequently reported response was a "boyfriend" or "girlfriend." As one youth said: "My boyfriend [was most helpful]. Before him, there was no one."

Various family members, most often a sibling, were also said to have been quite helpful to youth. Young women often named their boyfriend's family; indeed, these youth were more likely to name their boyfriend's family than their own parents as most helpful.

None of these participants named their (former) social worker as most helpful, even though it was evident from earlier questions that their social worker had helped and/or supported them when they first left care. However, one participant did include her former foster parent as someone who was most helpful.

A few participants spoke of a financial resource (e.g., an inheritance), a personal quality (e.g., inner strength or a feeling of confidence), or a goal-oriented activity (e.g., going to school) as something that helped them the most. Finally, one participant included her infant child among those who had been most helpful (she also named her sister and her family); this suggests that the baby was a key focus of this participant's life, and that, for her, transitioning from care coincided with transitioning into motherhood.

What Did You Need That You Didn't Have When You Left Care?

Participants' responses to this question reflected a wide variety of needs at the time of leaving care. Overall, most youth reported needing financial and/or material resources and basic knowledge or skills in order to live independently. Indeed, only one youth reported "having pretty much everything that [I] needed" when leaving care.

The most frequent response, stated by nearly half of participants, was a need for additional financial support or "backup" savings. Following this, a common need was for a driver's licence. Additional needs voiced by participants included: support in learning about various community resources and how to access them; assistance in finding safe housing; assistance in obtaining employment; assistance in obtaining medical or dental coverage; and material goods such as a vehicle, furniture, and food.

As well, two participants spoke of needing emotional support. Generally, the comments of these young people underscored the fact that their needs for financial, practical, and emotional support were intertwined.

Summary and Conclusion

As noted in the introduction, this study was unique within Canada in that it was a prospective, longitudinal exploration of the experiences of youth from government care, rather than a retrospective review, based on a series of face-to-face interviews with youth. Among our most notable findings was that several participants reported having no source of practical support, and one youth had no one who could be relied upon to provide emotional support. Although it is arguably positive that the majority of participants could identify a source of both practical and emotional support, the "bad news" reality was that at least half of the youth in this study were either without social support or had only one source of support. These young adults did not have a support network. They had, at most, one or two sources of support.

Another noteworthy finding was the importance of the participant's boyfriend or girlfriend and the boyfriend's family, in particular, as a source of both practical and emotional support. Apart from the Cashmore and Paxman (2006a) study, the importance of a partner and the partner's family in providing support has largely been overlooked in research on young people. This phenomenon should be investigated more thoroughly by practitioners and researchers to understand better what difference they make to young adults' sense of security, stability, and/or social connection. At the same time, given that our study was longitudinal and we were able to observe the flux and fragility in participants' personal relationships over time, we had questions about how enduring those relationships were, and/or how isolated and vulnerable youth might feel when this relationship was the only source of social, emotional, and financial support. What this likely speaks to is the need for practitioners to facilitate a wider supportive network for young adults, and to consider the partner's family as a potential ally or resource in this endeavour.

When asked to look back at who had helped them at the time that they left care, youth most frequently identified social workers or family members. This suggests that social workers were initially a strong source of both practical and emotional support for participants, and continued to fulfill this role in a voluntary capacity for a few participants. Nevertheless, it was family members and partners that many youth perceived to be the most helpful in the process of transitioning from care, and they were the ones who tended to remain part of the youth's support "network" over time.

Siblings were a more important source of family support for participants. It is likely that youths' relationships with their siblings offered a measure of safety inasmuch as they had a shared family history and possibly a shared experience of living in care. In view of our study's findings, practitioners are urged to explore ways to help sustain, nurture, and expand positive sibling relationships so as to be supportive over the long term.

With respect to the question of what youth said they most needed or could have used when they left care, the highly practical nature of youths' needs was striking. Even more striking was how basic these needs were, particularly in relation to the kinds of skills and resources that mainstream youth typically possess before they begin living on their own. For example, in this study, many participants identified having a driver's licence as something they wished they had achieved prior to leaving care. In B.C., under the graduated licensing program, this can take several years to complete, and at least for the first year, the process requires having an adult present in order to practise driving. Hence, a driver's licence requires the availability of several things: access to a vehicle, the financial resources to pay the costs associated with driving and test-taking, and a committed adult as guide and mentor. The desire of young people for additional financial resources post-care is not a surprise, and throughout the study, many young people expressed worries about their finances since leaving care. For many, the poverty that they fell into after leaving care was clearly a serious problem that made them vulnerable to a host of other negative and potentially tragic consequences.

Finally, youth in care need to feel ready to age out of care. This means, in part, having a strong supportive network and having continuity in their social connections (Cashmore & Paxman, 2006a; McCreary Centre Society, 2004, 2006; Samuels, 2008). This also means ensuring that they obtain the foundational resources, skills, and supports they identify as important in helping them get launched to living on their own. More importantly, this process needs to be a gradual and supported process, not unlike that experienced by their mainstream peers. To gauge whether youth are ready to leave care, we believe that practitioners need to work with youth to identify people who can become part of a true broad-based support network that includes both natural supports (i.e., family members, partners, partners' families, friends, co-workers, and support group members) as well as others, including former caregivers, social workers, support workers, teachers, counsellors, and those connected with other community-based resources.

19

Providing a Seamless Continuum of Care
Themes and Implications

Kathleen Kufeldt
Brad McKenzie

L egislation that allows the state to intervene in the lives of children and families is based on the principle of children's best interests: these include the rights of children to be protected from abuse and to receive a certain standard of care (i.e., to be free from neglect). When that intervention requires removal of children from their family, the state takes on parental responsibilities. Although public parenting is somewhat different from private parenting, it should achieve the same standards as those exercised by a responsible parent with adequate resources. However, state intervention and care of children does not always reach that goal. Unlike the experiences of children raised within their own families, children in care are subject to services that are highly fragmented and discontinuous. Part II presented research that examined services within the three major phases of state intervention: before, during, and after care. This concluding chapter begins by explaining what is meant by a *seamless* continuum of care. This is followed by a discussion, first of the difference between public and private parenting, and then of the messages conveyed by the chapters in this section. It concludes with implications for policy, practice, and research.

A Seamless Continuum

A relatively *seamless* continuum of care would contribute to continuity of care. Such a continuum would include preventive services, family support services, and placement within a kinship or friendship community, or in inclusive foster care when removal of a child is necessary, as well as support when returned home, and after care. Working toward seamlessness and continuity would do much to prevent the extent of hurt and damage that too many children currently experience. It should also help to prevent recidivism. The challenge in child welfare is to think of ways in which the current unravelled, partitioned, and discontinuous pathway through the system can be restitched into a seamless whole. Unless and until services are improved, they will be vulnerable to headlines such as Libin's "Critics say it's time to rein in child welfare agencies" (Libin, 2009, p. A1). A letter to the editor in response to Libin's article identified some of the real dilemmas that child welfare agencies face, including the inevitable pressures of the job and insufficient foster homes, and suggested that "We need to find an effective way for the child protection community to distinguish between parenting that is 'good enough' and parenting that calls for some intervention" (Monaghan, 2009, p. A13). The editors of this book would go further and assert that the majority of families whose children reach the attention of child welfare services could be assisted in being "good enough" parents if there were more worker time and resources spent on support and prevention. It is ironic that the least well resourced and serviced parts of the continuum are the beginning and the end, before and after care.

So what are the connecting threads that can be used to stitch the various parts together? First and foremost is the connection to family, friends, and community. If services can be brought to the family, and children maintained in their own homes, there is no broken link. When children enter care, continuing family connections can maintain the link. Similarly, when young people leave care, services should be designed in order to maintain a link to significant former care providers and workers in order to provide needed continuity and support.

Public versus Private Parenting

The "good enough" parent is first and foremost the attachment figure that all children need, a source of security, who usually provides the unconditional love that Bronfenbrenner (1979) described as the most essential need of children. Good parenting includes many practical and emotional tasks that parents provide for their children on a day-to-day basis. There are great similarities in what most people want for their children and what they do in order to achieve those goals. Parents want their children to be healthy, happy, to have friends; they would like them to know how to behave and to keep out of trouble, and they want them to grow up with skills, motivation, and abilities which will allow them to achieve a satisfactory lifestyle for themselves and their own families as they progress into adulthood. The challenge that faces agencies with child welfare and child protection responsibilities is to replicate the task of the good parent. Unless and until there is acknowledgement of the inherent differences between public and private parenting, it will not be easy to meet that challenge.

By Whom Are Children Parented?

The question of who is the parent is the first major difference. This does not arise in the ordinary family. Where divorce or separation occurs, parents may decide amicably the issue of custody, or the courts may decide for them. But neither ceases to be a parent, and the children know their parents. When children enter care, the issue of who does the parenting is much more complex. Most foster carers do a good job in parenting, but are limited in their abilities to (1) provide the children with a sense of permanence, (2) decide what is in the children's best interests, and (3) make decisions in most areas that affect the children's lives.

Permanence is an elusive goal, even when a child becomes a permanent ward. Admirable work and research by Maluccio and others (Barth, Courtney, Berrick, & Albert, 1994; Maluccio, Fein, & Olmstead, 1986) is available, but underutilized. Changes in legal status, workers, and placements interfere with children's abilities to put down roots and have the sense of permanence that children raised by their own parents take for granted. Decision-making is the purview of whoever is the child's worker at the time. Foster carers may know the child better, but it is not common practice to consult a foster parent, the children's own parents, or others, such as school personnel (Tuff, 2007). Yet foster carers and school personnel carry out most of the duties of the good parent. And as the developers of the *Looking After Children* protocols warned, "when responsibility for a child is divided among a number of people there is always the risk that necessary actions will be overlooked" (Parker, Ward, Jackson, Aldgate, & Wedge, 1991, p. 130).

How Is Their Progress Assessed?

Parents assess their children's progress in formal and informal ways. Good parents can tell whether their child is happy or sad, tired or hungry, sick or well, and will respond accordingly. They ensure that their children are well nourished, have sufficient sleep, time for play, and exposure to interesting experiences. On a more formal level, there will be immunizations as well as periodic medical and dental checkups. Once the child enters school, report cards and parent-teacher interviews inform them of progress. Family pictures assist in providing the child with a sense of history, continuity, and belonging.

The experience of the child in care is different, particularly where there are changes in foster carers and/or social workers. Research has shown that medical records and school records are not always well kept or accurate. Foster carers do not always have the child's history, and can miss subtle cues that may indicate the child's needs. Changes in foster homes very often trigger a change in schools, and reports of the child's progress may be missing. Children who initially came into care because of abuse may be relabelled later as the problem (Kufeldt & Klein, 1998). This is not conducive to good progress or accurate assessment.

How Are Plans Made for Children and by Whom?

Parents make plans for their children based on their knowledge of their needs, aspirations, and best interests. Ostensibly, for the child in care, plans are made by the child's social worker. These may, or may not, be endorsed by a family court judge. Plans are also subject to the availability of resources; too often these plans are crisis driven rather than developed purposively and proactively. Unlike plans made by a responsible parent, plans for young people in care may not necessarily be based on an intimate knowledge of what might be in their best interests. In Tuff's case (2007), a social worker she had never met before overruled the advice of her foster carers and school counsellor.

Who Checks That Plans Are Successfully Completed?

When plans do not work out in the way that was intended, parents will make the necessary adjustments. Checks and balances for the child in care depend on many factors:

- Does the child still have the same social worker?
- Has the foster care placement remained stable?
- Who is checking health and school progress?
- Does the agency have a systematic protocol for checking outcomes?
- Who is prepared to advocate for the child if difficulties occur?

The first national Canadian study using the *Looking After Children* protocols found deficiencies in outcomes for children in care but had this to say:

> It was very clear from the analysis of the data that those matters within the purview of the foster parents were well looked after ... It may well be that foster parents

could attend to many other aspects of the child's developmental needs if information and authority were shared. (Kufeldt, Simard, Vachon, Baker, & Andrews, 2000, p. 229)

Studies have shown that foster carers have a good capacity to work with social workers and to engage children's own parents in the care of their children (Champion & Burke, 2006; Kufeldt et al., 2000; Palmer, 1992, 1995; Parker et al., 1991). Clearly better outcomes could be achieved and heavy demands on social workers reduced if there were more sharing of the tasks, greater collegiality, and more acknowledgement of foster parents' and teachers' abilities.

The State of the Continuum of Care: What Does the Research Tell Us?

The first section on early intervention provides a number of important messages. It began with a discussion of differential response, and the need to develop a more accessible range of family-friendly services to support the well-being of children and their parents. Part of that approach might include bringing services closer to the day-to-day lives of children and families such as within schools, health centres, and family resource centres. Chapter 7 outlines some of the benefits of more accessible services; however, the challenge, if this approach is to be expanded, is do so in such a way that does not isolate workers from their support systems. Physical accessibility must be coupled with support services and personal approaches to families that transcend the investigative approach inherent in the child welfare system. Over thirty years ago Goldstein (1973) described an approach that could reduce power imbalance and promote partnership, but as Chapter 8 reminds us, too little has been achieved in the ensuing years. The search for a seamless approach will be futile if more efforts are not made to engage the whole family from first referral to case closure. *Projet famille* in Chapter 9 reminds us of the complexity and multi-dimensional nature of the problems that bring children and families to the attention of the child welfare system; the corollary, as they suggest, is to work with the whole system, in their case using the McMaster Model of Family Functioning.

The importance of family and family connections continues to pervade the next section dealing without out-of-home care. Kinship care and inclusive foster care respect the children's need to know and be connected to their roots. There is growing recognition of this fact, but, as these chapters show, widespread implementation is not yet a reality. There is also too little recognition of some of the differences between the needs of kinship and foster carers. In Chapter 13,

Swan and Twigg draw needed attention to the important fact that there are other children in the foster care system, the foster parents' own children. These children and foster children impact on each other through their interactions and the responses of the parents. The children of foster parents need to be recognized and included in collaborative practice. As in the earlier edition of this text, Anglin describes group care as a useful and often preferred resource for those children unable to benefit from family-based care. The out-of-home care section concludes with a review of adoption. Here, too, the theme of connection to family of origin is pervasive. Adoption is changing, and is more likely now to recognize the importance of prior relationships. Nevertheless, new challenges have emerged. These include international adoption, which separates children from family, language, and culture, and the lack of supports for adoptive parents who, often unwittingly, adopt children who challenge them with a range of special needs.

Finally, we come to the "end of the road" with respect to the care continuum—and here indeed it becomes unravelled, unless the young person has a family situation to return to that is now capable of providing support. Not surprisingly, Simard and Poirier, in Chapter 16, found that those most likely to return home were those who had ongoing contact during care. For the others the transition is too often abrupt, with little preparation for the realities of coping on one's own. Chapter 17 draws attention to the increasingly longer period in current society between adolescence and fully attained adulthood, now termed *emerging adulthood*. Young people from the care system, arguably the most fragile and in need of support, are too often denied the opportunity of this extension. As emphasized by Rutman and Hubberstey in the following chapter, they need a strong network of support and continuity in relationships and connections. The authors also suggest that these young people need to feel ready for independence. At the same time, many who feel ready cannot manage without ongoing support, and sadly, these young graduates of the child welfare system are overrepresented among street youth.

Implications for Policy, Practice, and Research

Policy

Parents do not abandon their children when they reach the age of majority. There are lifelong connections, and the availability of support to the extent of parental ability. When the state becomes parent, should there not be a similar commitment? Canada's National Youth in Care Network claims that the standard of *good enough parenting* has not been achieved in this country. In an open letter to the government of Canada, youth in care noted that the government is their parent, and raised questions about the quality of care being received from this parent (National Youth in Care Network, 2000). Extended parenting beyond the age of majority is not only desirable in developmental terms, but also may be cost-effective. Packard, Delgado, Fellmeth, and McCready (2008) completed a prospective cost-benefit study of a transition guardian plan program for former youth in foster care between the ages of 18 and 25 in California. The authors project a benefit to cost ratio of 1.5 to 1 when both input and reduced social costs are included in the calculations. United Kingdom experts (Parker et al., 1991; Ward, 1995) designed the *Looking After Children* protocols to improve outcomes by reflecting the core principles of parenting and partnership, with the added admonition that good outcomes are dependent on good parenting. The first national Canadian trial of their Assessment and Action Records (Kufeldt et al., 2000) attested to their ability to promote its philosophical underpinning, as the following vignette illustrates:

> The coordinator of the project in one agency received a call from a care leaver who had participated in the project. His call went something like this: "You remember that stuff we did, it was like you were being like my parents, yes? Well, I need to have some dental work done but can't afford it." The coordinator found some funds and the dental work was done. A year later the same young man called and said that he felt ready and thought he should go to University, could his old "parents" help? Fortunately this agency had a scholarship fund and he received the help he needed. (personal communication)

Although there is increased attention to the need for growing supports for youth aging out of child welfare care, not all agencies currently have the capacity to respond to such requests and as a result not all care leavers are as fortunate. After care services that are provided have specific conditions attached, are time-limited, and are usually confined to those who have been in permanent care.

Changes in policy that would promote better parenting of abused and neglected children would, we contend, reduce overall social service expenditures in the long run. More importantly, they would improve outcomes and provide a better quality of life for young people whose disadvantaged position is no fault of their own. Specific requirements are:

- flexibility in funding so that resources can be directed to the specific intervention required, whether this be family support, alternative care, or after care;

- early decision-making and early permanency planning to ensure that children have the opportunity to grow up in a stable home environment; and
- a reduction in the fragmentation of services through better coordination and collaboration.

The implementation of a guaranteed annual income would do much to reduce the involuntary neglect that can occur in families living in poverty. Taking children in need into care is not the answer. Providing parents who love their children and have aspirations for them with the means to fulfill their parental role would benefit children, families, and society itself.

Practice

It is imperative that child welfare services refocus on the child. Implicit in many of the chapters in this book is that services must become child-centred rather than agency-, program-, or even family-focused. With respect to the latter, we are not arguing here against family-focused services and support, only that a particular child's needs, including the need for alternative care, not be trumped by a focus on family preservation. And we have strongly emphasized that when it is necessary to take a child into care, this action should be accompanied by continuing family contact.

If one thinks in a child-centred way, then the program can be tailored to fit the child's needs rather than have the child fit the program. A case in point is the decision-making at the point of entry into care. Arbitrary decisions to remove a child are often made on the basis of what *degree* of risk emerges on a risk assessment scale. If one instead asks what *kind* of risk, and to which aspect of the child's development, it may be possible to develop a plan that is targeted, maintains continuity, and ensures the child's safety.

The range of possibilities is many if we focus on the child rather than the program. Over the years, innovative projects have been tested and found to be effective. Bringing them into mainstream practice does not necessarily follow. Some examples are the use of practical assistance to families to fulfill basic needs, with daycare or homemaker support if necessary (Pecora, 1995); five-day foster care (Loewe & Hanrahan, 1975); involvement of parents in group home care (Simmons, Gumpert, & Rothman, 1973), extended family care; and shared care with foster parents (Kufeldt & Allison, 1990; Maluccio & Sinanoglu, 1981).

Chapter 10 suggests ways in which the role of foster care can be expanded to reinforce connection and continuity. Such alternatives avoid the abrupt transition and loss of all that is familiar that too often occurs at the time of entering and leaving care.

The quality of service is dependent on quality of service providers. Child welfare and child protection work require more than entry-level qualifications. We recommend:

- that newly graduated workers serve a period of internship;
- that all schools of social work provide specialized training in child welfare, either within current curriculum or as a postgraduate certification;
- that child welfare agencies provide more comprehensive in-service training programs for their staff;
- that data collection be designed to reflect outcomes, not simply outputs; and
- that agencies commit to searching out and implementing services that reflect better practice, such as those highlighted in Part IV.

Research

Too little is known about either the short- or long-term outcomes of child welfare interventions, and the termination of federal funding for the Centre of Excellence for Child Welfare (effective March 2010) will not help in developing more evidence-based research in Canada. The use of the *Looking After Children* protocols in Canada, Australia, Sweden, and the United Kingdom is beginning to highlight where some of the deficiencies lie in the short term. Studies that have focused on adults who received care (e.g., Fanshel, Finch, & Grundy, 1990; Fanshel & Shinn, 1978; Kufeldt, 2003) provide some information on the consequences of changing policies. However, such studies remain few and far between. Experimental studies are inappropriate, but in Canada the National Longitudinal Survey of Children and Youth (NLSCY) can allow for natural comparisons. Australia and the United States have similar population-based studies that are also relevant. In this chapter we repeat the recommendation noted in Chapter 15 that Statistics Canada enter into partnership with child welfare authorities in order to include samples of fostered and adopted children in NLSCY. Research is needed to improve our understanding of the determinants and predictors of outcomes, both negative and positive. There is an urgent need to avoid the former and enhance the latter in order to choose the best pathway to adulthood for each individual child.

Indigenous Issues in Child Welfare

Introduction

It was clear to the editors, when preparing the first edition of this text, that greater attention should be devoted to the special concerns of Indigenous communities and their children. Part III focuses on some of these concerns. The contents of Chapter 20 are compelling in that they confirm the deleterious effects of colonization on Indigenous families, not only in Canada, but in the U.S., Australia, and New Zealand. The sad legacy is the disproportionate numbers of children of Indigenous descent within the child welfare systems of these countries. Chapter 21 traces the historical reasons for overrepresentation in Canada, and presents findings from the 2003 *Canadian Incidence Study of Reported Child Abuse and Neglect* (CIS–2003) that relate to this issue. These results provide empirical evidence for the concerns expressed by organizations such as the First Nations Child and Family Caring Society of Canada. These chapters provide the groundwork in identifying the many challenges faced by Aboriginal communities and the child welfare agencies that serve these communities. In turn, there are suggestions for actions that may help to redress the historical and contemporary effects of colonization in these communities. Recommendations include interventions that are based on a respect for culture and the traditional strengths of these communities, including engagement with kinship networks.

In Chapter 22, McKenzie and Shangreaux outline a general framework for "community caring" in First Nations child and family services. This approach incorporates community building principles, which are then illustrated by a case study that highlights results from one agency's experience in implementing this approach.

Chapter 23 is written by an Aboriginal scholar who focuses on the educational disadvantages faced by Indigenous children and youth in care. Using research based on the lived experiences of former Indigenous youth in care, Johnson links their growing awareness of the impact of colonization on their experiences in care and within the educational system to the need for social and educational supports that are respectful of culture. The star blanket serves as a powerful metaphor for the kinds of supports that need to be provided for current Indigenous children and youth in care.

The final chapter in Part III summarizes themes, describes some of the implications for research, policy, and practice, and provides recommendations important to building a better future for children of Aboriginal ancestry who receive services from the child and family welfare system.

20

Disproportionate Representation of Indigenous Children in Child Welfare Systems: International Comparisons

Clare Tilbury
June Thoburn

The overrepresentation of Indigenous children in the child welfare system is a major policy challenge for wealthy countries with colonized Indigenous populations. The legacy of colonization is evident in the huge gaps between Indigenous and non-Indigenous well-being on most social and economic indices. These inequalities are evident in the child welfare system, with Indigenous families much more likely to be subject to government surveillance and intervention than other families. Therefore, making effective responses to child maltreatment in Indigenous populations is a vital element of achieving social justice goals of equity, fairness, and non-discrimination.

Globalization has made an international perspective increasingly important in child welfare policy, practice, and research. Governments and researchers look toward developments in other countries in searching for policies and strategies to address complex social problems. This chapter compares the situation of Indigenous children in the child welfare systems of Canada, Australia, New Zealand, and the U.S. Using administrative data, levels of disproportionality and/or disparity are presented at two points: entry to the statutory child protection system, and placement in out-of-home care. While it is recognized that Indigenous peoples in different countries are unique, and local solutions are required, the chapter examines what can be learned from international comparisons.

A note on terminology: there are important political debates about terminology in relation to "race," "ethnicity," and "culture." In this paper, we use the term "Indigenous" in line with the *United Nations Declaration on the Rights of*

Indigenous Peoples to denote and recognize the sovereignty of the original owners of the lands subject to discussion. More than any other characteristic, it is sovereignty that distinguishes the position of Indigenous peoples from other racial or ethnic minority groups, and which imposes particular obligations on government. The term "Indigenous" also recognizes the shared oppression of Indigenous people caused by colonization. The process of colonization has been similar in all countries selected, involving dispossession of land, forcible relocation to prescribed geographical areas, unpaid labour, and racism. Notably for this chapter, it also involved the regulation of family life and childhood through the separation of children from their families (although not in New Zealand), institutional care, assimilation, and denial of cultural identity (Cross, Earle, & Simmons, 2000; Haebich, 2000; Keddell, 2007; McGillivray, 1997). This history compels us to consider the particular dimensions of Indigenous disproportionality in the child welfare system.

Literature Review

The possible reasons for the overrepresentation of Indigenous children in the child welfare system range from the macro level to the micro level. It is often explained with reference to macro factors such as the long-term social and economic impacts of colonization on Indigenous family life. These include problems such as poverty, high levels of drug and alcohol abuse and family violence, health and mental health conditions, unstable housing, and the intergenerational loss of parenting skills (Donald, Bradley, Day, Crichley, & Nuccio, 2003; Human Rights and Equal Opportunity Commission, 1997; Trocmé, Knoke, & Blackstock, 2004). Needs may be especially acute in rural or remote Indigenous reserves or communities with little sustainable employment and limited infrastructure in the form of education, social services, health services, or adequate housing. Therefore, Indigenous overrepresentation in child welfare reflects Indigenous disadvantage, and is consistent with other indicators showing that Indigenous children are worse off than non-Indigenous children (for example, educational participation and attainment, health, suicide rates, juvenile justice arrests, and incarceration).

If proportionately more Indigenous families experience hardships, live in disadvantaged communities, and have more unmet needs, then children and their parents are more likely to be in need of culturally appropriate support, practical assistance, and therapeutic services, and more of the children are likely to be at risk of harm. These structural factors can affect rates of entry into the family support and child protection systems. Regrettably, reliable data are not available from any jurisdiction on the comparative usage of family support services by Indigenous and non-Indigenous families. Where data are available, as with the formal child protection and out-of-home care systems, the above factors play a major part in explaining why Indigenous children are reported and may be substantiated more often as having been maltreated. Related influences on both entry rates and placement rates are that Indigenous parents may have less access to informal family and social supports (because extended families and communities have few resources), and formal support services may be less available or less effective (either insufficient to meet demand or lacking cultural competence in assisting Indigenous families) (Courtney et al., 1996; Donald et al., 2003).

A range of micro factors are also implicated in Indigenous overrepresentation in child welfare. These include discriminatory practices of reporters (such as police, teachers, and health workers); institutional racism or system biases such as a lack of cross-cultural competence, culturally inappropriate or inaccessible service delivery; Indigenous families being less likely to have legal representation or advocacy in decisions on removal and placement; and discriminatory practices of child welfare workers (Hines, Lemon, Wyatt, & Merdinger, 2004). Stereotypes may influence worker decisions in a range of ways. Although not comparable to the circumstances facing Indigenous populations, a review of research on the overrepresentation of Black children in the child welfare system in England points to issues such as poverty, language barriers, child-rearing differences, and discrimination in child and family assessments (Thoburn, Chand, & Procter, 2005; Chand & Thoburn, 2006). Differences in child-rearing, such as more laissez-faire supervision or the involvement of the extended family, may be viewed as deficits (Earle & Cross, 2001). It has been argued that, under Australian law, decisions about "the best interests of the child" in placement or reunification have minimized the importance of children's cultural identity to their well-being (Bamblett & Lewis, 2007). Such practices can result in higher placement rates, as well as children staying longer in care. The level of disproportionality is affected by length of stay, and African-American children have been found to leave care at a slower rate (Harris & Courtney, 2003). Other case factors may affect exit patterns, such as Indigenous children being more likely to be placed in kinship care placements, which tend to be more stable but often receive less support, and are associated with lower reunification rates (Hill, 2006; see Wulczyn, 2003, in relation to African-American children).

There have been mixed results from research efforts to disentangle the effects of race from the influences of poverty and hardship. Some studies examining disproportional representation have found that economic factors (poverty and receipt of welfare payments) are more statistically significant than race in determining child welfare involvement, but the interaction with other factors such as family structure, parental substance abuse, and mental ill-health is less clear (Hill, 2006; Miller, 2008). It has been pointed out that poverty and associated problems are not race-neutral (Needell, Brookhart, & Lee, 2003). In the case of Indigenous people, disadvantaged living conditions are a consequence of colonization. That is, the process of colonization produced alienation, marginalization, disempowerment, welfare dependency, deprived neighbourhoods and communities, and intergenerational poor parenting, and these conditions adversely impact upon children's well-being (Bamblett & Lewis, 2007; Blackstock & Trocmé, 2005; Blackstock, Trocmé, & Bennett, 2004). To some extent, the debate about causation highlights different perspectives on understanding causation and the extent to which both direct causes (the stated reasons for a child entering the care system, such as parental substance misuse or incarceration) and indirect causes and cumulative effects (the reasons behind high rates of substance abuse and incarceration for Indigenous people) are being investigated. Taking into account only direct or immediate causes misses effects that operate over time, or cumulative disadvantage. For example, there may be discrimination across generations, whereby discrimination against one generation can negatively affect health, work opportunities, or wealth accumulation to diminish opportunities in later generations; it can also operate across domains, such as living in a depressed neighbourhood, which lessens a person's chance of a job and good health care (Blank, Dabady, & Citro, 2004). The extent to which both individual and structural conditions are considered also reflects different theoretical positions, whether psychological, sociological, or ecological, and different political stances regarding the role of the state and how individual and social responsibilities are allocated.

It would seem to be important in addressing Indigenous overrepresentation to acknowledge the burden of history, but also to recognize the multiple individual and structural factors in operation today, to tackle both causes and symptoms, and to influence both policies and practice. This study aims to assist in understanding and responding to this complex issue through a cross-national examination of Indigenous disproportionality and disparity.

Method

Child welfare administrative data which identify the Indigenous status of children were collected from four countries: Canada, the U.S., Australia, and New Zealand. In the countries with federal systems of government, several provinces or states were also included: Manitoba and Alberta in Canada, Washington and California in the U.S., and New South Wales and Queensland in Australia. Data are presented on levels of disparity and disproportionate representation for children at entry to the statutory child protection system (subject to a child maltreatment substantiated investigation) and for children in out-of-home care. Data are for 2005–6 or as otherwise indicated.

These data are important for understanding broad trends and patterns, and provide contextual information for cross-national comparisons and initiatives. However, they have limitations. First, differences in legislation, policy, and service systems affect how child welfare data are collected. For example, the criteria for recording a report or substantiation, and what counts as out-of-home care, vary between jurisdictions. Second, the Indigenous status of children coming in contact with the child welfare system may not be accurately recorded. This is particularly problematic at the early stages of intervention, when there is less known about a child's background. Children who identify as multiracial are not always included in Indigenous counts. As a result, the levels of overrepresentation at report and investigation stages are likely to be undercounted. In the U.S., children may be subject to tribal jurisdiction under the *Indian Child Welfare Act 1978* (ICWA), so not all children of Indigenous heritage are included in states' routinely collected administrative data, also under-counting Indigenous disparity. A further limitation relates to cross-sectional out-of-home care data. Cross-sectional samples represent the "stock" of children subject to intervention, but not the "flow" of children through the system. These data can be biased in that cross-sectional samples of children in care generally contain a higher concentration of children who stay a long time (Wulczyn, 1996). For example, smaller disparities between children entering care compared to "in care" indicate that, to some extent, overrepresentation is a legacy of children taken into care up to 16 years earlier. Other limitations on the comparability of the data will be discussed later in the chapter.

The administrative data for the study were mostly publicly available, but some were obtained directly from government agencies and some reported in research. While national data are available in the U.S., there are issues with aggregating data across states. The "big picture" can overshadow both intrastate and interstate variances. For example, it is reported that there is no disproportional representation of Indigenous children in 31 states, whereas in six states Native American children are over three times more likely to be substantiated than other children (U.S. Department of Health and Human Services, Children's Bureau, 2006). Canada has no national child welfare data collection, so data here are from the 1998 *Canadian Incidence Study* (Trocmé et al., 2004) and other reported research. Data were also obtained from provincial agencies, although the mix of government and non-government service providers poses challenges to uniform data collection. Australia has national data, but again, it is not always reliably aggregated because of the differences between state jurisdictions. New Zealand has a national system, and aggregate data were able to be supplied.

Findings

Table 1 shows the level of disproportionate representation in out-of-home care. The disproportionality metric indicates the extent to which Indigenous representation in the child welfare system is proportionate to their representation in the population. It is calculated by dividing the percentage of Indigenous children in substantiations and out-of-home care by the percentage of Indigenous children in the total child population (0–17 years) (Hill, 2006). Indigenous overrepresentation is evident in all jurisdictions at both decision points. New Zealand, California, and the U.S. as a whole have relatively low levels of dis-

Table 1 *Indigenous Disproportionality: Percentage of Children in Substantiated Maltreatment Cases and Out-of-Home Care Who Are Indigenous*

Jurisdiction	Percent in Population (0–17 years)	Percent of Substantiated Cases	Disproportion-tality at Substantiation	Percent of Children in Out-of-Home Care	Disproportion-ality in Out-of-Home Care
Australia (2006–7)	4.5	20.2	4.5	27.7	6.2
Australia – Queensland (2006)	6.3	16.4	2.6	28.6	4.5
Australia – New South Wales (2006)	4.0	23.9	6.0	31.1	7.8
Canada (1998)	5.0	19.0	3.8	40.0	8.0
Canada – Alberta (2007)	9.3	na	na	54.0	5.8
Canada – Manitoba (2007)	25.9	na	na	85.4	3.3
New Zealand (2007)	24.0	46.0	1.9	47.0	1.9
United States (2003)	1.0	2.0	2.0	3.0	3.0
U.S. – Washington (2006)	2.1	12.8	6.1	13.3	6.3
U.S. – California (2006)	0.84	1.11	1.32	1.41	1.7

Sources: **Australia, Queensland, and New South Wales:** Australian Institute of Health and Welfare, 2007. (Due to jurisdictional differences, totals for the whole country are not as reliable as data for each state.) **Canada:** Blackstock et al., 2004. (Due to different legislation and data collection rules in different provinces, data for Canada as a whole are not as reliable as data for each province. Data for Canada are drawn from the 1998 *Canadian Incidence Study*, but sampling issues may affect the reliability of the estimates.) **Canada – Alberta:** Thoburn, 2007; **Canada – Manitoba:** Department of Family Services and Housing, 2008. **New Zealand:** Department of Child, Youth and Family Services, 2006, and New Zealand Ministry of Social Development, 2008. **United States:** Hill, 2007; **U.S. – Washington:** Washington State Department of Social and Health Services, 2006 and 2008; **U.S. – California:** Needell et al., 2007.

proportional representation (around 2.0), whereas Canada, Alberta, Washington, and Australia have relatively high levels (around 6.0). However, the separate reporting of data from the tribal agencies probably means that the data on U.S. jurisdictions is less reliable than that for New Zealand.

Table 2 shows disparity rates per 10,000 children in substantiations and out-of-home care. The disparity rate compares Indigenous with non-Indigenous children, and is the ratio between rates for the two groups. It is calculated by dividing the rate per 10,000 of Indigenous children in substantiations and out-of-home care by the rate for non-Indigenous children (Hill, 2006). Indigenous children are about twice as likely as non-Indigenous children to be subject to a substantiated maltreatment investigation in New Zealand and the U.S., three times more likely in Queensland, and around six times more likely in the other jurisdictions. Disparity in California, with a large Indigenous population (though still comprising only a small proportion of the total population), is relatively low at substantiation and in out-of-home care. At the other end of the spectrum, there is a stark contrast between placement rates for Indigenous and non-Indigenous children in Manitoba, with Indigenous children almost 17 times more likely to be in care. Indigenous children in Canada, Washington, and the Australian jurisdictions were over six times more likely to be in care.

Table 2 *Indigenous Disparity: Ratio Between Indigenous and Non-Indigenous Rates of Substantiated Maltreatment and Placement Out-of-Home*

Jurisdiction	Rate per 10,000 Substantiations for Non-Indigenous Children	Rate per 10,000 Substantiations for Indigenous Children	Disparity Rate for Substantiated Cases	Rate per 10,000 in Care for Non-Indigenous Children	Rate per 10,000 in Care for Indigenous Children	Disparity Rate Out-of-Home Care
Australia	58	318	5.5	44	361	8.2
Australia – Queensland	69	203	2.9	45	275	6.1
Australia – New South Wales	71	535	7.5	53	570	10.8
Canada	na	na	na	na	na	na
Canada – Alberta	na	na	na	na	na	na
Canada – Manitoba	na	na	na	50	843	16.9
New Zealand	92	251	2.7	35	93	2.7
United States	na	na	2.1	na	na	4.3
U.S. – Washington	33	227	6.9	47	336	7.1
U.S. – California	na	139	1.0	na	129	1.7

Note: Sources are identical to those identified for Table 1.

There are a few studies that test the "visibility hypothesis" of racial disparity, which is that rates of entry to care are higher in localities in which the minority group constitutes a small proportion of the population (that is, they are
more visible) (Hill, 2006). For example, American Indians are a small minority (1% of child population) in the U.S., but they experience higher levels of disproportionality and disparity than African-Americans, who are a large minority
group (15% of child population). In Australia, where Indigenous children comprise a small minority, disparity levels are high. However, there are no discern-
able patterns that relate to the size of the Indigenous population in our selected
jurisdictions: for example, in New Zealand and Manitoba, where Indigenous children are a large minority, there are relatively low and very high disparity rates
respectively.

Examining disproportionality and disparity at both substantiation and
placement shows how Indigenous representation can be affected by decisions
made after referral to child welfare authorities. It is notable that in Australia as
a whole, and in both states, the level of overrepresentation increases significantly between these two decision points. There are also slight increases in overrepresentation after referral in the U.S. as a whole and the two states. Research
in the U.S. has also shown this effect for African-American children—that having been reported, these children are more likely to be investigated and substantiated, less likely to receive in-home support services, more likely to be
placed in out-of-home care, and more likely to stay longer (Courtney et al.,
1996; Hill, 2006; Needell et al., 2003). A study in Washington showed that the
disproportionality of Indigenous children increased twofold between referral
and placements over two years' duration (Miller, 2008). The disparity that accu-
mulates within the child welfare system also suggests that the differences between
countries can be explained to some extent by policy and practice. Not all disparity relates to the gap in living standards and well-being; it also depends upon
the types of child welfare services provided.

Discussion

Governments have taken different legislative, policy, and practice approaches to
providing child welfare services, and to addressing the particular needs of Indigenous children and families. Concerns about Indigenous racial disparity levels
are expressed in all the jurisdictions discussed here, but some are tackling the
issue with more urgency and with more specific strategies than others, with
varying levels of devolution of control to Indigenous communities themselves.
A major focus has been legislation or policy that encourages culturally matched

placements. While it can be argued that this improves the quality of care within the system (though quantitative as opposed to case-related evidence is not yet clear), it does not appear to be having an impact on rates of entry to care.

In the U.S., the ICWA was a major reform, aimed at reducing the high numbers of American Indian children being removed from parental care. It affirms tribal sovereignty in dealing with family matters, but there are both legal and financial limits to tribal power (Hand, 2006). The ICWA establishes procedures enabling Indigenous oversight of child welfare interventions, rather than substantively reducing child maltreatment. It has increased culturally appropriate placements, but has also been accompanied by more children in care—partly attributed to greater awareness of child abuse and neglect, partly to limited resources for prevention, and partly to population growth (Nelson, Cross, Landsman, & Tyler, 1996). Moreover, there are ongoing jurisdictional difficulties. More than half of the U.S. Indian population lives off-reserve, so they are not subject to the ICWA, and not all states provide financial support for tribal placements (Nelson et al., 1996).

Canada has taken a different approach. Rather than separate legislation, governments have taken steps to devolve child welfare powers and functions to Indigenous agencies. While this has mainly occurred for on-reserve children and families, in the province of Manitoba Indigenous child and family agencies have been given authority to provide services province-wide (Hudson & McKenzie, 2003). However, it is argued that the forms of self-management or self-determination that are being used are limited in practice through legislative limits on powers, jurisdictional problems, and funding constraints (Blackstock & Trocmé, 2005). The quantum of government funding for Indigenous agencies is also a major issue in Australia (Bamblett & Lewis, 2007). Governments in both Australia and New Zealand have a legislative obligation to consult with Indigenous children's family and community representatives. For example, New Zealand's *Children, Young Persons and their Families Act 1989* aims to place responsibility and care in the hands of members of the family group (the "family, whanau, hapu, or iwi"). In practice, however, Indigenous families and/or agencies have limited powers in relation to decision-making in these countries compared to the situation for Indigenous children living on-reserve in Canada and the U.S. (Libesman, 2004).

Australia is moving in the opposite direction to devolution, with policies of self-determination taking a back seat to "mutual obligation" and "shared responsibility" to achieve child welfare goals (McCallum, 2005). The federal and some state governments have recently introduced or announced measures that aim to reduce Indigenous family violence and child maltreatment, particularly in rural and remote communities, through banning the supply and purchase of alcohol, increased policing, and withholding income security payments from parents who do not enforce school attendance and comply with other behavioural requirements. These measures are not contingent upon either individual or local community agreement (they may be imposed), and have not been accompanied by more early childhood, family support, or treatment services.

At the micro level, workforce development initiatives such as employing Indigenous staff, and cultural awareness training for non-Indigenous staff, have been implemented in most jurisdictions, along with strategies to improve the capacity and capability of Indigenous service providers. More trained Indigenous staff are needed to make Indigenous agencies a viable reality, and to enhance the cultural competence of statutory agencies. But however necessary these micro level strategies are, bolder action is necessary in order to tackle Indigenous disproportionality in child welfare.

Implications for Policy and Practice

Indigenous community representatives and agencies in these countries have called for more resources, more flexibility as to how resources are used, greater input into decision-making at policy and practice levels, and more comprehensive child and family welfare policies to respond to Indigenous disadvantage. Addressing material disadvantage must be a priority. Research has established the link between high levels of socio-economic disadvantage and related problems, and the overrepresentation of minority racial groups in the child welfare system (Trocmé et al., 2004). In addition to parental factors, these systemic conditions need to be dealt with if child abuse and neglect are to be reduced. In wealthy countries, it is the size of the gap between rich and poor that impacts on self-esteem and affects child well-being, as well as the lived experience of poverty, so the inequality gap must be narrowed to increase child well-being (Pickett & Wilkinson, 2007).

Governments need to look beyond the child protection and criminal justice systems for solutions—to health, housing, employment, mental health, substance abuse prevention programs, education, and domestic violence services—to develop more comprehensive responses for children and their families. Strategies must aim to improve the well-being of all Indigenous children, rather than targeting only those within the purview of child welfare agencies. Alternative strategies would involve adopting more preventative approaches, providing more intensive support to parents and extended families, more voluntary and non-stigmatizing family support placements, and community development initiatives (Cross, Earle, & Simmons, 2000; Libesman, 2004). Currently most government funding for child welfare goes to out-of-home care rather than family support or family wellness programs. There are clear limitations of socio-legal investigative responses, particularly in geographically remote townships where there are few social service agencies on the ground. These reactive responses suggest individual pathology or criminality as the causes of child maltreatment, ignoring social and community-level factors. Instead of relying upon child removal, there must be positive programs to improve family functioning and relationships. This includes greater recognition of Indigenous values, knowledge, and cultural practices in developing service models (Libesman, 2004).

Consideration must also be given to changes within the child welfare system to address cumulative disparities. Practice varies in different countries in respect of placement with relatives, long-term or permanent foster care, guardianship with relatives or "strangers," and adoption by relatives or "strangers." Only Canada, Britain, and the U.S. routinely use adoption without parental consent as a route out of care, and the U.S., and to a lesser extent Canada, are the only countries that encourage the legal adoption of young children by their kinship foster carers as a route out of care. The preferred "outcome" of adoption, particularly if it involves terminating parental rights, may not be suitable for Indigenous children and families or supported by Indigenous child welfare agencies or tribes under the ICWA (Barth, Webster, & Lee, 2002; Earle & Cross, 2001). In the U.S., although a reality in the lives of many children entering care (Courtney et al., 2005), long-term "part of the family" foster care is not recognized as permanent care. This is despite growing evidence of its effectiveness as a permanence option, especially for children of minority heritage (Thoburn, Norford, & Rashid, 2000). Long-term foster and kinship care and legal guardianship are more established routes to permanence in Australia and New Zealand, and the adoption of Indigenous children is very infrequent. This is linked with attitudes toward the family, the relationship between the family and the state, professional opinions about the ability of the state and voluntary organizations to provide positive out-of-home care, the characteristics of the children entering care, and child welfare history. This is one (we would argue positive) explanation for the higher rates in care in those countries which use kinship care and long-term culturally matched foster care when children cannot return to their families.

Recommendations for Further Research

Developing effective responses to Indigenous children's overrepresentation in the child welfare system needs to be informed by a thorough understanding of the scale and nature of the problem. As a starting point, it is important for all jurisdictions to collect reliable administrative data in order to better plan and provide the child welfare services and strategies that best fit the needs of their populations and contexts. Collecting data on entrants into the care system by ethnic group (not available from Canada, as a whole, and not reliable in some other jurisdictions) is a step that could quickly be taken. It is reasonably clear that the causes of disproportionality relate to a mix of individual, family, and system factors, associated with serious social disadvantage which is a consequence of colonization. A more detailed understanding of trends and patterns over time, and at multiple decision points, will assist in designing child welfare strategies. For example, while time series data are not reported in this chapter, the disparity gap has been widening in some of the countries under discussion, and this must be regarded as very concerning. Some jurisdictions do not know whether there are different entry patterns for Indigenous children depending on age, or whether there are different exit dynamics due to more complex child needs, more kinship care, or fewer reunification services for Indigenous children. In addition to reliable administrative data, detailed quantitative and qualitative research could be used to examine the micro and service factors in jurisdictions which have achieved lower disparity rates in the coercive child welfare systems, such as New Zealand and California.

As well as research on the causes of cumulative disproportionality (when overrepresentation increases the further a child gets into the system), it is also necessary to examine the effects of the child welfare system on Indigenous children and families to observe any differential outcomes. Indigenous agencies have raised particular concern about the social and emotional development of Indigenous children in placements with non-Indigenous carers, where they may lose touch with their Indigenous heritage (Earle & Cross, 2001; Human Rights and Equal Opportunity Commission, 1997). The evidence base on effective strategies to improve the process and outcomes of child welfare interventions for Indigenous children and families is limited. In fact, given the scale of the problem, it is remarkable how little research has been conducted. It is also vital to incorporate the voices of Indigenous children, families, and communities in research, capturing their experiences and aspirations, and to ensure Indigenous community engagement in the selection, implementation, and evaluation of programs (Cross et al., 2000).

Conclusion

The reasons for the overrepresentation of Indigenous children in the child welfare system are a combination of historical and current conditions that adversely affect children's well-being. In many jurisdictions, overrepresentation becomes further entrenched through decision-making after child welfare involvement. This is a long-standing problem. Government strategies to develop more effective and culturally sensitive responses to improve the welfare of Indigenous children, in the main, have not achieved desired outcomes.

Moderate gains may be achieved through concentrating on diversion from the system following a referral, and remedial action once in the system. But for countries in which the size of the disparity gap at entry to the statutory child welfare system is marked, it is more critical to address the underlying causes of family problems for Indigenous people. Concerted action must be taken to improve family living conditions and reduce maltreatment, in collaboration with Indigenous families and communities. Current approaches move too quickly from disadvantage and need to "child maltreatment," missing out the likely need for additional broadly based family support services. Given high levels of deprivation and disadvantage, one would expect Indigenous families to have more need for supportive family services, including out-of-home care as family support, as well as needing more protective services.

Notwithstanding that Indigenous status, in itself, does not "cause" overrepresentation independent of poverty and a range of parental factors, there are problems with child welfare legislation and policies that are "blind" to race. This denies the history and impact of colonization, unequal power relations between Indigenous and non-Indigenous peoples, and inequalities across multiple social and economic domains. Thus, it is not sufficient to provide Indigenous communities with the same level or types of services as others when their needs are so much greater and the pattern of their involvement with the child welfare system is so markedly different.

21

Understanding the Overrepresentation of First Nations Children in Canada's Child Welfare System

Vandna Sinha
Nico Trocmé
Cindy Blackstock
Bruce MacLaurin
Barbara Fallon

The overrepresentation of First Nations children in the child welfare system results from complex interactions between historical patterns, social policies, bureaucratic structures, and the needs of children, families, and communities. This chapter summarizes some of the major factors that have shaped child welfare services to First Nations communities, and provides a general framework for understanding the overrepresentation of First Nations children in Canada's child welfare system. Whenever possible, data are presented on First Nations families and children. However, because First Nations child welfare has been shaped by policies targeting the broader Aboriginal population, and because First Nations children constitute the majority of Aboriginal children, Aboriginal data are presented when First Nations-specific data are not available. This chapter also includes data from the *Canadian Incidence Study of Reported Child Abuse and Neglect* (CIS–2003) to examine the types of maltreatment associated with First Nations overrepresentation in the child welfare system and describe associated child and household characteristics. Implications for policy and future research are discussed in the final section.

Aboriginal children are significantly overrepresented in Canada's child welfare system; there are multiple studies which confirm this overrepresentation across provinces (see Table 1). The *Constitution Act* (1982) recognizes three groups of Aboriginal peoples: "Indians" (now commonly referred to as First Nations), Métis, and Inuit.[1] First Nations children constitute 64% of the Aboriginal child population (Statistics Canada, 2001, 2006c), and there is some

Table 1 *Overrepresentation of Aboriginal Children in Care in Selected Provinces, 1999–2006*

Province	Aboriginal Children as a Percentage of All Children	Aboriginal Children as a Percentage of All Children in Care	Year	Source
British Columbia	7	50	2006	a, b
Alberta	8	38	2001	c, d
	9	57	2006	b
Saskatchewan	23	67	1999	c, d
	25	70	2006	b
Manitoba	20	78	2000	e
	23	85	2006	b
Nova Scotia	3	16	2006	b
New Brunswick	4	13	2006	b

[a]Foster, 2007.
[b]National Council of Welfare, 2007, p. 86.
[c]Statistics Canada, 2006c.
[d]Farris-Manning & Zandstra, 2003.
[e]Aboriginal Justice Inquiry – Child Welfare Initiative, 2001, p. 7.

evidence that First Nations children may be more highly overrepresented in the child welfare system than other Aboriginal children. For example, Blackstock, Prakash, Loxley, and Wien (2005, p. 43) found the rate of out-of-home placements for status First Nations children (102 per 1000) in three sample provinces to be three times that for Métis children (33 per 1000), and almost 15 times the rate for other children (7 per 1000). Nationally, 5.5% of all First Nations children living on-reserve[2] were in child welfare care in 2003 (Indian and Northern Affairs Canada, 2005a, p. 61), a rate estimated to be "eight times that of all Aboriginal and non-Aboriginal children living in care off-reserve" (Auditor General of Canada, 2008, p. 2).

The History of First Nations Child Welfare in Canada

The arrival of European settlers and subsequent extension of colonial policies into First Nations communities disrupted traditional patterns of care among First Nations communities. Colonization brought with it practices that resulted in the removal of tens of thousands of First Nations children from their communities. The devastating history of First Nations child welfare in Canada can be divided into three stages: the period of residential schools, the "sixties scoop," and the contemporary period (Royal Commission on Aboriginal Peoples, 1996).

The Period of Residential Schools (1890–1950)

The residential school system was the primary mechanism of colonial efforts to force the assimilation of First Nations people into non-Aboriginal society. Schools started as small, church-based efforts, but quickly expanded, shifting to an American-inspired industrial format (Milloy, 1999). An 1894 amendment to the *Indian Act* required all First Nations children to attend residential schools, and officials enforced this law through methods such as apprehension of orphaned and neglected children, coercion of parents, and the removal of children by force (Fournier & Crey, 1997; Miller, 1996). At the height of the residential school period, approximately one-third of the Aboriginal children in Canada were enrolled, and, in some areas, peak enrolment was considerably higher (Miller, 1996, p. 142).

From their inception, the philosophy behind these schools was one of "protecting" children from the perceived evils of life in their home communities by "civilizing" and "Christianizing" them, while simultaneously protecting non-Aboriginal society from the perceived threat of First Nations communities by getting rid of "the Indian problem." In the words of Duncan Campbell Scott, Superintendent of Indian Affairs, the objective of "Indian education and advancement since the earliest times" was to ensure that "there is not a single Indian in Canada that has not been absorbed into the body politic and there is no Indian question, and no Indian Department" (cited in Miller, 1989, p. 207).

The education system was a major force in the quest to assimilate First Nations people. Poor attendance (due to conflicts with traditional life patterns, parental indifference, and the daily home to school travel time), as well as the cost of building schools in small communities, made day schools an inefficient socializing force. Accordingly, government and church officials favoured residential schools, which promoted assimilation by enforcing sustained geographic separation of children from their parents and communities (Royal Commission on Aboriginal Peoples, 1996).

Once living in the residential schools, children who had already suffered removal from their families and communities were subjected to further suppression of their cultures. They were forbidden from speaking their native languages or practising their religious customs, and punished if they disobeyed these rules. In addition, funding did not keep pace with the needs of a rapidly growing school system, and children lived in deteriorating and overcrowded buildings, suffering shortages of food, clothing, and medical attention. As the residential school system expanded in the early 1900s, tuberculosis and other diseases spread through the crowded schools, and many children died from preventable illnesses (Bryce, 1922). Writing during his tenure as deputy superintendent of Indian Affairs (1913–32), Duncan Campbell Scott estimated that 50% of the children who attended residential schools died (as cited in Miller, 1996, p. 133). Accounts from the time showed that, in many schools, children were also subject to physical abuse that included beating, strapping, chaining, lashing, and other forms of severe punishment. After residential schools began closing, there were also revelations of widespread sexual abuse (Milloy, 1999; Royal Commission on Aboriginal Peoples, 1996).

In the 1940s, a special joint committee of the House of Commons and Senate, assembled to review the *Indian Act*, recommended that the residential schools system be phased out. In its place, they advocated a policy of assimilation through inclusion of First Nations children in provincial schools whenever possible. Residential school closures began in the mid-twentieth century, but progress toward dismantling the school system was slow, and the last school did not close until 1998 (Milloy, 1999).

The Sixties Scoop (1950–1980)

The shift away from residential schools, along with legislative policy, set the stage for the second period of First Nations child welfare. During this period, responsibility for "protecting" First Nations children from the perceived ills of life in their communities—"crushing poverty, unsanitary health conditions, poor housing and malnutrition" (Johnston, 1983, p. 23)—shifted from the education system to the child welfare system. Between 1950 and 1980, the child welfare system, like the residential school system that preceded it, oversaw the removal of thousands of children from their homes and communities. This period is often referred to as the "sixties scoop," a play on the remorseful words of a B.C. worker who described herself and her colleagues as acting to "scoop children from reserves on the slightest pretext" (Johnston, 1983, p. 23).

A 1951 revision to the federal *Indian Act* set the stage for provincial child welfare agencies to extend their reach into First Nations communities (Sinclair, Bala, Lilles, & Blackstock, 2004). Section 88 of the *Indian Act* decreed that provincial laws applied to all "Indians in the province" (*Indian Act*, 1985); thus child welfare in First Nations communities was identified as a provincial responsibility. However, because section 88 did not provide additional funding for the extension of such services, most on-reserve child welfare services were initially provided only in instances of extreme emergency. A gradual shift began in the mid-1950s, when Indian and Northern Affairs Canada (INAC) began providing funds for some on-reserve services; somewhat later, INAC entered into bilateral agreements that provided federal funds to support provincial provision of child welfare services (INAC, 2007; Johnston, 1983). A 1975 Supreme Court decision affirmed provincial responsibility for providing child welfare services to First Nations families on-reserve (*Natural Parents v. Superintendent of Child Welfare*, reported at [1976] 2 S.C.R. 751), giving further impetus for the extension of provincial child welfare services to First Nations communities.

The extension of provincial services to reserves led to a steep growth in the number of Aboriginal children in care. For example, Aboriginal children grew from less than 1% of all children in the care of British Columbia's child welfare system in 1955 to 34% in 1964 (MacDonald, 1983, pp. 79–80). By 1980, status First Nations children, who made up 2% of the nation's child population, represented more than 10% of the children in care (Johnston, 1983).

Reports from this period suggest that First Nations children were removed from their communities in large numbers, sometimes with no justification other than poverty or cultural differences in parenting (Johnston, 1983). In the most dramatic cases, communities lost an entire generation of children. For example, between 1970 and 1980, roughly 80 children were removed from the Spallumcheen community of British Columbia, which had a total population of less than 400 (MacDonald, 1983, p. 88). Many of the children apprehended during this period were permanently removed from their homes and communities, and over 11,000 Aboriginal children—as much as one-third of the child population in some First Nations communities—were adopted between 1960 and 1990 (Royal Commission on Aboriginal Peoples, 1996). For most First Nations children, adoption meant separation from Aboriginal cultures as well as from their families. Between 70% and 85% of all First Nations children adopted between 1971 and 1980 were adopted by non-Aboriginal parents (Johnston, 1983, p. 57). The adoptive families included many in the United States; in Manitoba, the last province/territory to put a halt to the practice of cross-border adoptions, nearly one-quarter of all Aboriginal adoptees were placed with American families in 1981 (Johnston, 1983, p. 42).

During this second period of First Nations child welfare, responsibility for protection of Aboriginal children shifted to the child welfare system, but the basic approach established during the residential schools era continued. Like the residential school system, provincial/territorial child welfare systems oversaw the separation of First Nations children from their families and communities. With few exceptions, First Nations communities had no control over child welfare activities during this period; child welfare standards and practices originating in non-Aboriginal society were simply imposed on First Nations people. Thus, the "sixties scoop," which extended into the early 1980s, can be seen as an extension of a colonial legacy of disenfranchising and destabilizing First Nations communities.

The Contemporary Period (1980–Present)

The third phase in the evolution of First Nations child welfare in Canada involves the transfer of responsibility for delivery of child welfare from the provinces/territories to First Nations communities. Growing concerns about the scale of child removal and the treatment of Aboriginal children by the child welfare system, combined with increased activism by First Nations, laid the groundwork for the emergence of First Nations child and family service agencies in the early 1980s. As earlier noted, INAC had established some informal child welfare agreements with bands and tribal councils as early as the late 1960s (Johnston, 1983). Reviews of First Nations child welfare services in Ontario and Manitoba, which took place at the end of the 1970s, spurred the further development of First Nations child and family service agencies, and the number of agencies grew from four in 1981 to 29 by 1986 (Armitage, 1995, p. 125). The rapid growth and "ad hoc" nature of the agreements between INAC, the provinces, and First Nations communities led to a moratorium on recognition of new First Nations child and family service agencies in 1986 (INAC, 2007).

In 1991 INAC lifted the moratorium and established a federal funding formula, known as Directive 20–1, for supporting First Nations child and family service agencies (INAC, 2007). From 1990 to 2008, the number of First Nations child and family service agencies grew from 34 to 108, and by 2008, First Nations agencies provided at least partial services to 442 of 606 reserve communities served by INAC (Auditor General of Canada, 2008, p. 442).

Most First Nations child and family service agencies operate under a "delegated service model" in which provinces grant community-based agencies the authority to provide child welfare services in accordance with provincial child welfare legislation and standards (Blackstock, 2003).[3] Some First Nations agencies are limited to providing services after an investigation has been completed by provincial child welfare authorities; in 2008, however, 86 First Nations agencies were fully delegated to provide a comprehensive range of child welfare services, including investigations and placement (Felstiner, 2008).

The growth of First Nations agencies attests to the resilience of First Nations peoples and to their determination to regain full responsibility for the welfare of First Nations children. Many First Nations agencies have adopted programs or practices that favour preventative, community-based and culturally sensitive approaches, thus establishing a foundation for moving away from the focus on child removal (Blackstock, 2003; McKenzie & Flette, 2003). However, many challenges remain: the role granted to First Nations agencies is still constrained by provincial legislation, and, although there are a growing number of First

Nations agencies that serve families off-reserve, First Nations communities have still not secured the right to provide child welfare services for all First Nations children. Moreover, the ability of First Nations child and family service agencies to provide effective services to families within their jurisdictions is severely restricted by inadequate funding and by disputes between branches of the federal and provincial governments over funding responsibilities.

Major Challenges and Emerging Changes in First Nations Child Welfare

The growth of First Nations agencies has been a positive step towards decolonization, but the overrepresentation of First Nations children in the child welfare system has remained a persistent problem. Indeed, as the number of First Nations agencies has increased, so has the number of on-reserve First Nations children in care. For example, the percentage of the on-reserve child population in out-of-home care grew from 3.9% in 1996 to 5.5% in 2003—an increase of 67% (INAC, 2005a).

Several studies (First Nations Child and Family Caring Society of Canada, 2005; INAC, 2007; McDonald & Ladd, et al., 2000) have identified serious flaws in Directive 20–1 and existing agreements regarding the provision of services for First Nations children. These studies concluded that jurisdictional problems, the underfunding of services on reserves, and the failure to provide adequate resources for family support programs have contributed to the increasing number of First Nations children in care and prevented the effective and efficient provision of a more comprehensive range of child welfare services.

Jurisdictional Disputes

The provision of services for First Nations families is complicated by disagreements between federal and provincial governmental departments over who should bear the costs. The Auditor General of Canada (2008) found that INAC lacks agreements clarifying federal responsibilities with some provinces, and that some agreements which do exist are outdated and unclear about the division of responsibilities. In addition, there are disagreements between INAC and other federal agencies about on-reserve services. For example, Health Canada claims that INAC bears financial responsibility for providing on-reserve children with all services available to other children in care within a province, but INAC argues that it has no authority to fund Health Canada services. Cradock

(2005) found that jurisdictional disputes over the costs of caring for First Nations children are prevalent, with 393 disputes occurring in 12 sample First Nations agencies in a single year. These disputes can result in long delays for service delivery, sometimes with tragic results. The First Nations Child and Family Caring Society (FNCFS) advocates a policy that puts children first when disputes arise. FNCFS has advocated that federal and provincial governments adopt "Jordan's Principle" (MacDonald & Walman, 2005), which would require the government department first contacted by a family to provide services to First Nations status and Inuit children without delay or disruption, and to settle any disputes regarding the sharing of costs later. Jordan's Principle has received support from the House of Commons, the Canadian Medical Association (Mac-Donald & Attaran, 2007), and many other institutions, but it has yet to be fully implemented by respective governments.

Underfunding of Services on Reserves

The federal funding formula established by INAC in Directive 20–1 applies to all reserves in Canada with the exception of those in Ontario. First Nations communities in Ontario receive provincial funding, and the province is provided with a block grant pursuant to a 1965 agreement between the two levels of government. Directive 20–1 has two basic components: an annual contribution covering agency operating costs, and payments for services to children in care (INAC, 2005b). Because the Directive 20–1 formula is not tied to inflationary increases or to the actual work performed by child and family agencies, it severely underestimates the funds needed for services in First Nations communities. The formula, which has never been significantly revised, does not reflect changes in provincial legislation or normative standards of practice in the past 20 years (Auditor General of Canada, 2008). In addition, it does not provide for expenses incurred by agencies serving communities with high child in care rates (Auditor General of Canada, 2008), agencies serving remote communities, or those serving children with complex medical/mental health or developmental needs (MacDonald & Walman, 2005). The basic flaws in the formula established by Directive 20–1 were exacerbated by a freeze on inflationary increases implemented by INAC in 1995 (Auditor General of Canada, 2008), and Loxley (2005) estimated that over $110 million in additional funding would have been needed to maintain 1999 service levels between 1999 and 2005.

No Special Funding for Early Intervention and Prevention Services

Directive 20–1 does not fund prevention or supportive services for families who retain custody of their children; funding for such services must be taken out of already strained administrative budgets. There is growing support for the provision of preventative and supportive family services across Canadian communities (Trocmé & Chamberland, 2003), and the need for such services is particularly acute for First Nations families. In comparison with the non-Aboriginal population, First Nations people have higher rates of poverty (Canadian Council on Social Development, 2006) and more acute housing needs (Statistics Canada, 2006c). Parents with fewer financial resources face greater challenges in responding to the needs of their children; in addition, low income parents often experience more negative life experiences and have fewer coping resources than others (Kessler & Cleary, 1980; McLeod & Kessler, 1990).

For First Nations people, the risks associated with their living environment may be compounded by the intergenerational effects of colonial policies which dislocated entire communities, suppressed languages and cultures, disrupted functioning communal support systems, and separated generations of children from their families. These lasting effects may be seen at the individual, family, or community levels (Evans-Campbell, 2008). For example, child removal policies may have prevented transmission of healthy parenting, instilled doubts about traditional parenting, or resulted in negative behaviours acquired in abusive, neglectful, or culturally inappropriate settings (Horejsi, Craig, & Pablo, 1992).

Research on the needs of disadvantaged families suggests that they require programs designed to address co-occurring problems by providing specialized services, high levels of contact, individualized attention, continuity over time, and crisis supports (Cameron, 2003). The design and implementation of such projects is costly, and, given research that shows a lack of voluntary services in First Nations communities (Nadjiwan & Blackstock, 2003), agencies serving First Nations families require sufficient funding in order to offer these supportive and preventative services without compromising basic child protection functions.

Emerging Changes in First Nations Child Welfare

Recent developments may signal important changes in First Nations child welfare. INAC has acknowledged the negative impact of Directive 20–1, concluding that it "has likely been a factor in increases in the number of children in care and program expenditures because it has had the effect of steering agencies towards in-care options—foster care, group homes and institutional care because only these agency costs are fully reimbursed" (INAC, 2007, p. ii). In a move to replace Directive 20–1, INAC is introducing new funding agreements, which are more flexible and more closely linked to provincial requirements, across the country. Alberta First Nations agencies have already started shifting to a new funding model, and, on average, agency funding is expected to rise by 74%, with full implementation of the new formula in 2010 (Auditor General of Canada, 2008). Similar arrangements are also being introduced in other provinces.

While it is too early to assess whether the new funding arrangement will provide more adequate support for the services so desperately needed, the change does hold some promise of support for new programs to help First Nations communities and families keep their children at home or closer to home. In addition, the First Nations Child and Family Caring Society and the Assembly of First Nations have filed a complaint with the Canadian Human Rights Commission (CHRC) alleging that chronic underfunding of First Nations child welfare amounts to discriminatory treatment of First Nations children. An October 2008 decision accepted the complaint for hearing by a tribunal, and the CHRC process may also affect funding patterns for First Nations child and family service agencies (Assembly of First Nations, 2008b).

First Nations Maltreatment Investigations: The *Canadian Incidence Study of Reported Child Abuse and Neglect* (CIS–2003)

The *Canadian Incidence Study of Reported Child Abuse and Neglect* (CIS–2003) is the only national study to collect disaggregated data about maltreatment investigations involving First Nations children (see Chapter 1 for a detailed description of study design). It provides a portrait of investigations conducted in a context shaped by the history and challenges described above. The CIS–2003 sample included Aboriginal children served by a random sample of provincial/territorial agencies and those investigated by a convenience sample of eight First Nations agencies. As indicated in Figure 1, Aboriginal children comprised 15% of the CIS–2003 sample; 12% were First Nations children (status or non-status) and 3% were Métis or Inuit.

The results presented here are based on the information reported by Trocmé, MacLaurin, Fallon, Knoke, Pitman, and McCormack (2005). These findings focus on First Nations (status and non-status) children; comparisons are made with non-Aboriginal children in all provinces and territories except Quebec, because information about Aboriginal identity was not collected there in 2003.

Figure 1 *Aboriginal Representation in the CIS–2003 Sample*

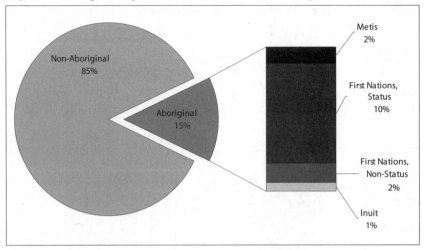

The final sample included 11,500 investigations for children, up to 15 years of age. The following analysis is based on weighted samples designed to reflect population estimates prepared by the First Nations Child and Family Caring Society using 2001 census data (see Trocmé et al., 2005).

In general, CIS–2003 results indicate that First Nations overrepresentation results from decisions made at multiple points in the child welfare investigation process. Figure 2 shows that the rate of child maltreatment investigations is much higher for First Nations children than for non-Aboriginal children (58.3 per 1000 vs. 44.1 per 1000). It also indicates that the substantiation rate for First Nations cases (30.2 per 1000) is higher than for non-Aboriginal cases (20.7 per 1000).

Multivariate analyses show that the difference in substantiation rates is explained primarily by the differences in caregiver functioning. Figure 3 shows the overrepresentation of First Nations children along other dimensions of the child welfare process. In comparison with non-Aboriginal children, First Nations children are more likely to have their cases stay open for services (64% of substantiated First Nations investigations vs. 41% for substantiated non-Aboriginal investigations), and more likely to be placed out of home, in kinship care (13% First Nations vs. 4% non-Aboriginal) and alternative care arrangements (16% First Nations vs. 7% non-Aboriginal). Multivariate analyses show that the difference in child welfare placement rates is not fully explained by maltreatment characteristics, child functioning concerns, household factors, or caregiver functioning concerns; it persists even in analyses controlling for these factors. Additional research is needed to explain this finding.

Figure 2 *Rates of Substantiated, Suspected, and Unsubstantiated Maltreatment for First Nations and Non-Aboriginal Children (CIS–2003)*

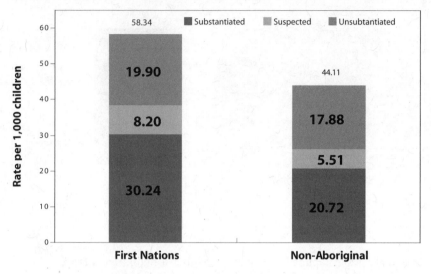

Figure 3 *Investigation History and Case Decisions for First Nations and Non-Aboriginal Investigations (CIS–2003)*

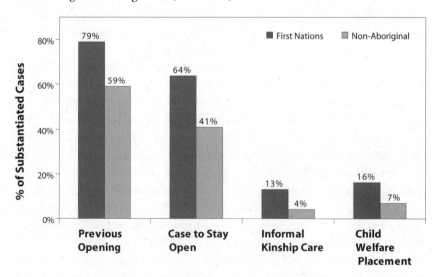

Figure 4 *First Nations and Non-Aboriginal Investigations by Substantiated Maltreatment Type (CIS–2003)*

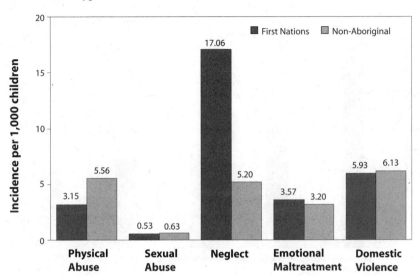

Figure 4, which presents First Nations and non-Aboriginal investigations by substantiated maltreatment type, demonstrates that the overrepresentation of First Nations children is driven by neglect cases. The rate of emotional maltreatment is slightly higher for First Nations children than for non-Aboriginal children, but rates of sexual abuse, physical abuse, and exposure to domestic violence are slightly lower. In contrast, neglect is the primary form of maltreatment in 56% of substantiated First Nations investigations, but accounts for only 22% of substantiated cases for the non-Aboriginal population. Physical neglect—in which a child is at risk of physical harm due to caregiver failure to provide adequate food, nutrition, or housing—is the primary neglect category; it accounts for 39% of substantiated First Nations neglect cases.

Figure 5 shows a pattern of income and housing need that is consistent with the high rate of First Nations physical neglect investigations. First Nations households involved in maltreatment investigations had lower incomes and poorer housing conditions than non-Aboriginal households. The percentage of First Nations households with unemployment or social assistance benefits as their primary income source was more than twice the percentage of non-Aboriginal families. The percentage of First Nations investigations involving families living in public housing was three times as high as the percentage of non-Aboriginal investigations for families living in public housing; as well, the

Figure 5 *First Nations and Non-Aboriginal Income and Housing Characteristics (CIS–2003)*

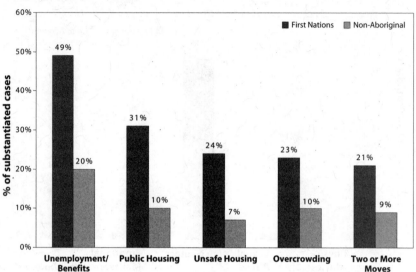

percentage of First Nations families who moved two or more times during the prior 12 months was double the percentage for non-Aboriginal families. Child and family service workers also reported that in comparison to non-Aboriginal children, a higher percentage of First Nations children lived in unsafe or overcrowded housing.

Figure 6 indicates worker ratings of concerns about First Nations female caregivers. In comparison with concerns about non-Aboriginal female caregivers, workers identified higher rates of alcohol abuse (55% for First Nations vs. 12% for non-Aboriginals) and drug/solvent abuse (33% for First Nations vs. 10% for non-Aboriginals) among First Nations caregivers. They also had more frequent concerns that female First Nations caregivers were maltreated as children, had cognitive impairments, participated in criminal activity, or had few social supports. Concerns noted for First Nations and non-Aboriginal male caregivers (not shown) revealed a similar pattern. In combination, caregiver alcohol abuse, caregiver history of being maltreated, and co-occurrence of multiple caregiver concerns provide the primary explanation for the difference in First Nations and non-Aboriginal rates of maltreatment substantiation.

Figure 6 *First Nations and Non-Aboriginal Female Caregiver Functioning Concerns*

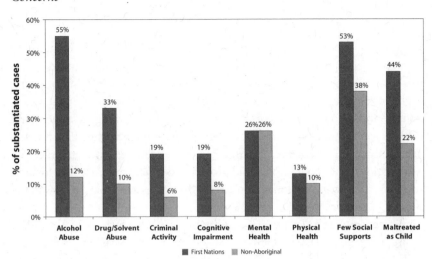

Implications for Policy and Future Research

The current overrepresentation of First Nations children in the child welfare system extends a pattern of state removal of First Nations children that is grounded in a colonial history of relations with mainstream society. More specifically, the CIS–2003 results suggest that the current overrepresentation is due, in large part, to the complex needs of First Nations families. First Nations children are more likely than non-Aboriginal children to come to the attention of child welfare authorities. The majority of First Nations investigations involve neglect, which may be tied to the low incomes and poor housing conditions of many First Nations families. Because child and family service workers identify a greater number of concerns about the caregivers of investigated First Nations children than about their non-Aboriginal counterparts, maltreatment is more likely to be substantiated in investigations involving First Nations children. Once substantiated, First Nations cases are more likely to stay open for ongoing services, and First Nations children are more likely to be placed in care than non-Aboriginal children with similar maltreatment and family characteristics.

Several policy recommendations, which flow from the discussion presented here, have been specified in prior reports and evaluations (Auditor General of Canada, 2008; First Nations Child and Family Caring Society of Canada, 2005; INAC, 2007; McDonald & Ladd, et al., 2000). First, increased flexibility in funding is needed in order to allow for the development of comprehensive preventative and supportive services that help keep First Nations children at home. Second, increased levels of funding are needed to cover preventative and supportive services, work mandated by provincial legislation, actual operations costs for agencies, cost adjustments for remoteness, costs of implementing and maintaining appropriate information management systems, and inflationary increases. Third, a solution to service delays caused by jurisdictional disputes is essential. In the short term, this means adopting Jordan's Principle of caring for children first and settling disputes afterwards. In the longer term, it means revising and refining agreements between provinces, federal agencies, and First Nations communities, placing a particular emphasis on increasing First Nations autonomy and their abilities to design and deliver child welfare services for all First Nations children. Fourth, child protection services must account for, and respond to, structural factors that place children at risk and may be beyond the control of families to address on their own.

There is also an urgent need for additional research which facilitates understanding of, and alternative approaches to addressing, the needs of First Nations children in the child welfare system. Further research is needed to understand the overrepresentation of First Nations children that has been explored in this paper. In particular, more research that follows child welfare cases beyond the investigation stage is required to understand the in-care trajectories and needs of First Nations children. In order to effectively address these needs, research which facilitates the development of culturally based programs/policies, and evaluates them according to appropriate standards, is also required. First Nations peoples have an increasing capacity to conduct their own research, and resources which support additional development of First Nations research capacity are essential to the emergence of a more comprehensive body of research on First Nations child welfare.

Notes

1 First Nations people can be divided into two categories: "status First Nations (status Indians)," who are entitled to certain rights and benefits because their First Nations identity is recognized by the Canadian government under the *Indian Act* (1985), and "non-status First Nations," whose First Nations identity is not recognized under the *Indian Act*.

2 In 2006, 46% of First Nations children (aged 0–14) lived off-reserve and 54% lived on-reserve (Statistics Canada, 2006c).

3 One notable exception is the Spallumcheen First Nation of British Columbia, which maintains sole jurisdiction over child welfare services to its members by means of a by-law that has been recognized by government (MacDonald, 1983).

22

From Child Protection to Community Caring in First Nations Child and Family Services

Brad McKenzie
Corbin Shangreaux

The negative effects of colonization on the well-being of Aboriginal children and families have been well documented both in this book and elsewhere (see among other sources Blackstock, 2003; McKenzie & Morrissette, 2003; Sinclair, Bala, Lilles, & Blackstock, 2004). These effects include parenting problems, addictions, and the overrepresentation of Aboriginal children in care. Although abuse, including sexual abuse, is a serious problem, most Aboriginal children are placed in care as a result of neglect (Blackstock, Prakash, Loxley, & Wien, 2005; Trocmé et al., 2005). Parental neglect, while not something to be condoned, is also related to structural factors in Aboriginal communities, such as inadequate housing, unemployment, and social exclusion (Assembly of First Nations, 2008a; Trocmé, Knoke, & Blackstock, 2004), or what is referred to here as "structural neglect."

Colonization has contributed to this pattern in two important ways. First, it is a causal factor in the prevailing pattern of inequality in social conditions that persists in Aboriginal communities. Second, institutional interventions—the residential school system, the "sixties scoop," and jurisdictional disagreements over responsibility (see Chapter 21; Fournier & Crey, 1997; McKenzie & Hudson, 1985)—have played a major role in contributing to the overrepresentation of Aboriginal children in care. There is no recent evidence that this pattern of overrepresentation is being reversed, even with the transfer of service delivery responsibility to First Nations child and family service agencies.

Although it is difficult to determine an accurate national count of Aboriginal children in care, among First Nations communities in Canada the number of First Nations children in out-of-home care at year-end increased by over 70% between 1995 and 2001 (McKenzie, 2002). Farris-Manning and Zandstra (2003) have estimated that between 30% and 40% of the 76,000 children in care in Canada in 2002 were Aboriginal. However, there has also been a national increase in child welfare service activity; between 1998 and 2003 the number of investigated children in Canada increased by 83%, and the number of children who experienced some type of alternative care placement increased by 56% (see Chapter 1). A more recent snapshot of one province (i.e., Manitoba) indicates that the number of children in care as of March 31, 2009, was 10.1% higher than the figure recorded a year earlier on that date (Rabson, 2009b, p. A4).

Policy and legislative changes that have placed more emphasis on child protection may explain some of these trends. The impetus for these changes has come from increasing evidence of the long-term negative effects of chronic neglect, recognition of the harm caused to children by interspousal violence, and growing recognition of the limitations of the family preservation movement. These changes have also been affected by public and political reaction to the deaths of children who had received service from or were in the care of the child welfare system. In turn, the shortcomings of an increasingly intrusive child welfare system have given rise to a more recent interest in differential response (see Chapter 6).

Alternative models of service delivery in Aboriginal child welfare which meet criteria associated with child well-being, keep children closer to home, reinforce their cultural identity, and reduce the number of children in care remain a continuing challenge in Canada. It is also self-evident that the ability of child welfare agencies to address the structural factors leading to child neglect is seriously restricted by current funding models and related legislative mandates. However, new models of service delivery can make a difference. Central to this goal is a shift in focus from a service model preoccupied with the child protection function to one that incorporates increased emphasis on prevention and family service and builds capacity for community caring.

Following a brief summary of relevant background, this chapter examines conceptual frameworks for child welfare service delivery, with special emphasis on a community caring orientation that has particular application in Indigenous communities. The model is then illustrated by a case study of one agency with data collected at three intervals over a 14-year period of time. Implications are highlighted in the final section.

Background

The historical effects of colonization on Indigenous people are not limited to Canada. Similar processes and related effects are found in other countries, including Australia, the United States, and New Zealand (Armitage, 1995; Horejsi, Craig, & Pablo, 1992; Love, 2006; Stanley, Tomison, & Pocock, 2003). In Canada, child welfare services were not provided on reserves in any comprehensive fashion until the 1980s (Ontario was the exception); intervention, when this occurred, was characterized by the removal and placement of First Nations children in non-Aboriginal resources. By the mid-1980s, First Nations resistance to the colonizing effects of these services, notably the loss of children from their families, communities, and culture, led to agreements to transfer jurisdictional control to First Nations communities. The service model that has evolved includes federal funding for First Nations children and families deemed to be a federal responsibility (i.e., living on reserves), recognition of provincial legislation and standards as the framework for service provision, and the delegation of responsibility, including agency governance, to First Nations communities. As noted in the previous chapter, by 2008 there were 108 agencies providing at least partial services under the delegated model to 442 of the 606 First Nations communities served by Indian and Northern Affairs Canada (INAC).

The transfer of jurisdictional control to Aboriginal authorities or agencies serving Aboriginal people living off-reserve has been a more recent development, but there are now such agencies in a number of major urban centres, including Toronto and Vancouver, with a mandate to provide a full range of child welfare services to Aboriginal children and families living in those cities. As well, a number of provinces have established Aboriginal agencies which provide child welfare services to Aboriginal children and families living off-reserve.

One of the more complex models is the provincial initiative launched in Manitoba in 1999 after the election of a New Democratic Party (NDP) government. This model, which evolved after extensive consultation with Aboriginal stakeholders, led to the establishment of four distinct authorities under new legislation. The *Child and Family Services Authorities Act* (2002) entrenched the right of Aboriginal people to receive services from agencies established under an authority governance structure composed of persons ratified by respective Aboriginal political organizations. Three of the new authorities are Aboriginal: First Nations North, First Nations South, and Métis. The other authority is known as the General Authority. Although the

General Child and Family Services Authority has primary responsibility for providing child welfare services to non-Aboriginal people, it also serves some Aboriginal people who express a preference to receive services from this authority. Each authority has a province-wide mandate (i.e., concurrent jurisdiction) to provide services to families and children from its cultural group anywhere in the province, and designated intake units are responsible for providing initial investigation services and determining the appropriate agency for ongoing services if such services are required.

Aboriginal jurisdictional control over child welfare services has potential advantages. First, it enables the development of more responsive community-based services that allow for incorporation of Aboriginal values, beliefs, and traditions, including more culturally appropriate practices. Second, it is more likely to lead to capacity-building initiatives at the community level. These can offer alternatives to conventional service models which have too often focused primarily on the continuing removal of Aboriginal children from their families, communities, and culture.

There are also limitations associated with current approaches to the transfer of jurisdictional control. Of particular significance are resource gaps in Aboriginal communities that have not been addressed by the transfer of jurisdictional control. For example, there are deficiencies in the funding formula for on-reserve services, including the lack of a designated allocation for prevention and family support services (First Nations Child and Family Caring Society of Canada, 2005). In Manitoba in 2008, the federal government spent only about 78 cents for on-reserve child welfare services for every dollar spent by the provincial government for services to children and families living off-reserve (Rabson, 2009b, p. A4). There have been recent efforts by the federal government in a number of regions to address this disparity by allocating additional funding for prevention and family support, but it is unclear whether these funds will be enough to make a difference.

Two related issues complicate the resource picture in Aboriginal communities. One is that these communities do not have the range of voluntary services available in more urban communities that can supplement government sponsored and funded therapeutic or support services for families. A second is the general lack of flexibility in funding that exists throughout the child welfare system, whereby funding is largely restricted to the support of children once they are admitted to care; thus it cannot be diverted to front-end services for families to allow children to remain at home.

Requirements to comply with provincial legislation and standards for child protection services are often defined as another limitation. This emphasis on compliance with child welfare standards is regarded as inconsistent with other legislative provisions that at least permit less disruptive family support services as a first step in intervention.

Finally, as noted in the introduction, it is apparent that the transfer of jurisdictional control has not reduced the overall numbers of Aboriginal children coming into care.

Despite these limitations, there are a number of innovations occurring in Aboriginal child and family services across the country. Many of these innovations are agency-based initiatives, and one of the reasons sometimes given for the absence of a more transformative paradigm of services in Aboriginal communities is that the transfer of jurisdictional authority has often led to the replication of the service orientation associated with child protection within dominant society. This orientation, and two other general frameworks for service delivery in child welfare, are considered next.

Frameworks for Service Delivery in Child Welfare

Two general frameworks which depict the organization of child welfare services in different countries are the child protection orientation and the family support or family services orientation. Characteristics of these two frameworks are summarized in Table 1. These orientations emerge from a comparative review of child welfare practice approaches in nine countries by Gilbert (1997). Gilbert concluded that countries with a "child protection" focus (e.g., England, Canada, and the United States) were legalistic in their approach, and applied most of their resources at the investigative end of the child protection process. Alternatively, western European countries, including Germany, Sweden, and Belgium, placed greater emphasis on the provision of family support services. A number of other authors (Connolly, 2004; Hill, Stafford, & Lister, 2002; Spratt, 2001) have elaborated on these orientations.

Such frameworks are helpful in describing general service orientations; however, it is important to note that the nature and scope of policy and practice in many jurisdictions often reflects some combination of these characteristics. In addition, differential response is evolving among many of those countries with a strong child protection orientation; its emergence has been driven by increased referrals for investigation of alleged abuse and neglect, higher numbers of children in care, and higher costs, resulting in some shift to a more family support orientation.

The community caring framework is a less well-recognized orientation, although its value is reinforced by research on community-building, the use of

Table 1 *Child Protection and Family Support Orientations in Child Welfare*

Child Protection	Family Support
Associated with child protection systems in the United Kingdom, Canada, the United States, and Australia, reflecting the following characteristics:	Associated with child protection systems in Belgium, France, Germany, and the Nordic countries, reflecting the following characteristics:
• Primary focus on investigation and placement, with extensive reliance on risk assessment instruments.	• Child protection services embedded within broader family support provisions where family services and supports are a first response.
• Family support services are poorly resourced, located largely outside the child welfare system, and poorly integrated with child protection functions.	• Increased resources devoted to early intervention and support, with these services linked to child protection services by an emphasis on partnerships and collaboration between services.
• Focus is on children's rights and protecting children from harm.	
• A more legalistic, bureaucratic, and adversarial response to child protection.	• Emphasis on family connections and flexible family-based service responses to address children's needs.
• Concentration of state resources on families identified as high risk.	• Less emphasis on coercive authority; state and families viewed as having shared responsibilities for child-rearing; more emphasis on partnerships with families.
	• Assistance is not restricted to those who reach a "threshold of risk"; services available to families at an early stage.

Source: Adapted from Connolly, 2004.

more community-oriented approaches, or a "whole of community" approach (Austin, 2005; McKenzie & Flette, 2003), and the old adage that "it takes a village to raise a child." The community caring model is particularly relevant to Indigenous communities that adopt a more holistic model of caring with an emphasis on connections to family, community, and culture. Professional knowledge and skills are required, but these must be linked to methods designed to engage and support formal and informal systems within communities in a partnership approach to service provision (see Table 2).

Although the community caring orientation builds on many of the perceived strengths of the family support framework, it also incorporates an emphasis on building community capacity where some of these traditional community supports have been lost. Examples of this orientation include the development of a healing circle approach to dealing with child sexual abuse on the Hollow Water reserve in Manitoba (Aboriginal Corrections Policy Unit, 1997), the approach to service provision developed by Lalum'utal'Smun'eem Child and Family Services in British Columbia (Brown, Haddock, & Kovach, 2002), the evolution of services in Tikinagan Child and Family Services (Brubacher, 2006), and the integration of child protection services within a public health model found in some maraes in New Zealand.

Table 2 *Community Caring Orientation*

Community Caring
Associated with smaller Indigenous communities, including Maori *maraes* in New Zealand/Aotearoa and Aboriginal communities in Canada, reflecting the following characteristics:
• Includes family support responses, but sees whole community as a "kind of family"; thus intervention builds on family support and child protection responses to emphasize community responsibility and strengths.
• In Indigenous communities, the approach often represents a form of resistance to the loss of Indigenous children, and the need to build local capacity and traditions as a form of "self-preservation."
• Uses conceptual models such as the "circle" and medicine wheel, along with a return to tradition, as a means of asserting strengths for "self-preservation."
• Jurisdictional control over child welfare services is an essential component in building community caring responses.
• Methods include family group conferencing, an increased role for local child and family services committees, more collaborative service responses, and a community-oriented practice approach.

There are strengths and weaknesses to each orientation that need to be considered in shaping a service model. Cameron (2006) has identified differences in the emphasis given to several service design characteristics. These differences are found in:

- the core values that are stressed;
- the boundaries that are placed around the service delivery system;
- the frequency and use of coercive authority; and
- the balance between relationship building and formal control mechanisms in carrying out child welfare functions.

To illustrate, core values may emphasize the rights of the child within a more individual context (i.e., child protection orientation) or the rights of the child in a more communal context (i.e., community caring orientation). Perception of the state's role in supporting families is somewhat different in each of these orientations. In addition, the boundaries of the child welfare system expand as one moves from a child protection to a family support or community caring orientation. The use of coercive authority is most prominent in the child protection orientation, although there is increasing agreement across all perspectives that the use of such authority should not be the primary method for engaging families. Indeed, the relative emphasis placed on investigation and the gathering of information for court-related actions influences the extent to which relationships between service providers and service users can be transformed from interactions clouded by power and control to those based on trust and mutual respect.

Although it may be difficult to find an appropriate balance among service activities across orientations, a community caring orientation, which incorporates a major emphasis on family support services without sacrificing the rights of children to protection from maltreatment, best represents the aspirations of Aboriginal communities that assume responsibility for the provision of child and family services. The next section summarizes the experiences of one agency in trying to develop a model based on these principles.

Integrating Community Caring Principles within an Aboriginal Child and Family Services Agency Background

West Region Child and Family Services (CFS) was established as a regional agency serving nine First Nations communities in western Manitoba in 1982; in 1985 it was approved as a fully delegated child and family services agency under the Manitoba *Child and Family Services Act*. The agency's governance structure includes a Board of Chiefs and local child and family services committees on each of its nine reserves. There are some centralized services, including a specialized child abuse unit and staff team responsible for the development of alternative care resources for children. However, most services are delivered by community-based teams, which include staff responsible for services pertaining to child protection and staff responsible for prevention and resource development activities. Each service delivery team works very closely with its local child and family services committee in the planning and delivery of services. The agency is guided by a vision statement which defines the agency as an extension of the kinship systems in the communities it serves, where families and communities live daily according to the teachings of the medicine wheel, and where there is a "circle of care" around every child. The medicine wheel serves as a framework for conceptualizing programs and services, and in 1998 the agency received the Peter F. Drucker Award for Canadian Nonprofit Innovation for its work in early intervention and family support based on medicine wheel teachings.

Between 1985 and 1990, increased expenditures required to support children in out-of-home care, particularly in off-reserve residential care facilities, and the questionable outcomes of some of these placements, led the agency to search for an alternative service model. A major priority was to secure increased control over the financial resources required to support children in out-of-home care in order to keep these children "closer to home" and to invest in a range of early intervention services that might prevent children from coming into care. In 1992, the agency negotiated the first flexible funding arrangement with the federal Department of Indian Affairs. Identified as "block funding" at the time, the agreement guaranteed the agency a negotiated amount for child maintenance, including the ability to carry forward surpluses, but required the agency to provide for children who needed out-of-home care within the annual allocated amount. In turn, the agency could spend anticipated or accumulated savings on new prevention, early intervention, and resource development initiatives that would have been impossible to fund without this arrangement. The flexible funding option for child maintenance pioneered by this agency is now more widely available to First Nations CFS agencies. However, it may not be appropriate for agencies in which it is difficult to predict ongoing child maintenance requirements, or for smaller agencies in which the amount of the grant provides limited flexibility in funding new programs or services.

The agency's experiences with flexible funding have been extensively evaluated. Reviews were completed in 1994 and 1999 (see McKenzie & Flette, 2003, for a summary of these results). Results summarized next are based primarily on a review of agency programs completed in 2005–6 (Shangreaux & McKenzie, 2006) and a follow-up report completed by Shangreaux (2008).

Results

Programs and Services

In fiscal year 2004–5, close to 40% of the agency's $5 million child maintenance allocation from the federal government was being used by the agency to establish and maintain alternative programs within the region and within member communities. These expenditures were allocated to three broad program initiatives: family support and preservation, alternative care, and community prevention. Agency programs are conceptualized as four circles of care: the *Staying at Home Circle of Care*, the *Circle of Alternate Care*, *Community Circles of Care*, and the *Family Restoration and Treatment Circle of Care* (see Figure 1).

The *Staying at Home Circle of Care* focuses on maintaining children in their own homes. It also reflects the overall orientation of the agency, which is to develop responses that minimize the level of intrusion of child welfare services on families and communities. This is operationalized by building programs and services that strengthen family networks, support children in their own homes, and provide a continuum of family support and preservation services. Since the inception of the pilot project, the overall rate of on-reserve children entering agency care declined from 10% in 1992–93 to 5.2% in 2003–4. This circle, which reflects the philosophical underpinnings of the family service orientation to service delivery, also informs the work within other caring circles or programs in the agency.

Figure 1 *Four Circles of Care at West Region Child and Family Services*

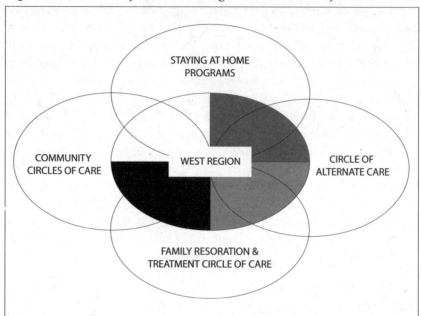

The *Family Restoration and Treatment Circle of Care* is an alternative service unit with specialized staff, established as a result of the flexible funding option, where the focus is on providing both practical and therapeutic support services to families in which children have special needs or in which children are at risk of being taken into care. Based on a 2004 survey, it was estimated that 212 children at medium to high risk were prevented from coming into care as a result of services provided by this unit and other community-based staff. Although the methodology used in this survey relies primarily on professional judgments about whether or not children would have entered care, the levels of risk attributed to the children served by the program were confirmed by more than one rater.

The *Circle of Alternate Care* has focused on developing foster, kinship, and residential care resources closer to home. In addition, a therapeutic foster care program (*Gai Gii Kweng*) was established. Training and support services for care providers emphasize the important role of culture and family connections in the provision of alternative care. "Closer to home" placements for children have been developed, and in 2004, 52% of the children in out-of-home care were placed with extended family, 47% were placed in homes within West

Region's communities, and 74% were in placement resources with at least one Aboriginal caregiver. In 2003–4, the *Gai Gii Kweng Program* provided services to 25 high-needs children.

It is the emphasis on *Community Circles of Care* that most reflects a community-building focus. This program includes an emphasis on early intervention and community prevention. However, building community capacity also involves the active engagement of community members in strengthening local networks of care.

Three general strategies are used within this circle of care. First, there is a major emphasis on engaging community volunteers. This includes the recruitment of community members, including Elders, as members on local child and family services committees, the provision of training, and the empowerment of these committees to play a role in child welfare decision-making at the community level. The community-building approach is also illustrated by the agency's efforts to regularly engage each community in operational planning and accountability workshops, which help to focus attention on emerging issues and service responses that can help support community efforts to address these issues.

A second and related strategy has been to fund positions for community prevention and special resource development initiatives. Community prevention workers have a wide range of responsibilities to promote educational workshops and to develop prevention-oriented programs targeted at families where children may be at risk. These activities are carefully planned with the local child and family services committee at the beginning of each year, and a budget is developed to support implementation. Funding for these activities is then provided to local communities to support these community-based prevention programs. In other circumstances, individuals have been hired to launch regionally-based initiatives. For example, a Special Needs Coordinator has worked to develop a community-based response to fetal alcohol spectrum disorder (FASD).

A third strategy has been the initiation of special projects, often as part of a coordinated community response with other community or regional partners. One example is the *Vision Seekers Program* offered in conjunction with other sponsors. This program incorporates life skills, occupational training, and wraparound services such as child care. Most adult students who enrol in the program are on social assistance, and many have had children who are at risk of future placement. Program outcomes have been positive. Most graduates have secured employment, and improved parenting outcomes, reducing the likelihood of future out-of-home placement, have been documented. Another example of a regional initiative is *Reclaiming Our Voices*. This is a special retreat program, available to individuals or families with addictions problems, where traditional and conventional intervention methods are combined to address the interrelated problems of addictions and inadequate parenting.

At the local level, more and more community members see the agency as a resource for supporting family wellness, family preservation, and family reunification, and less and less as a child protection agency to be feared.

Assessing Costs and Benefits

The alternative program model established by West Region CFS, which is based on principles associated with family connections and the use of a flexible funding option for resource development, gives rise to questions about the overall effects on children who are in care or may be at risk in the community. For example, it may be argued that a flexible funding option can lead to a reduction in services for these children because funds are diverted to alternative programs. There was no evidence that children in out-of-home care were being shortchanged in any way, or that risk factors for children remaining at home had increased (Shangreaux & McKenzie, 2006). In addition, the active engagement of parents and community members in agency programs, including the provision of alternative care homes, suggests a growing capacity to care for the most vulnerable members of these communities. This is not to suggest that persistent problems have been eradicated. The incidence of reported child abuse and neglect has declined over the years, but child protection concerns, often exacerbated by addictions issues, remain. And although the number of permanent wards has declined, the growing child population within communities presents programming challenges due to the gaps between local needs and the availability of both formal and informal community resources.

Assessing benefits in financial terms should not be the only yardstick used to evaluate program performance, but a general cost-benefit study of the alternative programs provided by this agency was completed in 2005 (Loxley and Deriviere, 2005b). Calculations may have overestimated the benefits from some programs in that future outcomes that might have occurred in the absence of alternative programs established by the agency cannot be substantiated empirically in the absence of a control group. For example, the rate of children in out-of-home care declined from 10% in 1992 to 5.2% in 2004, and based on the assumption that the 10% rate would have continued in the absence of alternative programs, the authors projected net cost savings of approximately $21 million over this 13-year period of time. Although it cannot be demonstrated that 10% of the children in these communities would have continued to come into care in the absence of alternative programming, it is of interest to note the differences in trends between West Region CFS and other First Nations CFS agencies in the province. These comparisons demonstrate significant cost savings from the alternative program model adopted by West Region CFS. For example, among all First Nations CFS agencies in Manitoba, there was a 26% increase in the number of paid days care and a 133% increase in child maintenance costs over a 10-year period to 2004. In West Region CFS there was a 17% increase in paid days care and a 66% increase in child maintenance costs over the same time period (Shangreaux & McKenzie, 2006).

Other cost-benefit projections calculated by Loxley and Deriviere (2005b) are based on annualized calculations. For example, the net benefits from working with high-risk children in their homes and diverting an estimated 212 from out-of-home placement was estimated at $2.9 million in 2004, and cost savings from the use of the *Gai Gii Kweng* program rather than higher cost residential care options in Winnipeg were estimated at $900,000 over a one-year period.

McKenzie and Shangreaux (2006) adopted a somewhat cautious approach in compiling projected cost savings (i.e., benefits) and then subtracting the costs of alternative care programming for the agency in 2004. Based on these calculations, it was estimated that the service model established by the agency produced a savings of approximately $1.5 million that would have been required to support children in care in the absence of the alternative programs established under the flexible funding arrangement.

Discussion

Case study results presented in the previous section demonstrate one First Nations CFS agency's efforts to integrate a more community caring orientation to its programs and services in ways that include an increased emphasis on family support and more community-based empowerment strategies. However, child protection functions are not neglected, and both the regionally-based child abuse team and community-based child protection workers help to ensure that this end of the service continuum receives adequate attention.

Although the flexible funding option provided resources for enabling the transition from a service model preoccupied by a child protection orientation, several other factors identified by Shangreaux and McKenzie (2006) have contributed to the agency's success. The community caring orientation has been influenced by the adoption of Ojibway teachings and the medicine wheel approach as guidelines for practice and service development. These guidelines are reflected in core values, the mission statement, and operating principles which are reinforced and applied to service planning in an ongoing manner. In turn, these attributes help to build an agency identity based on differences from conventional practice that are regarded as strengths by both the staff and the communities they serve.

Traditional teachings have been combined with a number of other qualities of well-functioning organizations that apply across cultures. First, there is a strong commitment to professional education and development; for example, the agency has played a leadership role in supporting staff to obtain professional social work degrees, and it also supports other forms of training and development. Second, it has developed a strong leadership team, which has remained relatively stable over time. Managers have promoted a common vision of services, fostered a team-oriented approach to program development and improvement, and advocated for changes to conventional practices, where necessary, to promote more culturally oriented service responses. For example, the agency was one of the first in the province to pay kinship carers the same payment rates as foster carers, and it has provided direct financial support to families when this was needed in order to facilitate family preservation or reunification plans. Third, the use of technology and management information systems to generate data, including cost analysis, for planning and program development has enabled the agency to become more proactive than reactive in anticipating needs or responding to current issues. The development of the *Gai Gii Kweng* program as an alternative to high-cost residential care in Winnipeg, and the development of the *Vision Seekers* program, are but two examples of the application of this approach to planning. Finally, one should not underestimate the importance of adequate resources. Although the data reviewed does indicate that cost savings can be realized over time, there must be sufficient resources to invest in community programs and services in the early stages, and agencies must have the flexibility to carry forward surpluses and use these resources to fund locally based initiatives. Of particular importance is the ongoing cost of alternative programs, and this has been a problem for West Region CFS. Operational costs for alternative programs increase over time, and it has been difficult to convince funders that allocations must keep pace with these inflationary factors in the same manner that child maintenance and other agency operating expenditures need to be adjusted for inflation, rate increases, or the increased costs for children with special needs.

Conclusion and Implications

Child protection services are important in child welfare, but this chapter demonstrates the value of integrating family support and community caring orientations as a means to altering the conventional role that child welfare can play in Indigenous communities. That role, heavily influenced by colonization and its preoccupation with child protection functions, is being challenged in many communities. Ongoing research can make a contribution to this transition, perhaps initially by focusing on examples of best practice and an analysis of the strengths and limitations of these innovations, both nationally and internationally. This is particularly important, because it reframes the role that child welfare services can play in these communities. Historically, that role has been associated with objectives related to assimilation and colonization; as it realizes objectives more clearly associated with family support and community-building, child welfare services can become more clearly associated with decolonization.

Certain limitations need to be recognized. First, this transformation will be ineffective without adequate attention to the need for high-quality child protection services, and the related agency supports, including adequate resources and well-trained staff. However, the current interest in differential response and the willingness of government to invest in alternative service models may help to support this transformation. Second, the introduction of alternative programs and models in child and family services is a limited response to the structural issues associated with poverty, poor housing, and related social problems that contribute to child neglect, and these gaps will remain until there is greater public policy attention to these factors in Aboriginal communities.

An important element in a more transformative paradigm for child welfare in Aboriginal communities is culture, and Shangreaux (2006) highlights the importance of traditions in promoting this transition. The use of the medicine wheel or other relevant cultural models can become frameworks for enhancing and operationalizing the core principles of the community caring orientation and the developmental planning and evaluation that must accompany this orientation to ensure its success. In the case of West Region CFS, the medicine wheel made an important contribution to new thinking about the role of child and family services, and provided guidance in balancing the requirements of provincial legislation and policies with a deep respect for culture. As noted by Shangreaux (2006),

> [t]he medicine wheel is widely used to describe humanity as interconnected and interdependent with one's family, community tribe, nation and all creation. It emphasises the importance of balance among all aspects of one's life, beginning with a spiritual core and expanding outward to the physical, emotional, intellectual, and social realms. (p. 5)

Using this framework, principles relevant to First Nations and Aboriginal child and family services are identified. Among these principles are the importance of the holistic approach, a balanced approach to intervention which emphasizes strengths and spirituality as well as problems, the need to strengthen kinship networks and interconnections between services and programs within communities, and the importance of hearing the voices of all community members, including children, young people, parents, and Elders in the development of community-based services. It is also noted that intervention programs must address issues related to the past, including historical trauma related to the residential schools. As an intervention method, the "sharing circle," which recognizes the strengths and gifts of individuals, can be incorporated, as appropriate, into decision-making and case planning processes.

23

Wrap a Star Blanket around Each One
Learning from the Educational Experiences of Indigenous Former Children in Care on Coast Salish Territory

Shelly Johnson (Mukwa Musayett)

The goal of the qualitative doctoral research project on which this chapter is based is to learn from 15 urban Indigenous former youth in care in ways that will help to develop a holistic, Indigenous child welfare educational model. By learning from the lived experiences of those that survived the child welfare and education systems, the hope is that one day all Indigenous children will be educated with adequate attention to their academic and cultural needs, and remain in the care of their family, community, or nation. My concern about the low educational outcomes of Indigenous children in government care in British Columbia has been shaped by my experience, first as an Indigenous social worker, supervisor, and manager, and more recently as a policy analyst, chief executive officer of a delegated urban child welfare agency, and university educator. Throughout these experiences I have witnessed, advocated, and struggled to help Indigenous children and youth in care to survive the failures of child welfare and education systems. This work continues. This chapter also reflects traditional values of respect and reciprocity in relationships by formally acknowledging the traditional territory on which the research was conducted and "giving back" research findings that may help to improve the lives of Indigenous children in care (ICIC) living on traditional Coast Salish territories in the urban communities of Victoria and Vancouver, B.C.

The term *Indigenous*, as it is used in this chapter, refers to those who inhabited or were descendants of those who inhabited a country or region before people with different ethnic origins arrived. These new arrivals became dominant through conquest, occupation settlement, or other means (United Nations

Permanent Forum on Indigenous Issues, 2007). The term *Aboriginal* is generally considered to have the same meaning in Canada, where it includes First Nations who are registered under the *Indian Act* (i.e., status Indians), those who are non-registered Indians or non-status, the Inuit, and Métis. Aboriginal people, then, include those with legal status as First Nations people and those who identify as having Aboriginal ancestry and are accepted as such within their community.

Why Is the Education of Indigenous Children in Care (ICIC) Important?

> Self-government has to start with education, whether it's an education of what our traditional systems were or how we merge what was once traditional governance to a more modern form governance. We have to be educated in both. We've been so displaced because of residential schools and foster homes. I felt like a fake Indian for 20 plus years. (Interview respondent, August 2009)

There are many reasons why education of ICIC is important to me. The most personal is based on my own First Nations identity and history. Upon entering my Saulteaux First Nations Treaty Four complex in Fort Qu'Appelle, Saskatchewan, visitors are greeted by a life-size mounted buffalo. Stonechild (2006) asserts that, historically, the buffalo provided much of the physical nourishment, as well as the emotional, mental, and spiritual support needed to sustain the health and well-being of Plains Indigenous families and communities. With the coming of European settlers to our Plains territories and the mass extermination of the buffalo, my ancestors could no longer depend on the buffalo to sustain them. Their lives were dramatically changed forever. Inscribed on a plaque affixed to the base of the buffalo is: "Education is our buffalo now." This is certainly true for me and my family. A blend of academic, cultural, and traditional education is the twenty-first-century buffalo that holds promise and opportunity for our ICIC, Indigenous communities, and nations. However, the decisions made by successive governments over time have created impediments to realizing that promise.

Within the urban Indigenous communities in Victoria and Vancouver, located on traditional Coast Salish territories, there is a diversity of Indigenous languages and cultural traditions. This urban Indigenous diversity creates both special resources and capacity challenges for urban Indigenous child welfare agencies and educational institutions. Specific challenges include the complexity of cultural and language revitalization important to rebuilding Indigenous children's cultural identities and reconnections with sometimes distant home communities. The historical destruction of Indigenous languages, cultures, families, and communities through the assimilative policies and practices associated with residential schools, as well as child welfare and educational institutions, makes it particularly difficult for these systems to repair this damage. This is perhaps the most important rationale for privileging the voices, and acting on the recommendations of, these former urban ICIC.

While their Indigenous identity can be strengthened through opportunities to learn about themselves through traditional and cultural education (Carrière, 2005; Sinclair, 2007a), my experience indicates that piecemeal or pilot opportunities are not enough to ensure academic success for all. To reduce dependency and increase academic and life success for ICIC, a holistic and long-term Indigenous model of educational support is required both during and after their experiences within the child welfare system. To do less will only ensure the continuance of B.C.'s educational failures for its most vulnerable children. This is not to suggest that the educational needs of ICIC should take precedence over those of non-Indigenous children in care, who are also disadvantaged educationally (Jackson, 2001; Kufeldt, Simard, Tite, & Vachon, 2003; Mitic & Rimer, 2002). Rather, it is to recognize that the educational needs of Indigenous children and youth in the B.C. child welfare system are unique as a result of historical, political, social, and economic circumstances, and that they require specially designed solutions.

An important professional reason for this focus is the current abysmal educational outcomes of the approximately 8,644 children in care in B.C., of which Indigenous children represent 54.5% (British Columbia Ministry of Children and Family Development, 2009). According to the B.C. Representative for Children and Youth (2007), currently only 7% (approximately 605) of all children in care in the province can expect to graduate from an academic secondary school stream within six years of entering Grade 8. This statistic appalled and shocked me into action. Why is this so? Indigenous, and indeed all children in care, deserve an education, don't they? What can be done to improve these outcomes? The lack of practice and policy relevant research on this issue is reflected in the limited amount of data available regarding the short- or long-term educational outcomes of ICIC in the province. This research gap precludes knowledge of how many urban ICIC are included in the 1.5% of success stories because specific data regarding these children is not readily available. What is evident is that between 2002–3 and 2007–8 (the most recent year for which B.C. statistics are available), the Aboriginal graduation rate in the province fluctuated between 45% and 50%, while the graduation rate of non-Aboriginal students was 73% (British Columbia Ministry of Education, 2009). It is simply unacceptable to do nothing with the knowledge that substantive educational improvements are urgently required to support children in care. This is particularly critical when the B.C. government reports that almost all children in its care fail to graduate from secondary school within six years of entering Grade 8, far below the average graduation rate for both Aboriginal and non-Aboriginal children in the province. To fail to take action is to be negligent in our duties to this particularly vulnerable population of children.

Literature Review

The Canadian National Youth in Care Network is the strongest voice for Canadian youth in care, and its 2001 study of 100 youth in care documented the actions, including meaningful engagement, resources, placement stability, and inclusion, that are required to create more positive school experiences and improve the outcomes for future youth in care. Unfortunately, the number of Indigenous youth included in the study is not identified. Mitic and Rimer (2002) provided an overview of the educational attainment of children in care in B.C. in 2001, and found that their academic performance was significantly lower than the general population of students. However, the study did not differentiate between the educational attainment of First Nations children in care that reside on-reserve, in urban communities or other off-reserve communities, and those who are Métis. Kufeldt, Simard, Tite, and Vachon (2003) used the *Looking After Children* approach developed in the United Kingdom to pilot a three-year research study in six Canadian provinces to address the question of how effective child welfare services are in meeting the needs of children in care. Their findings reinforce the work of British researchers (Parker, 1998; Parker, Ward, Jackson, Aldgate, & Wedge, 1991; Walker, 1994; Ward, 1995), who concluded that far greater priority must be given to the educational dimension in work with children in care. This theme is also expressed in the British research of Martin and Jackson (2002), who interviewed a group of 38 former youth in care identified as high educational achievers. Their findings indicate that these youth believed that supportive attitudes of social workers and teachers, ongoing financial support, and a "guardian angel" to support and encourage them in post-secondary education were key factors in achieving success.

Indigenous research in North America speaks to the issues of promoting access and achievement in education for urban Aboriginal populations (Archibald, 2008; Battiste & Barman, 1995; Baskin, 1997; Castellano, Davis, & Lahache, 2000; Kirkness & Barnhardt, 1991; Regnier, 1995; Silver et al., 2006;

Williams, 2000), for urban Aboriginal peoples with disabilities (Durst & Bluechardt, 2001), and for urban Aboriginal children in care (Brendtro, Brokenleg, & Van Bockern, 2001; Johnson, 2008). Much of the child welfare research written by Indigenous academics reflects a focus on issues relevant to on-reserve concerns such as jurisdictional issues and funding models (Bennett, Blackstock, & De la Ronde, 2005; Blackstock, 2008; Gough, Blackstock, & Bala, 2005; Kovachs, Thomas, Montgomery, Green, & Brown, 2007; Sinclair, Bala, Lilles, & Blackstock, 2004; Trocmé, Knoke, Shangreaux, Fallon, & MacLaurin, 2005). Non-Indigenous academics, such as Ball and Pence (2006) and Walmsley (2005), have highlighted the importance of Aboriginal issues in their publications on child welfare both in B.C. and Canada.

A comprehensive literature review undertaken by the B.C. Ministry of Education, Aboriginal Education Enhancement Branch (2008), identifies a number of issues that continue to affect Indigenous kindergarten to Grade 12 (K–12) learners. These issues include the existence of assimilation through deficit thought patterns that persist in hidden codes and structures in the education system; racism in schools; the need to reinforce Indigenous identities in schools; and acknowledgement that Indigenous students learn differently from non-Indigenous learners and may need to be treated differently in order to be treated fairly. Findings also suggest the critical need for Indigenous control of Indigenous education, and the need for Indigenous community involvement to support collective learning in the classroom. Essentially, the review calls for the development of long-term strategies that begin with those in charge of education becoming "students again themselves" (British Columbia Ministry of Education, 2008). This relearning about Indigenous education is critical, given the findings of the McCreary Centre Society (2007) report of street involved youth in B.C. Their 2006 survey of 762 street youth in nine B.C. communities found that Aboriginal youth were disproportionately represented among youth who were marginalized and street-involved, and that 40% of the surveyed youth had spent time in government care.

Although a number of articles, books, and reports with recommendations have been written, little improvement has occurred in the lives and educational attainment of ICIC. How can this be, given that over the past 15 years a number of B.C. child welfare advocacy or "watchdog" officers have been appointed to oversee the child welfare system, to write reports, and to publicly comment on gaps in programs and services for children and youth in government care? Many library shelves could be filled with reports generated by their offices, while the numbers of Aboriginal children in care have continued to increase, educational outcomes remain low, and the B.C. child welfare system seems doomed to lurch from crisis to crisis (Pivot Legal Society, 2009). More needs to be done, because what exists is obviously ineffectual in making significant systemic transformative change.

Rather than looking for answers in the child welfare and education systems that have created the crisis, it is time to pay attention to the work of Indigenous people who have experienced the B.C. and Canadian child welfare systems as either former youth in care or adoptees, or worked as social workers in trying to change it. Those who have offered recommendations about a way forward include Cree academic Raven Sinclair; Métis scholar Jeannine Carrière; Lauri Gilchrist; and Gitxsan advocate for First Nations children and families, Cindy Blackstock. Sinclair's dissertation (2007b) explores the problems identified in the literature concerning the adoption of Native children into non-Native families in Canada between the 1950s and the early 1980s. Carrière (2005, 2008) explores issues of connectedness and health for First Nation adoptees. Gilchrist's dissertation (1995) explores the experiences of Aboriginal street youth in Vancouver, Winnipeg, and Montreal, while Blackstock (2008, 2009a) has written extensively about funding models and jurisdictional child welfare issues.

Despite the fact that in Canada approximately 60% of the First Nations population lives in off-reserve areas (Statistics Canada, 2006c), until recently the experiences of urban Aboriginal peoples garnered little attention from non-Aboriginal Canadian policy researchers (Chataway, 2004; Hanselmann, 2003). A gap remains in the literature on the educational outcomes of urban Indigenous children and youth in care of the child welfare system. This is why it is important for me, an Indigenous academic with 25 years of child welfare practice, policy, and research experience, to undertake research on the B.C. experience. This special responsibility was brought to my attention by a Saulteaux elder before he journeyed on:

> Mukwa Musayett: the Creator made you this way and put you in that place for a purpose. So, when you do those things always ask yourself if they are good for your children and grandchildren. Always remember who you are in your heart. Never pick up something new and leave behind who you are, who we are and what we believe. (Saulteaux Elder Bones, November 2006)

Star Blanket Teachings and the Research Project

As a Saulteaux woman, my traditional teachings are that the sun and moon are placed in the sky by the Creator and represent our Grandfathers and Grandmothers. The Creator also placed stars in the sky, and the one that holds the most meaning for me is the one which shines most brightly in the east just before daybreak. Women in my family have replicated that star on a blanket as an eight-point symbol that has come to be known as a "lone star quilt" or "star blanket" pattern. Like other Saulteaux women, I have made and gifted many star blankets in celebration of special events and milestones. This signifies that the recipient's well-being is important and conveys honour and care for the person. Sometimes the design, colours, and placement in a star blanket pattern are clear in my imagination, dreams, or prayers, and offer a general idea of the finished project. Yet often the star blanket turns out differently than expected. At times changes happen because a specific material or colour cannot be found. Learning to trust that the right material will be found is another part of the star blanket process. Sometimes the process happens quickly. At other times it moves slowly with a deliberate, meandering pace. More than the mechanical pieces of planning, cutting, and sewing the star blanket, reflection and contemplation account for many of the hours involved from the inception of the idea to thinking about the person who will receive it, and my reasons for gifting it.

The star blanket process feels much like the way research is described by Wilson (2008), who asserts that research is ceremony and stresses the importance of developing and using Indigenous research methods. The process of making a star blanket became a metaphor for my qualitative research process. It helped to clarify relationships with ideas, and shapes the specific research process I used to explore the educational outcomes of 15 urban Indigenous former youth in care in B.C. This process includes a continuum of decision-making, from the inception of the idea through to the dissemination of the findings.

At this preliminary analysis phase, four issues are emerging. First, the newly co-created information contributes to a "star blanket child in care educational organization" that is Indigenous in its design, and helpful for the people it is meant to wrap around and support. Second, the process and final creation will be respectful and relevant in improving the educational and child welfare realities in the lives of urban Indigenous children and youth in care of the B.C. child welfare system because it includes the experiences and knowledge of former Indigenous youth in care. Third, it will help to protect my research helpers from further trauma, harm, or disruption in their lives, and prove to be a positive and healing development in their educational experiences. Fourth, this knowledge co-creation will help to develop more reciprocity and balance in the relationships between the academy and First Nations people, and guide us all toward a meaningful new day.

Learning from Urban Indigenous Former Children in Care

> When I was two I was adopted. When I was four I went into foster care. My mother promised that she'd come back for me, so I waited for her to return. All my time in school, I sat like a bump on a log, never learning to read or write, just waiting and staring out the window. I repeated Grade 1 twice and Grade 2. When I was 18 I was adopted again by my foster parents. Much later I went for upgrading on my own initiative. I searched for a long time and finally found my mom when I was 50 years old. (Urban Indigenous former youth in care, April 2009)

In the summer and fall of 2009 I interviewed 15 urban Indigenous former children in care about their educational experiences during and after their involvement in the B.C. child welfare system. The participants were either referred to me by workers in two urban Indigenous child welfare agencies located on traditional Coast Salish territories, or self-referred. Prior to enactment of the B.C. *Child, Family and Community Service Act* (CFCSA) (1996), the legal status of a child in permanent care was that of a "permanent ward." After the introduction of the CFCSA, it changed to that of a "continuing custody ward." While the legal terminology was revised, the B.C. Director of Child Protection continued to have legal guardianship responsibilities and obligations. With the exception of one interview that occurred on the traditional territory of the Secwepemc peoples, the interviews occurred on the traditional Coast Salish territory in the urban communities of Victoria and Vancouver, where all of the research participants lived while in care. Thirteen of the fifteen participants were status, registered Indian people as defined by the *Indian Act* (1985), and two were non-status. Of the nine urban Indigenous women and six men ranging in age from 24 to 55, only two had experienced an Aboriginal foster home or had an Aboriginal social worker or teacher while they were in care. All spent between nine and eighteen years as permanent legal wards or continuing custody wards of the government. Their educational attainment levels ranged from Grade 7 to one who had a graduate degree. Fourteen of the fifteen research participants had at least one parent who was legally required to attend a residential school. The remaining individual did not have access to this information. Fourteen of the interviews lasted approximately one to one and a half hours, and one lasted over four hours.

One of the recurring themes that negatively impacted their educational experiences was that of deep, intergenerational trauma, and unresolved grief and loss, as evidenced by this participant:

> The Creator had extra special plans for me. My people, I think, have suffered because of my absence ... I believe that today. Me and my family and my band were deprived of me. I wouldn't have a clue on trying to think how to get that back. (Respondent, August 2009)

The interview data indicate that the unresolved issues of cultural, familial, and spiritual grief and loss as a direct result of historical trauma, apprehension, and numerous placement experiences in care were obstacles to achieving academic success in school. Participants also pointed to a lack of emphasis and support from either the child welfare or education systems to address their unique educational needs and plans, both while they were in care and post-care. In addition, as the participants became aware of the generational effects of residential school traumas, they began to make important connections between those historical experiences and the educational challenges of ICIC in the current child welfare system.

An Indigenous Education Model for ICIC

> I would like to see an advocacy organization that has the authority to bring all the parties together, education and child welfare services, to share information, provide early intervention with lots of coordinated, targeted support and tutoring for our youth. They should have a mandate, an urban Aboriginal educational advocacy group for urban Aboriginal children in care. (Respondent, August 2009)

Two of the research questions asked of each Indigenous former child in care were: (1) Based on your experiences, what has helped to facilitate your educational success? (2) Is there anything that you think will help to improve the educational outcomes of urban ICIC that I didn't ask? The responses of each research participant were thoughtful, specific, practical, and, with political will and adequate funding, clearly achievable. Most telling was their individual and collective sense of responsibility and desire to help develop holistic educational and child welfare services, mentoring relationships, and advocacy to improve the educational outcomes for ICIC. Their suggestions included offering hope and "living proof" through their own experiences that life post-care for ICIC could ultimately bring an increased and welcome responsibility for personal decision-making and action that would provide a real sense of control in their lives.

The reflections of these research participants, combined with my own administrative, policy, and practice experience, became crystallized as a Saulteaux star blanket educational support model for ICIC. This developing model of a star blanket educational support organization could be symbolically and literally wrapped around each urban Indigenous child in care to help improve their current educational outcomes. The holistic nature of this star blanket model (identified in Figure 1) has numerous policy, practice, and research implications which are only briefly highlighted in this chapter. These will be further developed in the next phase of this research project.

The research participants were also clear that urban ICIC needed other "people to know that being in care doesn't make you a bad person, it's not your fault" (Respondent, August 2009); their reasons for being in care were largely structural (e.g., poverty; lack of safe, affordable housing; unemployment; lack of access to education), and based on decisions made by adults (i.e., judges, lawyers, social workers, police, parents) regarding parental addiction and abuse issues over which Indigenous children have no control.

Figure 1 *Star Blanket Model of an Urban Indigenous Child in Care Education Organization*

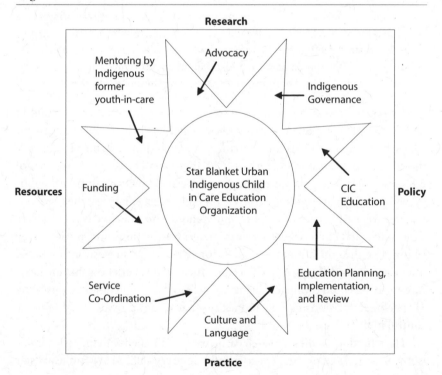

Implications

> I was in foster care since I was 3 going on 4. I learned that Aboriginal people were stupid and they didn't graduate and they were drunks and I would never amount to anything because I had Aboriginal heritage ... After I left care, I wouldn't go near social workers, they're the devil. So I had a really hard time to finish my degree. I got student loans and have $80,000 worth of student loan debt. (Respondent, August 2009)

What became evident through the research process is the disconnection between the child welfare and educational policies developed *to protect and educate* Indigenous children and youth and the experiences of these research participants. At best, their experiences provide many examples of the gaps between policies and practices. At worst, their experiences demonstrate the systemic failure of the services provided to Indigenous children by the dominant child welfare and education systems. These failures become readily apparent when we consider that most of the former ICIC came into care before school age and spent their entire childhood and a large part of their youth in the child welfare system. The evidence of failure both by child welfare and educational institutions to adequately address the unique educational needs of both Indigenous and non-Indigenous children in care raises serious questions about the parenting responsibilities exercised by provincial and federal governments.

The sentiment has been expressed by colleagues that "These are damaged and traumatized children. The education system has never been able to address the needs of Aboriginal students, much less kids in care, so what can you expect? They've got bigger issues than their marks in school." As an inexperienced young social worker, the first time I heard these comments I was shocked. As my experience grew, so did the level of my personal and professional disagreement with what I perceived to be the profound ignorance of some of my colleagues. For the most part, my efforts to model and focus my advocacy on improving educational outcomes through the provision of more intensive educational supports met with limited success. It seemed as though people at all levels of the child welfare and education systems were prepared to give up on these children. Yet, in my practice, some of the ICIC repeatedly demonstrated academic success when they had educational obstacles removed both during their time in care and after they left the system. My belief remains that if we can find ways to reduce or eliminate educational obstacles for all ICIC, they will prove to be much more academically successful than they are at present.

Policy-makers may argue that budgets are limited, particularly when the need for new programs is identified. However, we are discussing the fact that

B.C.'s most vulnerable children are denied access to opportunities that are open to the vast majority of the rest of the child and youth population. The responsibility rests squarely on the shoulders of governments to take seriously their role as "legal guardians and parents" and make the required funds and supports available whether ICIC are in care or wanting to access post-secondary supports after care. They also have a duty of care to address the long-standing negative stereotypes, attitudes, and lack of educational expectations of child welfare and education personnel. These constitute additional obstacles to the academic success of ICIC. In the long run, meeting such responsibilities is likely to be cost-effective in preventing future social costs for this population.

There is much that can be done to remove the educational obstacles that persist. The most urgent policy action that should be taken is to ensure that urban ICIC have an explicit *right to education* added to section 70, *Rights of children in care* (CFSCA, 1996). This *right to education*, which does not currently exist for any children in care in B.C., must be applicable on their entry into care, remain during their time in care, and extend for a reasonable period of time after they leave the child welfare system. To ensure that this right is realized, critical oversight and resources must flow to this key policy area. It is particularly critical that Indigenous children who spend most of their childhood in the child welfare system, and who experience little or no family support, receive educational supports and cultural reinforcement in the development of a positive Indigenous identity. This is not to say that all ICIC may choose to adopt a traditional, cultural, or spiritual path, but they deserve to have that choice. This is reinforced by a former ICIC who commented that:

> ... the sound of a running river or being up the mountains—all those things are nurturing to the spirit. Those are the things that will see you through hard times. Your physical body is going to let you down. Your mind is going to let you down. It's your spirit that will see you through. (Respondent, August 2009)

The most critical practice issue is a concerted focus on the unique educational and stable placement needs of ICIC. A place to start is the development of a holistic star blanket urban Indigenous child in care educational organizational model, as recommended by several of these research participants. This organization must be governed by Indigenous peoples and funded to coordinate services between the child welfare and education systems to improve the educational outcomes of ICIC. The organization must offer mentoring by Indigenous former youth in care, advocacy services, specialized educational assessments, and planning, implementation, and review services. As well, there must be opportunities lo learn Indigenous languages, cultural supports, and educational opportunities for ICIC to learn about their unique historical, legal, economic, and political realities. The federal and provincial governments must accept their responsibilities to fund the development and maintenance of such an organization until such time as the educational outcomes of ICIC equal those of children and youth outside the child welfare system.

From a research perspective, there are many opportunities to engage and support the work of such an organization, and to ensure that what "works" can be communicated to other agencies providing services to ICIC. In B.C. in 2009, there were 24 delegated Aboriginal, First Nations, and Métis child welfare agencies providing various levels of statutory child welfare services to Indigenous peoples living on-reserve and in urban communities, five more in the process of development, and one agency providing services under a band by-law model. Yet only 41% of all Indigenous children and youth in care are receiving services from these agencies (British Columbia Ministry of Children and Family Development, 2009). There is need for greater support for these children, but particularly for those who are not receiving services from Indigenous child welfare agencies.

All of the research participants in this study believe that government has specific responsibilities (primarily financial and legislative) to acknowledge and address the educational issues of these children. However, they do not believe that non-Indigenous government bureaucrats, social workers, foster parents, or teachers can be the only vehicle to provide the healing and support required to make a difference or to improve the educational outcomes of urban ICIC. Although they acknowledge the valued role that allies can provide, these research participants expressed the view that the coordinating and leadership role of an education support organization for ICIC must be undertaken by Indigenous people who have a shared history and understanding of being in care, or experience working in the child welfare or education systems. This does not mean that society is "off the hook," or somehow absolved from the effort and responsibility of focusing attention and resources on making changes to reduce dependency and improve the educational well-being of our most precious resources. Our entire society will be strengthened because we all stand to benefit from the results of improved educational outcomes for all of those who live on this land.

Conclusion

There is no single path on the journey to transform and improve the academic, traditional, and cultural educational outcomes of urban ICIC; indeed, it is an issue that invites transformative efforts in many educational and child welfare sites and work by many peoples. These efforts must encourage us all to become students again, to rethink and rediscover new ways of teaching and learning that will support vulnerable Indigenous children and youth in our educational and child welfare systems. Yet so much hope and promise exists in the words, experiences, and contributions of these 15 urban Indigenous people who have survived the B.C. child welfare and education systems. Perhaps as we look to the future, it is best to conclude this chapter with the voice of the youngest former ICIC participant, who spoke eloquently to the issue of who can be the leaders in addressing and healing the pressing educational issues for our urban ICIC. The simultaneous simplicity and complexity of her question invites reflection about who will benefit and who will be harmed if their voices are ignored and no substantive action is taken to improve the educational outcomes of urban ICIC.

> Over 50% of young people in care are Aboriginal, and that's huge. We need to listen to them and we need to give them power. If I'm Premier and I have all this power but I'm making decisions on behalf of them and they don't seem to be working, why aren't we giving them some of the power so they can make some of the decisions? (Respondent, August 2009)

24

Indigenous Issues in Child Welfare
Themes and Implications

Brad McKenzie
Kathleen Kufeldt

P art III touches on some of the current issues and developments in Indigenous child welfare. It is not fully comprehensive, as the nature and scope of services—particularly in Aboriginal child and family services in Canada—have expanded significantly over the last few years. Some new developments include the growth of Aboriginal-led services off-reserve and in large urban centres; these call for additional attention in the literature. Although there have been many changes, certain trends have remained remarkably consistent. One of these is the overrepresentation or disproportionality of Indigenous children in care, not only in Canada but in other countries such as Australia and New Zealand. This issue was outlined in Chapters 20 and 21.

The effects of colonization on Aboriginal people in Canada were discussed in Chapters 21 and 22. Chapter 22 outlined a service model in First Nations child and family services, along with supporting evidence to demonstrate its effectiveness, and Chapter 23 focused on the educational experiences of former Indigenous children in care. This chapter provides a summary of three key themes regarding Aboriginal child and family services that emerge from the preceding four chapters:

- disproportionality, colonization, and self-determination;
- service models and cultural continuity; and
- resilience and well-being.

Implications for research, policy, and practice are explored in the final section.

Disproportionality, Colonization, and Self-Determination

Although information on disproportionality from several countries is provided in Chapter 20, data from Canada on the overrepresentation of Aboriginal children in care are particularly important to consider. For example, the disparity rate for Aboriginal children in care in Manitoba was 16.9 in 2008 (i.e., an Aboriginal child was 16.9 times more likely to be placed in care than a non-Aboriginal child).

There are wide differences among countries in disparity rates; for example, both New Zealand and Canada have a significant minority of Indigenous children in their populations, yet the disparity rates are much lower in New Zealand than in Canada. It is difficult to identify the factors that influence this variation, although the experiences pertaining to colonialism in these two countries is somewhat different. For example, Maori children in New Zealand were largely spared from the residential and boarding school history common to Canada and Australia.

The colonization of Aboriginal people that took place in Canada can be described as involving two components: structural colonialism and cultural colonialism (McKenzie & Hudson, 1985). The structural component includes the appropriation of the land of Indigenous inhabitants, their relegation to reserves, and the removal of their traditional means of survival without adequate attention to the provision of meaningful alternatives. The cultural component involves the devaluation of traditional culture, including the marginalization of Indigenous ways of helping by the dominant society. Instruments of cultural colonialism include residential schools and mainstream health and child welfare services. Dependency is created because of the dual loss of economic self-sufficiency and traditional socio-cultural expressions of identity and well-being. It is recognized that many Aboriginal people have resisted these assimilative policies, and there has been a growth in cultural revival and self-determination as expressions of resilience. Nevertheless, many economic, social, and cultural challenges remain.

A number of models intended to increase the level of Aboriginal self-determination in child and family services have been identified (Mandell, Clouston Carlson, Fine, & Blackstock, 2007), and these are briefly summarized below.

- *Pre-mandated child and family services*: Agencies are established to provide prevention and family support services subject to agreements or contracts with provincial governments; however, a full range of child protection services is not offered. These types of agencies are most common in Ontario and British Columbia (B.C.), where they may evolve, after a period of time, into fully mandated agencies.

- *Band by-law model*: The *Indian Act* allows Indian band chiefs and councils to enact by-laws on-reserve, and in 1980 the Spallumcheen First Nation in B.C. passed a by-law giving them sole jurisdiction over child welfare services. The Minister of Indian and Northern Affairs Canada (INAC) has refused to recognize any further by-laws of this nature, and the Spallumcheen First Nation continues to operate the only child welfare service based on this model.

- *Self-government model*: This model recognizes the jurisdictional right of Aboriginal entities to enact laws pertaining to child welfare as long as these laws are consistent with provincial standards. This authority exists in the Nisga'a Treaty in B.C., although it has not yet been fully implemented. Certain provisions associated with the *Aboriginal Justice Inquiry–Child Welfare Initiative* in Manitoba, discussed below, reflect aspects of the self-government model.

- *Delegated model*: Distinctions are sometimes made between a tripartite model, a statutory model, and a delegated model. The tripartite model applies only to First Nations agencies on reserves where the agreement specifies the funding obligations of the federal government, along with accountability requirements to the provincial government with respect to child welfare legislation, regulations, and standards. The statutory model applies in Ontario, where both funding and service delivery in First Nations communities are subject to provincial law and regulations; in turn, the province receives funding directly from INAC for on-reserve services. In reality, there is little difference between these two models and the delegated model, in that in all cases it is the provincial government that delegates responsibility to Aboriginal agencies for the provision of services subject to provincial legislation. In all other provinces and territories except Ontario, on-reserve agencies receive funding for on-reserve residents from INAC.

The most common model in realizing self-determination in Aboriginal child welfare has been the delegated model. There are limitations to the delegated model, including the availability of adequate resources (see Chapter 21 and 22), government control over standards, and the difficulties in translating delegated power into improved services and better outcomes for children and families (Brown, Haddock, & Kovach, 2002). But it has given Aboriginal people an increased voice in developing their own child welfare services, and this is an important step in the decolonization process.

A key aspect of success is whether community empowerment is enhanced by greater self-determination, and three outcome-oriented measures have been suggested for assessing this (McKenzie, 1999). These include "the extent to which the community exercises a constructive influence over agency services and programs, the level of partnership arrangements between child and family services and other programs in community-building initiatives, and the degree to which the community is proactive in dealing with issues such as abuse or the need for prevention" (p. 211). Positive outcomes, including greater use of kinship care placements, more collaborative working relationships with families, and innovative service models, have been identified in many communities.

Although some of the limitations to the delegated service model, particularly in First Nations communities, have been externally imposed, there have also been examples of internal management problems related to funding and service provision. Financial mismanagement has included inappropriate expenditures and the use of child welfare funds for purposes unrelated to the needs of children and families. Some of the financial problems have been traced to political interference, often by chiefs and band councils, whereas service problems are more often related to the lack of training for front-line staff and supervisors. Using Manitoba as an example, remedial actions, including the appointment of new managers, have occurred as a result of external reviews with government working in collaboration with new First Nations child and family services authorities responsible for overseeing service delivery (Welch, 2009, 2010).

The transfer of jurisdictional control began in the 1980s, when the responsibility for on-reserve child welfare services began to be transferred to First Nations communities. This process has continued to evolve, and in more recent years it has been extended to Aboriginal people living off-reserve, including in major urban centres such as Toronto, Winnipeg, and Vancouver. As well, a broad range of child and family welfare services that provide both therapeutic and early intervention and support services have emerged, primarily in urban centres with a significant Aboriginal population.

One of the more interesting service delegation models for Aboriginal people living off-reserve has been established in Manitoba. Under the *Aboriginal Justice Inquiry–Child Welfare Initiative* described briefly in Chapter 22, three new Aboriginal authorities (the Southern First Nations Authority, the Northern First Nations Authority, and the Métis Authority) were created by legislation, and each new authority has the power to manage service delivery units for their respective populations throughout the province. A General Authority was also established which oversees services primarily to non-Aboriginal people in Manitoba. The provincial government followed an inclusive policy development approach in designing this model, whereby planning committee structures included equal representation from each political organization (i.e., the two First Nations governance bodies in the province, the Métis Society, and the provincial government). In general, a government-to-government process with Aboriginal partners evolved during the planning process, and decisions were generally respectful of Aboriginal aspirations. The new governance model, which includes separate boards for each authority appointed by their respective political organization, transfers considerable jurisdictional control for child welfare to Aboriginal organizations, and in general this has been a positive development. At the same time, several political and service delivery concerns have emerged. Political challenges have included situations in which Aboriginal political organizations have challenged the decision-making powers of authorities and their boards. Problems in service coordination and gaps in the quality of services have resulted in several reviews by the Office of the Children's Advocate. Although a number of these early implementation problems have been addressed, there are differing views about how well the new system is working.

The transfer of jurisdictional control for child welfare services has to date had little impact on reducing the general level of disproportionality. But it is important to note that there is some evidence that the rates of disproportionality vary among groups of Aboriginal people. For example, in one study in three provinces, the rate of out-of-home placements for First Nations children (102 per 1000) was more than three times the rate of Métis children (33 per 1000) and almost 15 times the rate for other children (7 per 1000) (Blackstock, Prakash, Loxley, & Wien, 2005, p. 43). And as noted in Chapter 21, 5.5% of First Nations children living on-reserve were in child welfare care in 2003, a rate estimated at eight times that for all Aboriginal and non-Aboriginal children in care off-reserve.

Trocmé, MacLaurin, Fallon, Knoke, Pitman, and McCormack (2005) have provided information on the differences between First Nations and non-Aboriginal children referred for investigation in the CIS–2003. First Nations children were more likely to be investigated, and these cases were more likely to result in a substantiated finding of abuse or neglect than for non-Aboriginal children (see Chapter 21). Of particular significance was the high rate of neglect in First Nations investigations (56% of substantiated First Nations cases vs 22% of substantiated cases for the non-Aboriginal population). Physical neglect—involving risk of physical harm due to the failure to provide adequate food, nutrition, or housing—was the primary neglect category, accounting for 39% of substantiated First Nations neglect cases. Consistent with these results, First Nations households involved in maltreatment investigations had lower incomes and poorer housing conditions than non-Aboriginal households. These data reinforce the connections between poverty, inequality, and neglect. With respect to Aboriginal people, it also reinforces the continuing impact of structural colonialism and the nature and scope of socio-economic disadvantages facing these communities.

Evidence that the social determinants of health, such as poverty and poor housing, contribute to disproportionality demonstrates the need to address these factors in preventing children from coming into care. These findings may also be linked to the length of time in care. Blackstock (2009b), in a comparative study of First Nations and non-Aboriginal children in care in Nova Scotia, found that there were few differences in the services provided to these groups of children. For both groups, poverty, overcrowded housing, and caregiver issues pertaining to substance abuse were the primary factors linked to difficulties in family reunification once children had been admitted to care. But it is also important to consider data summarized on the Assembly of First Nations website (2008a). These data indicate that almost one in four First Nations children were living in poverty in 2006, the rate of disabilities among First Nations children was almost double the rate for all Canadian children, overcrowded housing was double the Canadian rate, and the high school completion rate among First Nations youth was half the Canadian rate. Although these factors are linked to neglect and difficulties in reunification among all families, the higher frequency of these problems in Aboriginal communities is an important causal factor in the overrepresentation of Aboriginal children in the child welfare system.

Structural factors such as housing, employment, income, and food security are described by Loppie Reading and Wien (2009) as proximal determinants of health, whereas health care systems, educational systems, community infrastructures (including resources and capacities), and opportunities for cultural continuity are described as intermediate determinants of health. Service quality, capacity, and resources for children and families in Aboriginal communities are often underdeveloped, and it is the interactive effects between these intermediate determinants of health and the proximal determinants of health that make it more difficult to "close the gap" on the structural challenges facing Aboriginal communities.

Service Models and Cultural Continuity

Three of the most important factors to address in building capacity in Aboriginal child and family services are self-determination, institutional capacity, and cultural continuity. Issues pertaining to self-determination were briefly summarized in the previous section. The importance of cultural relevance is generally recognized, and traditional frameworks and practices have been incorporated into the service models that have evolved in many communities. For example, the medicine wheel framework is used quite often to conceptualize and guide service delivery, and the principles of self-determination and cultural relevance underpin the proposals advanced by Johnson for an urban educational support service for Indigenous children in care (Chapter 23). There is empirical support for the importance of traditional cultural practices in research on suicide conducted in British Columbia (Chandler & Lalonde, 1998). These researchers found that communities which had taken active steps to preserve and rehabilitate traditional culture had dramatically lower suicide rates than communities where this was not the case.

Chapter 22 describes a successful service model—based on principles associated with community caring and the medicine wheel framework—that has evolved in a First Nations agency serving several communities. There are other service models that appear to reflect improved outcomes for children. One example is Lalum'utul'Smun'een Child and Family Services in British Columbia, which has established a strengths-based model that involves community-based services and close connections with Elders (Brown et al., 2002). Another example is the model developed by Tikinagan Child and Family Services in northwestern Ontario. It is based on traditional teachings about customary care, along with a commitment to meeting the accountability requirements of its communities and the Ontario Ministry of Children and Youth Services (Brubacher, 2006).

Traditional beliefs and practices have also informed the development of smaller programs and specialized approaches to healing. For example, Sterling-Collins (2009) describes a holistic approach to supporting children with special needs, and Desmeules (2007) outlines a family group conferencing process applicable to Aboriginal children and families in north-central Alberta. Healing in an Aboriginal context is closely linked to spirituality and the circle concept, beginning with the individual and building outward to include family, communities, and society (Connors & Maidman, 2001). One example of this is the community-initiated healing circle approach to dealing with sexual abuse established in Hollow Water First Nation, Manitoba (Aboriginal Corrections Policy Unit, 1997).

A review of these service models suggests that several characteristics are associated with success. These are identified briefly below:

- *Commitment to community-based services:* This includes not only the decentralization of staff and service delivery responsibility, but also an investment in building community capacity and local initiatives through the use of a community development approach. This may be interpreted in different contexts as community building, community empowerment, or local capacity building.

- *The importance of traditional culture and the guidance of Elders:* Alfred (1999) has referred to this as "self-conscious traditionalism," in which traditional values are identified and consciously used to inform contemporary activities. Such values may be included in developing frameworks for practice (e.g., medicine wheel, customary care) that more closely represent and resonate with the strengths approach as defined by Aboriginal people. In addition, Elders are often used as a source of knowledge and guidance. Traditional Indigenous helping services may be combined with contemporary practices in helping.

- *Vision, leadership, and planning:* Successful service models appear to be associated with strong leadership and a commitment to planning. There is a common commitment within the agency to a service mission that reinforces cultural and community engagement as important components in service delivery. Accountability to community, agency stakeholders, and government is essential, and this helps to avoid problems commonly associated with political interference.

- *A focus on internal capacity:* This includes the availability of adequate resources, including staff. There is also significant investment in staff training and advanced professional education, as required, to build staff capacity for providing quality services across the continuum of care.

Resilience and Well-Being

There has been significant growth in the capacity of Aboriginal organization to provide culturally appropriate services to families and children, including the expansion of customary care and more preschool services for children in the early years. Between 1990 and 2008, the number of First Nations child and family services agencies grew from 34 to 108, and these agencies provided at least partial child welfare services to 442 of the 606 reserve communities served by Indian and Northern Affairs Canada in 2008 (Auditor General of Canada, 2008). The Truth and Reconciliation Commission headed by Justice Murray Sinclair, which is designed to hear the stories of those involved with or affected by residential schools, is now beginning its work. Aboriginal political organizations exert considerable influence on social policy issues, and the First Nations Child and Family Caring Society, under the leadership of Cindy Blackstock, has emerged as a key research and advocacy organization on First Nations child and family service issues. Within an Aboriginal world view, helping and wellness are based on a commitment to holism, which can be defined as achieving harmony and balance among the physical, mental, spiritual, and emotional components of one's being. Holism is also connected to the development of a positive Aboriginal identity, and the focus on identity and its association with traditional cultural connections has received increased attention in the literature on social work practice (McKenzie & Morrissette, 2003).

The developments noted above provide evidence of the resilience of Aboriginal people and communities. However, an important challenge is to move beyond problem analysis and an understanding of general service models to increased knowledge about the types of intervention that can improve outcomes for children and families. While improvements in education and employment have occurred for Aboriginal people in general, particularly in the urban context (Rabson, 2009a), Johnson (Chapter 23) notes that educational outcomes for former Indigenous children in care remain quite dismal.

There are also concerns about how outcomes are defined and measured within an Aboriginal cultural context. A participatory research study (McKenzie, Bennett, Kennedy, Balla, & Lamirande, 2009) involving four First Nations agencies in northwestern Ontario was conducted to explore culturally appropriate ways of assessing child welfare outcomes in their communities. The study identified three general problems that affect different levels of outcome assessment. One was the cultural relevance of instruments in use (primarily the LAC approach). Although there was general support for the developmental outcomes included in the LAC approach, respondents felt that questions and guidelines did not adequately represent cultural imperatives in the communities they served, or the cultural dimensions of services being delivered to children in care. Some adaptations had been made to the LAC instruments by adding culturally relevant questions, and in one case a new dimension on culture was proposed. However, these adaptations were not regarded as fully satisfactory. It is important to note that the cross-cultural relevance of outcome measures is often coloured by the process used in design and implementation, in that too often these measures are prescribed by central authorities with too few opportunities for Aboriginal input. This is an important issue to address both in relation to service design and evaluation. In a recent study, Filbert and Flynn (2010) examined the ability of the developmental assets emerging from the LAC Assessment and Action Records, and separate questions that assessed cultural assets, to explain variations in resilience among First Nations youth. Results suggest that higher levels of developmental assets were associated with increased resilience on all four criterion variables: pro-social behaviour, self-esteem, educational performance, and behavioural difficultness. Cultural assets were significantly related to fewer behavioural difficulties, but not with other resilience measures. Although these results generally support the cross-cultural use of the LAC developmental outcomes in assessing well-being, one should not conclude that cultural assets are unimportant. The questions used to assess cultural assets in this study were quite limited, and more work, in consultation with Aboriginal people, is required to better define this concept. One Australian Aboriginal leader in child welfare has noted that it is important to ensure that "culturally appropriate" services are "culturally effective," and attention to what and how cultural assets influence resilience may be an important step in this direction.

A second problem is the inadequacy of current approaches to assessing outcomes for in-home services to families. This is a more general problem in child welfare, but it is of particular importance in an Aboriginal context because of the focus on family preservation and reunification. Although outcome assessment measures, including LAC, are available for assessing the well-being of children and/or families, most are time-consuming or intrusive to use on a widespread basis. In addition, cultural relevance needs to be considered.

Finally, there is the question of community well-being raised by a focus on "community caring." The costs and benefits of programs which were included in the case study in Chapter 22 are important to consider. However, assessing more intangible community-based outcomes that go beyond program costs and benefits remains a challenge not only in child welfare but also in other programs. In addition, the interactive effects of policies and practices on community capacity building need to be considered. One example of this is how placing children in resources outside the community affects the educational system. In two Manitoba First Nations communities in 2008, between 50% and 60% of school-aged children were in alternative care placements in Winnipeg, leading to lost revenues for community-based schools that receive their funding based on enrolment figures each September. The annual loss in educational operating funds was estimated between $1 million and $2 million for each of these communities, and in one community all classes for kindergarten to Grade 2 were cancelled because there were no children for these grades (Shangreaux, 2009). Placement alternatives for children must be responsive to their needs, and in the short term it is not always possible to use local community resources. However, this example raises two important points. First, capacity building in establishing alternative resources is required to keep at least some children closer to home, and second, building infrastructure capacity in communities needs to consider the availability of resources for programs other than those directly related to child and family services.

Implications for Research, Policy, and Practice

There are a number of implications that emerge directly from the discussion of these major themes. Priorities identified here are organized under the three headings of research, policy, and practice.

Research

Although the *Canadian Incidence Study of Reported Child Abuse and Neglect* has helped to identify some of the characteristics of abuse and neglect involving Aboriginal children, this study does not yet include a representative sample of Aboriginal children and families reported to child welfare authorities, and so has limitations. Further research focused on understanding factors associated with disproportionality is necessary, but it is also important to identify communities where quality services to children and families are being provided in ways that appear to be reducing the proportion of children admitted to care. Understanding more about what works for whom will help to enhance service models that move us closer to "best practice" in these communities.

Additional research that focuses on developing better outcomes in Aboriginal child and family welfare, and applying successful measures, is also important. Special attention to in-home services for families and the outcomes for Aboriginal children in long-term care is required. As well, the cultural assets that ensure resilience, particularly in relation to children, need to be better understood.

Studies that examine more of the experiences of families and children receiving services from Aboriginal child and family service agencies will not only assist in understanding the relative benefits of self-determination in child and family services, but also identify policies and practices that can help to improve these services.

Research that has focused on Indigenous communities has often been criticized on methodological grounds, and for its failure to benefit these communities. An expectation arises, therefore, that research studies conducted in Aboriginal communities incorporate the principles of Aboriginal ownership, control, access, and possession (OCAP) (First Nations Centre, 2007). These ethical principles, which are now generally incorporated into national research protocols for government sponsored research, require the active engagement of

Aboriginal people in decisions regarding the control and utilization of research affecting their interests.

Policy

In a policy context, the problem of disproportionality is not easy to resolve. It is more complicated when one recognizes that a higher proportion of children in care may also mean that children in need of protection are being well served. For example, one might increase the threshold of risk for taking children into care, but in the absence of alternative services, too many children may be left in circumstances where they will be harmed. As discussed, the high frequency of neglect among referrals involving First Nations children reinforces the need for increased measures to address poverty and other socio-economic inequalities in Aboriginal communities.

An important development consistent with this theme may be to consider child welfare issues within a broader public health context. One strategy is to consider how the social determinants of health can provide direction to policy-related initiatives. As earlier noted, Loppie Reading and Wien (2009) provide a broad framework for examining how those social determinants influence the health outcomes of Aboriginal peoples. More specific attention to how these health determinants affect trends in Aboriginal child welfare is explored by McKenzie and Shangreaux (2010). The link between poverty (and related factors such as unemployment), poor housing, inadequate human services, and disproportionality is not new, but an emphasis on these linkages reinforces the importance of broader measures to address these health determinants as part of the solution. In addition, Loppie Reading and Wien's (2009) identification of self-determination, adequate community infrastructure, and opportunities for cultural continuity as important health determinants for Aboriginal peoples provides guidelines that need to be considered in advancing more specific policy initiatives. This focus needs to be considered within a health promotion framework that is broadly applicable to children, families and communities. At the same time, some issues affecting Aboriginal communities need special attention. For example, particular attention to the problems of FASD and suicide are required. As well, many prevention and early intervention programs, including those offered by non-government agencies, are either unavailable or under-resourced when compared with other communities.

A second strategy advanced by Loxley and Deriviere (2005a) uses the public health classification of primary, secondary, and tertiary prevention in discussing the continuum of care in Aboriginal communities. They note that the effectiveness of prevention is enhanced when an issue, such as FASD, is addressed at multiple levels by a combination of programs, including medical services, health education, Elder counselling, and support groups. A summary of best practices in prevention applicable to Aboriginal communities is provided in Loxley and Deriviere (2005a, pp. 132–8), although it is stressed that such programming must integrate cultural practices and collaborative working relationships with communities to be effective. However, none of the three levels of prevention can achieve maximum effectiveness unless the structural issues in these communities are addressed through capacity building programs designed to strengthen the infrastructure of Aboriginal child and family services agencies and their communities (Shangreaux, 2004). And only through adequate financial resources and a community-building approach can general development strategies dealing with the structural barriers to well-being, such as poverty, inadequate housing, addictions, and violence be adequately addressed. There has been little evidence of new investment designed to make a serious dent in the structural inequalities that affect Aboriginal communities, but the 2010 federal budget did include increased funding for on-reserve child welfare services (Rabson, 2010). Whether this will make a difference is not yet clear, but it could provide some support in addressing some of the funding deficiencies identified in Chapter 21, and help to facilitate the development of differential response systems in these communities. As noted in Chapter 22, increased resources and the ability to use them in a more flexible fashion can assist in establishing alternative support programs for children and families.

A critical policy issue pertains to jurisdictional disputes over the responsibility for service provision and funding. This issue is particularly relevant to First Nations services on-reserve. Although a common dispute is whether the federal or provincial government should provide or fund services, disputes also occur between departments within a single government or between agencies. Chapter 21 highlights how one survey of 12 First Nations agencies' records identified 393 incidents involving jurisdictional disputes over a one-year period of time. On many occasions these disputes can lead to significant delays in service, and in some cases the failure to provide needed services. This has led the First Nations Child and Family Caring Society (FNCFCS) (2005) to champion *Jordan's Principle*, named after a young child who died in hospital because federal government departments could not agree on which department would assume responsibility for the costs of providing home-based services. The "child first" policy advocated by the FNCFCS is that the government or department that receives a request for payment of services for a First Nations child will pay, without disruption or delay, to ensure services otherwise available to non-Aboriginal children in similar circumstances. The government or department then has the option of resolving final responsibility for funding the service or referring the matter to a dispute resolution process. While this principle has received some support, widespread adoption of *Jordan's Principle* would help to ensure timely and more equitable services to First Nations children caught in the middle of such disputes.

Practice

Some of the practice implications have been identified in our discussion of service models. New service models are being developed, and there is a variety of family support initiatives. One example includes an intensive family preservation program for parents and their children in a rural setting in Manitoba. In this residential program, designed for both parents and their children, teaching and support services focus on developing parenting skills and new problem-solving approaches over a six-week time period. Johnson (Chapter 23) provides a useful reminder that the child welfare system alone will not be sufficient to break the cycle of disadvantage. Quality education that is culturally appropriate will contribute to greater resilience.

We conclude by drawing special attention to two issues. The first is that of human resources, particularly in relation to training and professional education. Considerable efforts have been made to provide professional social work education to Aboriginal students in many universities, but there is demand for increased specialization in child welfare and the inclusion of more content on child welfare practices relevant to the Aboriginal service context. Ongoing professional training is also important, and both government and child welfare organizations must take an active leadership role in this area.

The second issue concerns the need to build capacity by increasing the level of coordination between service providers within communities. There are examples of this which capitalize on the principle of wraparound services, and an increased emphasis on building a community coordinated response is an important aspect of building community capacity.

The well-being of children and families requires attention to rights and responsibilities as well as needs, and as Prilleltensky and Prilleltensky (2006) have noted, this is highly dependent on relationships and the community in which one lives. Thus, the well-being of Aboriginal children and families cannot be achieved without also addressing the well-being of the organizations and communities that are connected to their daily lives.

Selected Practice Issues

Introduction

The practice issues presented in this section have been chosen for their particular relevance to current child welfare discourse, though for somewhat different reasons. In 2003 we commented: "Social work records are remarkable for the absence of information about fathers. One disturbing effect of the tendency toward mother blaming is the way that it avoids holding fathers accountable. This in turn makes it unlikely that services or treatment will be offered to them" (Kufeldt, Este, McKenzie, & Wharf, 2003, p. 402). Seven years later there has been little change—representing a serious gap in serving children. This topic, including some important research on the multi-faceted roles played by fathers, is addressed in Chapter 26. Chapter 27 addresses the flip side, mother blaming. At the same time, it—together with Chapter 28—offers some new insights into one of the most serious issues of our times, the prevalence of fetal alcohol spectrum disorder (FASD) in the child welfare population.

The beginning and end of Part IV present contrasting perspectives on contemporary challenges for social work education and practice. The first chapter deals with a dilemma at the micro level of practice: how can one approach certainty in such a complex field of practice? Decision-making at the front end of child protection is literally, at times, a life and death issue. In North America the use of risk assessment tools has become increasingly the route of choice, particularly at the managerial level. Chapter 25 provides a critical analysis of the strengths and weaknesses of these tools and their use in practice.

At the other end of the spectrum, Chapter 29 takes us from North America to developing countries and summarizes the macro level challenges facing social work. In our judgment it was important to include this perspective in the current text. Modern communications bring global issues to the consciousness of all of us. Social work, along with other professions (e.g., medicine and nursing), is increasingly engaged with the task of bringing training and development to countries struggling to improve the conditions of their citizens. In addition, developed countries are opening their doors to immigrants and refugees looking for a better life for their children. Understanding the conditions that newcomers have experienced is essential if social workers are to respond appropriately to these needs both at home and abroad. A brief review of themes and implications emerging from this section is provided in Chapter 30.

25

Risk Assessment in Child Welfare
Use and Misuse

Jan Christianson-Wood

C hild welfare workers face difficult decisions in attempting to meet what may be perceived as competing goals: safeguarding children and preserving family unity. The realities of child protection casework place pressure on workers to "get it right" when assessing risk, as there are potentially harmful consequences for children and families when we are wrong. For the child welfare worker faced with a situation of child abuse or neglect by a caregiver, trying to predict what might happen if the child's situation remains unchanged involves an assessment of risk. Thus, in a general way, risk assessment in child welfare can be described as an activity designed to prevent future harm to the child.

The ability to estimate the probability and severity of future harm is useful in such situations. Rycus and Hughes (2003) argue that best practice in these circumstances requires the use of formal risk assessment protocols based on the findings and conclusions of well-designed and implemented research. Shlonsky and Wagner (2005) caution that assessing risk in child welfare practice is similar to predicting the weather; a forecast of rain is not a certainty, but it does suggest when it is a good idea to carry an umbrella! This lack of precision in risk assessment is recognized by Cash (2001), who notes that

> risk assessment instruments are not a panacea for decision-making in child welfare. Decisions should optimally be made through a combination of both empirical evidence (science) and practice wisdom (art), as one without the other is incomplete. The synergy created by the art and science of risk assessment provides for a more holistic and effective assessment. (p. 825)

Controversies surrounding the use of risk assessment continue. At a general level are those that question the fundamental value of risk assessment, and express concerns about how risk assessment instruments narrow the decision-making focus to a limited set of factors defined by experts—a process that reinforces a top-down managerial approach to assessment in a field which cannot be regulated in this fashion (Callahan & Swift, 2006). Concerns are also raised about the predictive validity of risk assessment measures and the extent to which these are substituted for clinical judgement (Schwalbe, 2008). In addition, there are controversies surrounding the preferred type or model of risk assessment.

This chapter provides a brief examination of the context of risk assessment, and discusses two alternative approaches. It then focuses on the purpose of risk assessment in child protection, including a discussion of the potential for misuse of risk assessment in practice. Implications for research, policy, and practice are identified in the concluding section.

The Context

Risk assessment in child welfare work can be described "as a process for assessing the likelihood that a given person (usually a parent) will harm a child in the future" (Wald & Woolverton, 1990, p. 486). Risk assessment tools have become a focus of child welfare research and practice due to the difficulty in predicting under what conditions children who already have been abused or neglected will experience further maltreatment. Formal reviews of child welfare organizations, triggered by the deaths of children known to child protection services, typically focus on services delivered by individual workers, judged against practice standards and policies (Kanani, Regehr, & Bernstein, 2002; Reder & Duncan, 1999, 2004; Reder, Duncan, & Gray, 1993). Recommendations have tended to focus on lowering the threshold of risk required to protect children, as well as expanding the legal definitions of maltreatment to include future harm, thus justifying the use of risk assessment procedures to predict the future safety of children (Callahan & Swift, 2006). One consequence has been an increase in referrals for child abuse and neglect (see Chapter 1). Challenged by limited resources, this creates pressure on child welfare organizations to identify and focus service on children at most risk of harm, and to be more accountable for the services they provide and to whom. The methodology of choice has been risk assessment based on scientific knowledge as opposed to assessments based on value judgments.

Historically, risk assessment research has focused on the characteristics of parents or parent substitutes, as they were most often involved in specific acts of omission or commission (Ammerman & Hersen, 1990; Factor & Wolfe, 1990; Vondra, 1990). The prediction systems that emerged were built on the combined knowledge and opinions of experts regarding outcomes when certain characteristics were combined with particular events. This focus on caregiver characteristics is criticized by some as contributing to an inordinate focus on the "private troubles of families" as opposed to "public issues" such as poverty, race, gender, neighbourhood safety, and housing (Kufeldt, Este, McKenzie, & Wharf, 2003). The reality, however, is that assessing risk, and finding the most effective means of predicting future maltreatment, continue to be important aspects of protecting children.

Types of Risk Assessment Tools

The two main types of risk assessment instruments currently utilized in frontline child welfare practice are consensus-based models and actuarial models. These instruments are based on differing perspectives of risk assessment, and use different methods to process information. Actuarial risk assessment uses formal, repetitive information processing systems such as statistical analysis to identify predictive factors. In consensus-based systems, the variables used and their weightings are applied using an interpretive method which will vary from worker to worker and from case to case (Reid, 1997). Each is described below.

Consensus-Based Risk Assessment

Consensus-based instruments are constructed using the clinical judgments of experienced workers and the knowledge of experts. These are supported by literature reviews of research identifying factors associated with people who have abused or neglected children. The items included in a consensus-based risk assessment instrument reflect knowledge of child abuse and neglect that is both practice- and research-based, and linked to theories about why children are maltreated by their caregivers. These instruments assist workers in structuring information gathering about incidents of maltreatment, and provide documentation of the reasoning underlying the risk assessment results. Clinical judgment is used in determining risk levels (Baird & Wagner, 2000; Reid, 1997).

Criticisms of these instruments focus on the variability between instruments, including the type and number of items included, and their reliance on variables associated with a first known incident of maltreatment (D'Andrade, Austin, & Benton, 2005, 2008). They are also described as having less validity and reliability than actuarial instruments (Baird & Wagner, 2000; D'Andrade et al., 2005; Rycus & Hughes, 2003). In a review of risk assessment in child welfare, Rycus and Hughes (2003) express support for the use of validated consensus-based decision-making models to guide ongoing clinical assessments of safety and risk, family assessment, and service planning, but do not support their use for estimating the likelihood of future maltreatment.

Actuarial Risk Assessment

Actuarial instruments are developed from risk factors selected by the "empirical study of child protection cases and their future maltreatment outcomes" (Barber, Trocmé, Goodman, Shlonsky, Black, & Leslie, 2007). Risk factors are aggregated and statistically calculated to maximize the accuracy of predictions. Items or factors having a strong association with future maltreatment are identified and used to construct an instrument allowing workers to categorize families at varying levels of risk (Baird & Wagner, 2000). The instrument is scored in a mechanical manner to ensure consistency and to avoid modification by clinical judgment.

The actuarial tool dominating child welfare practice is the Structured Decision Making (SDM) risk assessment tool developed by the Children's Research Center in Wisconsin. The risk factors are derived from an empirical and retrospective analysis of cases in particular jurisdictions to predict risk for cases likely to be substantiated for maltreatment in the future. The factors included in the scales are subjected to further empirical analysis to produce a "weight," enabling the worker to add up the "weights" for each identified risk factor. The subsequent score determines the "level of risk," enabling users to deliver service based on an understanding of the probability of future harm. The retrospective analysis of cases will, of necessity, include information derived from the clinical context, as this is a component of child welfare files. The second part of the SDM process involves using "local" data, resulting in risk factors drawn from the community contexts in which the work is being done. While there will be similarities between jurisdictions, there may very well be differences that will affect the assessment of risk. At the same time, as research on the instrument has accumulated, there has been a growing confidence about the widespread applicability of items in the instrument. The SDM model, in addition to a risk assessment tool, also includes components to assist in screening, setting priorities for response, safety assessment, child needs and strengths assessment, family needs and strengths assessment, case planning, setting standards, and case reassessment. Not all tools in the SDM system are empirically based, e.g., the safety assessment and the child and family assessment tools combine research data, policy knowledge, and clinical knowledge and experiences (Child Welfare League of America [CWLA], 2005; Children's Research Center, 2008).

As child maltreatment is considered a low base rate phenomenon, it has been argued that actuarial classification is best suited to accurate prediction, and this is supported by research on actuarial instrument performance (Baird & Wagner, 2000; Barber et al., 2007). The relatively small set of case factors required to make a risk assessment is advantageous (D'Andrade et al., 2005, 2008), as is the reliability of these instruments; actuarial instruments are also less vulnerable to effects from the varying skill levels of individual workers than consensus-based instruments. Another argument for using actuarial models is that validation of consensus-based models takes place after implementation, while actuarial models are prospectively validated prior to implementation because of their statistical association with maltreatment.

Comparative Value of the Two Approaches

The reality is that knowledge and skill are necessary to use actuarial instruments despite the fact that they are based on the statistical association of particular factors with child maltreatment. As well, workers may be cautious about using an instrument that is not grounded in a causal theory of maltreatment (Schwalbe, 2004).

Consensus-based systems are criticized as requiring a higher level of education and experience in child protection, making them vulnerable to error when used by workers lacking training, knowledge, or experience, or not having access to competent supervision (Reder & Duncan, 2004; Wald & Woolverton, 1990). When using either type of instrument, workers must be able to recognize indicators of conditions, such as substance abuse, and also understand how their personal values impact on their interpretations of what they are seeing—or, in the case of the SDM system, how they interpret the definitions and criteria provided to guide workers in scoring. As noted by Rycus and Hughes (2003), there is no substitute for clinical knowledge and supervision. The clinician must therefore translate identified risk factors into an estimate of the probability that maltreatment will occur again, and what interventions may be required to address this risk. Indeed, the CWLA argues for clinically adjusted actuarial prediction where that is the tool of choice, to allow "for the consideration of plausible risk factors present in an individual case" (CWLA, 2005, p. 5). The SDM risk assessment tool provides workers, in agreement with their supervisors, with the ability to make such adjustments through the inclusion of "overrides."

Despite agreement that any instrument used to predict risk must be both reliable and valid, supporters of the two types of instruments differ on which approach best meets these criteria (Baumann, Law, Sheets, Reid, & Graham, 2005, 2006; Johnson, 2006a, 2006b).

Validity and Reliability

Knowing the accuracy of an instrument overall is important, but it also is important to know how often an instrument results in false positives (incorrectly scoring high risk) and false negatives (incorrectly scoring low risk) in order to understand where prediction errors are occurring. There is a value judgment required in determining how much error is acceptable in assessing risk, with the knowledge that false negatives leave children exposed to more harm or even death (Gelles, 1996). False positives subject families to intrusive intervention that may involve the removal of children. An instrument that is considered accurate should predict maltreatment recurrence at a rate between 65% and 85%. However, accuracy (validity) and consistency (reliability) are relative terms, as an instrument's ability to achieve a statistically significant level of accuracy means only that it can predict an event better than chance. The key questions are: How much better than chance, and what is the margin of error?

Reliability refers to the degree to which a risk assessment instrument results in similar decisions on similar cases. Inter-rater reliability refers to the degree to which different people using the same instrument will reach the same conclusion using the same information. The Structured Decision Making (SDM) system's actuarial risk assessment instrument, identified earlier, has been assessed as having much higher reliability than two consensus-based models (Baird, Ereth, & Wagner, 1999).

Problems can arise when workers are less consistent in some risk categories of the same instrument than in others; e.g., rating the same on high- or low-risk cases but demonstrating variability in the middle range of risk. When assessing the use of the instrument, it is necessary to decide if this degree of reliability is sufficient to ensure a child's safety. A lack of reliability in the application of any instrument has the potential to seriously compromise decisions regarding the safety of children (Baird et al., 1999).

Purpose and Use of Risk Assessment in Child Protection Work

Risk Assessment as Triage

Risk assessment is used in the triage of cases at intake during the investigative process, sometimes in combination with a safety assessment which assesses immediate danger to the child. The problem in assessing risk is to find a method for collecting and organizing known facts, extracting meaning from what has been gathered and producing a prediction of future harm. The resulting prediction assists child welfare agencies in making decisions that address legislative requirements and the best interests of the child. Workers and supervisors attempting to assess risk without the assistance of reliable and validated instruments or systems rely on their understanding of practice knowledge, or on "intuition" that is not necessarily reflective of evidence-based practice. Although they are not a substitute for skill and clinical knowledge, risk assessment systems are generally accepted as having the potential to contribute to better decisions than clinical judgment alone.

Risk Assessment as a Means of Setting Priorities

As resources decline and referrals increase, actuarial risk assessment is utilized at the "front end" of service delivery in order to classify families into categories of increasing risk, thus allowing agencies to focus service on where it is most needed. In their research, Barber et al. (2007) noted the significant increase of substantiated maltreatment cases in Ontario, and expressed support for the use of structured risk assessment to ration services (p. 1). With this information, child welfare agencies are able to concentrate on serving families at the highest risk of harming their children, guiding decisions to intervene, divert cases, or close them (Barber et al., 2007; Johnson, 2004; Schwalbe, 2004).

It is also possible that an increase in referrals could result in organizations deciding to raise the criteria related to risk factors in determining when a family would be eligible for particular services, potentially leaving children at risk of harm (English et al., 2000). In this regard, risk assessment has been criticized as benefiting organizations by providing a way to limit services to the most endangered children while reducing or eliminating service to a wider range of children and families (Saunders & Goddard, 1998). Nevertheless, providing services first to children assessed as being at highest risk is difficult to dispute, particularly when resources are limited. California's Family Risk Assessment instrument, which is based on the SDM model, focuses on opening and serving higher risk cases, as these are most likely to have occurrences or recurrences of maltreatment if effective services are not provided (Johnson, 2004, pp. 2–3).

Risk Assessment to Enable Appropriate Allocation of Services

Risk assessment is used also in Differential Response (DR), a model of service delivery described in Chapter 6. Differential response systems, or alternative response systems, as they are sometimes called, are dependent both on high quality risk assessment and on sound clinical assessments to ensure that families are matched with appropriate services. They are also dependent on the required services being available both in child welfare organizations and in the community. In such systems, more families can be directed to voluntary service providers in the community, or alternative services within agencies.

A number of Canadian jurisdictions are moving toward or have implemented SDM and/or DR systems which include actuarial risk assessment instruments. The appropriate use of risk assessment procedures will play an important role in determining whether the outcome of improved safety can be realized. Both SDM and DR share a common goal: greater safety for children through more effective and efficient service, in combination with the goal of greater accountability and transparency. Large-scale validation studies are needed to ensure that actuarial instruments deliver what they promise when used in these systems.

The Potential for Misuse in Risk Assessment

Greater reliance on formalized risk assessments may, on the face of it, appear to be consistent with the ability to offer more professionalized service. However, it is not problem-free. The literature on risk assessment in child welfare identifies a number of ways in which these instruments can be misused (see for example, Callahan, 2001; Callahan & Swift, 2006; Gillingham & Humphreys, 2009; Kufeldt et al., 2003; Saunders & Goddard, 1998; Wald & Woolverton, 1990). Examples of such misuse include using instruments for purposes other than those for which they were designed, and failing to address the impact of false negatives and false positives. Some of the "risks" in using risk assessment instruments inappropriately are identified below.

Risk Assessment and Individual Responsibility

Risk assessment procedures are criticized for shifting the emphasis and culpability for negative events from the agency to the worker. Workers are offered the assurance of objective certainty and legitimization in a work environment that is ambiguous and uncertain (Stanley, 2007).

The appeal of legitimization is understandable, as social workers are professionally and often physically vulnerable when engaged in work that is reactive and defensive (Stanley & Goddard, 2002). When children are injured or killed, there is, not surprisingly, little tolerance for such outcomes, leaving child welfare organizations facing public inquiries and questions about what appears to be a failure to give appropriate attention to important information (Munro, 2005). Typically, the cause is assigned to human error, individuals are identified and may be punished as a deterrent to others, professional independence is reduced with the introduction of new procedures, and monitoring is increased to ensure compliance (Munro, 2005; Reder et al., 1993; Reder & Duncan, 1999). Reder and Duncan (2004), in one response to this trend, call for a moratorium on inquiries, noting that 30 years of recommendations for change after the deaths of children in Great Britain have not led to any substantive changes.

Risk Assessment as Proxy for Change

Risk assessment is misused when it is substituted for meaningful change in how child welfare practice is conducted. As indicated by Munro (2005), there are factors affecting the assessment of risk that require consideration beyond what is usual in child welfare practice. Of particular importance is the process of implementing a new risk assessment system. These include attending to the reactions of front-line staff, including both legitimate concerns and resistance, and an acceptance by senior management that simply providing tools and compelling compliance may have the opposite effect of what was intended. For example, Gillingham and Humphreys (2009), in an Australian study, found significant inconsistencies in the utilization of SDM tools, including the risk assessment form, and a tendency to ignore results in the case planning process. Front-line staff must be given a voice in the implementation process, and have opportunities to explore how these tools affect both service to clients and their own workloads. In the absence of these considerations, using risk assessment processes may become just more forms to complete without any positive impact on practice.

Risk Assessment as Substitute for Training and Experience

Criticisms of risk assessment systems reflect an aspect of child protection work that should concern social workers. Organizations focus on systematizing and standardizing routine tasks to ensure that service (i.e., the output) is not affected significantly by the skill or experience of individual workers (i.e., the input). Procedures often appear to be substituted for professional judgment, limiting critical thinking, particularly in actuarial risk assessment. This occurs at the expense of developing clinical expertise in workers, and may lead to errors in decision-making, in addition to limiting the amount and scope of data collected and recorded for that purpose (D'Andrade et al., 2005, 2008; Ryan, Wiles, Cash & Siebert, 2005; Saunders & Goddard, 1998). A commitment to evidence-based practice acknowledges the need to demonstrate that *all* services are effective and efficient, including those requiring clinical judgment (Barber et al., 2007; Rycus & Hughes, 2003; Schwalbe, 2008; Shlonsky & Gibbs, 2004). Training and experience are essential elements in ensuring "best practice."

Risk Assessment as "Quick Fix"

Saunders and Goddard (1998) raise the question of who benefits from the use of standardized, structured risk assessment, in that it can be presented as a "relatively financially inexpensive 'quick fix' to difficult and distressing problems and system inadequacies" (p. 22). They argue that standardized risk assessment has the potential to divert an agency's attention and resources away from providing services to children who are the victims of present abuse in favour of predicting future abuse.

Despite their wide acceptance, concerns exist about how actuarial risk instruments may be misused, specifically by organizations unwilling or unable to provide sufficient human and material resources to protect children and assist families. The elimination or reduction of social service programs has resulted in an environment of scarcity for the most vulnerable families. Programs used by child welfare workers to support and strengthen families are often cut or underfunded to such a degree that children may not receive the range of services needed (Callahan & Swift, 2006; Reder & Duncan, 2004). What remains, Callahan and Swift (2006) argue, are programs intended to fix families, such as parenting skills programs.

Risk Assessment as New Technology

New systems of practice require careful planning and extensive training for management and workers, accompanied by research designed to ensure that implementation has been successful and that the risk assessment models chosen remain valid and reliable. The impact of large-scale and costly implementation initiatives requires that attention be directed to the inevitable impact on the lives of children and families, as well as the practice of workers and supervisors. New systems, including risk assessment systems, require additional time and effort, particularly in the training and implementation phase. Implementation issues are further complicated if new or untested technologies prove ineffective but are seen as too expensive to replace. Rycus and Hughes (2003) warn that the seemingly intractable problems of child welfare practice may leave us vulnerable to the promise of untested and unproven risk assessment models and technology.

Risk Assessment Philosophies

The question of how to best assess risk also brings forward consideration of the philosophies behind risk assessment. Saunders and Goddard (1998) support the use of contextual assessments of individual families through clinical judgment, and argue against individualized assessments of risk as described by Reid, Sigurdson, Christianson-Wood, and Wright (1996). Saunders and Goddard's argument is that risk assessment may be benevolent in intent but abusive in practice, as each child and family is unique. Actuarial methods, it is argued, may stereotype families through classification into risk categories, affecting the type and scope of services offered (Shlonsky & Wagner, 2005). Callahan and Swift (2006) note that the greater portion of time and money in child welfare is spent on investigations (of which an assessment of risk is a part) and on out-of-home placement as opposed to restoring balance to practice by providing supportive services to families. Philosophical differences such as these drive much of the debate and controversy surrounding the use of risk assessment tools.

Risk Assessment Is Not Infallible

The position that actuarial risk assessment is effective and efficient may not stand up under an examination of how accurately it predicts risk for a particular child in a particular situation (Callahan, 2001). It provides a classification of risk based on the *probability* of future harm, but not every family assessed as high risk or very high risk will go on to mistreat their children again. The limitations of risk assessment technologies must be acknowledged in the broader context of child welfare, as there are ethical and legal issues in failing to acknowledge these and their impact on children and families (Gelles, 1996; Rycus & Hughes, 2003).

Risk Assessment and Information

Schwalbe (2004) identifies a source of potential bias if risk assessment leads to mental shortcuts in processing information. These can lead workers to disregard key information, discount empirical information, or resist changing first impressions (Jagannathan & Camasso, 1996). Both consensus-based and actuarial risk assessments are vulnerable to misuse if the quality or quantity of information gathered is inadequate.

Risk Assessment for Assigning Service Categories

Shlonsky and Wagner (2005) note that risk assessment may be seen as a means of rationing services under conditions of high demand. Risk assessment procedures can be misused by organizations if risk ratings are linked to service provision; in such circumstances, shortages of human or material resources may lead to raising the threshold for children of families to "qualify" for protective services (Reder & Duncan, 2004; English et al., 2000). Conversely, risk ratings can be elevated by workers to ensure that families continue to receive services (Lyle & Graham, 2000).

Liability and Risk Assessment

Kanani, Regehr, and Bernstein (2002) reviewed the issue of liability for social workers in the aftermath of the deaths of children known to the child welfare system in Canada. They concluded that although social workers may feel under siege, they will not be held criminally culpable or civilly negligent if they act in good faith and according to accepted standards of practice, including the assessment of risk. D'Andrade et al. (2005) speculate that the same good faith immunity, which is extended to workers in the United States, could change if agency workers misused an agency's designated risk assessment instrument by failing to follow procedures when assessing risk. In addition, the agency could share in any liability if the instrument was not validated or if workers were not adequately trained in risk assessment. Conducting risk assessment as a defence against liability is inappropriate, and constitutes misuse unless the instrument is designed for that specific purpose rather than for the protection of children.

Conclusion and Implications

Any consideration of the use of risk assessment in child welfare raises questions about why a particular tool is chosen over others to predict future maltreatment. There are consequences for families and for workers if instruments are not valid and reliable; children may be left at risk of harm, while some families will experience unwarranted intrusion into their lives. At a more general level, Kufeldt et al. (2003) explore the effects of risk assessment on families, and argue that child welfare in Canada is moving toward a system preoccupied with the investigation of allegations of maltreatment and the removal of children upon substantiation. The focus on risk assessment contributes to deflecting attention from the role that structural issues, such as poverty, gender, and discrimination, play in the personal troubles of families.

Notwithstanding these cautions, risk assessment is a critical component of child welfare practice, and should be used with an appreciation and understanding of its strengths and limitations. This has implications for research, policy, and practice.

Research

There is limited research in Canada that has examined the impact of culture, race, or economic status on risk assessment. Research is needed to assess how a lack of services such as safe and affordable housing, daycare, parenting support services, or parent education services contributes to situations of increased risk for children and families.

Given the subjectivity and complexity involved in answering questions about human behaviour, can risk assessment instruments produce satisfactory results when used by workers of varying experience, education, and skill? Are scientific notions of objectivity, validity, and reliability sufficient when risk assessments are used to support potentially life-changing decisions for children and families? Outcome research is needed to help child welfare practitioners understand both the individual and systemic costs and benefits of risk assessment.

Risk assessment instruments cannot guarantee that results are accurate for each family assessed. It would be helpful to know if there are characteristics common to families who experience "false negatives" as compared to those who have "false positives." Another area of inquiry is whether there are characteristics of workers that are linked to false negatives and false positives. Large-scale validation studies are needed to improve the quality and quantity of knowledge about risk assessment application in Canada. As well, gaining an understanding of what it means when we "get it wrong" is an important step in improving risk assessment.

Policy

There are serious implications for child welfare policy-makers when implementing risk assessment systems. Clarity of purpose is important if risk assessment is intended to assist in allocating scarce resources. Family preservation is a desired outcome, but this requires that parents or caregivers demonstrate that their children will be safe at home. Child welfare has a history of improving services at the "front end," where families are scrutinized, yet failing to provide robust and extended service at the point where change is mandated. Ensuring that there is service to mitigate risk is critical to protecting children while supporting families.

Risk assessment has become increasingly appealing at the policy and managerial level. At these levels, it is promoted as a helpful adjunct to assessment and intervention. However, clear guidelines and protocols need to be established for its use. One investigation of decision-making in child protection found that inexperienced workers exhibited only superficial awareness of the concept of risk assessment; as a consequence, they were unable to weigh various factors and apply them to practice (Drury-Hudson, 1999). As Chapter 4 indicates, the majority of workers conducting investigations in the CIS–2003 study were relatively inexperienced. In this study the mean number of years of child protection experience for participating workers was 2.4, and many workers were not qualified social workers. Given both the uncertainty and complexity of risk assessment in child protection, service improvements require attention at the policy level to the important issues of staff recruitment, training, and retention.

Practice

Callahan and Swift (2006) note that the use of risk assessment moves child welfare practice in the direction of investigation and out-of-home placement. They see the introduction of differential response as a practice method that returns "some opportunities for judgment" to social workers (p. 214).

Good clinical judgment must accompany the use of risk assessment in child welfare work. Clinical judgment is needed to assess a family's situation and to produce an individualized case plan beyond the initial assessment of risk. Risk assessment, if done using a valid and reliable instrument, provides a degree of consistency in decision-making around maltreatment, helping to reduce the negative effects of idiosyncratic assessment or poor supervision. Despite these advantages, social workers should be aware of the limitations of risk assessment instruments and the potential impact on their practice.

In similar fashion, workers should be aware of their own needs for training, supervision, and support in order to offer quality service to children and families. If these are not present in their agencies, workers would do well to call on their agencies, professional associations, and unions to lobby for appropriate resources to respond to these needs. Adequate training, supervision, and support are essential elements in improving services and providing a rewarding practice environment for those committed to ensuring the safety of children and the health of families.

26

Engaging with Fathers in Child Welfare

Christopher Walmsley
Leslie Brown
Marilyn Callahan
Lena Dominelli
Susan Strega

Today, men are present in the lives of child welfare-involved children as resident or non-resident fathers, stepfathers, the mothers' partner, the mother's brother or father, and family friends. Yet the overwhelming focus of child welfare policy, practice, research, and education is mothers. This chapter explores why men and fathers are often not involved in child welfare services, describes how to encourage their involvement, and identifies some of the complexities of increased father involvement in child welfare. The chapter is based on a review of the literature and the authors' research.

Background
Isn't Parenting Really Mothering?

In Canada, the majority of first-level child protection social workers are women (see Chapter 4, which indicates that 82% of those participating in the 2003 CIS study were women), and historically child welfare has been viewed as a practice that takes place between women (Davies, 2005; Callahan & Walmsley, 2007; Scourfield, 2006). Until the end of World War II, almost all child welfare practitioners and administrators were women, but with the return of male war veterans, men began to enter the field of child welfare. Men are found today in the field as managers, parenting experts, and child development researchers, but research, education, and practice in child welfare has nevertheless remained focused on mothers.[1]

In our recent analysis of child protection practice, we found that social workers considered fathers irrelevant to both mothers and children 50% of the time (Strega, Brown, Callahan, Dominelli, & Walmsley, 2009). Men's potential violence may be a reason to avoid them in practice (Buckley, 2003), but clearly, social workers give little importance to involving fathers in planning for a child's care. In our society, caring work is constructed as feminized activity (Christie, 2006), and with the feminization of the child welfare workplace, men perceive social services as designed for women (Devault, Gaudet, Bolte, & St-Denis, 2005) or mother-centric (Ball & George, 2006). However, processes that exclude, marginalize, or render fathers invisible are not unique to child welfare. A study of popular parenting literature (Fleming & Tobin, 2005) found that although most books were written for the gender-neutral "parent," the adults portrayed with children were most frequently female (69%) in comparison to male (23%). In parent education materials, fathers are often depicted only in peripheral ways as sideline participants or helpers (Hodgins, 2007). A study of popular parenting materials in Britain and the United States also found fathers portrayed as doing little more than stepping in and helping, whereas mothers are viewed as the full-time parent (Sunderland, 2004). In parent education programs such as those found in Quebec's community-based health and social service centres, known as "Centres locaux de services communautaires" (CLSCs), only 18% offered self-help groups for future/new fathers, whereas about two-thirds offered programs for the gender-neutral parent (Richard et al., 2005). Parenting has traditionally been viewed as mothers' work, and even today, as fathers are portrayed "helping" at home, co-parenting still means "Mom's responsible, Dad helps out" (Carter & McGoldrick, 1999, p. 255). The gendering of parenting, which views child care as "mother's work," is expressed in child welfare practice by focusing on mothers and largely ignoring or excluding fathers.

Involved Fatherhood

Today, a growing popular and academic discourse argues the benefits of involved fatherhood. There are websites, research projects, father support programs, and father-specific education booklets available to encourage fathers to actively care for their children (Father Involvement Research Alliance website (n.d.); Fatherhood Institute website (n.d.); Devault et al., 2005; Hoffman, 2008; Nanaimo Men's Resource Centre, 2007). Since the publication of Michael Lamb's *The role of the father in child development* (1976), researchers have been interested in involved fatherhood. Since then, the benefits of increased father involvement have been argued to be: increased cognitive, emotional, relational, and physical well-being; higher measures of cognitive functioning; better relationships with peers and siblings; fewer health-related problems; less substance abuse among adolescents; lower rates of delinquency; less incarceration; less likelihood of becoming an unwed mother; and less likelihood of experiencing homelessness, receiving state benefits, or living in subsidized housing (Long, 2008). However, as Featherstone (2004) notes, disentangling whether poor outcomes for children in mother-led families are a result of father absence or the absence of a second parent are difficult, since the second parent is most often equated with being male. This raises the question of whether it is the male sex role that is essential or the fulfillment of economic, social, and emotional roles in child development (Featherstone, 2004).

Children can clearly benefit from the economic and social support of fathers, but the conditions under which fathers become active caregivers of their children also need to be understood. While a cultural shift may be occurring in which some fathers in heterosexual couples take primary responsibility for child care (Doucet, 2006), significant variations by class, culture, and employment status of the parents can also be found. In some dual income families, for example, when a mother's work requires some early morning or evening work or overnight travel, some fathers take more responsibility for household work and child care (Walsh, 2003b). The shift work of one partner can also demand that the father take more responsibility for child care in the home (Preston, Rose, Norcliffe, & Holmes, 2008). Yet, at times, increased father involvement in child care occurs only when circumstances demand it. These include when a man becomes a single father, after a couple's separation/divorce and the completion of a joint custody arrangement, or when a father is unemployed. Fathers who do become involved parents describe it as a "trial and error" process that they learned on the job, often by trying to be better than or different from the male figures in their lives (Steinberg, Kruckman, & Steinberg, 2000). Few supports, little mentoring, and considerable suspicion can greet the active caregiving father, and fathers often comment on the lack of educational resources specifically directed toward them.

Research on Fathers and Child Welfare

Studies that explore men's or fathers' participation in the lives of child welfare-involved children are not numerous. McKinnon, Davies, and Rains (2001) noted three dominant and sometimes overlapping constructions of men in the lives of Canadian teenage mothers. Men were seen as violent and irresponsible, as romantic attachments, or as involved in fathering. Scourfield (2003) described six constructions of men in the occupational discourse of child welfare social workers in the United Kingdom. Men were seen as a threat, as no use, as irrele-vant, as absent, as no different from women, and as better than women. Neither of these studies involved or interviewed men themselves. These studies and oth-ers (Strega et al., 2009; Swift, 1995b; Ryan, 2000) suggest there is a gendered occupational discourse in child welfare that supports absenting men and holds mothers responsible for the effect of men's behaviour on children. This dis-course fails to recognize that men have assets beyond economic support which could be beneficial to mothers and children, that some men could play more meaningful roles if given support and/or help to resolve their issues, and that oth-ers should not be ignored, as they may cause harm to mothers and children.

Research Method

The limited research about father involvement in Canadian child welfare sug-gested a multi-dimensional study, and we undertook several research strate-gies to identify more information about the role of fathers. These included a quantitative and qualitative analysis of child protection files, interviews with fathers whose children had child welfare involvement, an analysis of BSW cur-riculum materials, focus group interviews with social workers, and an exami-nation of child and family policies relevant to father involvement.

To understand better social workers' practice with fathers, we reviewed a ran-dom sample of 282 child protection case files in a mid-size Canadian city (Strega et al., 2009). We included birth/biological fathers, stepfathers, and men provid-ing emotional, financial, or social support to a child or children. The files were dated between 1997 and 2005, and were restricted to those files in which the mother was an adolescent (19 years of age or younger) at the time of the birth of at least one child. We were particularly interested in men who father children with adolescent mothers, as it is these mothers and their children who are more likely to be involved with child welfare services (Trocmé et al., 2005).

Results

Fathers in Child Protection Files

The mean age of mothers in the sample was 16 years, whereas the mean age of the first biological fathers was 19 and the mean age of the second biological fathers was 25. By "first biological father," we mean the first man to biologi-cally father the mother's child or children. "Second biological father" refers to the second man to do the same. Of these fathers, 25% to 30% were financially contributing to the mother and/or child. With respect to contact with their children, 49% of first biological fathers and 68% of second biological fathers had some contact with their children. Social workers' descriptions of fathers in formal and informal file recordings led us to create four analytic categories: father as risk, father as asset, father as risk and asset, and father as irrelevant. These categories were quantified based on social workers' expressed description of fathers (in both formal and informal file recordings), actions taken or not taken by social workers in relation to fathers (e.g., instituting or not instituting risk assessment procedures, including or excluding father in parenting assessments), and the number and type of social worker contacts or attempted contacts with fathers.

Our analysis of file data found that social workers considered almost 50% of fathers irrelevant to both mothers and children. Nearly 20% were viewed as a risk to mothers and children, while 20% were considered an asset. Over half (60%) of the fathers who were identified as a risk to children were not contacted by social workers, and similarly not contacted 50% of the time when they were considered a risk to mothers. They were contacted only 50% of the time when considered an asset to mothers, and contacted 75% of the time when viewed as an asset to children. Out of 29 first biological fathers identified as being violent toward mothers, 35% were currently contributing financial support, and 45% had contributed financially in the past. While child maltreatment concerns were noted for about 35% of first biological fathers, 47% of these fathers were not interviewed by social workers about these concerns. Our findings about the lack of contact with fathers, irrespective of whether they are perceived as risks or assets, are congruent with other studies of social work practice with fathers, as summarized by Daniel and Taylor (1999) and Risley-Curtiss and Heffernan (2003).

We conducted a further qualitative analysis of this file data to better understand the phenomenon of fathers' paradoxical presence and absence in child welfare (Brown, Callahan, Strega, Dominelli, & Walmsley, 2009). In previous studies (Rutman, Strega, Callahan, & Dominelli, 2002; Callahan, Brown, MacKenzie, & Whittington, 2004; Callahan, Rutman, Strega, & Dominelli, 2005; Strega, 2006), we had noted the active presence of fathers within the family, although it was often unacknowledged by child welfare workers. Frequently, there was a series of fathers coming and going, such as non-resident fathers who played a role in the lives of the women and children, and hidden fathers who were scarcely acknowledged because mothers were not willing to do so. We chose the word "ghost" to describe these fathers, as they *exist* in the lives of women and children in child welfare, but are *rarely seen* by social workers, even when present.

While ghosts may lack substance, they can appear and disappear unexpectedly. The malevolent ghosts of men who have been violent to mothers and children often engender fear, while the friendly ghosts of capriciously involved men are equally mysterious. Some fathers are seen clearly by child welfare workers as they are caring for their children, but we believe the majority of men are not seen. One social worker commented that she wouldn't open up the Pandora's box of "the father," as she had no resources to offer. Another stated that contacting fathers would double her workload.

Consistent with other research, we found that workers didn't hold fathers to account for their absence and their violence. If fathers are not in the home, they are not seen as "neglecting" their children for child welfare purposes (Scourfield, 2003; Swift, 1995b). If they are abusing their spouses, it is seen as a police matter or taken up in terms of a mother's responsibility to protect her children from this violence (Radhakrishna, Bou-Saada, Hunter, Catellier, & Kotch, 2001; Scourfield, 2003). Social workers have been found to routinely disregard dangerous men when assessing risk and family functioning (Munro, 1998; Stanley, 1997).

Cavanagh, Dobash, and Dobash (2007), who examined 26 fatal child abuse cases in which a child had been killed by a father or father figure, found that even when fathers perpetrated serious assaults they received minimal attention. Coohey and Zhang (2006) found that fathers who had physically abused their children were excluded from risk assessments, and Mayer, Dufour, Lavergne, Firard, and Trocmé (2003) noted that fathers are often left out of intervention plans. We found that whenever a parenting capacity assessment appeared in the files, only the mother had been assessed regardless of whether or not a man was actively participating in parenting. Many treatment or risk reduction plans involve instructing fathers to leave the home, and threaten the mother with the loss of her children if she is unable to effect this (Strega, 2006).

We further observed that mothers who live on the margins often have disincentives to identify the fathers of their children. Contiguous policies such as welfare provision and social housing make it difficult for women to identify fathers in their households for fear of jeopardizing their own and their children's benefits. As one father noted when talking about his girlfriend filling out her form for income assistance, "She put zero, zero, zero" when asked about income and his presence, even though he was living in the home and bringing in wages. Current welfare policies lack provision for poor non-custodial fathers to maintain adequate living space and resources to remain involved with their children. The number of children in the home or family unit determines income assistance needs, but children are rarely residing with their father.

It has also been noted that indigenous women in Canada were reluctant to ascribe paternity because both they and their children would be adversely affected by the children's loss of benefits under the *Indian Act* (Mann, 2005). Between 1985 and 1999, nearly one in five children born to registered Canadian Indians did not have their paternity designated (Blackstock, Clarke, Cullen, D'Hondt, & Formsma, 2004). The necessity of father invisibility in social welfare and social housing translates into father invisibility in child welfare.

Overall, social workers told three stories about fathers from our analysis of child protection files. They saw them as heroes, ghosts, or monsters. "Hero" fathers rarely came to the attention of social workers, and had such assets that they required no social work intervention. "Ghost" fathers were invisible men who moved in and out of children's lives and were subject to social work surveillance or control in case their interactions with children became "risky" or "dangerous." "Monsters" were deemed extremely dangerous, and social workers intervened to keep these men out of women's lives to protect both the mothers and children. If these men remained on the scene, mothers ran the risk of losing their children.

Interviews with Child Welfare-Involved Fathers

In order to understand fathers' experience of child welfare, we interviewed a purposive sample of 11 fathers whose children had child welfare involvement and who had "stepped up to the plate" and taken responsibility to care for their children (Strega et al., 2009). Yet they experienced child welfare services as an encounter with absolute power, felt an ongoing need to prove they were adequate parents, sometimes saw themselves as better caregivers than the women in their lives, and always felt under the surveillance of child welfare officials. At the same time, they wanted to be seen as both deserving and promising candidates for assistance by social workers. Other studies that interviewed young fathers found that they lacked education and economic advantages to financially support the mothers and their children (Glikman, 2004). They also felt unsupported, and rarely encouraged by social workers to become involved with their children (Speak, Cameron, & Gilroy, 1997; Tyrer, Chase, Warwick, & Angleton, 2005).

Fathering Content in the BSW Curriculum

We were curious about the role social work education might play in fathers' exclusion and lack of support from child welfare services. Our analysis of

Canadian bachelor's-level social work curricula found that students received little explicit education about fathers or fathering. From a two-thirds sample of Canadian schools of social work, we could identify only three courses at three schools (two francophone, one anglophone) where fathering content formed at least part of one class in a 13- to15-week BSW course. From 59 course outlines in six topic areas (child welfare, human development, family practice, human behaviour, family therapy, and Aboriginal studies), a total of four required readings related to fathers or fathering were found.

In a further analysis of fathering content, we examined textbooks required for human development, family practice, and child welfare courses. Human development texts made brief references to fathers, describing them as more active playmates than mothers, and as a potential compensatory attachment figure. Two family practice texts had extensive discussion of fathers and considered issues such as gender roles, household work, outside work, and changes that occurred for a couple with the birth of the first child, as well as divorce, single fathers, fathers from diverse cultural backgrounds, and gay fathers. However, these texts used United States society as the social context for the family, had U.S. publishers, and provided no Canadian content. Virtually all textbooks assigned to child welfare students made no reference to fathers; Swift's (1995b) Canadian study of child protection practice was the one exception (Walmsley, Strega, Brown, Dominelli, & Callahan, 2009). Swift found that social workers did not negatively assess fathers in comparison to mothers when considering household cleanliness or poor child care, and any contribution a father made was regarded as positive. Fathers could completely abandon their children with no comment at all by social workers, and the quantity, quality, or frequency of their financial input was generally not described. In general, social work students in Canada receive little education about fathering in spite of a growing list of reference material (Walmsley et al., 2009).

Discussion

Gender-Differentiated Practice

In light of our own research and our review of the literature, we conclude that social workers need to reconceptualize child welfare practice from gender-neutral, with its implicit focus on mothers, to gender-differentiated. That is, practice with women/mothers will be different from practice with men/fathers. To begin, child protection agencies need to acknowledge that fathers and fathering persons exist in the lives of child welfare-involved children, and should plan to include them at all stages of intervention. At a basic level, social workers need to search for contact information for both birth fathers and other significant father figures, record it in child protection files, and describe whether birth fathers or other father figures are actively involved with the child. More substantively, they need to take the necessary time to interview fathers and fathering persons to understand their role(s) within the family. Children's views about their relationships with both parents and fathering men in their lives need to be explored, and social workers need "to engage with fathers' versions of events in an open and exploratory way" (Family Rights Group, 2008). Follow-up communication and official correspondence should be sent to both mothers and fathers, and forms need to be designed to provide space for the views of fathers and not just those of "parents."

Resident and non-resident fathers should be systematically invited to attend child protection conferences and planning meetings. Social workers should also consider requiring men's participation in assessments and family interventions when they are involved with children. Scourfield (2003) argues that to not do so could be dangerous to mothers and children. Fathers' presence or absence should be routinely recorded in the file, and their views, when different from those of other family members or the child protection agency, should be noted in the file. To encourage fathers' participation in child protection conferences and meetings, social workers should take into account the distance fathers have to travel to the meeting (particularly in the case of non-resident fathers) and schedule them around fathers' work commitments. In general, fathers should be involved at all stages of the child protection process unless a specific and well-documented reason justifies their exclusion.

Social workers need to recognize the importance of positive father involvement, and be prepared to assist fathers in resolving issues that hinder their parenting ability, such as addictions, violence, unemployment, limited education, and mental health. When a father needs education or treatment, social workers can help maintain father involvement by searching for resources within a father's extended family to provide care for a child. These resources might be grandparents, aunts, uncles, and other extended family members. Their participation in planning for a child through a family group conference can ensure that a child grows and develops within a supportive family network.[2]

Euro-Canadian society has an idealized image of the "good father," but there are many different ways to be a father. Marginalized mothers often recognize men's day-to-day performance with their children as a more realistic and substantive definition of fathering (Haney & March, 2003) than the formal biological, institutional, and financial connections that policy-makers recognize. Today, men contribute to children's lives in a range of ways, and sometimes this is quite similar to the work of mothering (Doucet, 2006). In specific families, the allocation of tasks and responsibilities will be unique and can vary with time, and not reflect gender, class, or "race" assumptions (Ryan, 2000). Being able to identify the strengths of a man's engagement as a father, rather than simply his deficits, is key to gender-differentiated practice. Not all men at all times lack the capacity to have an active caring role with children. However, in a child welfare system attuned to the assessment of safety risks to children, men involved with children can become potential risks as perpetrators of abuse. In our research (Brown, Strega, Callahan, Dominelli, & Walmsley, 2009), fathers indicated that social workers often focused on problems, and saw their deficits and incapacities before they recognized any of their strengths. With support, encouragement, and recognition, more fathers will play active and positive roles with children. A father who receives support in making progress on his own issues will have a greater capacity to care for his children.

Multiple oppressions shape the identity and social world of some fathers whose children are involved with child welfare services. They are more likely to be young, poor, from racialized groups, unemployed, lack education and skills, and face greater disadvantages than other Canadian fathers. They may have been a child in care themselves and/or experienced violence, addictions, and abuse from parental figures in their growing years. A long history of social intervention in their family of origin can create a mix of suspicion, powerlessness, anger, and compliance in the present. At the same time, some of these men exert power and control over women and children through violence while simultaneously living out an intergenerational history of oppression that they still confront in daily life. Recognizing fathers' multiple oppressions, strengths, capacities for change, and the many ways of fathering is important to effective gender-differentiated practice.

Working with the Abusive or Violent Father

The reality of men's violence toward women and children presents the most complex challenge for practitioners engaging with fathers. As Featherstone (2003) notes:

> An agenda in relation to tackling family violence appears to have developed separately from that of engaging fathers. In this agenda, those who are violent are constructed as offenders who should be dealt with in the criminal justice system but they are often fathers and most frequently men. Are they the same fathers whose involvement are to be encouraged or are they different? (p. 248)

There is an extensive literature on fathering, men who batter, and the impact of violence on children, but little research considers men who batter as fathers (Guille, 2003; Peled, 2000). Studies about battering from the point of view of the male batterer are scarce, and "it is even more rare to find a study that explores their perspective regarding their children and their roles as fathers" (Guille, 2003, p. 155). As Scourfield (2006) says, "Abusive men are indeed the cause of most child protection concerns, often directly as abusers, or at least at one remove, perhaps as a threatening presence that affects a mother's parenting" (p. 441). At the same time, he also notes that "[m]ost children want contact with most fathers" (p. 441). Research on children with violent fathers has found that they are caught between strong opposing emotions, seeing either the good and loving father or the bad and abusive father, and are often unable to deal with the contradictions (Peled, 2000). At the same time, family policies have focused on maintaining family links, constructing fatherhood as non-violent, and seeing virtually any involvement by fathers as "good-enough" fathering (Eriksson & Hester, 2001).

Little research on the outcome of parenting education work with abusive men exists, and these men are simply "let off the parenting hook" (Peled, 2000). Mothers then become responsible for managing these men in their children's lives, and find themselves blamed when their children are harmed. Although some argue that social workers should work with abusive fathers (Scourfield, 2003), the difficulty is distinguishing situations where social work intervention with violent and/or abusive fathers would benefit mothers and children from situations where it would increase the risk of harm or further harm them.

Substantive research in this area is not available, but a number of cautionary practice principles can be identified from the existing literature. First, to engage with violent/abusive men, social workers should not put themselves at risk or endanger the safety of mothers and children (Daniel & Taylor, 2001). Second, initial intervention with abusive fathers should not focus on the development of child management skills, as the primary issues for these men are overly controlling behavior, a sense of entitlement, and self-centred attitudes. These issues need to be addressed successfully before parenting issues can be explored (Scott & Crooks, 2004). Intervention programs should assume that many men have little motivation to change. "Maltreating fathers typically do not seek intervention voluntarily, nor are they intrinsically motivated to change their parenting style" (Scott & Crooks, 2004, p. 101). As these authors suggest, abusive men may also justify their behavior on the basis of traditional gender stereotypes, and these attitudes need to be explicitly addressed in treatment as they provide an underlying framework for child maltreatment.

Third, abusive men also need to understand that the relationship they have with their children is not independent of the relationship they have with the children's mother. "Intervention needs to convey … that being a good father requires that they avoid or end abuse against their children's mother and that they develop a relationship with her that is respectful" (Scott & Crooks, 2004, p. 104). As little is known about the effectiveness of parenting intervention with abusive men, any attempt to intervene directly "should be based on a carefully designed model which takes into consideration the danger involved, and is fully agreed upon and co-ordinated with the children and the victim-survivor" (Peled, 2000, p. 33). Abusive fathers who attempt to rebuild relationships with their children also need to recognize that the relationship is complex and fundamentally damaged. They need to be patient to allow children adequate time to rebuild the trust that has been violated (Scott & Crooks, 2004).

While identifying safe conditions for fathers with a history of violence and abuse to re-engage with their families is important, there are some situations where families should be supported to end contact with fathers. These include "men who are withdrawing from their family, who have already caused substantial harm to their children, and who are actively avoiding services that challenge their behavior" (Scott & Crooks, 2004, p. 107). In other cases, where men may be able to benefit from services, they should have their contacts with their children supervised. Ending or limiting contact with fathers should involve a carefully developed retrospective and prospective assessment of the harm to children and mothers of ongoing contact.

Conclusion

Child welfare agencies that "see" fathers, and provide policy and practice guidance to their social workers about engaging with them, will in the long term reduce the risk of harm to children and mothers. However, further research is still needed to describe helpful social work intervention from a father's point of view, and to document effective father-inclusive practice. Policy change is also needed to differentiate gender-specific rights, roles, and responsibilities of mothers from fathers in relation to children's care, protection, and well-being. Adequate initial and ongoing training of social workers is required to enable them to effectively engage with fathers and respond well to violent, abusive, and controlling men. Social workers who create a space for fathers to reflect on their behaviour in intimate relationships and to heal from their traumas will enable them to become more positively involved with their children, and, ultimately, to have better ongoing relationships with children and grandchildren.

Notes

1   During the six-year period ending in 2007, only three papers about fathering were given at the annual Canadian Association for Social Work Education (CASWE) conference. In contrast, 21 papers about mothering were given in the same period. Child and adolescent psychology research shows a similar trend. Researchers focus on mothers and ignore fathers (Phares, 1992; Phares et al., 2005; Cassano et al., 2006). A search of the (U.S.) National Clearinghouse on Child Abuse and Neglect found 3,031 "mother" documents and 1,023 "father" documents—a 3:1 ratio. Similarly, a search of the National Clearinghouse on Family Violence (Public Health Agency of Canada) found 1,419 "mother" documents and 300 "father" documents, close to a 5:1 ratio.

2   The many specific suggestions in this section are derived from Featherstone, Rivett & Scourfield (2007), Daniel & Taylor (2001), the Family Rights Group (2008), Ferguson & Hogan (2004), Ryan (2000), and our own work (Brown, Strega, Callahan, Dominelli, & Walmsley, 2009).

27

Critical Issues of Practice and Protection in Relation to Families and Fetal Alcohol Spectrum Disorder

Dorothy Badry

The purpose of this chapter is to provide an overview of the broad social and political response to the issue of fetal alcohol spectrum disorder (FASD) as it relates to women's health research in Canada and child protection. It is critical to recognize that the myriad of disabilities caused by alcohol exposure in utero emerge from backgrounds where intergenerational child abuse and exposure to alcoholism are often historical problems. A particular focus on issues for families in relation to their involvement with the child welfare system will be presented through utilizing information gathered in a qualitative study from my doctoral research (Badry, 2008).

The topic of fetal alcohol syndrome (FAS) and fetal alcohol spectrum disorder (FASD) is one of great interest to all sectors in the health field. I purposely use both the terms FAS (Jones, Smith, Ulleland, & Streissguth, 1973) and FASD (O'Malley, 2000; Streissguth & O'Malley, 2000) because they in fact represent two very different phenomena. The term FAS represents a diagnostic category that identifies a severe consequence of alcohol exposure. Children diagnosed with this condition can have multiple disabilities such as cognitive delays, cardiac defects, and growth and developmental problems (Stratton, Howe, & Battaglia, 1996; Streissguth, 1997). Fetal alcohol spectrum disorder (FASD) is currently considered an umbrella term in which FAS is one of the conditions along the spectrum (Streissguth & O'Malley, 2000). The term FASD will be utilized throughout this chapter as it reflects current terminology, except in those cases where the reference is directly to a diagnosis of FAS.

I begin with a brief description of my own interest in the topic. Then, in order to illuminate the complexity of the issue of the birth of children diagnosed with FASD, the following sections are offered: background, the framing of FASD within society, alcohol use during pregnancy, and key Canadian studies. This is followed by a discussion of child protection issues, and I offer a profile of one birth mother from my study. Relevant literature is integrated throughout the chapter. The chapter ends with conclusions and recommendations.

Background

My interest in the area of FASD began in 1992, while working for Alberta Children's Services, when I met a 16-year-old youth who had been diagnosed with FAS. As knowledge about FASD became more available, child protection authorities began to recognize the complexity of the needs of both children and families who had problems related to substance misuse. I identified complex case management as an important construct for working with families over the short and long term. The focus of this chapter is primarily on birth mothers and their needs in relation to child welfare practice. This research represents a way to include the voices of women in the public discourse about FASD.

Within my inquiry of eight women, there were 28 pregnancies in total and 19 live births. Of these 19 children, 13 were in parental care and only one was an emancipated adult. Five children remain in the care of child welfare. The age of first pregnancy ranged from 15 to 18 years for seven of eight participants, while the age that drinking began ranged from 10 to 18 years.

Framing Fetal Alcohol Spectrum Disorder within Society

There is increased awareness of the complexity of FASD as a significant challenge to traditional child welfare practice. According to Floyd, Ebrahim, Tsai, O'Connor, and Sokol (2006), "Prevalence rates of FAS range from 0.3 to 2.0 cases per 1,000 live births depending on the methodology used, and the subpopulations assessed" (p. 149). Alberta Health Services (2007) estimates that 9 of every 1000 births have fetal alcohol spectrum disorder in Canada. Research of children in the care of child welfare agencies in Manitoba estimated that 17% of children in care have a fetal alcohol spectrum disorder (Fuchs, Burnside, Marchenski, & Mudry, 2005). Concerns for children with FASD, in relation to child welfare, is that they come into care at a younger age than other children and become permanent wards of the government more quickly (Fuchs, Burnside, Marchenski, Mudry, & De Riviere, 2008). Variance amongst prevalence rates exists, as there is no coordinated approach in Canada to gathering this information.

Fetal alcohol spectrum disorder (FASD) in contemporary Western society has become overtly represented as a moralized disability (Armstrong, 1998, 2003; Poole, 2003). The preventable nature of FASD frames it as a social problem that affects everyone, and public recourse lies in targeting conceiving women for prevention campaigns. If FAS were simply preventable by abstention from alcohol during pregnancy, why do children continue to be born with this problem? Discourse on prevention suggests that pregnant women, if they do not refrain from alcohol, must be held responsible—ethically, socially, morally, medically, and politically—for any alcohol-related difficulties the child experiences.

Women who are alcohol addicted often become separated from their children due to child welfare involvement, contributing to issues of loss and grief, rendering them more vulnerable to their addictions, and silencing their voices. The treatment of alcoholism is not a service integrated into child welfare practice, and women who require treatment are forced to place their children in foster care voluntarily, or have them apprehended. The family voice has not been heard in relation to FASD as a disability because birth mothers are often disenfranchised, and because this topic is one that still represents shame and blame. As a prevailing discourse, women are held responsible for causing a preventable disability.

Alcohol Use During Pregnancy

There is massive denial in contemporary Western society about the use of alcohol as a serious problem. An introduction to alcohol use and alcoholism within the family and society is a factor leading to intergenerational substance abuse. Alcohol is a teratogen, defined as an "agent or factor causing malformation of an embryo" (*Oxford English Dictionary*, 2001, p. 1478). There is a tendency not to view the use of alcohol as the ingestion of poison, but rather as a personal and social stimulant, a socially acceptable practice.

Alcohol consumption during pregnancy presents a conundrum to society. Armstrong and Abel (2000) highlight concerns about the "reinvigoration of the temperance mentality in American life," and identify FAS as a problem of "moral panic" (p. 276). This raises the concern of the politics of issues of gender-based "social control" (p. 280), and, subsequently, the responsibility women hold for the future. In the flurry of activities focused on educating and informing the public about FASD, the voices of birth mothers have been absent in the discourse. Radomsky (1995) uses the metaphor of lost voices to apply to Aboriginal women, women living in poverty, and women dealing with domestic violence and other forms of oppression, culturally and within society.

Armstrong and Abel (2000) have flagged a concern about identifying "moral disorder" in women through the diagnosis of their children with FAS (p. 276). The notion of maternal-fetal conflict (Poole, 2003) has harsh implications for women. Astley, Bailey, Talbot, and Clarren (2000) suggest that birth mothers of children diagnosed with FAS are often separated from their children through child welfare apprehension. This contributes to their being pushed further to the outside and placed on the margins in relation to the lives of their children. From a policy perspective, creating effective responses and programs remains a challenge.

Key Canadian Studies

The "G" case of 1997 was a pivotal one in Canadian legal history, riveting public attention to dominant issues of power, control, and personal autonomy between the individual and the state. Ms. G, an Aboriginal woman who was five months pregnant, had been confined to a Manitoba jail cell. She had previously given birth to other children affected by substance use during pregnancy, and had now been ordered into treatment to prevent further substance use while she was expecting. Her incarceration was subsequently deemed unconstitutional in a court challenge. As well as being widely publicized in the Canadian media, it became the subject of an analysis that served to broadly inform policy and practice for pregnant women using substances (Rutman, Callahan, Lundquist, Jackson, & Field, 2000). The authors identified concerns and provided key recommendations for supporting women in these circumstances, including key paradigm shifts:

- from a moralizing/medical model to a harm reduction/health promotion philosophy;
- from a child welfare mandate as protection-focused to one that emphasized supporting families; and
- from viewing child apprehension as a failure on the mother's part to a failure of the system/community to provide what was needed (Rutman et al., 2000, p. iv).

Poole (2003) authored a seminal paper about FASD that highlighted the need for a response to the problem of alcohol and substance abuse from a harm reduction as well as a women's health perspective. "Since the impact of FASD cannot be reversed," she stated, "it is extremely important to focus efforts on prevention" (2003, p. 1). Focusing only on alcohol use contributes to the stigmatization of women while not addressing problems related to addiction. Poole further suggested that it is important to remove the current focus from Aboriginal women, as substance misuse is not a culturally based problem.

Child Protection Issues

If the term *prenatal substance abuse* is used, a woman is immediately implicated as guilty and placed within a dichotomous framework where harm/control of her body is weighed against harm/control to the fetus. Framing the issue of FASD from a child protection standpoint immediately places a mother in conflict with this system because of negative perceptions related to alcohol use and pregnancy. The welfare of children is considered to be a public issue. One of the expected roles of women as mothers is to protect their children from harm. Through a societal lens, and driven by a dominant medical response to this issue, women who drink during pregnancy are causing undue harm to their unborn children. One of the problems with this position is that not all women who drink during pregnancy give birth to children with FASD. However, women who do give birth to children with FASD are perceived as unfit, portrayed as irresponsible and even malevolent. The "unhealthy" womb has become a heavily contested space.

The importance of child protection intervention in families who are actively impacted by alcoholism cannot be underestimated. A study that examined young children in care with complex needs and multiple vulnerabilities suggested that 80% might have had prenatal alcohol exposure. Factors cited in the removal of children from parental care broadly included "neglect and parental incapacity" (Vig, Chinitz, & Shulman, 2005, p. 147). Aronson suggested that "even though early fostering did not appear to eliminate the harmful effects of exposure to alcohol in utero, foster care seems to be the most favorable alternative for children whose biological mothers, despite vigorous attempts at psychological support, continue to abuse alcohol and have severe personal psychological problems. Children prenatally exposed to alcohol who remain in biological families … remain at continued risk" (1997, p. 24).

When the physical and emotional needs of children are not met due to active alcoholism, child protection services are required. Each family needs to be assessed on an individual basis in terms of determining the specific needs for protection. Yet there is a generalized belief in child welfare practice that children of alcoholic women are better off in care. This may not always be the case, as models have emerged that work with high-risk women to offer support while children remain in their care. One example that demonstrates the possibility of alternative responses is Sheway in downtown Vancouver. This program helps women to engage with health care systems, and has produced promising results for women and children, including improved nutritional status, decreased homelessness, increased birth weights, and decreased child apprehension (Poole, 2007).

The hunt for information on women's use of alcohol during pregnancy as the explanation for their children's problems is a phenomenon that has emerged within child protection investigations, as diagnosis of FASD relies on the confirmation of exposure. After their children are apprehended by child welfare authorities and mothers are identified as potentially neglectful, abusive, and unable to care for their children, they are subjected to questioning during events, such as child protection investigations, in which they feel vulnerable. Women who are alcoholic, or struggle with both alcohol and drug use problems, are frequently asked by authorities such as child welfare to disclose their history of alcohol use during pregnancy. Women may be reluctant to reveal information regarding their substance use, and often underreport this information due to fear of authorities, fear of judgment, and fear of the consequences of disclosing this information (Poole, 2003; Rutman et al., 2000; Tait, 2000).

One of the key areas in which problems arise in child welfare practice is the relationship between child welfare workers and birth mothers. Child welfare practice has evolved into a brokerage model rather than direct service provision, moving further away from a model of relational theory that is critical in working with vulnerable mothers and children (Grant, Ernst, Pagalilauan, & Streissguth, 2003). Child protection timelines and policies related to permanency planning often do not allow sufficient time to develop trusting relationships between families and caseworkers. The underlying reason for resistance to child welfare intervention is that women who are the birth mothers of children with FASD are very vulnerable themselves (Leischner, Johnson, Mallet, Sam, & Thio-Watts, 2001; Poole, 2003; Rutman et al., 2000; Tait, 2000). Consequently, children with FASD and their birth mothers are in conflict with the system. Understanding pre-existing vulnerabilities of women in these circumstances is important in relation to developing effective working relationships between families and child welfare authorities. Poole and Salmon—co-leaders of the Prairie Northwest FASD Network Action Team on FASD Prevention from a Women's Determinants of Health perspective—suggest that a trauma-informed response should guide intervention (Poole, 2007).

My Research

A qualitative approach was utilized in my research with eight birth mothers of children diagnosed with FAS. Qualitative approaches propose that new concepts and viewpoints be grounded in the lives of people, thus offering a broader understanding of human experience (Denzin & Lincoln, 2003). I contend that women do not intend to become birth mothers of children with FAS, as this diagnosis becomes a reflection of a lifetime of challenges faced by women. It became clear through my research that women did not connect the use of alcohol during pregnancy with potential harm to the fetus, partly because alcohol misuse was a problem prior to the pregnancy for all sorts of reasons—mostly negative.

Four of the eight women I interviewed had both a mother and father who were alcoholic and had traumatic histories. The issue of alcohol consumption during pregnancy was represented, at times, as a way to cope with past life experiences. Pregnancies were unplanned, stressful, and represented difficult times for the women. Most had experienced domestic violence and abuse which contributed to low self-worth. Poverty, lack of psychosocial supports, and involvement with the child welfare system were highlighted as problematic and traumatic events in their lives.

In the following section, the voice of one woman participant is highlighted.

A Profile of One Birth Mother: Nora

Life Themes Trauma and abandonment in family of origin, abuse, violence, child diagnosed with FAS, low self-worth, fighting with others, didn't know how to grow up, sexual abuse by father, sexual assault by others, suicide attempt, domestic violence, alcohol abuse, father of child not involved, child welfare involvement, experience of abortion.

Nora (pseudonym) is in her late thirties and currently cares for her young adult daughter, who has a diagnosis of FAS. Her child was apprehended by child welfare at six months of age and was returned to her care at the age of 18. It was clear that this separation from her child had taken a toll on her well-being.

Nora was raised by maternal grandparents after her mom died when she was eleven years old. She was sexually abused by her father, whom she described as "diddling" her and subsequently abandoning her after the death of her mother. Nora described herself as "devastated" in life. She presented her way of dealing with life as putting things into "different baskets" in order to be able to cope. Nora completed two years of high school and has had many jobs, including kitchen work and working in various stores. She currently lives on a disability pension and works part-time.

Nora had multiple experiences of violence in her relationships with male partners as an adolescent and adult. She described having a long history of depression that she believed was a "family trait" that had been passed down. She experienced suicidal ideation and made one attempt by taking an overdose of sleeping pills. She was sexually assaulted at age 17, and had three pregnancies at ages 18, 19, and 20, resulting in two abortions and one live birth. Nora still struggles with depression, but highly values the fact that she now cares for her daughter, who is a young adult.

A pattern of cumulative losses was evident in Nora's life. She lost her mother, was sexually abused by her father and step-grandfather, sexually assaulted with two subsequent abortions, had her child taken away, experienced loss in relationships, and had severe depression and low self-esteem. Nora said that she felt she did not know how to grow up. This is an important comment that warrants further attention, as women who give birth to FASD children often come from homes where their mother, father, or both were alcoholic. Nora stated, "People look down on me." She described being sexually assaulted more than once, and blamed herself because she was "hanging around with the wrong people." Nora struck me as being sad. Although she expressed satisfaction with having her daughter back in her life, I perceived a tangible emptiness, or perhaps a lack of vibrancy, in her tone of voice, in her presence. Nora suggested "paternal alcohol syndrome" as partially responsible for the diagnosis of her child. The father's use of alcohol was a concern, as men in the lives of such women often encourage alcohol use. This issue is rarely raised in the literature, yet offers a way to counter the dominant notion that women are solely responsible for giving birth to children diagnosed with FASD (Gearing, McNeill, & Lozier, 2005).

Nora stated, "I waited 18 years to parent." When I interviewed Nora, the experience of having lost her child as an infant to child welfare apprehension, and subsequently returned as an adult by the system, emerged as a baffling process. This experience weighed heavily as unresolved grief. There was a great depth of sadness, and experiences of loss and trauma permeated our conversation. With Nora, there was a deep sense of vulnerability that was somewhat mediated by having a relationship with her daughter. It appeared that caring for her daughter presently creates a fragile truce with the past. Nora represented the voices of women who are often marginalized and silenced. The voices of women such as Nora have a great deal to contribute to our understanding of the lives of birth mothers.

Given Nora's experience, early intervention would have been required in order to support her experiencing a different life trajectory. The notion of culpability becomes shaky when one reviews in depth the lives of birth mothers of children with FAS. Perhaps listening to the voices of women, dealing with historical trauma, offering more compassionate interventions through child welfare, and alternative treatment resources that include women staying involved with their children, if possible, will support change. A system that believes women have the capacity to care for their children and relates to them from this perspective has the opportunity to engage women with their children's lives, rather than distancing them. Rethinking child welfare practice with birth mothers of children with FASD is an ongoing process, as more knowledge develops through research and dissemination of models of practice. The construct of social justice is one that demands all voices be heard, even the disenfranchised voices of birth mothers of children with FAS.

Conclusions and Recommendations

This study generated a number of recommendations regarding intervention with birth mothers. The pivotal recommendation relates to child protection: Interventions by child welfare authorities in my province have a primary focus on the protection of the child—despite the Alberta *Child, Youth and Family Enhancement Act* (2005), which signals that support and protection must be provided to the entire family in times of crisis. There is an evident gap between the policy intent and the practices of health and social workers in that such workers often do not have the capacity or mandate to provide the intensive support/care required to address the problems of the birth mother of a child diagnosed with FASD. Health and child welfare systems tend to offer short-term rather than long-term supports for families. The state's child protection system seems to prefer to focus on the needs of the child in isolation from the needs of the birth mother. Although a focus on the child is essential, approaching practice from a trauma- and addiction-informed position would enhance developing relationships with mothers who become involved with child welfare authorities.

There is a need for the government and supportive agencies to harmonize and align policy and practices related to the care of children and families regarding issues of alcohol and substance misuse, and associated problems such as child neglect/abuse and domestic violence. Of further benefit would be a change in approach whereby child welfare agencies and health care systems could become places that women can turn to for help within their own communities, and thus work in partnership with care systems long before there is cause for intervention. An important message to policy-makers, implementers, and evaluators, as well as to support practitioners, would be the need to work collaboratively. A trauma-informed, woman-centred approach to care must be implemented within child welfare, health, and welfare support systems (Boyd & Marcellus, 2007; Poole, 2003; Rutman et al., 2000).

The utilization of the Parent-Child Assistance Program (P-CAP) would be beneficial; its intent is the prevention of alcohol-affected births. This program offers intensive support over three years for women who have given birth to children with FASD, used alcohol and/or drugs, and are potentially at risk for further births (Grant, Ernst, Streissguth, & Porter, 1997). To suggest that women merely refrain from alcohol to prevent FASD is too simplistic a response. A comprehensive response such as that of P-CAP is critical for prevention. Positive outcomes of these programs include family stability, effective treatment for social problems, including substance abuse and psychosocial issues, and involvement in work or educational opportunities.

Awareness of and training with dealing with addictions, especially alcohol, should be required in social work school curricula, and certainly for practitioners in the health and child welfare systems. Education and training on the complex issues faced by birth mothers in terms of their rights and entitlements would support more informed responses from health and social service systems.

Women also deserve to be treated by health and social service systems in ways that respect their worth and dignity as human beings and citizens. Helpers must rise above the perception of blameworthy harm on the part of birth mothers and endeavour to develop an informed response that considers them as women who have complex, traumatic histories, often including cumulative loss. Engaging with the mother-child dyad requires strong clinical skills and minimizes the use of a punitive approach (Marcellus, 2008). In my research, all eight women started consuming alcohol as teenagers, and all became pregnant as teens, with the exception of one birth mother who had been assessed as infertile and had her first pregnancy at age 31. This suggests that it is important to pay attention to drinking patterns and sexual behavior of adolescents, as well as the availability of accessible alcohol within the family home.

Unfortunately, policies on child apprehension and time in care often prohibit women with long-term substance misuse problems from achieving their goals within limited time frames. Working with birth mothers is a long-term versus a short-term process, and this must be considered in evolving models of practice. An approach grounded in compassion, utilizing a women-centred approach and trauma-informed responses, will greatly enhance casework with birth mothers.

28

Children with Disabilities in Care in Manitoba

Don Fuchs

Children with disabilities are overrepresented in the child and family service system, and there is increasing concern about their growing numbers in care (Fudge Schormans & Brown, 2006). Because of additional risk factors associated with disability, these already vulnerable children have a greater potential than other children for requiring the support or protection of a child welfare agency. In Manitoba, it has been shown that one-third of children in care fall within a broad definition of disability (Fuchs, Burnside, Marchenski, & Mudry, 2005).

This chapter presents some of the major results to date from a program of research which was focused on children with disabilities in care of the child welfare system in Manitoba. The program of research was initiated in 2005 to examine the profiles of the children with disabilities, and continues to examine issues such as pathways in care, transitioning out of care, and the economic impact of children in care with fetal alcohol spectrum disorder (FASD). Although the general research program covers all children in care with disabilities, this chapter focuses more specifically on children with FASD. Information on the disadvantages faced by children with FASD, and the general placement and legal status patterns of these children, are examined. In addition, the chapter provides preliminary information on how the cost of children in care with FASD compares to other children in care (Fuchs, Burnside, Marchenski, & Mudry, 2009), and presents implications of the findings for research, policy, and practice.

Children with Disabilities in the Manitoba Child Welfare System

The first stages of this research program focused on identifying the profiles of children in care with disabilities. The results of this initial research found that approximately one-third of Manitoba's children in care have a disability, and most of these have multiple disabilities (Fuchs et al., 2005). Intellectual disability was the most frequently identified, followed by mental health disabilities. In children with multiple disabilities, the most common co-occurrence involved intellectual and mental health disabilities.

Most of the children with disabilities came into care as a result of situations related to the conduct or the incapacity of their parents to fulfill a parental role rather than as a result of issues related to the conduct of the child. The majority (69%) were permanent wards, although 13% were in care under a Voluntary Placement Agreement.

Prenatal substance abuse was the origin of disability for one-third of the children with disabilities, and was a suspected cause for an additional 17%. If suspected FASD was included, more than half of children in care with disabilities were disabled as a result of prenatal substance abuse (Fuchs et al., 2009).

The majority of the children in care with disabilities were not able to learn at an age-appropriate rate or to use language in an age-appropriate way (Fuchs et al., 2005). Most of these children were not able to achieve age-appropriate independence, emotional modulation, interpersonal interaction, or awareness of risk. Aggressive behaviour was also problematic for many of the children with disabilities, and often caused a great deal of difficulty in finding appropriate placements. Other problems associated with behaviour included sexually inappropriate behaviour and conflict with the law (Gough & Fuchs, 2006).

Overrepresentation of Aboriginal Children with Disabilities in Care

The general overrepresentation of Aboriginal children in the Canadian child welfare system is documented in Part III of this book, and elsewhere (Trocmé, Knoke, & Blackstock, 2004); it is argued that overrepresentation is related to structural factors, including poverty, arising from the loss of language, culture, and family connections that can be attributed, at least in part, to colonization, the legacy of residential schools, and the response of the mainstream child welfare system (Trocmé, Knoke, Shangreaux, Fallon, & MacLaurin, 2005). Coping with these disconnections has been challenging, to say the least, and many Aboriginal people and communities struggle with the poverty that is so often related to other social problems such as substance misuse, family violence, and child neglect.

The rate of disabilities for Aboriginal people has been reported to be twice as high as that of the non-Aboriginal population in Canada (Standing Committee on Human Resources Development and the Status of Persons with Disabilities, 2003). First Nations families who live on reserves are also disadvantaged in receiving services for their children with disabilities, since reserves fall under federal jurisdiction and social services are typically provided by provinces and territories. For these reasons, there is a greater risk that Aboriginal children with disabilities will come into care.

In examining the culture of origin of children with disability in care, the researchers found that First Nations children comprised 69% of all children with disabilities in care. This is generally consistent with the overall rate of First Nations children in care with the Manitoba child welfare system. First Nations children in care receive services both on and off reserves, but those on reserves are disadvantaged because funding for services to children with disabilities in First Nations communities is quite limited. This difference becomes even greater as they reach adulthood, since adult services for persons with disabilities are not available for those living on reserves. Individual bands provide for their members as they are able and see fit, but this is more difficult because of limited funds and restricted access to support services for children and families with disabilities. The extended families of many children in care live on reserves. The lack of on-reserve services means that difficult choices must be made for some of the children and youth with disabilities: they could remain in their communities with access to an extended family network, but with limited access to professional services, or they could be placed in substitute care outside their communities, where they would receive specialized services but lose some of the supports that might be available from family.

Children in Care with FASD in Manitoba

As part of their program of research, Fuchs and his colleagues found that a significantly high proportion (17%) of all the children in care were affected by (diagnosed or suspected) fetal alcohol spectrum disorder (FASD). Children with a diagnosis of FASD present agencies with an array of complex and variable needs that are a result of their compromised neurological biology, their family system, and the psychosocial environmental implications of both those factors. FASD was diagnosed in approximately 34% of children in care with disabilities. In addition, the researchers found that 81% of the children with FASD were First Nations (Fuchs et al., 2005).

The proportion of boys to girls among those diagnosed with FASD (61% boys and 39% girls) was very close to the 60:40 male–female ratio found in the general disability population of children in care in Manitoba (Fuchs et al., 2005). It is also consistent with the overrepresentation of males with intellectual disability in the general Canadian population.

In most cases, children with FASD (88%) had co-occurring disabilities. Intellectual and mental health disabilities were the most frequently noted combination (Fuchs et al., 2009). The most commonly occurring combination of cognitive and mental health disabilities was FASD and Attention Deficit Hyperactivity Disorder (ADHD).

An overwhelming majority of children with FASD (89%) were in the permanent care of a child welfare agency—compared to 61% of the general population of children with disabilities in care.

The reasons for children with FASD coming into care were predominantly related to a difficult parental situation; 62% of children came into care because of the parents' conduct, or the parents' incapacity to fulfill their parental role (Fuchs et al., 2005). Only 6% of the children with FASD came into care because of reasons that were related to the child's condition or the child's conduct. By comparison, in the non-FASD population, 54% of children were in care for reasons related to parental care, and 18% were in care for reasons related to the child's conduct or conditions.

The Placement Trajectories of Children in Care with FASD in Manitoba

The second phase of this program of research was focused on examining the trajectories of children with FASD in the care system. The findings clearly demonstrated that children with FASD come into care earlier and become permanent wards more quickly than other children (Fuchs et al., 2009). In addition, they also indicated that children who were diagnosed with FASD enter care at an earlier age, tend to become permanent wards, and spend a greater proportion of their lives in care (Fuchs et al., 2009). These factors place additional responsibility on child welfare agencies, as they must assume the role of substitute parent for the majority of the individual's childhood years. Children in care are known to be disadvantaged and face additional risks to their successful adaptation to adulthood. These risks represent a major challenge to child and family service agencies, which represent the caring capacity of the community.

The duty of providing responsible substitute parental care to the rapidly growing number of children in care with FASD carries a major fiscal commitment.
The magnitude and extent of this fiscal commitment is discussed later.

To further understand the factors that were driving the demand for in-care
services for children with FASD, the researchers examined some of the data of
the Addictions Foundation of Manitoba (AFM) relating to women of child-
bearing age. The study found that in 2005–6, more than 1,200 adult women of
child-bearing age were assessed as in need for alcohol addictions services (Fuchs
et al., 2009). These women tended to be single, unemployed, many with less
than a high school education, and of low economic status; half had a history of
emotional or mental health issues. They were mothers to 2,500 children, but were
not currently custodial parents to all of their children. Many of those women
(about one-third) were already involved with a child welfare agency. Only 25%
of the women reported being in a relationship; the majority were solely responsible for the care of children.

The potential for children to be affected by alcohol, biologically as a result
of prenatal exposure, and socially and environmentally by postnatal exposure
to alcoholism, remains significant. Prevention of prenatal and postnatal exposure to alcohol could have a dramatic effect on costs to the child welfare system,
as well as on the human toll. Even if prevention efforts were able to reduce the
number of children entering the system, actual numbers of children with FASD
in the system would continue to rise for some time as a result of new diagnoses
of FASD for children currently in care, admissions to care of children already
exposed to prenatal alcohol abuse and subsequently diagnosed with FASD, and
few children with FASD leaving the system except through reaching the age of
majority. There is no foreseeable reduction in the number of children with
FASD requiring the resources of the child welfare system. In fact, the evidence
presented would indicate that numbers of children with disabilities in care are
increasing at an alarming rate.

Because children with FASD enter the child welfare system at a younger age
and spend a greater proportion of their lives in care than other children, their
needs present an additional challenge to the child welfare system. The data on
the increasing number of children coming into care, and the prevalence data
from the AFM, would indicate that there is a high degree of urgency for health,
education, and child welfare systems to develop effective integrated health and
service policy and programs to respond to the special needs of the growing
numbers of children and families with FASD.

Issues Relating to Youth Transitioning Out of Care

It is not enough to plan for the needs of children solely while they are in care. Every year increasing numbers of children who have been identified with FASD are transitioning out of care and into the community or the adult service system. The shift to independence is difficult for all children in care, but particularly for those with disabilities. This is due in part to the significant differences in the structure of service delivery for children and adults (Geenen, Powers, Hogansen, & Pittman, 2007; Child and Youth Officer for British Columbia, 2006b; Child Welfare League of America, 2007). The move to independence for youth with FASD is further complicated by the nature of their disability (Serge, Eberle, Goldberg, Sullivan, & Dudding, 2002; Reid & Dudding, 2007). They are often not eligible for services related to cognitive impairments because their level of intellectual functioning is above the eligibility criteria (Massachusetts Society for the Prevention of Cruelty to Children, 2005). There are few if any adult services directly related to FASD. As adults, their disability tends to be invisible, but their behaviour can present many challenges. Long-term planning for children with FASD needs to incorporate special attention to their transition into adulthood (Schibler & McEwan-Morris, 2006).

Within their research program, Fuchs, Burnside, Marchenski, and Mudry (2008) examined the issues of children with FASD who essentially grew up in the care of the child and family service system in Manitoba. The purpose of this research was to examine the evidence of the transition planning that had occurred for young people with FASD who had recently aged out of the child welfare system in Manitoba. This project examined the Child and Family Services administrative database to study issues related to "aging out" of care for youth who had been identified as having a diagnosis or suspected diagnosis of FASD.

A review of the literature on youth transitions out of care (Fuchs et al., 2008) disclosed that a number of factors would support the success of any youth leaving care. Briefly summarized, those placement factors that supported resiliency included the stability of residential placements, the stability of school placements, and attachment to a significant mentoring adult. Transition plans need to address the particularly problematic outcome areas of employment, income, housing, social relationships, and mental health. Further, especially for those managing FASD, agency care needs to be replaced by a structured environment that includes the support of a one-on-one advocate/mentor.

In the third phase of their research program, the researchers conducted a file review of a sample of youth (n=27) with FASD who were permanent wards aged 16 years or more. The review examined the case summaries, placement histories, and case recordings. The researchers focused on gathering information on transition planning, placements, and legal status. They found that placement stability was clearly an issue for this age group of children in care (Fuchs et al., 2008). Furthermore, they found that while stability in placements is always important, as children age, placement stability has increasing impact on educational continuity (Reilly, 2003; Romney, Litrownik, Newton, & Lau, 2006). Without placement stability in later adolescence, the process of transitional planning becomes more difficult. As demonstrated by the file review, this sample of children with FASD tended to have stable placements in their early years, but faced increasing instability as they entered adolescence, a time critical for both their education and transition planning (Fuchs et al., 2008).

This later instability also reduced the likelihood of establishing enduring relationships with foster parents or teachers, reducing the pool of possible adults who might serve as the advocate/mentor that has been characterized as important to successful transition (Schibler & McEwan-Morris, 2006). Workers who might have filled the role of mentor appeared to be even more changeable than placements. Given the dramatic changes to the administration of children's services in Manitoba in the past four years, and some subsequent growing pains marked by a higher than usual staff turnover, it is perhaps understandable that children have had a higher than desirable number of workers. All these factors have served to increase the risk of poor transition outcomes for this group of youth.

In Manitoba there is provision in the child welfare system to extend services to permanent wards beyond the age of majority (18 years) to assist them in the transition out of care. During this period the youth are identified as having "Transitional Planning Status." The study on youth transition out of care found that use of this status was minimal in a group where disability would have tended to impede both school progress and social maturity. One would expect such factors to automatically trigger use of Transition Planning provisions (Fuchs et al., 2008b). Much more study is needed to understand the factors inhibiting such support, as well as those that would assist with the transition for the increasing number of youth with FASD as they age out of care.

Economic Costs of Children in Care with FASD

The study of the pathways of children with disability in care (Fuchs et al., 2009) led the researchers to expand the focus of their program of study to learn more about the social and economic costs of growing up in the care of the child welfare system. In their examination of these factors, Fuchs, Burnside,

Marchenski, Mudry, & DeRiviere (2008) found, not surprisingly, that providing for children with FASD within the child welfare system was more expensive than providing for other children in care. The special needs rate for this group of children was higher than for children in general, and costs were further increased because children with FASD tended to be in the system longer than other children. As this group of children is more reliant on the child welfare system for parenting, agency care has a greater impact on their success, or lack of it. Without adequate measures of success, it is difficult to establish the effectiveness of the current investment in care for children with FASD. Children in care in general, and children with disabilities in particular, face the risk of poor adult outcomes. Children in care with disabilities are, therefore, doubly challenged. The separation of systems to support children in care and children with disabilities increases the challenge of meeting the needs of children with FASD. Children living on reserves are at an even greater disadvantage because of lack of funding for services.

The higher average special rate cost of care for this group merits even greater attention when considered in the light of previous research. The studies undertaken demonstrated that children who received a diagnosis of FASD had come into care for the first time at a significantly earlier age (2.5 years) than both children with no disability (3.6 years) and children with other disabilities (4.3 years) (Fuchs et al., 2009). Their legal and placement histories confirmed that permanent wards with FASD spent on average three-quarters of their childhood in the care of an agency, or about 15% more than any other permanent wards. Therefore, not only were the daily special rate costs higher for this group of children, but they were also extended over a longer period of time. The costs of maintaining these children in care, therefore, are significantly higher than for other children (Fuchs et al., 2009).

Given what has been learned in previous studies of the population of children with FASD in care in Manitoba (Fuchs et al., 2005, 2009), cost analysis suggests a strong need for consideration of issues related to the provision of foster care, issues related to the service needs of this population, issues related to service delivery, and issues related to culturally appropriate approaches to prevention.

Implications for Service Delivery, Policy, and Prevention

The rate of disability for children in care in Manitoba is much higher than the rate for Manitoba as a whole, and even higher than the rate for the general population of children in Canada (Fuchs et al., 2009). This extremely high rate raises many questions. The first is to ask what conditions prevail in Manitoba that may be different from other provinces. The second is to determine what the incidence rates are across other provinces. In part, results may reflect the vulnerability to maltreatment experienced by children with disabilities. Children with disabilities have been reported to experience maltreatment at a rate three times that of children with no disability (Fudge Schormans & Brown, 2006).

With one in three children in the child welfare system in Manitoba having at least one disability, and the majority of the children having two or more disabilities, there is an urgent need for preventive measures. Social workers need to be aware of the different types of disabilities and the services available for them. In addition, they need to appreciate the additional stressors faced by families caring for a child with a disability, especially when the evidence indicates that many of these children require behavioural supervision. Children with disabilities who are in care have unique needs that require adaptations, personal supports, and special services (Romney et al., 2006). To enable foster parents and other direct care providers to meet these needs, child welfare agencies must provide them with culturally appropriate family support and training programs to enhance their understanding of their foster child's disability and how it affects the child.

Social workers need to be aware of the possibility that children for whom they are providing service may be alcohol-affected. Workers need to know the characteristic physiology and behaviour patterns that are an indication of the condition, and pursue the assessment of children suspected of having this disability. In addition to understanding how this disability affects the child's functioning and service needs, workers need to be trained to recognize and help alleviate the additional stressors faced by families caring for a child with FASD. Because children with FASD come into care earlier and spend more of their life in placement, workers must recognize the even more critical role of permanency planning for them. There are some services available in the community for children with FASD and/or their families. Workers need to know about the availability of services in their region, and to be able to advocate for FASD-related services for both children in care and children in danger of coming into care and their caregivers.

Similarly, expertise related to FASD is critical for foster parents and other direct service providers. They must be prepared to manage the unique needs of children with this condition. Recognizing the long-term placement needs of these children, foster parents need to be able to make a long-term commitment to their care. They must be aware of the additional stresses that may result from caring for children with FASD, and develop some reliable stress management strategies. In summary, social workers, foster parents, and other service providers must be prepared to provide the kind of care that best supports children presenting with this configuration of needs.

There is an urgent need for the development of FASD expertise in order to provide adequately for the needs of alcohol-affected children. Whether this means increasing the expertise within child welfare services or integrating FASD services with other service providers, it is essential to have knowledge and skill related to FASD available to every affected child in care. This might include hiring policies that require coursework in FASD for social workers, core module training in FASD for workers on the job, or the creation of specialist positions to provide consultation and connection to external services. It might also include closer connection with early intervention programs, and collaboration with Manitoba's Children's Special Services program, to benefit from their expertise in managing disability. The availability and accessibility of such services and resources in remote and isolated communities must also be addressed. This will require the involvement of federally funded programs for on-reserve communities.

The review of the number of women of child-bearing age who are involved with the Addictions Foundation of Manitoba gives a cursory indication of the scope of addiction issues among women in Manitoba. The potential for children to be affected by alcohol both before and after birth is significant. The child welfare system appears to be a primary intervenor with this high-risk population. Policy direction and resource allocation are needed to respond to the prevalence and complex needs of this group. Though beyond the scope of child welfare services, the AFM data emphasize the importance of prenatal alcohol prevention programs and the pressing need for supports for women and families. They also indicate the importance of early childhood intervention and identification of children and families requiring support.

The availability of FASD diagnostic services is problematic in most jurisdictions across Canada. These services for children of all ages are fundamental to service planning and provision. Early identification and provision of appropriate support for children and their families has been shown to greatly improve the successful developmental outcomes for children with FASD. Manitoba has high quality assessment services, but these services are not available to everyone. Assessment services for alcohol and drug exposed children are often located in larger urban settings. These access barriers to diagnostic and support service resources continue to negatively affect children with FASD and their families, particularly in First Nations communities.

Within Manitoba and elsewhere, there is a need to develop service models which function across sectoral divisions to encompass the provision of early childhood intervention and child care, family supports, vocational/employment strategies, independent living supports, and affordable housing. Integrated service delivery on this scale would make social inclusion of persons with FASD possible. In addition, an integrated approach would reduce the demand on the overly subscribed child welfare system and provide greater access to the range of appropriate services required by the children and families with FASD disabilities.

A particularly serious gap in services exists for children living on reserves. There are no diagnostic resources available in First Nations communities. Provincial disability services to support children and families are not provided to any reserve residents. Children are too often required to leave family and community to access services, and often have to come into care to receive disability services. In addition, federal funding does not extend to special services for children with disabilities. Both families and agencies struggle to provide essential services to children with disabilities who are disadvantaged by funding structures unresponsive to their needs. In estimating the cost of providing services to children with FASD, a significant oversight occurs if we do not recognize that many children do not represent a direct cost not because they do not need service, but because no service is available to them.

Conclusion

The care of children with disabilities, particularly FASD, is of significant concern to child welfare systems across Canada. It is said that of all disabilities, FASD, as with some others, is preventable. Yet there is strong evidence that the number of children coming into care with disabilities is growing at an alarming rate. The high prevalence of intellectual disabilities, including FASD, among Aboriginal children, especially First Nations children, indicates a compelling need to establish and expand programs that emphasize the importance of not drinking any alcohol if a pregnancy is being planned, or, especially, during pregnancy. There is a need for accessible, culturally appropriate prenatal programs and family supports for families with children with disabilities to prevent these children from coming into care, as well as to meet their needs while in care. There is an urgent social and economic need for primary, secondary, and tertiary prevention programs that are culturally appropriate and are targeted to address the needs of various at-risk individuals and groups.

In addition, the data on the increasing number of children coming into care, and the prevalence data from the Addictions Foundation of Manitoba, would indicate that there is an urgent need for the health, education, and child welfare service systems to develop effective integrated health and service policies and programs to respond to the special needs of the growing numbers of children and families with FASD and other disabilities. Since an increasing number of children with FASD are spending over 70% of their childhood in care, there is a great need for child welfare agencies to rethink their roles as they serve "in loco parentis"—enabling them to provide appropriate parental nurturance to meet the special needs of these children. Child and family service agencies and social work professionals need to be effective brokers and case advocates in assisting children with disabilities to gain access to the services they need to meet their multiple and complex needs. They need skills in accessing care across rigid sectoral boundaries that present many barriers. These barriers limit the resources available to the children and families affected. Finally, the development of home-based services could serve to reduce the numbers of children who enter the care system.

Meeting the needs of children with FASD and other disabilities in care presents a number of challenges. Four in particular are associated with providing care for children in this group: the length of time they are in care; their special developmental needs; their needs as they transition out of care; and the number of affected children that will continue to enter the system and require care. Each of these challenges is a factor that increases the demand on resources available for children in care in Canada. There is an urgent need for innovative research and development activities aimed at formulating policy, programs, and service initiatives to systematically address these four areas.

29

Child Welfare Challenges for Developing Nations

Myrna McNitt

This chapter explores the child welfare challenges in developing nations by considering some of the major systemic factors that relate to the practice of child welfare and child protection. The overarching challenge is that of developing humane policies and programs in ways that do not replicate models of colonialism. The United Nations *Convention on the Rights of the Child* provides a framework for the discussion that follows, and evidence from research is used to understand and explore policy and practice in developing questions.

The goal of the United Nations *Convention on the Rights of the Child* (CRC), which was ratified November 20, 1989, is to set international standards for health care, education, as well as legal, civil, and social services. The CRC's basic premise, as stated in its preamble, is that children are individuals with rights, but who "by reason of his (sic) physical and mental immaturity, needs special safeguards and care, including appropriate legal protection, before as well as after birth" (as quoted from the United Nations *Declaration on the Rights of the Child* (1959) in the *Convention on the Rights of the Child*, United Nations Office of the High Commissioner for Human Rights, 1989). The CRC states that children have the right to survival, full development, protection from harm and exploitation, and participation in family and social life. Cantwell (2005) identifies those principles that apply to children without parental care:

- Family-based solutions are generally preferable to institutional placements.
- National (domestic) solutions are generally preferable to those involving another country.

- Permanent solutions are generally preferable to inherently temporary ones.
- Alternative care should have a range of options. (p. 4)

Despite the 30-year history of the Convention, children in developing nations are vulnerable to a wide range of conditions that limit their rights and prevent healthy growth and development.

Child Maltreatment and Neglect

Children are abused and neglected worldwide. In India, a two-year study commissioned by the Ministry of Women and Child Development found that 53% of the 2,200 surveyed children between the ages of 5 and 12 reported one or more forms of sexual abuse, with two out of three children physically abused (Pandey, 2008).

The International Society for the Prevention of Child Abuse and Neglect (ISPCAN), with UNICEF, sampled 72 nations for their perception of child maltreatment. Daro (2006), in this work for ISPCAN and UNICEF, found that the most common definition of maltreatment was neglect or abuse (physical and sexual) by a parent or caretaker. However, other forms included "forcing a child to beg, child infanticide, and abuse within a school or detention facility" (p. 13).

Neglect is the most common form of child maltreatment. Extreme neglect is defined as having a history of sensory deprivation in one or more domains of development (e.g., minimal exposure to language, touch, and social interactions) (Perry, 2001). Extreme neglect leads to disorganization of the brain's functioning at particularly sensitive times of development for the child, and thus a lag in social, emotional, and cognitive development (Perry, 2001; Rutter & English and Romanian Adoptees Study Team, 1998). In all forms of abuse or neglect, the child's development is derailed when the significant adult fails to meet the child's needs. Neglect and abuse interfere with academic progress, social relationships and competence, self-concept, and emotional and behavioural functioning (Cicchetti & Toth, 2000; Appleyard, Egeland, van Dulmen, & Stroufe, 2005; Thrane, Hoyt, Whitbeck, & Yoder, 2006; Windsor, Glaze, Koga, & Bucharest Early Intervention Project Core Group, 2007). Substance misuse increases the risk for physical, emotional, and sexual abuse (Vungkhanching, Sher, Jackson, & Parra, 2004).

It is also important to understand child maltreatment by looking through a wider lens at abuse in institutionalized systems of care outside the family. Institutional abuse of children occurs in many forms. Educators in many parts of the world use harsh physical discipline to manage children in school. Child care workers in orphanages may use unacceptable discipline or sexually exploit children. Children may be subjected to multiple forms of extreme neglect by being restrained, or denied food or access to bathrooms. Under these conditions the very young and disabled are at highest risk. The risk of abuse and neglect for children in developing countries is further exacerbated by systemic issues.

Systemic Challenges within Developing Countries

The conditions that erode children's rights and weaken the fabric of family life in developing countries include chronic poverty, the pandemic health crisis HIV/AIDS, human trafficking and migration, violence from armed conflict, and all forms of abuse, neglect, and maltreatment. Most of these conditions co-occur, creating conditions of cumulative risk.

The Impact of Poverty

The World Bank, in 2008, defined poverty in developing countries as persons living on less than $1.25 to $2.00 US per day. Based on this criterion, the number of persons living in poverty is estimated at over 1.4 billion worldwide (World Bank, 2008). Extreme poverty occurs when individuals are too poor to obtain adequate nutrition and health care, protection from the elements, and access to education. Poverty is multi-dimensional, impacting all aspects of family life and inhibiting the family's ability to care for its children. An added concern is the 50% of disabilities that are preventable and directly linked to poverty (Department for International Development, 2000, p. 3).

Progress to eradicate poverty is threatened by current economic crises, including the crisis in international banking, the war on terrorism, and lack of affordable petroleum for agricultural production. The poor are hardest hit in times of social and economic volatility. They have few available resources to protect themselves from the soaring costs of food and fuel. An example of the depths of such deprivation is that of slum dwellers in Haiti who have resorted to eating mud cakes as a primary staple of their diet (Carroll, 2008, p. 17). This is a far cry from the three pillars of food security defined by the World Food Summit of 1996: food availability, food access, and food use. The Summit defined food security as existing "when all people at all times have access to sufficient, safe, nutritious food to maintain a healthy and active life" (World Health Organization, 2008). Women are particularly vulnerable to conditions of poverty, and with children they represent "75% of the world's population" (Luthra, 2005, p. 4); throughout the world there remains an unacceptably high death rate for women and children, with 10 million deaths of children under the age of 5

(Black, Morris, & Bryce, 2003). Neonatal deaths are also of major concern. Over 98% of the 4 million neonatal deaths occur in developing nations (Costello, Francis, Byrne, & Puddephatt, 2001; Lawn, Cousens, Zupan, & Lancet Neonatal Survival Steering Team, 2005).

Added to the direct risks to health and safety is the vulnerability to human trafficking and child labour. The poor are lured by promises of money for the family and a better life for the individual, free from poverty (Hodge, 2008). Children are used as child labour to support the meagre existence of the family. An estimated 158 million children aged 5 to 14 (i.e., one in six children in the world) are engaged in child labour, often working in dangerous conditions (UNICEF, n.d.).

Child welfare challenges in developing nations cannot be addressed without examining the far-reaching issues of poverty, as child welfare practitioners are key case managers linking families to life-saving care, be it food, medicine, or protection from the elements. An example of an ecologically based holistic intervention, using the strengths of the community to reverse poor outcomes for children and families at risk, is a program in Mozambique. There, the World Food Programme assists women, children, and HIV/AIDS patients by distributing cash and vouchers that allow families to purchase nutritionally enhanced food from local and other community-based support services (World Food Programme, 2008).

Child welfare practitioners have critical decisions to make when families cannot be preserved due to poverty. Child rescue comes into play when poverty sets up conditions in which children will die without intervention. Families neglect children—but so do nations. The global community and national governments are culpable for failing to address the larger contextual issues of poverty.

Disease

Developing nations are faced with other extreme health concerns. Nations are responsible for developing policies and programs that promote the well-being of children, including their health care and disease prevention. Much progress was made in the 1980s with worldwide coverage at 80% of infants immunized against polio, diphtheria-tetanus-pertussis (DTP), and measles. However, by 2000, less than 50% of the infants in sub-Saharan Africa had received their third DTP vaccine (Clemens & Jodar, 2005). In addition to the familiar diseases of childhood, HIV/AIDS, malaria, tuberculosis, and other major diseases are endemic in many countries. Forty per cent of persons living in developing nations are at risk of contracting malaria, 300 million individuals have acute malaria, and 1 million die each year (Centers for Disease Control and Prevention, n.d.). Children under the age of five are most vulnerable. Those infected with malaria are at risk of developing permanent mental and physical disabilities, with about one in 10 children suffering from neurological impairment after cerebral malaria, including epilepsy, learning disabilities, and loss of coordination (Jones, 2002). Tuberculosis often co-occurs with HIV/AIDS, and tuberculosis kills 1.7 million people annually (United Nations Millennium Project, 2005, p. 29).

The United Nations estimates that there are 15 million children orphaned by AIDS, with 25 million persons infected (UNAIDS, n.d.; UNAIDS, UNICEF et al., 2004). HIV/AIDS is transmitted in many forms, but the most innocent victims are infants exposed during and shortly after birth. Less than 10% of children orphaned or made vulnerable by AIDS receive any support; less than 10% of pregnant women are offered services to prevent HIV transmission to their infants; and less than 5% of young HIV-positive children in need of treatment are receiving it (UNAIDS, n.d., home page).

Antiretroviral (ARV) medication is not affordable or available to all persons infected with HIV/AIDS. The effectiveness of ARVs is closely related to good nutrition. Parents infected with HIV/AIDS often need to choose between taking a casual or day labour job to pay for food and rent and attending a health clinic to obtain medication, and those patients who fail to maintain dose compliance are dropped from health care services. The end result is that too many children are becoming orphaned.

The term "orphan" varies in sub-Saharan Africa. Many of the countries in this region recognize a child under the age of 18 who has lost one or both parents as an orphan. A child may be an orphan if one parent is deceased and a total orphan if both parents are dead. In addition, these nations embrace a working term of "vulnerable children" that includes children in need of social protection, children at high risk for infection when compared to other children, and those living in conditions of poverty. Protective care for AIDS orphans is necessary, along with other forms of assistance. At a minimum this requires consistent access to adequate nutrition, clean water, sanitation, and health care for all members of the family. In Uganda, multigenerational households foster the orphans: one in four families care for one child, and many have ten or more children in their care. The household heads are most often women: widows, grandmothers, aunts, siblings, or extended kin (Okong'o, 2004).

HIV/AIDS orphans are often cared for in child-headed households. Child-headed households are defined as those where children under the age of 18 assume responsibility for the care and maintenance of its members. This living arrangement for children without parental care has allowed for children to remain in their home and community, but there are related risks. Children are vulnerable to exploitation in the form of forced labour, sexual abuse, and dropping out of school. They are often stigmatized as "social orphans" along with their real orphan status (Ansah-Koi, 2006).

It is important to understand HIV/AIDS as a social-emotional problem as well as a medical one. Families with one or more members infected by HIV/AIDS suffer social exclusion, and when death occurs the grieving may be without community support. Culture, social stigma, and poverty converge on families coping with HIV/AIDS. Disease impacts on children's lives directly and indirectly. Child welfare practitioners need to understand the complex interplay of the various factors when considering appropriate interventions.

Natural Disasters

Entire family systems are vulnerable to natural disasters. These may take the form of a tsunami, hurricane, earthquake, flood, or drought. In June 2008, a cyclone in Burma affected between 2.5 million and 5.5 million people (May, 2008). That same year, earthquakes hit Western China, with 51,151 confirmed dead, 5 million homeless, 300,000 injured, and 4,000 children orphaned (Weaver, 2008). Some disasters impact entire regions. The December 26, 2004 tsunami in Asia created a human tragedy on a scale that remains difficult to comprehend, with 170,000 people killed in Aceh (Indonesia), 35,000 in Sri Lanka, 16,000 in India, and 9,000 in Thailand (Marks, 2007). When this happens, recovery takes years.

Catastrophic natural events call for a crisis response from the international community. Social workers employed or volunteering for international non-governmental organizations, such as the International Red Cross, are often first responders. After a natural disaster it is not only the loss of life, property, and affiliation that stresses families, but other protection issues. Women and children are particularly vulnerable and need protection from sexual violence, exploitation, and trafficking (Kälin, 2005). Child welfare practitioners are challenged to respond to the need for safe care for children immediately after this kind of crisis. This need must be considered in the context of broader goals pertaining to recovery. Connecting with family and engaging elders in telling coping stories of historical survival is a healing process for children and community. It assists in mitigating devastating losses.

Child welfare practitioners need to advocate for concrete services and trauma relief for the victims. External pressure from developed nations often encourages international adoption as the first choice. This is but one option, and not necessarily the best. Keeping children connected to natural supports during a time of tragedy is important in helping them understand the event. Family-based care through kin or informal foster arrangements gives children a sense of safety while long-term permanency options can be explored, either on a case-by-case basis or through a change in national policy.

War, Civil Unrest, and Violence

In many countries, including Sierra Leone, the Democratic Republic of Congo, Iraq, Liberia, the occupied Palestinian territories, and northern Uganda, children are subject to the horrors of war, with estimates of over 300,000 children involved in government or rebel forces in over 30 armed conflicts in the world. They work as soldiers, runners, guards, sex slaves, cooks, or spies (UNICEF, 2002). A study of girls in the Philippines identified poverty, living in a combat zone, dropping out of school, and being marginalized in their family as risk factors in their recruitment as child soldiers (Keairns, 2003).

A further concern is the fact that children living in areas of conflict are not always safe. Children have protection under international law, but during conflicts they are killed or maimed, sexually abused, deprived of basic education and health services, abducted, and recruited as active combatants in armed conflict (Otunnu, 2004). Interviews with children in the Ivory Coast, Southern Sudan, and Haiti uncovered a disturbing pattern. The children interviewed highlighted many different types of abuse, including trading food for sex, rape, child prostitution, pornography, indecent sexual assault, and trafficking for sex. Children identified fear of retribution from the adults by way of withholding aid as the reason for not reporting the abuse (Csáky, 2008).

Violent behaviour has serious effects, both immediate and post-traumatic stress. Children living with family or community violence develop overactive and hypersensitive stress responses creating behavioural patterns of fight, flight, or freeze. This compromised use of the brain occurs under conditions of armed conflict, and critically derails the well-being of children (Perry, 1997). Living with high levels of survival stress creates an altered brain state in which cognitive and emotional energy is used to survive and not thrive.

Social workers can play an important role in assessing more equitable distribution of aid and prevention services during times of conflict. They can also help to protect children from being recruited as child soldiers or exploited in other ways. Social workers trained in trauma work are able to assist those who were once child soldiers or victimized to help them understand and process the lived experience and re-enter community life. Contemporary social work education should include specific training on the mental health needs of children and families exposed to war and civil unrest.

Moving across Borders

Migrants

Each year millions of children and families move across national borders without permission. They seek political asylum from all forms of persecution, but struggle to meet basic needs for food, housing, health care, employment, and education. Forced to live in the shadows, they have little legal protection and often face discrimination and exploitation. Frequently they lack the documentation (certificates of birth, death, marriage, or national identity) often required by receiving countries. Obtaining permission to remain is complicated by difficulties in understanding legal processes. Cultural differences, such as coming from a tradition of child or arranged marriages, may be in conflict with the values of the host country.

Post-migration births of children cause other problems. These children may have the right to citizenship in the country of their birth, but their parents may have no right to remain. Deportation hearings may take days or years. If the parents are detained, the child may be placed in foster care.

When child welfare services become involved in cases of illegal immigration, it is important to assess the parents' ability to provide for the child as well as the barriers they face in obtaining food, health care, employment, and education.

Trafficking

Human trafficking is often likened to modern-day slavery. The United Nations estimates that 12.3 million persons live in forced labour, bonded labour, forced child labour, or sexual servitude. The *2007 Trafficking of Persons Report* indicates that approximately 800,000 people have been trafficked across national borders; in addition, millions have been trafficked in their own countries, with 80% of transnational victims being women and girls (United States Department of State, 2007). Approximately 50% of these individuals are minors.

There are few social workers and caregivers trained to provide services for trafficked children. Children taken into protective custody will often run away or refuse to participate in the legal processes. It is not uncommon for child victims to form a trauma bond with aggressors, and to be confused as to whom they should trust. Inadequate victim services have resulted in poor outcomes despite the best intervention efforts. Long-term secure detention facilities are a remedy used for older adolescents and adults, but detention serves to further fragment families and often violates human rights.

There is some evidence that training in this type of work can make a difference. In Ecuador, for example, students on placement from the Chicago-area Dominican University participated in the rescue of 11 girls aged 13 to 17 from forced sex trade in a brothel. These girls were taken to a safe house, and therapeutic work enabled them to safely reunite with their families (Ceaser, 2008).

International adoption is sometimes associated with trafficking, violating the rights of children and parents. Adopters willing to pay high fees contribute to making children into commercial commodities. Birth mothers are often poor and illiterate and can be manipulated into signing a release, particularly if they receive a promise of money.

Asylum-Seeking

Children and adolescents seeking asylum from a life of war, conflict, and violence—such as those from Burma or the Lost Boys of Sudan—require protection from the international community. International non-governmental organizations often recruit foster families to assist the children in resettlement. However, foster families in developed nations have difficulty comprehending the effects of experiences such as starvation, or witnessing extreme violence, rape, and murder. These foster families need training in what to expect from a child exposed to prolonged trauma. They also benefit from developing an appreciation for the young person's birth culture.

In addition, foster families need their own support network, as the repeated exposure to the story of the young person seeking asylum places them at risk for vicarious trauma (compassion fatigue). The young persons in their care have grown up too soon, and are not typical teenagers. They need assistance to return to school and integrate into other aspects of community life. Part of the direct work by social workers involves listening to the story of the migration and the conditions leading to the need for asylum. These workers, and the foster parents, can help the young person make sense of the experience and create a narrative of hope. Where appropriate, they may be able to assist in reuniting family members.

Child Welfare Practice in Developing Countries

Developing nations look for best practice models to create child welfare systems. Kessler, Gira, and Poertner (2005) define "best practice" as making use of practice wisdom, emulating systems, utilizing expert advice, following the guidelines of evidence-based practice, and professional knowledge. Practices should be consistent with the values of the CRC. Practice wisdom in child welfare stresses the importance of understanding child development, attachment, loss and grief, trauma, behavioural concerns, and the need for lasting connections.

Family Preservation

Family preservation services are intended to provide relief to families during times of crisis. Maternal support services, feeding programs, wellness clinics, and community-based rehabilitative care for the disabled are but a few examples of responses to family preservation found in Africa and Asia. As noted in *Care Matters*, a report to the Parliament of the United Kingdom, family preservation focuses on children on the edge of care (Department for Children, Schools, and Families, 2006). Family breakdown is often a result of real or perceived systemic inequities such as resource allocation limiting opportunities for education, employment, and safe housing. Ideally, family preservation works to strengthen how the community responds to the needs of families (Manalo & Meezan, 2000).

Family preservation is consistent with the CRC standards in keeping children connected with family and community. Workers face difficulty in deciding when to preserve a family and when not to—that is, when it is not in the interests of the child. Although family preservation purists contend that the family should be maintained at all costs, this is not best practice, and misrepresents the positive elements of family preservation.

Kinship Care

When families cannot be preserved, placing the child with kin is considered to be best practice. Kinship is defined as relationships that a child has by blood, law, or affinity. The use of kinship care has increased in developed nations due to the difficulty in recruiting sufficient numbers of foster carers and the growing awareness of the importance of continuing relationships for the child within the extended family unit. However, Farmer and Moyers (2005) note that standards of practice in how to best assess and support kinship carers have lagged behind the development of kinship care placements.

Kinship care is consistent with the pattern of care in many developing nations. In Namibia, South Africa, and Zimbabwe, grandparents are guardians for 60% of AIDS orphans, while in Botswana, Malawi, and Tanzania, 50% of AIDS orphans live in grandparent-headed households (Tewodros, 2003). The CRC supports the use of kinship care for children whose parents are deceased, ill, or unavailable, as it provides continuity of attachment relationships (Bowlby, 1980, 1988). In developing nations, it is important to understand the child's relationship and attachment to kinship systems. This reliance on family groups stands in contrast to the parental dyad common in most developed countries.

Institutions, Children's Homes, Orphanages, and Group Homes

Most developing nations have relied on the use of congregate care. This care may take the form of institutions, children's homes, orphanages, and group homes. They are characteristically run by shift staff with a low caregiver to child ratio. The staffs are usually women, poorly trained and poorly compensated for their work.

Children raised in congregate care experience developmental lags in one or more significant areas: physical, emotional, social, and cognitive, with weakened attachment, a higher rate of inattentiveness and hyperactivity, and reading delays (Browne, Hamilton-Giachritsis, Johnson, & Ostergren, 2006; Roy & Rutter, 2006; Smyke, Dumitrescu, & Zeanah, 2002).

Developing nations working toward membership in the European Union are expected to develop services that reflect the principles found in the CRC and human rights standards. Romania, as part of its process to enter the European Union, took steps to deinstitutionalize children through foster care and domestic adoption placements, and in 2004 passed a law restricting the placement of children under two in institutions (Parliament of Romania, 2004). The only exception was children who were "severely disabled." Yet many questions remain, particularly in relation to the quality of care for children with disabilities, and a report by Ahern et al. (2006) noted severe institutional abuse of children. Although all children have a right to grow up in a family, simply closing the doors of children's homes without standards of practice which will promote safe care and inclusion is not the answer.

Family Foster Care

As developing nations rely less on institutions and orphanages, the development of family foster care emerges as a major practice issue. In developed nations, foster care has been fraught with various problems, including evidence of abuse by some caregivers, as well as neglect by the state in supporting carers and providing adequate monitoring to ensure quality care. Some ask the question: "Given the problems of foster care in developed nations, is it a reasonable solution for developing nations?"

Children raised in institutional care suffer from the lack of close contact with a significant caregiver. Family-based care is a viable option for children when it is of high quality. Quality family care promotes the development and well-being of children. It is essential that foster carers be assessed for safe care and trained to meet the cognitive, emotional, and behavioural challenges of the children.

When a child is in foster care, the child welfare practitioner is expected to conduct child and family assessments. To assure quality and consistency in this work it is important to utilize tools that are not only respectful but are based on evidence. In a three-year study of Canadian children in care, it was found that consistent use of the *Looking after Children* Assessment and Action Records (AARs) promoted resiliency in children and improved outcomes (Kufeldt, McGilligan, Klein, & Rideout, 2006). The use of this tool is a shared process between the social worker, child, and carer. The goal is permanency for the child through the use of positive communication and planning.

Adoption

A particularly contentious area in child welfare is that of international adoption. There are those who believe it should be abolished, and that resources should focus on developing children's services. Abolitionists view international adoption as a neo-colonialist construct in which rich nations benefit from the human pain of the developing nations. They argue that healthy children receive the benefit of international adoption, whereas the "hard to place" remain behind. In a second group are the pragmatists. They accept the place of international adoption as a genuine service in child welfare, but promote standards to eliminate abuse. A third group comprises the promoters. Promoters contend that international adoption gives children from desperate circumstances a chance at life in the homes of loving families (Masson, 2001).

Adoption is not only a legal process but a cultural one as well. Domestic adoption in some countries is viewed as the extended family taking on the responsibility of care for kin, not permanent care by unrelated persons. Johnson (2002) discusses the impact of culture on adoption in China. China has had a one-child policy for many years, and Chinese Confucian patriarchal thinking values sons over daughters for the purpose of passing on the family name. Female babies are at very high risk for abandonment, and once abandoned are viewed by society as having no identity.

The *Hague Convention on Protection of Children and Co-operation in Respect of Intercountry Adoption* (1993) established standards for the practice of international adoption in member countries. The *Hague Convention* promotes the value of family life for the children, and notes that domestic adoption may not offer some children a permanent home, whereas international adoption will. *Hague Convention* standards instruct member nations to act in the best interests of the child. If a child is to be adopted, the child must not be a victim of abduction, sale, or trafficking. The CRC supports the position of the *Hague Convention* and is opposed to any practice that exploits or manipulates with money or goods. Child welfare practitioners need to carefully assess the legal status of the child and how the release from the birth parent was obtained before proceeding with an international adoption. It is imperative to work with legitimate agencies that understand human rights as well as national laws regarding adoption.

Training and Development for Social Workers

Social workers in developing nations require knowledge and skills to work in many settings and differing roles. They must understand pluralism and be able to meet the many demands of diverse groups (Potocky, 1997). They may practise as administrators for international non-governmental agencies, as international humanitarians advocating for standards of protection, as community organizers or social development workers. They may be child protection workers investigating circumstances of abuse, neglect, or oppression, or first responders and mental health workers helping to heal the effects of trauma. All of these possible roles require a rigorous education and post-graduate experiences under the supervision of qualified professional social workers. Spending time in the classroom or in practice learning does not fully prepare a person to be a professional social worker. Students need to link theory with practice to prepare them for the multiple roles involved in international social work.

As an example, Dominican University—located just outside of Chicago— offers a graduate social work curriculum which is globally focused and family centered. The university engages in the international exchange of professors and students with developing nations such as South Africa, India, Latvia, and Mexico. Immersion into global practice is an essential part of professional development, and training must include, as it does in Dominican University, service overseas. Dominican University works to support the mission of the International Association of Schools of Social Work (IASSW) by the "engagement of a community of social work educators in international exchange of information and expertise" (International Association of Schools of Social Work website, n.d.).

Problems of practice often involve ethical dilemmas. The International Federation of Social Workers (IFSW) describes common ethical concerns related to conflicting interests, role conflicts as helpers and controllers, the demand for efficiency, and limitations in resources (International Federation of Social Workers website, n.d.). Due diligence in the protection of children should be the guiding value for both social workers and national governments. A key component in the education of social workers desiring to practise in child welfare is helping them understand their legal and ethical responsibilities.

Conclusion

All nations have a responsibility to meet the mandate of the CRC and care for its vulnerable citizens. Without addressing the daunting challenges of poverty, disease, violence, natural disasters, human trafficking and migration, and all forms of maltreatment, children remain at risk of losing their families and community. The social work profession has an ethical duty to respond in calling for a vision to transform child welfare by advancing best practice models, exemplars of humane child welfare policy, and research agendas focused on the well-being of children.

There is sufficient knowledge of the challenges, as well as a plethora of existing models of good practice and humane policies. Nations need to apply what is known. Children's needs are best met in the least restrictive placement. Family-based solutions are preferable to institutional care as long as the family supports the child's physical, emotional, and intellectual development. Child welfare services must be delivered by social workers rigorously trained in child development, assessment, and standards of protection. Lessons from research and practice are the road map for the way forward.

30

Selected Practice Issues: Themes and Implications

Kathleen Kufeldt
Brad McKenzie

The chapters in Part IV have varied content and so, unlike other parts of this text, do not have connecting themes. Rather, as noted in the Introduction, they have been chosen for their relevance to critical issues in current child welfare discourse. These are:

- risk management;
- mother blaming;
- forgotten fathers;
- children with special needs; and
- the challenge of practising social work across cultures and in different milieus.

This chapter provides a brief discussion of each of these issues, with recommendations for research, policy, and practice.

Risk Management

The perennial problem in the child welfare field is managing competing values. As Bala points out in the Introduction to this book, there is tension between parental rights in the *Canadian Charter of Rights and Freedoms* and the rights of children to protection from harm. The social workers charged with managing this delicate balance are themselves caught in a dilemma. Their desire to support and enhance their clients' well-being is juxtaposed against legal responsibilities requiring them to investigate allegations of neglect and abuse and to present evidence in court. Yet this is the context in which social workers have to make crucial decisions. Some, as Chapter 4 indicates, have limited experience. As indicated in the Introduction to Part IV, the use of risk assessment tools has become increasingly the route of choice to improve the reliability and validity of these decisions. Chapter 25 provides a balanced overview of the value of these tools, and in some sense echoes conclusions drawn in the review of Zachary Turner's death at his mother's hands. Dr. Markesteyn's comments are worth repeating.

> I digress briefly to a discussion I had about risk assessment tools with my round-table of experts. These are some of their remarks: "There are a variety of things one uses as tools. One of them may be a risk assessment. But it ultimately never replaces the ability to understand the information that one collects and to make judgments based on that ... I watch practice where people explain-away or attempt to explain-away what they've done based on this tool. Well no, because no tool that we know of, ever says 'with this, do this'...." I drew certain conclusions from this discussion:
> - no one tool is fool proof;
> - too heavy a reliance on the check-list approach limits the development of assessment skills;
> - time spent on documenting and computerizing a time consuming exercise may take away time from the important other work that must be done; and
> - the tool itself may have questionable validity; in turn, worker evaluation may be based on the wrong criteria and, therefore, limit the worker's learning. (Markesteyn & Day, 2006, pp. 205–6)

Markesteyn's cautions should not be taken lightly. Excessive dependence on such tools can deflect workers' attention from other indicators. In Zachary's case, the fact that his mother was charged with murdering his father, and that she attributed slapping her young daughter to the stress this caused, were apparently not considered as risk factors.

Some jurisdictions have introduced *Signs of Safety* principles and approaches based on the work of Turnell (2004) as a complement to actuarial risk models. The *Signs of Safety* approach attempts to integrate strengths-based questioning based on the solution-focused model to the assessment of safety in interactions with families. For example, statements of harm pertaining to the children are expressed to the family, and a safety network or plan is created from the dialogue that results in order to ensure that risk is reduced to a tolerable level. Despite the growing popularity of this approach, there is no clear consensus about how it fits within a service model based on a formalized approach to risk assessment, nor is there enough evidence yet of its effectiveness in ensuring safety and reducing risk. However, its particular focus on documenting constructive practice interventions as described by front-line workers, parents, and children, and its use of appreciative inquiry in defining "better practice," is a positive antidote to the "problem saturated focus" of many assessment approaches in child welfare. This model's focus on strengths may well hold considerable promise both in connecting with families and in improving services in child protection.

Mother Blaming

Recognition of the tendency in child welfare intervention to blame mothers has been a relatively recent development (Callahan, 1993; Swift, 1995b, 1995c). A positive offshoot of that realization is the growing body of literature that demonstrates the efficacy of working *with* mothers rather than in a spirit of alienation (Callahan, Lumb, & Wharf, 1994; Cameron, 2003; Peirson, Nelson, & Prilleltensky, 2003). Chapter 27 reinforces this view by identifying not only the futility of such an approach, but also its failure to understand the wider context of parental failure and the possible inter-generational effects that flow from this.

Forgotten Fathers

Little has changed since 2003, as Chapter 26 attests. Social work records continue to be remarkable for their absence of information about fathers. Foster fathers are generally treated as peripheral to social work interaction with children and foster mothers, and this pattern extends to the paternal relatives of the child. For example, Zachary Turner's father had been murdered, but his paternal grandparents were not accorded any standing by child welfare authorities (Bagby, 2007; Markesteyn & Day, 2006).

Forgetting about fathers and their extended family limits the possible kinship resources available for children. Dr. Fernandez of the University of New South Wales has found that many children in foster care are interested in their fathers. She is in the ninth year of a longitudinal study of children in foster care (2006b; 2007a; 2008a), and in a recent paper (Fernandez, 2009) provides some interesting information about both birth and foster fathers. As in other studies, many children had no contact at all with their birth fathers. For example, 56% had no contact, and another 28% saw their father infrequently (i.e., once a month, every few months, or on holidays). But many children expressed interest in seeing their fathers and establishing a connection. One eight-year-old made the poignant comment that she had never had a real dad, only "false dads." With respect to foster fathers, Fernandez found that the nature of the relationship with the foster father appeared to have an important developmental influence. For those children where she had noted good foster father cohesion at the first interview, over time these children appeared to experience fewer relationship problems with carers, improved relationship skills, and fewer conduct problems (Fernandez, 2009).

Clearly there are many benefits to be gained by remembering that children have fathers. Walmsley and his colleagues provide some new insights, and these are important to consider for the study of both the benefits of inclusion and reasons for current exclusion of fathers.

Children with Special Needs

Chapter 27 provides new insights into the antecedents of fetal alcohol spectrum disorder (FASD), and Chapter 28 highlights its prevalence in the child welfare population. The latter information is no cause for surprise given widespread assumptions that the children's mothers are responsible for the disability and perhaps not fit to care for their children. In addition, the challenge of caring for any child with a disability adds significant strain on family resources.

There is a dual message contained in these chapters. The first line of defence should be prevention through education and support. However, when FASD has been identified as the precipitating problem, it may still be possible to maintain the family through provision of appropriate supports. If that is not possible, then, as Fuchs suggests in Chapter 28, these children deserve early permanency planning to stabilize their lives and optimize their life chances. Indeed, these same principles apply to all children with special needs.

Practising Social Work in a Global Community

Modern communications and means of travel have expanded the frontiers of social work. Social workers from the developed countries are now being asked to practise their skills and bring aid to children and families living in very different conditions and within different cultural norms. At home there are the challenges of serving a growing immigrant and refugee population. Chapter 29 presents a summary of systemic factors prevalent in less well-developed countries. And as McNitt points out, it is important that we do not fall into the trap of replicating colonialism—an issue discussed in Part III of this book. By the same token, it is important for social workers to understand the background and culture of immigrant and refugee families who come to the attention of child welfare authorities. Where cultural practices violate the values and standards of the host country (e.g., genital mutilation, subjugation of women), social workers must play a dual role—educating parents and children about their rights and responsibilities in the host country, and intervening to ensure that the rights of these children are protected.

Concluding Comments

The practice issues addressed in Part IV have implications for social work education. Our suggestion is that social work degree programs should include certain elements that we highlight here in summary fashion only:

- The practice of social work is both art and science. There is no one tool that can assist in a foolproof way in determining how clients should be served. As Chapter 25 ably demonstrates, child welfare is a complex field of practice that requires knowledge, experience, and a good sense of the strengths and limitations of available assessment and evaluation tools.
- Children are born into families, and "family" has continuing importance for children who, for whatever reason, have to be raised in substitute care. Moreover, these families include not only father and mother, but also the extended clan or family members such as grandparents, aunts, uncles, and cousins. The kinship network has value, not only to the child, but to the social work agency because it expands the range of available resources that can play a role in helping both the child and the parent. The extended family can also assist in maintaining links and attachments to the child's cultural heritage.
- Preparation for work in child welfare should include education about the causes and effects of various disabilities, particularly those related to children with FASD.
- Social work education must include exposure to the multicultural nature of contemporary practice and the systemic issues that affect families' abilities to care for their own.

In closing, we reiterate that child welfare is a particularly challenging field of practice, not one to be assigned to the novice. Yet, as Chapter 4 shows, a good proportion of workers are relatively inexperienced. The wide-ranging nature of the issues covered in this section illustrates only a few of the challenges that workers face. Decisions to be made do at times have life or death implications.

In the medical field, such decisions are not left in the hands of neophytes, but follow a period of internship, and ongoing access to specialized consultation when required. We suggest the same for work in child protection. Without adequate education, training, a period of internship, and quality supervision, child welfare systems will continue to fail too many children and families.

The Search for Best Practice

Introduction

Part IV identified and discussed some selected practice issues. This section includes six chapters based on research regarding best practice, and in so doing offers some optimistic directions for improvement of the child welfare system. The common focus in these chapters is the desire to effect practice that will provide better outcomes for children and youth. The opening chapter promotes family-based practice, but differs from the others in that it is conceptually rather than empirically based. The fact that we open with this chapter in no way negates the message conveyed in Chapter 19, which was that child welfare services must be child-centred. Indeed, in Part II, family contact emerged strongly as the primary linking thread throughout the continuum of care. The family cannot be ignored, and even when children cannot live in safety within their family, they still need that sense of connection. In addition, there is ample research to support the importance of working with the family before, during, and after care. Thus, Chapter 31 reviews the literature on family-centred practice and provides guidelines for the implementation of this approach in child welfare.

The *Looking After Children* (LAC) practice model continues to generate the interest shown in the earlier edition of this text (Kufeldt & McKenzie, 2003a). Chapters 32, 33, and 34 reinforce this interest, now well entrenched in Australia and showing promise in Canada. Chapter 34 not only discusses the use of LAC as a guided practice model for children in care, but also includes the Australian experience with guided practice with families known as Supporting Children and Responding to Families, or SCARF. It appears that Barnardos Australia is in the forefront with respect to proactive planning for the children and families it serves.

Chapter 35 provides an approach to working with troubled youth that is refreshingly different from the traditional focus on the presenting problem. Rather than focusing on a potentially stigmatizing fact, it engages with youth to help them identify their strengths and assets, those that are intrinsic and those derived from family and community. The model is clear and well conceptualized, and there is evidence of promising results from early use of this model.

The outcomes indicator matrix presented in Chapter 36 encapsulates some of the core components of the LAC model, though in more summary fashion. Its potential value lies in its ability to aggregate readily available data in order to evaluate an agency's effectiveness. The authors also provide an example of its use in one agency. If adopted by all child welfare authorities in Canada, it has the potential to provide a barometer of the current state of affairs with respect to meeting the needs of children in care.

Policy-makers and researchers in the United Kingdom continue to work in partnership to improve outcomes for children in need. The LAC model was absorbed into an ambitious tripartite assessment framework (Department of Health, Department for Education and Employment, and Home Office, 2000, p. 89; Kufeldt, 2003, p. 275). LAC assesses and monitors children's developmental needs; the other two components address parenting capacity and family and environmental factors which are known to affect the safety and well-being of children. The more recent development is the national promotion of a holistic Integrated Children's System. Scott, a key player in these activities, provides a summary of some of the implementation experiences with this system in Chapter 37. A summary of themes and implications pertaining to best practice is presented in the final chapter.

31

Family-Centred Child Welfare Practice

Alexandra Wright
Diane Hiebert-Murphy

This chapter applies family-centred practice (FCP) concepts to the front-line child welfare context. It is recognized that child welfare practice occurs on a continuum, ranging from the least restrictive (or voluntary) to the most restrictive (or involuntary) services, often based on a range of legal sanctions. The basic premise of this chapter is that FCP principles and skills can improve child welfare practice by providing the worker with an approach to practice that is based on respect, builds on family strengths, emphasizes safety, is culturally respectful and appropriate, and empowers families. The chapter begins with a brief review of FCP and its relevance as a "best practice" approach to child welfare. Through a summary of key elements of FCP, the chapter provides an FCP model applicable to child welfare work. Although the value of community-based work and the need for an overall organizational support of family-centred service planning and provision are recognized (Cameron, 2003; Glisson & Green, 2005; Wharf, 2002), this discussion is limited to the integration of FCP within front-line child welfare practice.

Background

There has been growth in the support of FCP as a valued and effective approach to social service provision. Family-centred practice has been identified as relevant to a range of helping professions, including nursing (Hutchfield, 1999), occupational therapy (Bazyk, 1989), speech and language therapy (Crais, 1991), physiotherapy (Chiarello, Effgen, & Levinson, 1992), and more recently social work (Hiebert-Murphy, Trute, & Wright, 2008). Family-centred practice is considered an effective and best practice approach to service provision (Law et al., 2003; Loxley & Deriviere, 2005a), with demonstrated benefits for service users (Dunst, Trivette, & Hamby, 2007; Trute & Hiebert-Murphy, 2007; Van Riper, 1999).

Family-centred practice is well-established in voluntary services, particularly childhood disability (e.g., Dunst, Trivette, & Deal, 1994a; King, Law, King, Kertoy, Hurley, & Rosenbaum, 2000). It is less frequently extended, however, to mandated services such as child welfare (Henry & Purcell, 2000). Within the child welfare field, FCP is most frequently applied within family preservation and family support services (e.g., Cole, 1995; McCroskey & Meezan, 1998) and alternative care (e.g., Lewandowski & Pierce, 2004; McFadden, 1996). Connolly (2006) refers to FCP in the context of family group conferencing, and notes the difficulty in balancing responses "to family preservation needs and meeting the care and safety needs of a child" (p. 354). While some authors (McCroskey & Meezan, 1998; Tracy & Pine, 2000) have recommended the incorporation of FCP in child welfare, there is little conceptual or empirical literature regarding the application of FCP when working directly with families involved with mandated child protection services who are not involved in family support/preservation/reunification programs.

A Family-Centred Practice Model

Family-centred practice is considered more than a technique; it is a way of conceptualizing intervention with families that guides practice (Powell, 1996). It is a philosophy of working with families that emphasizes family strengths, empowerment, partnership, and the use of family service plans (Bailey & Simeonsson, 1988; Dunst et al., 1994a; King, Law, King, & Rosenbaum, 1998). The family's needs and desires are the basis for all services, and must be the focus on case, organizational, and system levels (Dunst, Johanson, Trivette, & Hamby, 1991). Family-centred practice is not limited to the relationship between the service coordinator and the family, but also refers to procedural aspects of service provision. For example, on a service coordination level, accuracy in documentation, the use of an "individualized family service plan" (IFSP), and clinical evaluation reflect FCP (Bailey & Simeonsson, 1988; Dunst, Trivette, & Deal, 1988). On a program level, FCP entails the provision of flexible, comprehensive services (Dunst, Trivette, & Deal, 1994b; Shelton & Stepanek, 1995); local, accessible services (Dunst et al., 1994b; Stroul, 1995); the implementation of resource-based approaches (as opposed to service-based approaches); program evaluation (Dunst et al., 1988); and the inclusion of families' perceptions in the evaluation of services (Park & Turnbull, 2003).

Based on information identified by the following authors (Bailey, McWilliam, Winton, & Simeonsson, 1992; Bailey & Simeonsson, 1988; Busca & Crystal, 1999; Dunst et al., 1994a; Dunst et al., 1988; Rosenbaum, King, Law, King, & Evans, 1998), the general principles associated with FCP are summarized below:

- Service provision and policies focus on families (as opposed to an individual child).
- The worker respects parents and children, and works in partnership with families (a collaborative approach to service provision). The relationship is based on trust.
- The worker listens to parents and children, and recognizes that parents know their children best; parents have a central role to play in determining what is best for their children.
- The worker works from a strengths-based perspective with a goal of empowering families and mobilizing families to access required resources, using both formal and informal support to meet family needs.
- The worker recognizes that all families are different, and services provided should be based on the family's needs, not based on "one size fits all" generic service availability (individualized, needs-based services).
- The worker corroborates that identified service needs are accessible and available (service providers must ensure that there are sufficient community resources available to support the family).
- Services provided are culturally sensitive, ecologically based, and coordinated.
- Services are normalized (as opposed to stigmatized).
- The worker provides sufficient information to families to enable informed decisions.

While individual components of this FCP model are not new concepts to child welfare practice, when considered as a whole, the FCP model reflects a distinctive approach to working with families.

The Application of Family-Centred Practice to Child Welfare

There are at least six child welfare practice stages: intake, investigation, assessment (including risk assessment), intervention, evaluation, and closure (Falconer & Swift, 1983; Maidman, 1984). The focus of this discussion is on the application of an FCP model for assessment and intervention in all stages of child welfare practice.

Assessment

Intake and investigation are the first stages in the child welfare process. These stages initially focus on collecting information from a referral source, and this information assists the worker in understanding the appropriateness of the referral, the specific child welfare needs of the family, the immediacy and severity of the alleged harm to the child (when relevant), and the motivation of the referral source (Falconer & Swift, 1983). Intake allows the worker to assess the validity of the report and gather information necessary to begin the process of decision-making. Information collected is rooted in an ecological perspective, which views a service user in the context of his/her family, community, and larger society (Lovell & Thompson, 1995). The worker documents all information and checks agency records to ascertain whether any previous information exists on the child/family (or if the file is currently open). From an FCP perspective, intake sets the context for the initial contact with the family, and begins to identify potential family needs that must be further assessed.

Family-centred practice recognizes that the welfare of a child is intricately intertwined with the welfare of the family (Tracy & Pine, 2000), and stresses the importance of building and sustaining an effective relationship with the family (McCroskey & Meezan, 1998). FCP requires that child welfare workers take responsibility for engaging with families and actively work toward developing trust in the working relationship. Building trust requires that workers respect the confidentiality of family members (and clarify the circumstances in which confidentiality cannot be promised), and follow up on all commitments. Families need to know that workers can be depended upon to complete agreed-upon tasks.

In intake and investigation meetings, workers avoid imposing their understanding of the situation with no, or superficial, family involvement. Workers actively listen to family members' points of view or understanding of issues, and respond with honesty and respect. Whenever possible, FCP involves the participation of all family members, even though some may be involuntary service users. Consequently, when a worker is arranging an initial meeting with a family, all family members are welcome. Workers ask each member about his/her understanding of the situation and perceived options to successfully resolve it. Workers must be honest with families about concerns and expectations based on the legal mandate or an ethical consideration of the safety and well-being of family members.

An FCP model in child welfare emphasizes the importance of working in partnership with families whenever possible, even when faced with the challenge of working with involuntary service users. There are seven major operatives when engaging with families to identify family needs (Dunst et al., 1988):

1. Be positive and proactive in arranging the first contact with the family.
2. Take time to establish rapport with the family before beginning the interview.
3. Begin by clearly stating the purpose of the interview.
4. Encourage the family to share aspirations as well as concerns.
5. Help the family clarify concerns, and define the precise nature of their needs.
6. Listen empathetically and be responsive throughout the interview.
7. Establish consensus regarding the priority needs.

Throughout assessment, the worker attempts to establish and maintain positive rapport, which sets the foundation for a positive working relationship. Interpersonal communication skills are critical. In the initial meeting the family may express many emotions (such as confusion, mistrust, fear, and/or relief). During this meeting the worker, using an FCP approach, explains her/his role and takes time to hear each family member's concerns, goals, and questions. Non-negotiable and negotiable items are clearly identified. Whenever possible, questions are answered immediately and honestly; when additional clarification is required, the worker makes a commitment to find the information and respond promptly. The worker explains to the family what she or he can do as well as what she or he is unable to do (e.g., return a child immediately, allow an alleged offender to move back with the family). In addition, as part of relationship building and assessment, the worker meets with all individuals identified as belonging to the "family," including individuals living outside of the family home, extended family members, and/or adopted members. Involving all relevant family members in assessment establishes the family as the focus and sets the tone for future intervention.

Assessment is a constant process (Brown, 2002) that is grounded in an ecological perspective. Thus there is an awareness of the relationship between the service user, the family, the community, the larger society, and how a person adapts to, and interacts with, his/her environment (Bronfenbrenner, 1977; Maidman, 1984). This perspective incorporates an anti-oppressive approach that recognizes that structural oppression can negatively impact parenting (Mullaly, 2002).

According to Bailey and Simeonsson (1988), there are five principal assessment domains within FCP: (a) child needs and characteristics likely to affect family functioning, (b) parent-child interactions, (c) family needs, (d) critical events, and (e) family strengths. The assessment examines needs of individuals and families within each of these areas, even if this exploration goes beyond the referred "problem." For example, a specific problem or issue may be the focus of the referral (such as child maltreatment); however, other issues such as food, clothing, and shelter; safety; medical needs; education needs; discipline methods; emotional support; and interactions between family members can also comprise aspects of the assessment. The assessment includes an examination of the service user's understanding of the situation, and identifies strengths as well as problems and potential areas for change. Assessments always include the identification of sources of support in formal and informal support networks (Tracy & Pine, 2000), which may include nuclear family members, kin, informal networks, social organizations, professionals, and policy-makers (Dunst et al., 1988). Genograms and ecomaps (to detail the family's current and potential sources of resources and social support) can be useful visual assessment tools (Dunst et al., 1988).

An FCP approach to assessment enhances a more traditional child welfare approach as it underscores the importance of family strengths and functioning, recognizes the complexity of families, and acknowledges that the child's best interests are met through a positively functioning family. Many models of family functioning are available to provide a framework for the assessment of family functioning. For example, the McMaster Model of Family Functioning (MMFF) (Epstein, Ryan, Bishop, Miller, & Keitner, 2003) identifies six dimensions of family functioning useful for the assessment of effective or ineffective family functioning:

1. family members' ability to problem-solve;
2. family members' ability to communicate;
3. family members' ability to fulfill family roles;
4. the family's range of affective responsiveness;
5. the extent of affective involvement by family members; and
6. patterns of behaviour control.

Walsh's family resilience framework (Walsh, 2003a) narrows target areas for assessment to the family's belief systems, the family's organizational patterns, and the family's ability to communicate and problem-solve. These models provide a basis for assessment in child welfare cases, as they recognize the importance of family roles, transitions, patterns, histories, and coping.

When working in the child welfare context, family functioning is assessed and, where evidence of ineffective functioning exists, solutions for change are ascertained and prioritized. An FCP child welfare assessment includes an assessment of current family functioning, family needs and goals, issues that the family considers important (goals to which family members are willing to commit energy and time), family strengths (what the family does well, skills that can help mobilize resources), and resources likely to support the family in meeting identified needs. The worker makes note of and acknowledges the positive aspects of family functioning (including daily routines), anecdotes shared by family members, and strengths reflected in the family's physical, social, and recreational environments. The worker strives to "rephrase and reframe" negative comments in a positive manner (Dunst et al., 1988).

Family-centred practice recognizes the importance of cultural identity and the need to provide services that are culturally appropriate and respectful. In child welfare this means that practices and policies should recognize the diversity in society and incorporate culturally appropriate approaches. This is an issue of particular importance to Canada's Aboriginal and newcomer populations. In the context of working with Aboriginal people, McKenzie and Morrissette (2003) provide a framework for "respectful" social work practice based on the recognition of an Aboriginal world view, the effects of colonization, the value of cultural knowledge and tradition in healing, and the diversity within Aboriginal culture. These themes are echoed in the works of other authors who identify an Aboriginal world view as an important element of Aboriginal culture (Connors & Maidman, 2001; Cross, 1998; Gosek, 2002). Gross (1995) cautions against assuming that Aboriginal practices are applicable to all Aboriginal people; this assumption runs the risk of missing individual needs and priorities. Others caution against generalization because of the great variation in Aboriginal culture (Gosek, 2002; McKenzie & Morrissette, 2003). From an FCP perspective, when engaging with a family, the worker explores the family's cultural background, individual members' cultural identities, and aspects of the particular family that define its unique culture (e.g., family values, spirituality). It is only when the family's culture is understood that an appropriate intervention plan can be developed.

It is also important to recognize the diversity among families, and to respond to the priorities of families within their unique family culture. When engaging with families, workers must acknowledge that there is no one "normal" family (Epstein et al., 2003; Walsh, 2003a), and that it is common for families to experience difficulties at different times in their lives, due to a wide range of stressors such as racism, sexism, addictions, life cycle transitions, chronic illnesses, or unemployment (McGoldrick & Carter, 2003). It is critical for workers to impress upon the family that, with appropriate supports, positive family functioning can be achieved and sustained in the presence of significant stressors so that all family members have the opportunity to develop and thrive.

Intervention

An FCP model of practice requires that the worker take a proactive and positive role to empower families to make positive change and meet specified goals (Dunst et al., 1988). Family-centred practice requires that workers engage with the family with the goals of enabling, empowering, and strengthening families, thereby helping families to identify solutions. Family-centred child welfare workers promote positive family functioning by working in partnership with the family and engaging in shared decision-making. This approach encourages co-operation and, to the extent possible, shared responsibility. A family-centred child welfare worker offers help in response to family-identified needs, and permits the family to decide whether to accept or reject help (informing the family of the consequences of decisions). The worker also ensures that the cost of receiving services (i.e., low self-esteem or financial) are lower than the benefits of receiving services. The benefits may include experiencing an increased sense of competence and an increased sense of safety of family members, as well as tangible benefits such as improved housing or child care services. Whenever possible, reciprocity between the family and the worker is supported. For example, family members are encouraged to share their knowledge of community programs or resources in their network that can help address family needs.

Support or services offered need to be congruent with the family's appraisal of needs, even in the context of a mandated child protection order. In these cases, the worker delineates non-negotiable issues (i.e., safety of a child) while working with the family on family-identified needs. In addition, support provided to the family is normative, and, as much as possible, non-stigmatizing, with the worker emphasizing that many families experience problems and that the family has the capabilities to ensure that members' physical and emotional needs are met. Intervention strategies should also promote the family's use of informal support. Families can be encouraged to engage with external supports such as extended family, school resources and activities, or spiritual supports. These resources respect the family's culture, enhance family well-being, and encourage the integration of the family within their community.

Important principles are empowerment, building on family resilience, and the use of participatory practice approaches wherever possible. The goal is to empower families to problem-solve and maintain positive family functioning without the intervention of a child welfare agency. Consequently, the family-centred child welfare worker encourages family members to learn and integrate behaviours that promote independence and develop capacity, increasing members' abilities to meet their own needs.

Within child welfare practice, information collected in the assessment phase provides the basis for service intervention and the evaluation of effectiveness (Tanner & Turney, 2006). Based on the needs identified in the assessment, a contract is developed between the family members and the worker (and other relevant people, including community members when appropriate), in order to identify specific goals and tasks necessary for positive change. The worker clarifies the purpose of her/his role, and specifies non-negotiable items with the family members. To the greatest extent possible, the service provider works in partnership with the family to define the problems/issues, set priorities, identify goals, and establish a service plan/contract (Falconer & Swift, 1983; Maidman, 1984).

Service contracts, or what are referred to as individualized family support plans (IFSPs), are an important aspect of FCP. The plan specifies the "what, how, and when" of intervention (Maidman, 1984, p. 48). A model IFSP might include the following information (Dunst et al., 1988, pp. 132–3):

1. The name of the case coordinator.
2. A statement of the child's strengths and current levels of functioning.
3. A statement of the family's strengths, and qualities that define their unique family functioning style.
4. The specific "early intervention" services to be used by the family, and the dates the services are started and ended.
5. A list of family-identified needs, concerns, aspirations, and projects in order of priority.
6. A statement of the sources of support, and resources that will be mobilized to meet needs.
7. A statement of the actions that will be taken to mobilize resources, and the role the family will play in actualizing the plan.
8. A procedure for evaluating the extent to which needs are met.

Consistent with the emphasis on service planning and follow-up, a clearly written IFSP sets out expectations and desired outcomes as well as identifying negotiable and non-negotiable issues. Strengths of individual family members and the family as a whole are noted and incorporated into the intervention plan. The worker clarifies the role of collateral service providers and the role of the family's social support system in the intervention plan. The IFSP also specifies the responsibilities for the worker as well as the family in implementing the plan. In agreement with family members, time frames and methods for evaluating success are recorded. An up-to-date IFSP provides the basis for the examination of process issues and outcomes during follow-up meetings.

While developing the IFSP, the worker is challenged to engage the family and, as much as possible, collaborate with the family on the plan. In cases where the parent is unable to agree to a contract, the worker then uses what Rooney (1992) describes as an "involuntary" case plan, which details requirements and associated consequences. Ultimately, every service user has the right to not work with an agency, and by exercising this right, the person is making a choice even if there are related consequences to that choice. However, a worker strives to help parents identify potential benefits to their children and family of engaging with the child welfare agency, and informs them of the outcome of choosing not to participate. Forrester, McCambridge, Waissbein, and Rollnick (2008) found that when faced with resistance by parents, social workers often employed a confrontational and aggressive communication style and were likely to impose their agenda on the families without attending to parents' concerns. The authors found that there was little empathy in the workers' responses, and argue that workers need to develop skills that encourage relationship building and trust, ultimately to ensure better outcomes for children.

Workers applying an FCP model to child welfare promote partnership by listening respectfully to family members' understanding of issues and their proposed solutions to overcome challenges, ideally working together to arrive at a solution that reflects the family's agenda as well as satisfying legal requirements. This approach is in contrast with the more "top-down" model of working with families, where the worker presents a family with a list of required services in which specific family members must participate in order to address identified problems. In FCP, once non-negotiable issues are delineated, family members and workers engage in a collaborative process that explores options for building and sustaining positive family functioning. This is consistent with the empowerment principle noted earlier, in which families are helped to identify choices when considering possibilities for change, including choices that are available within the wider community.

Family-centred practice involves a shift from a problem-based approach to a strengths-based approach, working toward positive solutions. This requires that workers view the family as resilient, or having "the ability to withstand and rebound from disruptive life challenges" (Walsh, 2003a, p. 399). The worker engages with the family in ways that build on family strengths and successes, in an effort to help them become more effective in dealing with crises and ongoing stressors. While specific difficulties within the family that result in harm to children are not ignored, workers engage with families to build a plan based on existing strengths that can be mobilized to support desired changes. For example, in the situation of a family in which parental substance abuse has left the children unsupervised and at risk of harm, the worker ensures that the assessment and intervention plan addresses the addiction and other areas of concern by building on what the family and individual members do well, positive family coping skills, and available supports.

Resources within the individuals, within the family, within the family's social network, and within the broader community are all considered in the formulation of a plan that addresses both family-identified needs and child welfare concerns. For example, if parents are leaving children at risk of harm due to weekend binging, the parents' willingness to address the addiction, as well as to develop a safety plan for the children, can be explored. A safety plan may be established based on shared agreement that the children's safety is a concern; thus an appropriate friend or extended family member may be identified as a resource for caring for the children should the parents be unable to provide appropriate supervision.

It is important to acknowledge that working in child welfare often involves working with involuntary service users. Pressure to be involved may stem from the justice system in which the service user is legally directed to be involved, or from other pressure such as family and friends, referral sources, or the child welfare agency. Involuntary clients may include a parent or guardian of the child who has been suspected or convicted of abusive or neglectful behaviour, or other family members such as the non-offending parent or children. Rooney (1992) advises that workers must be aware of hidden agendas and cross-purposes when working with involuntary service users, as some may "sabotage" the helping relationship and may provide inaccurate, dishonest information as well as failing to buy into the contracting process. Falconer and Swift (1983) note that typical reactions of parents when involved in a child protection investigation include "denial, hostility, apathy and depression, fear, extreme compliance, and occasionally, co-operation" (p. 86). Other family members may perceive it to be in the family's best interests to hide or manipulate information, lie, or misinform the worker and collateral service providers, in order to avoid outcomes such as separation, charges being laid, and/or the placement of a child in alternative care. In these cases the worker may use various techniques to overcome resistance (Cingolani, 1984; Rooney, 1992). Rooney (1992) advocates the use of both "more intrusive" compliance-oriented methods (punishment and inducement) and "less intrusive" (and more preferable) persuasion methods when working with involuntary clients. Fundamentally, an important role of the worker is to remind the service user of his/her right to non-compliance and related consequences.

Despite the challenges of working with involuntary clients, an FCP model remains a viable approach (McCroskey & Meezan, 1998). Regardless of the behaviour of family members, the worker must continue to work in a respectful manner with parents and children, building on strengths to arrive at an acceptable solution. In some situations, safety concerns (e.g., in cases in which there is severe violence) and/or the diminished capacity of the family member (e.g., when there are significant mental health issues or severe cognitive impairment) may prevent the establishment of a partnership. To the extent that it is possible and does not compromise safety, the goal of FCP is to work toward engagement and empowerment, recognizing that partnership is a process that exists along a continuum and may take some time to develop. The challenge for the worker is to attempt to remain involved with the service user, look for opportunities to advance engagement, and identify small steps that can be taken toward collaboration.

Even when a family member presents as unable or unwilling to engage with the worker, it is still possible to apply a family-centred approach by using honesty and respect when explaining the outcomes of the choices the individual is making. When a reluctant family member is willing to engage with the worker on some level, then the door is open to ensure that non-negotiable issues are identified and acknowledged, and other areas of focus, such as the person's aspirations and personal goals, are explored. When meeting with the service user, workers must maintain honesty about what they can and cannot do, and clearly identify options that are available as well as goals or tasks that are not negotiable. Under no circumstances can a child's best interests and safety be sacrificed in order to maintain engagement with family members. For example, a worker and family members may agree that one of the goals is for the family to remain together. The worker may assert, however, that in order to achieve this goal, certain conditions must be met, such as one parent refraining from disciplining the children or certain family members not being alone together. The worker can then engage with the family in working through the specific challenges associated with meeting the conditions.

Evaluation is based on the plan as written in the contracted IFSP. The evaluation of intervention effectiveness includes both an examination of the process of services provided as well as the outcomes realized (Mather & Lager, 2000). Evaluation requires that the worker meet with the family (or identified members) on a regular basis to jointly examine the specific goals and tasks outlined in the IFSP, and discuss any issues arising that create obstacles to attaining positive results (Falconer & Swift, 1983). Based on regular evaluations, problems that may arise are incorporated into a modified service plan. The worker and family continue to meet regularly to ensure that people are meeting the tasks as identified in the IFSP, to ensure that as new needs arise they are incorporated into the IFSP, and to problem-solve when difficulties are faced. Thus family members share feedback on their specific tasks and goal attainment, identifying outcome successes or challenges that require further work. Feedback from other collateral service providers also contributes information on which to evaluate the need for further involvement. Termination or closure occurs when goals have been attained and family functioning is stable. The worker meets with the family and acknowledges successes as well as areas that require further support (Mather & Lager, 2000).

Conclusion

This chapter has summarized the benefits of applying an FCP model of practice to direct child welfare service provision. Critical elements of FCP that are particularly relevant for direct practice in child welfare include the emphasis on the worker engaging with families based on respect and trust, workers taking a proactive approach when working with families with the goal of empowering families using a strengths-based perspective, recognizing the importance of culture and culturally appropriate services, and working in partnership with families to the greatest extent possible to develop and implement an intervention plan, based on choice.

While our focus has been on front-line practice, it is important to acknowledge that this practice occurs within a broader context. Many factors have been identified as impediments to good practice in child welfare, including high caseloads, general resource limitations, inadequate training, and poor supervision (CWLA, 2006). The implementation of an FCP model in child welfare has important organizational, system, and policy implications. Organizations must support the engagement of workers with families. This requirement translates into manageable workloads, continuity in worker-family relationships, and adequate education and training for workers. Organizations must also work to ensure inter- and intra-agency policy and service coordination. An FCP policy lens needs to be applied on organizational, system, and legislative levels to ensure that the family and family needs remain the focus of intervention, and family members should have a voice in all levels of policy and program planning. An FCP approach also requires that preventative, community-based services be available to provide needed supports for families. Funders have a responsibility to ensure that sufficient resources are available to child welfare organizations, and to the communities in which the organizations exist, to enable them to provide family-centred services to families. Although these community and organizational responses are important in ensuring an effective family-centred service model, the absence of a more comprehensive response need not prevent the incorporation of FCP principles within any specific agency's service model.

32

Using *Looking After Children* Data to Link Research to Policy and Practice in Out-of-Home Care

Sarah Wise
Ruth Champion

This chapter looks at linking research to policy and practice in out-of-home care. It sets out the prerequisites for evidence-based decision-making; that is, evidence relevant to policy and practice, available when needed and communicated in a way which maximizes its use. The quality of relationships between key stakeholders is stressed as essential in meeting these requirements. It draws on the *Looking After Children* Outcomes Data Project, recently conducted in the Australian state of Victoria, to highlight how evidence can be produced and utilized to best effect. The aims, methods, and findings from the *Looking After Children* Outcomes Data Project are outlined. Impacts of the findings in the areas of policy and practice are discussed.

An Evidence-Based Approach to Policy and Practice

Evidence-based policy and practice is a paradigm for promoting good outcomes by basing interventions on the best available knowledge of "what works" (Gray & McDonald, 2006; Witkin & Harrison, 2001). The idea of allowing evidence to determine or inform policy and practice decision-making has its origin in the scientific movement of the early twentieth century, and has since spread to a wide range of disciplines, including child and family welfare. An evidence-based approach is critical in achieving good outcomes and avoiding unintended consequences (Petersen, 2006), and thus clearly serves the best interests of service users and the public. At the same time, political pressure to show greater accountability and effectiveness have been key drivers in bringing evidence to the forefront of policy and practice (Lewig, Arney, & Scott, 2006). Thus, a rigorous, evidence-based approach to policy and practice has wide support (Buysse & Wesley, 2006).

Evidence can play a useful and even decisive role in policy and practice decisions, and can also condition the environment in which decisions are made. However, there are many factors aside from established knowledge that play a role in decision-making. A growing literature examining research utilization identifies three factors that influence whether an evidence-based approach will take centre stage: the nature and extent of the evidence; timing and circumstance; and the effectiveness of research dissemination (Banks et al., 2009).

Nature and Extent of the Evidence

For evidence-based decision-making to occur, there must first be enough quality research to form an evidence base. A key issue here is the *standard* of evidence appropriate for policy and practice decisions. Different forms of evidence are not all equally informative, and they present a hierarchy of research methods in terms of their ability to reliably and directly inform policy and practice (Thyer, 2004). Randomized control trials are considered the "gold standard" for a well-informed policy and practice decision (Boruch, de Moya, & Snyder, 2002). However, in the child and family welfare field, this method of research is rarely conducted, because it is unethical to withhold services that respond to child abuse and neglect for the purpose of establishing a control group. There is also a lack of research adopting longitudinal methodologies, as well as research that quantifies impacts and controls for simultaneous influences on outcomes.

It should be noted, however, that there is active debate about the authority of scientific evidence in this field; that is, what constitutes appropriate methodology, and what should count as evidence. Given that service provision in child and family welfare operates within a complex socio-political context, some commentators suggest that knowledge gained from practitioners' experience as well as a host of non-experimental research approaches should be used as evidence (Humphreys, Berridge, Butler, & Ruddick, 2003).

Timing and Circumstance

The time involved in producing detailed research involving data gathering can clash with the political need for speed. Even when there is a need for good evidence, it will tend not to be used unless it is available when practitioners and policy-makers need it. For policy formation, this often means the appropriate stage of policy development and the budget cycle. Other contextual factors that influence the take-up of research include the learning culture within relevant systems or organizations, as well as individual factors such as "innovativeness," values, vested interests, and personalities (Barwick, Boydell, Stasiulis, Ferguson, Blase, & Fixsen, 2005).

Dissemination of Knowledge

Even within an environment that is open to evidence, for social science research to be applied in policy-making and practice it must be *proactively* communicated in a relevant, compelling, and accessible way, and presented in a language that is familiar to decision-makers and practitioners (Davies, 2003; Theis et al., 2000). The relevant knowledge transfer literature also suggests that for wide diffusion, dissemination approaches need to be specifically tailored to suit the target audience (Scullion, 2002).

Evidence-based advice for policy and practice also needs to reach the right people, such as ministers, departmental secretaries, and senior public servants, as well as operational and program managers. Dissemination to the broader public may also be important to affect community attitudes and perceptions. Here, engagement with community stakeholders such as not-for-profit organizations and other groups who aim to influence decisions made by government on behalf of a special interest may be of particular importance.

Building Relationships to Maximize Research Utilization

Several authors have suggested that a stable, interactive relationship between researchers, policy-makers, and practitioners is the key mechanism through which research utilization takes place (Walter, Nutley, & Davies, 2003; Landry, Amara, & Laamary, 2001). Close working relationships are thought to lead to the right evidence at the right time, because researchers develop a better understanding of the priorities, interests, and information needs of policy-makers and practitioners, and because research users learn the language, methods, and constraints operating within the environment of research. Personal interaction with researchers may also promote research use through better understanding of the quality of the research evidence and the application of research findings to programs and policies (Innvaer, Vist, Trommald, & Oxman, 2002).

The *Looking After Children* Outcomes Data Project, which was initiated by the Victorian Department of Human Service (DHS), is a case example of researchers, policy-makers, and practitioners working together to generate timely and relevant knowledge to inform funded models of service delivery in out-of-home care.

Although the research project was established through a process of external contracting, both research and policy teams showed a high level of respect, goodwill, co-operation, and engagement in order to achieve the aims of the project. Two issues were important. First, there was a shared history and common understanding of the *Looking After Children* (LAC) approach, and a mutual desire to unlock the potential of the practice records as tools for evaluation and outcomes monitoring. Second, the government contract manager established very close contact with the lead investigator, encouraged frank dialogue on all aspects of the project, and demonstrated a willingness to incorporate the researchers' perspective in framing the research task. The contractual arrangements also permitted publication of the results of the research, which created incentives for the researchers to make robust findings.

The commitment and co-operation shown within the community sector was also vital to the project's success. Agency participation was strictly on an opt-in basis, so there was a genuine commitment to explore whether the LAC records could produce client data that would assist innovation at a systems and individual agency level. Allowing government personnel access to client information at an agency level showed a real commitment to the idea that responsibility for corporate parenting and children's futures is shared across the whole system.

What follows is a description of the research, policy, and practice context within which the project came about, a brief description of the project aims, methods, and findings, followed by a discussion of how the results have been disseminated and used in policy and practice to date.

The *Looking After Children* Outcomes Data Project

Looking After Children is a comprehensive system for gathering information, making plans, and reviewing children's cases—that is, to ensure that what is known about good parenting is integrated into casework practice. The centrepiece of the *Looking After Children* framework is the Assessment and Action Records (AARs). These records focus on the child's development across seven life areas (health, education, emotional and behavioural development, family and social relationships, identity, social presentation, and self-care skills) across six different age formats (< 12 months, 1–2 years, 3–4 years, 5–9 years, 10–14 years, and 15 years and older).

Project Aims

In 2007, a project commenced in the Australian state of Victoria to aggregate information recorded on paper-based AARs from approximately 46 community service organizations (CSOs) providing home-based and residential care services. The specific aims of the project were:

1. to construct an annotated electronic database from individual-level data recorded on the AARs in hard copy format;
2. to identify approximately 30 outcome measures for analysis; and
3. to identify whether the LAC tools produce the appropriate management information that government and agencies need in order to monitor service effectiveness.

A further purpose of the project was to provide a confidential report to each of the participating CSOs, which would present the agency's data on the selected measures, compared with the state as a whole. This was designed to assist with the engagement of CSOs in the project, and to develop a learning culture across placement and support services where research and evidence is privileged.

The Research Context

The overall shortage of Australian research (Cashmore, Higgins, Bromfield, & Scott, 2006), combined with difficulties capturing data through primary research, was an important dynamic in the establishment of the *Looking After Children* Outcomes Data Project. At present, there is a considerable knowledge gap for sound policy and practice decisions in out-of-home care. Quantitative studies concerning children's development tend to be cross-sectional in nature, and few studies involve standardized measures or objective assessments, or involve children directly. While the U.S. Longitudinal Studies of Child Abuse and Neglect (LONGSCAN) (Litrownik, Newton, Mitchell, & Richardson, 2003), the Canadian National Longitudinal Survey of Children and Youth (NLSCY), and the National Survey of Child and Adolescent Well-Being (NSCAW) (NSCAW Research Group, 2003) are notable exceptions, research involving objective assessments, and child reports and studies that collect longitudinal data, tend to be small-scale and descriptive in nature.

Several authors (e.g., Berrick, Frasch, & Fox, 2000; Knight et al., 2000; Rutter, 2000) have related the paucity and poor quality of research on children in out-of-home care to difficulties in recruitment and other methodological and ethical challenges that are peculiar to this sample group (Wise,

2007). Indeed, previous efforts in out-of-home care research have highlighted a multitude of challenges in design, sampling and recruitment (NSCAW Research Group, 2002, 2003; Kotch, 2000; Berrick et al., 2000; Heptinstall, 2000; Gilbertson & Barber, 2002), and instrumentation (Hunter et al., 2002; Berrick et al., 2000).

In Australia, there is also the issue of research infrastructure and funding for research in child and family welfare. There have been some noteworthy developments of late,there is no systematic framework for research in relation to out-of-home care, and currently no funding scheme exists that is designed specifically to support research in this area, such as sponsorship from the state and territory departments with statutory responsibility for children in care.

The Policy and Practice Context

A defining feature of the Victorian out-of-home care system is the use of the U.K. *Looking After Children* framework (Parker, Ward, Jackson, Aldgate, & Wedge, 1991) to assess individual child needs and to inform or revise the child's Care and Placement Plan (Champion & Burke, 2006). A collaborative implementation process has been underway since 2002 in Victoria to use the LAC system as a practice tool to guide the routine assessment of the developmental needs of children in foster care and residential care, and to stimulate provision of services and inputs in response to identified needs (see Champion & Burke, 2006). While voluntary throughput data collated by CSOs suggests variable implementation across the state, the LAC approach has generally wide support among the community service organizations whose task it is to ensure that the AARs are completed by the care team with the active, age-appropriate involvement of the child.

Although the Assessment and Action Records of the LAC framework were designed first and foremost for use in practice, they have meaning at the aggregate level and thus have the potential to produce quite powerful performance data. As discussed earlier in the chapter, the potential to aggregate client information captured through implementation of LAC had been recognized within government and in research settings for some time (Wise, 2003a). Indeed, various researchers have used information collected from the LAC schedules in studies of the needs and experiences of children in public care (Bailey, Thoburn, & Wakeham, 2002; Brandon, Lewis, Thoburn, & Way, 1999; Thoburn, Norford, & Rashid, 2000; Ward & Skuse, 2002), including those conducted in Australia (Fernandez, 2006b; Wise, 2003a).

Perhaps due to the perceived difficulty in collecting reliable data from the AARs used in the course of everyday practice, research studies conducted in the U.K. have generally opted to adapt the schedules and implement them separately from the normal assessment and review of children's cases. However, research studies conducted in Canada, as well as jointly with Barnardos Australia, have used the AAR as the primary research tool (e.g., Cheers, Kufeldt, Klein, & Rideout, 2007; Klein, Cheers, Kufeldt, Kelly-Egerton, & Rideout, 2006; Kufeldt, Simard, Vachon, Baker, & Andrews, 2000). Indeed, in one Canadian province, a modified version of the AARs (see Flynn & Ghazal, 2001) has been implemented as an instrument for outcomes monitoring. The Ontario *Looking After Children* Project (ONLAC) has assessed 600 to 800 children and adolescents in care across all 53 Children's Aid Societies (CAS) in the province annually since 2001 (Flynn, Ghazal, Legault, Vandermeulen, & Petrick, 2004).

The possibility of the Victorian government establishing a system to capture LAC data was strengthened through participation in the seventh International LAC conference in Sydney in 2006. The conference gave examples of how LAC data were being utilized in out-of-home care systems overseas. At the same time, there were ongoing efforts to enhance the data warehousing facility and reporting functionality of CRIS/SP. CRIS/SP is a comprehensive electronic client information system now being used by the Department of Human Services child protection services and CSO placement and support services. Thus, the climate was favourable for getting the project off the ground, as the long-term objective of the LAC Outcomes Data Project was to incorporate revised versions of the AARs within the CRIS/SP environment.

Methodology

Data Retrieval

In March 2007, all CSOs providing out-of-home care were invited by DHS to participate in the current project. CSOs agreeing to participate in the project were given instructions to forward de-identified copies of current AARs to the Placement and Support Unit of the DHS Children, Youth and Families Division via the DHS Quality Enhancement worker located in each region (the AARs are completed every six months for children 0–4 years old, and annually for children aged 5 years and above). CSOs replaced the AAR front sheets (containing the child's name and other personal identifying information) with a cover sheet containing non-identifying information about the child's gender, age, placement type, region, and CSO.

Sample

Out of a possible 46 regionally based services providing out-of-home care in Victoria, 32 services participated in the project. These included all the larger agencies, which provide the overwhelming majority of placements. On the whole, the non-participating services were the smaller agencies with limited infrastructure and administrative resources. Examination of LAC implementation data suggests that failure to update existing AARs may have been a barrier to participation. Moreover, while several Aboriginal-controlled service providers had agreed to participate in this project, returns were received from only one such agency. Whether this relates to the cultural appropriateness of the AAR content and the method of data documentation (recording information versus oral knowledge transfer) is unclear.

The final sample comprised 614 children from all eight DHS regions, of whom 488 were in home-based care, 109 were in residential care, and 10 were in a lead tenant service. This represents slightly more than half of the children who had been in care for at least three months, or long enough to have been reasonably expected to have had an AAR completed, and 31% of *all* Victorian children in foster care, residential care, or lead tenant care at the time the AARs were collected. The sample was evenly distributed across the age range; 25% were under 5 years, 21% were aged 5–9 years, 29% were aged 10–14 years, and 25% were aged 15 years or more. Fifty-five per cent of the sample were male.

Data Aggregation

Data aggregation involved the construction of an electronic database of the approximately 1,000 data items recorded on each of the AARs, and entry of data recorded on the 614 completed AARs. The process of database development was quite complicated. It involved identifying items within each AAR that were common across other formats, as well as items that applied to more than one age format. In order to identify and merge common items across AAR formats, a metadata table was created as a source document. The metadata table included all aar items across all age formats, and ensured that the same field names were used for equivalent items across the different age formats, ready for later analysis.

Item wording sometimes varied across the different AAR age formats. Where appropriate, these items were treated as equivalent. For example, wording of the "child read to on a daily basis" measure is slightly different for children aged 1–2 years and 3–4 years. For children aged 1–2 years, the item wording is, "How frequently is the child read to, shown picture books or told stories?", whereas the wording for children aged 3–4 years is "How often is the child read to?"

Development of the Outcome Measures

A systematic process was undertaken whereby an initial set of 55 measures was identified for preliminary analysis, and ultimately reduced to 29 based on response rates and item variance. A minimum 85% response rate was required for all items included in the final analysis.

For sheer manageability, as well as to enhance measurement rigour, some composite measures were constructed from the mean of individual item ratings. For example, the "attainment of outcome objectives" items that appear at the end of each life area were combined to summarize the achievement of well-being objectives. There was good internal consistency reliability for these measures.

Some outcomes of inherent interest (e.g., height and weight data, and some education outcomes) were not included in the final set of measures due to missing data. These findings are useful, however, in highlighting where specific items need modification for sense and clarity, or where new measures need to be developed.

Analysis and Findings

Statistical analysis was undertaken to describe outcomes for the sample as a whole. Results (see Table 1) indicate the proportion of all cases that fell into a particular response category (e.g., "Had illness/accident in last year," or "Has a special friend").

At the end of each of the seven well-being sections, items are included to assess the attainment of specific developmental goals, such as "The child has had continuity of care" in the Family and Social Relationships section. The number of these outcome objectives items differs across the developmental domains and across the AAR age formats. In order to derive a single measure of the attainment of outcome objectives, the means of ratings for individual items on all outcome objectives were calculated to produce a score ranging between 0 and 1, where 0 = none of the outcome objectives met and 1 = all of the outcome objectives met. Where all outcome objectives were met in only a small proportion of cases, the attainment of outcome objectives was measured in terms of whether more than half of the outcome objectives had been met ($M \leq 0.5$).

All 614 cases were included in these calculations (including those that were coded "don't know" or "missing"); that is, responses were not based only on valid/known responses. Percentages may therefore underestimate the actual proportion of cases that fall within a particular response category.

Logistic and Poisson multivariate regression techniques (Tabachnick & Fidell, 2001) were used to show the odds of a particular outcome occurring

Table 1 *Proportion of Cases That Fell into 29 Outcome Response Categories (N = 614)*

Well-Being Domain and Related Outcome Response Category	Proportion of Cases
Health	
All health outcome objectives met[a]	59%
Had illness/accident in the last year	40%
Immunizations up-to-date for age	62%
Had recent medical review	86%
Adolescent low-risk health behaviour (10–17 years)[a]	53%
Education	
More than half education outcomes objectives met[a]	41%
Owns more than 10 books (3–17 years)	64%
Child read to on a daily basis	68%
Identity	
More than half identity outcomes objectives met[a]	65%
Life story book being completed (0–14 years)	74%
Child is teased/picked on (3–17 years)	39%
Knowledge of why in care (3–17 years)	85%
Family and social relationships	
More than half family and social relationships outcomes objectives met[a]	62%
Number of main carers	M = 4.6
Presence of adult that child can turn to in a crisis (5–17 years)	81%
Regular contact with at least one family member[a]	76%
Has a special friend (5–17 years)	86%
Child sees friends outside school (5–14 years)	70%
Social presentation	
All social presentation outcome objectives met[a]	62%
Child/carer thinks the child appears well cared for	80%
Adjusts behaviour to different situations (5–17 years)	63%
Child always has suitable clothes (10–17 years)	48%
Emotional and behavioural development	
One or both emotional and behavioural development outcome objectives met[a]	52%
Criminal activity (10–17 years)	26%
High relationships with others score[a]	34%
High concentration and behaviour score (3–17 years)[a]	31%
Low anxiety and worries score[a]	36%
Self-care	
Self-care objective met (1–17 years)	50%
High daily living skills score (1–17 years)[a]	34%

[a]Denotes composite measure.

according to DHS region, child age, child gender, and placement type, while simultaneously controlling for the confounding effects of these covariates.

Consistent with other research in this area, poorer outcomes were observed among older children and children in residential care compared to younger children and children in home-based care. Age effects were noted in relation to out-of-home care status, risky health behaviour, illnesses/accidents, number of books has/owns, teased/picked on, number of main carers, and life storybook completed. Care type effects were noted in relation to immunization status, risky health behaviour, attainment of education objectives, teased/picked on, attainment of family and social relationships objectives, number of main carers, attainment of emotional and behavioural development objectives, relationships with others, anxiety/worries, and seeing friends outside school. By comparison, few effects of gender and DHS region were noted. The adjusted odds ratios and *p*-values for all the regression analyses are presented in the report provided to DHS by the Australian Institute of Family Studies (Wise & Egger, 2008).

Dissemination and Utilization of Research Findings

Key findings from this project were presented at a well-publicized statewide launch and forum, which was very much directed at a policy and practice audience. After a formal presentation there was general discussion around the significance of some of the findings, and where work needs to be undertaken at a state-wide level to enhance children's long-term life chances. Researchers, policy-makers, and program managers were all in attendance, so there was an opportunity for all stakeholders to delineate the key policy and practice messages. A series of regional workshops was also undertaken, following the same basic format. Again, linkages between research, policy, and practice were at the forefront of these meetings. The consultant's full report was also made publicly available on the DHS website for the widest possible dissemination and access.

As discussed earlier, participating out-of-home care service providers were given their own individual data for comparison with regional and statewide findings, and have undertaken their own discussion and follow-up of the findings from this study with their own management teams and staff. Findings have been provided to the out-of-home care service sector with the understanding that these provide baseline information about how children in care are faring now as a consequence of their previous life experiences, and that these findings should be used to inform future efforts to achieve better futures for these children.

As well as enhancing understanding of the broader application of LAC data among local service providers, and providing baseline data for management and planning purposes, the project appears to have generated momentum around evidence-based practice more generally. For example, dissemination of the findings has heightened the interest amongst practitioners, service managers, and policy-makers in comparing the circumstances of children in care to looked after children in other jurisdictions and in the community more generally.

Higher levels of usage and participation in LAC processes in the period immediately following the release of the project findings also suggests increased stakeholder support for *Looking After Children* as a tool for good practice, and to routinely and systematically aggregate and analyze outcomes data derived from the AARs.

It was especially opportune that during May 2008, the Minister for Community Services announced a review of the state's out-of-home care system in the context of rising costs and increasing pressures on the service system due to declining foster care numbers, increasing lengths of stay in care, and the increasing complexity of the needs of the children and adolescents in the Victorian care system. Findings from the current project were used as evidence of how children in care in the state of Victoria were faring. Without these outcome data, the knowledge base that informed the out-of-home care review would have been far less robust.

While it is still too early to report on the results of the government review, which is intended to inform government policy directions over the medium to longer term, it is reasonable to suggest that the findings from the project added considerable weight to the review's capacity to suggest areas for further development, especially in relation to improving the educational opportunities for children in care, promoting more therapeutic approaches to ensuring their well-being, and redressing the impact of previous trauma and abuse, as well as reducing the likelihood of ongoing negative life experiences while in the care of the state.

The impact of this project is limited because it involves the aggregation and analysis of data obtained at one period of time only. However, plans are underway to revise the AARs to enhance their quality and utility for supporting both good practice and service management and monitoring for eventual incorporation within the CRIS/SP environment. By continuing the current process of outcomes monitoring, and streamlining data collection and aggregation processes, the Department of Human Services and individual agencies will have systematic data to consider the effects their services are having on children in out-of-home care and how best to respond. Outcomes monitoring will also enable services to consider whether particular investments have proven their worth, or whether alternatives are indicated.

Conclusion

The *Looking After Children* Outcomes Project demonstrates that when conditions are favourable, and when researchers, policy-makers, and practitioners are able to talk the same language and work in close partnership toward a common aim, positive impacts are possible. Prior to this study, the capacity to derive and utilize information from the AARs about how groups of children were faring in care was not well developed or understood, at least in the Victorian context. There was also very little evidence to systematically assess whether or not out-of-home care services were doing well or improving over time, or what aspects of the systems worked more or less well.

Although information collected in the course of routine practice is not perfect, and work still needs to be done to refine the AARs and related data aggregation processes, the potential to use practice data for a system of outcomes monitoring is very real. There is, and will continue to be, great demand for more focused and fine-grained research and analysis in the out-of-home care field. However, establishing a data collection process that actively involves policy-makers and practitioners will certainly build the evidence base and should lead to better use of evidence in practice and policy decisions, to promote the best interests of current and future generations of children and young people unable to live with their own families.

33

The *Looking After Children* Approach in Quebec: An Evaluation of the Experiences of Youth, Caseworkers, and Foster Parents

Marie-Andrée Poirier
Marie-Claude Simard
Véronique Noel
Béatrice Decaluwe

Placement in out-of-home care, and particularly placement in foster families, has an important role in the continuum of services offered to young people and families in difficulty. In Quebec, in 2007–8, almost 31,900 young people were referred to the *Centres Jeunesse* (Association des Centres Jeunesse du Québec [ACJQ], 2008). A significant proportion of these children were placed in substitute care. On March 31, 2008, approximately 11,914 young people were in substitute care. More than half, or 6,887, of these children were living with foster families (ACJQ, 2008).

The use of foster care presents major challenges: When children are placed away from their own homes, how does the responsible agency ensure that they are provided with opportunities for optimal development? How can conditions be put in place that protect the children but at the same time allow them to develop their competencies, to dream, and to have fulfilling lives as future young adults? There are no simple answers to these questions.

Recent studies indicate that the placement practices most likely to encourage the child's optimal development are those in which particular attention is paid to the following aspects: a detailed evaluation of the child's needs, proper care planning, listening attentively to the child, the presence of supportive foster parents, positive school and social experiences, and good collaboration among the different adult actors involved (Pecora & Maluccio, 2000; Ward & Rose, 2002). In light of such findings, it is important that the protection system encourage innovative approaches with the aim of providing these conditions. It was precisely from this perspective that the *Looking After Children* (LAC) approach was developed in

England at the end of the 1980s. The province of Quebec has implemented LAC in four Centres Jeunesse since 2003. (It should be noted here that when LAC was introduced in Quebec, the French name—S'occuper des enfants [SOCEN]—was used. In this chapter, however, the abbreviation LAC will be used.)

Implementation of LAC was accompanied by a research project. The first phase, which ended in June 2006, was aimed at evaluating the implementation conditions of LAC, as well as the perceptions of the children, the foster parents, and the workers on the repercussions of the approach (Poirier et al., 2007). This chapter presents the principal results of this first evaluation phase. The first section briefly introduces the approach, presenting its philosophy, objectives, and methods. The second section presents the results of a study on the implementation of LAC in Quebec. The chapter concludes with discussion of the essential conditions needed to promote and facilitate the implementation of LAC by child protection agencies.

The *Looking After Children* Approach

The main goal of LAC is to support the development of children in foster care by determining their needs, potential, and personal aspirations as a basis for care planning (Ward, 1995). Lack of evaluation and of care planning had been identified; LAC was developed to promote positive outcomes for children in care. It enables workers and foster parents to gain a deeper knowledge of the children in care, and to improve care planning.

LAC is an ecosystemic approach that considers the child more holistically (Poirier, Simard, Dumont, & Richard, 2005). It differs from traditional foster care approaches by its emphasis on a rigorous evaluation of the child's progress in multiple areas of development: health, education, emotional and behavioural development, identity, family and social relations, self-presentation, and self-care skills. According to Ward (2000), it is essential to consider these dimensions in order to achieve adequate health and development goals for children in substitute care. In addition, the concept of resilience is an element of the theoretical framework underpinning LAC (Lemay & Ghazal, 2007). Thus, the approach aims to provide the conditions that will allow optimal development for children in foster care. Specifically, the approach emphasizes the children's strengths and competencies and directs them toward positive and validating experiences. It also promotes the children's involvement in the needs assessment and care planning that affect them.

One of the main tools used in LAC is the Assessment and Action Record (AAR). This tool is used to evaluate the needs of the child in the developmental dimensions outlined above, and to document achievement of developmental objectives and the effectiveness of services and support given to the child (Lemay & Ghazal, 2007). The original British AAR was adapted for Canadian use, in both English and French, in 1997. This version was revised once more in 2000. The tool currently used in Quebec is the second Canadian adaptation, AAR-C (Flynn, Ghazal, Legault, Vendermeulen, & Petrick, 2004). The Canadian version changed the original AAR, designed for six age groups, into eight age groups (0–12 months, 1–2 years, 3–4 years, 5–9 years, 10–11 years, 12–15 years, 16–17 years, and 18–21 years). However, the revised tool retains the same developmental dimensions and most of the service quality monitoring questions as the original British version.

The AAR is an assessment tool intended to be used in the form of a conversation between the child, the foster parents, and the social worker (Lemay & Ghazal, 2007)—an instrument that facilitates translating the assessment of the child's needs into paths of concrete action (Ward, 1995). It was designed to target the conditions for intervention required by the specific situation of a child in foster care. The appropriate use of the AAR helps achieve the plan of care. In addition, administering the AAR allows the worker to identify the roles and responsibilities of the people involved in the care of the child relative to the targeted goals in the care plan. Finally, used on an annual basis, the AAR makes it possible to evaluate the child's progress and to adjust the care plan. Thus, it ensures systematic follow-up of the of the child's changing situation.

LAC in Quebec and Its Evaluation

Methodology

The project relied on two data collection techniques: telephone interviews and face-to-face interviews with the children, the foster parents, and the workers.

The Telephone Interviews

Telephone interviews were conducted with all the social workers (n=31) and foster parents (n=72) involved in the project. These interviews were based on a questionnaire designed to obtain their points of view on the following aspects: the LAC approach, the training, the AAR and its use, the problems in implementing LAC, and the repercussions of using the AAR. The questionnaire varied slightly according to whether it was addressed to workers or foster parents. It included closed questions permitting Likert scale responses, and short open-ended questions. The data were processed by descriptive and bivariate analysis (using Pearson's chi-square, χ^2), allowing comparison between the points of view of the workers and the foster parents. The information obtained in the open-ended questions was analyzed using qualitative methods in order to present the participants' experiences in greater detail.

The Face-to-Face Interviews

The evaluation strategy also included semi-structured, face-to-face individual interviews with youth between 8 and 16 years of age (n=16), social workers (n=15), and foster parents (n=16) randomly selected from all the participants in the project. The interviews with the foster parents and the workers elicited perceptions of the factors that either facilitated or hampered the implementation of LAC, their degree of satisfaction with the approach, and their evaluations of both positive and negative effects. The interviews with the youth aimed to elicit their perceptions of the content of the AAR, its utilization, and its effects. The interviews were taped and transcribed in full. A content analysis technique was applied to the data. The analysis of the material gathered allowed us to present the viewpoints of each group and to compare them.

Principal Results Concerning Implementation Issues

Training

Training is the principal means of disseminating the LAC approach. Initial training is essential for all the workers and foster parents involved in LAC, and should also be given to the supervisors who follow workers in the project. The training curriculum used in Quebec was based on Ontario developments (Lemay, Byrne and Ghazal, 2006; Lemay and Ghazal, 2007). Since the beginning of the project, 26 of the 31 social workers (84%) and 41 of the 72 foster parents (57%, a significant difference) had received appropriate training. The two groups were almost unanimous in stating that the training gave them a good understanding of the philosophy of the approach. However, similar to the results of a Scottish study (Wheelaghan, Hill, Lambert, Borland, & Triseliotis, 1999), some of the workers and foster parents felt that the time allocated to the AAR practice exercises was insufficient. Moreover, some workers said they didn't feel fully prepared to use the AAR immediately after training.

Several foster parents emphasized in the face-to-face interviews that the training sessions allowed them to have contact with other foster parents, and to discuss their experiences and impressions regarding the project. For their part, workers mentioned the relevance of undergoing training with foster parents, and exchanging ideas with them about perceptions of the LAC approach and the administration of the AAR. Some social workers emphasized the relevance of providing training to the supervisors and resource workers (social workers assigned to the foster family), so that they could integrate the approach more fully, better understand its implications for the children in care, and become more aware of the value of LAC.

Several workers and a few foster parents said that the training was an excellent means of promoting the approach. It served to convince the foster parents of the potential benefits of LAC, not only for the child, but also for the foster family. According to one worker:

> It's important in the training sessions that the foster families see the benefits of the approach—that it isn't done to evaluate them, but to support them and to support the child. Training must be used to promote LAC in a positive way.

Support

Several studies have reported the positive effects of support, particularly that of supervisors and managers, in the implementation of LAC (Kufeldt, Simard, Vachon, Baker, & Andrews, 2000; Pantin, Flynn, & Runnels, 2006; Wheelaghan et al.,1999). In the following section, we will explore the workers' and foster parents' views on the quality of the support given to them during the first two years of the project implementation.

Support Provided to Workers and Foster Parents
In the telephone interviews, the majority (77%) of the workers said they felt their participation in the LAC project was supported by their supervisors. In the face-to-face interviews, they detailed aspects of their supervisors' support, recognition of the importance of the LAC approach, a better distribution of their caseloads, discussion of the project in team meetings, and the fostering of interest in the project among workers who were not using the approach. Slightly less, though nearly two-thirds (65%), said they felt supported by their colleagues at work. More than two out of three (71%) reported having discussed their experiences of LAC during meetings at work, and 81% said they had shared their experiences with colleagues.

Support Offered to Foster Parents
In the telephone interviews, 90% of the foster parents answered that they could speak freely about their experiences in the project when they met with social workers. Concerning the support given them, 86% said that they felt supported

by their resource worker during their participation in the project. In the face-to-face interviews, however, some foster parents said they had perceived a lack of involvement on the part of certain resource workers. According to one foster parent: "The resource worker should be more involved, because there are some things she doesn't know (about LAC). If I call her with certain questions (about LAC), she doesn't necessarily know the answers."

A small percentage of the foster parents (25%) felt supported by other foster parents. Only 38% had shared their experience with other foster parents involved in the project. Some underlined the importance of holding meetings for foster parents to allow them to discuss their experiences.

Comparison of the data from the workers and from the foster parents show that the latter group were more likely to feel isolated, with few opportunities to share their experiences with other foster parents; thus they received significantly less support from their peers. This feeling of isolation among foster families has been expressed for a long time, and not only within the context of the LAC project. Ways should be found, taking into account their daily reality and availability, to allow foster parents to meet together more often.

Practice Conditions

A little more than half of the social workers (55%) considered that their working conditions facilitated the implementation of LAC. Working conditions included their roles, their various responsibilities, and the utilization of other intervention tools (i.e., plan of care). Questions were asked specifically about their workload. The workers were almost unanimous (90%) in answering that using the AAR increased their workload. Less than one-quarter (23%) felt that their caseloads had been adjusted to take their participation in the project into account. This adjustment partly reduced the impact of the increased workload associated with the use of the AAR. In the face-to-face interviews, several workers said that the AAR took up a lot of time in their schedules, and that no adjustment had been made to facilitate this aspect of implementing the approach. They stressed that caseloads needed to be reduced in order to be able to apply the approach effectively.

During the telephone interviews, 86% of the foster parents said that their situation was taken into account in their participation in the project. Interviewed in person, some foster parents added that their availability was respected when the time came to fill out the AAR. Only 38% of the foster parents felt that administering the AAR increased their daily tasks. In the face-to-face interviews, the foster parents said that, in their opinion, the workers had overly heavy workloads, and not enough time to properly carry out follow-up after filling out the AAR, and that worker caseloads should be reduced.

A statistically significant higher proportion of foster parents (85%), compared to workers (58%), considered that the atmosphere at the Centre Jeunesse encouraged the use of LAC [χ^2 (1) = 8,617, p<.01]. On the other hand, 90% of workers, compared to 86% of foster parents, said that the management personnel at the Centre Jeunesse supported them in the implementation of LAC.

Principal Results Pertaining to the Effectiveness of the Approach

This section presents the participants' evaluation of the effectiveness of using the AAR in relation to the children's needs assessment, the quality of parenting, and the drafting of a care plan.

The Children's Needs Assessment

The majority of the foster parents (83%) and the workers (94%) said that the AAR increased their knowledge of the children's needs. With respect to the children's progress, the majority of both workers (93%) and foster parents (71%) found that the use of the AAR produced positive results. The face-to-face interviews carried out with the foster parents, workers, and youth allowed for an exhaustive discussion about the effects of the AAR in relation to responding to the children's needs, the exploration of rarely discussed subjects, and placing the focus on the children's strengths, competencies, and hopes for the future.

Responsiveness to the Child's Needs

The foster parents and the social workers emphasized that filling out the AAR provided a context for the children to express their needs concretely. In particular, they were able to verbalize their feelings about various family or social situations and articulate their wishes. In the words of one worker: "It allowed us to know more specifically what the child wanted. Without the AAR, we wouldn't have known these things." The youth said that the AAR helped them to know themselves better, because it gave them time to think things over, to ask themselves questions, and to be aware of certain realizations. Among other things, they learned more about their identity and origin, their future possibilities, their personality, their tastes, strengths, and values.

The Exploration of Rarely Discussed Subjects

Several foster parents, workers, and children stated that filling out the AAR encouraged discussion of aspects of the child's life that were otherwise difficult to talk about, such as the family of origin, past history, drug use, and sexual relations. It also encouraged discussion of things that were taken for granted or overlooked. One worker said: "Sometimes, there are great discoveries. The youth come out with things, and even the foster parent says: 'Hey, look at that—how come you've been with us for five years and you never told us that?' So, it seems that taking the time to stop and think makes them question certain things." Some of the youth interviewed said that the AAR session allowed them to talk about subjects that they wouldn't dare bring up in other contexts. One 11-year-old girl said that responding to the AAR encouraged her to express her negative feelings about her foster family. It was the first time she had talked about this: "After filling out the AAR, a lot of things happened. My worker realized we weren't happy there. I don't know if she moved us to another foster family because of that, but she moved us." In contrast, other youth interviewed said that certain subjects or questions in the AAR made them feel uncomfortable.

Placing the Focus on the Children's Strengths and Competencies

As mentioned earlier, the concept of resilience is basic to the LAC approach; one of the objectives of the AAR is to place the emphasis on the children's strengths and competencies and direct them toward positive, validating experiences. It is still too early to evaluate whether the young participants in the LAC implementation project have had more experiences of this nature. However, it was clear from the interviews that several youth had enjoyed answering questions about their strengths and achievements. Statements by the foster parents and workers also revealed that the AAR brings out the children's positive aspects, competencies, and strengths. They said that LAC allowed them to have high expectations for the child and to believe in his or her potential. Therefore, this aspect of the AAR helps to ensure that intervention is not limited to targeting the children's weaknesses and problems. The AAR is a tool that not only measures resilience but encourages it.

Quality of Parenting

The LAC approach considers the quality of parenting to be an essential element in the welfare of children in foster care. The foster parents in our project were questioned about the effects of the AAR on their awareness of their responsibilities as foster parents, and on their participation in the decisions concerning the child. Approximately three out of four foster parents responded that, in their view, using the AAR gave them a better idea of their responsibilities as parents. The majority (72%) said that using the AAR allowed them to play a more active role in decisions concerning the child. In the face-to-face interviews, several foster parents said that filling out the AAR gave them the impression of being listened to, and that their knowledge of the child was taken into consideration in the drawing up or modification of the care plan.

Foster parents frequently expressed their views about the AAR's contribution to their awareness of appropriate child-rearing practices. In the face-to-face interviews, several said that the AAR identified what needed improvement, allowing them to enhance the quality of their parenting. A number of foster parents stated that the AAR brought out the fact that their points of view differed from those of the children in their care, and some said they adjusted their viewpoints in consequence, and began to re-examine certain child-rearing practices. The following excerpt from an interview with one foster parent illustrates this aspect:

> When we filled out the AAR, I was sure he'd answer that he felt comfortable with me. I had the impression that everything was fine, but it came out that, no, he still feels like a stranger in our home. What can we do about that? Can we do something to help him?

Care Planning

In the telephone interviews, certain questions allowed us to evaluate the workers' and foster parents' views on the effects of the use of the AAR on care planning. The majority of the workers said that the AAR helped to set more precise objectives, and therefore facilitated establishing the care plan. Other questions explored the extent to which filling out the AAR increased the involvement of the various actors (parents, children, foster parents) in drawing up or reviewing the care plan. Three out of four workers (77%) found that the children had become more involved in drawing up or reviewing their care plans since the beginning of the LAC project. In addition, 75% of the foster parents and 87% of the workers said that the foster parents had become more involved in drawing up the care plan since the project began.

The face-to-face interviews with the foster parents, the workers, and the youth allowed exhaustive discussion about the repercussions of the AAR on care planning. Their answers brought out the following elements: the structure provided by the AAR, the AAR's contribution to the care planning itself, and its effect on the youths' involvement in it.

The Structure Provided by the AAR

Regarding the AAR's contributions to their practice, several workers said it had helped them in their work with foster families, as it contributed to making better-informed decisions about the children. Using the AAR facilitated the identification of needs, indicated paths to follow that might not have been envisaged otherwise, structured the planning of the children's care, and was a concrete support for the workers in their response to the identified needs. One foster parent expressed it this way: "I think she used [the AAR] to support us. Take sports, for example. I think the worker wasn't really aware of the importance of sports in my youngster's life. After filling out the AAR, she even obtained funding for his sports activities. They supported us in this because they saw the results." Some workers, however, did not find that using the AAR particularly helped them in their work with the foster children. They said there was not much change when they had already been following the child for a considerable period of time before the project. As the tool did not reveal any significant new information about the child, it had little influence on their practices.

The Contribution of the AAR to Care Planning

Most of the workers and foster parents interviewed said that a care plan was prepared for all the children who filled out the AAR. Several workers underlined that the AAR facilitated drawing up the care plan, as it highlighted all the pertinent information needed for this. Some of these workers said that it helped in creating a care plan that focused on the children's strengths. Some foster parents reported that the AAR helped to respond to the needs that were identified. The AAR indicated whether the children were doing well in the different aspects of their lives. If this was not the case, it identified the aspects to be worked on, changed, or improved. Moreover, a few foster parents were critical of the fact that the AAR identified various needs which had not necessarily been met. Lack of resources seemed to be the principal reason for the lack of response to those needs.

The Involvement of Youth in Care Planning

The youths' answers revealed that they knew very little about the use of the AAR in the drawing up of their care plans. Moreover, only a few youth claimed to know what a care plan was, or whether they had one. The data raise several questions about the involvement of the youth in this aspect of their care. To be able to effectively put into practice LAC's emphasis on encouraging the youths' involvement, we must gain a better understanding of what occurs in the process of translating the observations made when filling out the AAR into a clear and goal-oriented care plan. There is evidence that the children are not involved in this process, even though the care plan directly concerns them. This result echoes what Francis found during the implementation of LAC in Scotland: "A high proportion of youth commented that they didn't have a care plan, or were unaware of its existence" (2002, p. 456). It also reflects the statements of some of the youth interviewed in an Australian study, who said they lacked an understanding of how the information would be used and the role they were to have in the planning process (Wise, 2003b, p. 11).

Discussion and Conclusion

Carrying out this evaluation allowed us to document the experiences of the respective actors involved in the project, to identify the elements that either facilitated or hampered the implementation of LAC, and to appreciate the degree of satisfaction among the children, the workers, and the foster parents with respect to the approach and its effects.

The results obtained underline the importance of carrying out adequate promotion of the approach among all the actors before soliciting their participation. We believe that agencies wishing to implement LAC should carry out activities to improve the understanding of the project among children in care, foster parents, and the personnel of the Centre Jeunesse. Training is also a crucial aspect in the implementation of an approach like LAC. As Pantin, Flynn, and Runnels (2006) have said, the quantity and quality of training influences the degree of acceptance of the LAC principles and the use of the AAR by workers. Beyond the initial training, we consider that the essential conditions necessary for the successful implementation of such an approach include ongoing training and support of participants.

The implementation evaluation identified the importance of providing enhanced support to workers and foster parents. This result is in agreement with Pantin et al. (2006), who maintain that encouragement from supervisors has a significant influence on the degree of acceptance of LAC and the AAR by workers, as well as on the successful integration of the approach within their daily practice. In this sense, it is essential that the Centre Jeunesse ensure that workers involved in LAC have regular meetings to discuss the approach and its integration into regular practice. Some agencies have developed specific strategies—for example, creating a team of LAC resource persons available to answer questions and host discussions about the approach within the agency. Others have integrated discussions on the LAC approach into regular work-team meetings. Whatever strategy is chosen, it must be adapted to the workers' work context in order to have long-term viability.

Support for the foster parents involved in LAC remains an important challenge. Due to their daily routines, foster families tend to be more isolated, and have fewer occasions to meet with each other. Nonetheless, it is essential that the establishments implementing LAC ensure that the foster parents involved in the project are given the opportunity to meet and exchange their ideas and experiences.

In their statements, the youth made us aware that further efforts must be made if we want to carry the LAC philosophy forward in Quebec; that is, we must allow the youth to be more involved. Concrete means to give them more say in decisions that concern them must be put in place. Among other things, they could participate in the training sessions for workers and foster parents (Francis, 2002; Jones, Clark, Kufeldt, and Norrman, 1998); some of the questions in the AAR could be modified to bring out their viewpoints and interests; and finally, the adults (foster parents and workers) could be trained to encourage a real dialogue with the children using the questions in the AAR (Francis, 2002).

The participants identified numerous positive outcomes related to the application of this approach. These were mostly linked to the evaluation of the needs of the children, the parental support and supervision, and the intervention planning and collaboration. These results are promising, and in tune with what was observed elsewhere regarding LAC (Jones et al., 1998). Nevertheless, some participants (foster parents and workers) have voiced criticism over the length of the AAR, as well the relevance and the redundancy of some questions. Finally, the face-to-face interviews with foster parents and workers brought out the fact that changes in practice are closely linked to the integration of the LAC philosophy rather than to the use of the AAR alone. As Lemay and Ghazal (2007) noted, "LAC is not merely a documentation system or even a yearly assessment tool; it is a proactive service approach ... that should change the way people do their jobs and monitor outcomes" (p. 113).

Besides the issues related to the participants' evaluation of the approach and the implementation conditions, a number of questions remain unanswered. Following the implementation of the approach, do we see concrete effects on the practices of workers and foster parents? Will children who are involved in the LAC project for several years do better than other children living in foster families? To be able to answer these questions, a second phase of the evaluation of the LAC project in Quebec is anticipated. The objective of the second phase is to document the effects of the utilization of the approach on the practices of foster parents and workers, as well as on the well-being of the children in care.

Acknowledgements

The implementation project and the evaluation were made possible by the financial support of the National Crime Prevention Strategy (NCPS) of the Canadian government, in collaboration with the Ministère de la Sécurité Publique du Québec.

34

Guided Practice in Australia: Research, Implementation, and Child and Family Perspectives on *Looking After Children* and the Assessment Framework

Deirdre Cheers
Elizabeth Fernandez
Jude Morwitzer
Sue Tregeagle

The search for best practice in Australian child welfare services is, as elsewhere in the world, affected by multiple factors. Policies and processes for the assessment and provision of services to children identified as at risk of abuse and neglect in Australia are subject to eight individual state and territory government sets of legislation. There are no national standards for intervention, and a fragmented service system exists (Clare, 2003). Furthermore, planning for children and services is made more difficult by the unhelpful division of responsibility for children between state/territory governments (child protection and out-of-home care) and the Australian government (family law, income support, health, education, and housing). This chapter provides a description of the Australian research and implementation experience of the *Looking After Children* (LAC) and *Supporting Children and Responding to Families* (SCARF) systems. It includes the experience of both service providers and service users (children and families using the LAC and SCARF systems). Australian implementation of these systems has also informed the development and use of information and communication technology (ICT) in relation to guided practice. The utilization of computerized systems for workers and managers is included in the discussion.

Australian child welfare services have been in crisis for some time. Reports of children and young people at risk have risen consistently over the past 10 years. In 2006–7, 62.7 per 1000 children and young people[1] were reported to statutory child protection departments, an increase of 15.8% over the previous 12-month period. The number of children and young people in out-of-home care placements has been steadily rising to a reported figure of 5.8 per 1000 children at June 30, 2007 (Australian Institute of Health and Welfare, 2008)—an increase of 9.4% from the previous year. Attempts to reform services have been reported as unsuccessful, with each Australian state and territory conducting individual inquiries into systemic failures (Cashmore & Ainsworth, 2004).

Against such a background, government and non-government agencies have sought solutions for improving practice to assist in producing better outcomes for individual children and young people. One such initiative has been the move to implement systems of guided practice. This chapter will present and discuss the adaptation and implementation of the United Kingdom (U.K.) systems *Looking After Children* (LAC) and *Framework for the Assessment of Children in Need and their Families* (known in Australia as *Supporting Children and Responding to Families*, or SCARF). These research-based projects were undertaken in collaboration with the University of New South Wales and funded by the Australian Research Council and the non-government agency Barnardos Australia.

After describing the research, the chapter concludes with a discussion of the implications of the use of guided practice systems, including how implementation can be enhanced, workers supported, service user participation strengthened, and ICT used to improve practice.

Guided Practice: Toward a Definition

In Australia, as elsewhere, interventions to bring children into protective care present a serious challenge to practitioners, policy-makers, and researchers. The pressing need to develop methods of assessing and monitoring outcomes of child protection interventions derives from an expanding body of global research on the experience of children and young people in care and those leaving care. This is coupled with the urgent need to establish accountability in the context of well-publicized child deaths and systemic failures in child welfare systems (Cashmore & Ainsworth, 2004; Parton, 2004).

The pattern of children experiencing discontinuities and disruptions as a result of placement breakdown is documented in research studies, which point to the costly repercussions for children and the community in terms of adult outcomes (Berridge & Cleaver, 1987; Rowe, Hundleby, & Garnett, 1989; Department of Health, 1991; Packman & Randall, 1989; Sinclair, Wilson, & Gibbs, 2005; Stein, 2008). Studies undertaken in Australia and overseas point to the educational deficits children bring to care, and which are exacerbated by the care experience and lack of planning (Cashmore, Paxman, & Townsend, 2007; Heath, Colton, & Aldgate, 1994; Jackson, 1989; Kufeldt, Simard, Tite, & Vachon, 2003; Pecora et al., 2006). Research attention has moved beyond the question of placement continuance and stability toward concern with long-term developmental outcomes (Parker, Ward, Jackson, Aldgate, & Wedge, 1991; Ward, 1995).

Guided practice represents a new approach to social work with children and families—introducing the external "expert" to what have previously been autonomous, professional child welfare relationships. Guided practice systems encapsulate a new emphasis on evidence-informed decisions, receiving increasingly significant attention in the area of child protection over the past 10 years (Kessler, Gira, & Poertner, 2005; Macdonald, 2004; Newman, 1999; Plath, 2006). Cheers' (2006) research into evidence-based practice in out-of-home care (OOHC) found that Australian practitioners strongly identified the link between research evidence and guided practice. Participants in this study viewed the terms "guided practice" and "evidence-based practice" as largely interchangeable. In Australia, LAC and SCARF represent frameworks built on research evidence, and incorporate summarized research findings to facilitate evidence-informed decision-making. The LAC and SCARF systems combine elements of assessment, intervention, and review in child protection.

The development of guided practice systems such as LAC and SCARF arose out of research (see Yeatman & Penglase, 2004, for a review) highlighting practice contributing to poor outcomes for children in OOHC, which included the lack of monitoring of health and educational achievement despite poor outcomes, little participation of children in decision-making, and low quality relationships between workers and children in care. Yet there is little evidence of the issues behind children's poor developmental outcomes being systematically addressed.

LAC and SCARF in Australia

LAC was developed in the U.K. in direct response to research evidence indicating trends reflective of negative outcomes for children in the care system (Jackson & Kilroe, 1996). The lack of a knowledge base to inform the debate on outcomes for children prompted the U.K. Department of Health at the time to commission a working group to study the issue. The result of their work (Parker et al., 1991) signalled a new way of guiding practice with children and young people in care. A substantive body of well-funded U.K. research that followed has informed Australian research and development, as similar trends were of concern (Clare, 2003).

Findings from Australian research into out-of-home care (Cashmore & Paxman, 2006b; Delfabbro, Barber, & Cooper, 2000; Fernandez, 1996) revealed high levels of placement disruption, consequent discontinuities in schooling and marginal educational outcomes, as well as high turnover of staff. Homelessness, mental health problems, and unemployment characterized the after care experience of Australian children and young people.

The U.K. development of LAC, followed by the *Framework for the Assessment of Children in Need and their Families* (Department of Health, 2000), generated immediate interest in Australia (Clare, 1997; Clare, 2003; Owen, Jones, & Corrick, 1998; Wise, 2003b). Pilot implementation projects of the LAC Assessment and Action Records (AARs) by government departments in the states of Victoria (Wise, 1999) and Western Australia (Clare & Peerless, 1996) were quickly followed by full implementation of the LAC system by the large non-government child and family agency, Barnardos Australia, commencing in 1997. By 2000, research and development of SCARF as the Australian adaptation of the U.K. *Framework for the Assessment of Children in Need and their Families* was also well underway.

Electronic systems were an integral part of the LAC and SCARF research and implementation projects in Australia, and these were designed to facilitate practice and research. Review and development of LAC and SCARF is ongoing. With rapid advances in technology, electronic systems for recording and aggregating data are continually enhanced. ICT, as discussed later, can be used not just to record and aggregate data, but to create processes which enable interactive client participation within the systems.

Research Methods

Research underpinning LAC and SCARF in Australia was principally funded by the Australian Research Council (ARC). An initial three-year (1997–99) collaborative grant was made to the University of New South Wales (UNSW) and Barnardos for the *Looking After Children: Pathways in Care* project. This provided funds for research pertaining to LAC implementation in Australian states and territories, and a concurrent longitudinal study of children in care in New South Wales. SCARF implementation research was supported by a further ARC grant in 2000 (Fernandez & Romeo, 2003); in addition, a doctoral research partnership between Barnardos and the University of Western Sydney Social Justice and Social Change Research Centre was established. This latter collaboration permitted an exploration of service users' experiences with the long-term use of the LAC and SCARF systems by examining LAC- and SCARF-based interventions in two states (Tregeagle & Mason, 2008; Tregeagle & Treleaven, 2006). It focused on service user participation, the relevance of assessment, planning and recording processes, and their interest in using ICT (Tregeagle, 2007).

Methods used in relation to LAC research were designed to facilitate and monitor the implementation process in addition to optimizing the potential for collection of outcome-related data. Strategies included:

- Assessment of the legislative context of implementation and adaptation of the materials to legislation and practice contexts.
- Development of an e-system—the *Looking After Children* Electronic System (LACES)—to facilitate electronic completion of LAC records in daily practice and aggregation of data for service planning.
- Five focus groups to canvass views of caseworkers and senior and middle managers on the LAC materials and experiences of implementation.
- Audit of usage of LAC materials (450 records) to monitor patterns of record completion (Dixon, 2001).
- Audit of 90 LAC Assessment and Action Records focusing on the domain of education (Fernandez, 1999).
- Longitudinal study of 60 children in long-term care, incorporating the LAC domains of emotional and behavioural development, family and social relationships, education, and identity, complemented with relevant standardized measures. This study is now in its ninth year, and results have been reported by Fernandez (2006a, 2007a, 2008a, 2008b).

Direct caseworker participation was essential to the implementation of both LAC and SCARF. The perceptions of LAC implementation by Barnardos frontline workers and managers were elicited through the five focus groups which were conducted by independent researchers from the University of New South Wales. A predetermined set of open-ended questions focused on gains, challenges, and drawbacks of the framework, and the implementation experience. Focus groups proved to be an appropriate methodology for gathering information about the change process, as outcomes are contingent on the perception, attitudes, and experiences of those experiencing change.

The SCARF system was tested and refined in six Barnardos family support teams. The comprehensive research and implementation strategy included adaptation of the system to the Australia practice context, consultative and training strategies with managers and staff, development of an electronic database audit of 200 case files, and research into staff and user perceptions regarding use of the SCARF system (Fernandez & Romeo, 2003; Tolley, 2005).

Doctoral research conducted under the auspices of the University of Western Sydney (Tregeagle, 2007) involved service users who had used either LAC or SCARF for between one and eight years, and who had completed their involvement with the child welfare agency. It involved 32 participants (children, young people, and parents) from a range of agencies in New South Wales and the Australian Capital Territory, utilizing qualitative methods. Research design involved consultation with representative groups of service users, including the NSW Association for Young People in Care (now the CREATE Foundation at <http://www.create.org.au>), and also included Aboriginal service providers. An advisory group of mothers using family support services was consulted, and an Aboriginal service user was trained as co-researcher. Participants were reimbursed for their time and offered a variety of ways to contribute, such as direct participation in feedback groups or online discussion. The majority of participants took part in semi-structured interviews. University of Western Sydney academic staff were involved in coding of the transcripts of semi-structured interviews and group meetings.

LAC Research Results

The decision made by Barnardos to implement LAC as a full guided practice case management system consistent with the original U.K. plan, rather than just the Assessment and Action Records, as in other implementations (Wise, 2003b; Kufeldt, Simard, Thomas, & Vachon, 2005), was to ensure that all children in care experienced the full benefits and potential of LAC in terms of assessment, planning, and review. A number of factors indicated the need for a full and comprehensive case management system in Australia, rather than just an assessment tool for children in out-of-home care, including:

- a weakening of confidence in the public care of children;
- emerging new legislation emphasizing principles of partnership with parents, and children's participation (e.g., the *New South Wales Children and Young Persons (Care and Protection) Act 1998*);
- the attention given by independent bodies (e.g., Community Services and Children's Commissioners) to consumer participation of children and young people in care.

Focus groups provided valuable insights on:

- the strengths of LAC;
- the adequacy of training and constraints arising from time scales;

- the communication and feedback on implementation issues;
- the refinement of record adaptations with respect to legislation and practice;
- interagency issues; and
- the transition to the e-system (LACES).

The Australian LAC implementation experience highlights the tensions between theory and practice, and the challenges of managing innovation and change (Salveron, Arney, & Scott, 2006). Selected results from this experience follow.

Identified Strengths

The majority of practitioners and managers endorsed LAC and its principles, and some acknowledged the effects on practice related to assessment, case planning, and case review. Despite concerns and frustrations, several positives were acknowledged. The potential for accountability and for guiding practice is reflected in the following comment:

> Philosophically the concept is great. For me the thing that comes to mind is accountability ... especially the Care Plan. There are reminders about who is going to do what by when, and I like that.

The importance of documenting the positives for the benefit of the young person was further highlighted:

> A young person was making a comment that when they were looking at their (government department) file that all that was documented were the negatives and the crises and the bad things ... whereas with LAC you get achievements, you get places to document that. I think it's a good record for them to go back to ... it balances their life a bit more.

The potential to ensure that information is not lost when cases are referred on was another identified strength. One caseworker expressed this by recounting how workers carry information in their heads, and that such information may be lost in the event of caseworker or placement change.

The LAC framework also appeared to make practitioners more outcome-focused:

> What I've noticed is that it does actually bring you back and make you think of outcomes for kids, or something that is affecting the young person in care that you may not have noticed before.

493

In general, LAC training was well received. Training groups which included a mix of Barnardos staff, carers, and invited professionals from other organizations were favoured. Inclusion of young people as presenters had a strong impact, and reinforced the significance of the system for service users. Respondents felt the need for time to be spent on the practicalities of completing LAC records, consistent interpretation of questions, and application to specific situations.

Several participants expressed the view that managers were very supportive and flexible during the change process. Support from managers was critical in operationalizing the system and maintaining workers' commitment. Integral to the success of the process was the provision of practical advice on completing assessments and the interpretation of questions, offering flexibility with time frames to complete forms, monitoring and adjusting workloads, and sustaining levels of supervision.

Teams were given substantial control within broad implementation time frames as to how they chose to implement certain parts of the LAC system, and this, combined with additional resources (such as the ability to reduce caseloads and extra administrative support), was of considerable assistance. Common guidelines for overall implementation, combined with regular meetings both within and across program teams, allowed for local decision-making.

Reaction to implementation was even more positive when the LAC Planning and Placement records were computerized and the *Looking After Children* Electronic System (LACES) made available. Electronic recording matched usual work practices of word processing and the use of information technology for record-keeping. The LAC Assessment and Action Records were not computerized as part of the project, as it was felt this would restrict the use of this record as a "conversation" with children and young people in care.

Commenting on the computerized version of LAC, practitioners spoke positively about the consultation process preceding implementation, the opportunity to choose to participate in the piloting of LACES, and the accessibility of IT support: "I felt that LACES was taken on a lot easier because you felt that you were consulted."

Reported Barriers

The implementation was perceived generally to be time-consuming, with many workers wanting to simultaneously continue to use old systems—a clear "change management" issue. Workers reported a sense of feeling overwhelmed, being burdened by the demands of a new system, and requiring shifts in ways of thinking. Issues such as these, coupled with meeting deadlines for LAC record completion, dominated staff responses in the first year of implementation at Barnardos Australia.

This experience of LAC implementation must be evaluated in the context of its complexity. In contrast to other Australian (Champion & Burke, 2006; Clare & Peerless, 1996; Wise, 1999) and overseas pilots (Clark & Burke, 1998; Flynn & Biro, 1998; Kufeldt, Cheers, Klein, & Rideout, 2007), Barnardos implemented the full LAC system, including the Planning and Placement Records and the Assessment and Action Records. As a direct result of this, operational expertise developed in relation to guided practice. Difficulties, doubts, and intricacies emerged and were discussed and resolved with the combined knowledge and resources of management, front-line workers, and direct care providers (residential and foster carers).

LAC, SCARF, and Participation

Research findings indicated that the majority of service users had positive experiences using guided practice. Nevertheless, there were a variety of experiences, and participants identified a number of issues requiring further consideration.

Service Users' Views of Guided Practice Assessment

The research explored service users' (N=32) views of the appropriateness of assessment when LAC and SCARF were used. This included views on the goals of intervention and the values underpinning the systems. The majority of service users described workers as having a good understanding of their problems. Service users particularly appreciated the practical assistance received. Parents and children using SCARF valued the assistance they received with problems related to poverty and social isolation. Young people using LAC also readily acknowledged the practical support that they had received. However, young people who were living independently raised concerns about the limited amount of support they experienced when leaving care, and spoke of needing more guidance about living independently. A number of parents using SCARF also felt that not all workers appreciated the depth of their financial difficulties, including budget management. Some Aboriginal families described workers as not fully appreciating the impact of extended family obligations on their circumstances.

The majority of service users spoke of the importance of emotional and social assessment and support in interventions. Young people using LAC mentioned the central importance of contact with their workers when they had limited family contact and/or few stable friendships. Parents using SCARF frequently raised the importance of workers encouraging them in their parenting role. However, not all service users ultimately received adequate support from their workers. One young woman whose family had used SCARF spoke of needing more support than she received. Her experience raised questions regarding the level of participation of young parents in SCARF-based family interventions. Some users spoke of not getting along with individual workers, and asking the agency for a change of worker. The individual values of workers seemed to have had a greater impact on clients in SCARF-based interventions than on interventions using LAC.

Most service users described the values underpinning assessment as acceptable to them. One significant area of difference, however, concerned the physical punishment of children (an issue covered in SCARF). While some parents acknowledged the need to change their behaviour, others disagreed with attempts to alter their approach to discipline. A concern, evident in both SCARF and LAC, involved questions on drugs and alcohol use; service users described avoiding these questions or misleading workers in the answers that they provided.

Service Users' Views of Guided Practice Processes

The research explored service users' experiences with the planning processes involved in guided practice, and the extent to which they felt able to participate in the LAC and/or SCARF intervention. Few service users commented on formal planning processes such as reviews, time limits on decision-making, or interagency collaboration; they were more likely to identify the relationship with their worker as the critical issue in assistance provided. They frequently acknowledged the importance of workers' reliability in developing a positive working relationship. Although reliability may not necessarily be the result of guided practice, making workers accountable for their actions and for the review of decisions is a central issue in the use of LAC and SCARF.

Not all service users reported positive relationships with their workers all the time. In addition to a small number who had sought to change workers, three participants described avoiding engagement with workers. In two situations, young men in long-term foster care resented the use of guided practice because it made them feel that they were "not normal." They reported that using LAC was stigmatizing, and did not want contact from workers beyond the provision of financial support. In a second situation, a mother using a SCARF-based model described the focus of the intervention as too strongly directed at her children and not adequately focused on her needs. Service users did not raise problems of the confidentiality of information sought; however, they did raise the issue of circulation of information within families as a privacy issue.

Service Users' Views of LAC and SCARF Documentation

Service users were asked about the impact of the documentation required in LAC and SCARF forms on their relationship with workers. This has been identified as an area of considerable concern in social work literature on guided practice systems (Francis, 2002; Munro, 2001). It was apparent from the research interviews that LAC and SCARF records were used in many different ways with service users—sometimes workers had given forms to participants to complete, whereas other workers had completed the forms alone without any service user involvement. Those service users who had used the forms directly often found that they were a source of insight and understanding, and were useful in correcting workers' misunderstandings of their situation. For other service users, however, the level of literacy required by the forms, and discomfort with paperwork, were problematic. Many identified the LAC and SCARF records as predominantly for the use of the worker and agency, and requested more user-friendly formats such as the use of cartoons, colour, and computer-based communication. Some service users did not want to keep copies of records, as they found it upsetting to be reminded of past events; others found it hard to keep track of paperwork.

Service users were asked about their interest in using ICT to communicate with workers, given the widespread use of computers and the Internet and the future development of LAC and SCARF. Many service users saw ICT as potentially useful, and younger people were particularly interested in the idea. It was apparent, however, that access to this technology was limited; although most of those in foster care had access to the Internet, most families in SCARF programs did not. It was also apparent that the way computers are used for communication is very different among service users (who used Instant Messaging) and workers (who used e-mail). There were also individual differences in the use of computers, depending on service user age (e.g., older participants reported being less comfortable with computers).

Overall, service users described positive experiences with assessment and planning processes in interventions using the LAC and SCARF systems. This is a significant finding given critics' concerns that guided practice systems could undermine professional autonomy and client-worker relationships (Garrett, 2003). It is also of interest to note that ongoing evaluation of child welfare programs using guided practice has directly involved service users in research on their experience of LAC (Fernandez, 2006a, 2007a, 2008a, 2008b) and SCARF (Fernandez, 2004, 2006b, 2008a).

Workers' Views of LAC and SCARF

Guided practice systems such as LAC and SCARF were developed in response to concerns arising from poor planning and monitoring of outcomes for children. Workloads initially increased in implementing and adapting to the systems; however, training, management support, and communication and feedback in the implementation phase resolved many of these issues. Guided practice was seen to offer clear advantages to workers in their practice. First, the system provided an accessible and explicit link to evidence-based good practice in planning. Second, it provided a vehicle to document the case management process of children and families in their involvement with the agency, so that information about them was not lost or disregarded. Finally, the system focused practice attention, in a holistic manner, on the individual needs of each child and family and their well-being.

Key Learnings

The Australian research and practice initiatives described in this chapter have made guided practice materials readily available across Australian states and territories, expanding knowledge of new ways of providing care and protection intervention. The theoretical approach underpinning LAC and SCARF has ensured a focus on the interventions required to improve specific outcomes and the overall well-being for children, young people, and families.

The experience of implementing LAC and SCARF in Australia also highlights the importance of attention to change management processes. In order to maximize effective implementation of guided practice, extensive and robust preparatory consultation processes are required. In this experience, additional resources and administrative support helped to ensure the successful implementation of guided practice.

Participation at all levels, not just of paid staff but also of service users, was found to be crucial for optimal use of guided practice. As evidenced by the Australian experience of implementing LAC and SCARF, approaches to participation must include staff training to raise awareness about the importance of ensuring that the voice of the service user is heard. It is not reasonable to expect that recipients of care and protection interventions will automatically accept plans and interventions made as a result of professional assessment without an opportunity to participate. The service user voice must be heard, and guided practice systems provide for this—in case management, in care planning, and in review.

Information technology as a component of guided practice is important, but ICT systems must be practitioner-friendly, and information relevant to management must be integrated within the system rather than a separate component. The ability to separate out reports for middle and senior managers is also advantageous in facilitating supervisory processes. As well, innovative use of ICT provides future possibilities for service user participation, and for improving practice.

Conclusion

This chapter has outlined the implementation of guided practice in Australia, pertaining to *Looking After Children* (LAC) and the *Assessment Framework* (known in Australia as SCARF) systems. Adaptation of these systems to the Australian child welfare legislative and practice context has been responsive to the needs of Australian workers, managers, and service users, and has attempted to address systemic difficulties in Australian child and family welfare.

From the outset of the guided practice research initiative by Barnardos Australia, there was a clear understanding of the reasons for implementation of the LAC and SCARF systems. The research represented an attempt to introduce theory and research evidence to guide outcome-focused practice with children and families. As well, the research brought the voices of consumers into assessment and decision-making processes within a service context where there was little evidence of practice protocols for engaging service users in these activities (Milner & O'Byrne, 1998). The findings reported in this chapter indicate how the guided practice systems SCARF and LAC can engage service users, and how such feedback can result in modifications to such systems. This, in turn, reinforces the importance of a participatory approach to research and implementation.

The widespread use of LAC and SCARF in Australia also provides a unique opportunity to develop more consistency in practice across the care and protection sector, and reflects a direct attempt to influence the Australian national policy agenda in child welfare. Embracing the innovative use of information technology to assist, supplement, and enhance social work practice, LAC and SCARF have forged ahead of case management systems which focus predominantly on the aggregation of data and compilation of case file notes.

The overall aim of the implementation of LAC and SCARF in Australia was to use the application of guided practice to enhance the quality of social work intervention to improve outcomes for children, young people, and their families. Direct practice implications also include the value of such systems in setting minimum standards in a largely unregulated policy and practice environment. Further implications include the importance of client participation as a direct means of improving decision-making, planning, and outcomes within a transparent and therefore accountable case management system. The goals of the original research project were to introduce and evaluate a guided practice framework in the New South Wales child welfare context; these goals are now moving in the direction of developing an Integrated Children's System (see Cleaver et al., 2008, and Chapter 37), which will encourage more joint planning and collaborative approaches to intervention.

Note

1 This figure should be treated with caution, as it is based on aggregated data from each state and territory in Australia, and each of these have different legislation, policies, and practices. Thus, the data from each jurisdiction are not necessarily comparable. Numbers for each jurisdiction are reported by the Australian Institute of Health and Welfare (2008).

35

Resiliency: Embracing a Strength-Based Model of Evaluation and Care Provision

Tyrone Donnon
Wayne Hammond

S tress, hardship, and misfortune resulting from personal or situational experiences can affect children and adolescents as well as adults. While some may develop serious and long-term educational, psychological, and social problems, a greater number grow up to lead healthy and productive lives in adulthood (Masten & Garmezy, 1985; Werner, 1989). In a problem-focused society, where the call for action through targeted intervention programs stems from specifically identified problems, the acknowledgement and promotion of children's strengths appear to contradict our general understanding of how to address societal concerns about child and adolescent development (Masten, Best, & Garmezy, 1990; Masten & Coatsworth, 1998). Grounded in research on resilience, protective factors, prevention, and human development, Resiliency Canada has established a strength-based, resiliency framework used to identify 10 domains of influence that promote healthy, caring, and productive children and adolescents (Donnon, Hammond, & Charles, 2003; Donnon & Hammond, 2007a).

In an effort to address this preoccupation with a restricted focus on the identification and treatment of at-risk behaviours, Resiliency Canada has worked with more than 50 communities and 25,000 Grade 3 to 12 students from across the country to design and develop the Child Resiliency and Youth Resiliency: Assessing Developmental Strengths (CR:ADS and YR:ADS) questionnaires. The resulting 10-factor model is used to define an individual's resiliency profile, which includes a framework consisting of 31 indicators of developmental strengths. Although the foundation for understanding the factors that encourage the development of resiliency is derived from sound theory and extensive research, the success of resiliency profiling stems from a shared vision among various social service stakeholders and community members in the establishment of a positive, strength-based approach to addressing the needs of all children.

In this chapter we present a strength-based model of evaluation that focuses on the identification and development of resiliency in children and youth in care. The resiliency factors and developmental strengths framework presented below reflect fundamental elements found to be essential for all children to become productive and responsible adults in society. In particular, the completion of the CR:ADS and YR:ADS questionnaires produces corresponding resiliency profiles as the first step in engaging children and youth in a participatory process. The Child and Youth Resiliency Profiles provide a comprehensive summary of where individuals perceive their intrinsic and extrinsic strengths to exist. Focused on a model of resiliency that emphasizes the importance of empowering the individual, this approach provides an opportunity for both the child and caregiver to identify an appropriate plan of action that builds capacity through strengths. Using the questionnaires as a repeated measure, the resiliency profiles provide the benefit of directing and monitoring individual growth while highlighting where programs and organizations work best in the development of resiliency for the children and youth they serve.

Contextualizing Resiliency Development

In a review of the literature and research on the development of resiliency, stress-resistant or "invulnerable" children and youth share common characteristics operating as two broad sets of resiliency factors:

- *Extrinsic* factors such as family, peers, school, and community; and
- *Intrinsic* factors or personality characteristics such as empowerment, self-control, cultural sensitivity, self-concept, and social sensitivity.

These factors generally include a number of associated components, or what we refer to as strengths, that support and promote the development of children's coping skills. For example, the family resiliency factor consists of six developmental strengths that focus on the characteristics of a supportive family (caring family, effective family communication, adult family members as role models, and family support), with explicit expectations for future growth (parental involvement in school, and high expectations). As shown in Table 1, the family-based factor (i.e., "Parental Support & Expectations"), with six developmental strengths, is identified as a key extrinsic component of the resiliency framework, as are school-related ("Commitment to Learning at School" and

"School Culture"), community ("Community Cohesiveness"), and peer ("Peer Relationships") factors. In particular, the developmental strengths that contribute to resiliency exist within the individual and through the situational and relational experiences related to family, peers, school, and community. Using a holistic approach to understanding the resiliency factors that contribute to child and adolescent development, Table 1 describes the extrinsic and intrinsic strengths related to child and adolescent resiliency.

Table 1 *List and Description of the 31 Developmental Strengths*

Resiliency Factors	Developmental Strength and Description
Extrinsic Factors	
Parental support & expectations	**Caring family:** Family provides a nurturing, caring, loving home environment
	Family communication: Can communicate with family openly about issues/concerns
	Adult family members as role models: Family provides responsible role models
	Family support: Family provides trust, support, and encouragement regularly
	Parental involvement in schooling: Family are active in providing help/support
	High expectations: Family encourages youth to set goals and do the best he/she can
Peer relationships	**Positive peer relationships:** Friendships are respectful and viewed positively by adults
	Positive peer influence: Friendships are trustworthy and based on positive outcomes
Community cohesiveness	**Caring neighbourhood:** Youth live in a caring and friendly neighbourhood
	Community values youth: Adults in the community respect youth and their opinions
	Adult relationships: Adults try to get to know the youth and are viewed as trustworthy
	Neighbourhood boundaries: Neighbours have clear expectations for youth
Commitment to learning at school	**Achievement:** Youth works hard to do well and get the best grades in school
	School engagement: Youth is interested in learning and working hard in the classroom
	School work: Youth works hard to complete homework and assignments on time
School culture	**School boundaries:** School has clear rules and expectations for appropriate behaviours
	Bonding to school: Youth cares about and feels safe at school
	Caring school climate: School environment and teachers provide a caring climate
	High expectations: School/Teacher encourages goal setting and to do the best they can
Intrinsic Factors	
Cultural sensitivity	**Cultural awareness:** Youth has a good understanding of and interest in other cultures
	Acceptance: Youth respects others' beliefs and is pleased about cultural diversity
	Spirituality: Youth has strong spiritual beliefs/values that play an important role in life
Self-control	**Restraint:** Believes that it is important to restrain from the use of substances
	Resistance skills: Is able to avoid or say "no" to people who may place them at risk
Empowerment	**Safety:** Youth feels safe and in control of his/her immediate environment
Self-concept	**Planning and decision-making:** Is capable of making purposeful plans for the future
	Self-efficacy: Youth believes in their abilities to do many different things well
	Self-esteem: Youth feels positive about his/her self and future
Social sensitivity	**Empathy:** Youth emphasizes with others and cares about other people's feelings
	Caring: Youth is concerned about and believes it is important to help others
	Equity & social justice: Believes in equality and that it is important to be fair to others

Unlike the extrinsic nature of some factors, through which children deal with external forces beyond their direct control (e.g., actions of their peers, school's expectations for homework and behaviour, people's indifference to children in their community), intrinsic factors are defined by the internal perceptions or mental constructs children develop about themselves and their personal capacity to cope with stress and adversity. Although living in an at-risk neighbourhood with peer relationships that encourage the abuse of alcohol and drugs are external detriments to a child's development, having the "resistance skills" and "restraint" to say "no" can be more important in the long term (i.e., "Self-control" factor). Correspondingly, children who indicate that they have high "Self-Concept" related to the intrinsic strengths identified with having strong "self-esteem," "self-efficacy," and "planning and decision-making" skills are more able to deal with the confrontations they will experience throughout their lives.

Where there exists a combination of both intrinsic and extrinsic strengths, children are able to cope with adversity more effectively than those who experience fewer of the developmental strengths. This becomes apparent when developmental strengths are compared with an individual's corresponding attitude and behaviour indicators. As demonstrated in the next section below, higher categories of combined intrinsic and extrinsic strengths experienced by adolescents correspond to more positive or constructive use of time and less engagement in at-risk behaviours or activities.

Resiliency Models: Understanding the Developmental Strengths Framework

Although protective factors or "invulnerable" youth have been studied for years by researchers in a variety of disciplines, only in the past few years has the concept of resiliency been presented as a viable scientific construct (Christiansen & Evans, 2005; Donnon & Hammond, 2007a; Fergus & Zimmerman, 2005; Garmezy, Masten, & Tellegen, 1984; Luthar, Cicchetti, & Becker, 2000; Masten et al., 1988; Rutter, 1990). We acknowledge that an individual's ability to overcome and thrive despite exposure to stress-related or adversarial situations is a reflection of that person's resilience or resiliency development. There are currently four models of resiliency proposed (Fergus & Zimmerman, 2005; Hollister-Wagner, Foshee, & Jackson, 2001):

1) the *compensatory model* states that each risk and protective factor acts independently and directly on predicted outcomes, but they combine cumulatively to compensate for each other;

2) the *risk-protective model* emphasizes the presence or absence of the protective factor as a moderator in predicting the relationship that will exist between risk and outcome;

3) the *protective-protective* model expands on the interactive risk-protective model by positing that the risk and outcome relationship decreases with each protective factor present; and

4) the *challenge model* purports a curvilinear relationship between the risk factor and predicted outcome. In this model, low levels of risk act as learning experiences that encourage the development of coping strategies, and may actually weaken problem behaviour outcomes initially (Brooks et al., 2001; Hawkins, Catalano, & Miller, 1992). With increased risk levels, however, the problem behaviour escalates in an almost exponential or curvilinear relationship, indicating the diminishing returns that come from having very few or no protective factors in an individual's resiliency profile.

Support for a Protective-Protective Model of Resiliency

We have observed that the additive effects of both intrinsic and extrinsic strengths enable children and adolescents to cope with adversity more effectively than those who experience fewer developmental strengths (Donnon & Hammond, 2007b). The completion of the self-reported CR:ADS (Grades 3 to 6 reading level) or YR:ADS (Grades 7 to 12 reading level) questionnaire results in a total resiliency score that will range from between 0 and 31 developmental strengths. For example, a Youth Resiliency Profile may show that an adolescent with only a few extrinsic strengths (e.g., a supportive and caring school) is able to overcome adversity due to an abundance of intrinsic developmental strengths (e.g., high self-concept, self-control, and social sensitivity). In understanding the influence of these resiliency factors, we combine the resiliency profiles of children and adolescents into one of the six developmental strength categories from least (i.e., 00–05 category, indicating 5 or less of the total 31 developmental strengths) to most resilient (i.e., 26–31 category, where a child or youth reports having most or all 31 of the developmental strengths).

Our findings consistently show that children with a greater number of self-reported developmental strengths (i.e., those in the 26–31 DS category) correspondingly engage in more positive or constructive use of their time (Figure 1) and are less likely to engage in at-risk behaviours (Figure 2). The bar graphs illustrate the relationship between the six developmental strength categories and the average number of behaviours engaged in by adolescents 13 to 18 years of

Figure 1 *Linear Relationship between Developmental Strengths Categories and Average Number of Constructive Behaviours Engaged in by Adolescents (n = 6,000)*

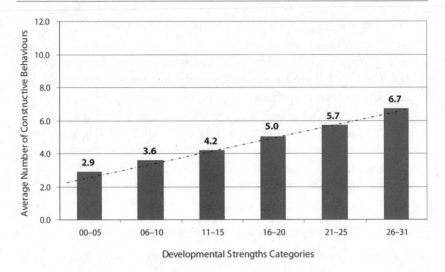

Figure 2 *Linear Relationship between Developmental Strengths Categories and Average Number of At-Risk Behaviours Engaged in by Adolescents (n = 6,000)*

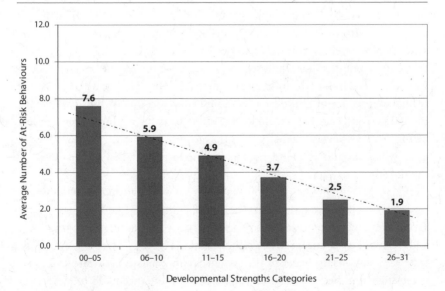

age (n = 6,000). In each case, up to 18 attitudinal or frequency (e.g., hours/week, monthly) questions are used to determine whether or not the adolescents have engaged in up to 12 constructive (e.g., success in school, values diversity, helps others, maintains good health, volunteerism, exhibits leadership, resists danger, delays gratification, overcomes adversity) or at-risk (e.g., substance abuse such as alcohol, tobacco, and illegal drugs, antisocial behaviour, violence, school problems, vandalism, gambling) behaviour patterns as measured by the YR:ADS questionnaire. In particular, when the total effect of resiliency factor exposure is compared with problem behaviour outcomes, the findings support the additive influence of developmental strengths as purported by the protective-protective model of resiliency. A similar linear relationship is also found for constructive behaviours: an increase in developmental strength category reflects a corresponding increase in the engagement of children and adolescents in more constructive behaviour patterns.

Using Resiliency Assessment to Connect Developmental Strengths with Program Outcomes

Resiliency Canada developed and introduced the concept of assessing the Resiliency Profile of children and adolescents as a focus on understanding how these resiliency strengths, and the dynamics involved in their development, lead to more productive and better outcomes for all children. In addition to maintaining the integrity of the CR:ADS and YR:ADS questionnaires through sound psychometric testing, activities to date have focused on the evolutionary development of the resiliency assessment protocols for use in strength-based approaches to children's services and program evaluation outcomes.

Empowering Children and Adolescents through a Participatory Process

Many individuals and their families are faced with barriers and challenges that hinder their ability to engage in a constructive and health-oriented lifestyle. They are often overwhelmed by their circumstances, and cope in ways that lead to a crisis or engagement in high-risk behaviours. As a result, many of these individuals and their families come in contact with service provision agencies involuntarily, and with the assumption that their "problem(s) will be solved." However, the traditional approach of "problem solving" or "crisis intervention" tends to meet only the immediate needs of the clients, and does not engage the child or adolescent in a participatory manner that leads to the development of the resiliency factors or strengths required for a long-term strategy of establishing a healthier lifestyle.

Based upon a strength-based approach to child and family development, the use of the resiliency assessment questionnaires provides an opportunity to invite children into a participatory intervention that focuses on meaningful engagement and change (Bartle, Couchonnal, Canda, & Staker, 2002; Cameron & Cadell, 1999). It is assumed that any real therapeutic benefits will only occur if the child perceives it as meaningful by understanding and directing the intervention provided (Prochaska, DiClemente, & Norcross, 1992). Since the resiliency questionnaire is designed to assess the individual's perception of reality, the resulting baseline profile of his or her strengths provides the basis for a meaningful "therapeutic action plan" that reflects both the needs identified and is relevant to the child's circumstances. When children are provided with a copy of their personalized Resiliency Profile, many are initially surprised to have the opportunity to use this summary to illustrate their developmental strengths and be subsequently asked what they feel would be the best approaches to build capacity with specific strengths.

As shown in the example of a Youth Resiliency Profile for a 15-year-old male in a group home setting (Figure 3), the family resiliency factor has a number of developmental strengths that would allow him to express his concerns about family communication, family support, parental involvement in school, and family members as role models. Correspondingly, an explanation of the strong peer influence and relationships as strengths may lead to an understanding of the weaker strengths found in school and with his family as a reflection of low self-control skills and self-esteem when it comes to dealing with expectations at home and in school academically. Using the Resiliency Profile summary, the young man may express an initial desire to do better at school, allowing the caregiver to work with him to identify strategies to reconnect with the school and teachers through additional tutoring or involvement with extracurricular activities. With time and repeated resiliency assessments at regular intervals, growth in some developmental strengths may lead to further initiatives and desires to build capacity in other resiliency factors.

Figure 3 *Example of a Youth Resiliency Profile for a 15-Year-Old Male in a Mentoring Program*

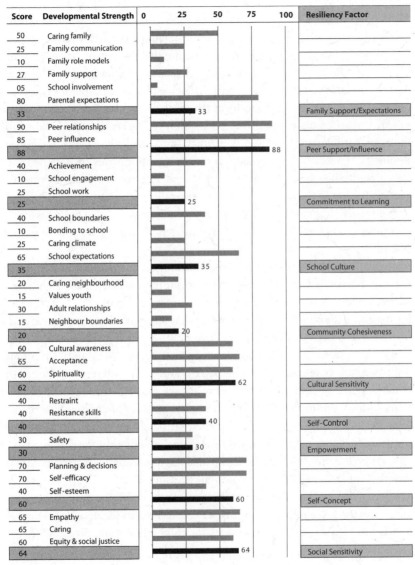

Score	Developmental Strength	0	25	50	75	100	Resiliency Factor
50	Caring family						
25	Family communication						
10	Family role models						
27	Family support						
05	School involvement						
80	Parental expectations						
33			33				Family Support/Expectations
90	Peer relationships						
85	Peer influence						
88						88	Peer Support/Influence
40	Achievement						
10	School engagement						
25	School work						
25			25				Commitment to Learning
40	School boundaries						
10	Bonding to school						
25	Caring climate						
65	School expectations						
35			35				School Culture
20	Caring neighbourhood						
15	Values youth						
30	Adult relationships						
15	Neighbour boundaries						
20		20					Community Cohesiveness
60	Cultural awareness						
65	Acceptance						
60	Spirituality						
62				62			Cultural Sensitivity
40	Restraint						
40	Resistance skills						
40				40			Self-Control
30	Safety						
30			30				Empowerment
70	Planning & decisions						
70	Self-efficacy						
40	Self-esteem						
60				60			Self-Concept
65	Empathy						
65	Caring						
60	Equity & social justice						
64				64			Social Sensitivity

Using Resiliency Development to Achieve Performance Outcome Measures

Although there are a variety of assessment tools available to measure therapeutic change, they are typically focused on problem or psychosis identification (e.g., anxiety, hysteria, depression) and require that the person administering the tool and interpreting the results be a chartered psychologist or a doctoral degree specialist in the field of practice. The resiliency assessment protocols, however, have been designed to meet the same psychometric rigour of other normed instruments without the confusion of using standardized statistical measures for interpretation (i.e., T-Scores). In particular, the Child and Youth Resiliency: Assessing Developmental Strengths questionnaires are designed and developed to be used by front-line caregivers, and require basic training in administration of the questionnaire, interpretation of Resiliency Profiles, and strength-based approaches in working with children and adolescents to address their needs collaboratively within the parameters of the services and programs provided.

In identifying appropriate outcome indicators, it is important to emphasize that what is being measured is whether or not there has been any significant change or benefit as a result of the particular service or program. In a mentoring program, the objective is to have an adult mentor provide a caring and supportive role model to a child in order to develop a better self-concept (e.g., higher self-esteem, self-efficacy, planning, and decision-making). Resultant improvements in relationships with parents and peers, and reconnecting with school, denote measurable change in resiliency factors, attitudes, and behaviours resulting from the program. The actual number of children who complete the mentoring program (or even their satisfaction with various aspects of the program) does not tell us anything about whether or not the children benefited from the program, and hence is considered to be more of an operational function (*output*) rather than an *outcome* measure.

In establishing a strength-based protocol for the collection of resiliency outcome measures, the following points are emphasized in the design and implementation of an evaluation framework for child services and programs:

1) focus on a single-system design using the CR:ADS or YR:ADS questionnaires as a standardized measurement;

2) identify general program- and client-specific strengths related to the focus of the service or program provided (e.g., a wilderness expedition may lead to greater self-concept strengths, but growth in other resiliency factors such as family, school, or community could be anticipated); and

3) establish an assessment schedule that may potentially reflect change over time using pre-/post-testing and a repeated measures evaluation framework (e.g., on intake, three-month, program exit, and six-month follow-up).

To maintain consistency in the collection of data or information concerning outcome measures, it is important that the staff involved with the process be adequately trained and qualified to administer and interpret the Resiliency Profile summaries. With ongoing monitoring of the evaluation framework, components of any program may require revisions to accommodate changes that occur as a result of various outcome measurement findings. These modifications may have implications for specific short- or long-term outcomes, or may even extend back to the principal goals for providing the program to clients in the first place.

From a program perspective, an aggregate report of findings based on clients' outcome results will require a fairly lengthy period of time to accumulate adequate and similar subgroupings (e.g., boys vs. girls) of measurement scores. What may become apparent with time is that a particular service or approach adopted in the program may have a greater influence or benefit than others when dealing with some presenting issues or concerns. This information or understanding becomes important in making programming decisions about how best to meet the needs of the client, and, at the same time, maximize the benefits in using the resources allocated to the program. As such, the use of the resiliency assessment questionnaires, Resiliency Profile summaries, and subsequent strength-based "plans of action" derived for each child can be designed to act as an all-encompassing evaluation instrument for both intrinsic and extrinsic short-term, intermediate, and long-term outcomes.

Discussion

There is a concern that many children are not being provided with a broad support system that promotes adequate caring and supportive relationships in their homes, schools, and communities (Jessor, Van Den Bos, Vanderryn, Costa, & Turbin, 1995; Kupersmidt & Coie, 1990). Particularly in large urban areas, it has become difficult to establish appropriate guidance or positive opportunities for children and adolescents to receive constant and consistent nurturing of the values, beliefs, and competencies they need to become independent, contributing members of society. During the past decade, research has shown that policies and programs for youth that focus on preventing specific youth behaviour problems (e.g., vandalism, drug abuse, violence), without attention to contextual factors, generally are unable to report any long-term benefits (Hawkins et al., 1992; Herman-Stahl & Petersen, 1996; Scales & Leffert, 1999).

Correspondingly, programs that involve the multi-faceted context of young people's lives, including influences from family, school, and community, have been more successful (Cameron & Cadell, 1999).

Child and youth resiliency can be defined as the capability of children and adolescents to cope successfully in the face of stress-related, at-risk, or adversarial situations. Resiliency Canada's primary goal is to provide an understanding, through applied and scientific research, of why some children and youth are more resilient than others in the face of adversity. Based on this research, and the literature on resiliency and youth development, the 31 developmental strengths framework identifies the protective factors that encourage and enhance the well-being and development of all youth in our communities. The Resiliency Profile consists of 31 developmental strengths that focus on five external factors (Parental Support and Expectations, Peer Relationships, Community Cohesiveness, Commitment to Learning at School, and School Culture) and five internal factors (Cultural Sensitivity, Self-Control, Empowerment, Self-Concept, and Social Sensitivity), that contribute to the enhancement of child and adolescent development. Resiliency Canada's research consistently demonstrates that children and adolescents with greater numbers of resiliency factors and developmental strengths are less likely to be involved with at-risk behaviours or risk-taking activities. Correspondingly, children and adolescents who have a strong resiliency profile are more likely to be involved with a greater number of positive and constructive behaviours. The resiliency profile derived from children and adolescents has been largely attributed to the use of a strength-based approach as the catalyst to inform, engage, and unite school and community-based members in subsequent efforts to promote core developmental strengths. The use of the resiliency assessment protocol as part of a strength-based approach to child service and program delivery also provides the opportunity to monitor and evaluate real change through repeated measures and child-led engagement in resiliency profile interpretation and intervention initiatives.

Implications for Policy, Practice, and Research

Currently, we have seen an increased demand on organizations to be "accountable" for the services and programs they provide to children and families in our communities. Although being accountable has a variety of meanings, the premise of the work that we do in the human service, health care, and other related sectors implies that we need to be responsible for what we do with our clients. As such, the most critical component of this responsibility is our commitment to deliver services and programs that are effective and beneficial to the participants. From a strength-based perspective, the use of aggregated CR:ADS and YR:ADS questionnaires administered at schools and within communities has been used specifically to assist educators and service sector providers in defining the strengths of the children and adolescents based on aggregated School or individual Child/Youth Resilience Profiles. This not only allows stakeholders the opportunity to look at the profiles of the children they serve, but also to highlight the strengths of their programs and identify areas where their clients may potentially benefit from additional services or resources provided by other child care organizations.

The Resiliency Canada national mandate seeks to motivate and equip individuals, organizations, and their leaders to embrace a strength-based culture that nurtures the resiliency development of children, adolescents, and families. The developmental strengths framework takes a holistic approach that looks at the resiliency factors supporting and encouraging our children to adopt positive attitudes and healthy lifestyle choices. By acknowledging the strengths that currently exist within our children and their families, the focus is to make every effort toward using a positive, strength-based approach to building the capacity of everyone to nurture the development of resiliency.

In support of this initiative, the resiliency assessment questionnaires have been used to:

- Assist provincial and local educators in monitoring indicators related to student well-being;
- Set priorities and strategies for programs and services;
- Provide a common framework for cross-sector collaboration;
- Provide both quantitative and qualitative data sources for grant writing;
- Provide positive, outcomes-focused data for reports to funding agencies; and
- Incorporate child, youth, and family needs in organizational and community planning.

Resiliency Canada presents the developmental strengths framework as a viable model to understanding the major components that contribute to the resiliency development and well-being of children, adolescents, and adults in our communities. Currently, research in the development and testing of an Adult Resiliency framework and adult's/parent's perception of child resiliency measures has shown promising results. Using the Child and Youth Resiliency Profiles in a variety of program settings is being explored in such settings as adolescent group homes, children in foster care, and through school-based mentoring programs. Educated in the strength-based approach to using the resiliency profiles to establish participatory relationships with the children, child care providers have found this method empowering for both themselves and the children they serve. Further research will continue to focus on the effectiveness and efficacy of using the resiliency assessment process and strength-based protocols in a variety of child and family services and programs.

36

The National Child Welfare Outcomes Indicator Matrix (NOM) and Its Application in a Child Welfare Agency

Nico Trocmé
Tonino Esposito
Meghan Mulcahy
Lorry Coughlin
Barbara Fallon
Bruce MacLaurin
Aron Shlonsky

Across Canada, social service providers are increasingly being asked to evaluate the outcomes of their interventions. These outcomes occur at different levels: the broad system level, including provincial and national perspectives; the program or agency performance level; and the clinical practice level. Program and system level measurement pose a particular challenge in the field of child welfare, where service standards and reporting systems vary by jurisdiction. In Ontario, for example, legislation defines a child as a person under the age of 18; however, children in need of protection can enter the system only if they are under 16, and data collected on children and families reflect this age threshold. And in Alberta, children up to the age of 18 may be admitted to care, and statistics track unique children. In addition, Canadian child welfare information systems are primarily used to report service activities such as the number of case openings per year. These month- or year-end counts provide limited information about child service trajectories and outcomes.

The National Child Welfare Outcomes Indicator Matrix (NOM) (Trocmé, MacLaurin, & Fallon, 2000) was developed through a series of national consultations initiated by the Provincial and Territorial Directors of Child Welfare and Human Resources Development Canada to serve as a common framework for tracking outcomes for children and families receiving child welfare services. Designed to reflect the complex balance that child welfare authorities maintain between a child's immediate need for protection, a child's long-term requirement for a nurturing and stable home, the family's potential for growth, and the community's capacity to meet a child's needs, the NOM includes four nested domains: child safety, child well-being, permanence, and family and community support (see Figure 1).

The 10 NOM indicators were selected on the basis of information that could be readily obtained from available administrative client data. Together they provide a rudimentary measure of the complex issues common to families involved with Canadian child welfare services, and should not be examined in isolation lest, for example, one be emphasized to the exclusion of another.

The NOM is intended for use by child welfare managers to inform decision-making, programming, and policy development. It is not designed to guide clinical decision-making, differentiating it from frameworks such as *Looking After Children* (LAC), which includes an *Assessment and Action Record* used with children in care in order to monitor developmental outcomes and match services to identified needs. The NOM framework guides the development of baseline outcome measures used by agencies to track trends, generate agency-specific knowledge, and inform future programs and policies.

Figure 1 *National Child Welfare Outcomes Indicator Matrix (NOM): Ecological Framework*

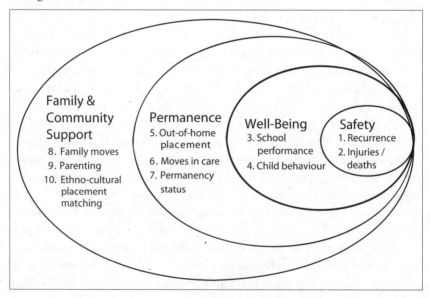

This chapter presents an updated version of the NOM and a revised set of indicators based on pilot testing conducted by various groups across Canada.[1] In the following pages we first describe the rationale, relevant research, and operational definition informed by the NOM for each of the 10 indicators. We then explain how a project of Montreal's anglophone child welfare agency, Batshaw Youth and Family Centres (BYFC), has been refining and applying the indicators for use by the agency.

National Child Welfare Outcomes Indicators

Safety

Recurrence of Maltreatment

Child welfare services are designed first and foremost to protect children from further victimization. Rates of recurrence are a key indicator of how successfully child welfare services have protected children from further abuse or neglect. In Quebec, Hélie (2005) found that 9% of child welfare-involved children were re-reported in the first 12 months, and 22% were re-reported in the four years following the index incident.

Recurrence can be measured in a number of ways relative to (1) the period of time over which data are collected, (2) the types of events counted as recurrent, and (3) the types of cases that are considered to be at risk of recurrence. The NOM measure of recurrence is the proportion of children who are investigated as a result of a new allegation of abuse or neglect within one year following closure of their child welfare file.

Serious Injuries and Deaths

Situations in which children known to child welfare authorities are seriously injured as a result of abuse or neglect are reviewed with care to minimize the chance of such situations recurring. While these tragedies remain relatively rare, systematic tracking and monitoring is required. Canadian police services document an average of 35 children per year killed by their parents, a figure that has remained stable over the past 30 years (Trocmé, Lajoie, Fallon, & Felstiner, 2007). The 2003 cycle of the *Canadian Incidence Study of Reported Child Abuse and Neglect* (CIS) found that 10% of victims had suffered some type of physical harm, representing an estimated 10,222 children across Canada (Trocmé, Fallon, MacLaurin, Daciuk, Felstiner et al., 2005). Three per cent of victims sustained harm severe enough to require medical care (for a breakdown of types of injuries, see Trocmé et al., 2007).

A number of challenges arise in tracking child injuries and fatalities. Under-detection is a problem in many instances. When tracking deaths of children receiving child welfare services, it is important to distinguish between maltreatment-related deaths and deaths of medically fragile children who may be placed in child welfare care because of their special needs. While serious injuries are systematically documented in child protection case files, data on injuries are not often aggregated or analyzed at an administrative level. Finally, it should be noted that because serious injuries and deaths are relatively rare, trends need to be examined over several years before they can be considered significant.

The NOM measures fatalities as the percentage of children who die while in the care of child welfare services, distinguishing between natural, accident, suicide, homicide, and/or undetermined causes of death. Some jurisdictions are additionally tracking data on child injury. The physical harm codes developed for the CIS–2003 provide an example of a simple checklist for describing the type and severity of injuries: (1) bruises, cuts, and scrapes; (2) burns/scalds; (3) broken bones; (4) head trauma; (5) fatality; and (6) other health condition (Trocmé et al., 2005). For each type of injury the CIS measures severity according to whether the child required medical care.

Well-Being

School Performance

Helping victims of maltreatment requires not only ensuring their physical safety but also that they have the opportunity to reach their full potential. Victims of child abuse and neglect are at significant risk for developmental, cognitive, and academic delays. A study in British Columbia examined a cross-sectional sample of 3,523 school-aged children between the ages of 6 and 19, and found that approximately 50% of children in permanent care in Grades 10 and 12 were behind at least one grade compared to children in the general population who had no involvement with child welfare services (Mitic & Rimer, 2002).

School performance is a good indicator of cognitive functioning for school-aged children. Performance can be measured as age-to-grade ratio, achievement on standardized tests (e.g., math and English), placement in special education classes, school attendance, and assessed risk of failure. While test scores may more accurately measure specific skills, age-to-grade ratio is the most feasible information to collect for child welfare services, especially for children receiving home-based services. Developmental information is not routinely available for preschoolers; however, consideration should be given to including regular developmental assessments for these children. The NOM measure for school performance is the proportion of children placed in out-of-home care who are in school and in the grade appropriate for their age. For older youth out of school, high school completion rates or the number of completed years of schooling are recommended.

Child Behaviour

Abused and neglected children are at high risk of developing emotional and behavioural problems at home, at school, and in the community. Children with emotional and behavioural problems tend to spend longer periods of time in out-of-home care, experience more placement disruptions, and are less likely to be reunified with their family of origin (Keil & Price, 2006). In an Ontario study (Burge, 2007) of a random sample of 429 children who were permanent wards, the prevalence rate of mental disorders was 31.7%.

Except in those jurisdictions where the *Looking After Children* materials are used, standardized measures of child emotional and behavioural functioning are not generally applied in child welfare settings. Documenting the rates of emotional and behavioural problems, as well as referrals to and the outcome of supportive services, is a priority for child welfare authorities.

A four-stage strategy is suggested for monitoring outcomes related to child emotional and behavioural problems: (1) document the specific problems identified in children (i.e., using the CIS–2003 child functioning codes); (2) track the proportion of children with emotional and behavioural problems who are referred to specialized services; (3) document the service completion rates for these children; and (4) report on rates of improvement, to the extent to which these are documented by the specialized services.

Permanence

Out-of-Home Placement

Legislation in every province and territory requires that children be served wherever possible in their own home. However, out-of-home placement may be required when leaving children at home poses significant risk, or when placement can give families needed respite. While placement is not an inherently negative outcome on an individual basis—indeed, for some children, it may be the only feasible option—high rates of out-of-home placement on an aggregate basis indicate a lack of effective home-based service options or unacceptable living conditions that should be addressed as a priority over removal.

According to estimates from the CIS–2003, 8% of victims of maltreatment were placed in out-of-home care during the first six to eight weeks of contact with child welfare authorities. The United States foster care data archive indicates that young children, especially infants, face the highest risk of placement with, on average, twice the rate reported for older children (Wulczyn, Hislop, & Harden, 2002). As a broader community health indicator, out-of-home placement rates are an important indicator of the overall well-being of children in a community.

Most jurisdictions report on the number of children in out-of-home placement at year-end, a method of tracking placements that undercounts the experience of most placed children who come into out-of-home care for relatively short periods of time. Placement rates are best understood in terms of a dynamic "case flow" calculation that tracks children receiving services over a set period of time. The NOM tracks the percentage of children who had at least one investigation begin in the fiscal year who were placed in out-of-home care within 12 months from the start of the first investigation. In order to exclude respite care and emergency placements, out-of-home placements lasting less than 72 hours are not counted.

Moves in Care

When children are separated from their families through out-of-home care, a stable placement experience assists them in developing and maintaining family, peer, and community relationships, and encourages a sense of belonging and identity. While some placement changes may be beneficial, multiple and unplanned placements have been associated with negative outcomes for children, including increased behaviour problems and poor academic performance (Barth, Lloyd, Green, James, Leslie et al., 2007; Unrau, Seita, & Putney, 2008). A four-year longitudinal study of 717 children who entered foster care in Saskatchewan found that 71% of children experienced only one out-of-home placement. The average number of moves for children who experienced more than one out-of-home placement was 2.3, and only 10% of these had more than four (Rosenbluth, 1995). The NOM tracks the number of placement changes experienced by children placed in out-of-home care during the fiscal year. Placements shorter than 72 hours are excluded from this measure, as are initial placements, initial family reunification, and planned respite.

Permanency Status

Lasting reunification with family is the primary goal for most children placed in out-of-home care, and a majority of children will return home within less than a year of initial placement. However, for some children, reunification is not possible, and stable alternatives such as permanent foster care, kinship care, and adoption must be pursued. Of the 289,000 children exiting foster care in the United States in 2006, 53% were reunified, 17% were adopted, 11% were placed with relatives, and 9% emancipated (United States Department of Health and Human Services, 2008). The average length of foster care placement was 20.9 months.

The primary challenge in measuring the time it takes to achieve permanency lies in determining when a situation becomes truly permanent, given that any planned permanent placement or reunification can always break down. In fact, the actual permanence of a placement can only be completely established once a youth has reached majority. Since a growing number of Canadian jurisdictions have set time frames for leaving children in temporary care (24 months for older children, 12–18 months for younger), the NOM tracks placed children forward for up to three years, assessing the relative permanence of reunification or placement at the three-year point. The NOM permanency status measure counts cumulative days in out-of-home care until a child is reunified, permanently placed with kin, adopted, emancipated, or placed in a permanent foster home.

Family and Community Support

Family Moves

Frequent moves in residence are a source of significant stress for families receiving child welfare services. Housing instability is caused by a range of factors, including lack of affordable, good quality housing, employment changes, lifestyle, and other family crises (Courtney, McMurtry, & Zinn, 2004; Crowley, 2003). Frequent moves can result in the loss of peer and social support networks for parents. For children, changes in residence and associated school changes may adversely affect their well-being, academic achievement, and ability to form supportive social networks. Sudden or unplanned moves pose a particular risk of emotional or psychological harm.

Children in families experiencing housing problems have been reported to be at increased risk of child welfare involvement and out-of-home placement (Courtney et al., 2004; Gewirtz, Hart-Shegos, & Medhanie, 2008). The results of the CIS–2003 indicate that close to a third of families substantiated for abuse or neglect moved at least once in the year prior to being reported, and 11% moved twice or more (Trocmé et al., 2005). In a study in Wisconsin comparing 480 families receiving in-home child welfare services to 494 families with children placed in out-of-home care, Courtney et al. (2004) report that "parents whose children have been removed were almost twice as likely as parents receiving in-home safety services to have been evicted, almost twice as likely to have been doubled up in housing with family or friends, and nearly three times as likely to have been homeless" (p. 404).

Changes of address are systematically recorded by child welfare services. Although data on previous addresses are often deleted from updated child welfare files, retaining this information would enable tracking this indicator of family stability. Changes in postal code could be used to approximate the distance between old and new addresses, an indicator of the likely social disruption accompanying moves. The NOM measures the percentage of families receiving services during a fiscal year that move at least once during that period.

Parenting

The quality of parenting is a significant concern in many cases of child abuse and neglect. Most children involved with child welfare will not be placed in foster care, while others will be reunited with their families after a relatively brief out-of-home placement. For these families, the provision of timely and appropriate services is essential for redressing the problems experienced by parents. Improvement in parenting is associated with a reduced risk of recurrent maltreatment, as well as better long-term outcomes for children (Barth, Landsverk, Chamberlain, Reid, Rolls, et al., 2005; Casanueva, Martin, Runyan, Barth, & Bradley, 2008).

The CIS–2003 documented caregiver functioning issues and reported that in 79% of cases of substantiated maltreatment involving 4,398 female caregivers, at least one functioning issue was identified, including being a victim of domestic violence (51%), lack of social supports (40%), and mental health issues (27%). For the 2,324 male caregivers, at least one functioning concern was noted in 72% of cases, with lack of social supports (33%), alcohol abuse (30%), mental health issues (18%), and maltreatment as a child (18%) noted the most often (Trocmé et al., 2005).

Measuring and improving parenting is limited by the lack of clear criteria describing what constitutes good parenting, and by a dearth of evidence-based interventions capable of addressing the complex issues faced by parents involved with child welfare services (Schmidt, Cuttress, Lang, Lewandowski, & Rawana, 2007). Because standardized measures of parenting are not routinely used by most child welfare service providers, the strategy being developed for the NOM focuses on tracking parenting problems. A four-stage strategy is suggested: (1) document the specific problems facing parents (i.e., using the CIS–2003 parent risk codes); (2) track the proportion of parents with problems who are referred to specialized services; (3) identify service completion rates for these parents; and (4) report on rates of improvement, to the extent that these are documented by service providers.

Ethnocultural Placement Matching

When children must be removed from their biological families, child welfare services attempt to place them as much as possible within their community, including with extended family, individuals emotionally connected to the child, or in a family of a similar religious or ethnocultural background. For Aboriginal children, this preference is specifically stated in most provincial and territorial statutes. However, a review conducted by the British Columbia Children's Commissioner (1998) indicated that only 2.5% of Aboriginal children in care were placed in Aboriginal homes.

Implementing a community placement policy can be a challenge, especially when such placements are not available. Difficulties in finding matched placements may not only lead to more disruptive experiences for placed children, but are also indicative of problems in recruiting foster families from these children's communities, and of limited engagement with those communities (Higgins, Bromfield, & Richardson, 2005; Rubin, Downes, O'Reilly, Mekonnen, Luan et al., 2008).

Given that placement matching for First Nations children is legislated in most jurisdictions, the NOM measure tracks the proportion of placed First Nations children in homes where at least one of the caregivers is First Nations. This indicator can be further explored by differentiating children placed in kinship care and those receiving services from First Nations child welfare agencies.

Child welfare agencies serving other significant ethnocultural or faith communities may, in like manner, define groups for whom similar placement matching issues arise. Categorizations should be simple, so as to support meaningful data collection, and developed in consultation with the specific communities.

Methodological Considerations

Moving from Management to Client-Centred Information System

Canadian child welfare information systems are primarily designed as management information systems directed toward financial accounting. The most commonly reported service statistics are the number of case openings per year and the number of children in care at year-end, statistics that provide limited information about service patterns. A case opened and closed three times during the year is indistinguishable from three cases each opened and closed once.

Neither the proportion of cases reopened nor the proportion of children investigated and subsequently placed in care can be derived from such statistics. To further complicate matters, many jurisdictions maintain separate databases for children in the community and children in care.

A child tracking system links each service event to the child(ren) and family(ies) served by that event, and the path of each child and family within the service system is recorded. This allows accurate reporting of statistics such as the proportion of investigated children admitted to care and the average number of placement changes.

Direct and Proxy Outcome Measures

Standardized observational and self-report instruments are the most accurate ′nd comprehensive methods for measuring outcomes. While such measures provide useful information for clinical and research purposes, they are lengthy to complete and are not easily interpreted as aggregate measures. In addition, self-report measures are not designed to be used in potentially adversarial child protection contexts. There is also a risk of measurement bias if these instruments are first introduced as performance measures rather than as tools to assist in clinical assessments.

Case events, such as adoption, grade completion, and address changes, can be used as proxy outcome measures. These system-based indicators are salient and easy to collect; however, the extent to which they truly reflect child outcomes must be carefully analyzed. Interpretation requires examination of the rationale for linking case events to specific outcomes and consideration of confounding events. A decrease in the proportion of children in age-appropriate grades could just as well indicate lower academic functioning as it could reflect changes in grading policies or the introduction of standardized tests. Given the limitations of such measures, they are best interpreted by examining multiple indicators, as recommended by the NOM.

In summary, optimizing the administrative use of client information systems enables child welfare agencies to better understand and respond to the children and families they serve. The 10 relatively simple indicators described provide a feasible model of outcome measurement consistent with an ecological model of social service delivery. In the next section, we describe a project being undertaken by Batshaw Youth and Family Centres (BYFC) that involves the application of the NOM indicators.

Using NOM to Establish Local Child Welfare Outcomes Measures

The Evidence-Based Management (EBM) project[2] is a three-year SSHRC-funded knowledge-mobilization initiative designed to develop and evaluate a model for supporting the use of research as a management tool in child welfare organizations. The project was conceived and developed jointly by McGill University's Centre for Research on Children and Families (CRCF) and BYFC following a request by BYFC for assistance in developing the agency's capacity to make better use of research to monitor the impact of its services and support the development of more effective services.

Now in its third year, the EBM project is helping BYFC develop a knowledge utilization infrastructure, in part by making better use of client service information systems to explore child welfare outcomes. The initiative emphasizes: the production of relevant and timely information through well-integrated partnerships between researchers, policy-makers, and service providers; and continuously evolving a research culture in which agency decision-making is informed by the research evidence base.[3] Responses to these questions must be accurate, informed to the full extent possible by local staff expertise, and provided in a timely fashion (e.g., weeks or months, not years), avoiding time-consuming and resource-intensive supplementary data collection procedures.

Three core project groups have been established to develop and operationalize the outcome indicators: (1) a technical workgroup which includes academics, a statistician, and the agency information systems coordinator; (2) a reference group, made up of child welfare managers; and (3) an external research group to conduct further in-depth analyses of the data.

The Technical Workgroup

The indicator workgroup meets to: (1) review existing research on child welfare outcomes in order to assist the reference group in defining agency-specific indicators; (2) review system-level data issues, such as establishing the system variables needed for the extraction of data on specific outcome indicators; and (3) analyze and report back on data to the reference group. Over the past three years, data on recurrence of child victimization, academic achievement, placement rate, moves in care, time in care, court involvement, worker continuity, and recidivism rates of youth criminal justice have been extracted and analyzed.

The EBM Reference Group

The reference group meets monthly to: (1) explore the reported data from a variety of perspectives, including caseworker, manager, and policy-maker; (2) discuss and agree upon a baseline measure for the outcome indicator in question; and (3) review and authorize the internal and external dissemination of the outcome data, including how to best present the data (i.e., tables, graphs, descriptive text, or a combination) for interpretation and application by front-line practitioners.

Data analysis was advanced through discussions between the reference group and the technical workgroup regarding the extent to which the data provided usefully portrayed child and family outcomes. For example, when investigating the likelihood that a child would experience a recurrent incident of abuse or neglect, the technical workgroup generated data on child re-victimization and presented it to the reference group, which decided: (1) at what stage of service (report, investigation, or ongoing services) a child was considered re-victimized; (2) whether to include data on children who previously received child welfare services; (3) whether to include data on children re-victimized while receiving services; and (4) the time frame in which re-victimization could occur (i.e., 12, 24, or 36 months). As a result of the ongoing dialogue between the two groups, and after providing descriptive data on the various possibilities, BYFC defined recurrence of child victimization as the proportion of children who had at least one substantiated recurrent event of maltreatment within 12 months of their file closing.

The EBM External Research Group

While the data generated from the EBM indicators provides BYFC with the ability to track trends over time, it does not provide a comprehensive overview of factors associated with the outcome (i.e., number of recurring incidents, predictors of recurrence, and the child and family characteristics associated with recurrence). As a result, the EBM baseline data is available to external research partners (i.e., *l'Institut de Recherche pour le Développement Social des Jeunes* [IRDS] and the *Association des Centres Jeunesse du Québec* [ACJQ]) for detailed analysis. Dr. Sonia Hélie and her research team at IRDS are currently conducting in-depth survival analysis of recurrence data in order to obtain a deeper understanding of the phenomena, including the influence of case factors such as age, type of maltreatment, and duration of services on rates of recurrence. Results of this research are made available to the reference group, and used to answer additional research questions that arise as the group explores baseline recurrence data.

The Information System

In order to generate context-specific knowledge on the selected outcome indicators, the EBM project promotes a rapid research-to-practice feedback loop that builds on pre-existing administrative systems and data collection instruments. BYFC uses a fully computerized client information system, which is part of the province-wide *Plateforme Intégration Jeunesse* (PIJ) information system. PIJ is one of the most comprehensive children and youth services information systems in North America, but to date its full capacity has been underutilized. PIJ is primarily used by front-line social workers to record individual client information. Managers have made limited use of its capacity as a management tool beyond case volume and case processing statistics.

Demonstration of the Potential of One Indicator: Recurrence of Child Victimization

Recurrence of child victimization was one of the first indicators developed by the reference group. In order to measure rates of recurrence, clear distinctions between substantiated and unsubstantiated incidents of child victimization first need to be made. Unsubstantiated events may indicate an absence of child abuse and neglect. Alternatively, unsubstantiated events may relate to a sub-threshold of severity, deficient evidence of maltreatment, inadequate abuse and neglect screening criteria, high worker caseloads, time constraints, or a lack of available resources (Trocmé, Knoke, Fallon, & MacLaurin, 2009; Fluke, 2009). Notwithstanding the importance of examining rates of unsubstantiated reports of child re-victimization, rates of substantiated recurring victimization remain indicative of children who continue to be at risk of abuse and neglect after receiving child welfare services.

In Quebec, the youth protection system intervenes when a child has been abandoned, neglected, abused psychologically, sexually, or physically, or has serious behavioural problems (La Direction des communications du Ministère de la Santé et des Services Sociaux du Québec, 2007). Based on these criteria, the EBM group defined recurring child victimization as including any substantiated report of neglect, physical abuse, sexual abuse, behavioural problems, and abandonment that occurred within 12 months of file closing.

In order to measure re-victimization, a list was compiled of all cases closed after receiving child welfare services in fiscal years 2002–3 through 2006–7. Of those cases, children who experienced a retained, substantiated incident of child victimization within 12 months of their file closing were identified. Children older than 17 years were excluded since they would have been too old to be re-reported within the follow-up period. Duplicate reports of incidents of child re-victimization are not counted as a recurrence.

Descriptive results reveal that the recurrence rate was relatively stable in the last five years, with approximately 15% of all children experiencing a recurring incident of child victimization within 12 months of their file closing. This first set of cross-tabular analyses helped draw attention to specific subgroups of children at risk of experiencing a recurring incident of child victimization. For instance, in 2005–6, most recurring incidents of child victimization occurred for children whose initial reason for substantiation was neglect (13.7%; n=51 recurring cases) and behavioural problems (21.7%; n=20 recurring cases). Re-victimization rates in cases involving sexual abuse (n=5) or abandonment (n=0) cannot be meaningfully analyzed over a single year, given the relatively small number of such cases, and can be better understood when followed for several consecutive years.

Of the cases recurring in 2005–6 (n=80 of 529 closed cases), close to half (n=39) were children aged 11 years and older, and three-quarters (n=60) were aged 6 years and older. The recurrence rate was lowest for children up to 1 year old (8.5%; n= 7 recurring cases), and highest for children aged 11 and older.

Patterns of recurring child victimization in closed child welfare cases have not been well documented in Quebec. Many service providers measure recurrence retrospectively using data on families with previous child welfare involvement. This overestimates chronic situations, and fails to take into consideration families who are never re-reported. Recurrence is more accurately measured prospectively by tracking cases forward over a defined period of time, capturing both recurrent and non-recurrent child victimization. The prospective, baseline re-victimization indicator used by BYFC identifies factors associated with an increased chance of a recurrent incident of child victimization. These findings have significant implications for understanding risk of child re-victimization at the initial evaluation of a case and when a case is recommended for closure.

The full potential of the indicators as management tools will emerge when comparing data on multiple indicators over various years. The rich case level data lends well to multivariate modelling, which will assist managers in understanding the factors associated with poor outcomes.

Conclusion and Future Directions

The NOM is proposed as a first step in an incremental process of developing meaningful, valid, and reliable outcome measures for child welfare. The 10 selected outcome indicators rely primarily on case events as proxy indicators of outcomes, and can be used by decision-makers to inform effective program and policy development. As the clinical use of standardized measures develops, it will be possible to replace these proxy indicators with more sophisticated measures. Success of the evidence-based management strategies can be assessed in terms of the extent to which decision-makers make more use of research, develop quality assurance and outcome tracking mechanisms, and eventually create a demand for more research on effective services to help abused and neglected children. Until then, the NOM provides a theoretically grounded ecological framework which relies on improvements to the structure of information systems rather than the introduction of new instruments. This strategy respects the feedback rule for developing effective information systems: provide those who collect information with relevant aggregated analyses based on their data before making new information requests. As Canadian child welfare information systems continue to evolve, so too will the quality of data collection and analysis.

Notes

1 These include work done by (1) the Federal–Provincial–Territorial Outcomes Coordinating Committee; (2) a Social Sciences and Humanities Research Council (SSHRC)–funded Knowledge Impact in Society (KIS) initiative (Trocmé and colleagues); and (3) analytic support from McGill University's Centre for Research on Children and Families, funded by a Centre of Excellence for Child Welfare (CECW) Public Health Agency of Canada grant. Additional partners include the Canada Foundation for Innovation (CFI) and the Bell Canada Child Welfare Research Unit.

2 The EBM Project is funded by an SSHRC grant under the KIS program, which supports "university-based strategic knowledge mobilization initiatives that systematically enable non-university stakeholder communities to benefit from existing academic research knowledge in the social sciences and humanities" (SSHRC–KIS Transformation Program description, n.d.). Additional partners include the CECW, l'Institut de Recherche pour le Développement Social des Jeunes (IRDS), the Association des Centres Jeunesse du Québec (ACJQ), the University of Toronto, the University of Calgary, and the Alberta Ministry of Children and Youth Services.

3 Consistent with the knowledge mobilization strategies of the Canadian Health Services Research Foundation (Lomas, 2000), the EBM initiative promotes research driven by questions decision-makers are faced with in their day-to-day activities.

37

Implementing the Integrated Children's System in the United Kingdom
A Summary of the Main Findings

Jane Scott

The Integrated Children's System was designed in early 2000 as part of the U.K. government's ongoing reform program for children's services in England and Wales. It was designed to ensure that assessment, planning, and decision-making led to good outcomes for children in need and their families. It built on earlier developments such as *Looking After Children* (Parker, Ward, Jackson, Aldgate, & Wedge, 1991; Ward, 1995) and the *Framework for the Assessment of Children in Need and their Families* (Cleaver & Walker, 2004). The research underpinning its development aimed to explore the extent to which the Integrated Children's System provided the foundation for achieving better outcomes for children.

Improving outcomes for children has been a priority for U.K. governments for over two decades, from the *Children Act 1989* through to recent policy developments such as *Every Child Matters: Change for Children* (Department for Education and Skills, 2005), with global outcomes of ensuring that children are healthy, safe, and reach their potential. These outcomes transcend political differences and the changing political structures within the U.K., including the emergence of a devolved Scottish Parliament and Welsh Assembly in the early 2000s.

During the 1980s and 1990s, concerns were beginning to emerge about what happened to children looked after away from home—children for whom a local authority had assumed a degree of parental responsibility—when they matured into adults. Many struggled to achieve educationally and maintain employment, struggled with relationships and their mental and physical health, and often appeared in other communities such as those of prison or of poverty. However, research identified that no consistent approach was in place in many organizations to measure outcomes for looked-after children (Department of Health and Social Security, 1985).

Research led by Roy Parker and subsequently Harriet Ward identified seven developmental areas or dimensions in a child's life considered critical to achieving satisfactory outcomes (Parker et al., 1991; Ward, 1995): health, education, identity, social presentation, family and social relationships, emotional and behavioural development, and self-care skills. This led to the development of *Looking After Children: Good Parenting, Good Outcomes* (referred to as LAC), a set of materials to assess, plan, record, and review children's progress. The materials were introduced to social services departments in England and Wales from 1995 on.

While the *Looking After Children* program was being implemented, there was growing concern about families, referred through the child protection system, who did not meet the criteria for child protection services but were nevertheless struggling and in need of support (Department of Health, 1995; Department of Health, Social Care Group, 1997). This led to a national debate on the level and types of services that should be offered to vulnerable children.

It was argued that services should be needs-led, and assessment was thought critical to identifying needs and informing the development of services required to meet those needs. This led to the development and implementation of the *Framework for the Assessment of Children in Need and their Families* (Department of Health, Department for Education and Employment, and the Home Office, 2000; National Assembly for Wales, 2001). Its aim was to provide a framework to gather and record information systematically to analyze, understand, and plan to meet the families' needs effectively. Implementation of the *Assessment Framework* was undertaken in England for completion by the end of March 2001, and begun in Wales in 2001.

Development of the Integrated Children's System

Looking After Children and the *Assessment Framework* were each the subject of pilots and evaluation studies which gathered information about implementation and its impact on practice. This was done through snapshot and longitudinal audits, consultations with key stakeholders such as carers, children, and young people, and interviews with those working in social care (Moyers, 1997; Peel, 1998; Scott, 1999, 2000; Cleaver and Walker, 2004). By the early 2000s, both studies had reported, with common messages emerging.

Generally, each set of materials supported practitioners in gathering and recording information about the needs of children, and improved confidence in decision-making and practitioners' abilities to monitor progress. Both sets of materials were thought to increase the involvement of families in social work processes through the clarification of such processes and the development of useful information leaflets for families. The materials were also said to strengthen inter-agency working through an increased understanding of the roles and responsibilities of agencies, increased communication, and a shared approach to, and improved collaboration in, assessments of children.

Many felt, however, that no explicit link existed between these two conceptual frameworks, which operated within the same children's department and often involved the same families. This resulted in some duplication of information gathered. Practitioners also commented that it was difficult to measure a child's progress or the impact of services over time if the child moved between the child protection system and becoming looked after. To fully understand the impact of interventions on a child or young person, a coherent approach was required which gathered information across the three domains of child development, parenting capacity, and family and environmental factors, and on the services planned and delivered from all agencies.

Consequently, the government decided to bring the two approaches together and produce a comprehensive methodology to assess the needs of children and families. The same theoretical framework would underpin all social care interventions with children and their families, whether support was offered in the form of supporting families in their home or through placement in foster or residential care. This was to become known as the Integrated Children's System (ICS).

The development of the Integrated Children's System was also informed by the findings of two significant inquiries in relation to safeguarding children, which have had a considerable impact on policy and practice. The first was the Victoria Climbié Inquiry (Laming, 2003), and the second concerned the conviction of Ian Huntley, a known sex offender, for the murder of two children (House of Commons, 2004). Both identified concerns about the gathering, storing, and sharing of information within and between agencies.

Throughout the development of the children's services reform agenda, there has been a strong and prevailing theme about the importance of improving information sharing within and across key agencies working with children and young people, in whatever sector or capacity. There have been clear statements from the government (Department for Education and Skills, 2006; Welsh Assembly Government, 2006) that good information sharing is seen as the key to successful collaborative working across children's services to improve the outcomes for children and young people.

At the same time, there has been equal emphasis on the promotion of integrated services and multi-agency working. Diverse models for multi-agency working have evolved, including Children's Trusts, Sure Start Children's Centres in England, and the Children and Young People's Framework Partnerships and Flying Start program in Wales.

The development of the Integrated Children's System also took account of national data requirements for children's services which the government had previously mapped out, refined, and related to key social care processes from point of first contact through to referral, assessment, planning, intervention, review, and case closure. The data requirements were incorporated into the ICS, and a series of recording tools, known as the exemplars, were designed to illustrate how this data could be captured as each process was undertaken. The exemplars themselves were the subject of extensive consultations with practitioners and managers, working across services provided to vulnerable children, who informed their development and content. By 2003, it was thought necessary to pilot the ICS to further understand both the complexities of translating this approach into practice and its subsequent impact on practice.

Piloting the Integrated Children's System

The key aims of the Integrated Children's System were:

- to ensure that necessary information is gathered and recorded systematically across services through the key processes of information gathering, assessment, planning, intervention, and review;
- to provide a common and coherent set of processes from first contact with a child and family through to assessment, decision-making, and subsequent interventions to review;
- to build a picture of a child, and the needs of the child, within the context of his or her family and environment;
- to contribute to a common language to describe children's needs and circumstances which can be used by all those concerned with children's well-being; and
- to focus on outcomes for children.

As the ICS was designed as an electronic system, it also aimed to address duplication of assessments undertaken by different agencies, practitioners' skills in analyzing information and in using information technology, and problems with the accessibility and structure of electronic information systems, particularly their ability to produce outputs that could genuinely support practice.

In 2003, two studies were funded to explore use of the ICS. The first, and the focus of this chapter, was a 30-month study led by Royal Holloway, University of London, in partnership with Loughborough, Cardiff, and Open Universities, to look at the issues of multi-agency working. It aimed to provide information to those preparing for implementation, and to identify how the ICS impacted on social work practice, inter-agency working, and information sharing. The second was a 24-month study led by the University of York which explored the issues relating to one agency, namely, social work.

Four pilot sites, representing large rural areas and urban conurbations, participated in the research. Each site immediately audited practice and business processes, IT provision, and staff skills to identify the scale of the change necessary to implement the Integrated Children's System. The authorities took different approaches to implementation, but each incurred costs; all had to tailor or develop their IT systems, release staff for training, and provide ongoing support. The research team alone provided training to more than 700 staff.

Methodology

The research aimed to explore the impact of the Integrated Children's System on practice, insights into how the authorities had implemented the system, and at what points in the delivery of services to children and families implementation resulted in the greatest challenge or change. To do so, the research team gathered information prior to its introduction (Audit 1) to establish a baseline, and again at least three months after implementation (Audit 2). In the first audit, the information was gathered from a sample of children's social care case files; for the second audit, the main source was the information contained within each authority's ICS. The structured sample included case files of children in need and living at home, children in need of protection, those looked after away from home, and young people looked after and preparing for independence.

A total of 150 cases (577 records) was scrutinized in Audit 1, and 143 (785 records) in Audit 2. Only the data from three pilot sites were included in the final analysis, as one site had delayed implementation beyond the time frame of the research.

Information about the impact on collaborative working and information sharing was gathered through the following methods: a scrutiny of blank recording formats used by partner agencies, such as health, education, police, and youth justice, to identify information regularly gathered on individual children; interviews with and questionnaires distributed to service providers and looked-after young people; multi-agency workshops; and field trips to explore the IT used to support the system. Again, data were gathered pre- and post-implementation, and this chapter summarizes some of the key findings; for a fuller discussion, see Cleaver et al. (2008).

Findings

Impact on Social Work Practice

The findings suggest that the degree of change experienced by practitioners was not uniform across children's social care, and that the impact of the Integrated Children's System on practice varied.

Where the ICS made few changes to the records for recording referrals and assessments of *children in need* previously introduced as part of the *Assessment Framework* in 2000, change was experienced to a lesser degree and there was little impact on most aspects of recording practice. Nonetheless, improvements were found in relation to increased recording about whether parents were aware of referrals to children's services, and the outcome of the referral was recorded in more cases.

Change was experienced to a greater degree when new formats were introduced where none or a variety had existed before. This was particularly evident for those working with *children in need of protection*. Before the introduction of the ICS, there was no specific format to ensure that information on some key child protection processes was recorded systematically and consistently across children's services. As a result, it was sometimes difficult to locate information, and when a record was found the quantity and quality of the information varied between cases.

The Integrated Children's System introduced major changes to child protection processes, and it was likely that arrangements required to take account of such changes were not fully established within local authorities during the early stages of implementation. As a result, the impact of change was great, and much of the feedback received by the research team was concerned with increases in paperwork, too much information to record, and meetings and child protection case conferences taking much longer. Nevertheless, audits of social work case files prior to the implementation of the ICS showed that, in general, less information had previously been recorded about children than about their parents or other relevant adults, and that sibling groups had often been considered together. As researchers observed in one case:

The record notes that the three children in this family had suffered serious neglect. The authorities intervened and the appropriate processes were put in place to protect the children, but in the subsequent assessments audited by the research team, a total of 15 words were recorded which related to the needs of these three children compared with far more information recorded about the parents. Admittedly, this was an extreme case, but the tendency to focus more on the needs and circumstances of the parents and other relevant adults compared with children, was consistent across all authorities. (Cleaver et al., 2008, p. 88)

Children within the same family rarely experience abuse in the same way depending on their age, gender, birth position within the family, and relationships with members of the family and with peers (Cleaver, Unell, & Aldgate, 1999; Dunn & McGuire, 1992; Jones & Ramchandani, 1999). However, it was clear from the child protection records that after implementation of the ICS, greater consideration was given to individual children within sibling groups, and more information was recorded about the needs of children which began to readdress the balance of attention between children and parents. Inevitably, of course, this tended to increase practitioner time recording information, and was viewed by some as increased bureaucracy.

The greatest degree of change was experienced by those completing ICS records that replaced an existing system—namely, those relating to *children looked after*. The ICS aimed to address some of the criticism to emerge from the implementation of *Looking After Children*, such as the lack of historical information available about those who enter the care system but have been known to services, and the difficulty in recording information about the parents' capacity to meet the needs of their child and the impact of wider family and environmental issues. In order to address such comments, the previous LAC records underwent radical changes, including a recommendation that all children entering care should have an up-to-date assessment.

The Integrated Children's System has had a mixed impact on the quantity and quality of recording information on looked-after children. An up-to-date core assessment of children who became looked after had resulted in comprehensive baseline information about children's needs being gathered for a greater proportion of children entering the care system. However, there continued to be little consistent and regular assessment of the progress of looked-after children, confirming findings from the audits of *Looking After Children* a decade previously (Moyers, 1997; Scott, 1999).

Generally, improvements were noted in planning for looked-after children, which broadened from a narrower focus on a child's health, education, and family relationships to emotional and behavioural development, and social relationships. This was particularly so for the plans for *young people preparing for independence*. Audits 1 and 2 found that plans took account of the young person's needs in terms of health, education, employment or training, finance, and accommodation, and recorded the supports he or she needed. However, before implementation, the young person's family and social relationships, and emotional and behavioural development, were rarely addressed in the assessment or plan, despite findings from research that isolation and mental health are key factors associated with successful transition to independence (Marsh & Peel, 1999; Stein, 2004). Indeed, young people themselves observed that planning should be about "life planning and not leaving home planning," and promote emotional and mental well-being (A National Voice, 1999). Both these issues were more explicitly addressed in case records completed post-implementation.

The findings also suggest a mixed impact on the recording of reviews for looked-after children. Review chairs welcomed the increased emphasis on outcomes and a more child-centred approach. However, practitioners reported that the changes to some existing records made it more difficult to locate and record information.

Impact on Recording: Social Workers' and Managers' Perceptions

The impact of the Integrated Children's System on social work practice has been significant. The system was thought to increase the amount of time social work practitioners and managers spent using IT. This was partly due to the change from handwritten to predominantly electronic recording, a new process with which practitioners needed to become familiar.

The Integrated Children's System is not an IT system in itself, but the volume and complexity of the information collected in the course of work with children in need and their families means that its use needs to be underpinned by appropriate information technology that is readily accessible to users.

The pilot authorities' projects showed that implementation required local authorities to address wider issues in the development of their IT systems. Single data entry, text handling, data cloning, and information sharing between agencies were all raised as important questions to be resolved. It also highlighted the need to improve the provision of hardware as well as the functionality of the system, and to consider the relationship between the roles of administrative staff and practitioners in their use of IT.

Not only did social workers acknowledge the need to change the way in which they recorded information about children and families, but many also reported changes in the structure of reports and assessments produced and received; some changes were welcomed (greater focus and less narrative), while others were not (unnecessary paperwork). Managers, however, reported that records were easier to access, and helped them to carry out their role more effectively.

Some practitioners were concerned that the system was unable to provide family-friendly documentation. This owed much to the stage of implementation at the point of the research. There had been little time for local authorities to review the way they generated information for children and families from their electronic systems, although work on resolving this had begun.

By the end of the study, the general conclusion of the three pilot authorities was that their IT systems were meeting most of the ICS requirements, though a lack of familiarity and difficulties in functioning, such as the speed of systems saving and printing information, continued to hamper practitioners' uptake and use of the system.

Impact on Collaborative Working and Information Sharing

Practitioners from children's social care, education, health, police, and youth justice were asked to assess the impact of the Integrated Children's System on inter-agency working. Their views were sought on four areas of inter-agency work:

- policy and practice;
- information sharing;
- clarification of roles and responsibilities; and
- the quality of inter-agency working.

Again, data were collected pre- and post-implementation.

In all, 131 professionals participated before implementation of the ICS, and 78 following implementation. This was through a combination of interviews, questionnaires, and focus groups.

Generally, and regardless of the area of inter-agency work under consideration, most professionals who responded assessed that their position had changed little as a result of the ICS. When change was reported, comments were received mainly from health and education, identifying a greater clarity of roles and responsibilities; the implementation of the ICS generated more discussions about improvements in practice. A few thought differently, with one colleague from education reporting that it had resulted in more confusion over roles and responsibilities, while one health professional considered that it had negatively affected the quality of inter-agency working, but did not give further details.

The findings from this study reinforced previous research on the factors that support good information sharing and inter-agency collaboration (Birchall & Hallett, 1995; Kroll & Taylor, 2003), such as an understanding and respect for the roles and responsibilities of other services; good communication; regular contact and meetings; common priorities; inter-agency training; and clear guidelines and procedures for working together.

Personal contacts and professional networks emerged as key to guiding collaborative work and information sharing. Professionals identified a number of ways that enabled such personal contacts to develop, including inter-agency training, regular meetings, joint working arrangements, and multi-agency forums. Personal contacts enabled professionals to more easily clarify or resolve matters, such as the issue of what information could be shared and in what circumstances. However, such contacts needed to be set within a formal framework of clear policies and procedures. Where policies and procedures were not in place, information sharing relied on personal contacts, leading to the potential for inconsistencies in practice, and situations in which legislation and guidance could be open to misinterpretation.

Not unexpectedly, the barriers identified by practitioners were often in circumstances in which many of the factors described above were not in place. A common observation was the difficulty in making the initial contact. Different working structures could become a barrier; for example, school timetables made contacting teachers difficult, and highly structured working practices could hamper contact with family doctors. Crucially, a lack of feedback to those who had referred children or shared information to inform an assessment impacted on many practitioners' reluctance to share information in the future.

Information sharing and collaborative working varied depending on the issue under discussion. Practitioners reported that information sharing was most effective when there were safeguarding concerns about a child, when a child was disabled, or when there were concerns over a child's health or education. Information sharing was less effective when there were concerns over the effects on a child of social exclusion, poverty, and housing. When concerns related to the parents, such as parental mental health, drug and alcohol abuse, learning disabilities, or domestic violence, information sharing was seen as least effective. Professionals from children's and adult services were often reluctant to share information. Infrequent contact between the two services meant that the informal relationships supporting information sharing had not developed;

in addition, adult services were not always viewed as being child-focused (see also Cleaver, Nicholson, Tarr, & Cleaver, 2007), and the protocols for information sharing between children and adult services had not always been agreed to.

The scrutiny of 169 recording formats, submitted by health (92), education (59), youth offending (13), and the police (5), showed that agencies collect a core of the same or similar data items about children and young people with whom they work. However, the variety of ways in which information is both understood and recorded will perhaps need further discussion.

The research identified that all agencies asked for the name of the child, but that this took 20 different forms, including pupil's name, patient's name, forename, your name, young person's name, child's name, and name of young person. Similarly, most formats recorded the child's gender, but six different terms were used, including Male, Female, Male/Female, M/F, and Boy/Girl.

These examples seem trivial, as practitioners will give the same meaning to terms such as name or gender. However, other expressions, such as *child's home address, health surveillance*, or *developmental checks*, are open to different interpretations; indeed, professional discipline, training, and experience affect how practitioners use and understand the same words. Some terms have specific meaning to those with a medical background, but are understood differently by those from social work or education. This can result in a lack of consistency in how terms are interpreted. From the scrutiny of blank formats, for example, it was unclear whether the term *immunization* related to all immunizations, or to immunizations relevant to the child's age; whether *developmental checks* related to the child's current age, developmental history, or developmental assessments; and whether information about *educational achievement* related to examinations sat, to examination results, to both, or to the assessment of educational need.

More generally, the ICS had acted as a catalyst for change. The occurrence of a closer relationship between children's social care, health, and education tended to reflect the emphasis within the participating authorities on improving collaborative working. One pilot site developed an electronic exchange of information between schools and children's social services; nominated members of staff within the schools had access to restricted ICS database information on children in social services; and this initiative was subsequently extended to health, with police and probation services also expressing an interest in developing pilots. A second pilot site had developed protocols for sharing information about the health of looked-after children between health and children's social care.

Conclusion

The Integrated Children's System was developed to support effective practice with children and families by providing a more structured and systematic approach to the processes of direct work, and recording underpinned by good information systems. The development of the conceptual framework was deeply rooted in research, guided by national policy and legislation, and messages from practice that took account of the views of those delivering and receiving services.

The implementation and translation of the ICS into practice has been challenging, and, at the time of the research, has had a variable impact on practice. An overarching finding was that the strategy and timing of the implementation process affected practice. During the early stages, when practitioners were learning new processes, practice temporarily deteriorated. However, once implementation was complete, the pilot authorities identified a number of positive changes to practice, as well as areas of greater challenge.

Improvements to practice were noted in terms of planning. More plans were available for all children in receipt of some service or support, and the general focus of plans on the key areas of health, education, and family relationships had broadened to more consistently include emotional well-being and social relationships. The ICS has put in place a framework that has helped to rebalance the focus of attention in child protection cases from mainly parents to both children and parents, and to consider individual children rather than sibling groups. The ICS has also introduced a framework to gather information about all aspects of a child's life when entering care in order to measure progress over time and to plan effectively if the child returns home.

The increase in inter-agency collaboration was greatest between health, education, and children's social care, and to a lesser degree between these agencies and the police and youth offending teams. The findings suggest that improved inter-agency collaboration was dependent on the existing culture of inter-agency working, the approach to implementing the ICS, and the stage of development. Implementation of the ICS has often provided the catalyst or impetus for further change.

Inevitably, however, improvements were not uniform across children's services. For example, where significant changes to well established local systems were introduced, such as those for looked-after children, the impact was varied. There have been concerns that improvements in recording practice have come at the expense of an increase in the amount and complexity of paperwork or inputting information on IT systems, or of increased bureaucracy.

The ICS has often been, and continues to be, part of the discussion about the role and direction of professional social work in the future. Rightly or wrongly, some practitioners have seen it as contributing to the increasing burden of IT on social workers, reducing their time available for direct work with children and families. Many of these issues have been part of the wider debate for more than two decades, which at times can seem polarized between those who advocate a structured recording system and those who advocate a greater emphasis on direct work; yet the two are not incompatible. As the research has shown, attention to recording could benefit outcomes for children, young people, and their families.

However, the implementation of a highly structured system may have brought into sharp relief the debate about what levels of information should be collected and recorded in order to make informed decisions about children's lives. It will be important to ensure that the principles underpinning the conceptual framework of the ICS—principles that were based on research, policy, and most importantly, messages from practice—are not lost. In time, these debates should be separated out to ensure that changes or revisions to the ICS do not lose sight of this; perhaps in light of these challenges the last word should be given to Winston Churchill: "Success is not final, failure is not fatal: it is the courage to continue that counts."

38

The Search for Best Practice: Themes and Implications

Kathleen Kufeldt
Brad McKenzie

S ome key themes emerge from this exploration of the search for best prac- tice. The first, and arguably the most important, is the growing recogni- tion that child welfare, and child protection in particular, should reflect how well society looks after its children. Looking after children well cannot be achieved without attention to family, hence the second theme of advocacy for family-cen- tred practice. A third theme that is gaining increasing prominence in child wel- fare research is that of promotion of resilience. Recurring as a theme throughout is the importance of evaluating outcomes, and therefore the need for mecha- nisms to achieve that goal. And a final consideration is the challenge of ensur- ing that research, policy, and practice work in harmony. This is taken up in the section on implications.

Looking After Children

Parker and his colleagues (Parker, Ward, Jackson, Aldgate, & Wedge, 1991) con- ceived the *Looking After Children* approach to child welfare practice. It was the first focused attempt to improve outcomes for children in care by targeting the here and now: what needs to be done on a day-to-day basis to enhance children's development. Three chapters in this section discuss the implementation of this system. In the first edition of this text, Jones (2003) described the iterative nature of its development and thus its ability to connect research and policy to actual practice—what is happening at the interface between child welfare serv- ices and the children looked after. The core component is the Assessment and

Action Record that guides practice. The encouraging note is that the emphasis on "good parenting" that the *Looking After Children* (LAC) protocols promote has a dual value. It focuses attention in a proactive fashion on the individual child's developmental needs; at the same time it identifies more general deficiencies in services, and provides agencies with solid information that can be used to improve its services (see, for example, Flynn, Lemay, Ghazal, & Hébert, 2003).

Apart from the proven ability of LAC to improve the quality of care, two particular aspects are worthy of note. These are the potential use of LAC to transform child welfare from a reactive residual service to a more proactive one, as identified above, and the richness of the information provided when data are aggregated (Cleaver et al., 2008; Kufeldt, Simard, Vachon, Baker, & Andrews, 2000; Ward, 1995). Although LAC has been well-established as an approach to "better practice," implementation in Canada is not yet firmly entrenched in practice.

The Importance of Family and Family-Centred Practice

There is ample evidence throughout this book that the best interests and healthy development of children cannot be attained without recognition of the importance of family. Prevention and early intervention programs that engage families can contribute to family preservation. Where maintaining the child within the family is not possible, continued connection with family is desirable, as the earlier chapters on foster care and adoption demonstrate. Scott, in Chapter 37, describes how the United Kingdom's initiatives have expanded beyond the initial development of LAC, first to develop an assessment framework that includes the broader context of parental capacity as well as family and environmental factors, and more recently the promotion of an Integrated Children's System. LAC itself promotes the ideal of partnership between social workers, foster carers, and child's family. Brousseau and her colleagues, in Chapter 9, describe parental involvement as a key component in family restoration, and Chapter 31 in this section walks the reader through the "how to" of family-centred practice.

Resilience

The concept of resilience is gaining increasing prominence in the child welfare discourse (Flynn, Dudding, & Barber, 2006; Gilligan, 1999; Masten, 2001; Masten & Coatsworth, 1998; Masten & Reed, 2002). Of particular value is its shift of focus, including intervention, from the problematic aspects of children's lives to ascertaining and promoting strengths. Gilligan (1999) identifies three key qualities, or components of resilience, that foster care can promote: "a sense of having a secure base in the world, self esteem and self efficacy" (p. 107). Klein, Kufeldt, and Rideout (2006) extend his thesis and present in tabular form common risk and protective factors that affect resilience. These relate to individual traits as well as family, school, and community features. They then demonstrate the link between these factors and the content of the LAC Assessment and Action Records. This is reinforced empirically, using a case study from their research, to illustrate how the use of LAC can promote resilience not only for the children but also for the workers charged with the demanding task of protecting children in care (Kufeldt, McGilligan, Klein, & Rideout, 2006). Chapter 35 reinforces the value of this strength-based approach, and how these can shift services from a problem focus to building on protective factors. In that chapter Donnon and Hammond demonstrate how positive developmental outcomes can be achieved by identifying and utilizing developmental strengths that are similar to those identified in LAC.

Research in the past has identified negative outcomes emanating from child protection and foster care. Such results have tended to identify children needing care as potential problems to be "treated." The growing recognition that these are children who need, and deserve, optimal parental care is a welcome shift. The examples of best practice in this section provide direction for improving outcomes in the future.

Evaluation

In order to improve outcomes for children who need care it is important to understand and be able to measure outcomes. To date, much of outcome research has been retrospective. Newer approaches provide hope that evaluation can be concurrent; they can not only provide information about the here and now, but promote interventions that can actually lead to better outcomes. The Donnon and Hammond model (Chapter 35), and the LAC Assessment and Action Records, both provide positive, outcomes-focused data that can in turn be used in iterative fashion to affect policy. Scott, in Chapter 37, demonstrates the compatibility between good practice, structured record-keeping, and positive outcomes. This in turn can affect policy in a positive direction. In Chapter 36, a set of outcome-oriented indicators are outlined that are relatively easy to collect, with some adaptation to existing data management systems.

It is interesting to note that emerging best practice approaches include indicators that can be used to evaluate the results of child welfare services, not simply in terms of outputs, but with respect to the effects on children themselves. This is a promising development in such a complex field.

Implications for Policy, Practice, and Research

The chapters in this section together demonstrate the value of guided practice in improving the quality of interventions. They also reinforce the usefulness of empiricism in affecting policy. There are barriers to be overcome, as Canadians have discovered when promoting LAC. A national study, involving six provinces and completed in 2000, showed promise, but various personnel changes at the federal and provincial levels, as well as within the project, affected momentum.

One exception is the considerable progress achieved in Ontario. A brief discussion of factors that have influenced progress in that province may help to illuminate the ingredients of successful integration of research, policy, and practice. At the outset, four of the larger Children's Aid Societies were involved simultaneously in a national as well as a provincial project (Flynn & Biro, 1998; Flynn & Ghazal, 2001; Kufeldt et al., 2000). The national project (Kufeldt et al., 2000) was funded by Health and Welfare Canada. Two of the key players in the United Kingdom initiative, Helen Jones and Harriet Ward, were engaged to provide consultation throughout as well as the initial training. Ontario participants invited to participate in the training included not only the project's designated Children's Aid Society project coordinators but also representatives from the government's Crown Ward Review panel, the provincial study team (Flynn & Biro, 1998), and the Ontario Association of Children's Aid Societies (OACAS). Crown Ward reviewers and the OACAS were enthusiastic, and became champions of the method. The OACAS in particular, in consultation with the provincial government, has continued to promote LAC as a best practice, with Robert Flynn of the University of Ottawa, provincial investigator in consecutive provincial projects, managing the aggregation and analysis of data (e.g., see Flynn, Lemay, Ghazal, and Hébert, 1993). As noted above, the national initiatives faltered, but Flynn was successful in obtaining funding for further provincial studies.

The Assessment and Action Records are now mandatory in Ontario for children and youth who have been in care one year or more, and LAC is an important element in raising the quality of care. The age of independence for youth is under discussion, and there are many who advocate raising it from 18 to 24. Capacity is also building for longitudinal research, and agencies are being trained in the use of statistical packages so they can do their own data analysis. These advancements enable the use of data on three levels (clinical, agency, and central administration) in order to influence those three levels of practice. This has potential to truly integrate research, policy, and practice. None of this would have been possible without co-operation between government, agencies, the OACAS, and academia.[1] Such co-operation mirrors that in the successful arrangements in Australia, as illustrated in Chapters 32 and 34.

Nevertheless, progress is not always smooth. Scott describes the hurdles facing the United Kingdom's efforts in developing its Integrated Children's System. To offset some of the resistance to more complex forms of outcome research, Trocmé and his colleagues offer a more limited set of outcome indicators that management can use to evaluate its services. The description of developments in Ontario, the NOM project described in Chapter 36, and the contributions from Australia demonstrate the value of partnership between policy-makers, practitioners, and researchers. Although there is yet some distance to go, this partnership, and the integration of research, policy, and practice on which it is based, are key elements in improving services for children and families.

Note

1   The editors wish to thank Bernadette Gallagher and Myra Hurst of OACAS for an informative discussion regarding the use of LAC in Ontario.

PART VI

The Future of Child Welfare

Introduction

In this final section we focus on the future of child welfare. In Chapter 39 we identify some of the critical issues to be faced if children and families are to receive the quality of service that we would wish for our own. These issues range from micro-level concerns such as attention to all key stakeholders, including fathers and foster carers, to problems at the macro level. Macro-level factors include structural factors that affect the ability of families to care for their children, and the challenges posed by the increased diversity of populations served.

In Chapter 40 we return to the eight-point research agenda developed fifteen years ago by Hudson and Galaway (1995). Doing so enables us to assess the progress achieved in the intervening years and to determine what might be the future directions for research, policy, and practice.

39

Critical Issues in Current Practice

Kathleen Kufeldt
Brad McKenzie

When we contemplate the issues still to be faced in child protection and child welfare, there is room for optimism but not for complacency. Our optimism is inspired by increasing recognition not only of the complexity of this field of practice, but also of the issues that have yet to be addressed in any comprehensive way. There is no room for complacency unless and until they cease to be problematic.

Forgotten Fathers

In the first edition of this book we wrote of the stigmatization of women and the forgotten voices of various stakeholders. This edition includes research that helps to address that imbalance. For instance, Badry (Chapter 27) provides insight into the backgrounds of mothers of fetal alcohol-affected children. Currently stigmatized and blamed, when given a voice they emerge as victims themselves who may yet have much to offer their children if drawn into partnership with the providers of service. Fathers, on the other hand, continue to be absent from the child welfare discourse. Social work records provide little information about them. Despite the acknowledged value of inclusive foster care, contact with family for children in care is not always vigorously pursued; contact with fathers receives even less attention. Children lose this possible source of support and continuity; they lose their paternal grandparents and other relatives as well. Chapter 26 draws attention to this gap, and identifies some recommendations about how this imbalance can be addressed. The inherent bias in child protection toward holding mothers accountable but forgetting fathers is compounded by the lack of attention to the importance of foster fathers. Fostering is primarily viewed as women's work. An encouraging note is that Fernandez's (2009) longitudinal study identifies the value of foster father engagement. This knowledge needs to be more widely disseminated, and research in this area expanded, to promote a change in practice.

Forgotten Foster Carers

The lack of attention to fathers is paralleled by a failure to utilize the potential of foster carers to assist in case planning and to promote the well-being of the children. It appears that, as with other "women's work" such as daycare and care of the elderly, foster care remains seriously undervalued. This undervaluation is not only monetary but relates as well to a failure to include the foster family as valuable partners in the care of and planning for the child. Yet it is this family that has most potential for healing or hurting the child or young person in placement. A closely related issue is the well-being of the foster carer's own family. Swan and Twigg, in Chapter 13, draw needed attention to the children of foster carers. They are part of the parenting circle provided to children coming into care, but their contributions—and their own needs—have for the most part been ignored.

Ambiguity of purpose also hinders full exploitation of the potential contribution of foster families. Chapter 10 indicates some of the ways in which foster families can be recruited as partners for change and in enhancing long-term goals for children in care. The growing use of the *Looking After Children* (LAC) Assessment and Action Records shows promise in this regard. Where properly used, they encourage co-operation and collaboration between all involved in the responsibilities of parenting children and young persons in care.

Children's Best Interests and Parental Rights: Maintaining a Balance

A particularly critical issue is the need to maintain a balance in child protection between the rights of children and the rights of their parents. Section 7 of the *Canadian Charter of Rights and Freedoms* has been invoked to uphold the rights of parents in child welfare proceedings (Thomas, 2003). Yet upholding parental rights can at times be a life and death issue, as has been the case for many children such as Matthew Vaudreuil (Gove, 1995) and Zachary Turner (Bagby, 2007; Markesteyn & Day, 2006). Gove's inquiry reflects patterns very similar to those identified in investigations of child deaths in the United Kingdom (House of Commons Health Committee, 2003; Laming, 2009; Parton, 2003). Concerns have included lack of inter-agency communication and co-operation, the provision of voluntary services when protective procedures were needed, and, as with Zachary Turner, inadequate risk assessment. The compelling messages that have emerged from the research presented in this text are:

- child welfare services, and particularly child protection, must be administered in a child-centred way;
- the child as the central focus can and should be maintained without severing family ties;
- the safety of the child and the likelihood of positive outcomes are enhanced when family, foster carers, health, school, and other services work in collaboration and with open communication; and
- differential response systems will allow more services to be targeted to where the need exists.

However, the positive intentions of differential and alternative response systems are lost if there is no parallel commitment to meeting the needs of families diverted from the investigative and protection route. The general practice is to divert families to voluntary services in the community. Such services are too often under-resourced and lack the capacity to meet the needs of all families who are referred.

The Voices of Youth

A promising development in the child welfare field is that of allowing the voice of youth to be heard. Pioneering work began in the United Kingdom with a *Who Cares? Conference,* and the development of the *Who Cares? Society.* These efforts were replicated in Calgary in 1979, the Year of the Child, with a conference for Alberta youth in care (Allison & Johnson, 1981). At that conference the seeds were sown for Canada's now flourishing National Youth in Care Network (Andrews & Manser, 2001; <http://www.youthincare.ca>). The Network has produced fine research of its own to advance advocacy, particularly in the area of education. Similar organizations have sprung up in other countries, and many provinces have provincial affiliates of the national body. It is also encouraging to see the efforts of some child welfare agencies in reaching out to youth. For example, within the General Child and Family Services Authority in Manitoba, a Youth Engagement Strategy has been developed as part of its operational plan. Each agency within the authority has undertaken activities to implement this strategy within its own jurisdiction, and to provide ongoing reports to ensure that youth in care have a voice about the services they need.

Another positive development is the expansion of Child and Youth Advocate Offices, which have now been established in most Canadian jurisdictions. The major purpose of these offices is to ensure that children's rights are upheld both in general terms and in the particular, as they have the ability and mandate to respond to concerns expressed by individual children. MacLean and Howe (2009) provide a useful summary of the characteristics of advocacy offices across Canada. As these authors note, children affected by the child welfare system are a primary focus, but several provincial offices have a broader mandate extending beyond child welfare to include children affected by other government services (e.g., children in the juvenile justice system and/or the education system).

Although most offices have roles that include both individual or case advocacy in response to complaints and systemic or policy advocacy in response to the broader issues affecting the rights of children, there is significant variation in the emphasis on these two roles among offices. For example, Saskatchewan, Manitoba, and British Columbia have been more active in recent years in releasing reports on systemic issues. In a few provinces these offices have taken on responsibilities for reviewing service delivery issues pertaining to child deaths. Although most offices have independent legislation, child and youth advocacy functions are set out in Alberta and in Manitoba, and in a few provinces provisions are included pertaining to the Ombudsman. MacLean and Howe note that all child advocacy offices have played a valuable role in promoting the rights of children and responding to the voices of children; however, these offices have little influence on matters falling within federal jurisdiction, such as divorce and custody, immigration and refugees, and a number of general issues affecting First Nations children living on reserves.

Equally encouraging is the existence of the flourishing Cape Breton University Children's Rights Centre. Executive director Katherine Covell and her colleague Brian Howe have done sterling work in raising awareness and understanding of children's rights in Canada (Covell & Howe, 2001; Howe & Covell, 2007).

At the grassroots level, the implementation of the LAC records enables children 10 years and up to have a direct voice in the assessment of progress and the care planning that occurs. There are limitations, however. LAC is not in universal use. Where it is part of agency work, its use tends to be confined to those who have been in care for more than a year. Yet the occasion of coming into care is as puzzling and confusing to young people as many of the events that occur afterwards. Involvement at an early stage might do much to alleviate anxiety and contribute to better planning. Another limitation is the failure to ensure that children and youth in care have the opportunity to meet with their worker without others present. There have been complaints from young people that they were questioned in the presence of an abusive parent or with foster carers present. Such instances inhibit their ability to speak frankly and freely.

Although much remains to be done, significant strides have been made in the last 15 years in ensuring that children and young people have a voice in how they are cared for.

Risk Assessment or Needs Assessment?

A logical corollary to the various messages conveyed in this text is that *comprehensive* assessment is crucial at the moment a child first comes to the attention of child welfare services. We deliberately stress that any assessment should be comprehensive, and this would extend well beyond the use of safety and risk assessment tools currently in use. As Markesteyn and Day (2006) conclude:

> In the search for tools to guide practice, it is generally acknowledged that there is no tool that can be used in the absence of competent worker judgment. Any tools, such as "safety assessment" and "risk management systems", should be used to enhance, if not substantiate, the professional judgment of the social worker as cases become more complex and demanding. They are not intended and should not become a substitute for competency. (Volume II, p. 97)

Gillingham and Humphreys (2009) note a further caution about the use of risk assessment tools. In an ethnographic study, they found that some risk assessment scores were manipulated to support workers' own judgment, rather than their being the primary source of assessment.

Child safety issues suggest a focus on determining risk; alternative family support responses suggest that the priority should be on identifying needs. A truly comprehensive assessment would include both factors. It would also entail conferring with all those with an interest in the child, or who might be in possession of information that can contribute to a full and complete assessment (e.g., health personnel, teachers, etc). In Chapter 25, Christianson-Wood notes that good risk assessment is both art and science. We would add that this also applies to assessment in general within the child welfare field. The application of any scientific method is only as good as the ability of the person using it. As Markesteyn and Day (2006) point out, no technical tool or method is a substitute for competency. A comprehensive assessment should not only identify the degree of risk, but also family and child needs, along with the actions required to prevent harm and to enhance child development and well-being. This requires well-educated and experienced professionals at the front line in child welfare.

Prevention

In the first edition of this book there were dedicated chapters on prevention and family support related to the theme of family wellness (MacLeod & Nelson, 2003), and the Family Wellness Project funded in Ontario by Human Resources Development Canada in the late 1990s (Cameron, 2003; Pancer et al., 2003; Peirson, Nelson, & Prilleltensky, 2003). The current focus has shifted some-what from family wellness initiatives to differential response, resilience, and broader policy attention to early years programming. Prevention and family support emerge as an important theme in differential response (Chapter 6), where it was noted that this reform may increase the level of support services to some families, although it is not a substitute for ensuring availability of a wide range of outreach and community prevention services. Prevention as com-munity-building in Aboriginal communities was discussed in Chapter 22, while Chapter 24 identified the importance of linking prevention to socio-economic improvements in order to realize long-term changes to the incidence rate of neglect in these communities. Approaches to resilience vary significantly. Many focus on individual attributes that reinforce resilience; resilience is also reinforced by community resources and family-centred practice.

One of the difficulties with many prevention programs is the ability to demonstrate positive outcomes and cost-effectiveness. Early results invariably seem promising, as was the case in many family preservation programs, and a broad reach early intervention for young children and their families, known as *Sure Start*, in the United Kingdom. Evaluation over the longer term has been less compelling. This may have to do with the persistence of systemic disadvantage and inadequate follow-through. Many of the lessons reported earlier about promising programs still apply. Unfortunately, there has been no widespread effort to act on this knowledge, and to implement new approaches based on this information.

The book edited by Prilleltensky, Nelson, and Peirson (2001) provides one of the most comprehensive descriptions of the links between programs to pro-mote family wellness and programs to prevent child maltreatment. They out-lined an ecological wellness framework that connects child, parent and family, community and society, and includes examples of resources, values, policies, and programs to not only prevent child maltreatment but also promote family and community well-being. Some of the programs and interventions to achieve these outcomes are in place, but there continue to be serious gaps.

The intervention framework outlined by these authors is a promotion-prevention-protection continuum. At the promotion level, proactive universal policies and programs, such as accessible child care, need to be available to all families. At the prevention level, policies and programs need to target families at high risk of maltreatment. For example, this may include home visiting and parent support services that will reach all those parents who are more at risk of neglecting or abusing their children. Protection services provided to those families where maltreatment has occurred is the final level, and these services are to be designed to prevent further maltreatment from occurring. Current protection services, and extended services based on a differential response model, are examples of this emphasis. The involvement of services and programs from outside the child welfare system is important at all levels, but particularly important at the promotion and prevention ends of the continuum. Improved policy and program coordination, along with evidence from the research about what works, are important in realizing the goals associated with this framework.

Primary Prevention or Promotion

Broad support services available to all families are important to the promotion component of the continuum, but increased intervention pertaining to poverty and other structural barriers is also essential. Chapters 21, 22, and 24 documented the connections in Aboriginal communities between structural issues, such as poverty and poor housing, and child neglect. Wharf (in Kufeldt, Este, McKenzie, & Wharf, 2003) discusses how the private troubles in child welfare interventions largely overshadow public issues, such as poverty, that are major causes of child maltreatment. In some respects this is old news. For example, in 1975, the National Council of Welfare observed that "one of the fundamental characteristics of the child welfare system has not changed appreciably over the years; its clients are still overwhelmingly drawn from the ranks of Canada's poor" (National Council of Welfare, 1975, p. 2). Even though most families in poverty do not neglect their children, poor children are vastly overrepresented in the child welfare system, and this remains as true today as it was then.

Recently there has been increased attention to the importance of the social determinants of health (Fernandez, MacKinnon, & Silver, 2010; Senate of Canada—Subcommittee on Population Health, 2009; see also Chapter 24); these are an important focus in poverty reduction and the promotion of family wellness. Yet there are somewhat contradictory policy directions at work in Canada on this issue. On the one hand there has been increased attention to the importance of poverty reduction, particularly in some provinces, promoted by advocacy groups and broadly-based anti-poverty coalitions like Campaign 2000. There have also been modest improvements to the Canada Child Tax Benefit and Working Income Tax Benefit for low-income families. On the other hand, income inequality is growing in Canada (Osberg, 2008), and the social costs of child poverty in Canada are estimated at approximately $40 billion annually (Finn, 2007).

Recent reforms in Canada have included reductions in the Goods and Services Tax (GST), some reduction in income tax, and reduced corporate taxes. Although some of these were initiated prior to the 2008 recession, the combined effects of lower taxation revenues and increased government investment in infrastructure designed to stimulate the economy following the recession have resulted in a new era of operating deficits. There is a real risk that deficit concerns at both the federal and provincial levels will place poverty reduction on the back burner, and lead to lower investment in programs that can make a difference to vulnerable families.

A powerful advocate for reframing our approaches to child neglect is Garbarino (1992, 1995; Garbarino & Kostelny, 1992). In his research he has plotted abuse and neglect incidence in terms of geographical location to identify what he refers to as toxic environments. In these and later texts he challenges readers to move from a victim-blaming stance to examining the systemic forces that affect children and families. Thus he provides powerful arguments for allocating resources toward creating nurturing communities.

Secondary Prevention or Early Intervention

We have argued elsewhere that the shift to differential response may promote greater attention to the concrete needs of families who are receiving child welfare services. It is also apparent that community work and community-based services in child welfare are essential to building community capacity in addressing goals related to prevention and child and family well-being. Wharf (in Kufeldt et al., 2003) has also argued that child welfare workers should give greater attention to reporting about the social conditions faced by the families receiving child welfare services. Child welfare practice, as it is currently organized, involves seeing parents and children on an individualized basis, with limited opportunities to see how often their situations are shared by others, and how the more general social disadvantages they face affect their ability to cope. More efforts need to be made to bring parents or families together for social support or problem-solving purposes. In addition, the collection and compilation of more data is necessary in strengthening arguments for policies that will address these structural needs and help to prevent child maltreatment.

MacLeod and Nelson (2003) completed a meta-analysis of evaluation studies conducted on early intervention and family support programs. The 56 programs included in this analysis conform more to the notion of secondary prevention or selectively targeted programs in that they are designed to reach families who are at higher risk of maltreating their families. Some of the general outcomes emerging from this study are noted below.

- Intensive family preservation programs that are flexible, consumer-driven, strengths-based, and accompanied by social support are more beneficial.
- Home visitation programs that are longer than six months, proactive rather than reactive, and begin early (prenatally or at birth) are more effective.
- Proactive interventions are generally more effective than reactive programs.
- These types of intervention are not a cure for poverty.

Cameron (2003), in his discussion of programs that work, notes that one shot, unidimensional interventions are not good enough, and that comprehensive programs with multiple components tailored to the needs of families are more effective.

The work by Cameron and his colleagues from the *Partnerships for Children and Families Project* at the Faculty of Social Work, Wilfrid Laurier University, has been instrumental in drawing attention to best practices in early intervention and support. Results from the final report of a recent research project that examined the impact of institutional settings on front-line practice note that service providers at decentralized, more accessible service delivery sites were able to establish a higher proportion of co-operative and appreciative helping relationships with children and parents (Cameron, Hazineh, & Frensch, 2010; see also Chapter 7). As well, parents at accessible sites, which were co-located with other services, described being connected with a much broader range of services and supports, and were more likely to rate these services and supports as sufficient to meet their needs than those at more centralized delivery sites. Parents at more accessible sites were also more likely to accept the involvement of the child welfare agency with their family and more likely to be satisfied with the services they received. These findings reinforce the value of community-based services and collaborative partnerships as important attributes in the development of helpful early intervention programs.

Tertiary Prevention or Protection

There are also serious questions related to the efficacy of the reactive or tertiary prevention end of the child welfare continuum, a primary focus of this text. Coady, Cameron, and Adams (2007) identify system design issues (see also Chapter 7) in arguing that the Anglo-American child protection framework sees all challenges faced by families as relevant only to the extent of their influence on the parenting environment for their children. The problems of individuals are largely isolated from the social environment in which they are located. This contrasts with some of the child and family welfare systems in continental Europe, which focus more directly on family wellness and seldom if ever sever links between children and families, and where many families are offered higher levels of assistance from the state and community to raise their children. More flexible response systems, increased use of intermediary services (e.g., mediation, family group conferences, other community organizations), family-friendly placement options (e.g., joint placements for parents and children where feasible, increased use of kinship networks), and a strengths-based, supportive approach to building relationships with families are advocated.

In Canada, in 2000, the Canadian Association of Social Workers (CASW) launched the project *Creating Conditions for Good Practice* in child welfare. It analyzed 983 surveys from child welfare workers across the country (Herbert, 2007), and identified factors that would encourage good practice as well as some of the challenges and the complexities of child welfare work. Its findings reinforce comments made elsewhere in this book, and in the conclusions we draw later in this chapter. They include the need for job-specific training for all new staff, increased fiscal resources, more services to meet the needs of children and families, and visible supports for good practice.

Other concerns consistent with those identified in this book include the undervaluation of child protection practice in social work education, the need for good clinical supervision, manageable caseloads, and staff who are both competent and qualified. Further criticism included the need for increased engagement with community agencies and organizations, and the failure to learn from or implement recommendations emanating from reviews. A meeting with the National Youth in Care Network resulted in the following recommendations from their representatives:

- have smaller caseloads;
- listen to youth;
- do not give up on young people;

- be better advocates; and
- above all, remember that a social worker should be someone who cares.

Herbert noted a decline over time in the value of child welfare work in the public domain, and little awareness of why child welfare intervention is required. She also commented on the fact that much is known about creating environments where children will prosper, including poverty reduction, but there seems little political will to make it happen.

Diversity Issues

A major challenge for social work in general, and child welfare in particular, is the widening of populations served. Aboriginal people were the original inhabitants of what is now known as Canada; these descendants are often recognized as "first peoples," and therefore somewhat distinct from other racial and ethnic groups in Canada. As documented by Blackstock (2003) and others in this book, the issue of colonialism sets Aboriginal people somewhat apart from other groups. However, intermarriage, along with differences in language, culture, and traditions among First Nations and between First Nations and other Aboriginal groups (see Chapter 23) demands respect for the principle of diversity in designing and implementing programs and services with both Indigenous people and other populations in Canada.

Canada and other developed countries have become host to growing immigrant and refugee populations, and different patterns of child-rearing, as well as views about the rights of children, can pose special challenges in intervention and relationship building within these communities. This further aggravates the dilemmas and controversies that plague child welfare more generally.

There are also other diversity issues, including the design and provision of services to those who are developmentally or physically challenged or those with differing sexual and identity orientations. Part III was devoted to Indigenous issues in child welfare. We comment briefly on other selected diversity issues here in an effort to encourage more attention to, and recognition of, these and other diversity issues within the field of child welfare.

Growing Immigrant Populations

Canada, like many countries in the Western world, is affected by an increasing immigrant and refugee population. Many adjust well to their new country. Some struggle to find work, and to have professional qualifications accepted by their new country (Este & Ngo, 2006). There may be cultural clashes, and cultural differences can emerge within different generations of the same family. For some families the conflicts may emerge for children in their adolescent years around issues related to supervision and autonomy. For others, contact with the child welfare system may be precipitated by inappropriate disciplinary measures which trigger allegations of abuse based on Canadian laws and customs. Adjustment is more difficult for refugee families, and in many cases, children and youth have been affected by the trauma of war and related violence (see Chapter 29). For some, even those who have spent time in refugee camps, survival meant belonging to a gang, and that experience is played out in gang activities in their new environment.

When children of immigrant families enter the care system, there is the further problem of maintaining connections not only with family but with their language and cultural roots. There has been limited attention to issues pertaining to cultural continuity, and the need for cultural competence in child welfare practice with immigrant and refugee children, families, and communities (Este, in press).

International Development

In addition to problems on the domestic front, there are pressing problems elsewhere in the world, some linked to peacekeeping initiatives, some to appeals from Third World countries calling for humanitarian aid. Countries are no longer isolated or insulated from one another, and international development work for the social work profession has become increasingly complex.

The challenge in assisting developing nations is to avoid repeating the mistakes made with respect to Indigenous people around the world. Despite knowledge of the past, considerable funds are expended in establishing orphanages rather than promoting family-based care. Nor is international adoption the ideal solution: it is more likely than not to remove the healthiest children, and it deprives the child and the kinship network of their right to ongoing relationships. Chapter 29 contributes to the discourse by outlining the real challenges that must be addressed if the children of developing nations are to receive the quality of care and enhanced life chances that all children deserve. There are clear implications for social work education.

A somewhat specialized but very important issue is the sexual exploitation of children. This is a global issue that is often referred to as the "commercial sexual exploitation of children" (Barnitz, 2001). Exploitation takes several forms, including child pornography, targeting particular children over the Internet, and trafficking children for sexual purposes. Advocacy groups have been developed to address this issue, and new laws have been passed, but a more coordinated local and global response is needed to address this issue.

Services for Lesbian, Gay, Bisexual, Transgendered, and Questioning Youth

There is limited research in the child welfare field that focuses on the needs of lesbian, gay, bisexual, transgendered, questioning, or two-spirited youth in the Canadian context. However, the Child Welfare League of America and the Lambda Legal Defense and Education Fund launched a joint initiative in 2002 to document the needs of LGBTQ youth in the United States. This project, called "Fostering Transitions," was designed to gain a better understanding of the needs, resources, and competencies required to support LGBTQ youth (Woronoff & Estrada, 2006).

Sexual orientation develops at an early stage, but these children and youth face a number of special challenges. These include lack of acceptance, negative responses or abuses from both family members and peers, and reluctance to disclose their gender orientation because of the fear of how others will respond. Positive identity development, a challenge for all adolescents, is much more difficult in these circumstances. Four adjustment phases have been identified for gay/lesbian youth (Cooley, 1998):

- sensitization: discovering same-sex feelings of attraction;
- identity confusion: reacting to the same-sex attraction;
- identity assumption: discovering that one is gay; and
- commitment: adopting the gay/lesbian identity.

Within the child welfare system, appropriate responses are hampered by the lack of recognition of both sexual and identity orientation issues among youth, and uncertainty among workers about how best to respond to youth in care, and others receiving services, who have questions about these issues. Also important is the need to educate caregivers about how to respond to LGBTQ children in their care, or children who may identify as such during their placement experience.

Ryan (2009) notes that it should not be assumed that families will not be supportive to their LGBTQ children, and there are more resources now than in the past, both in the community and online, to assist youth and those seeking advice on how to be supportive. However, much more needs to be done to increase the capacity of the child welfare system to respond to these youth. In one U.S. study, Ragg, Patrick, and Ziefert (2006) report on results from interviews with 21 youth who had received child welfare services. Based on these interviews, a number of practice competencies were identified. These were:

- "tuning in" to understand how the youth experiences life in the system;
- helping the youth resolve challenges with his or her sexual identity;
- advocating for standards of respect inclusive of gay and lesbian youth;
- responding to each youth as an individual separate from his or her sexual identity group;
- searching for, and supporting, strengths in the young person;
- affirming the youth's internal experiences and struggles;
- normalizing the young person's feelings;
- remaining open by avoiding too much judgment and advice-giving;
- remaining engaged in a supportive fashion; and
- keeping an open mind in order to explore new situations and feelings with the youth.

Education and Training of Child Welfare Workers

The pervasive message emerging from this coverage of the various aspects of child welfare research, policy, and practice is the complexity of this field. This is compounded by the difficulty in achieving good outcomes, or indeed consensus about desired outcomes.

There are dilemmas related to the three arms of research, policy, and practice. Research is needed; however, good research is dependent on access to children and families served, and this is not a straightforward process. Policy intentions are too often subverted by unanticipated, unintended consequences. Front-line practice is arguably the most complex of all social work tasks, particularly in child welfare, yet is too often carried out by workers with limited experience and without adequate training, education, and supervision.

Although some schools of social work offer specialized courses in child welfare, and a few offer a child welfare specialization, there are no required courses in child welfare, despite the fact that many graduates will at least begin their careers in this field. Too many do not stay, overwhelmed not only by the stressful nature of this work, but also by excessive bureaucratic demands. For example, various studies have demonstrated that a greater proportion of time is spent on documentation than on face-to-face contact with clientele. Yet as Scott reminds us in Chapter 37, record-keeping is important and has value. Nevertheless, it is essential to ensure a balance between record-keeping for planning and accountability purposes and time for direct service provision. It is also incumbent on management to ensure that required documentation has direct value to service providers. Good examples of such are contained in Chapters 32 and 35.

As noted elsewhere, decision-making in child protection is very often a life and death issue, and this does require precise documentation. In addition, any decision or intervention in childhood has lifelong consequences for those most affected by the decision. Should we not therefore allocate this work to the best and most experienced of workers? Should we not establish internships before new workers are expected to make these life and death decisions?

The critical issues noted in this chapter have been summarized in a disaggregated form, but progress on these and other issues discussed in the book will be enhanced by more attention to the interface between policy, practice, and research. We focus on this theme in the final chapter after first giving attention to how dominant theories in child welfare and research methodologies must inform these connections. We then update the eight-point research agenda originally developed by Galaway and Hudson in 1995.

40

The Policy, Practice, and Research Connection: Are We There Yet?

Kathleen Kufeldt
Brad McKenzie

This final chapter examines the current policy, practice, and research connection. As indicated, we begin with a summary of the theoretical underpinnings of child welfare research and practice, followed by discussion of methodological challenges inherent in social work research. After exploring the state of the art with respect to connecting research, policy, and practice, we conclude, as in the 2003 edition, by using Galaway and Hudson's (1995) eight-point research agenda as a barometer of progress.

Theory-Building

The noted pioneer in the professionalization of child welfare practice, Norman Polansky, once declared that there is nothing as practical as a good theory. Time has proven him correct as we observe the evolution of new and better ways of serving children and families. It is encouraging to note the increasingly solid theoretical basis for child welfare research, and indeed for innovative and effective practice.

A primary underpinning for all our endeavours continues to be that of attachment theory. This theory has been further enriched by Bowlby's efforts to embed it within ethology. In doing so, he has drawn on the work of ethologists such as Lorenz, who explored activity within the animal kingdom—colourfully illustrated by his encounter with the greylag goose (Lorenz, 1952, 1966). The connection between attachment and ecological theories has enhanced our understanding of attachment as a necessary survival mechanism (Bowlby, 1988,

1990). Without secure attachment, the young child, like the young gosling, will not fare well. In infancy, lack of secure attachment may be manifested by "failure to thrive"; in older children, by a variety of behavioural indicators. In designing the *Looking After Children* Assessment and Action Records, Parker and his colleagues have used attachment and developmental theory well in their identification and operationalization of the necessary steps to healthy adulthood (Parker, Ward, Jackson, Aldgate, & Wedge, 1991).

Bronfenbrenner (1979) and Garbarino (1992), in turn, have influenced social work activity in positive ways through their explanation and application of ecological theory. Ecological theory draws attention to the different levels within human systems, from individual through to intermediate and macro societal systems. As noted in Chapter 37, application of this theory is very much in evidence in the design of the Integrated Children's System (ICS) in the U.K. In a radical departure from locating problems within an individual, ICS draws attention not only to children's developmental progress, but also to family variables and to strengths and stressors within the larger environment (meso- and macro-systems).

Biddle's conceptualization of role theory (1966, 1979) has contributed to a clearer understanding of the complexity of foster care. It assists in bringing clarity to the somewhat different roles of foster family and family of origin parenting. The theory sheds light on the difference, yet interconnectedness, of the roles and obligations of the members of the foster care role-set: child, foster carers, family, and social workers. This in turn contributes to role consensus, with congruency of perceptions and expectations. Such consensus and congruency is necessary if all members of the role-set are to work in harmony for the well-being of the child.

Role theory, together with attachment theory, has influenced the expanded application of inclusive foster care (see Chapter 10). The various examples of best practice within this text draw on knowledge of child development theory and resilience. Writers such as Leibenberg, Masten, and Ungar (Leibenberg & Ungar, 2009; Masten, 2001; Masten, Best, & Garmezy, 1990; Ungar, 2004) are becoming well known as proponents of the value of resilience theory. In turn, resilience theory is emerging as a valuable component of best practice design (see Chapter 35, as well as Flynn, Dudding, & Barber, 2006; Klein, Kufeldt, & Rideout, 2006). McAuley, Pecora, and Rose (2006) echo similar theoretical underpinnings, and make apt use of Erikson's stage theory (1968, 1985) in addressing effective interventions for young people leaving care.

Methodological Challenges

As the preceding paragraphs indicate, the underlying theoretical bases for child welfare practice are relatively well developed. In order to ensure that they are entrenched in research in ways that enhance both policy and practice, there are challenges to overcome. This section addresses some of the methodological challenges. In brief, they consist of:

- the need to make explicit the theoretical background of any research or demonstration project;
- barriers associated with sampling;
- balancing quantitative and qualitative methods;
- use and misuse of statistical analysis;
- issues related to generalization; and
- translation of findings into policy and practice.

Explaining Theory

Despite strong theoretical foundations, there is a tendency in social work research to assume that these foundations are well understood by consumers of the research. Hence, too often, the theory is implicit. This may not obstruct the consumers' understanding of the messages contained therein; however, this limitation often interferes with the consolidation or advancement of theory-building in the field of child protection and child welfare.

Barriers to Obtaining Adequate and Appropriate Samples

Sampling in child welfare research is, in the first place, very dependent on engagement and partnership with child welfare agencies. The success of the CIS reported in Chapters 1 to 5 was made possible through successful negotiations with the 13 different child welfare authorities in Canada, as well as with potential funders—no easy task. Another sampling challenge is that of accessing a full range of indicators. For instance, the National Child Welfare Outcomes Indicator Matrix featured in Chapter 36 was originally designed to reflect data that would be readily available, thus limiting its scope. Over time, some of these indicators have expanded to reflect the need for additional information.

Access to children is even more complicated. Parental consent is required. In the case of permanent wards of the government, this consent must come from a Director of Child Welfare. Access to temporary wards normally requires consent from the Director and from the children's parents. A survey of runaway and homeless youth (Kufeldt & Nimmo, 1987) was initially stalled by an ethics committee on the grounds that there was no intention to first seek parental consent. Clearly, young people who have run from an abusive situation, whether at home or in care, could not be expected to agree to such a condition. For children in care, frequent moves can be a further inhibitor.

If the study is commissioned by a government department in the first place, however, many hurdles can be overcome. For example, a study of former wards of the government (Kufeldt, Simard, Tite, & Vachon, 2003) was possible because of the government's ability to search databases such as motor vehicle registrations and addresses of former foster carers in order to find graduates of their system. Such records are not available to the average researcher.

Many studies are affected by high rates of attrition in the sample group. The ability to follow young people longitudinally is compromised by the extreme mobility of children and youth during and after care. The gold standard of research design, comparison of experimental to control groups, is generally impossible because of ethical considerations. This limitation is usually non-negotiable. A further limitation, related more particularly to qualitative research, although also to survey research that involves interviewing, is its labour-intensive nature. In a climate of restricted financial resources, such studies tend to be limited to quite small samples. Increasingly, the counter-response is to build knowledge through triangulation of evidence.

Quantitative versus Qualitative Methods

In the earlier stages of social work and child welfare research there was considerable debate about the superiority of quantitative methods over qualitative methods. The former is necessary to describe populations, particularly when representative samples can be obtained. In child welfare, qualitative methods are also important. In a very real sense, such studies put flesh on the bones of the more abstract numerical data. They are also able to establish validity, not through generalization obtained on the basis of statistical probability tests (i.e., external validity), but through a more in-depth understanding of experiences and the particular phenomena under investigation (i.e., internal validity).

As well, it is worth remembering that fruitful research passes through several stages. The first level is that of random observation, which offers at some point the emergence of predictable patterns. At this stage, case studies of small samples or even a single case study can provide an example of perceived patterns. This in turn can be used to justify investment of agency and funding resources to further explore the issues at a higher stage of research design. Some of our chapters use mixed methods, and there is a growing trend to recognize the value of this approach. Those that include the voice of consumers carry with them an immediacy and persuasiveness that can engage and influence policy change. A particularly fruitful development in child welfare research is the expanded use of participatory action research. It blends the rigour of the research community with the authenticity of the consumer. When well done, it can have an immediate impact on front-line practice, and, from the grass roots up, on policy development.

Use and Misuse of Statistical Analysis when Generalizing Results

Sampling limitations do in turn limit the range of statistical analyses available. In order to disseminate findings through peer reviewed publications, some academics are tempted to use parametric statistics with non-parametric samples. It is essential that researchers observe the restrictions of their data and report accurately on the strengths and limitations of their findings and recommendations. We owe this to the populations that we wish to serve. Subject to methodological considerations and the strength of our evidence, we will at times be able to offer clear recommendations; at other times our recommendations should be tentative and subject to stated limitations and cautions. Chapter 3 is a good example of drawing conclusions with adequate attention to the strengths and limitations of both the data and results from the method of analysis utilized in the study. At a different end of the sampling perspective, Chapter 13 demonstrates how the synthesis of several small sample studies can be used to offer explanation and prediction.

Despite the limitations outlined above, the gradual building of knowledge through testing in small-scale demonstrations, and evaluation of existing programs, is leading us to the development of efficient and effective interventions. Examples are to be found in Part V, which examines the search for best practice.

Translating Findings into Policy and Practice

In social work and child welfare, the task goes beyond the accumulation of knowledge and small improvements to interventions. We need also to have findings enshrined in policies that reduce harm and support best practice. Davies (2003) eloquently described the discrepancy between the needs of policy-makers for short, succinct reports with clear recommendations and the researchers' imperative to produce lengthy, exhaustive reports that may necessarily include disclaimers and limitations based on sampling and analysis procedures. She also pointed out that sometimes acceptance is based on chance—the timeliness of a study report that happens to address a current urgent problem facing decision-makers. The ideal situation is one in which there is close co-operation between policy-makers and researchers, with due attention to involvement of consumers. Canada's major funding body, the Social Sciences and Humanities Research Council (SSHRC), has recognized this fact, and for the past few years has been promoting increased partnership between academic researchers and the communities they serve.

The Eight-Point Research Agenda: Taking Stock and Looking Forward

In the final chapter of the first edition of this book (Kufeldt & McKenzie, 2003b), we used as an organizing framework the eight-point research agenda identified by Galaway and Hudson (1995). Once again we return to this agenda. It allows us to take stock and to express a vision for the future. In each case we offer a brief synthesis of where we are, and our recommendations as to where we need to go in the search for an effective child and family welfare system.

Child Welfare Outcomes

Despite some progress, as indicated earlier, the issue of child welfare outcomes continues to be problematic. One reason is the lack of specification of purpose. In 1995, Galaway and Hudson declared: "Immediate attention needs to be given to specifying the purposes of child welfare services in terms of what is intended to be accomplished" (p. 369). This has not happened. Yet unless we know exactly what it is that we wish to achieve, then measurement of outcomes will continue to be elusive. Furthermore, it becomes difficult to identify appropriate methods if the desired end is unclear.

As Chapter 37 indicates, the United Kingdom has made much greater progress than Canada in attacking this problem. It has identified its purpose as meeting the needs of children more globally than within the narrower definition of "protection." In the process, it has developed legislation and policy directed toward the integration of research, policy, and practice. Nevertheless, as Scott points out in that chapter, translation of the well-designed Integrated Children's System (ICS) into practice is not a smooth process: the debate can become polarized between those who advocate the kind of structured recording methods that such a system requires, and those who argue that this might detract from direct service work. Research demonstrates that attention to structured recording such as that required by the ICS and by LAC can promote both more effective service and better outcomes for children, young people, and their families; however, the burden of documentation on service providers, given the high caseloads that exist in many jurisdictions, also requires attention.

Part of the problem, at least in North America, appears to be the dissonance between research, policy, and practice. One would expect that the core of evaluation and measurement of outcomes should be whether children have fared better as a result of child welfare intervention. To date there is a shortage of research to provide an answer to that question. Indeed, ethical issues limit the use of control groups in evaluation research, which could help provide more definitive information about what works for whom. To illustrate the apparent dissonance we briefly highlight current policy imperatives and the actual progress of children at the receiving end of child welfare interventions.

Policy Imperatives

The current focus of policy directives in Canada is on family preservation and family reunification. These would be laudable goals if used in a discriminating fashion. Family preservation and family reunification require:

- knowledge of which families are likely to benefit;
- sufficient qualified workers to ensure adequate monitoring of children's safety;
- allocation of resources both practical and supportive to maintain families;
- continued support, services, and monitoring for reunited families; and
- accessible family counselling services.

Research, including studies of runaway and homeless youth, has established that family breakdown is a risk factor for the children involved, and that family reunification is not a straightforward matter (Bullock, Little, & Millham, 1993; Kufeldt & Nimmo, 1987; Maluccio, Fein, & Davis, 1994; Walberg & Mrozek, 2009). Yet there are no public services dedicated to family preservation, or to after care. Private and non-government organizations, most not easily accessible to the poor and marginalized, are the only resources. Children are too often damaged before families receive help.

Is family preservation in children's best interests at all times? Not necessarily: there is a growing litany of children who die at the hands of parents because of adherence to the goals of family preservation or family reunification. Some children enter care later and more damaged than in the past. Some oscillate between alternative care and family care. This policy imperative is partly driven by documentation of poor outcomes for graduates of foster care. Adults surveyed in one Canadian study certainly did not fare as well as the general population, based on a number of criteria (Kufeldt, 2003). Despite this, the majority of respondents (71%) believed coming into care was the right decision.

In summary, there continues to be an urgent need for clarity regarding the purpose of child welfare services. In tandem with that need is the requirement to pay greater attention to what research is telling us. Based on that research, actual practice should be informed by:

- knowledge of indicators of success or failure of the family of origin;
- the need to reduce the aspects of foster care that impact negatively on children (e.g., frequent changes of workers, foster carers, schools, etc.); and
- a focus on permanency planning as soon as possible after a child comes to the attention of child welfare services.

Child Development

The good news is the expansion of attention to the developmental needs and well-being of children in care. In contrast to practice directed toward current policy imperatives is the increased focus of the research community on the developmental progress of children at the receiving end of child welfare interventions. There is ample evidence in this book that translating these findings into practice can directly affect children's development, and, even more importantly, can promote the resilient personality that all parents wish for their children. We note that the use of *Looking After Children* (LAC) continues in various parts of the world, including Canada. Hammond (see Chapter 35) has said that earlier exposure to the LAC method influenced his increasing focus on resilience and the positive attributes of child and youth coping mechanisms. This in turn inspired the model that he and his colleague describe in their chapter (personal communication). As well, Wise and Champion, in Chapter 32, describe the very positive partnership that has developed around LAC in the state of Victoria, Australia, where the experience has been one of successfully linking research, policy, and practice. It can be done, but as in Australia (see also Chapter 34), it requires dedicated partnerships between policy-makers, practitioners, and the research community.

The policy imperatives have merit so long as child development outcomes are not compromised. The United Kingdom's ICS, and the Differential Response (DR) system on this side of the Atlantic, are promising developments. We recommend:

- that understanding of and use of these systems be promoted at all levels;
- that they be properly resourced;
- that evaluation of outcomes be child-centred; and
- that a feedback loop be established such that policy and practice become evidence-based.

Specification of Programs and Interventions

Considerable progress has occurred since Galaway and Hudson identified this challenge to the child welfare community in 1995. There is a very encouraging move toward guided practice and evidence-based practice. One such approach, LAC, is clearly taking hold in various parts of the world. In Canada, Ontario is moving toward mandatory use of the approach. Partnerships of government services with NGOs, such as that illustrated in Chapter 34, expand available expertise and enable localization of services. This is particularly important in work with First Nations communities. Guided practice and evidence-based practice are now part of the discourse in child welfare. The next step in "walking the talk" is to bring such practice into widespread use.

Comparative Approaches to Organizing and Delivering Services

An example of progress made is that the repeated waves of the *Canadian Incidence Study* (CIS) provide the opportunity to study the effects of different organizational arrangements and changes in policy. Findings emerging from service innovations in Aboriginal child and family services provide examples of best practice in these contexts and serve as useful comparisons to conventional practice in mainstream services. As well, Cameron and his colleagues (see Chapter 7) provide new insights on the benefits and limitations of community-based service delivery models. Although available data is accumulating, it has yet to be fully exploited, let alone applied to the redesign of existing services. It could also be considerably enriched if it were augmented by consumer surveys. To that end we would repeat our 2003 recommendation that "youth, parents, and foster parents be surveyed to obtain their opinion on which arrangements have been most helpful to them" (Kufeldt & McKenzie, 2003a, p. 434).

We also recommend that comparative studies be undertaken using the LAC Assessment and Action Records to monitor and compare progress of children left in their own homes, returned home, or remaining in foster care.

Evaluations of Programs and Program Components

There are examples in the preceding chapters, as well as in our earlier text, of ways and means of evaluating programs. However, most studies focus on time-limited projects rather than on the overall service system. In addition, most are retrospective. However, there is a growing body of available data; for example, the CIS now has three waves of data. Chapter 36 provides an outcome matrix based on existing data that can be adopted for local use. These data may not provide the full picture, but they provide valuable insights on critical issues that can be helpful to decision-makers. Aggregation of LAC data, which is occurring in Ontario, could be expanded to other jurisdictions, and help to provide more information on the effects of interventions on the children themselves. Scott, in Chapter 37, repeats some of the messages embedded in chapters included in the first edition of this book (Davies, 2003; Jones, 2003) with respect to using data in iterative fashion to inform policy and practice. It is timely now for Directors of Child Welfare in Canada to promote a dynamic interplay between available data, policy directions, and managerial decisions in order to monitor and improve the well-being of the children, youth, and families who are being served. This requires an iterative process and partnerships with the research community which appear more common in other countries. If this process is combined with continued attention to actual outcomes, it will allow for more comprehensive evaluations of child welfare interventions.

The 13 Canadian Provincial and Territorial Directors of Child Welfare meet together annually. We recommend that they add to their meeting at least one day with key representatives of the research community, within which the policy, practice, and research connections can be examined and evaluated.

Institutionalizing Innovations and Research

Galaway and Hudson (1995) suggested an "agency research plan that can help ensure that research is carried out in a purposeful way in the agency setting" (p. 371). The Australian and United Kingdom experiences included in preceding chapters give cause for optimism. In Canada there are examples of productive partnerships, but we are not yet at the level of institutionalizing promising approaches. This is particularly true with respect to prevention programs. Crises occur, and studies are commissioned, but too often crisis containment takes precedence over attention to existing evidence of what might constitute good practice, or indeed the very recommendations contained in these reports. It is important that new approaches not be seen as burdensome, but rather as positive guided practice. The final report of the national Canadian pilot of LAC had this advice regarding implementation of a new approach:

> Observations of experiences on both sides of the Atlantic suggest that a move towards full implementation should proceed gradually (probably somewhat slowly). There is one line of thought that suggests that full implementation could be started on a specific date and workers would be expected to come on line immediately. The argument is that everyone will have to do it, so it is best just to get it done. British experience, and indeed change theory itself, would advise more caution. The risk with the top down approach is that workers may not have time to take ownership of a new method, and indeed a change in the whole culture of child welfare work. When workers feel coerced, the philosophy gets lost and a quality project and full compliance are jeopardized. Our preferred approach would be to set a date for the implementation process to begin. Prior to that date, workers, supervisors and foster parents would receive orientation and training in this approach, as well as in the correct methods to fill out and use the forms. When the implementation date occurs, targeted groups could be designated and others (all remaining existing cases) gradually be brought on line. This could occur by having workers complete one new file per month until existing caseloads are on line. Another alternative would be to start using *Looking After Children* materials at logical points in the case management process (e.g., when a case review is required, when preparing information for court, transferring child to an adoption caseload, etc.). (Kufeldt, Simard, Vachon, Baker, & Andrews, 2000, p. 233)

Despite these observations, we are moving closer to the required iteration between research, policy, and practice. We noted earlier the value of partnership between researchers, funders, and service providers. The challenge is for greater openness on the part of agencies to admit researchers through their doors, and for researchers to design the work in such a way that it does not impose undue burdens on workers, whose time and energies are stretched to the limit. Agencies and researchers also require continued investment in research and development by both federal and provincial governments. Society as a whole values scientific research: partnerships in the child welfare field have the challenge of convincing the general public of the value of investing in children.

Longitudinal Research

The level of knowledge of longer term outcomes for those young people who grow up in care is still very limited. We are not aware of any new Canadian study since that reported in our earlier text on graduates of guardianship care (Kufeldt, 2003). That study indicated that, although in the aggregate young adult care leavers did less well than their peers, there were success stories. Coupled with anecdotal evidence, it also suggests that it takes longer for care leavers to achieve well-functioning adulthood. Unless and until there is investment in high quality prospective longitudinal research, it will not be possible to identify the antecedents of adult outcomes.

The Australian Tracking Study was a two-year longitudinal study. Though too short to provide information on long-term outcomes, it did provide some useful information on short-term psychological adjustment and testing of the assumptions and predictors of returning home (Knott & Barber, 2005). The most promising study to date is that of the Australian researcher Elizabeth Fernandez. Her longitudinal study began with her work on the implementation of LAC, and documentation of its outcome data is now augmented by other tests. This is likely to reinforce the validity and reliability of this long-term tracking study. The study is now in its ninth year, and it is because of a successful partnership with Barnardos Australia that funding has been continued for this research.

Canada's *National Longitudinal Survey of Children and Youth* (NLSCY) does not provide adequate information on either foster children or adopted children, as these groups are small percentages of the total child and youth population. We recommend that Statistics Canada partner with the Directors of Child Welfare to obtain purposeful samples for this much-needed work.

Studies of Gatekeeping

Hudson and Galaway (1995) asked how key decisions are made in child welfare. The answer was elusive in 2003, and continues to be so today. Decisions ought to be based on the circumstances of the situation, and there is evidence that these factors are important (Chapter 3). Yet there are a number of other factors, including geographical location and worker characteristics, which have some influence. In addition, standardized instruments, such as risk assessment tools, can be misused because the information is not connected to clinical expertise (Chapter 25).

Gatekeeping decisions, nevertheless, are critical. At times they are literally life and death decisions. The consequences for a particular child and family will always have far-reaching consequences. Despite this, such decisions are too often carried out by relatively inexperienced workers. This is in contrast to medicine, where there is an extended internship and the availability of expert consultation and/or second opinions when the intervention is uncertain or serious consequences from a procedure or treatment may occur. The decision to take a child into care (major surgery for a family) or to concentrate on family preservation (less intrusion) is one that requires similar experience and expertise. We recognize that supervision is available in the child welfare system, and that reviews are commissioned to enhance the quality of decision-making. With respect to the latter, a number of Child Advocacy Offices investigate cases where a child death that has some connection to the provision of public services has occurred. As valuable as these reviews are, they are conducted after the event. In addition to reviews of "what went wrong," we recommend a more proactive approach that includes additional attention to intensive training, internship, and clinical supervision of workers within the child welfare system.

Unintended Consequences

In 1995 Galaway and Hudson asked some serious questions. "Are there conditions under which interventions worsen the conditions for children and families?… Are there unintended consequences from cross cultural adoptions or closed adoption?" (p. 371). We know that the most extreme unintended consequence, the death of a child, does happen. More recent research on adoption is beginning to provide some answers. Adoption at one time was presumed to be a simple solution to infertility and to unplanned pregnancy. Chapter 15 explored some of the key issues pertaining to adoption, and other chapters identified some of the adverse effects from both historical and contemporary interventions with First Nations and other Aboriginal communities. Knott and Barber (2004) examined assumptions regarding placement stability and found that within the first eight months of care, placement change might be a positive action. Not surprisingly, the *reason* for the change was the important determining factor. The challenge is to improve the ability of those on the front line to be aware and to anticipate the possibility of unintended consequences. Whatever decision is made will have long-term effects on the child being served, as well as the child's family. Will this decision enhance or inhibit the long-term developmental outcomes? There is an integral connection here with our earlier comments regarding the seriousness of gatekeeping functions. Child protection is a highly charged, complex task that requires well-educated, highly skilled, and experienced social workers.

Disproportionate Representation of Indigenous Children in the Child Welfare System

The eight-point research agenda reviewed above provides a broad and still relevant framework for considering research in child welfare. However, we introduce a ninth point in this edition of the book that pertains to ever-growing concerns about the disproportionate number of Indigenous children admitted to care. This is a Canadian problem, but as demonstrated in Chapter 20, it is a problem in other countries as well. Some data are available on the nature and scope of this issue, but there are significant gaps in information available across jurisdictions, even within Canada. For example, the number and rate of Aboriginal children in care is often qualified as a "best estimate." Although the connections between colonization and overrepresentation are well recognized, it is only recently, through analysis of CIS data, that causality has been explored empirically (see Chapter 21). This is a serious indictment in a system where an Aboriginal child can be as much as 17 times more likely than a non-Aboriginal child to enter the child welfare system (Chapter 20). There is much to be learned by comparisons across jurisdictions both within Canada and between Canada and other countries.

Cross-comparisons of disproportionality, however, should not be limited to examination of rates of families receiving services or children in care. First, advanced research on causality, including colonization and socio-economic disadvantages, and secondary factors, such as reporting patterns and caregiver factors (e.g., addictions and parenting capacity), is important. Analysis of data from the CIS in Canada (Chapters 21 and 24) has made a beginning contribution to understanding how these issues contribute to overrepresentation. However, the 1998 and 2003 samples for this study included a limited sample of First Nations and other Aboriginal agencies; as well, the proportions of Aboriginal children included in these samples were significantly lower than the proportion of Aboriginal children in care. Continuing efforts to understand the characteristics of Aboriginal children receiving child welfare services from both Aboriginal and non-Aboriginal agencies is recommended.

While focus on these aspects of disproportionality is important, critical attention must be devoted to answering the question of what works for whom, and under what conditions. Chapter 22 discusses one service model that has been evaluated on several occasions, and there has been some growth in the literature on culturally appropriate services (e.g., Carrière & Richardson, 2009; Desmeules, 2007; Sterling-Collins, 2009). However, knowledge development so far is based largely on descriptive studies of small-scale programs or conceptual models that have yet to be fully tested. More comprehensive evaluations are required, and knowledge development would benefit from more attention to international comparisons with programs in countries such as the U.S., Australia, and New Zealand.

Research and evaluation strategies pertaining to disproportionality also require attention to a number of the points in Galaway and Hudson's (1995) eight-point agenda, including the need to clearly specify programs and interventions. As noted in Chapter 24, attention to these issues must also be infused with respect for cultural differences, and research that observes OCAP (Aboriginal ownership, control, access, and possession) principles.

Conclusion

As we contemplate this now 15-year-old research agenda, we note that some progress has been made, but there is yet no cause for complacency. The welfare and protection of children is still a fragile reality for too many. The good news is that we are developing greater knowledge of what needs to be done to ensure healthy development for all. The challenge is to make that a reality.

The Policy, Practice, and Research Connection: Are We There Yet? Where To from Here?

A clear and consistent connection between research, policy, and practice has yet to be realized, though there are promising developments in some jurisdictions. The United Kingdom has been a leader in promoting a close connection between these three branches of child welfare service. It has invested considerable resources into the commissioning of research to enlighten policy directions, and child welfare services around the world have benefited from its initiatives. Chapter 37 provides an update on more recent progress, although within that chapter is the caution that practice does not necessarily fall into line with research-based policy initiatives. Part of the explanation may lie not only in the demanding and stressful nature of this field of practice, but also in the human resistance to change, and hence the need to pay attention to change theory when instigating reform. Chapter 32 demonstrates how one Australian state achieved success in forming the connection within its *Looking After Children* Outcomes Data Project. As its authors indicate, success depends on a high level of mutual respect and collaboration. The project gained co-operation at the practice level through offering an opt-in opportunity. This is similar to the strategy used with front-line workers in the first national Canadian LAC project, and is in contrast to the United Kingdom's top-down approach. An added value was the permission given to the researchers to publish their results, as publication bans on the part of providers can inhibit the engagement of researchers.

An ingredient emerging in other successful research, policy, and practice initiatives is championship from a non-governmental agency such as Barnardos in Australia (see Chapter 34) and the Ontario Association of Children's Aid Societies (see Chapter 38).

Also encouraging is the growing interest in evidence-based practice and the use at the practice level of tools such as LAC and the resilience model described in Chapter 35, which not only enhance practice but also produce positive, outcomes-focused data. These data, when aggregated, provide significant information to evaluate policy and to guide policy development and change whenever necessary. We will have achieved a well-functioning policy, practice, and research connection when a solid, co-operative, and iterative partnership between all three is the norm—but this is no simple matter.

We referred earlier to the development of the Integrated Children's System (ICS) in the United Kingdom. It began with an excellent partnership between policy and research communities that was well supported by national funding. This partnership has evolved over a significant period of time in the U.K., including research that led to the development of the 1989 *Children Act* and the LAC system of assessing outcomes, the development of a common assessment framework, and the more recent focus on this integrated children's system. Resistance noted at the grassroots practice level in Chapter 37 may have to do with too much change too quickly, and with reaction to what is regarded as a change imposed from the top. Successes elsewhere, including examples in this book about the use of LAC, have benefited from collaborative partnerships between government, academia, and non-governmental organizations (NGOs).

Productive connections between the research, policy, and practice domains remain elusive in many jurisdictions. Their achievement depends on a number of factors:

- the existence of charismatic leadership from at least one sector committed to collaboration;
- the availability of funding and other supports to introduce best practice approaches; and
- engagement of those at the practice level in participatory research and policy consultation.

In addition, strong lines of communication between the three sectors are important in enhancing these elements. Too often each seems to operate in isolation from the others. For example, inquiries into the avoidable deaths of children elicit reaction and policy changes from the senior management level, but in some cases these may not be entirely reflective of the recommendations within these reports. Indeed, the implementation of recommendations often renders the work of those on the front line more complex and less client-centred.

An illustration of this dilemma comes from Parton (2003), who compared two public inquiries into high-profile deaths of children in England that occurred 30 years apart. A discouraging finding was the many similarities between the two reports, including the failure to communicate directly with the children. Parton notes that "we should not underestimate the considerable complexity that has come to characterize the child protection system, and child welfare more generally" (p. 32). He concludes by arguing that professionals involved in this work should be paid more, and be expected to acquire more qualifications in responding to these complaints. If we consider the information regarding the qualifications and experiences of child welfare workers in Chapter 4, we have a long way to go in meeting the complex demands within the field of child welfare today. The question is whether child welfare work is undervalued because it is not yet well understood by those with the power to introduce needed changes.

As we consider the connections between research, policy, and practice, there is both good and bad news. There is evidence of increased research and the use of research for policy development, even if problems remain in how these two domains can be better integrated. There is evidence of more investment in research and evaluation within the Canadian child welfare field, and some of this funding has been specifically targeted to university-community research partnerships. However, the failure of the federal government to extend funding for the Centre of Excellence for Child Welfare will leave a serious gap in Canada's voice to create a national child welfare research agenda, and to collaborate closely on policy and practice development.

Connections between the research and policy domains and the practice domain are a particular challenge. There are a number of reasons for this, including increased workloads for front-line workers, new responsibilities, and the potential lack of fit between policy changes and the needs of both staff and service users on the front line. Perhaps the more recent emphasis on evidence-based practice within child welfare may encourage better connections between these domains.

There is intuitive appeal to the concept of evidence-based practice (EBP) in child welfare in that it implies a more disciplined approach to policy-making, program development, and practice. Services grounded in quality of care considerations, focused on outcomes, and cost-effective in nature are seen as a welcome reprieve from a "flavour of the month" approach to adopting new ideas and innovations in the field. This focus on EBP is closely connected to the notion of "best practice," which has become part of the new lexicon in child welfare. Indeed, we are guilty of encouraging this in that Part V of this book is devoted to the theme of "best practice."

Two broad issues raise concerns about EBP (Usher & Wildfire, 2003). One is clarity about what constitutes EBP in the field; that is, how it should be defined within child welfare. This concern relates to the fact that the evidence base is at an early stage of development in child welfare, and research generated in the field is not based primarily on strong research designs. A second, but related, concern is the implication that EBP gives researchers significant influence, if not primary control, in setting the practice research agenda. Such an approach is inconsistent with the development of more community-based service models, where there is recognition that service must be context-driven to a significant degree, and that more participatory, collaborative approaches are essential in understanding what works best for whom. Coupled with this focus is recognition of the limits of technical knowledge, and our assertion that assessment and intervention in child welfare comprise both art and science.

Evidence-based practice, for some, is equated with the application of intervention methods associated with empirically demonstrated positive outcomes in controlled practice settings (O'Hare, 2005). The relevance of such outcomes in different contexts, however, is open to question. Others connect it to the use of standardized screening and assessment tools along with practice guidelines or criteria, which are often set out as practice standards (Steenrod, 2005). In this case, supporting evidence for standards may be incomplete or not critically examined relative to the intended population. Thus, changes in the evidence base will produce new definitions of what might be more accurately described as "better" rather than "best" practice. This recognition leads to an interpretation of EBP as decisions made based on the best available evidence at that time, even if that evidence lacks the rigour associated with experimental designs.

A partial answer to the definition dilemma may be found in O'Hare's effectiveness-focused approach to EBP, in which the emphasis is on evaluating interventions in everyday practice. Two variations of this process-oriented approach are identified. One owes its origin to earlier proponents of empirical practice, in which the focus is on evaluating one's practice through qualitative case analysis and/or single subject designs to monitor and evaluate results. The problem with this approach, at least as it developed historically, was that little attention was paid to the knowledge and related decision-making criteria that guided the initial choice of intervention. A second approach, which O'Hare regards as preferable, involves the use of existing outcome research, and applying the findings of outcome research to unique or particular contexts with adequate recognition of the importance of flexibility and practice wisdom. Thus, practitioners need to adjust intervention based on consumer feedback and ongoing evaluation. In this model, EBP involves the integration of current best evidence, clinical expertise or practice knowledge, and client preference.

EBP is relevant to the clinical or direct practice context, but it can also inform policy and program choices at the organizational level. For example, Chapter 25 reviewed the use of risk assessment tools from an evidence-based perspective that is consistent with O'Hare's recommendation, and the LAC approach provides an evidence base for both clinical and program level decisions. As well, Chapter 36 describes how the development of data on the effectiveness of interventions can promote EBP in an organization through a collaborative problem-solving process between researchers and organizational decision-makers.

It is recognized that the integration of research, policy, and practice remains a challenge, but without increased attention to the interface between these domains, and how knowledge from each domain can inform the others, best practice in child welfare will remain more of a dream than a reality. One of the measures in Canada that could help to promote the increased utilization of research would be to incorporate child welfare questions and concerns within the National Longitudinal Survey of Children and Youth (NLSCY). Conferences and symposia that include representatives from all three domains also help to promote a common understanding of issues and potential solutions. There are a number of ongoing provincial, national, and international conferences, and at the international level the ongoing cycle of conferences focusing on the LAC approach is a particular example of this. Although these are important, a national conference which includes representatives from policy-makers (such as Directors of Child Welfare and ministers), researchers, practitioners, and service users (e.g., foster parents and youth in care) has not occurred for over a decade. The periodic sponsorship of national symposia focused on research, policy, and practice in child welfare, with participation from these stakeholders, along with provincial or regionally organized conferences designed along the same lines, can help to promote better connections between research, policy, and practice. In the latter category, the Prairie Child Welfare Consortium has sponsored several conferences of this type, attracting a wide range of participants from Alberta, Saskatchewan, and Manitoba.

In closing, we draw on the message embedded in the United Kingdom's *Looking After Children* initiatives that looking after children well requires attention to parenting, partnership, and outcomes, and that good parenting enhances the likelihood of good outcomes.

REFERENCES

Aboriginal Corrections Policy Unit. (1997). *The four circles of Hollow Water.* Ottawa: Supply and Services Canada.

Aboriginal Justice Inquiry—Child Welfare Initiative (AJI–CWI). (2001, August). *Promise of hope: Commitment to change. Child and family services in Manitoba.* Retrieved September 5, 2008, from <http://www.aji-cwi.mb.ca/pdfs/promiseof hope.pdf>.

Adoption Council of Canada. (2005). China leads adoption statistics for 2004. <http://www.adoption.ca/news/050527stats04.htm>.

Adoption Council of Canada. (2009). *About CWK.* <http://www.canadaswaiting kids.ca/about.html>.

Ahern, L., Rosenthal, E., Bauer, E., Levy, R., McGowan, K., & Okin, R. (2006). *Hidden suffering: Romania's segregation and abuse of infants and children with disabilities.* A Report by Mental Disability Rights International. Washington, DC: Mental Disability Rights International. Originally retrieved March 25, 2009; accessible at <http://www.mdri.org/PDFs/reports/romania-May%209%20final_with%20 photos.pdf>.

Aichhorn, A. (1935). *Wayward youth.* New York: Viking.

Albert, V., Iaci, R., & Catlin, S. N. (2004). Facing time limits and kinship placements. *Families in Society: The Journal of Contemporary Social Services, 85*(1), 63–70.

Alberta Health Services and Alberta Alcohol and Drug Abuse Commission. (2007). Estimating the rate of FASD and FAS in Canada. Originally retrieved January 7, 2009; accessible at <http://www.aadac.com/547_1224.asp>.

Alderson, P. (2000). Children as researchers: The effects of participation rights on research methodology. In P. Christensen & A. James (Eds.), *Research with children: Perspectives and practices* (pp. 241–57). New York: Falmer Press.

Alfred, T. (1999). *Peace, power, righteousness: An Indigenous manifesto.* Don Mills, ON: Oxford University Press.

Allison, J., & Johnson, J. (1981). *Say hi to Julie.* Calgary: Who Cares Society.

Alston, P. (Ed.). (1994). *The best interests of the child: Reconciling culture and human rights.* Oxford: Clarendon Press.

Alwon, F., & Reitz, A. (2000). Empty chairs: As a national workforce shortage strikes child welfare, CWLA responds. *Children's Voice, 9*(6), 35–7.

American Humane Association and Family Group Decision Making Committee (2010). *Guidelines for family group decision making in child welfare.* Englewood, CO: American Humane Association. <http://americanhumane.org/assets/docs/protecting-children/PC-fgdm-guidelines.pdf>.

Ammerman, R. T., & Hersen, M. (1990). Research in child abuse and neglect: Current status and an agenda for the future. In R. T. Ammerman & M. Hersen (Eds.), *Children at risk: An evaluation of factors contributing to child abuse and neglect* (pp. 3–19). New York: Plenum Press.

A National Voice. (1999). *Response to Me, survive out there?: The report on the findings of a young people's consultation conference.* London: Author.

Anderson, K. (1998). A Canadian child welfare agency for urban natives: The clients speak. *Child Welfare, 77*(4), 441–60.

Andrews, Y. M., & Manser, L. (2001). *From the roots up: A National Youth in Care Network historical research project.* Ottawa: National Youth in Care.

Anglin, J. P. (2002). *Pain, normality and the struggle for congruence: Reinterpreting residential care for children and youth.* Binghamton, NY: Haworth Press.

Ansah-Koi, A. (2006). Care of orphans: Fostering interventions for children whose parents die of AIDS in Ghana. *Families in Society: The Journal of Contemporary Social Services, 87*(4), 555–64.

Antle, B. F., Barbee, A. P., & van Zyl, M. A. (2008). A comprehensive model for child welfare training evaluation. *Children and Youth Services Review, 30*(9), 1063–80.

Appleby, T. (2006, April 8). Jeffrey's grandparents guilty of murder. *The Globe and Mail*, p. A1.

Appleyard, K., Egeland, B., van Dulmen, M., & Stroufe, A. (2005). When more is not better: The role of cumulative risk in child behavior outcomes. *Journal of Child Psychology and Psychiatry, 46*(3), 235–45.

Archibald, J. (2008). *Indigenous storywork: Educating the heart, mind, body and spirit.* Vancouver: University of British Columbia Press.

Arendell, T. (1999). *Hegemonic motherhood: Deviancy discourses and employed mothers' accounts of out-of-school time issues* (Working Paper No. 9). Berkeley: Center for Working Families, University of California, Berkeley.

Argent, H. (Ed.). (2002). *Staying connected: Managing contact arrangements in adoption.* London: British Association for Adoption and Fostering.

Armitage, A. (1995). *Comparing the policy of Aboriginal assimilation: Australia, Canada, and New Zealand.* Vancouver: University of British Columbia Press.

Armstrong, E. M. (1998). Diagnosing moral disorder: The discovery and evolution of fetal alcohol syndrome. *Social Science and Medicine, 47*(12), 2025–42.

Armstrong, E. M. (2003). *Conceiving risk, bearing responsibility: Fetal alcohol syndrome and the diagnosis of moral disorder.* Baltimore: Johns Hopkins University Press.

Armstrong, E. M., & Abel, E. (2000). Fetal alcohol syndrome: The origins of a moral panic. *Alcohol and Alcoholism, 35*(3), 276–82.

Armstrong, S., & Slaytor, P. (Eds.). (2001). *The colour of difference.* Sydney, Australia: Federation Press.

Arnett, J. J. (2000). Emerging adulthood: A theory of development from the late teens through the twenties. *American Psychologist, 55*(5), 469–80.

Arnett, J. J. (2006). Emerging adulthood: Understanding the new way of coming of age. In J. J. Arnett & J. Tanner (Eds.), *Emerging adults in America: Coming of age in the 21st century* (pp. 3–20). Washington, DC: American Psychological Association Press.

Arnett, J. J. (2007). Afterward: Aging out of care—Toward realizing the possibilities of emerging adulthood. In V. Mann-Feder (Ed.), *Transition or Eviction: Youth Exiting Care for Independent Living.* Special issue of *New Directions for Youth Development, 113*, 151–61.

Aronson, M. (1997). Children of alcoholic mothers: Results from Goteborg, Sweden. In. A. K. Streissguth & J. Kanter (Eds.), *The challenge of fetal alcohol syndrome: Overcoming secondary disabilities* (pp. 15–24). Seattle: University of Washington Press.

Assembly of First Nations. (2008a). *Make poverty history: The First Nations plan for creating opportunity.* Originally retrieved October 1, 2008; accessible at <http://www.afn.ca/article.asp?id=2903>.

Assembly of First Nations. (2008b). National chief praises decision regarding human rights complaint on child welfare. Retrieved May 5, 2009, from <http://media.knet.ca/node/5542>.

Association des Centres Jeunesse du Québec (ACJQ). (2008). *La bonne mesure au bon moment. Bilan des directeurs de la protection de la jeunesse 2008.* Québec: Centres jeunesse du Québec.

Astley, S. J., Bailey, D., Talbot, C., & Clarren, S. (2000). Fetal alcohol syndrome (FAS) primary prevention through FAS diagnosis: Identification of high-risk birth mothers through the diagnosis of their children. *Alcohol and Alcoholism, 35*(5), 499–508.

Atkinson, G. J. (1988). *Coming to terms.* Unpublished master's thesis, University of Calgary.

Auditor General of Canada. (2008). First Nations child and family services program—Indian and Northern Affairs Canada. In Office of the Auditor General of Canada, *May report of the Auditor General of Canada.* Originally retrieved August 15, 2008; accessible at <http://www.oag-bvg.gc.ca/internet/English/parl_oag_200805_04_e_30700.html>.

Austin, S. (2005). Community-building principles: Implications for professional development. *Child Welfare, 84*(2), 105–22.

Australian Institute of Health and Welfare. (2005). *Child protection Australia 2003–04.* Child Welfare Series No. 36. AIHW Cat. No. CWS 24. Canberra: Author. <http://www.aihw.gov.au/publications/index.cfm/title/10095>.

Australian Institute of Health and Welfare. (2006). *Child protection and out-of-home care performance indicators.* Child Welfare Series No. 41. AIHW Cat. No. CWS 29. Canberra: Author. < http://www.aihw.gov.au/publications/index.cfm/title/10224>.

Australian Institute of Health and Welfare. (2007). *Child protection Australia 2005–06.* Child Welfare Series No. 40. AIHW Cat. No. CWS 28. Canberra: Author. < http://www.aihw.gov.au/publications/index.cfm/title/10383>.

Australian Institute of Health and Welfare. (2008). *Child protection Australia 2006–07.* Child Welfare Series No. 43. Cat. No. CWS 31. Canberra: Author. < http://www.aihw.gov.au/publications/index.cfm/title/10566>.

Badry, D. (2008). *Becoming a birth mother of a child diagnosed with fetal alcohol syndrome.* Unpublished doctoral thesis, University of Calgary.

Bagby, D. (2007). *Dance with the devil: A memoir of murder and loss.* Toronto: Key Porter Books.

Bailey, D., Jr., McWilliam, P. J., Winton, P. J., & Simeonsson, R. J. (1992). *Implementing family-centered services in early intervention: A team-based model for change.* Cambridge, MA: Brookline Books.

Bailey, D., Jr., & Simeonsson, R. (1988). *Family assessment in early intervention.* Englewood Cliffs, NJ: Macmillan.

Bailey, S., Thoburn, J., & Wakeham, H. (2002). Using the "Looking After Children" dimensions to collect aggregate data on wellbeing. *Child and Family Social Work, 7,* 189–201.

Baird, C., Ereth, J., & Wagner, D. (1999). *Research-based risk assessment: Adding equity to CPS decision making.* Madison, WI: Children's Research Center.

Baird, C., & Wagner, D. (2000). The relative validity of actuarial- and consensus-based risk assessment systems. *Children and Youth Services Review, 22*(11/12), 839–71.

Bala, N. (1999–2000). Reforming Ontario's *Child and Family Services Act:* Is the pendulum swinging back too far? *Canadian Family Law Quarterly, 17,* 117–73.

Bala, N. (2001). The Charter of Rights and family law in Canada: A new era. *Canadian Family Law Quarterly, 18*(3), 373–428.

Bala, N., Zapf, M. K., Williams, R. J., Vogl, R., & Hornick, J. P. (Eds.). (2004). *Canadian child welfare law: Children, families and the state* (2nd ed.). Toronto: Thompson Educational Publishing.

Ball, J., & Pence, A. (2006). Transforming knowledge through trust and respect. In *Supporting Indigenous children's development: Community-University partnerships* (pp. 79–93). Vancouver: University of British Columbia Press.

Bamblett, M., & Lewis, P. (2007). Detoxifying the child and family welfare system for Australian Indigenous peoples: Self determination, rights and culture as the critical tools. *First Peoples Child and Family Review, 3*(3), 43–56.

Banks, D., Hazen, A. L., Coben, J. H., Wang, K., & Griffith, J. D. (2009). Collaboration between child welfare agencies and domestic violence service providers: Relationship with child welfare policies and practices for addressing domestic violence. *Children and Youth Services Review, 31*(5), 497–505.

Banks, G. (2009). *Evidence-based policy-making: What is it? How do we get it?* Public lecture at Australian National University, February 2009. Accessible via <http://www.pc.gov.au/speeches/cs20090204>.

Barber, J. G., & Delfabbro, P. H. (2004). *Children in foster care.* New York: Routledge.

Barber, J. G., & Delfabbro, P. H. (2006). Psychosocial well-being and placement stability in foster care: Implications for policy and practice. In R. J. Flynn, P. M. Dudding, & J. G. Barber (Eds.), *Promoting resilience in child welfare* (pp. 157–72). Ottawa: University of Ottawa Press.

Barber, J., Trocmé, N., Goodman, D., Shlonsky, A., Black, T., & Leslie, B. (2007). *The reliability and predictive validity of consensus-based risk assessment.* Toronto: Centre of Excellence for Child Welfare.

Barnitz, L. (2001). Effectively responding to the commercial sexual exploitation of children: A comprehensive approach to prevention, protection, and reintegration services. *Child Welfare, 80*(5), 597–610.

Barnsley, J., & Ellis, D. (1992). *Research for change: Participatory action research for community groups.* Vancouver: Women's Research Centre.

Barth, R. P. (1993). Fiscal issues and stability in special-needs adoptions. *Public Welfare, 51*(3), 21–8.

Barth, R. P., & Berry, M. (1987). Outcomes of child welfare services since permanency planning. *Social Service Review, 61*, 71–90.

Barth, R. P., & Berry, M. (1988). *Adoption and disruption: Rates, risks, and responses.* New York: Aldine de Gruyter.

Barth, R. P., Courtney, M. E., Berrick, J. D., & Albert, V. (1994). *From child abuse to permanency planning: Child services pathways and placements.* New York: Aldine de Gruyter.

Barth, R. P., Guo, S., Green, R. L., & McCrae, J. S. (2007). Kinship care and nonkinship foster care: Informing the new debate. In R. Haskins, F. Wulczyn, & M. B. Webb (Eds.), *Child protection: Using research to improve policy and practice* (pp. 187–206). Washington, DC: Brookings Institution.

Barth, R. P., Landsverk, J., Chamberlain, P., Reid, J. B., Rolls, J. A., Hurlburt, M. S., et al. (2005). Parent-training programs in child welfare services: Planning for a more evidence-based approach to serving biological parents. *Research on Social Work Practice, 15*(5), 353–71.

Barth, R. P., Lloyd, E. C., Green, R. L., James, S., Leslie, L. K., & Landsverk, J. (2007). Predictors of placement moves among children with and without emotional and behavioral disorders. *Journal of Emotional and Behavioral Disorders, 15*(1), 46–55.

Barth, R.P., Webster, D., & Lee, S. (2002). Adoption of American Indian children: Implications for implementing the Indian Child Welfare and Adoption and Safe Families Acts. *Children and Youth Services Review, 24*(3), 139–58.

Bartle, E. E., Couchonnal, G., Canda, E. R., & Staker, M. D. (2002). Empowerment as a dynamically developing concept for practice: Lessons learned from organizational ethnography. *Social Work, 47*(1), 32–43.

Barwick, M. A., Boydell, K. M., Stasiulis, E., Ferguson, H. B., Blase, K., & Fixsen, D. (2005). *Knowledge transfer and evidence-based practice in children's mental health.* Toronto: Children's Mental Health Ontario.

Baskin, C. (1997). Mino-Yaa-Daa: An urban community based approach. *Native Social Work Journal, 1*(1), 55–67.

Bath, H., Atkin, S., & Boswell, D. (2008). *Transforming care: The meaning and practice of trauma-informed care.* Canberra: Thomas Wright Institute.

Battiste, M., & Barman, J. (Eds.). (1995). *First Nations education in Canada: The circle unfolds.* Vancouver: University of British Columbia Press.

Baumann, D., Law, J. R., Sheets, J., Reid, G., & Graham, J. C. (2005). Evaluating the effectiveness of actuarial risk assessment models. *Children and Youth and Services Review, 27,* 465–90.

Baumann, D., Law, J. R., Sheets, J., Reid, G., & Graham, J. C. (2006). Remarks concerning the importance of evaluating actuarial risk assessment models: A rejoinder to Will Johnson. *Children and Youth Services Review, 28*(6), 715–25.

Bazyk, S. (1989). Changes in attitudes and beliefs regarding parent participation and home programs: An update. *American Journal of Occupational Therapy, 43*(11), 723–8.

Beaudoin, A., Brousseau, M., Drapeau, S., Saint-Jacques, M.-C., Simard, M., Turcotte, D., et al. (2e éd.) (2006). *L'intervention de soutien des services psychosociaux pour les parents qui vivent des situations difficiles.* Québec: Université Laval, Centre de recherche JEFAR, Partenariat de recherche: Jeunes et familles à risque.

Bednar, S. (2003). Elements of satisfying organizational climates in child welfare agencies. *Families in Society: The Journal of Contemporary Social Services, 84*(1), 7–12.

Beeman, S. K., & Boisen, L. (1999). Child welfare professionals' attitudes toward kinship foster care. *Child Welfare, 78*(3), 315–37.

Belsky, J. (1984). The determinants of parenting: A process model. *Child Development, 55,* 83–96.

Bennett, M., Blackstock, C., & De la Ronde, R. (2005). *A literature review and annotated bibliography on aspects of Aboriginal child welfare in Canada* (2nd ed.). Ottawa: First Nations Child & Family Caring Society of Canada.

Benzies, K., & Mychasiuk, R. (2009). Fostering family resilience: A review of the key protective factors. *Child and Family Social Work, 14*(1), 103–14.

Berrick, J. D. (1997). Assessing quality of care in kinship and foster family care. *Family Relations, 46*(3), 273–80.

Berrick, J. D., Frasch, K., & Fox, A. (2000). Assessing children's experiences of out-of-home care: Methodological challenges and opportunities. *Social Work Research, 24*(2), 119–27.

Berridge, D., & Cleaver, H. (1987). *Foster home breakdown*. Oxford: Blackwell.

Berry, M., Charlson, R., & Dawson, K. (2003). Promising practices in understanding and treating child neglect. *Child and Family Social Work, 8*(1), 13–24.

Besharov, D. J., & Laumann, L. A. (1996). Child abuse reporting. *Society, 33*(4), 40–6.

Besharov, D. J., & Laumann, L. A. (1997). Don't call it child abuse if it's really poverty. *Journal of Children and Poverty, 3*(1), 5–36.

Biddle, B. J. (1979). *Role theory: Expectations, identities, and behaviors*. New York: Academic Press.

Biddle, B. J., and Thomas, E. J. (Eds.). (1966). *Role theory: Concepts and research*. New York: Wiley.

Biddle, J. K. (1996). The stories of adolescent mothers: Hearing the voices in context and community. *Dissertation Abstracts International, The Humanities and Social Sciences, 56*(8), 3329–30.

Birchall, E., & Hallett, C. (1995). *Working together in child protection*. London: Her Majesty's Stationery Office.

Black, R. E., Morris, S. S., & Bryce, J. (2003). The Bellagio Study Group on Child Survival: Where and why are 10 million children dying every year? *The Lancet, 361* (9376), 2226–34.

Black, T., Trocmé, N., Fallon, B., & MacLaurin, B. (2008). The Canadian child welfare system response to exposure to domestic violence investigations. *Child Abuse and Neglect, 32*(3), 393–404.

Blackstock, C. (2003). First Nations child and family services: Restoring peace and harmony in First Nations communities. In B. McKenzie & K. Kufeldt (Eds.), *Child welfare: Connecting research, policy, and practice* (pp. 331–42). Waterloo, ON: Wilfrid Laurier University Press.

Blackstock, C. (2008). Reconciliation means not saying sorry twice: Lessons from child welfare. In M. B. Castellano, L. Archibald, & M. DeGagné (Eds.), *From truth to reconciliation: Transforming the legacy of residential schools* (pp. 164–78). Ottawa: Aboriginal Healing Foundation.

Blackstock, C. (2009a). The occasional evil of angels: Learning from the experiences of Aboriginal peoples and social work. *First Peoples Child and Family Review, 4*(1), 28–37.

Blackstock, C. (2009b). *When everything matters: Comparing the experiences of First Nations and non-Aboriginal children removed from their families in Nova Scotia from 2003 to 2005*. Unpublished doctoral dissertation, Factor-Inwentash Faculty of Social Work, University of Toronto, Toronto.

Blackstock, C., Clarke, S., Cullen, J., D'Hondt, J., & Formsma, J. (2004). *Keeping the promise: The Convention on the Rights of the Child and the lived experience of First Nations children and youth*. Ottawa: First Nations Child & Family Caring Society of Canada.

Blackstock, C., Prakash, T., Loxley, J., & Wien, F. (2005). Summary of findings. In First Nations Child & Family Caring Society of Canada, *Wen: de (We are coming to the light of day)* (pp. 7–59). Ottawa: First Nations Child & Family Caring Society of Canada.

Blackstock, C., & Trocmé, N. (2005). Community based child welfare for Aboriginal children: Supporting resilience through structural change. *Social Policy Journal of New Zealand, 24*, 12–33.

Blackstock, C., Trocmé, N., & Bennett, M. (2004). Child maltreatment investigations among Aboriginal and non-Aboriginal families in Canada. *Violence Against Women, 10*(8), 901–16.

Blanchard, C. J. (1999). *Relationship of services and family reunification in New Jersey.* Unpublished doctoral dissertation, Yeshiva University, New York.

Blank, R. M., Dabady, M., & Citro, C. F. (Eds.). (2004). *Measuring racial discrimination: Panel on methods for assessing discrimination.* Washington, DC: National Academies Press.

Bloom, R. B. (1992). When staff members sexually abuse children in residential care. *Child Welfare, 71*(2), 131–45.

Bodnarchuk, J., Patton, D., & Reick, T. (2006). *Adolescence without shelter: A comprehensive description of issues faced by street youth in Winnipeg.* Winnipeg: Addictions Foundation of Manitoba. <www.afm.mb.ca/Research/documents/StreetYouth Report.pdf>.

Boer, F., & Spiering, S. M. (1991). Siblings in foster care: Success and failure. *Child Psychiatry and Human Development, 21*(4), 291–300.

Boone, L. (1999, October 7). More options [Letter to the editor, editorial page]. *Times-Colonist*, Victoria, BC.

Boruch, R., de Moya, D., & Snyder, B. (2002). The importance of randomized field trials in education and related areas. In F. Mosteller & R. Boruch (Eds.), *Evidence matters: Randomized trials in education research* (pp. 50–79). Washington, DC: Brookings Institution.

Boutilier, L., & Rehm, D. (1993). Family reunification in a community-based mental health center. In B. A. Pine, R. Warsh, & A. N. Maluccio (Eds.), *Together again: Family reunification in foster care* (pp. 51–64). Washington, DC: Child Welfare League of America.

Bowlby, J. (1971). *Attachment.* Vol. 1 of *Attachment and loss* [3 vols.]. New York: Penguin.

Bowlby, J. (1980). *Loss: Sadness and depression.* Vol. 3 of *Attachment and loss* [3 vols.]. London: Penguin.

Bowlby, J. (1988). *A secure base: Clinical applications of attachment theory.* London: Routledge.

Bowlby, J. (1990). *The making and breaking of affectional bonds.* London: Routledge.

Boyd, M., & Norris, D. (1999). The crowded nest: Youth adults at home. *Canadian Social Trends* (Catalogue No. 11-008). Ottawa: Statistics Canada.

Boyd, S., & Marcellus, L. (2007). *With child: Substance use during pregnancy. A woman centred approach.* Halifax: Fernwood.

Brandon, M., Lewis, A., Thoburn, J., & Way, A. (1999). *Safeguarding children with the Children Act 1989.* London: Stationery Office.

Brendtro, L., Brokenleg, M., & Van Bockern, S. (2001). *Reclaiming youth at risk: Our hope for the future.* Bloomington, IN: National Educational Service.

Brendtro, L., & du Toit, L. (2005). *Response ability pathways: Restoring bonds of respect.* Cape Town: Pretext Publishers.

Brick, J. M., & Morganstein, D. (1996). WesVarPC: Software for computing variance estimates from complex designs. *Proceedings of the 1996 Annual Research Conference* (pp. 861–6). Washington, DC: U.S. Bureau of the Census.

British Columbia Children's Commission. (1998). *Children's Commission annual report, 1996/1997.* Victoria, BC: Author.

British Columbia Ministry of Children and Family Development. (2009, August). *Aboriginal children in care.* Victoria, BC: Author.

British Columbia Ministry of Education. (2009, February). *Aboriginal report 2003/04–2007/08: How are we doing?* Retrieved August 12, 2009, from <www.bced.gov.bc.ca/abed/perf2008.pdf>.

British Columbia Ministry of Education, Aboriginal Education Enhancement Branch. (2008, February). *Shortcomings and successes: Understanding and addressing the complex challenge of Aboriginal education.* Victoria, BC: Author.

British Columbia Representative for Children and Youth. (2007). *Joint special report: Health and well-being of children in care in British Columbia (Report 2 on Educational Experiences and Outcomes).* Victoria, BC: Author.

Britner, P. A., & Mossler, D. G. (2002). Professionals' decision-making about out-of-home placements following instances of child abuse. *Child Abuse and Neglect, 26*(4), 317–32.

Broad, B., Hayes, R., & Rushforth, C. (2001). *Kith and kin: Kinship care for vulnerable young people.* London: National Children's Bureau.

Bronfenbrenner, U. (1977). Toward an experimental ecology of human development. *American Psychologist, 32*(7), 513–31.

Bronfenbrenner, U. (1979). *The ecology of human development. Experiments by nature and design.* Cambridge, MA: Harvard University Press.

Brook, J. S., Brook, D. W., de La Rosa, M., Whiteman, M, Johnson, E., & Montoya, I. (2001). Adolescent illegal drug use: The impact of personality, family, and environment factors. *Journal of Behavioral Medicine, 24*(2), 183–203.

Brousseau, M. (2000). *La perception du fonctionnement familial de parents négligents et non négligents et les facteurs familiaux, parentaux et environnementaux associés.* Québec: Laboratoire de recherche, École de service social, Université Laval.

Brousseau, M., & Morel, E. (2006). *Le fonctionnement familial: Représentations de praticiens sociaux et pratiques centrées sur la famille en négligence.* (Rapport de recherche.) Québec: Centre jeunesse de Québec—Institut Universitaire.

Brousseau, M., & Simard, M. (2000). Fonctionnement familial et négligence envers des enfants. In M. Simard & J. Alary (Eds.), *Comprendre la famille. Actes du 5e symposium québécois de recherche sur la famille* (pp. 141–62). Sainte-Foy: Presses de l'Université du Québec.

Brown, E., Bullock, R., Hobson, C., & Little, M. (1998). *Making residential care work: Structure and culture in children's homes.* Aldershot, UK: Ashgate.

Brown, L., Callahan, M., Strega, S., Dominelli, L., & Walmsley, C. (2009). Manufacturing ghost fathers: The paradox of father presence and absence in child welfare. *Child and Family Social Work, 14*(1), 25–34.

Brown, L., Haddock, L., & Kovach, M. (2002). Watching over our families: Lalum'utul' Smun'een Child and Family Services. In B. Wharf (Ed.), *Community work approaches to child welfare* (pp. 131–51). Peterborough, ON: Broadview Press.

Brown, L., Strega, S., Callahan, M., Dominelli, L., & Walmsley, C. (2009). Engaging fathers in child welfare. In S. Strega & J. Carrière (Eds.), *Walking this path together: Antiracist and anti-oppressive child welfare practice* (pp. 238–56). Halifax: Fernwood.

Brown, R. A., & Hill, B. A. (1996). Opportunity for change: Exploring an alternative to residential treatment. *Child Welfare, 75*(1), 35–57.

Brown, V. (2002). *Child welfare: Case studies.* Toronto: Allyn and Bacon.

Browne, K. (2005). A European survey of the number and characteristics of children less than three years old in residential care at risk of harm. *Adoption and Fostering, 29*(4), 23–33.

Browne, K., & Chou, S. (2008). Child rights and international adoption: A response to critics. *Adoption and Fostering, 32*(2), 69–74.

Browne, K., Hamilton-Giachritsis, C., Johnson, R., & Ostergren, M. (2006). Overuse of institutional care for children in Europe. *British Medical Journal, 332*, 485–7.

Browne, K., & Lynch, M. (1998). The challenge of child neglect. *Child Abuse Review, 7*(2), 73–6.

Brubacher, M. (2006). *Coming home: The story of Tikinagan Child and Family Services.* Sioux Lookout, ON: Tikanagan Child and Family Services.

Bryce, P. H. (1922). *The story of a national crime.* Ottawa: James Hope & Sons.

Buckley, H. (2003). *Child protection work: Beyond the rhetoric.* London: Jessica Kingsley Publishers.

Buckley, H. (2005). Neglect: No monopoly on expertise. In J. Taylor & B. Daniel (Eds.), *Child neglect: Practice issues for health and social care* (pp. 113–30). London and Philadelphia: Jessica Kingsley Publishers.

Bullock, R. (1995). Return home as experienced by children in state care and their families. In J. Hudson & B. Galaway (Eds.), *Child welfare in Canada: Research and policy implications* (pp. 298–307). Toronto: Thompson Educational Publishing.

Bullock, R., Gooch, D., & Little, M. (1998). *Children going home: The re-unification of families.* Aldershot, UK : Ashgate.

Bullock, R., Little, M., & Millham, S. (1993). *Going home: The return of children separated from their families.* Aldershot, UK: Dartmouth Publishing.

Burge, P. (2007). Prevalence of mental disorders and associated service variables among Ontario children who are permanent wards. *Canadian Journal of Psychiatry, 52*(5), 305–14.

Busca, S., & Crystal, N. (1999). *Family-centered services in the Winnipeg Children's Program at the Society for Manitobans with Disabilities: An evaluation.* Winnipeg: Authors.

Butcher, A. (2004). Foster care in Australia in the 21st century. *Developing Practice, 11,* 42–54.

Buxton, B. (2004). *Damaged angels: A mother discovers the terrible cost of alcohol in pregnancy.* Toronto: Knopf Canada.

Buysse, V., & *Wesley,* P. W. (Eds.). (2006). *Evidence-based practice in the early childhood field.* Washington, DC: Zero to Three Press.

Callahan, M. (1993). Feminist approaches: Women recreate child welfare. In B. Wharf (Ed.), *Rethinking child welfare in Canada* (pp. 172–209). Toronto: McClelland & Stewart.

Callahan, M. (2001). Marilyn Callahan replies. Debate: Risk assessment in child protection services. *Canadian Social Work Review, 18*(1), 155.

Callahan, M., Brown, L., MacKenzie, P., & Whittington, B. (2004). Catch as catch can: Grandmothers raising their grandchildren and kinship care policies. *Canadian Review of Social Policy, 54,* 58–78.

Callahan, M., Lumb, C., & Wharf, B. (1994). *Strengthening families by empowering women: A joint project of the Ministry of Social Services and the School of Social Work.* Victoria, BC: School of Social Work, University of Victoria.

Callahan, M., Rutman, D., Strega, S., & Dominelli, L. (2005). Looking promising: Contradictions and challenges for young mothers in care. In D. Gustafson (Ed.), *Unbecoming mothers: Women living apart from their children* (pp. 185–209). Binghamton, NY: Haworth Press.

Callahan, M., Strega, S., Rutman, D., & Dominelli, L. (2003). *The experience of young mothers in/from care.* Ottawa: Child Welfare League of Canada.

Callahan, M., & Swift, K. (2006). Back to the present. In A. Westhues (Ed.), *Canadian social policy: Issues and perspectives* (4th ed.) (pp. 203–21), Waterloo, ON: Wilfrid Laurier University Press.

Callahan, M., & Walmsley, C. (2007). Rethinking child welfare reform in British Columbia: 1900–60. In L. Foster & B. Wharf (Eds.), *People, politics, and child welfare in British Columbia* (pp. 10–33). Vancouver: University of British Columbia Press.

Cameron, G. (2003). Promoting positive child and family welfare. In K. Kufeldt & B. McKenzie (Eds.), *Child welfare: Connecting research, policy, and practice* (pp. 79–99). Waterloo, ON: Wilfrid Laurier University Press.

Cameron, G. (2006, November). *Progress on the path to a child and family service system.* Presentation to Manitoba Association of Social Workers Symposium on Child Welfare, Winnipeg.

Cameron, G., & Cadell, S. (1999). Fostering empowering participation in prevention programs for disadvantaged children and families: Lessons from ten demonstration sites. *Canadian Journal of Community Mental Health, 18*(1), 105–21.

Cameron, G., Hazineh, L., & Frensch, K. (2010). *Transforming front-line child welfare practice: The impact of institutional settings on services, employment environments, children and families (Summary of final report).* Waterloo, ON: Faculty of Social Work, Wilfrid Laurier University. Accessible via <http://www.wlu.ca/pcfproject>.

Cameron, G., & Hoy, S. (2003). *Summary: Stories of mothers and child welfare.* Waterloo, ON: Partnerships for Children and Families Project, Faculty of Social Work, Wilfrid Laurier University.

Canadian Council on Social Development. (2006). *The progress of Canada's children and youth.* Retrieved August 17, 2008, from <http://www.ccsd.ca/pccy/2006/tools.htm>.

Canadian Mothercraft Society. (n.d.). *Growing healthy Canadians: A guide for positive child development.* Retrieved October 18, 2006, from <http://www.growing healthykids.com/>.

Canadian Paediatric Society. (2006). Transracial adoption. *Paediatrics and Child Health, 11*(7), 443–7.

CANGRANDS. (2008). *National kinship support for caregivers across Canada.* Retrieved November 30, 2008, from <http://www.cangrands.com>.

Cantwell, N. (2005). The challenges of out-of-home care. *Early Childhood Matters, 105,* 4–14.

Carpenter, S. C., & Clyman, R. B. (2004). The long-term emotional and physical well-being of women who have lived in kinship care. *Children and Youth Services Review, 26*(7), 673–86.

Carrière, J. (2005). *Connectedness and health for First Nation adoptees.* Doctoral dissertation, University of Alberta, Edmonton. (Proquest Digital Dissertations, 1014322421. AATNR08619.)

Carrière, J. (2008). Maintaining identities: The soul work of adoption and Aboriginal children. *Pimatisiwin: A Journal of Aboriginal and Indigenous Community Health, 6*(1), 61–80.

Carrière, J., & Richardson, C. (2009). From longing to belonging: Attachment theory, connectedness, and Indigenous children in Canada. In S. McKay, D. Fuchs, & I. Brown (Eds). *Passion for action in child and family services: Voices from the prairies* (pp. 49–67). Regina: Canadian Plains Research Center.

Carroll, R. (2008, July 29). Haiti: Mud cakes become staple diet as cost of food soars beyond a family's reach—With little cash and import prices rocketing half the population faces starvation. *The Guardian.* Originally retrieved September 30, 2008; now accessible at <http://www.guardian.co.uk/world/2008/jul/29/food.internationalaidanddevelopment>.

Carter, B., & McGoldrick, M. (1999). *The expanded family life cycle: Individual, family, and social perspectives* (3rd ed.). Toronto: Allyn and Bacon.

Casanueva, C., Martin, S. L., Runyan, D. K., Barth, R. P., & Bradley, R. H. (2008). Parenting services for mothers involved with child protective services: Do they change maternal parenting and spanking behaviors with young children? *Children and Youth Services Review, 30*(8), 861–78.

Cash, S. (2001). Risk assessment in child welfare: The art and the science. *Children and Youth Services Review, 23*(11), 811–30.

Cashmore, J., & Ainsworth, F. (2004). *Audit of Australian out-of-home care research.* Sydney: Child and Family Welfare Association of Australia and Association of Children's Welfare Agencies.

Cashmore, J., Higgins, D. J., Bromfield, L. M., & Scott, D. A. (2006). Recent Australian child protection and out-of-home care research: What's been done and what needs to be done? *Children Australia, 31*(2), 4–11.

Cashmore, J., & Paxman, M. (2006a). Predicting after-care outcomes: The importance of "felt" security. *Child and Family Social Work, 11*, 232–41.

Cashmore, J., & Paxman, M. (2006b). Wards leaving care: Follow up five years on. *Children Australia, 31*(3), 18–25.

Cashmore, J., Paxman, M., & Townsend, M. (2007). The educational outcomes of young people 4–5 years after leaving care: An Australian perspective. *Adoption and Fostering, 31*(1), 50–61.

Cassano, M., Adrian, M., Veits, G., & Zeman, J. (2006). The inclusion of fathers in the empirical investigation of child psychopathology: An update. *Journal of Clinical Child and Adolescent Psychology, 35*(4), 583–9.

Castellano, M. B., Davis, L., & Lahache, L. (2000). Conclusion: Fulfilling the promise. In M.B. Castellano, L. Davis, & L. Lahache (Eds.). *Aboriginal education: Fulfilling the promise* (pp. 251–5). Vancouver: University of British Columbia Press.

Cautley, P. W. (1980). *New foster parents: The first experience.* New York: Human Sciences Press.

Cavanagh, K., Dobash, R., & Dobash, R. P. (2007). The murder of children by fathers in the context of child abuse. *Child Abuse and Neglect, 31*, 731–46.

Ceaser, M. (2008, July 25). Notes from academe: A dark window on human trafficking. *Chronicle of Higher Education, 54*(46), 1–5.

Center for Child and Family Policy. (2006). *Multiple Response System (MRS) evaluation report to the North Carolina Division of Social Services.* Durham, NC: Author.

Originally retrieved October 17, 2009; now accessible at <http://childandfamily policy.duke.edu/pdfs/pubpres/MRS_FinalReport-06.pdf>.

Centers for Disease Control and Prevention. (n.d.). *Malaria* (topic home page). Retrieved June 22, 2009, from <http://www.cdc.gov/malaria/>.

Chahine, Z., van Straaten, J., & Williams-Isom, A. (2005). The New York City neighborhood-based services strategy. *Child Welfare 84*(2), 141–52.

Chai, J. (2005, July 21). *Forced removal of Romani children from the care of their families.* Paper produced for the European Roma Rights Center. <http://www.errc.org/cikk.php?cikk=2290>.

Chamberlain, P., & Moore, K. (1998). Models of community treatment for serious juvenile offenders. In J. Crane (Ed.), *Social programs that work* (pp. 258–76). New York: Russell Sage Foundation.

Chamberlain, P., & Reid, J. B. (1998). Comparison of two community alternatives to incarceration for chronic juvenile offenders. *Journal of Consulting and Clinical Psychology, 66*(4), 624–33.

Champion, R., & Burke, G. (2006). Implementing *Looking After Children* as a collaborative practice and policy framework in Victoria, Australia. In R. J. Flynn, P. M. Dudding, & J. G. Barber (Eds.), *Promoting resilience in child welfare* (pp. 368–89). Ottawa: University of Ottawa Press.

Chand, A., & Thoburn, J. (2006). Child protection referrals and minority ethnic children and families. *Child and Family Social Work, 11*(4), 368–77.

Chandler, M., & Lalonde, C. (1998). Cultural continuity as a hedge against suicide in Canada's First Nations. *Transcultural Psychiatry, 35*(2), 191–219.

Chandler, S., & Giovannucci, M. (2004). Family group conferences: Transforming traditional child welfare policy and practice. *Family Court Review, 42*(2), 216–31.

Chapman, M. V., Wall, A., & Barth, R. P. (2004). Children's voices: The perceptions of children in foster care. *American Journal of Orthopsychiatry, 74*(3), 293–304.

Charles, K., & Nelson, J. (2000). *Permanency planning : Creating life long connections. What does it mean for adolescents?* Tulsa, OK: National Resource Center for Youth Development, University of Oklahoma.

Chataway, C. (2004). Aboriginal development: The process is critical to success. In J. White, P. Maxim, & D. Beavon (Eds.). *Aboriginal policy research: Setting the agenda for change* (2 vols.), vol. 2 (pp. 65–86). Toronto: Thompson Educational Publishing.

Cheers, D. (2006). *Evidence based practice in out of-home care.* Unpublished master's thesis, University of Sydney, New South Wales, Australia.

Cheers, D., Kufeldt, K., Klein, R., & Rideout, S. (2007). Comparing caring: Preliminary findings of an international research project based on the use of the *Looking After Children* system in Canada and Australia. *Children Australia, 32*(2), 21–8.

Chenitz, W. C., & Swanson, J. M. (1986). *From practice to grounded theory: Qualitative research in nursing.* Menlo Park, CA: Addison-Wesley.

Chiarello, L., Effgen, S., & Levinson, M. (1992). Parent-professional partnership in evaluation and development of individualized family service plans. *Pediatric Physical Therapy, 4*(2), 64–9.

Child and Youth Officer for British Columbia. (2006a). *Health and well-being of children in care in British Columbia: Report 1 on health services utilization and mortality.* Victoria, BC: Child and Youth Officer for British Columbia and Office of the Provincial Health Officer.

Child and Youth Officer for British Columbia. (2006b). *A bridge to adulthood: Maximizing the independence of youth in care with Fetal Alcohol Spectrum Disorder.* Victoria, BC: Author. <http://www.llbc.leg.bc.ca/public/pubdocs/bcdocs/406749/bridgeadulthood.pdf>.

Child and Youth Officer for British Columbia. (2006c). *Special report: Heshook-ish Tsawalk: Towards a healthy state of interdependence in the child welfare system.* Victoria, BC: Author. <http://www.rcybc.ca/Groups/Archived%20Reports/heshook_ish_tsawalk_special_report.pdf>.

Child, Family and Community Service Act (CFCSA). (1996). R.S.B.C. 1996, c. 46. Victoria, BC: Queen's Printer.

Children, Young Persons, and Their Families Act 1989 (New Zealand). (1989). Wellington, NZ: Government of New Zealand.

Children's Action Alliance (Arizona). (2005). *Transitions: Building better lives for youth leaving foster care.* Originally retrieved November 9, 2008; accessible at <http://www.azchildren.org/MyFiles/PDF/_CAA_Transitions_FosterCare_.pdf>.

Children's Research Center. (2008). *The Structured Decision Making model: An evidence based approach to human services.* Retrieved October 15, 2008, from <http://www.nccd-crc.org/crc/crc/c_sdm_about.html>.

Child Welfare Information Gateway. (2008). *Differential response to reports of child abuse and neglect.* Washington, DC: Children's Bureau, U.S. Department of Health & Human Services. <www.childwelfare.gov/pubs/issue_briefs/differential_response>.

Child Welfare League of America. (2000). *Child Welfare League of America standards of excellence for kinship care services.* Washington, DC: Author.

Child Welfare League of America. (2001). *The child welfare workforce challenge: Results from a preliminary study.* Washington, DC: Author.

Child Welfare League of America. (2005). *A comparison of approaches to risk assessment in child protection and brief summary of issues identified from research on assessment in related fields.* Arlington, VA: Author. Accessible via <http://www.cwla.org/>.

Child Welfare League of America. (2006). *Guidelines for computing caseload standards.* Retrieved April 20, 2006, from <http://www.cwla.org/programs/standards/caseloadstandards.htm>.

Child Welfare League of America. (2007). *Hearing on disconnected and disadvantaged youth*. Testimony to the Subcommittee on Income Security and Family Support. <http://www.cwla.org/advocacy/fostercare070619.htm>.

Child Welfare Secretariat (Ontario). (2005). *Child welfare transformation 2005*. Toronto: Ministry of Children and Youth Services.

Child Welfare Secretariat (Ontario). (2006). *Linking child welfare and the children's service system in Ontario: A policy framework for communities*. Toronto: Ontario Ministry of Children and Youth Services.

Child, Youth and Family Evaluation Unit (New Zealand). (2003). *Researching kinship and foster care in Aotearoa*. Wellington, NZ: Department of Child, Youth and Family, Government of New Zealand.

Chou, S., & Browne, K. (2008). The relationship between institutional care and the international adoption of children in Europe. *Adoption and Fostering, 32*(1), 40–8.

Christenson, B., Curran, S., DeCook, K., Maloney, S., & Merkel-Holguin, L. (2008). The intersection between differential response and family involvement approaches. *Protecting Children, 23*(1/2), 88–95.

Christian, S. (2002). Supporting and retaining foster parents [electronic version]. *NCSL State Legislative Report, 27*(11), 1–11.

Christiansen, E. J., & Evans, W. P. (2005). Adolescent victimization: Testing models of resiliency by gender. *Journal of Early Adolescence, 25*(3), 298–316.

Christie, A. (2006). Negotiating the uncomfortable intersections between gender and professional identities in social work. *Critical Social Policy, 26*(2), 390–411.

Cicchetti, D., & Lynch, M. (1993). Toward an ecological/transactional model of community violence and child maltreatment: consequences for children's development. [Review]. *Psychiatry, 56*(1), 96–118.

Cicchetti, D., & Toth, S. L. (2000). Developmental processes in maltreated children. In D. J. Hansen (Ed.), *Nebraska symposium on motivation*, Vol. 46: *Motivation and child maltreatment* (pp. 85–160). Lincoln: University of Nebraska Press.

Cingolani, J. (1984). Social conflict perspective on work with involuntary clients. *Social Work, 29*, 442–6.

Clare, M. (1997). The UK Looking After Children project: Fit for out-of-home care practice in Australia?. *Children Australia, 22*(1), 29–35.

Clare, M. (2003). "Good enough parenting" when government is "the parent." *Children Australia, 28*(4), 19–24.

Clare, M., & Peerless, H. (1996). *An evaluation study of the UK Looking After Children materials*. Unpublished report for the Out-of-Home, Preventative and Alternative Care Committee, University of Western Australia, Perth, Australia.

Clark, R., & Burke, G. (1998). *Looking After Children: An evaluation of the Victorian pilot program*. Unpublished report prepared for the Children's Welfare Association of Victoria, Melbourne, Australia.

Clarke, A. M., & Clarke, A. D. B. (1976). *Early experience: Myth and evidence.* London: Open Books.

Clarke, A. M., & Clarke, A. D. B. (2000). *Early experience and the life path.* London: Jessica Kingsley Publishers.

Clarke, A. M., & Clarke, A. D. B. (2003). *Human resilience: A fifty year quest.* London: Jessica Kingsley Publishers.

Cleaver, H., Nicholson, D., Tarr, S., & Cleaver, D. (2007). *Child protection, domestic violence and parental substance misuse: Family experiences and effective practice.* London: Jessica Kingsley Publishers.

Cleaver, H., Unell, I., & Aldgate, J. (1999). *Children's needs—parenting capacity: The impact of parental mental illness, problem alcohol and drug use, and domestic violence on children's development.* London: Stationery Office.

Cleaver, H., & Walker, S., with Meadows, P. (2004). *Assessing children's needs and circumstances: The impact of the assessment framework.* London: Jessica Kingsley Publishers.

Cleaver, H., Walker, S., Scott, J., Cleaver, D., Rose, W., Ward, H., et al. (2008). *The Integrated Children's System: Enhancing social work and inter-agency practice.* London: Jessica Kingsley Publishers.

Clemens, J., & Jodar, L. (2005). Introducing new vaccines into developing countries: Obstacles, opportunities and complexities. Nature Medicine, 11, S12–S15. Originally retrieved March 25, 2009; accessible at <http://www.nature.com/nm/journal/v11/n4s/full/nm1225.html>.

Cliffe, D., & Berridge, D. (1992). *Closing children's homes: An end to residential childcare?* London: National Children's Bureau.

Coady, N., Cameron, G., & Adams, G. R. (2007). Fundamental considerations for child and family welfare. In G. Cameron, N. Coady, & G. R. Adams (Eds.), *Moving toward positive systems of child and family welfare* (pp. 347–71). Waterloo, ON: Wilfrid Laurier University Press.

Coates, R. B., Miller, A. D., & Ohlin, L. (1978). *Diversity in a youth correctional system: Handling delinquents in Massachusetts.* Cambridge, MA: Ballinger.

Cockburn, G. (1994). The *Children, Young Persons and their Families Act 1989*: Past, present and future. In R. Munford & M. Nash (Eds.), *Social work in action* (pp. 85–103). Palmerston North, New Zealand: Dunmore Press.

Cole, E. (1995). Becoming family centered: Child welfare's challenge. *Families in Society: The Journal of Contemporary Social Services, 76*(3), 163–72.

Collins, D., & Colorado, P. (1988). Native culture and child care services. In G. Charles & P. Gabor (Eds.), *Issues in child and youth care practice in Alberta* (pp. 83–94). Lethbridge, AB: Lethbridge Community College.

Collins, M. E. (2001). Transition to adulthood for vulnerable youth: A review of research and implications for policy. *Social Service Review, 75*(2), 271–91.

Collins, M. E., Amodeo, M., & Clay, C. (2007). Training as a factor in policy implementation: Lessons from a national evaluation of child welfare training. *Children and Youth Services Review, 29*(12), 1487–1502.

Conley, A. (2007). Differential response: A critical examination of a secondary prevention model. *Children and Youth Services Review, 29*(11), 1454–68.

Connolly, M. (2003). *Kinship care: A selected literature review.* Wellington, NZ: Department of Child, Youth and Family Services, Government of New Zealand.

Connolly, M. (2004). *Child and family welfare: Statutory responses to children at risk.* Christchurch, New Zealand: Te Awatea Press.

Connolly, M. (2006). Up front and personal: Confronting dynamics in the family group conference. *Family Process, 45*(3), 345–57.

Connors, E., & Maidman, F. (2001). A circle of healing: Family wellness in Aboriginal communities. In I. Prilleltensky, G. Nelson, & L. Peirson (Eds.), *Promoting family wellness and preventing child maltreatment: Fundamentals for thinking and action* (pp. 349–416). Toronto: University of Toronto Press.

Constitution Act, 1982, being Schedule B to the *Canada Act 1982* (U.K.), 1982, c. 11. Retrieved August 20, 2008, from <http://www.solon.org/Constitutions/Canada/English/ca_1982.html>.

Convention on Protection of Children and Co-operation in Respect of Intercountry Adoption (U.N.). (1993). Hague Conference on Private International Law, Final Act of the Seventeenth Session, May 29, 1993, 32 I.L.M. 1134.

Coohey, C., & Zhang, Y. (2006). The role of men in chronic supervisory neglect. *Child Maltreatment, 11*(1), 27–33.

Cooley, J. J. (1998). Gay and lesbian adolescents: Presenting problems and the counselor's role. *Professional School Counseling, 1*(3), 30–4.

Cordero, A. E. (2004). When family reunification works: Data-mining foster care records. *Families in Society: The Journal of Contemporary Social Services, 85*(4), 571–80.

Costello, A., Francis, V., Byrne, A., & Puddephatt, C. (2001). *State of the world's newborns: A report from Saving Newborn Lives.* Washington, DC: Save the Children.

Côté, J. E. (2006). Emerging adulthood as an institutionalized moratorium: Risks and benefits in identity formation. In J. E. Arnett. & J. Tanner. (Eds.), *Emerging adults in America: Coming of age in the 21st century* (pp. 85–116). Washington, DC: American Psychological Association.

Council on the Aging (COTA). (2003). *Grandparents raising grandchildren: A report commissioned by the Ministry of Children and Youth Affairs Australia.* Melbourne: Author.

Courtney, M. E. (1994). Factors associated with the reunification of foster children with their families. *Social Service Review, 68*(1), 81–108.

Courtney, M. E. (1995). Reentry to foster care of children returned to their families. *Social Service Review, 69*(2), 226–41.

Courtney, M. E., Barth, R. P., Berrick, J. D., Brooks, D., Needell, B., & Park, L. (1996). Race and child welfare services: Past research and future directions. *Child Welfare, 75*(2), 99–137.

Courtney, M. E., & Dworsky, A. (2005). *Midwest evaluation of the adult functioning of former foster youth: Outcomes at age 19. Executive summary.* Chicago: Chapin Hall Center for Children, University of Chicago.

Courtney, M. E., & Dworsky, A. (2006). Early outcomes for young adults transitioning from out-of-home care in the USA. *Child and Family Social Work, 11*(3), 209–19.

Courtney, M. E., Dworsky, A., Ruth, G., Keller, T., Havlicek, J., & Bost, N. (2005). *Midwest evaluation of the adult functioning of former foster youth: Outcomes at age 19.* Chicago: Chapin Hall Center for Children, University of Chicago.

Courtney, M. E., & Heuring, D. H. (2005). The transition to adulthood for youth "aging out" of the foster care system. In D. W. Osgood, E. M. Foster, C. Flanagan & G. R. Ruth (Eds.), *On your own without a net: The transition to adulthood for vulnerable populations* (pp. 27–67). Chicago: University of Chicago Press.

Courtney, M. E., McMurtry, S. L., & Zinn, A. (2004). Housing problems experienced by recipients of child welfare services. *Child Welfare, 83*(5), 393–422.

Covell, K., & Howe, R. B. (2001). *The challenge of children's rights for Canada.* Waterloo, ON: Wilfrid Laurier University Press.

Cradock, G. (2005). Extraordinary costs and jurisdictional disputes. In First Nations Child and Family Caring Society of Canada, *Wen:de (We are coming to the light of day)* (pp. 178–207). Ottawa: First Nations Child and Family Caring Society of Canada.

Craft, J. L., & Bettin, C. A. (1991). Case factor selection in physical abuse investigations. *Journal of Social Service Research, 14*(3), 107–23.

Craig, B. (2001). *Annotated bibliography on transitions to independence.* Unpublished paper.

Crain, J., & Tonmyr, L. (2007). Differential response models of child protection and implications for the *Canadian Incidence Study of Reported Child Abuse and Neglect—2008. Canada's Children,* Summer, 21–6.

Crais, E. R. (1991). Moving from "parent involvement" to family-centered services. *American Journal of Speech-Language Pathology, 1*, 5–8.

Cross, T. (1998). Understanding family resiliency from a relational world view. In H. I. McCubbin, E. A. Thompson, A. I. Thompson, & J. E. Fromer (Eds.), *Resiliency in Native American and immigrant families* (pp. 143–57). Thousand Oaks, CA: Sage.

Cross, T., Earle, K. A., & Simmons, S. (2000). Child abuse and neglect in Indian country: Policy issues. *Families in Society: The Journal of Contemporary Social Services, 81*(1), 49–58.

Crosson-Tower, C. (2006). *Exploring child welfare: A practice perspective.* 4th ed. Toronto: Allyn & Bacon.

Crowe, K. (2007). Using youth expertise at all levels: The essential resource for effective child welfare practice. In V. Mann-Feder (Ed.), *Transition or eviction? Youth exiting care for independent living.* Special issue of *New Directions in Youth Development, 113,* 139–49.

Crowley, S. (2003). The affordable housing crisis: Residential mobility of poor families and school mobility of poor children. *The Journal of Negro Education, 72*(1), 22–38.

Crush, L. (2006). The state of child protection mediation in Canada. *Canadian Family Law Quarterly, 24,* 191–221.

Csáky, C. (2008). *No one to turn to: The under-reporting of child sexual exploitation and abuse by aid workers and peacekeepers.* London: Save the Children.

Culbertson, J. L., & Schellenbach, C. (1992). Prevention of maltreatment in infants and young children. In D. J. Willis, E. W. Holden and M. Rosenberg (Eds.), *Prevention of child maltreatment: Developmental and ecological perspectives* (pp. 44–77). New York: Wiley.

Curry, D., McCarragher, T., & Dellmann-Jenkins, M. (2005). Training, transfer, and turnover: Exploring the relationship among transfer of learning factors and staff retention in child welfare. *Children and Youth Services Review, 27*(8), 931–48.

Damant, D., Lapierre, S., Lebossé, C., Thibault, S., Lessard, G., Hamelin-Brabant, L., et al. (2010). Women's abuse of their children in the context on domestic violence: Reflection from women's accounts. *Child and Family Social Work, 15*(1), 12–21.

D'Andrade, A., Austin, M. J., & Benton, A. (2005). *Risk and safety assessment in child welfare: Instrument comparisons.* Berkeley: Center for Social Services Research, School of Social Welfare, University of California, Berkeley.

D'Andrade, A., Austin, M. J., & Benton, A. (2008). Risk and safety assessment in child welfare: Instrument comparisons. *Journal of Evidence-Based Social Work, 5*(1/2), 31–56.

Daniel, B., & Taylor, J. (1999). The rhetoric versus the reality: A critical perspective on practice with fathers in childcare and protection work. *Child and Family Social Work, 4*(3), 209–220.

Daniel, B., & Taylor, J. (2001). *Engaging with fathers: Practice issues for health and social care.* London: Jessica Kingsley Publishers.

Daro, D. (1988). *Confronting child abuse: Research for effective program design.* New York: Free Press.

Daro, D. (Ed.). (2006). *World perspectives on child abuse* (7th ed.). Chicago: International Society for the Prevention of Child Abuse and Neglect.

Daro, D., & McCurdy, K. (1994). Preventing child abuse and neglect: Programmatic interventions. *Child Welfare, 73*(5), 405–30.

Davies, C. (2003). Policy development: Making research count. In K. Kufeldt & B. McKenzie (Eds.), *Child welfare: Connecting research, policy, and practice* (pp. 377–86). Waterloo, ON: Wilfrid Laurier University Press.

Davies, L., Collings, S., & Krane, J. (2003). Making mothers visible: Implications for social work practice and education in child welfare. *Journal for the Association for Research on Mothering, 5*(2), 158–69.

Davies, L., & Krane, J. (1996). Shaking the legacy of mother blaming: No easy task for child welfare. *Journal of Progressive Human Services, 7*(2), 3–22.

Davies, L. & Krane, J. (2006). Collaborate with caution: Protecting children, helping mothers. *Critical Social Policy, 26*(2), 412–25.

Davies, M. (2005). Welfare amazons or handmaidens of the state? Welfare field workers in rural British Columbia, 1935–1942. In D. Purvey & C. Walmsley (Eds.) *Child and family welfare in British Columbia: A history* (pp. 195–234). Calgary: Detselig.

Davis, I. P., Landsverk, J., Newton, R., & Ganger, W. (1996). Parental visiting and foster care reunification. *Children and Youth Services Review, 18*(4/5), 363–82.

De Boer, C., Cameron, G., & Frensch, K. M. (2007). Siege and response: Reception and benefits of residential children's mental health services for parents and siblings. *Child and Youth Care Forum, 36*(1), 11–24.

Delfabbro, P. H., Barber, J. G., & Cooper, L. (2000). Placement disruption and dislocation in South Australian substitute care. *Children Australia, 25*(2), 16–20.

Delfabbro, P. H., Barber, J. G., & Cooper, L. (2003). Predictors of short-term reunification in South Australian substitute care. *Child Welfare, 82*(1), 27–51.

DeMause, L. (Ed.). (1976). *The history of childhood.* London: Souvenir Press.

Denzin, N., & Lincoln, Y. (Eds.) (2003). *Collecting and interpreting qualitative materials* (2nd ed.). Thousand Oaks, CA, and London: Sage.

DePanfilis, D. (1999). Intervening with families when children are neglected. In H. Dubowitz (Ed.), *Neglected children: Research, practice, and policy.* (pp. 211–36). Thousand Oaks, CA: Sage.

DePanfilis, D. (2006). *Child neglect: A guide for prevention, assessment and intervention.* Washington, DC: U.S. Department of Health and Human Services, Department for Children and Families.

DePanfilis, D., & Dubowitz, H. (2005). Family connections: A program for preventing child neglect. *Child Maltreatment, 10*(2), 108–23.

DePanfilis, D., Glazer-Semmel, E., Farr, M., & Meek, G. F. (1999). *Family connections intervention manual.* Baltimore: University of Maryland, School of Social Work.

DePanfilis, D., & Zuravin, S. (1999). Epidemiology of child maltreatment recurrences. *Social Service Review, 73*(2), 218–39.

DePanfilis, D., & Zuravin, S. (2001). Assessing risk to determine the need for services. *Children and Youth Services Review, 23*(1), 3–20.

Department for Children, Schools, and Families (U.K.). (2006). *Care matters: Transforming the lives of children and young people in care [Green paper].* Originally retrieved September 11, 2008; now accessible via <http://publications.education.gov.uk/>.

Department for Children, Schools, and Families (U.K.), MTFCE Implementation Team. (2008). *Multidimensional treatment foster care in England (MTFCE): Annual project report.* London and Manchester: MTFCE Implementation Team.

Department for Education and Skills (U.K.). (2005). *Every child matters: Change for children.* London: Department for Education and Skills.

Department for Education and Skills (U.K.). (2006). *Information sharing: Practitioners' guide.* London: Department for Education and Skills.

Department for International Development (U.K.). (2000). *Disability, poverty and development.* London: Author.

Department of Child, Youth and Family Services (New Zealand). (2006). *Annual report 2006.* Wellington, NZ: Government of New Zealand.

Department of Family Services and Housing (Manitoba). (2008). *Annual report 2006–07.* Winnipeg, MB: Government of Manitoba.

Department of Health (U.K.). (1991). *Patterns and outcomes in child placement: Messages from current research and their implications.* London: Her Majesty's Stationery Office.

Department of Health (U.K.). (1995). *Child protection: Messages from research.* London: Her Majesty's Stationery Office.

Department of Health (U.K.), Social Care Group. (1997). *Responding to families in need: Inspection of assessment, planning and decision-making in family support services.* London: Department of Health.

Department of Health, Department for Education and Employment, and Home Office (U.K.). (2000). *Framework for the assessment of children in need and their families.* London: Stationery Office.

Department of Health and Social Security (U.K.). (1985). *Social work decisions in child care: Recent research findings and their implications.* London: Her Majesty's Stationery Office.

Desmeules, G. (2007). A sacred family circle: A family group conferencing model. In I. Brown, F. Chaze, D. Fuchs, J. Lafrance, S. McKay, & S. Thomas Prokop (Eds.), *Putting a human face on child welfare: Voices from the prairie* (pp. 161–88). Toronto: Centre of Excellence for Child Welfare/Prairie Child Welfare Consortium.

Devault, A., Gaudet, J., Bolte, C., & St-Denis, M. (2005). A survey and description of projects that support and promote fathering in Canada: Still work to do to reach fathers in their real-life settings. *Canadian Journal of Community Mental Health, 24*(1), 5–17.

Dickenson, M. (2008). *The invisible children in foster care: Providing support to "children who foster."* Unpublished manuscript.

Dickinson, N., & Perry, R. (2002). Factors influencing the retention of specially educated public child welfare workers. *Journal of Health and Social Policy, 15*(3/4), 89–103.

Differential Response Sub-Committee of Ontario Children's Aid Society Directors of Service. (2004). *A differential service response for child welfare in Ontario.* Toronto: Ontario Association of Children's Aid Societies.

Dill, K. (2009). *Finding the best home.* Unpublished doctoral dissertation, Factor-Inwentash Faculty of Social Work, University of Toronto, Toronto.

Dingwall, R., Eeklaar, J., & Murray, T. (1983). *The protection of children: State intervention and family life.* Oxford, UK: Basil Blackwell.

La Direction des communications du Ministère de la Santé et des Services sociaux du Québec. (2007). *Your child's situation has been reported to the DYP: What do you need to know now?* Originally retrieved November 1, 2008; accessible at <http://publications.msss.gouv.qc.ca/acrobat/f/documentation/2007/07-838-02A .pdf>.

Dixon, D. (2001). *Looking After Children* in Barnardos Australia: A study of the early stages of implementation. *Children Australia, 26*(3), 27–32.

Dixon, J., Wade, J., Byford, S., Weatherly, H., & Lee, J. (2006). *Young people leaving care: A study of costs and outcomes.* York, UK: Social Work Research & Development Unit, University of York. <http://www.york.ac.uk/inst/spru/research/pdf/ leaving.pdf>.

Dominelli, L., Strega, S., Callahan, M., & Rutman, D. (2005). Endangered children: Experiencing and surviving the state as failed parent and grandparent. *British Journal of Social Work, 35*(7), 1123–44.

Dominican University. (2009). Graduate School of Social Work, River Forest, IL. Home page at <http://www.dom.edu/>.

Donald, K. L., Bradley, L., Day, P., Crichley R., & Nuccio, K. E. (2003). Comparison between American Indian and non-Indian out-of-home placements. *Families in Society: The Journal of Contemporary Social Services, 84*(2), 267–74.

Donnon, T., & Hammond, W. (2007a). A psychometric assessment of the self-reported Youth Resiliency: Assessing Developmental Strengths questionnaire. *Psychological Reports, 100,* 963–78.

Donnon, T., & Hammond, W. (2007b). Understanding the relationship in between resiliency and bullying in adolescence: an assessment of youth resiliency from five urban junior high schools. *Child and Adolescent Psychiatric Clinics of North America, 16*(2), 449–71.

Donnon, T., Hammond, W., & Charles, G. (2003). Youth resiliency: Assessing students' capacity for success at school. *Teaching and Learning, 1*(2), 23–8.

Doorbar, P. (1999). The children of foster carers. In A. Wheal (Ed.), *The RHP companion to foster care* (pp. 183–7). Dorset, UK: Russell House Publishing.

Doucet, A. (2006). *Do men mother?: Fathering, care, and domestic responsibility.* Toronto: University of Toronto Press.

Downs, S., Moore, E., McFadden, E. J., Michaud, S. M., & Costin, L. B. (2004). *Child welfare and family services: Policies and practice.* (7th ed.). Boston: Allyn & Bacon.

Drake, B., Jonson-Reid, M., Way, I., & Chung, S. (2003). Substantiation and recidivism. *Child Maltreatment, 8*(4), 248–60.

Drake, B., & Zuravin, S. (1998). Bias in child maltreatment reporting: Revisiting the myth of classlessness. *American Journal of Orthopsychiatry, 68*(2), 295–304.

Drapeau, S., Simard, M., Beaudry, M., & Charbonneau, C. (2000). Siblings in family transitions. *Family Relations, 49*(1), 77–85.

Drasgow, F., & Schmitt, N. (2002). *Measuring and analyzing behavior in organizations.* San Francisco, CA: Jossey-Bass.

Drolet, M., & Sauvé-Kobylecki, M. (2007). Perceptions d'intervenantes sur l'approche *S'occuper des enfants* et son outil, le *Cahier d'évaluation et de suivi* : Pour mieux saisir des contraintes organisationnelles. *Service social, 53*(1), 25–39.

Drury-Hudson, J. (1999). Decision making in child protection: The use of theoretical, empirical and procedural knowledge by novices and experts and implications for fieldwork placement. *British Journal of Social Work, 29*(1), 147–69.

Dubowitz, H. (Ed.). (1999). *Neglected children: Research, practice, and policy.* Thousand Oaks, CA: Sage.

Dubowitz, H., Feigelman, S., Zuravin, S., Tepper, V., Davidson, N., & Lichenstein, R. (1992). The physical health of children in kinship care. *American Journal of Diseases of Children, 146*(5), 603–10.

Dufour, S., & Chamberland, C. (2004). The effectiveness of selected interventions for previous maltreatment: Enhancing the well-being of children who live at home. *Child and Family Social Work, 9*(1), 39–56.

Dufour, S., Chamberland, C., & Trocmé, N. (2003). *A state-of-knowledge review: What is the effectiveness of child welfare interventions?* Centre of Excellence for Child Welfare. Accessible via <http://www.cecw-cepb.ca/publications/635>.

Dumbrill, G. C., & Maiter, S. (2003). Child protection clients designing the services they receive: An idea from practice. *Child and Family: A Journal of the Notre Dame Child and Family Institute, 7*(1), 5–10.

Dunn, J., & McGuire, S. (1992). Sibling and peer relationships in childhood. *Journal of Child Psychology and Psychiatry, 33*(1), 67–105.

Dunne, G., & Kettler, L. (2008). Grandparents raising grandchildren in Australia: Exploring psychological health and grandparents' experience of providing kinship care. *International Journal of Social Welfare, 17*(4), 333–45.

Dunst, C., Johanson, C., Trivette, C., & Hamby, D. (1991). Family oriented early intervention policies: Family-centered or not? *Exceptional Children, 58*(2), 115–26.

Dunst, C., Trivette, C., & Deal, A. (1988). *Enabling and empowering families. Principles and guidelines for practice.* Cambridge, MA: Brookline Books.

Dunst, C., Trivette, C., & Deal, A. (1994a). Enabling and empowering families. In C. Dunst, C. Trivette, & A. Deal (Eds.), *Supporting and strengthening families.* Vol. 1: *Methods, strategies and practices* (pp. 2–11). Cambridge, MA: Brookline Books.

Dunst, C., Trivette, C., & Deal, A. (1994b). Resource-based family-centered intervention practices. In C. Dunst, C. Trivette, & A. Deal (Eds.), *Supporting and strengthening families*. Vol. 1: *Methods, strategies and practices* (pp. 140–51). Cambridge, MA: Brookline Books.

Dunst, C., Trivette, C., & Hamby, D. (2007). Meta-analysis of family-centred helpgiving practices research. *Mental Retardation and Developmental Disabilities, 13*(4), 370–8.

Durst, D., & Bluechardt, M. (2001). *Urban Aboriginal persons with disabilities: Triple jeopardy!* Social Policy Research Unit, University of Regina.

Earle, K. A., & Cross, A. (2001). *Child abuse and neglect among American Indian/Alaska Native children: An analysis of existing data*. Seattle: Casey Family Programs.

Eddy, J. M., Bridges Whaley, R., & Chamberlain, P. (2004). The prevention of violent behavior by chronic and serious male juvenile offenders: A 2-year follow-up of a randomized clinical trial. *Journal of Emotional and Behavioral Disorders, 12*(1), 2–8.

Efron, B. (1982). *The jackknife, the bootstrap and other resampling plans*. Philadelphia: Society for Industrial and Applied Mathematics.

Egypt charges 11 in baby buying scheme. (2009, January 21). *Calgary Herald*, p. A16.

Ehrle, J., & Geen, R. (2002). Kin and non-kin care—Findings from a national survey. *Children and Youth Services Review, 24*(1/2), 15–35.

Eldridge, S. (1999). *Twenty things adopted kids wish their parents knew*. New York: Bantam Dell.

Eldridge, S. (2003). *Twenty life-transforming choices adoptees need to make*. Colorado Springs, CO: Pinon Press.

Eldridge, S. (2009). *20 things adoptive parents need to succeed*. New York: Bantam Dell.

Ellis, L. (1972). Sharing parents with strangers: The role of the group home foster family's own children. *Child Welfare, 51*(3), 165–70.

Emlen, A. C., Lahti, J., Downs, G., McKay, A., & Downs, S. (1979). *Outcomes of permanency planning for children in foster care*. Portland, OR: Portland State University.

English, D. J., Marshall, D., Brummel, S., Novicky, R., & Coghlan, L. (1998). *Decision-making in CPS: A study of effectiveness*. Final report, phase II: *Social worker interviews*. Olympia, WA: Department of Social and Health Services, Children's Administration, Management Services Division, Office of Children's Administration Research .

English, D. J., Marshall, D., Brummel, S., & Orme, M. (1999). Characteristics of repeated referrals to child protective services in Washington state. *Child Maltreatment, 4*(4), 297–307.

English, D. J., Thompson, R., Graham, J., & Briggs, E. (2005). Toward a definition of neglect in young children. *Child Maltreatment, 10*(2), 190–206.

English, D. J., Upadhyaya, M. P., Litrownik, A. J., Marshall, J. M., Runyan, D. K., Graham, J., et al. (2005). Maltreatment's wake: The relationship of maltreatment dimensions to child outcomes. *Child Abuse and Neglect, 29*(5), 597–619.

English, D. J., Wingard, T., Marshall, D., Orme, M., & Orme, A. (2000). Alternative responses to child protective services: Emerging issues and concerns. *Child Abuse and Neglect*, 24(3), 375–88.

Epstein, N. B., Baldwin, L. M., & Bishop, D. S. (1983). The McMaster family assessment device. *Journal of Marital and Family Therapy*, 9(2), 171–80.

Epstein, N. B., Ryan, C. E., Bishop, D. S., Miller, I. W., & Keitner, G. I. (2003). The McMaster model: A view of healthy family functioning. In F. Walsh (Ed.), *Normal family processes: Growing diversity and complexity* (3rd ed.), (pp. 581–607). New York: Guilford Press.

Erickson, M. F., & Egeland, B. (1996). The quiet assault: A portrait of child neglect. In L. Berliner, J. Briere, S. Bulkley, C. Jenny, & T. Reid (Eds.), *The handbook of child maltreatment* (pp. 4–20). Newbury Park, CA: Sage.

Erickson, M. F., Egeland, B., & Pianta, R. (1989). The effects of maltreatment on the development of young children. In D. Cicchetti & V. Carlson (Eds.), *Child maltreatment: Theory and research on the causes and consequences of child abuse and neglect* (pp. 647–84). Cambridge, MA: Cambridge University Press.

Erikson, E. H. (1968). *Identity, youth, and crisis.* New York: W. W. Norton.

Erikson, E. H. (1985). *The life cycle completed.* New York: W.W. Norton.

Eriksson, M., & Hester, M. (2001). Violent men as good-enough fathers?: A look at England and Sweden. *Violence Against Women*, 7(7), 779–98.

Espejo, R. (Ed.). (2002). *Adoption: Opposing viewpoints.* San Diego: Greenhaven Press.

Este, D. (2009). Cultural competency and social work practice in Canada: A retrospective examination. *Canadian Social Work Review*, 24(1), 93–104.

Este, D., & Ngo, H. (2006). The professional re-entry of immigrants. *Journal of International Migration and Integration*, 7(1), 27–51.

Éthier, L. S., Couture, G., Lacharité, C., & Gagnier, J.-P. (2000). Impact of a multidimensional intervention programme applied to families at risk for child neglect. *Child Abuse Review*, 9(1), 19–36.

Evans-Campbell, T. (2008). Historical trauma in American Indian/Native Alaska communities: A multilevel framework for exploring impacts on individuals, families, and communities. *Journal of Interpersonal Violence*, 23(3), 316–38.

Factor, D., & Wolfe, D. (1990). Parental psychopathology and high-risk children. In R. T. Ammerman & M. Hersen (Eds.), *Children at risk: An evaluation of factors contributing to child abuse and neglect* (pp. 171–99). New York: Plenum Press.

Falconer, N., & Swift, K. (1983). *Preparing for practice: The fundamentals of child protection.* Toronto: Children's Aid Society of Metropolitan Toronto.

Fallon, B., Trocmé, N., MacLaurin, B., Knoke, D., Black, T., Daciuk, J. et al. (2005). *Ontario incidence study of reported child abuse and neglect—2003: Major findings.* Toronto: Centre of Excellence for Child Welfare, Faculty of Social Work, University of Toronto.

Family Rights Group. (2008). *Fathers Matter 2—Further findings on fathers and their involvement with social care services.* Originally retrieved July 9, 2008; accessible at <http://www.frg.org.uk/pdfs/Fathers%20Matter%202%20publication.pdf>.

Fanshel, D., Finch, S. J., & Grundy, J. F. (1990). *Foster children in a life course perspective.* New York: Columbia University Press.

Fanshel, D., & Shinn, E. B. (1978). *Children in foster care: A longitudinal investigation.* New York: Columbia University Press.

Farmer, E. (1996). Family reunification with high risk children: Lessons from research. *Children and Youth Services Review, 18*(4/5), 403–24.

Farmer, E., & Moyers, S. (2005). *Children placed with family and friends: Placement patterns and outcomes.* (Report to the Department for Education and Skills: Executive Summary.) Bristol, UK: School for Policy Studies, University of Bristol. Originally retrieved September 11, 2008; accessible at <http://www.education.gov.uk/research/data/uploadfiles/RW83.pdf>.

Farmer, E., & Moyers, S. (2008). *Kinship care: Fostering effective family and friends placements.* London: Jessica Kingsley Publishers.

Farris-Manning, C., & Zandstra, M. (2003). Children in care in Canada: Summary of current issues and trends and recommendations for future research. In Child Welfare League of Canada, *The welfare of Canadian children: It's our business* (pp. 54–72). Ottawa. Retrieved January 5, 2009, from <http://www.cwlc.ca/policy/welfare_e.htm>.

Farrow, F. (1997). *Child protection: Building community partnerships.* Cambridge, MA: Harvard University Press.

Fatherhood Institute Website. (n.d.). Retrieved May 21, 2009. <http://www.fatherhoodinstitute.org>.

Father Involvement Research Alliance. (n.d.). Retrieved May 21, 2009. <http://www.fira.ca>.

Featherstone, B. (2003). Taking fathers seriously. *British Journal of Social Work, 33*(2), 239–54.

Featherstone, B. (2004). Fathers matter: A research review. *Children and Society, 18*, 312–19.

Featherstone, B., Rivett, M., & Scourfield, J. (2007). *Working with men in health and social care.* Thousand Oaks, CA: Sage.

Felstiner, C. (2008). Survey of First Nations child and family service agencies. Unpublished internal memo for *Canadian Incidence Study of Reported Child Abuse and Neglect—2008.*

Fergus, S., & Zimmerman, M. A. (2005). Adolescent resilience: A framework for understanding healthy development in the face of risk. *Annual Review of Public Health, 26*, 399–419.

Ferguson, H., & Hogan, F. (2004). *Strengthening families through fathers: Developing policy and practice in relation to vulnerable fathers and their families.* Dublin:

Department of Social and Family Affairs. <http://www.welfare.ie/publications/fathers_fams/contents.html>.

Fernandez, E. (1996). *Significant harm: Unravelling child protection decisions and substitute care careers of children.* Avebury, UK: Ashgate.

Fernandez, E. (1999, September). *The educational outcomes: The challenge for children in care.* Paper presented to Fourth International Conference on *Looking After Children.* Oxford: University of Oxford.

Fernandez, E. (2004). Effective interventions to promote child and family wellness: A study of outcomes of intervention through Children's Family Centres. *Child and Family Social Work, 9*(1), 91–104.

Fernandez, E. (2006a). *Children's wellbeing in care: Evidence from a longitudinal examination of outcomes.* Paper presented at the Association of Children's Welfare Agencies Conference/7th International *Looking After Children* Conference, Sydney, Australia.

Fernandez, E. (2006b). Supporting families: Tracking interactions between families and professionals in Sydney, Australia. *International Journal of Child and Family Welfare, 9*(1/2), 26–40.

Fernandez, E. (2007a). How children experience fostering outcomes: Participatory research with children. *Child and Family Social Work, 12*(4), 349–59.

Fernandez, E. (2007b). Supporting children and responding to their families: Capturing the evidence on family support. *Children and Youth Services Review, 29*(10), 1368–94.

Fernandez, E. (2008a). Unravelling emotional, behavioural and educational outcomes in a longitudinal study of children in foster care. *British Journal of Social Work, 38*(7), 1283–1301.

Fernandez, E. (2008b). Psychosocial wellbeing of children: A longitudinal study of outcomes. *Child Indicators Research, 1*(3), 303–20.

Fernandez, E. (2009, July). Children's wellbeing in care—Evidence from a longitudinal study of outcomes. Presentation at 15th IFCO International Conference (*Linking Global Foster Care*), Dublin, Ireland.

Fernandez, E., & Romeo, R. (2003). *Implementation of the framework for the assessment of children and their families: The experience of Barnardos Australia.* Sydney: University of New South Wales.

Fernandez, L., MacKinnon, S., & Silver, J. (Eds.) (2010). *The social determinants of health in Manitoba.* Winnipeg: Canadian Centre for Policy Alternatives—Manitoba.

Fessler, A. (2006). *The girls who went away: The hidden history of women who surrendered children for adoption in the decades before Roe v. Wade.* New York: Penguin Books.

Filbert, K. M., & Flynn, R. J. (2010). Developmental and cultural assets and resilient outcomes in First Nations young people in care: An initial test of an explanatory model. *Children and Youth Services Review, 32*(4), 560–4.

Finkelhor, D., & Jones, L. (2006). Why have child maltreatment and child victimization declined? *Journal of Social Issues, 62*(4), 685–716.

Finn, E. (2007). Ending child poverty has economic as well as moral benefits. *CCPA Monitor, 14*(2), 4.

First Nations Centre. (2007). *OCAP: Ownership, control, access and possession*. Sanctioned by the First Nations Information Governance Committee, Assembly of First Nations. Ottawa: National Aboriginal Health Organization.

First Nations Child and Family Caring Society of Canada. (2005). *Wen:de (We are coming to the light of day)*. Ottawa: Author.

Fisher, P. A., & Chamberlain, P. (2000). Multidimensional treatment foster care: A program for intensive parenting, family support, and skill building. *Journal of Emotional and Behavioral Disorders, 8*(3), 155–64.

Fleming, L., & Tobin, D. (2005). Popular child-rearing books: Where is Daddy? *Psychology of Men and Masculinity, 6*(1), 18–24.

Floyd, R. L., Ebrahim, S., Tsai, J., O'Connor, M., & Sokol, R. (2006). Strategies to reduce alcohol-exposed pregnancies. *Maternal Child Health Journal, 10* (Supplement 1). Originally retrieved April 7, 2006; accessible at <http://tarjancenter.ucla.edu/upload/Strategies%20to%20Reduce%20Alcohol-Exposed%20Pregnancies.pdf>.

Fluke, J. D. (2009). Allegory of the cave: On the theme of substantiation. *Child Maltreatment, 14*(1), 69–72.

Fluke, J. D., Parry, C., Shapiro, P., Hollinshead, D., Bollenbacher, V., Baumann, D., & Davis-Brown, K. (2001). *The dynamics of unsubstantiated reports: A multi-state study. Final report.* Englewood, CO: American Humane Association.

Flynn, R. (2003). *Resilience in transitions from out-of-home care in Canada: A prospective longitudinal study*. Unpublished research proposal.

Flynn, R. J., & Biro, C. (1998). Comparing developmental outcomes for children in care with those for other children in Canada. *Children and Society, 12*(3), 228–33.

Flynn, R. J., Dudding, P. M., & Barber, J. G. (Eds.). (2006). *Promoting resilience in child welfare*. Ottawa: University of Ottawa Press.

Flynn, R. J., & Ghazal, H. (2001). *Looking After Children in Ontario: Good parenting, good outcomes–Assessment and Action Record* [Second Canadian adaptation developed under licence from Department of Health (London: Her Majesty's Stationery Office, 1995.)] Ottawa: Centre for Research on Community Services, University of Ottawa.

Flynn, R. J., Ghazal, H., Legault, L., Vandermeulen, G., & Petrick, S. (2004). Use of population measures and norms to identify resilient outcomes in young people in care: An exploratory study. *Child and Family Social Work, 9*(1), 65–79.

Flynn, R. J., Lemay, R., Ghazal, H., & Hébert, S. (2003). PM3: A performance measurement, monitoring, and management system for child welfare organizations. In

K. Kufeldt & B. McKenzie (Eds.), *Child welfare: Connecting research, policy and practice* (pp. 319–30). Waterloo, ON: Wilfrid Laurier University Press.

Folaron, G. (1993). Preparing children for reunification. In B. A. Pine, R. Warsh, & A. N. Maluccio (Eds.), *Together again: Family reunification in foster care* (pp. 141–54). Washington, DC: Child Welfare League of America.

Foli, K., & Thompson, J. R. (2004). *The post-adoption blues: Overcoming the unforeseen challenges of adoption.* Emmaus, PA: Rodale.

Forrester, D., McCambridge, J., Waissbein, C., & Rollnick, S. (2008). How do child and family social workers talk to parents about child welfare concerns? *Child Abuse Review, 17*(1), 23–35.

Forsythe, P. W. (1989). Family preservation in foster care: Fit or fiction? In J. Hudson and B. Galaway (Eds.), *Specialist foster family care: A normalizing experience* (pp. 63–73). New York: Haworth Press.

Foster, L. T. (2007). Trends in child welfare: What do the data show? In L.T. Foster & B. Wharf (Eds.) *People, politics, and child welfare in British Columbia* (pp. 34–65). Vancouver: University of British Columbia Press.

The Fostering Network. (2003). Listening to young people: Foster care—the way forward. *Voices from Care*, March, 6–40.

Fournier, S., & Crey, E. (1997). *Stolen from our embrace: The abduction of First Nations children and the restoration of Aboriginal communities.* Vancouver: Douglas and McIntyre.

Fox, W. (2000). *The significance of natural children of foster families.* Social Work Monographs (Serial No. 184). Norwich, England: School of Social Work and Psychosocial Studies, University of East Anglia.

Frame, L., Berrick, J. D., & Brodowski, M. L. (2000). Understanding reentry to out-of-home care for reunified infants. *Child Welfare, 79*(4), 339–69.

Francis, J. (2002). Implementing the "Looking After Children in Scotland" materials: Panacea or stepping-stone? *Social Work Education, 21*(4), 449–60.

Freeman, J., Levine, M., & Doueck, H. (1996). Child age and caseworker attention in child protection service investigations. *Child Abuse and Neglect, 20*(10), 907–20.

Frengley, S. (2007). *Kinship care: Roots or grafts?* Unpublished master's thesis, University of Otago, Dunedin, New Zealand.

Frensch, K. M., Cameron, G., & Hazineh, L. (2005). *A study of three community and school-based models of child welfare service delivery in Ontario: An exploration of parents', service providers', and community experiences.* Waterloo, ON: Partnerships for Children and Families Project, Faculty of Social Work, Wilfrid Laurier University.

Freymond, N., & Cameron, G. (2006). Learning from international comparisons of child protection, family service, and community caring systems of child and family welfare. In N. Freymond & G. Cameron (Eds.), *Towards positive systems of child and family welfare: International comparisons of child protection, family service, and community caring systems* (pp. 289–317). Toronto: University of Toronto Press.

Freymond, N., & Cameron, G. (2007). Mothers and child welfare placements. In G. Cameron, N. Coady, & G. Adams (Eds.), *Moving toward positive systems of child and family welfare: Current issues and future directions* (pp. 79–114). Waterloo, ON: Wilfrid Laurier University Press.

Friend, C., Shlonsky, A., & Lambert, L. (2008). From evolving discourses to new practice approaches in domestic violence and child protective services. *Children and Youth Services Review, 30*(6), 689–98.

Fryer, G. E., Jr., Miyoshi, T., & Thomas, P. (1989). The relationship of child protection worker attitudes to attrition from the field. *Child Abuse and Neglect, 13*(3), 345–50.

Fuchs, D., Burnside, L., Marchenski, S., & Mudry, A. (2005). *Children with disabilities receiving services from child welfare agencies in Manitoba.* Toronto: Centre of Excellence for Child Welfare. Accessible via <http://www.cecw-cepb.ca/publications/577>.

Fuchs, D., Burnside, L., Marchenski, S., & Mudry, A. (2008). *Transition out-of care: Issues for youth with FASD.* Toronto: Centre of Excellence for Child Welfare. Accessible via <http://www.cecw-cepb.ca/publications/626>.

Fuchs, D., Burnside, L., Marchenski, S., & Mudry, A. (2009). *Children with FASD involved with the Manitoba child welfare system: The need for passionate action.* Toronto: Centre of Excellence for Child Welfare. Accessible via <http://www.cecw-cepb.ca/publications/1140>.

Fuchs, D., Burnside, L., Marchenski, S., Mudry, A., & De Riviere, L. (2008). *Economic impact of children in care with FASD, Phase 1: Cost of children in care with FASD in Manitoba.* Toronto: Centre of Excellence for Child Welfare. Accessible via <http://www.cecw-cepb.ca/publications/590>.

Fudge Schormans, A., & Brown, I. (2006). An investigation into the characteristics of the maltreatment of children with developmental delays and the alleged perpetrators of this maltreatment. *Journal on Developmental Disabilities, OADD 20th Anniversary Issue*, 131–51.

Fuller-Thomson, E. (2006). Grandparent caregiving among First Nations Canadians. In B. J. Hayslip, Jr., & J. H. Patrick (Eds.), *Custodial grandparenting: Individual, cultural and ethnic diversity* (pp. 183–98). New York: Springer.

Galaway, B., & Hudson, J. (1995). The directions for future research. In J. Hudson & B. Galaway (Eds.), *Child welfare in Canada: Research and policy implications* (pp. 368–72). Toronto: Thompson Educational Publishing.

Garbarino, J. (1992). *Children and families in the social environment* (2nd ed.). New York: Aldine de Gruyter.

Garbarino, J. (1995). *Raising children in a socially toxic environment.* San Francisco, CA: Jossey-Bass Publishers.

Garbarino, J., & Collins, C. (1999). Child neglect: The family with a hole in the middle. In H. Dubowitz (Ed.), *Neglected children: Research, practice, and policy* (pp. 1–23). Thousand Oaks, CA: Sage.

Garbarino, J., & Kostelny, K. (1992). Child maltreatment as a community problem. *International Journal of Child Abuse and Neglect, 16*(4), 455–64.

Garmezy, N., Masten, A. S., & Tellegen, A. (1984). The study of stress and competence in children: A building block for developmental psychopathology. *Child Development, 55*(1), 97–111.

Garrett, P. M. (2003). *Remaking social work with children and families: A critical discussion on the "modernisation" of social care.* London: Routledge.

Gaudet, J., & Chagnon, F. (2003). *Étude des besoins prioritaires en matière de programmes chez les adolescents au Centre jeunesse de Montréal-Institut universitaire.* Document de travail. Montréal : Direction des services professionnels et de la recherche, Centre jeunesse de Montréal—Institut universitaire.

Gaudin, J. M., Jr. (1993). Effective interventions with neglectful families. *Criminal Justice and Behaviour, 20*(1), 66–89.

Gaudin, J. M., Jr. (1999). Child neglect: Short-term and long-term outcomes. In H. Dubowitz (Ed.). *Neglected children: Research, practice, and policy* (pp. 89–108). Thousand Oaks, CA: Sage.

Gaudin, J. M., Jr., & Dubowitz, H. (1997). Family functioning in neglectful families: Recent research. In J. D. Berrick, R. P. Barth, & N. Gilbert (Eds.), *Child welfare research review*, Vol. 2 (pp. 28–62). New York: Columbia University Press.

Gauthier, L., Stollak, G., Messe, L., & Arnoff, J. (1996). Recall of childhood neglect and physical abuse as differential predictors of current psychological functioning. *Child Abuse and Neglect, 20*(7), 549–59.

Gearing, R., McNeill, T., & Lozier, F. (2005, August). Father involvement and fetal alcohol spectrum disorder: Developing best practices. *Journal of Fetal Alcohol Spectrum International, 3*:e14. Originally retrieved October 12, 2007; accessible at <http://www.motherisk.org/FAR/econtent_commonDetail.jsp?econtent_id=90>.

Geen, R. (2003a). Finding permanent homes for foster children. The Urban Institute, Series A, No. A-60, 1–5. < http://www.urban.org/uploadedpdf/310773_A-60.pdf>.

Geen, R. (2003b). Kinship care: Paradigm shift or just another magic bullet? In R. Geen (Ed.), *Kinship care: Making the most of a valuable resource* (pp. 231–60). Washington, DC: Urban Institute Press.

Geen, R. (2003c). Kinship foster care: An ongoing, yet largely uninformed debate. In R. Geen (Ed.), *Kinship care: Making the most of a valuable resource* (pp. 1–23). Washington, DC: Urban Institute Press.

Geenen, S., Powers, L., Hogansen, J., & Pittman, J. (2007). Youth with disabilities in foster care: Developing self-determination within a context of struggle and disempowerment. *Exceptionality, 15*(1), 17–30.

Gelles, R. (1996). *The book of David: How preserving families can cost children's lives.* New York: Basic Books.

Gergen, K. (1999). *An invitation to social construction.* London: Sage.

Gewirtz, A., Hart-Shegos, E., & Medhanie, A. (2008). Psychosocial status of homeless children and youth in family supportive housing. *American Behavioral Scientist, 51*(6), 810–23.

Gibb, B. E., Chelminski, I., & Zimmerman, M. (2007). Childhood emotional, physical, and sexual abuse, and diagnoses of depressive and anxiety disorders in adult psychiatric outpatients. *Depression and Anxiety, 24*(4), 256–63.

Gibbs, D., & Wildfire, J. (2007). Length of service for foster parents: Using administrative data to understand retention. *Children and Youth Services Review, 29*(5), 588–99.

Gilbert, N. (1997). *Combating child abuse: International perspectives and trends.* Oxford: Oxford University Press.

Gilbertson, R., & Barber, J. G. (2002). Obstacles to involving children and young people in foster care research. *Child and Family Social Work, 7*(4), 253–8.

Gilchrist, L. (1995). *Aboriginal street youth in Vancouver, Winnipeg and Montreal.* Doctoral dissertation, University of British Columbia, Vancouver. (Proquest Digital Dissertations, 742854381. AAT NN05963.)

Gillespie, J. M., Byrne, B., & Workman, L. (1995). An intensive reunification program for children in foster care. *Child & Adolescent Social Work Journal, 12*(3), 213–28.

Gillingham, P., & Humphreys, C. (2009). Child protection practitioners and decision-making tools: Observations and reflections from the front line. *British Journal of Social Work* (Advance Access), 1–19.

Gilligan, R. (1999). Promoting resilience in children in foster care. In G. Kelly & R. Gilligan (Eds.), *Issues in foster care: Policy, practice and research* (pp. 107–26). London: Jessica Kingsley Publishers.

Giovannoni, J., & Becerra, R. (1979). *Defining child abuse.* New York: Free Press.

Glaser, B. G. (1978). *Theoretical sensitivity.* Mill Valley, CA: Sociology Press.

Glaser, B. G. (1992). *Basics of grounded theory analysis.* Mill Valley, CA: Sociology Press.

Glaser, B. G. (1998). *Doing grounded theory: Issues and discussions.* Mill Valley, CA: Sociology Press.

Glaser, B. G. (Ed.). (1993). *Examples of grounded theory: A reader.* Mill Valley, CA: Sociology Press.

Glaser, B. G. (Ed.). (1994). *More grounded theory methodology: A reader.* Mill Valley, CA: Sociology Press.

Glaser, B. G., & Strauss, A. L. (1967). *The discovery of grounded theory: Strategies for qualitative research.* Chicago, IL: Aldine de Gruyter.

Gleeson, J. P., & Hairston, C. F. (Eds.). (1999). *Kinship care: Improving practice through research.* Washington, DC: Child Welfare League of America Press.

Glikman, H. (2004). Low-income fathers: Contexts, connections and self. *Social Work*, *49*(2), 195–206.

Glisson, C., & Green, P. (2005). The effects of organizational culture and climate on the access to mental health care in child welfare and juvenile justice system. *Administration and Policy in Mental Health and Mental Health Services Research, 33*(4), 433–48.

Goerge, R. M. (1990). The reunification process in substitute care. *Social Service Review, 64*(3), 422–57.

Goldstein, H. (1973). *Social work practice: A unitary approach.* Columbia: University of South Carolina Press.

Goldstein, J., Freud, A., & Solnit, A. J. (1973). *Beyond the best interests of the child.* New York: Free Press.

Goldstein, J., Freud, A., & Solnit, A. J. (1979). *Before the best interests of the child.* New York: Free Press.

Goodman, C., & Silverstein, M. (2002). Grandmothers raising grandchildren: Family structure and well-being in culturally diverse families. *Gerontologist, 42*(5), 676–89.

Goodson, I. F., & Sikes, P. (2001). *Life history research in educational settings: Learning from lives.* Buckingham, UK: Open University Press.

Gordy-Levine, T. (1990). Time to mourn again. In A.N. Maluccio, R. Krieger, & B.A. Pine (Eds.), *Preparing adolescents for life after foster care* (pp. 53–72). Washington, DC: Child Welfare League of America.

Gosek, G. (2002). *Towards an understanding of suicide among Aboriginal people.* Unpublished master's thesis, Faculty of Social Work, University of Manitoba, Winnipeg.

Gough, P. (2006). *Kinship care.* CECW Information sheet No. 42E. Toronto: Centre of Excellence for Child Welfare. Retrieved August 29, 2008, from <http://www.cecw-cepb.ca/sites/default/files/publications/en/KinshipCare42E.pdf>.

Gough, P., Blackstock, C., & Bala, N. (2005). *Jurisdiction and funding models for Aboriginal child and family service agencies.* CECW Information Sheet No. 30E. Toronto: Centre of Excellence for Child Welfare. Retrieved February 12, 2009, from <http://www.cecw-cepb.ca/sites/default/files/publications/en/Jurisdiction andFunding30E.pdf>.

Gough, P., and Fuchs, D. (2006). *Children with FASD-related disabilities receiving services from child welfare agencies in Manitoba.* Manitoba: Centre of Excellence for Child Welfare. Accessible via <http://www.cecw-cepb.ca/publications/430>.

Gove, T. J. (1995). *Report of the Gove Inquiry into child protection in British Columbia.* Vol. 1: *Matthew's story.* Victoria, BC: Government of British Columbia.

Goyette, M. (2007). Promoting autonomous functioning among youth in care: A program evaluation. In V. Mann-Feder (Ed.), *Transition or Eviction: Youth Exiting Care for Independent Living.* Special issue of *New Directions for Youth Development, 113,* 89–106.

Graef, M., & Hill, E. (2000). Costing child protective services staff turnover. *Child Welfare, 79*(5), 517–33.

Grant, T., Ernst, C., Pagalilauan, G., & Streissguth, A. (2003). Post-program follow-up effects of paraprofessional intervention with high-risk women who abused alcohol and drugs during pregnancy. *Journal of Community Psychology, 31*(3), 211–22.

Grant, T., Ernst, C., Streissguth, A., & Porter, J. (1997). An advocacy program for mothers with FAS/FAE. In A. Streissguth & J. Kanter (Eds.), *The challenge of fetal alcohol syndrome: Overcoming secondary disabilities* (pp. 102–12). Seattle, WA: University of Washington Press.

Grasso, A., & Epstein, I. (1988). Management by measurement: Organizational dilemmas and opportunities. *Administration in Social Work, 11*(3–4), 89–100.

Gray, M., & McDonald, C. (2006). Pursuing good practice? The limits of evidence-based practice. *Journal of Social Work, 6*(1), 7–20.

Greaves, L., Varcoe, C., Poole, N., Morrow, M., Johnson, J., Pederson, A., et al. (2002). *A motherhood issue: Discourses on mothering under duress.* Ottawa: Status of Women Canada.

Greenwald, C. A. (1998). *Characteristics of social workers and families that affect family reunification outcomes.* Unpublished doctoral dissertation, California State University, Long Beach, CA.

Gross, E. R. (1995). Deconstructing politically correct practice literatures: The American Indian case. *Social Work, 40*(2), 206–13.

Guérard, G. (2008). *Mastering the conflict game: Getting ahead by exploring the hidden life of organizations.* Montreal: Éditions Yvon Blais.

Guille, L. (2003). Men who batter and their children: An integrated review. *Aggression and Violent Behavior, 9*, 129–63.

Gustafson, D. L. (2005). The social construction of maternal absence. In D. L. Gustafson (Ed.), *Unbecoming mothers: The social production of maternal absence* (pp. 23–44). New York: Haworth Clinical Press.

Haebich, A. (2000). *Broken circles: Fragmenting Indigenous families 1800–2000.* Fremantle, Australia: Fremantle Arts Centre Press.

Hand, C. A. (2006). An Ojibwe perspective on the welfare of children: Lessons of the past and visions for the future. *Children and Youth Services Review, 28*(1), 20–46.

Haney, L., & March, M. (2003). Married fathers and caring daddies: Welfare reform and the discursive politics of paternity. *Social Problems, 50*(4), 461–81.

Hanselmann, C. (2003). Ensuring the urban dream: Shared responsibility and effective urban Aboriginal voices. In D. Newhouse & E. Peters (Eds.), *Not strangers in these parts: Urban Aboriginal peoples* (pp. 167–77). Retrieved August 12, 2009, from <http://www.policyresearch.gc.ca/doclib/AboriginalBook_e.pdf>.

Hansen, B. (2008). *The brotherhood of Joseph: A father's memoir of infertility and adoption in the 21st century.* New York: Modern Times.

Hansen, M. E., & Hansen, B. A. (2005). *The economics of the adoption of children from foster care.* Working Paper No. 2005-10. Washington, DC: Department of Economics, American University.

Harnack, A. (Ed.) (1995). *Adoption: Opposing viewpoints.* San Diego: Greenhaven Press.

Harris, M. S., & Courtney, M. E. (2003). The interaction of race, ethnicity, and family structure with respect to the timing of family reunification. *Children and Youth Services Review, 25*(5/6), 409–29.

Hawkins, J. D., Catalano, R. F., & Miller, J. Y. (1992). Risk and protective factors for alcohol and other drug problems in adolescence and early adulthood: Implications for substance abuse prevention. *Psychological Bulletin, 112*(1), 64–105.

Hazel, N. (1981). *A bridge to independence.* Oxford: Blackwell.

Heath, A., Colton, M., & Aldgate J. (1994). Failure to escape: A longitudinal study of foster children's educational attainment. *British Journal of Social Work, 24*(3), 241–60.

Hegar, R. (2005). Sibling placement in foster care and adoption: An overview of international research. *Children and Youth Services Review, 27*(7), 717–39.

Heidbuurt, J. (1995). *All in the family home: The biological children of parents who foster.* Unpublished master's thesis, Wilfrid Laurier University, Waterloo, ON.

Helfer, R. E., & Kempe, C. H. (1968). *The battered child.* Chicago: University of Chicago Press.

Hélie, S. (2005). *Fréquence et déterminants de la récurrence du signalement en protection de la jeunesse: Analyse de survie d'une cohorte montréalaise.* Montréal : Université du Québec à Montreal.

Henry, J., & Purcell, R. (2000). Exploring the tensions: Being family-centered with parents who abuse/neglect their children. *Infant-Toddler Intervention: The Transdisciplinary Journal, 10*(4), 275–285.

Heptinstall, E. (2000). Gaining access to looked after children for research purposes: Lessons learned. *British Journal of Social Work, 30*(6), 867–72.

Herbert, M. (2007). Creating conditions for good practice: A child welfare project sponsored by the Canadian Association of Social Workers. In I. Brown, F. Chaze, D. Fuchs, J. Lafrance, S. McKay, & S. T. Prokop (Eds.), *Putting a human face on child welfare: Voices from the prairie* (pp. 223–50). Toronto: Centre of Excellence for Child Welfare/Prairie Child Welfare Consortium.

Herman-Stahl, M., & Petersen, A. C. (1996). The protective role of coping and social resources for depressive symptoms among young adolescents. *Journal of Youth and Adolescence 25*(6), 733–53.

Hetherington, R., & Nurse, T. (2006). Promoting change from "child protection" to "child and family welfare": The problems of the English system. In N. Freymond & G. Cameron (Eds.), *Towards positive systems of child and family welfare: International comparisons of child protection, family service, and community caring systems* (pp. 53–83). Toronto: University of Toronto Press.

Hiebert-Murphy, D., Trute, B., & Wright, A. (2008). Patterns of entry to community-based services for families with children with developmental disabilities: Implications for social work practice. *Child and Family Social Work, 13*(4), 423–32.

Higgins, D. J., Adams, R. M., Bromfield, L. M., Richardson, N., & Aldana, M. S. (2005). *National audit of Australian child protection research 1995–2004*. Melbourne: National Child Protection Clearinghouse, Australian Institute of Family Studies.

Higgins, D. J., Bromfield, L., & Richardson, N. (2005). *Enhancing out-of-home care for Aboriginal and Torres Strait Islander young people*. Melbourne, Australia: National Child Protection Clearinghouse, Australian Institute of Family Studies.

Hildyard, K., & Wolfe, D. (2002). Child neglect: Developmental issues and outcomes. *Child Abuse and Neglect, 26*(6/7), 679–95.

Hill, L. F. (2005). Family group conferencing: An alternative approach to placement of Alaskan Native children under the Indian Child Welfare Act. *Alaska Law Review, 22*(1), 89–112.

Hill, M., Stafford, A., & Lister, P. G. (Eds.). (2002, March). *International perspectives on child protection: Report of a Seminar for the Scottish Executive Child Protection Review: Protecting Children Today and Tomorrow*. Glasgow: Centre for the Child & Society, University of Glasgow.

Hill, R. B. (2006). *Synthesis of research on disproportionality in child welfare: An update*. Seattle, WA: Annie E. Casey Foundation.

Hill, R. B. (2007). *An analysis of racial/ethnic disproportionality and disparity at the national, state, and county levels*. Seattle, WA: Annie E. Casey Foundation.

Hines, A. M., Lemon, K., Wyatt, P., & Merdinger, J. (2004). Factors related to the disproportionate involvement of children of color in the child welfare system: A review and emerging themes. *Children and Youth Services Review, 26*(6), 507–27.

Hoagwood, K. (1997). Interpreting nullity: The Fort Bragg experiment—a comparative success or failure? *American Psychologist, 52,* 546–50.

Hobbs, N. (1982). *The troubled and troubling child*. San Francisco: Jossey-Bass.

Hodge, D. (2008). Sexual trafficking in the United States: A domestic problem with transnational dimensions. *Social Work, 53*(2), 143–52.

Hodgins, B. (2007). *Father involvement in parenting young children: A content analysis of parent education programs in BC*. Unpublished master's project, University of Victoria, Victoria, BC.

Hoffman, D., & Rosenheck, R. (2001). Homeless mothers with severe mental illnesses and their children: Predictors of family reunification. *Psychiatric Rehabilitation Journal, 25*(2), 163–9.

Hoffman, J. (2008). *Daddy, I need you: A father's guide to early childhood brain development*. Carleton, ON: Father Involvement Initiative—Ontario Network. Accessible via <http://www.cfii.ca/daddy_i_need_you>.

Höjer, I. (2004). What happens in the foster family? A study of fostering relationships in Sweden. *Adoption and Fostering, 28*(1), 38–48.

Höjer, I. (2007). Sons and daughters of foster carers and the impact of fostering on their everyday life. *Child and Family Social Work, 12*(1), 73–83.

Höjer, I. (2008). Sharing the care? Birth parents' perception of foster care placements. In *Care matters: Transforming lives—Improving outcomes* (pp. 46–8). Loughborough, UK: Centre for Child and Family Research, Loughborough University.

Höjer, I., & Nordenfors, M. (2003). *Growing up with foster siblings.* In *Childhoods in late modern society.* Göteburg, Sweden: Göteborgs universitet, institutionen för socialt arbete, Skriftserien 2003:1.

Holland, S., & O'Neill, S. (2006). We had to be there to make sure it was what we wanted: Enabling children's participation in family decision-making through the family group conference. *Childhood: A Global Journal of Child Research, 13*(1), 91–111.

Hollister-Wagner, G. H., Foshee, V. A., & Jackson, C. (2001). Adolescent aggression: Models of resiliency. *Journal of Applied Social Psychology, 31*(3), 445–66.

Holman, R. (1975). The place of fostering in social work. *British Journal of Social Work, 5*(1), 3–29.

Horejsi, C., Craig, B., & Pablo, J. (1992). Reactions by Native American parents to child protection agencies: Cultural and community factors. *Child Welfare, 71*(4), 329–42.

Hornberger, S. & Briar-Lawson, K. (2005). Advancing 21st century child welfare through community building. *Child Welfare, 84*(2), 101–4.

Horwath, J. (2007). *Child neglect: Identification and assessment.* New York: Palgrave Macmillan.

House of Commons (U.K.). (2004). *Bichard Inquiry Report.* London: Stationery Office.

House of Commons Health Committee (U.K.). *See* Laming, H., Baron.

Howe, D. (1995). *Attachment theory for social work practice.* Basingstoke, UK: Palgrave Macmillan.

Howe, D. (1997). *Patterns of adoption: nature, nurture and psychosocial development.* Oxford: Wiley-Blackwell.

Howe, R. B., & Covell, K. (2007). *A question of commitment: Children's rights in Canada.* Waterloo, ON: Wilfrid Laurier University Press.

Howell, J., Kelly, M. R., Palmer, J., & Mangum, R. (2004). Integrating child welfare, juvenile justice, and other agencies in a continuum of services. *Child Welfare, 83*(2), 143–56.

Hudson, J., & Galaway, B. (Eds.). (1995). *Child welfare in Canada: Research and policy implications.* Toronto: Thompson Educational Publishing.

Hudson, P., & McKenzie, B. (2003). Extending Aboriginal control over child welfare services: The Manitoba Child Welfare Initiative. *Canadian Review of Social Policy, 51*, 49–66.

Human Resources Development Canada. (2000). *Federal/Provincial Working Group on Child and Family Services Information.* Ottawa: Author.

Human Rights and Equal Opportunity Commission (Australia). (1997). *Bringing them home: Report of the National Inquiry into the Separation of Aboriginal and Torres Strait Islander Children from their Families*. Sydney: Author.

Humphreys, C., Berridge, D., Butler, I., & Ruddick, R. (2003). Making research count: The development of "knowledge-based practice." *Research, Policy and Planning, 21*(1), 41–9.

Hunt, J. (2009). Family and friends care. In G. Schofield & J. Simmonds (Eds.), *The child placement handbook: Research, policy and practice* (pp. 102–19). London: British Association for Adoption and Fostering.

Hunter, W. M., Cox, C. E., Teagle, S., Johnson, R. M., Mathew, R., Knight, E. D., et al. (2002). *Measures for assessment of functioning and outcomes in longitudinal research on child abuse*. Vol. 2: *Middle childhood*. Chapel Hill, NC: LONGSCAN Coordinating Center, University of North Carolina at Chapel Hill.

Hutchfield, K. (1999). Family centred care: A concept analysis. *Journal of Advanced Nursing, 29*(5), 1178–87.

Indian Act. (1985). R.S.C. 1985, c. I-5, s. 88. Originally retrieved August 19, 2008; accessible at <http://laws.justice.gc.ca/eng/I-5/index.html>.

Indian and Northern Affairs Canada. (2005a). Basic departmental data 2004. Originally retrieved August 25, 2008; now accessible at <http://www.collections canada.gc.ca/webarchives/20071115212333/http://www.ainc-inac.gc.ca/pr/sts/bdd04/bdd04_e.html>.

Indian and Northern Affairs Canada. (2005b). *First Nations child and family services: National program manual*. Retrieved August 25, 2008, from <http://www .ainc-inac.gc.ca/hb/sp/fncf/pubs/fnc/fnc-eng.pdf>.

Indian and Northern Affairs Canada, Departmental Audit and Evaluation Branch. (2007). *Evaluation of the First Nations child and family services program*. Retrieved August 25, 2008, from <http://www.ainc-inac.gc.ca/ai/arp/aev/pubs/ev/06-07/06-07-eng.pdf>.

Inkelas, M., & Halfon, N. (1997). Recidivism in child protection services. *Children and Youth Services Review, 19*(3), 139–61.

Innvaer, S., Vist, G., Trommald, M., & Oxman, A. (2002). Health policy-makers perceptions of their use of evidence: A systematic review. *Journal of Health Services Research & Policy, 7*, 239–44.

International Association of Schools of Social Work Website (n.d.). Retrieved September 11, 2008, from <http://www.iassw-aiets.org/>.

International Federation of Social Workers Website. (n.d.). Retrieved September 11, 2008. <http://www.ifsw.org/>.

International Social Service/International Reference Centre for the Rights of Children Deprived of their Family (ISS/IRC). (2008a). Exposing myths about the number of adoptable children and the need for more precision when defining who is adoptable. *ISS/IRC Monthly Review No. 10/2008*, p. 1. Accessible via <http://www.iss-ssi.org/>.

International Social Service/International Reference Centre for the Rights of Children Deprived of their Family (ISS/IRC). (2008b). The ISS/IRC has published a study on the adoption of older children. *ISS/IRC Monthly Review No. 10/2008*, p. 7. Accessible via <http://www.iss-ssi.org/>.

Internet baby's new parents cannot be prosecuted. (2009, January 21). *Calgary Herald*, A17.

Iwaniec, D., Larkin, E., & Higgins, S. (2006). Research review: Risk and resilience in cases of emotional abuse. *Child and Family Social Work, 11*(1), 73–82.

Jack, S., Dudding, P., Brooks, S., Tonmyr, L., Dobbins, M., Fox, C., et al. (2007). Understanding the uptake and utilization of research evidence by administrators in Ontario Children's Aid Societies. *Canada's Children, 13*(2), 42–5.

Jackson, A. (1996). The reconnections and family admission programs: Two models for family reunification within Melbourne, Australia. *Community Alternatives, 8*(1), 53–75.

Jackson, M. (1988). *The Maori and the criminal justice system. A new perspective: He Whaipaanga Hou. (Part 2)*. Wellington, NZ: Policy and Research Division, Department of Justice, Government of New Zealand.

Jackson, S. (1989). Educating children in care. In B. Kahan (Ed.), *Child care and research, policy and practice* (pp. 133–51). London: Hodder and Stoughton.

Jackson, S. (1994). Educating children in residential and foster care. *Oxford Review of Education, 20*(3), 267–79.

Jackson, S. (Ed.). (2001). *Nobody ever told us school mattered: Raising the educational attainments of children in public care*. London: British Agencies for Adoption and Fostering.

Jackson, S., & Kilroe, S. (Eds.). (1996). *Looking After Children: Good parenting, good outcomes*. London: Stationery Office.

Jagannathan, R., & Camasso, M. J. (1996). Risk assessment in child protective services: A canonical analysis of the case management function. *Child Abuse and Neglect, 20*(7), 599–612.

Jayaratne, S., Faller, K. C., Ortega, R. M., & Vandervort, F. (2008). African American and white child welfare workers' attitudes towards policies involving race and sexual orientation. *Children and Youth Services Review, 30*(8), 955–66.

Jessor, R., Van Den Bos, J., Vanderryn, J., Costa, F. M., & Turbin, M. S. (1995). Protective factors in adolescent problem behaviour: Moderator effects and developmental change. *Developmental Psychology, 31*(6), 923–33.

Johnson, K. (2002). Politics of international and domestic adoption in China. *Law & Society Review, 36*(2), 379–96.

Johnson, M. M. (1998). Family engagement practices in residential group care: Differences between public and private cases. *Child and Youth Care Forum, 27*(2), 139–48.

Johnson, S. (2008). Learning over thunder and lightning: Shouldn't children in care have the right to an education? *Perspectives, 30*(1), 18–19.

Johnson, W. (2004). *Effectiveness of California's child welfare Structured Decision-Making (SDM) model: A prospective study of the validity of the California Family Risk Assessment.* Madison, WI: Children's Research Center.

Johnson, W. (2006a). The risk assessment wars: A commentary response to 'Evaluating the effectiveness of actuarial risk assessment models' by Donald Baumann, J. Randolph Law, Janess Sheets, Grant Reid, & J. Christopher Graham. *Children and Youth Services Review, 28*(6), 704–14.

Johnson, W. (2006b). Post-battle skirmish in the risk assessment wars: Rebuttal to the response of Baumann and colleagues to criticism of their paper, 'Evaluating the effectiveness of actuarial risk assessment models'. *Children and Youth Services Review, 28*(9), 1124–32.

Johnson, W., & L'Esperance, J. (1984). Predicting the recurrence of child abuse. *Social Work Research and Abstracts, 20*(2), 21–6.

Johnston, P. (1983). *Native children and the child welfare system.* Toronto: Canadian Council on Social Development in association with James Lorimer & Co.

Jones, D. P. H., & Ramchandani, P. (1999). *Child sexual abuse: Informing practice from research.* Oxford: Radcliffe Medical Press.

Jones, G. (2002). *The youth divide: Diverging paths to adulthood.* York, UK: Joseph Rowntree Foundation.

Jones, H. (2003). The relationship between research, policy, and practice in delivering an outcome-led child welfare service. In K. Kufeldt & B. McKenzie (Eds.), *Child welfare: Connecting research, policy, and practice* (pp. 367–76). Waterloo, ON: Wilfrid Laurier University Press.

Jones, H., Clark, R., Kufeldt, K., & Norrman, M. (1998). *Looking After Children*: Assessing outcomes in child care. The experience of implementation. *Children and Society, 12*(3), 212–22.

Jones, I. (2002). Neurological damage from malaria. Retrieved September 17, 2008, from <http://malaria.wellcome.ac.uk/doc_wtd023883.html>.

Jones, K. L., Smith, D., Ulleland, C., & Streissguth, A. (1973). Pattern of malformation in offspring of chronic alcoholic mothers. *The Lancet, 1301*(7815), 1267–71.

Jones, L. (1998). The social and family correlates of successful reunification of children in foster care. *Children and Youth Services Review, 20*(4), 305–23.

Jones, M. B. (1993). *Birthmothers: Women who have relinquished babies for adoption tell their stories.* Chicago: Chicago Review Press.

Jonson-Reid, M., Drake, B., Chung, S., & Way, I. (2003). Cross-type recidivism among child maltreatment victims and perpetrators. *Child Abuse and Neglect, 27*(8), 899–917.

Jonson-Reid, M., Drake, B., & Kohl, P.L. (2009). Is the overrepresentation of the poor in child welfare caseloads due to bias or need? *Children and Youth Services Review, 31*(3), 422–7.

Juby, C., & Scannapieco, M. (2007). Characteristics of workload management in public child welfare agencies. *Administration in Social Work, 31*(3), 95–109.

Kabacoff, R. I., Miller, I., Bishop, D. S., Epstein, N. B., & Keitner, G. I. (1990). A psychometric study of the McMaster Family Assessment Device in psychiatric, medical, and nonclinical samples. *Journal of Family Psychology, 3*(4), 431–9.

Kadushin, A., & Martin, J. (1988). *Child welfare services* (4th ed.). New York: Macmillan.

Kälin, W. (2005, July). Natural disasters and IDPs' rights. *Forced Migration Review,* Special issue: *Tsunami: Learning from the humanitarian response,* 10–11. Retrieved August 12, 2008, from <http://www.fmreview.org/FMRpdfs/Tsunami/03.pdf>.

Kanani, K., Regehr, C., & Bernstein, M. (2002). Liability considerations in child welfare: Lessons from Canada. *Child Abuse and Neglect, 26*(10), 1029–43.

Kaplan, S., Pelcovitz, D., & Labruna, V. (1999). Child and adolescent abuse and neglect research: A review of the past 10 years. Part I: Physical and emotional abuse and neglect. *Journal of the American Academy of Child and Adolescent Psychiatry, 38*(10), 1214–22.

Keairns, Y. (2003). *The voices of girl child soldiers, Philippines.* New York: Quaker United Nations Office.

Keck, G. C., & Kupecky, R. M. (1995). *Adopting the hurt child: Hope for families with special needs kids.* Colorado Springs, CO: Pinon Press.

Keddell, E. (2007). Cultural identity and the Children, Young Persons, and Their Families Act 1989: Ideology, policy and practice. *Social Policy Journal of New Zealand, 32,* 49–71.

Keil, V., & Price, J. M. (2006). Externalizing behavior disorders in child welfare settings: Definition, prevalence, and implications for assessment and treatment. *Children and Youth Services Review, 28*(7), 761–79.

Kelly, G. (2002). Outcome studies of foster care. In G. Kelly & R. Gilligan (Eds.), *Issues in foster care: Policy, practice and research* (pp. 59–84). London: Jessica Kingsley Publishers.

Kempe, C. H., Silverman, F. N., Steele, B. F., Droegemueller, W., & Silver, H. K. (1962). The battered child syndrome. *Journal of the American Medical Association, 181,* 17–24.

Kerr, D. C. R., Leve, L. D., & Chamberlain, P. (2009). Pregnancy rate among juvenile justice girls in two randomized controlled trials of multidimensional treatment foster care. *Journal of Consulting and Clinical Psychology, 77*(3), 588–93.

Kessler, M. L., Gira, E., & Poertner, J. (2005). Moving best practice to evidence-based practice in child welfare. *Families in Society: The Journal of Contemporary Social Services, 86*(2), 244–50.

Kessler, R., & Cleary, P. D. (1980). Social class and psychological distress. *American Sociological Review, 45,* 463–78.

King, G., Law, M., King, S., Kertoy, M., Hurley, P., & Rosenbaum, P. (2000). *Children with disabilities in Ontario: A profile of children's services. Part 2: Perceptions about family-centred service delivery for children with disabilities.* Hamilton, ON: Can-Child Centre for Childhood Disability Research, McMaster University.

King, G., Law, M., King, S., & Rosenbaum, P. (1998). Parents' and service providers' perceptions of the family-centredness of children's rehabilitation services. In M. Law (Ed.), *Family-centred assessment and intervention in pediatric rehabilitation* (pp. 21–40). Birmingham, NY: Haworth Press.

Kirk, H. D. (1964). *Shared fate: A theory of adoption and mental health.* New York: Free Press of Glencoe.

Kirk, H. D. (1981). *Adoptive kinship: A modern institution in need of reform.* Toronto: Butterworths.

Kirk, H. D. (1984). *Shared fate: A theory and method of adoptive relationships* (2nd ed.). Port Angeles, WA: Ben-Simon Publications.

Kirk, H. D. (1988). *Exploring adoptive family life: The collected adoption papers of H. David Kirk* (B. J. Tansey, Ed.). Port Angeles, WA: Ben-Simon Publications.

Kirkness, V. J., & Barnhardt, R. (1991). First Nations and higher education: The four R's—respect, relevance, reciprocity, responsibility. *Journal of American Indian Education. 30*(3), 1–15. Retrieved August 12, 2009, from <http://jaie.asu.edu/v30/V30S3fir.htm>.

Klein, R. A., Cheers, D., Kufeldt, K., Kelly-Egerton, A., & Rideout, S. (2006, August). *Looking After Children in the looking glass: Insights from a matched sample in Canada and Australia.* Paper presented at the Association of Children's Welfare Agencies Conference/7th International *Looking After Children* Conference, Sydney, Australia.

Klein, R. A., Kufeldt, K., & Rideout, S. (2006). Resilience theory and its relevance for child welfare practice. In R. J. Flynn, P. M. Dudding, & J. G. Barber (Eds.), *Promoting resilience in child welfare* (pp. 34–51). Ottawa: University of Ottawa Press.

Kligman, G. (1998). *The politics of duplicity: Controlling reproduction in Ceausescu's Romania.* Berkeley: University of California Press.

Kline, M. (1995). Complicating the ideology of motherhood: Child welfare law and First Nation women. In M. A. Fineman & I. Karpin (Eds.), *Mothers in law: Feminist theory and the legal regulation of motherhood* (pp. 118–41). New York: Columbia University Press.

Knight, E. D., Runyan, D. K., Dubowitz, H., Brandford, C., Kotch, J., Litrownik, A. J., et al. (2000). Methodological and ethical challenges associated with child self-report of maltreatment: Solutions implemented by the LongSCAN consortium. *Journal of Interpersonal Violence, 15*(7), 760–75.

Knott, T., & Barber, J. (2005). *Do placement stability and parental visiting lead to better outcomes for children in foster care? Implications from the Australian Tracking Study.* CECW Information Sheet No. 19. Toronto: Centre of Excellence for Child Welfare. Accessible via <http://www.cecw-cepb.ca/publications/462>.

Kohl, P. L., Barth, R. P., Hazen, A. L., & Landsverk, J. A. (2005). Child welfare as a gateway to domestic violence services. *Children and Youth Services Review, 27*(11), 1203–21.

Kominkiewicz, F. B. (2004). The relationship of child protection service caseworker discipline-specific education and definition of sibling abuse: An institutional hiring impact study. *Journal of Human Behavior in the Social Environment, 9*(1/2), 69–82.

Kotch, J. B. (2000). Ethical issues in longitudinal child maltreatment research. *Journal of Interpersonal Violence, 15*(7), 696–709.

Kovachs, M., Thomas, R., Montgomery, M., Green, J. & Brown, L. (2007). Witnessing wild woman: Resistance and resilience in Aboriginal child welfare. In L. T. Foster & B. Wharf (Eds.), *People, politics, and child welfare in British Columbia* (pp. 97–116). Vancouver: University of British Columbia Press.

Krane, J., & Davies, L. (2000). Mothering and child protection practice: Rethinking risk assessment. *Child and Family Social Work, 5*(1), 35–45.

Kroger, J. (1996). *Identity in adolescence: The balance between self and other* (2nd ed.). London: Routledge.

Kroll, B., & Taylor A. (2003). *Parental substance misuse and child welfare.* London: Jessica Kingsley Publishers.

Krueger, R. A. (1988). *Focus groups: A practical guide for applied research.* Newbury Park, CA: Sage.

Kufeldt, K. (1979). Temporary foster care. *British Journal of Social Work, 9*(1), 49–66.

Kufeldt, K. (1982). Including natural parents in temporary foster care: An exploratory study. *Children Today, 11*(5), 14–16.

Kufeldt, K. (1991). Foster care: A reconceptualization. *Community Alternatives: International Journal of Family Care, 3*(1), 9–17.

Kufeldt, K. (1993). Inclusive foster care: Implementation of the model. In B. McKenzie (Ed.), *Current perspectives on foster family care* (pp. 84–100). Toronto: Wall & Emerson.

Kufeldt, K. (1995). Inclusive care, separation management and role clarity in foster care: The development of theoretical constructs. In J. Hudson and B. Galaway (Eds.), *Canadian child welfare: Research and policy implications* (pp. 337–50). Toronto: Thompson Educational Publishing.

Kufeldt, K. (2003). Graduates of guardianship care: Outcomes in early adulthood. In K. Kufeldt & B. McKenzie (Eds.), *Child welfare: Connecting research, policy, and practice* (pp. 203–16). Waterloo, ON: Wilfrid Laurier University Press.

Kufeldt, K., & Allison, J. (1990). Fostering children—Fostering families. *Community Alternatives: International Journal of Family Care, 2*(1), 1–17.

Kufeldt, K., & Armstrong, J. (1993). *Empowering families in an inclusive care model.* Paper presented at the 17th Western Canadian Conference on Family Practice, Vancouver, May 27–29.

Kufeldt, K., Armstrong, J., & Dorosh, M. (1995). How children in care view their own and their foster families: A research study. *Child Welfare, 74*(3), 695–715.

Kufeldt, K., Armstrong, J., & Dorosh, M. (1996). Connection and continuity in foster care. *Adoption and Fostering, 20*(2), 14–20.

Kufeldt, K., Cheers, D., Klein, R., & Rideout, S. (2007). *Looking After Children in government care in Australia and Canada: Final report.* Fredericton: University of New Brunswick.

Kufeldt, K., Este, D., McKenzie, B., & Wharf, B. (2003). Critical issues in child welfare. In K. Kufeldt, & B. McKenzie (Eds.). *Child welfare: Connecting research, policy, and practice* (pp. 395–428). Waterloo, ON: Wilfrid Laurier University Press.

Kufeldt, K., & Klein, R. (1998). *Review of children in care in Newfoundland and Labrador: 1984–1995.* St. John's: Government of Newfoundland and Labrador.

Kufeldt, K., McGilligan, L., Klein, R., & Rideout, S. (2004, August). *Looking After Children: A case study of its ability to promote resilient children and resilient workers.* Paper presented at 6th International *Looking After Children* Conference, *Promoting Resilient Development in Children Receiving Care,* Ottawa.

Kufeldt, K., McGilligan, L., Klein, R., & Rideout, S. (2006). *Looking After Children* and its ability to promote resilient children and resilient workers: A case study. *Families in Society: The Journal of Contemporary Social Services, 87*(4), 565–74.

Kufeldt, K., & McKenzie, B. (Eds.). (2003a). *Child welfare: Connecting research, policy, and practice.* Waterloo, ON: Wilfrid Laurier University Press.

Kufeldt, K., & McKenzie, B. (2003b). Conclusions and directions for the future. In K. Kufeldt & B. McKenzie (Eds.), *Child welfare: Connecting research, policy, and practice* (pp. 429–38). Waterloo, ON: Wilfrid Laurier University Press.

Kufeldt, K., & Nimmo, M. (1987). Youth on the street: Abuse and neglect in the eighties. *Child Abuse and Neglect, 11*(4), 531–43.

Kufeldt, K., Simard, M., Thomas, P., & Vachon, J. (2005). A grass roots approach to influencing child welfare policy. *Child and Family Social Work, 10*(4), 305–14.

Kufeldt, K., Simard, M., Tite, R., & Vachon, J. (2003). The *Looking After Children in Canada* Project: Educational outcomes. In K. Kufeldt & B. McKenzie (Eds.), *Child welfare: Connecting research, policy, and practice* (pp. 177–89). Waterloo, ON: Wilfrid Laurier University Press.

Kufeldt, K., Simard, M., & Vachon, J. (2002). Parental separation from children who enter the child welfare system. *Canadian Journal of Community Mental Health,* Special Supplement, No. 4, Summer, 39–48.

Kufeldt, K., Simard, M., & Vachon, J. (2003). Improving outcomes for children in care: Giving youth a voice. *Adoption and Fostering, 27*(2), 8–19.

Kufeldt, K., Simard, M., Vachon, J., Baker, J., & Andrews, T.-L. (2000). *Looking After Children in Canada: Final report.* Submitted to the Social Development Partnerships Division, Human Resources Development Canada. Saint John, NB, and Québec: University of New Brunswick and Université Laval.

Kufeldt, K., Simard, M., Vachon, J., Baker, J., & Andrews, T.-L. (2001). *S'occuper des enfants au Canada: Rapport final.* Fredericton: University of New Brunswick.

Kufeldt, K., & Stein, M. (2005). The voice of young people: Reflections on the care experience and the process of leaving care. In J. Scott and H. Ward (Eds.) *Safeguarding and promoting the wellbeing of children, families and communities* (pp. 134–48). London: Jessica Kingsley Publishers.

Kupersmidt, J. B., & Coie, J. D. (1990). Preadolescent peer status, aggression, and school adjustment as predictors of externalizing problems in adolescence. *Child Development, 61*(5), 1350–62.

Lamb, M. (Ed.). (1976). *The role of the father in child development.* New York: Wiley.

Laming, H., Baron. (2003). *The Victoria Climbié Inquiry.* London: Stationery Office.

Laming, H., Baron. (2009). *The protection of children in England: A progress report.* London: Stationery Office.

Landry, R., Amara, N., & Laamary, M. (2001). Utilization of social science research knowledge in Canada. *Research Policy, 30,* 333–49.

Landsman, M. J. (2001). Commitment in public child welfare. *Social Service Review, 75*(3), 386–419.

Landsman, M. J. (2002). Rural child welfare practice from an organization-in-environment perspective. *Child Welfare, 81*(5), 791–819.

Landsverk, J., Davis, I., Ganger, W., Newton, R., & Johnson, I. (1996). Impact of child psychosocial functioning on reunification from out-of-home placement. *Children and Youth Services Review, 18*(4/5), 447–62.

Lapierre, S. (2008). Mothering in the context of domestic violence: The pervasiveness of a deficit model of mothering. *Child and Family Social Work, 13*(4),454–63.

Law, M., Hanna, S., King, G., Hurley, P., King, S., Kertoy, M., & Rosenbaum, P. (2003). Factors affecting family-centred service delivery for children with disabilities. *Child: Care, Health & Development, 29*(5), 357–66.

Lawder, E. A., Poulin, J. E., & Andrews, R. G. (1986). A study of 185 foster children 5 years after placement. *Child Welfare, 65*(3), 241–51.

Lawn, J. E., Cousens, S., Zupan, J., & Lancet Neonatal Survival Steering Team. (2005). 4 million neonatal deaths: When? Where? Why? *The Lancet, 365* (9462), 891–900.

Lawrence, B. (2004). *"Real" Indians and others: Mixed-blood urban Native peoples and Indigenous nationhood.* Vancouver: University of British Columbia Press.

Leathers, S. J. (2002). Parental visiting and family reunification: Could inclusive practice make a difference? *Child Welfare, 81*(4), 595–616.

Le Blanc, M. (1995). Y a-t-il trop d'adolescents placés en internat aux Centres jeunesse de Montréal? *Revue canadienne de psycho-éducation, 24*(2), 93–120.

Legault, L., Flynn, R. J., Artz, S., Balla, S., Dudding, P., Norgaard, V., et al. (2004). *Looking After Children:* Implementation and outcomes in Canada. *Journal of Child and Youth Care Work, 19,* 159–69.

Lehman, C. M., Liang, S., & O'Dell, K. (2005). Impact of flexible funds on placement and permanency outcomes for children in child welfare. *Research on Social Work Practice, 15*(5), 381–8.

Lehman, C. M., Liang, S., O'Dell, K., & Duryea, M. (2003). *Evaluation of Oregon's Title IV-E Waiver Demonstration Project, Final report.* Portland, OR: Portland State University, Child Welfare Partnership, Graduate School of Social Work.

Lehtonen, R., & Pahkinen, E. J. (1995). *Practical methods for design and analysis of complex surveys.* Chichester, UK: Wiley.

Leibenberg, L., & Ungar, M. (2009). *Researching resilience.* Toronto: University of Toronto Press.

Leischner, C., Johnson, V., Mallet, B., Sam, J., & Thio-Watts, M. (2001). *Creating solutions: Women preventing FAS: Understanding women's substance misuse.* Prince George, BC: Northern Family Health Society.

Lemay, R., Byrne, B. A., & Ghazal, H. (2006). Managing change: Implementing *Looking After Children* at Prescott-Russell Services to Children and Adults. In R. J. Flynn, P. M. Dudding, & J. G. Barber (Eds.), *Promoting resilience in child welfare* (pp. 316–36). Ottawa: University of Ottawa Press.

Lemay, R., & Ghazal, H. (2007). *Looking After Children: A practitioner's guide.* Ottawa: University of Ottawa Press.

Lero, D., Ashbourne, L., & Whitehead, D. (2006). *Inventory of policies and policy areas influencing father involvement.* Guelph, ON: Father Involvement Research Alliance.

Leschied, A. W., MacKay, R., Raghunandan, S., Sharpe, N., & Sookoor, M. (2007). *Empowering families, strengthening and protecting children: Introducing a kinship program and a family group conferencing program at the Children's Aid Society of London and Middlesex.* London, ON: Children's Aid Society of London and Middlesex/Faculty of Education, University of Western Ontario.

Leschied, A. W., Whitehead, P. C., Hurley, D. & Chiodo, D. (2003). *Protecting children is everybody's business: Investigating the increased demand for service at the Children's Aid Society of London and Middlesex.* London, ON: University of Western Ontario.

Leslie, L., Landsverk, J., Ezzet-Lofstrom, R., Tschann, J. M., Slymen, D. J., & Garland, A. F. (2000). Children in foster care: Factors influencing outpatient mental health service use. *Child Abuse and Neglect, 24*(4), 465–76.

Levy, A., & Kahan, B. (1991). *The Pindown experience and the protection of children: The report of the Staffordshire child care inquiry.* Stafford, UK: Staffordshire County Council.

Lewandowski, C., & Pierce, L. (2004). Does family-centered out-of-home care work? Comparison of a family-centered approach to traditional care. *Social Work Research, 28*(3), 143–51.

Lewig, K., Arney, F., & Scott, D. (2006). Closing the research-policy, research-practice gaps: Ideas for child and family services. *Family Matters, 74*, 12–19.

Lewis, J. (2005, December 23). Jeffrey's legacy is whatever we can learn. *Globe and Mail*, p. A21.

Libesman, T. (2004). Child welfare approaches for Indigenous communities: International perspectives. *Child Abuse Prevention Issues, 20*, 1–39.

Libin, K. (2009, June 13). State as mother. *National Post*, pp. A1, A13.

Lindsey, D. (1994). *The welfare of children*. New York: Oxford University Press.

Litrownik, A. J., Newton, R., Mitchell, B., & Richardson, K. K. (2003). Long-term follow-up of young children placed in foster care: Subsequent placements and exposure to family violence. *Journal of Family Violence, 18*(1), 19–28.

Lloyd, C., King, R., & McKenna, K. (2004). Generic versus specialist clinical work roles of occupational therapists and social workers in mental health. *Australian and New Zealand Journal of Psychiatry, 38*(3), 119–24.

Loar, L. (1998). Making visits work. *Child Welfare, 77*(1), 41–58.

Loewe, B., & Hanrahan, T. E . (1975). Five-day foster care. *Child Welfare, 54*(1), 7–20.

Lohrbach, S., Sawyer, R., Saugen, J., Astolfi, C., Schmitt, K., Worden, P., et al. (2005). Ways of working in child welfare: A perspective on practice. *Protecting Children, 20*(2/3), 93–100.

Loman, L. A., & Siegel, G. L. (2004a). *Minnesota alternative response evaluation: Final report*. St. Louis, MO: Institute of Applied Research.

Loman, L. A., & Siegel, G. L. (2004b). *Differential response in Missouri after five years: Final report*. St. Louis, MO: Institute of Applied Research. <http://www.iarstl.org/papers/MODiffResp2004a.pdf>.

Loman, L. A., & Siegel, G. L. (2005). Alternative response in Minnesota: Findings of the program evaluation. *Protecting Children, 20*(2/3), 78–92.

Lomas, J. (2000). Using "linkage and exchange" to move research into policy at a Canadian foundation. *Health Affairs, 19*(3), 236–40.

Long, D. (2008). *All fathers matter: Towards an inclusive vision for father involvement initiatives in Canada*. Guelph, ON: Father Involvement Research Alliance.

Loppie Reading, C., & Wien, F. (2009). *Health inequalities and social determinants of Aboriginal peoples' health*. Prince George, BC: National Collaborating Centre for Aboriginal Health.

Lorenz, K. Z. (1952). *King Solomon's ring: New light on animal ways*. New York: Crowell.

Lorenz, K. Z. (1966). *On aggression*. London: Methuen.

Love, C. (2006). Maori perspectives on collaboration and colonization in contemporary Aotearoa/New Zealand child and family welfare policies and practices. In N. Freymond & G. Cameron (Eds.), *Towards positive systems of child and family welfare: International comparisons of child protection, family service, and community caring systems* (pp. 235–68). Toronto: University of Toronto Press.

Lovell, M. L., & Thompson, A. H. (1995). Improving the organization and delivery of child welfare services: Themes, policy implications, and research agenda. In J. Hudson & B. Galaway (Eds.), *Child welfare in Canada: Research and policy implications* (pp. 91–8). Toronto: Thompson Educational Publishing.

Lowry, M. (1998). Commentary 2. In D. J. Besharov, M. Lowry, L. Pelton, & M. Weber, Four commentaries: How can we better protect children from abuse and neglect? *The Future of Children, 8*(1), 123–6.

Loxley, J. (2005). Losses on INAC operations funding due to lack of inflation adjustment. In First Nations Child & Family Caring Society of Canada, *Wen:de (We are coming to the light of day)* (pp. 224–6). Ottawa: First Nations Child & Family Caring Society of Canada. Originally retrieved August 20, 2008; now accessible at <http://www.fncfcs.com/sites/default/files/docs/WendeReport.pdf>.

Loxley, J., & Deriviere, L. (2005a). Promoting community and family wellness: Least disruptive measures and prevention. In First Nations Child & Family Caring Society of Canada, *Wen: de (We are coming to the light of day)* (pp. 114–45). Ottawa: First Nations Child & Family Caring Society of Canada.

Loxley, J., & Deriviere, L. (2005b, July). *Final report on cost benefit analysis: West Region Child and Family Services.* Unpublished. Rolling River, MB: West Region Child and Family Services.

Luongo, G. (2007). Re-thinking child welfare training models to achieve evidence-based practices. *Administration in Social Work, 31*(2), 87–96.

Luthar, S. S., Cicchetti, D., & Becker, B. (2000). The construct of resilience: A critical evaluation and guidelines for future work. *Child Development, 71*(3), 543–62.

Luthra, R. (2005, June 1). Safe motherhood: A matter of human rights and social justice. *UN Chronicle, 42*(2), 14–16. Accessible via <http://www.thefreelibrary.com/UN+Chronicle/2005/June/1-p57>.

Lyle, C. G., & Graham, E. (2000). Looks can be deceiving: Using a risk assessment instrument to evaluate the outcomes of child protection services. *Children and Youth Services Review, 22*(11/12), 935–49.

Macdonald, G. (2004, September). *Evidence based child protection: What it is and what it isn't.* Keynote address, ISPCAN, 15th International Congress on Child Abuse and Neglect, Brisbane, Queensland, Australia.

MacDonald, J. A. (1983). The Spallumcheen Indian Band by-law and its potential impact on Native Indian child welfare policy in British Columbia. *Canadian Journal of Family Law, 4*(1), 75–96.

MacDonald, K. A., & Walman, K. (2005). Jordan's Principle: A child first approach to jurisdictional issues. In First Nations Child & Family Caring Society of Canada, *Wen:de (We are coming to the light of day)* (pp. 87–112). Ottawa: First Nations Child & Family Caring Society of Canada.

MacDonald, N., & Attaran, A. (2007). Jordan's Principle: Governments' paralysis. *Canadian Medical Association Journal, 177*(4), 321.

MacLean, R., & Howe, R. B. (2009). *Brief report on Canada's provincial children and youth advocacy offices: Highlights of functions and recent activities.* Sydney, NS: Children's Rights Centre, Cape Breton University.

MacLeod, J., & Nelson, G. (2003). A meta-analytic review of programs for the promotion and prevention of child maltreatment. In K. Kufeldt & B. McKenzie (Eds.), *Child welfare: Connecting research, policy and practice* (pp. 133–45). Waterloo, ON: Wilfrid Laurier University Press.

Maidman, F. (Ed.). (1984). *Child welfare: A sourcebook of knowledge and practice.* New York: Child Welfare League of America.

Malamuth, N. M., Sockloskie, R. J., Koss, M. P., & Tanaka, J. S. (1991). Characteristics of aggressors against women: Testing a model using a national sample of college students. *Journal of Consulting and Clinical Psychology, 59,* 670–81.

Maluccio, A. N. & Fein, E. (1983). Permanency planning: A redefinition. *Child Welfare, 62*(3), 195–201.

Maluccio, A. N., Fein, E., & Davis, I. P. (1994). Family reunification: Research, findings, issues, and directions. *Child Welfare, 73*(5), 489–504.

Maluccio, A. N., Fein, E., & Olmstead, K. A. (1986). *Permanency planning for children: Concepts and methods.* New York: Tavistock Publications.

Maluccio, A. N., & Sinanoglu, P. A. (1981). *The challenge of partnership: Working with parents of children in foster care.* New York: Child Welfare League of America.

Manalo, V., & Meezan, W. (2000). Toward building a typology for the evaluation of services in family support programs. *Child Welfare, 79*(4), 405–29.

Mancuso, R. (1998). With the best of intentions: New York State's child protection system and the laws used to mask the real reasons for organizational failure. *Journal of Human Behavior in the Social Environment, 1*(4), 57–72.

Mandell, D., Clouston Carlson, J., Fine, M., & Blackstock, C. (2007). Aboriginal child welfare. In G. Cameron, N. Coady, & G. R. Adams (Eds.), *Moving toward positive systems of child and family welfare* (pp. 115–59). Waterloo, ON: Wilfrid Laurier University Press.

Mann, M. (2005). *Indian registration: Unrecognized and unstated paternity.* Ottawa: Status of Women Canada.

Mann-Feder, V. (2007). Issue editor's notes. In V. Mann-Feder (Ed.), *Transition or Eviction: Youth Exiting Care for Independent Living.* Special issue of *New Directions for Youth Development, 113,* 1–8.

Mann-Feder, V., & Garfat, T. (2006) Leaving residential placement: A guide to intervention. *Relational Child and Youth Care Practice, 19*(40), 66–72.

Mann-Feder, V., & Guérard, G. (2008). *Organizational factors in the transition to independent living.* Unpublished manuscript.

Mann-Feder, V., & White, T. (2004). Facilitating the transition to independent living: Reflections on a program of research. *International Journal of Child and Family Welfare, 6*(4), 198–204.

Marcellus, L. (2008). (Ad)ministering love: Foster families caring for infants with prenatal substance exposure. *Qualitative Health Research, 18*(9), 1220–30.

Markesteyn, P. H., & Day, D. C. (2006). *Turner Review and Investigation.* St. John's, NL: Government of Newfoundland & Labrador.

Marks, K. (2007, December 26). The big question: Three years on from the Boxing Day tsunami, have the countries recovered? *The Independent.* Retrieved March 28, 2008, via <www.independent.co.uk>.

Marris, P. (1974). *Loss and change.* New York: Random House.

Marris, P. (1987). *Loss and change* (rev. ed.). New York: Routledge, Kegan & Paul.

Marris, P. (1996). *Politics of uncertainty: Attachment in private and public life.* New York: Routledge.

Marsh, P., & Peel, M. (1999). *Leaving care in partnership: Family involvement with care leavers.* London: The Stationery Office.

Martin, F. (2003). Knowing and naming "Care" in child welfare. In K. Kufeldt & B. McKenzie (Eds.), *Child welfare: Connecting research, policy, and practice* (pp. 261–71). Waterloo, ON: Wilfrid Laurier University Press.

Martin, G. (1993). Foster care: The protection and training of carers' children. *Child Abuse Review, 2*(1), 15–22.

Martin, G., & Stanford, D. (1990). *Children who foster.* York, UK: Natural Children's Support Group.

Martin, P., & Jackson, S. (2002). Educational success for children in public care: Advice from a group of high achievers. *Child and Family Social Work, 7*(2), 121–30.

Mason, K., Kirby, G., & Wray, R. (1992). *Review of the Children, Young Persons, and Their Families Act 1989: Report of the Ministerial Review Team to the Minister of Social Welfare* (*Mason Report*). Wellington, NZ: Government Printer.

Massachusetts Society for the Prevention of Cruelty to Children. (2005). *18 and out: Life after foster care in Massachusetts.* <http://www.mspcc.org/document.doc?id =168>.

Masson, J. (2001). Intercountry adoption: A global problem or a global solution. *Journal of International Affairs, 55*(1), 141–66.

Masten, A. S. (2001). Ordinary magic: Resilience processes in development. *American Psychologist, 56*(3), 227–38.

Masten, A. S., Best, K. M., & Garmezy, N. (1990). Resilience and development: Contributions from the study of children who overcome adversity. *Development and Psychopathology, 2*, 425–44.

Masten, A. S., & Coatsworth, J. D. (1998). The development of competence in favorable and unfavorable environments: Lessons from research on successful children. *American Psychologist, 53*, 205–20.

Masten, A. S., & Garmezy, N. (1985). Risk, vulnerability, and protective factors in developmental psychpathology. In B. Lahey & A. Kazdin (Eds.), *Advances in clinical child psychology*, Vol. 8 (pp. 1–52). New York: Plenum Press.

Masten, A. S., Garmezy, N., Tellegen, A., Pellegrini, D. S., Larkin, K., & Larsen, A. (1988). Competence and stress in school children: The moderating effects of individual and family qualities. *Journal of Child Psychology and Psychiatry, 29*, 745–64.

Masten, A. S., Obradovic, J., & Burt, K. B. (2006). Resilience in Emerging Adulthood: Developmental perspectives on continuity and transformation. In J. E. Arnett & J. Tanner (Eds.), *Emerging Adults in America; Coming of age in the 21st century* (pp. 173–90). Washington, DC: American Psychological Association.

Masten, A. S., & Reed, M. J. (2002). Resilience in development. In C. R. Snyder & S. J. Lopez (Eds.), *Handbook of positive psychology* (pp. 74–88). Oxford: Oxford University Press.

Mather, J., & Lager, P. (2000). *Child welfare: A unifying model of practice.* Belmont, CA: Wadsworth/Thomson Learning.

Maughan, A., & Cicchetti, D. (2002). Impact of child maltreatment and interadult violence on children's emotion regulation abilities and socio-emotional adjustment. *Child Development, 73*(5), 1525–42.

Maunders, D., Liddell, M., Liddell, M., & Green, S. (1999). *Young people leaving care and protection: A report to the National Youth Affairs Research Scheme.* Hobart: Australian Clearinghouse for Youth Studies.

May, M. (2008). Burma: Thousands of children orphaned by Nargis. Inter Press Service (IPS) News Agency. Originally retrieved August 12, 2008; accessible at <http://ipsnews.net/news.asp?idnews=42661>.

Mayer, M., Dufour, S., Lavergne, C., Firard, M., & Trocmé, N. (2003, May). *Comparing parental characteristics regarding child neglect: An analysis of cases retained by child protection services in Quebec.* Paper presented at the 3rd World Health Congress (Child and Youth Health), Vancouver.

Mayer, M., Lavergne, C., Tourigny, M., & Wright, J. (2007). Characteristics differentiating neglected children from other reported children. *Journal of Family Violence, 22*(8), 721–32.

McAdams, D. P. (1993). *The stories we live by: Personal myths and the making of the self.* New York: Guilford Press.

McAuley, C., Pecora, P. J., & Rose, W. (2006). *Enhancing the well-being of children and families through effective interventions.* London: Jessica Kingsley Publishers.

McCallum, D. (2005). Law and governance in Australian Aboriginal communities: Liberal and non-liberal political reason. *International Journal of Children's Rights, 13*, 333–50.

McCallum, S. P. (1995). *Safe families: A model of child protection intervention based on parental voice and wisdom.* Unpublished doctoral thesis, Wilfrid Laurier University, Waterloo, ON.

McCreary Centre Society. (2004). *Healthy youth development: Highlights from the 2003 Adolescent Health Survey III.* Vancouver: Author.

McCreary Centre Society. (2006). *Building resilience in vulnerable youth*. Vancouver: Author.

McCreary Centre Society. (2007). *Against the odds: A profile of marginalized and street-involved youth in BC* [series of five individual pamphlets]. Vancouver: Author.

McCroskey, J., & Meezan, W. (1998). Family-centered services: Approaches and effectiveness. *The Future of Children, 8*(1), 54–71.

McDonald, R., & Ladd, P. (2000). *Joint national policy review of First Nations child and family services*. Ottawa: Assembly of First Nations and Indian and Northern Affairs Canada.

McFadden, E. J. (1985). Practice in foster care. In J. Laird & A. Hartman (Eds.), *A handbook of child welfare* (pp. 585–616). New York: Free Press.

McFadden, E. J. (1996). Family-centered practice with foster-parent families. *Families in Society: The Journal of Contemporary Social Services, 77*, 545–58.

McGillivray, A. (1997). Therapies of freedom: The colonization of Aboriginal childhood. In A. McGillivray (Ed.), *Governing childhood* (pp. 135–99). Aldershot, UK: Dartmouth.

McGoldrick, M., & Carter, B. (2003). The family life cycle. In F. Walsh (Ed.) *Normal family processes: Growing diversity and complexity* (3rd ed.) (pp. 375–98). New York: Guilford Press.

McKenzie, B. (1993). *Current perspectives on foster family care for children and youth*. Toronto: Wall & Emerson.

McKenzie, B. (1999). Empowerment in First Nations child and family services: A community-building process. In W. Shera & L. Wells (Eds.), *Empowerment practice in social work: Developing richer conceptual foundations* (pp. 196–219). Toronto: Canadian Scholars' Press.

McKenzie, B. (2002). *Block funding child maintenance in First Nations child and family services: A policy review* (Final Report). Winnipeg: Faculty of Social Work, University of Manitoba.

McKenzie, B., Bennett, M., Kennedy, B., Balla, S., & Lamirande, L. (2009). *An exploratory regional study on child welfare outcomes in Aboriginal communities: Final Report*. Thunder Bay, ON: Association of Native Child and Family Services Agencies of Ontario.

McKenzie, B., & Flette, E. (2003). Community building through block funding in Aboriginal child and family services. In K. Kufeldt & B. McKenzie (Eds.), *Child welfare: Connecting research, policy, and practice* (pp. 343–53). Waterloo, ON: Wilfrid Laurier University Press.

McKenzie, B., & Hudson, P. (1985). Native children, child welfare, and the colonization of Native people. In K. Levitt & B. Wharf (Eds.), *The challenge of child welfare* (pp. 125–41). Vancouver: University of British Columbia Press.

McKenzie, B., & Morrissette, V. (2003). Social work practice with Canadians of Aboriginal background: Guidelines for respectful social work. In A. Al-Krenawi & J.R.

Graham (Eds.), *Multicultural social work in Canada: Working with diverse ethno-racial communities* (pp. 251–82). Don Mills, ON: Oxford University Press.

McKenzie, B., & Shangreaux, C. (2006, November). *From child protection to community caring in First Nations child and family services.* Presentation at World Forum on Child Welfare, Vancouver.

McKenzie, B., & Shangreaux, C. (2010). Aboriginal child welfare and health outcomes in Manitoba. In L. Fernandez, S. MacKinnon, & J. Silver (Eds.). *The social determinants of health in Manitoba* (pp. 127–38). Winnipeg: Canadian Centre for Policy Alternatives.

McKinnon, M., Davies, L., & Rains, P. (2001). Taking account of men in the lives of teenage mothers. *Affilia, 16,* 80–99.

McLeod, J. D., & Kessler, R. C. (1990). Socioeconomic status differences in vulnerability to undesirable life events. *Journal of Health and Social Behavior, 31*(2), 162–72.

McMurtry, S. L., & Lie, G.-Y. W. (1992). Differential exit rates of minority children in foster care. *Social Work Research and Abstracts, 28*(1), 42–8.

Melville, L. (2003). *Children and young people in New Zealand: Key statistical indicators.* Wellington, NZ: FAIR Centre of Barnardos.

Mendes, P., & Moslehuddin, B. (2003). Graduating from the child welfare system: An overview of the UK leaving care debate. *Youth Studies Australia, 22*(4), 37–43.

Messing, J. T. (2006). From the child's perspective: A qualitative analysis of kinship care placements. *Children and Youth Services Review, 28*(12), 1415–34.

Meston, J. (1988). Preparing young people in Canada for emancipation from child welfare. In E.V. Mech (Ed.), *Independent living services for at-risk adolescents* (pp. 129–38). Washington, DC: Child Welfare League of America.

Mewshaw, M. (2006). *If you could see me now: A chronicle of identity and adoption.* Columbia, MO: Unbridled Books.

Miller, I. W., Epstein, N. B., Bishop, D. S., & Keitner, G. I. (1985). The McMaster Family Assessment Device: Reliability and validity. *Journal of Marital and Family Therapy, 11*(4), 345–56.

Miller, I. W., Kabacoff, R. I., Epstein, N. B., Bishop, D. S., Keitner, G. I., Baldwin, L. M., et al. (1994). The development of a clinical rating scale for the McMaster model of family functioning. *Family Process, 33*(1), 53–69.

Miller, I. W., Ryan, C. E., Keitner, G. I., Bishop, D. S., & Epstein, N. B. (2000). The McMaster Approach to Families: Theory, assessment, treatment and research. *Journal of Family Therapy, 22,* 168–89.

Miller, J. (1991). Child welfare and the role of women: A feminist perspective. *American Journal of Orthopsychiatry, 61*(4), 592–8.

Miller, J. R. (1989). *Skyscrapers hide the heavens: A history of Indian–White relations in Canada.* Toronto: University of Toronto Press.

Miller, J. R. (1996). *Shingwauk's vision: A history of native residential schools.* Toronto: University of Toronto Press.

Miller, M. (2008). *Racial disproportionalty in Washington State's child welfare system.* Olympia: Washington State Institute for Public Policy (Document no. 08-06-3901).

Millham, S., Bullock, R., Hosie K., & Haak, M. (1986). *Lost in care.* Aldershot, UK: Gower.

Milloy, J. (1999). *A national crime: The Canadian government and the residential school system, 1879–1986.* Winnipeg: University of Manitoba Press.

Milner, J., & O'Byrne, P. (1998). *Assessment in social work.* London: Macmillan.

Ministerial Advisory Committee on a Maori Perspective for the Department of Social Welfare (New Zealand). (1986). *Puao-te-ata-tu (Day break).* Wellington, NZ: Government Printer.

Minkler, M., & Fuller-Thomson, E. (2005). African American grandparents raising grandchildren: A national study using the Census 2000 American Community Survey. *Journals of gerontology (Series B, Psychological sciences and social sciences) 60*(2), S82–92.

Minkler, M. & Roe, K. (1993). *Grandmothers as caregivers: Raising children of the crack cocaine epidemic.* Newbury Park, CA: Sage.

Mitic, W., & Rimer, M. (2002). The educational attainment of children in care in British Columbia. *Child and Youth Care Forum, 31*(6), 397–414.

Moles, K. (2008). Bridging the divide between child welfare and domestic violence services: Deconstructing the change process. *Children and Youth Services Review, 30*(6), 674–88.

Molgat, M. (2007). Do transitions and social structures matter? How "Emerging Adults" define themselves as adults. *Journal of Youth Studies, 10*(5), 495–516.

Monaghan, D. (2009, June 17). The state and our kids. [Letter to the Editor]. *National Post*, p. A13.

Morgan, D. L. (1988). *Focus groups as qualitative research.* Newbury Park, CA: Sage.

Morgan, D. L. (1993). *Successful focus groups: Advancing the state of the art.* Newbury Park, CA: Sage.

Moyers, S. (1997). *Report of an audit of the implementation of Looking After Children in Year 1: 1995/6.* Leicester, UK: University of Leicester.

Mullaly, B. (2002). *Challenging oppression: A critical social work approach.* Don Mills, ON: Oxford University Press.

Munro, E. (1998). Improving social workers' knowledge base in child protection work. *British Journal of Social Work, 28*, 89–105.

Munro, E. (2001). Empowering looked-after children. *Child and Family Social Work, 6*(2), 129–37.

Munro, E. (2005). Improving practice: Child protection as a systems problem. *Children and Youth Services Review, 27*(4), 375–91.

Munro, E. R., Stein, M., & Ward, H. (2005). Comparing how different social, political and legal frameworks support or inhibit transitions from public care to independence in Europe, Israel, Canada and the United States. *International Journal of Child and Family Welfare, 8*(4), 191–201.

Myles, J. (2005). *Postponed adulthood: Dealing with the new economic inequality.* Ottawa: Canadian Council on Social Development. Originally retrieved November 9, 2008; now accessible at <http://www.ccsd.ca/pubs/2005/pa/pa.pdf>.

Nadjiwan, S., & Blackstock, C. (2003). *Caring across the boundaries: Promoting access to voluntary sector resources for First Nations children and families.* Ottawa: First Nations Child & Family Caring Society of Canada.

Nanaimo Men's Resource Centre. (2007). *Dads make a difference* (2nd ed.). Nanaimo, BC: Nanaimo Men's Resource Centre.

National Assembly for Wales. (2001). *Framework for the assessment of children in need and their families.* London: Stationery Office.

National Association of Black Social Workers. (2003). *Preserving families of African ancestry: A position paper adopted by the NABSW steering committee, January 10, 2003.* <http://www.nabsw.org/mserver/PreservingFamilies.aspx>.

National Council of Welfare. (1975). *Poor kids.* Ottawa: Author.

National Council of Welfare. (1979). *In the best interests of the child.* Ottawa: Author. Accessible via <http://www.ncw.gc.ca/>.

National Council of Welfare. (2007). *First Nations, Métis and Inuit children and youth: Time to act.* Ottawa: Author. Accessible via <http://www.ncw.gc.ca/>.

National Survey of Child and Adolescent Well-Being Research Group. (2002). Methodological lessons from the National Survey of Child and Adolescent Well-Being: The first three years of the USA's first national probability study of children and families investigated for abuse and neglect. *Children and Youth Services Review, 24*(6/7), 513–41.

National Survey of Child and Adolescent Well-Being Research Group. (2003). *National Survey of Child and Adolescent Well-Being (NSCAW): One year in foster care, Wave 1 data analysis report.* Washington, DC: U.S. Department of Health and Human Services.

National Youth in Care Network. (2000, October 17). *Dear Mom and Dad.* [An open letter presented to the Government of Canada.] Ottawa: Author.

National Youth in Care Network. (2001). *Who will teach me to learn? Creating positive school experiences for youth in care.* Originally retrieved January 12, 2009; now accessible via <http://www.crin.org/bcn/index.asp>.

Natural Parents v. Superintendent of Child Welfare (1975), [1976] 2 S.C.R. 751, 60 D.L.R. (3rd) 148 (Supreme Court of Canada).

Needell, B., Brookhart, M.A., & Lee, S. (2003). Black children and foster care placement in California. *Children and Youth Services Review, 25*(5/6), 393–408.

Needell, B., Webster, D., Armijo, M., Lee, S., Cuccaro-Alamin, S., Shaw, T., et al. (2007). *Child welfare services report for California*. Retrieved February 14, 2008, from University of California, Berkeley, Center for Social Services Research website at <http://cssr.berkeley.edu/CWSCMSreports/>.

Nelson, G., Laurendeau, M.-C., Chamberland, C., & Peirson, L. (2001). A review and analysis of programs to promote family wellness and prevent the maltreatment of preschool and elementary-school-aged children. In I. Prilleltensky, G. Nelson, & L. Peirson (Eds.), *Promoting family wellness and preventing child maltreatment: Fundamentals for thinking and action* (pp. 220–72). Toronto: University of Toronto Press.

Nelson, K., Cross, T., Landsman, M. J., & Tyler, M. (1996). Native American families and child neglect. *Children and Youth Services Review, 18*(6), 505–21.

Newman, T. (1999). *Evidence-based child care practice. Highlight No. 70*. London: National Children's Bureau.

New Zealand Ministry of Social Development. (2008). Data supplied by Planning and Business Analysis Unit, Child Youth and Family Service on March 4, 2008.

Nixon, K. L., Tutty, L. M., Weaver-Dunlop, G., & Walsh, C. A. (2007). Do good intentions beget good policy? A review of child protection policies to address intimate partner violence. *Children and Youth Services Review, 29*(12), 1469–86.

Nixon, P. (2007). *Relatively speaking: Developments in research and practice in kinship care*. Dartington, UK: Research in Practice. Originally retrieved June 14, 2009.

Norrington, S. (2002). *The forgotten children in child welfare: Caregivers' children*. Unpublished master's thesis, McMaster University, Hamilton, ON.

Nuske, E. (2004). *Beyond the doubled edged sword: The contradictory experiences of biological children in foster families*. Originally retrieved June 19, 2006; now accessible via <http://www.aifs.gov.au/afrc/bibs/siblings.html>.

Nuske, E. (2006). *Double edged sword: A contradictory experience. A phenomenological study of the lived experience of natural children of foster families*. Unpublished doctoral dissertation, Southern Cross University, Sydney, Australia.

Odell, T. (2008). Promoting foster carer strengths: Suggestions for strengths-based practice. *Adoption and Fostering, 32*(1), 19–28.

O'Hare, T. (2005). *Evidence-based practice for social workers: An interdisciplinary approach*. Chicago: Lyceum.

Okamura, A., & Jones, L. (2000). Reprofessionalizing child welfare services: An evaluation of a Title IV-E training program. *Research on Social Work Practice, 10*(5), 607–21.

Okong'o, M. (2004, September 1). Helping foster families in Uganda. *UN Chronicle*. Originally retrieved September 30, 2008; now accessible via <http://www.thefreelibrary.com/UN+Chronicle/2004/September/1-p57>.

O'Malley, K. (2000). *A new diagnostic classification: FASD*. Originally retrieved March 28, 2003; now accessible at <http://www.come-over.to/FAS/FASD-OMalley.htm>.

Ontario Association of Children's Aid Societies. (2008). *Children in care statistics.* Originally retrieved August 29, 2008, from <http://www2.oacas.org/>.

Ortez, M. J., Shusterman, G. R., & Fluke, J. D. (2008). Outcomes for children with allegations of neglect who receive alternative response and traditional investigations: Findings from NCANDS. *Protecting Children, 23*(1/2), 57–70.

Osberg, L. (2008). *A quarter century of economic inequality in Canada: 1981–2006.* Toronto: Canadian Centre for Policy Alternatives.

Osborn, A., & Bromfield, L. (2007). *Young people leaving care.* Research Brief No. 7. Melbourne: Australian Institute of Family Studies. Originally retrieved November 9, 2008; accessible at <http://www.aifs.gov.au/nch/pubs/brief/rb7/rb7.pdf>.

Osgood, D. W., Foster, E. M., Flanagan, C., & Ruth, G. R. (2004). *Why focus on the transition to adulthood for vulnerable populations?* Research Network Working Paper No. 2. The Network on Transitions to Adulthood. Originally retrieved November 9, 2008; accessible via <http://www.transad.pop.upenn.edu/publications/wp.html>.

Osgood, D. W., Foster, E. M., Flanagan, C., & Ruth, G. R. (2005). Introduction: Why focus on the transition to adulthood for vulnerable populations? In D.W. Osgood, E.M. Foster, C. Flanagan, & G.R. Ruth (Eds.), *On your own without a net: The transition to adulthood for vulnerable populations* (pp. 1–26). Chicago: University of Chicago Press.

Otunnu, O. (2004, March 1). Protecting children in times of war: How to develop an effective monitoring and reporting system. *UN Chronicle, 41*(1), 68–70. Accessible via <http://www.thefreelibrary.com/UN+Chronicle/2004/March/1-p57>.

Owen, L., Jones, D., & Corrick, H. (1998). Implementing *Looking After Children* in Australia. *Childhood and Society, 12*(3), 240–1.

Oxford English Dictionary. (2001). New York: Oxford University Press.

Packard, T., Delgado, M., Fellmeth, R., & McCready, K. (2008). A cost-benefit analysis of transitional services for emancipating foster youth. *Children and Youth Services Review, 30*(11), 1267–78.

Packman, J., & Randall, J. (1989). Decision-making at the gateway to care. In O. Stevenson (Ed.), *Child abuse: Public policy and professional practice* (pp. 88–109). Hemel Hempstead, UK: Harvester.

Palmer, S. E. (1992). Including birth families in foster care: A Canadian–British comparison. *Children and Youth Services Review, 14*(5), 407–25.

Palmer, S. E. (1995). *Maintaining family ties: Inclusive practice in foster care.* Washington, DC: Child Welfare League of America.

Palmer, S. E. (1996). Placement stability and inclusive practice in foster care: An empirical study. *Children and Youth Services Review, 18*(7), 589–601.

Pancer, M., Nelson, G., Dearing, B., Dearing, S., Hayward, K., & Peters, R. De V. (2003). Promoting wellness in families and children through community-based interventions: The Highfield Community Enrichment Project. In K. Kufeldt &

B. McKenzie (Eds.), *Child welfare: Connecting research, policy, and practice* (pp. 111–21). Waterloo, ON: Wilfrid Laurier University Press.

Pandey, G. (2008). Abuse of Indian children "common." BBC News website. Retrieved August 18, 2008, from <http://news.bbc.co.uk/2/hi/south_asia/6539027.stm>.

Pantin, S., Flynn, R. J., & Runnels, V. (2006). Training, experience and supervision: Keys to enhancing the utility of the Assessment and Action Record in implementing *Looking After Children*. In R. J. Flynn, P. M. Dudding, & J. G. Barber (Eds.), *Promoting resilience in child welfare* (pp. 281–96). Ottawa: University of Ottawa Press.

Park, J., & Turnbull, A. (2003). Service integration in early intervention: Determining interpersonal and structural factors for its success. *Infants and Young Children, 16*(1), 48–58.

Parker, E. (2006). *Children and social policy; "Identity, rhetoric and reality."* Social Work Monographs (Serial No. 220). Norwich, UK: School of Social Work and Psychosocial Studies, University of East Anglia.

Parker, R. A. (1998). Reflections on the assessment of outcomes in child care. *Children and Society, 12*(3), 192–201.

Parker, R. A. (Ed.). (1980). *Caring for separated children: Plans, procedures, and priorities.* London: Macmillan.

Parker, R. A., Ward, C., Jackson, S., Aldgate, J., & Wedge, P. (Eds.). (1991). *Looking after children: Assessing outcomes in child care.* London: Her Majesty's Stationery Office.

Parkes, C. M., Stevenson-Hinde, J., & Marris, P. (1991). *Attachment across the life cycle.* New York: Routledge.

Parliament of Romania. (2004). Law No. 272/2004, Art. 24. *Romania Official Gazette,* Part 1, No.557. Retrieved June 15, 2009, from <http://www.salvaticopiii.ro/romania/copiii_romania/legislatie/Legeacopilului_272.pdf>.

Part, D. (1993). Fostering as seen by the carers' children. *Adoption and Fostering, 17*(1), 26–31.

Partenariat familles en mouvance et dynamique intergénérationnelles. (2005). *Agir sur les politiques familiales. La recherche: Un outil indispensable. Fiches synthèses de transfert des connaissances.* <http://partenariat-familles.ucs.inrs.ca/DocsPDF/FichesAPFROI.pdf>.

Partnerships for Children and Families Project. Lyle S. Hallman Faculty of Social Work, Wilfrid Laurier University, Waterloo, ON. <http://www.wlu.ca/pcfproject>.

Parton, N. (2003, July). *From Maria Colwell to Victoria Climbié: Reflections on a generation of public inquiries into child abuse.* Plenary paper presented at BASPCAN conference. <http://www.gptsw.net/papers/clwlclmbi.pdf>.

Parton, N. (2004). From Maria Colwell to Victoria Climbié: Reflections on public inquiries into child abuse a generation apart. *Child Abuse Review, 13*(2), 80–94.

Parton, N., & Mathews, R. (2001). *New directions* in child protection and family support in Western Australia: A policy initiative to re-focus child welfare practice. *Child and Family Social Work, 6*(2), 97–113.

Pat Doorbar & Associates. (1996). *We're here too: The view on fostering of the natural children of foster parents.* Originally retrieved October 2, 2008.

Pauzé, R., Toupin, J., Déry, M., Mercier, H., Joly, J., Cyr, M., et al. (2004). *Portrait des jeunes âgés de 0 à 17 ans référés à la prise en charge des Centres jeunesse du Québec, leur parcours dans les services et leur évolution dans le temps.* Sherbrooke, QC: Groupe de recherche sur les inadaptations sociales de l'enfance, Université de Sherbrooke, Université de Montréal, et Université du Québec en Outaouais.

Pecora, P. J. (1989). Evaluating risk assessment systems: Methodological issues and selected research findings. In P. Schene & K. Bond (Eds.), *Research issues in risk assessment for child protection* (pp. 47–59). Denver, CO: American Humane Association.

Pecora, P. J. (1991). Investigating allegations of child maltreatment: The strengths and limitations of current risk assessment systems. *Child and Youth Services, 15*(2), 73–92.

Pecora, P. J. (1995). Assessing the impact of family-based services. In J. Hudson & B. Galaway (Eds.), *Child welfare in Canada: Research and policy implications* (pp. 100–12). Toronto: Thompson Educational Publishing.

Pecora, P. J., Briar, K., & Zlotnik, J. (1989). *Addressing the program and personnel crisis in child welfare* (Technical Assistance Report, Commission on Family and Primary Associations). Silver Springs, MD: National Association of Social Workers.

Pecora, P. J., & Maluccio, A. N. (2000). What works in family foster care. In M. Kluger, G. Alexander, & P. Curtis (Eds.), *What works in child welfare?* (pp. 139–56). Washington, DC: Child Welfare League of America.

Pecora, P. J., Williams, J., Kessler, R. C., Hiripi, E., O'Brien, K., Emerson, J., et al. (2006). Assessing the educational achievements of adults who were formerly placed in family foster care. *Child and Family Social Work, 11*(3), 220–31.

Peel, M. (1998). *Report of an audit of the implementation of Looking After Children in Year 2: 1996/7.* Leicester, UK: University of Leicester.

Peirson, L., Nelson, G., & Prilleltensky, I. (2003). Expanding the frontiers in family wellness and prevention. In K. Kufeldt & B. McKenzie (Eds.), *Child welfare: Connecting research, policy, and practice* (pp. 101–9). Waterloo, ON: Wilfrid Laurier University Press.

Peled, E. (2000). Parenting by men who abuse women: Issues and dilemmas. *British Journal of Social Work, 30*, 25–36.

Pelton, L. (1989). *For reasons of poverty: A critical analysis of the public child welfare system in the United States.* New York: Greenwood Publishing Group.

Pendreigh, B. (2002). Leaping the fence of Australia's past. <http://www.iofilm.co.uk/feats/interviews/r/rabbit_proof_fence_2002.shtml>.

Perks, R., & Thomson, A. (Eds.). (1998). *The oral history reader.* London: Routledge.

Perry, B. (1997). Incubated in terror: Neurodevelopmental factors in the "cycle of violence." In J. Osofsky (Ed.), *Children, youth and violence: The search for solutions* (pp. 124–48). New York: Guilford Press.

Perry, B. (2001). The Neuroarcheology of childhood maltreatment: The neurodevelopmental costs of adverse childhood events. In K. Franey, R. Geffner & R. Falconer (Eds.), *The cost of child maltreatment: Who pays? We all do* (pp. 15–37). New York: Haworth Press.

Pertman, A. (2000). *Adoption nation: How the adoption revolution is transforming America.* New York: Basic Books.

Peters, J. (2005). True ambivalence: Child welfare workers' thoughts, feelings and beliefs about kinship foster care. *Children and Youth Services Review, 27*(6), 595–614.

Petersen, A. (2006). Conducting policy-relevant developmental psychopathology research. *International Journal of Behavioral Development, 30*(1), 39–46.

Petr, C. G., & Entrikin, C. (1995). Service system barriers to successful reunification. *Families in Society: The Journal of Contemporary Social Services, 76*(9), 523–32.

Phares, V. (1992). Where's poppa? The relative lack of attention to the role of fathers in child and adolescent psychopathology. *American Psychologist, 47*(5), 656–64.

Phares, V., Lopez, E., Fields, S., Kamboukos, D., & Duhig, A. (2005). Are fathers involved in pediatric psychology research and treatment? *Journal of Pediatric Psychology, 30*(8), 631–43.

Pickett, K. E., & Wilkinson, R. G. (2007). Child wellbeing and income inequality in rich societies: Ecological cross sectional study. *British Medical Journal, 335*(7629), 1080–7. doi:10.1136/bmj.39377.580162.55.

Pilkington, D. (2002). *Rabbit-proof fence: The true story of one of the greatest escapes of all time.* New York: Hyperion.

Pine, B. A., Warsh, R., & Maluccio, A. N. (1993). *Together again: Family reunification in foster care.* Washington, DC: Child Welfare League of America.

Pivot Legal Society. (2009, May). *Hands tied: Child protection workers talk about working in, and leaving, BC's child welfare system.* Retrieved June 1, 2009, from <http://www.pivotlegal.org/pdfs/Pivot_HandsTied.pdf>.

Plath, D. (2006). Evidence-based practice: Current issues and future directions. *Australian Social Work, 59*(1), 56–72.

Plummer, K. (2001). *Documents of life 2: An invitation to critical humanism.* London: Sage.

Poirier, M.-A., Dumont, R., Simard, M.-C., Richard, A.-M., Chamberland, C. & Normandeau, S. (2007). *Le projet SOCEN au Québec: Rapport d'évaluation.* Quatrième rapport intérimaire présenté à l'Association des centres jeunesse du Québec.

Poirier, M.-A., Simard, M.-C., Dumont, R., & Richard, A.-M. (2005). L'approche s'occuper des enfants (SOCEN): Une initiative visant le développement des enfants placés en famille d'accueil. *Intervention, 123*, 28–36.

Poland, D., & Groze, V. (1993). The effects of foster care placement on biological children in the home. *Child and Adolescent Social Work, 10*(2), 153–64.

Poole, N. (2003). *Mother and child reunion: Preventing fetal alcohol spectrum disorder by promoting women's health.* Vancouver: Centre for Excellence in Women's Health. Accessed July 30, 2010 at <www.cewh-cesf.ca/PDF/bccewh/FASbrief.pdf>.

Poole, N. (2007). Improving outcomes for women and their children: Evaluation of the Sheway program. In N. Poole & L. Greaves, L. (Eds.), *Highs and lows: Canadian perspectives on women and substance use* (pp. 247–8). Toronto: Centre for Addiction and Mental Health.

Potocky, M. (1997). Multicultural social work in the United States: A review and critique. *International Social Work, 40*(3), 315–26.

Powell, J. Y. (1996). A schema for family-centered practice. *Families in Society: The Journal of Contemporary Social Services, 77*(7), 446–8.

Powell, M., & York, R. (1992). Turnover in county public welfare agencies. *Journal of Applied Social Sciences, 16*(2), 111–27.

Preston, V., Rose, D., Norcliffe, G., & Holmes, J. (2008). Shift work, childcare, and domestic work: Divisions of labour in Canadian paper mill communities. In M. Kimmel, A. Aronson, & A. Kaler (Eds.), *The gendered society reader*, Canadian edition (pp. 143–57). Toronto: Oxford University Press.

Prilleltensky, I., Nelson, G., & Peirson, L. (Eds.). (2001). *Promoting family wellness and preventing child maltreatment: Fundamentals for thinking and action.* Toronto: University of Toronto Press.

Prilleltensky, I., Peirson, L., & Nelson, G. (2001). Mapping the terrain: Framework for promoting family wellness and preventing child maltreatment. In I. Prilleltensky, G. Nelson, & L. Peirson (Eds.), *Promoting family wellness and preventing child maltreatment: Fundamentals for thinking and action* (pp. 3–40). Toronto: University of Toronto Press.

Prilleltensky, I., & Prilleltensky, O. (2006). *Promoting well-being: Linking personal, organizational, and community factors.* Hoboken, NJ: John Wiley.

Proch, K., & Howard, J. A. (1986). Parental visiting of children in foster care. *Social Work, 31*(3), 178–81.

Prochaska, J. O., DiClemente, C. C., & Norcross, J. C. (1992). In search of how people change: Application to addictive behavior. *American Psychologist, 47*(9), 1102–14.

Pron, N. (2006, April 8). Abusers convicted, inquest ordered. *Toronto Star*, p. A1.

Public Health Agency of Canada. (2010). *Canadian incidence study of reported child abuse and neglect—2008: Major findings.* Ottawa: Author.

Rabson, M. (2009a, March 11). Aboriginals making strides: Report. *Winnipeg Free Press*, p. A7.

Rabson, M. (2009b, August 11). More kids in agency care. *Winnipeg Free Press*, p. A4.

Rabson, M. (2010, March 5). New cash for on-reserve child welfare may loom. *Winnipeg Free Press*, p. A6.

Radhakrishna, A., Bou-Saada, I., Hunter, W., Catellier, D., & Kotch, J. (2001). Are father surrogates a risk factor for child maltreatment? *Child Maltreatment, 6*(4), 281–9.

Radomsky, N. (1995). *Lost voices: Women, chronic pain, and abuse*. New York: Haworth Press.

Rae-Grant, Q., & Moffat, P. J. (1971). *Children in Canada: Residential care*. Toronto: Leonard Crainford for the Canadian Mental Health Association.

Ragg, D. M., Patrick, D., & Ziefert, M. (2006). Slamming the closet door: Working with gay and lesbian youth in care. *Child Welfare, 85*(2), 243–65.

Raychaba, B. (1993). *Pain, lots of pain: Violence and abuse in the lives of young people in care*. Ottawa: National Youth in Care Network.

Raymond, B. B. (2007). *The baby thief: The untold story of Georgia Tann, the baby seller who corrupted adoption*. New York: Carroll & Graf.

Raynor, L. (1980). *The adopted child comes of age*. London: George Allen & Unwin.

Reagh, R. (1994). Public child welfare professionals: Those who stay. *Journal of Sociology and Social Welfare, 21*(3), 69–78.

Reder, P., & Duncan, S. (1999). *Lost innocents: A follow-up study of fatal child abuse*. London: Routledge.

Reder, P., & Duncan, S. (2004). Making the most of the Victoria Climbié Inquiry Report. *Child Abuse Review, 13*(2), 95–114.

Reder, P., Duncan, S., & Gray, M. (1993). *Beyond blame: Child abuse tragedies revisited*. London: Routledge.

Reed, J. A. (1994). We live here too: Birth children's perspectives on fostering someone with learning disabilities. *Children & Society, 8*(2), 164–73.

Register, C. (1991). *"Are those kids yours?": American families with children adopted from other countries*. New York: Free Press.

Regnier, R. (1995). The sacred circle: An Aboriginal approach to healing education at an urban high school. In M. Battiste & J. Barman (Eds.), *First Nations education in Canada: The circle unfolds* (pp. 313–29). Vancouver: University of British Columbia Press.

Reid, C. (2007). The transition from state care to adulthood: International examples of best practices. In V. Mann-Feder (Ed.), *Transition or Eviction: Youth Exiting Care for Independent Living*. Special issue of *New Directions for Youth Development, 113*, 33–49.

Reid, C., & Dudding, P. (2006). *Building a future together: Issues and outcomes for transition-aged youth*. Ottawa: Centres of Excellence for Children's Well-Being, Child Welfare League of Canada, and National Youth in Care Network. Accessible via <http://www.cecw-cepb.ca/publications/568>.

Reid, C., & Dudding, P. (2007). Building a future together: A summary of issues for transition-aged youth exiting state care. In Child Welfare League of Canada (Ed.), *The welfare of Canadian children: It's our business* (pp. 142–51). Ottawa: Author.

Reid, G. (1997). Key CPS decisions: Case selection. In T. D. Morton & W. Holder (Eds.), *Decision making in children's protective services: Advancing the state of the art.* (pp. 76–85). Duluth, GA: Child Welfare Institute.

Reid, G., Sigurdson, E., Christianson-Wood, J., & Wright, A. (1996). Risk assessment: Some Canadian findings. *Protecting Children, 12*(2), 24–31.

Reilly, T. (2003). Transition from care: Status and outcomes of youth who age out of foster care. *Child Welfare, 82*(6), 727–46.

Reinharz, S., with L. Davidman. (1992). *Feminist methods in social research.* New York: Oxford University Press.

Richard, L., Pineault, R., D'Amour, D., Brodeur, J.-M., Séguin, L., Latour, R., et al. (2005). The diversity of prevention and health promotion services offered by Québec Community Health Centres: A study of infant and toddler programmes. *Health and Social Care in the Community, 13*(5), 399–408.

Richardson, J. (2008, November). *Differential response literature review.* Urbana, IL: Children and Family Research Center, School of Social Work, University of Illinois at Urbana-Champaign.

Risley-Curtiss, C., & Heffernan, K. (2003). Gender biases in child welfare. *Affilia, 18*(4), 395–410.

Robinson, E. B. (2002). A response to *The Colour of Difference.* <http://www.clova publications.com/_data/docs/2002%20the%20colour%20of%20difference2.pdf>.

Robinson, E. B. (2003). *Adoption and loss: The hidden grief* (rev. ed.). Christies Beach, Australia: Clova Publications.

Rolock, N., & Testa, M. (2007). Stability of family life: At home and in substitute care. In N. Rolock & M. Testa (Eds.), *Conditions of children in or at risk of foster care in Illinois: An assessment of their safety, permanence, and well-being* (pp. 2.1–2.9). Urbana, IL: Children and Family Research Center, School of Social Work, University of Illinois at Urbana-Champaign.

Romney, S., Litrownik, A., Newton, R., & Lau, A. (2006). The relationship between child disability and living arrangement in child welfare. *Child Welfare, 85*(6), 965–84.

Rooney, R. H. (1992). *Strategies for work with involuntary clients.* New York: Columbia University Press.

Rosenbaum, P., King, S., Law, M., King, G., & Evans, J. (1998). Family-centred services: A conceptual framework and research review. *Physical and Occupational Therapy in Pediatrics, 18*(1), 1–20.

Rosenberg, E. B. (1992). *The adoption life cycle: The children and their families through the years.* New York: Free Press.

Rosenbluth, D. (1995). Moving in and out of foster care. In J. Hudson and B. Galaway (Ed.), *Child welfare in Canada: Research and policy implications* (pp. 233–44). Toronto: Thompson Educational Publishing.

Rossi, P. H., Schuerman, J., & Budde, S. (1999). Understanding decisions about child maltreatment. *Evaluation Review, 23*(6), 579–98.

Rowe, J., Hundleby, M., & Garnett, L. (1989). *Child care now: A survey of placement patterns.* London: British Agencies for Adoption and Fostering.

Roy, P., & Rutter, M. (2006). Institutional care: Associations between inattention and early reading performance. *Journal of Child Psychology and Psychiatry, 47*(5), 480–7.

Royal Commission on Aboriginal Peoples (RCAP). (1996). *Report of the Royal Commission on Aboriginal peoples.* Ottawa: Author.

Rubin, D. M., Downes, K. J., O'Reilly, A. L. R., Mekonnen, R., Luan, X., & Localio, R. (2008). Impact of kinship care on behavioral well-being for children in out-of-home care. *Archives of Pediatrics and Adolescent Medicine, 162*(6), 550–6.

Rubin, S. (1972). Children as victims of institutionalization. *Child Welfare, 51*(1), 6–18.

Russell, T. (2004). Personal communication to the authors, May 10, 2004. Cited in D. Rutman, C. Hubberstey, & A. Feduniw, *When youth age out of care—Where to from there? Final report based on a three year longitudinal study.* Victoria, BC: School of Social Work, University of Victoria.

Rutman, D., Barlow, A., Alusik, D., Hubberstey, C., & Brown, E. (2003). Supporting young people's transitions from government care. In K. Kufeldt & B. McKenzie (Eds.), *Child welfare: Connecting research, policy, and practice* (pp. 227–38). Waterloo, ON: Wilfrid Laurier University Press.

Rutman, D., Callahan, M., Lundquist, A., Jackson, S., & Field, B. (2000). *Substance use and pregnancy: Conceiving women in the policy making process.* Ottawa: Status of Women Canada.

Rutman, D., Hubberstey, C., Barlow, A., & Brown, E. (2005). *When youth age out of care: A report of baseline findings.* Victoria, BC: School of Social Work, University of Victoria.

Rutman, D., Hubberstey, C., & Feduniw, A. (2007). *When youth age out of care—Where to from there? Final report based on a three-year longitudinal study.* Victoria, BC: School of Social Work, University of Victoria.

Rutman, D., Strega, S., Callahan, M., & Dominelli, L. (2002). "Undeserving" mothers? Practitioners' experiences working with young mothers in/from care. *Child and Family Social Work, 7*(3), 149–59.

Rutter, M. (1990). Psychosocial resilience and protective mechanisms. In J. Rolf, A. S. Masten, D. Cicchetti, K. H. Nuechterlein & S. Weintraub (Eds.), *Risk and protective factors in the development of psychopathology* (pp. 181–214). New York: Cambridge University Press.

Rutter, M. (2000). Children in substitute care: Some conceptual considerations and research implications. *Children and Youth Services Review, 22*(9/10), 685–703.

Rutter, M., & English and Romanian Adoptees Study Team. (1998). Developmental catch-up, and deficit, following adoption after severe global early privation. *Journal of Child Psychology and Psychiatry, 39*, 465–76.

Ryan, C. (2009). *Helping families support their lesbian, gay, bisexual and transgender (LGBT) children.* Washington, DC: National Center for Cultural Competence, Georgetown University Center for Child and Human Development.

Ryan, C. E., Epstein, N. B., Keitner, G. I., Miller, I. W., & Bishop, D. S. (2005). *Evaluating and treating families: The McMaster approach.* New York: Routledge.

Ryan, J. P., Garnier, P., Zyphur, M., & Zhai, F. (2006). Investigating the effects of caseworker characteristics in child welfare. *Children and Youth Services Review, 29*(9), 993–1006.

Ryan, M. (2000). *Working with fathers.* Abingdon, UK: Radcliffe Medical Press.

Ryan, S., Wiles, D., Cash, S., & Siebert, C. (2005). Risk assessments: Empirically supported or values driven? *Children and Youth Services Review, 27*(2), 213–25.

Ryburn, M. (1993). A new model for family decision making in child care and protection. *Early Child Development and Care, 86*(11), 1–10.

Rycraft, J. (1994). The party isn't over: The agency role in the retention of public child welfare caseworkers. *Social Work, 39*(1), 75–80.

Rycus, J. S., & Hughes, R. C. (2003). *Issues in risk assessment in child protective services.* Columbus, OH: North American Resource Center for Child Welfare.

Salveron, M., Arney, F., & Scott, D. (2006). Sowing the seeds of innovation: Ideas for child and family services. *Family Matters, 73*, 39–45. Melbourne: Australian Institute of Family Studies.

Samantrai, K. (1992). Factors in the decision to leave: Retaining social workers with MSWs in public child welfare. *Social Work, 37*(5), 454–8.

Samuels, G. (2008). *A reason, a season, or a lifetime: Relational permanence among young adults with foster care backgrounds.* Chicago: Chapin Hall Center for Children, University of Chicago.

Saunders, A. (2005, March 5). CYF child has fifteen homes in a year. *The Dominion*, p. 5.

Saunders, B., & Goddard, C. (1998, June). *A critique of structured risk assessment procedures: Instruments of abuse?* Ringwood, Australia: Australian Childhood Foundation & Caulfield East, Australia: National Research Centre for the Prevention of Child Abuse, Monash University.

Sawyer, R., & Lohrbach, S. (2005a). Differential response in child protection: Selecting a pathway. *Protecting Children, 20*(2/3), 44–53.

Sawyer, R., & Lohrbach, S. (2005b). Integrating domestic violence intervention into child welfare practice. *Protecting Children, 20*(2/3), 62–77.

Scales, P. C., & Leffert, N. (1999). *Developmental assets: a synthesis of the scientific research on adolescent development.* Minneapolis: Search Institute.

Scannapieco, M., & Hegar, R. (1999). Kinship foster care in context. In R. Hegar & M. Scannapieco (Eds.), *Kinship foster care: Policy, practice and research* (pp. 1–13). New York: Oxford University Press.

Schene, P. A. (1998). Past, present, and future poles of child protective services. *The Future of Children*, 8(1), 23–38.

Schene, P. A. (2001a). Making differential response work: Lessons learned. *Best Practice/Next Practice*, Spring, 15–19.

Schene, P. A. (2001b). Meeting each family's needs: Using differential response in reports of child abuse and neglect. *Best Practice/Next Practice*, Spring, 1–14.

Schene, P. A. (2006). Forming and sustaining partnerships in child and family welfare: The American experience. In N. Freymond & G. Cameron (Eds.), *Towards positive systems of child and family welfare: International comparisons of child protection, family service, and community caring systems* (pp. 84–117). Toronto: University of Toronto Press.

Schibler, B., & McEwan-Morris, A. (2006). *"Strengthening our youth": Their journey to competence and independence.* Winnipeg: Office of the Children's Advocate. Accessible via <http://www.childrensadvocate.mb.ca/>.

Schmid, J., & Goranson, S. (2002). Family group conferencing: An effective tool in planning for children's safety and well-being. *OACAS Journal*, 46(4), 19–23.

Schmid, J., Tansony, R., Goranson, S., & Sykes, D. (2004). Family group conferencing: Doorway to kinship care. *OACAS Journal*, 48(4), 2–7.

Schmidt, F., Cuttress, L. J., Lang, J., Lewandowski, M. J., & Rawana, J. S. (2007). Assessing the parent–child relationship in parenting capacity evaluations: Clinical applications of attachment research. *Family Court Review*, 45(2), 247–59.

Schorr, L. B. (1997). *Common purpose: Strengthening families and neighbourhoods to rebuild America.* New York: Doubleday.

Schwalbe, C. S. (2004). Re-visioning risk assessment for human service decision making. *Children and Youth Services Review*, 26(6), 561–76.

Schwalbe, C. S. (2008). Strengthening the integration of actuarial risk assessment with clinical judgment in an evidence based practice framework. *Children and Youth Services Review*, 30(12), 1458–64.

Schwartz, A. E. (2002). Societal value and the funding of kinship care. *Social Service Review*, 76(3), 430–59.

Scott, J. (1999). *Report of an audit of the implementation of Looking After Children in Year 2: 1997/8.* Leicester, UK: University of Leicester.

Scott, J. (2000). *Report of a longitudinal audit of the implementation of Looking After Children by local authorities which implemented Looking After Children in Year 1: 1995/6.* Leicester, UK: University of Leicester.

Scott, K., & Crooks, C. (2004). Effecting change in maltreating fathers: Critical principles for intervention planning. *Clinical Psychology: Science and Practice*, 11(1), 95–111.

Scourfield, J. (2001). Constructing women in child protection work. *Child and Family Social Work, 6*(1), 77–87.

Scourfield, J. (2003). *Gender and child protection.* Houndmills, Basingstoke, UK: Palgrave Macmillan.

Scourfield, J. (2006). The challenge of engaging fathers in the child protection process. *Critical Social Policy, 26*(2), 440–9.

Scullion, P. (2002). Overcoming barriers to research utilization. *British Journal of Therapy and Rehabilitation, 9*(10), 408.

Scully, A. (1986). *Special needs adoption.* Unpublished master's thesis, University of Calgary.

Seaberg, J. R. (1981). Foster parents as aides to parents. In A. N. Maluccio & P. Sinanoglu, (Eds.), *The challenge of partnership: Working with parents of children in foster care* (pp. 209–20). Washington, DC: Child Welfare League of America.

Sedlak, A. (1991). *National incidence study and prevalence of child abuse and neglect: 1988* (rev. ed.). Rockville, MD: Westat.

Senate of Canada—Subcommittee on Population Health. (2009). *A healthy, productive Canada: A determinant of health approach (Final report).* Ottawa: The Senate. Retrieved November 15, 2009; accessible via <http://senate-senat.ca/health-e.asp>.

Serge, L., Eberle, M., Goldberg, M., Sullivan, S., & Dudding, P. (2002). *Pilot study: The child welfare system and homelessness among Canadian youth.* Ottawa: National Secretariat on Homelessness. Accessible via <http://www.cecw-cepb.ca/publications/596>.

Shangreaux, C. (2004). *Staying at home: Examining the implications of least disruptive measures in First Nations child and family services agencies.* Ottawa: First Nations Child & Family Caring Society of Canada.

Shangreaux, C. (2006, November). *Integrating Medicine Wheel teaching into First Nations and Aboriginal child welfare practice.* Unpublished paper. Winnipeg: Author.

Shangreaux, C. (2008, July). *Strengthening and protecting the future of our children* (Follow-Up Report on the 2005 Evaluation West Region Child and Family Services Alternatives Services Continuum). Rolling River, MB: West Region Child and Family Services.

Shangreaux, C. (2009). *Southeast Child and Family Services 2009/2010 federal operations plan.* Winnipeg: Southeast Child and Family Services.

Shangreaux, C., & McKenzie, B. (2006, March). *West Region Child and Family Services flexible funding option service plan: 2005–2010.* Rolling River, MB: West Region Child and Family Services.

Shelton, T., & Stepanek, J. (1995). Excerpts from family-centered care for children needing specialized health and developmental services. *Pediatric Nursing, 21*(4), 362–4.

Shlonsky, A. (2008, November). *Siblings in foster care: What do we know, what do we need to know, and how might this influence practice in child welfare?* Paper presented at the Sibling Relationships Conference: Practice and Research Together, Ottawa.

Shlonsky, A., & Berrick, J. D. (2001). Assessing and promoting quality in kin and non-kin foster care. *Social Service Review, 75*(1), 60–83.

Shlonsky, A., & Gibbs, L. (2004). Will the real evidence-based practice please stand up? Teaching the process of evidence-based practice to the helping professions. *Brief Treatment and Crisis Intervention, 4*(2), 137–53.

Shlonsky, A., & Wagner, D. (2005). The next step: Integrating actuarial risk assessment and clinical judgment into an evidence-based practice framework in CPS case management. *Children and Youth Services Review, 27*(4), 409–27.

Shusterman, G. R., Hollinshead, D., Fluke, J. D., & Yuan, Y-Y. T. (2005). *Alternative responses to child maltreatment: Finding from NCANDS.* Washington, DC: U.S. Department of Health and Human Services, Office of the Assistant Secretary for Planning and Evaluation. <www.aspe.hhs.gov/hsp/05/child-maltreat-resp/>.

Silber, K., & Dorner, P. M. (1990). *Children of open adoption.* San Antonio, TX: Corona.

Silver, J., Hay, J., Klyne, D., Ghorayshi, P., Gorzen, P., Keeper, C., MacKenzie, M., & Simard, F. (2006). *In their own voices: Building urban Aboriginal communities.* Halifax: Fernwood.

Silverman, A. R. (1993). Outcomes of transracial adoption. *The Future of Children, 3*(1), 104–18.

Simard, G. (1989). *La méthode du focus group.* Laval, QC: Mondia.

Simard, M.-C. (2007). *La réunification familiale des adolescents placés en ressource de réadaptation : Étude des facteurs prédictifs.* Unpublished doctoral dissertation, School of Social Work, McGill University, Montreal.

Simard, M., & Vachon, J. (1990). Perceptions des parents du succès ou de l'échec de la réinsertion familiale d'enfants placés. *Intervention, 87,* 15–23.

Simmons, G., Gumpert, J., & Rothman, B. (1973). Natural parents as partners in child care placement. *Social Casework, 54*(4), 224–32.

Sinclair, I. (2005). *Fostering now: Messages from research.* London: Jessica Kingsley Publishers.

Sinclair, I., Gibbs, I., & Wilson, K. (2004). *Foster carers: Why they stay and why they leave.* London: Jessica Kingsley Publishers.

Sinclair, I., Wilson, K., & Gibbs, I. (2005). *Foster placements: Why they succeed and why they fail.* London: Jessica Kingsley Publishers.

Sinclair, M., Bala, N., Lilles, H., & Blackstock, C. (2004). Aboriginal child welfare. In N. Bala, M. K. Zapf, R. J. Williams, R. Vogl, & J. Hornick (Eds.), *Canadian child welfare law: Children, families and the state* (2nd ed.) (pp. 199–244). Toronto: Thompson Educational Publishing.

Sinclair, R. (2007a). Identity lost and found: Lessons from the sixties scoop. *First Peoples Child and Family Review, 3*(1), 65–82.

Sinclair, R. (2007b). *All my relations. Native transracial adoption: A critical case study of cultural identity.* Unpublished doctoral dissertation. Faculty of Social Work, University of Calgary.

Smith, B. D. (2003). How parental drug use and drug treatment compliance relate to family reunification. *Child Welfare, 82*(3), 335–65.

Smith, N. A. (1999). *Understanding the lack of family reunification success for chemically dependent mothers and their children: A presentation of consumer and service provider perspectives.* Unpublished doctoral dissertation, State University of New York, Albany, NY.

Smyke, A., Dumitrescu, A., & Zeanah, C. (2002). Attachment disturbances in young children. I: The continuum of caretaking casualty. *Journal of the American Academy of Child and Adolescent Psychiatry, 41*(8), 972–82.

Spar, D. L. (2006). *The baby business: How money, science, and politics drive the commerce of conception.* Boston: Harvard Business School Press.

Speak, S., Cameron, S., & Gilroy, R. (1997). *Young, single, non-residential fathers: Their involvement in fatherhood. Child and Family Social Work.* York, UK: Joseph Rowntree Foundation.

Spears, W., & Cross, M. (2003). How do "children who foster" perceive fostering? *Adoption & Fostering, 27*(4), 38–45.

Spratt, T. (2001). The influence of the child protection orientation on child welfare practice. *British Journal of Social Work, 31*(6), 933–54.

Springer, K. W., Sheridan, J., Kuo, D., & Carnes, M. (2007). Long-term physical and mental health consequences of childhood physical abuse: Results from a large population-based sample of men and women. *Child Abuse and Neglect, 31*(5), 517–30.

Standing Committee on Human Resources Development and the Status of Persons with Disabilities. (2003). *Building a brighter future for urban Aboriginal children.* Ottawa: House of Commons. Originally retrieved October 23, 2005; accessible via <http://www.parl.gc.ca/>.

Stanley, J., & Goddard, C. (2002). *In the firing line: Violence and power in child protection work.* Chichester, UK, and New York: Wiley.

Stanley, J., Tomison, A. M., & Pocock, J. (2003). Child abuse and neglect in Indigenous Australian communities. Child Abuse Prevention Issues, Discussion Paper No. 19 (Spring). Melbourne: Australian Institute of Family Studies, National Child Protection Clearinghouse. <http://www.aifs.gov.au/nch/pubs/issues/issues19/issues19.html>.

Stanley, N. (1997). Domestic violence and child abuse: Developing social work practice. *Child and Family Social Work, 2*(3), 135–45.

Stanley, T. (2007). Risky work: Child protection practice. *Social Policy Journal of New Zealand, 30,* 163–77.

Statistics Canada. (2001). *Census of Canada,* 2001. Retrieved August 23, 2008, from <http://www12.statcan.ca/english/census01/home/index.cfm>.

Statistics Canada. (2006a). *Census families by number of children at home, by province and territory (2006 Census).* Accessed July 2008 at <http://www40.statcan.ca/l01/cst01/famil50g.htm>.

Statistics Canada. (2006b). *Family portrait: Continuity and change in Canadian families and households in 2006. National portrait: Individuals.* Originally retrieved November 9, 2008; accessible at <http://www12.statcan.gc.ca/census-recensement/2006/as-sa/97-553/index-eng.cfm>.

Statistics Canada. (2006c). *Aboriginal Peoples in Canada in 2006: Inuit, Métis and First Nations, 2006 Census.* Retrieved August 23, 2008, from <http://www12.statcan.ca/english/census06/analysis/aboriginal/pdf/97-558-XIE2006001.pdf>.

Statistics New Zealand. (June 2005). *New Zealand Income Survey.* Wellington, NZ: Government of New Zealand.

Statistics New Zealand. (2007). *2006 Census of population and dwellings.* Originally retrieved October 3, 2008; accessible at <http://www.stats.govt.nz/Census/2006CensusHomePage.aspx>.

Steenrod, S. (2005). The relationship between managed care and evidence-based practices in outpatient substance abuse programs. *Best Practices in Mental Health, 1*(1), 31–46.

Steering Committee for the Review of Commonwealth/State Service Provision (Australia). (2006). *Report on government services 2006. Chapter 15: Protection and support services.* Canberra: Government of Australia. < http://www.pc.gov.au/__data/assets/pdf_file/0005/87440/60-chapter15-only.pdf>.

Stein, M. (2004). *What works for young people leaving care?* Barkingside, UK: Barnardos.

Stein, M. (2006). Research review: Young people leaving care. *Child and Family Social Work, 11*(3), 273–9.

Stein, M. (2008). Transitions from care to adulthood: messages from research. In M. Stein & E. Munro (Eds.), *Young people's transitions from care to adulthood: International research and practice* (pp. 289–306). London: Jessica Kingsley Publishers.

Steinberg, S., Kruckman, L., & Steinberg, S. (2000). Reinventing fatherhood in Japan and Canada. *Social Science and Medicine, 50*(9), 1257–72.

Steinhauer, P. D. (1991). *The least detrimental alternative: A systematic guide to case planning and decision making for children in care.* Toronto: University of Toronto Press.

Sterling-Collins, R. (2009). A holistic approach to supporting children with special needs. In R. Sinclair, M. A. Hart, & G. Bruyere (Eds.), *Wicihitowin: Aboriginal social work in Canada* (pp. 65–88). Halifax: Fernwood.

Stevenson, O. (2007). *Neglected children and their families* (2nd ed.). Oxford: Blackwell.

Stewart, D. W., & Shamdasani, P. N. (1990). *Focus groups: Theory and practice.* Newbury Park, CA: Sage.

Stonechild, B. (2006). *The new buffalo: The struggle for Aboriginal post-secondary education in Canada.* Winnipeg: University of Manitoba Press.

Stratton, K., Howe, C., & Battaglia, F. (Eds.). (1996). *Fetal alcohol syndrome: Diagnosis, epidemiology, prevention and treatment.* Washington, DC: Institute of Medicine and National Academy Press.

Strauss, A. L. (1987). *Qualitative analysis for social scientists.* New York: Cambridge University Press.

Strauss, A. L., & Corbin, J. (1990). *Basics of qualitative research: Grounded theory procedures and techniques.* Newbury Park, CA: Sage.

Strega, S. (2006). Failure to protect: Child welfare interventions when men beat mothers. In R. Alaggia & C. Vine (Eds.), *Cruel but not unusual: Violence in Canadian families* (pp. 237–66). Waterloo, ON: Wilfrid Laurier University Press.

Strega, S., Brown, L., Callahan, M., Dominelli, L., & Walmsley, C. (2009). Working with me, working at me: Fathers' narratives of child welfare. *Journal of Progressive Human Services, 19*(2), 1–20.

Streissguth, A. (1997). *Fetal alcohol syndrome: A guide for families and communities.* Baltimore: Paul H. Brookes Publishing.

Streissguth, A., & Kanter, J. (1997). *The challenge of fetal alcohol syndrome: Overcoming secondary disabilities.* Seattle: University of Washington Press.

Streissguth, A., & O'Malley, K. (2000). Neuropsychiatric implications and long-term consequences of fetal alcohol spectrum disorders. *Seminars in clinical neuropsychiatry, 5*(3), 177–90.

Strolin-Goltzman, J., Auerbach, C., McGowan, B. G., & McCarthy, M. L. (2008). The relationship between organizational characteristics and workforce turnover among rural, urban, and suburban public child welfare systems. *Administration in Social Work, 32*(1), 77–91.

Stroul, B. (1995). Case management in a system of care. In B.J. Friesen & J. Poertner (Eds.), *From case management to service coordination for children with emotional, behavioral, or mental disorders. Building on family strengths* (pp. 3–25). Baltimore: Paul H. Brookes.

Strug, D., & Wilmore-Schaeffer, R. (2003). Fathers in the social work literature: Policy and practice implications. *Families in Society: The Journal of Contemporary Social Services, 84*(4), 503–11.

Sundell, K., & Vinnerljung, B. (2004). Outcomes of family group conferencing in Sweden: A 3-year follow-up. *Child Abuse and Neglect, 28*(3), 267–87.

Sunderland, J. (2004). *Gendered discourses.* New York: Palgrave Macmillan.

Surbeck, B. C. (2003). An investigation of racial partiality in child welfare assessments of attachment. *American Journal of Orthopsychiatry, 73*(1), 13–23.

Swan, T. (2000). *Care providers' children share their experiences.* Unpublished report, Faculty of Social Sciences, McMaster University, Hamilton, ON.

Swan, T. (2002). The experience of foster caregivers' children. *Canada's Children,* Spring, 13–17.

Swift, K. (1995a). An outrage to common decency: Historical perspectives on child neglect. *Child Welfare, 74*(1), 71–91.

Swift, K. (1995b). *Manufacturing "bad mothers": A critical perspective on child neglect.* Toronto: University of Toronto Press.

Swift, K. (1995c). Missing persons: Women in child welfare. *Child Welfare, 74*(3), 486–502.

Swift, K. (1998). Contradictions in child welfare: Neglect and responsibility. In C. T. Baines, P. M. Evans & S. Neysmith (Eds.), *Women's caring: Feminist perspectives on social welfare* (2nd ed.) (pp. 160–90). Toronto: Oxford University Press.

Swift, K. (2003). *Canadian child welfare: Trends and issues in placement and reporting.* Retrieved July 2008 from <http://www.sws.soton.ac.uk/cwab/Guide/KRCanada.rtf>.

Tabachnick, B. G., & Fidell, L. S. (2001). *Using multivariate statistics* (4th ed.). Needham Heights, MA: Allyn & Bacon.

Tait, C. (2000). Aboriginal identity and the construction of fetal alcohol syndrome. In L. J. Kirmayer, M. E. Macdonald, & G. M. Brass (Eds.), *Culture and Mental Health Research Unit Report No. 10: The Mental Health of Indigenous Peoples* (pp. 95–111). Montreal: McGill University. Originally retrieved February 2, 2003.

Tanner, J. (2006). Recentering during emerging adulthood: A critical turning point in lifespan human development. In J. Arnett & J. Tanner (Eds.), *Emerging adults in America; Coming of age in the 21st century* (pp. 21–55). Washington, DC: American Psychological Association.

Tanner, K., & Turney, D. (2006). Therapeutic interventions with children who have experienced neglect and their families in the UK. In C. McAuley, P. Pecora, & W. Rose (Eds.), *Enhancing the well-being of children and families through effective interventions: International evidence for practice* (pp. 118–30). London: Jessica Kingsley Publishers.

Tapsfield, R., & Collier, F. (2005). *The cost of foster care: Investing in our children's future.* London: The Fostering Network; British Association of Adoption and Fostering.

Teare, J. F., Becker-Wilson, C., & Larzelere, R. E. (2001). Identifying risk factors for disrupted family reunifications following short-term shelter care. *Journal of Emotional and Behavioral Disorders, 9*(2), 116–22.

Teare, J. F., Furst, D. W., Peterson, R. W., & Authier, K. (1992). Family reunification following shelter placement: Child, family, and program correlates. *American Journal of Orthopsychatry, 62*(1), 142–6.

Teare, J. F., Peterson, R. W., Authier, K., Schroeder, L., & Daly, D. L. (1998). Maternal satisfaction following shelter placement: Child, family and program correlates. *Child and Youth Care Forum, 27*(2), 125–38.

Terling, T. (1999). The efficacy of family reunification practices: Reentry rates and correlates of reentry for abused and neglected children reunited with their families. *Child Abuse and Neglect, 23*(12), 1359–70.

Terling-Watt, T. (2001). Permanency in kinship care: An exploration of disruption rates and factors associated with placement disruption. *Children and Youth Services Review, 23*(2), 111–26.

Testa, M. (2008, April). *Kinship care and permanency outcomes.* Paper presented at the *Kinship Care and Permanency Outcomes: Practice and Research Together* Conference, Oshawa, ON.

Tewodros, A. (2003). *Forgotten families: Older people as carers of orphans and vulnerable children.* London: International HIV/AIDS Alliance and HelpAge. Retrieved October 1, 2008, from <http://www.crin.org/docs/Forgotten%20Families.pdf>.

Theis, M., Erickson, W., Lloyd-Jones, T., Gandelsonas, C., Kalra, R., Khiabany, G., et al. (2000). *Improving knowledge transfer: Communication for development.* Originally retrieved July 20, 2006, from website of Max Lock Centre, University of Westminster, London.

Thériault, E. (2003). Introduction. In Kufeldt, K. & McKenzie, B. (Eds.), *Child welfare: Connecting research, policy, and practice* (pp. 1–9). Waterloo, ON: Wilfrid Laurier University Press.

Thoburn, J. (1994). *Child placement: Principles and practice* (2nd ed.). Aldershot, UK: Ashgate.

Thoburn, J. (2007). *Globalisation and child welfare: Some lessons from a cross-national study of children in out-of-home care.* Norwich, UK: Social Work Monographs, School of Social Work and Psychosocial Studies, University of East Anglia. (Individual country profiles are accessible via Prof. Thoburn's web page at <http://www.uea.ac.uk/swp/people_old/jthoburn?mode=print>.)

Thoburn, J., Chand, A., & Procter, J. (2005). *Child welfare services for minority ethnic families: The research reviewed.* London: Jessica Kingsley Publishers.

Thoburn, J., Norford, L., & Rashid, S. P. (2000). *Permanent family placement for children of minority ethnic origin.* London: Jessica Kingsley Publishers.

Thomas, P. (2003). Charter implications for proactive child welfare services. In K. Kufeldt & B. McKenzie (Eds.), *Child welfare: Connecting research, policy, and practice* (pp. 355–66). Waterloo, ON: Wilfrid Laurier University Press.

Thomlison, B., Maluccio, A. N., & Abramczyk, L. W. (1996). The theory, policy, and practice context of family reunification: An integrated research perspective. *Children and Youth Services Review, 18*(4/5), 473–88.

Thomlison, B., Maluccio, A. N., & Wright, L. W. (1996). Protecting children by preserving their families: A selective research perspective on family reunification. *International Journal of Child and Family Welfare, 2*(2), 127–36.

Thompson, D., Siegel, G., & Loman, L. A. (2008). The Parent Support Outreach Program: Minnesota's early intervention track. *Protecting Children, 23*(1/2), 23–9.

Thompson, S. J., Safyer, A. W., & Pollio, D. E. (2001). Differences and predictors of family reunification among subgroups of runaway youths using shelter services. *Social Work Research, 25*(3), 163–72.

Thorpe, M. B., & Swart, G. T. (1992). Risk and protective factors affecting children in foster care: A pilot study of the role of siblings. *Canadian Journal of Psychiatry, 37*(9), 616–22.

Thrane, L., Hoyt, D. Whitbeck, L., & Yoder, K. (2006). Impact of family abuse on running away, deviance, and street victimization among homeless rural and urban youth. *Child Abuse and Neglect, 30*(10), 1117–28.

Thyer, B. (2004). What is evidence-based practice? *Brief Treatment and Crisis Intervention, 4*(2), 167–76.

Timmer, S. G., Sedler, G., & Urquiza, A. J. (2004). Challenging children in kin versus nonkin foster care: Perceived costs and benefits to caregivers. *Child Maltreatment, 8*(3), 251–62.

Tizard, B. (1977). *Adoption: A second chance.* London: Open Books.

Tolley, S. (2005). SCARF (Supporting Children and Responding to Families): A family casework model with client and worker friendly assessment, planning and review tools, *National Child Protection Clearinghouse Newsletter, 13*(2), 16–19.

Tonmyr, L., Jack, S., Brooks, S., Kennedy, B., & Dudding, P. (2008). Utilization of the *Canadian Incidence Study of Reported Child Abuse and Neglect* in First Nations child welfare agencies in Ontario. *First Peoples Child and Family Review, 4*(1), 38–46.

Tracy, E., & Pine, B. (2000). Child welfare education and training: Future trends and influences. *Child Welfare, 79*(1), 93–113.

Tregeagle, S. (2007). The complex digital divide: Information and communication technology use amongst Australian child welfare service users. *Children Australia, 32*(4), 9–16.

Tregeagle, S., & Mason, J. (2008). Service user experience of participation in child welfare case management. *Child and Family Social Work, 13*(4), 391–401.

Tregeagle, S., & Treleaven, L. (2006). Key questions in considering guided practice for vulnerable Australian children. *Australian Journal of Social Issues, 41*(3), 359–68.

Triseliotis, J., Borland, M., & Hill, M. (2000). *Delivering foster care.* London: British Agencies for Adoption & Fostering.

Trocmé, N. (1996). Le rôle des facteurs de classe et de genre dans la sélection de stratégies de recherche, d'intervention et de prévention de la maltraitance des enfants. In F. Ouellet & M. Clément (Eds.). *Violences dans les relations affectives: Représentations et interventions. Actes du Colloque tenu à Chicoutimi le 23 mai 1995 dans le cadre du 63e congrès de l'ACFAS. Réflections, 4*, 7–34). Montréal: CRI-VIFF.

Trocmé, N., & Chamberland, C. (2003). Re-involving the community: The need for a differential response to rising child welfare caseloads in Canada. In N. Trocmé, D. Knoke, & C. Roy (Eds.), *Community collaboration and differential response* (pp. 45–56). Ottawa: Child Welfare League of Canada.

Trocmé, N., Fallon, B., MacLaurin, B., Daciuk, J., Felstiner, C., Black, T., et al. (2005). *Canadian incidence study of reported child abuse and neglect—2003: Major findings*. Ottawa: Minister of Public Works and Government Services Canada / *Étude canadienne sur l'incidence des signalements de cas de violence et de négligence envers les enfants—2003. Données pricipales*. Ottawa: Ministre de Travaux Publics et Services gouvernementaux Canada.

Trocmé, N., Fallon, B., MacLaurin, B., & Neves, T. (2005). What is driving increasing child welfare caseloads in Ontario? Analysis of the 1993 and 1998 Ontario Incidence Studies. *Child Welfare, 84*(3), 341–62.

Trocmé, N., Knoke, D., & Blackstock, C. (2004). Pathways to the overrepresentation of Aboriginal children in Canada's child welfare system. *Social Service Review, 78*(4), 577–600.

Trocmé, N., Knoke, D., Fallon, B., & MacLaurin, B. (2009). Differentiating between substantiated, suspected, and unsubstantiated maltreatment in Canada. *Child Maltreatment, 14*(1), 4–16.

Trocmé, N., Knoke, D., Shangreaux, C., Fallon, B., & MacLaurin, B. (2005). The experience of First Nations children coming into contact with the child welfare system in Canada: *The Canadian Incidence Study on Reported Abuse and Neglect*. In First Nations Child & Family Caring Society of Canada, *Wen:de (We are coming to the light of day)* (pp. 60–86). Ottawa: First Nations Child & Family Caring Society of Canada.

Trocmé, N., Lajoie, J., Fallon, B., & Felstiner, C. (2007). *Injuries and deaths of children at the hands of their parents*. CECW Information Sheet No. 57E. Toronto: University of Toronto, Faculty of Social Work. Originally retrieved October 15, 2008; accessible at <http://www.cecw-cepb.ca/sites/default/files/publications/en/Injuries 57E.pdf>.

Trocmé, N., MacLaurin, B., & Fallon, B. (2000). Canadian child welfare outcomes indicator matrix: An ecological approach to tracking service outcomes. *Journal of Aggression, Maltreatment and Trauma, 4*(1), 165–90.

Trocmé, N., MacLaurin, B., Fallon, B., Daciuk, J., Billingsley, D., Tourigny, M., et al. (2001). *Canadian incidence study of reported child abuse and neglect: Final report*. Ottawa: Minister of Public Works and Government Services Canada.

Trocmé, N., MacLaurin, B., Fallon, B., Knoke, D., Pitman, L., & McCormack, M. (2005). *Understanding the overrepresentation of First Nations children in Canada's child welfare system: An analysis of the Canadian incidence study of reported abuse and neglect (CIS-2003)*. Toronto: Centre for Excellence for Child Welfare. Accessible via <http://www.cecw-cepb.ca/publications/606>.

Trocmé, N., McPhee, D., & Tam, K. K. (1995). Child abuse and neglect in Ontario: Incidence and characteristics. *Child Welfare, 74*(3), 563–86.

Trute, B., & Hiebert-Murphy, D. (2007). The implications of "working alliance" for the measurement and evaluation of family-centered practice in childhood disability services. *Infants and Young Children, 20*(2), 109–19.

Tuff, R. (2007). A Canadian foster care story. *IFCO Informer*, Issue 1, 8–9.

Turcotte, D., Trocmé, N., Dessureault, D., Hélie, S., Cloutier, R., Montambeault, E., et al. (2007). Étude sur l'incidence et les caractéristiques de la maltraitance signalée à la Direction de la protection de la jeunesse au Québec. La situation en 2003. (Rapport de recherche.) Québec: Ministère de la Santé et des services sociaux du Québec.

Turnell, A. (2004). Relationship-grounded, safety-organised child protection practice: Dreamtime or real-time option for child welfare? *Protecting Children, 19*(2): 14–25.

Turney, D. (2000). The feminizing of neglect. *Child and Family Social Work, 5*(1), 47–56.

Tweddle, A. (2005). *Youth leaving care—How do they fare?* Briefing paper prepared for the Modernizing Income Security for Working Age Adults (MISWAA) Project (Ontario). <http://www.laidlawfdn.org/sites/default/files/resources/Youth_Leaving_Care_report.pdf>.

Tweddle, A. (2007). Youth leaving care: How do they fare? In V. Mann-Feder (Ed.), *Transition or Eviction: Youth Exiting Care for Independent Living*. Special issue of *New Directions for Youth Development, 113*, 15–31.

Twigg, R. (1993). *What price foster care: The effects of the foster care experience on the foster parent's own children*. Unpublished doctoral dissertation, Smith College School for Social Work, Northampton, MA.

Twigg, R. (1994). The unknown soldiers of foster care: Foster care as loss for the foster parents' own children. *Smith College Studies in Social Work, 64*(3), 297–313.

Twigg, R. (1995). Coping with loss: How foster parents' children cope with foster care. *Community Alternatives: International Journal of Family Care, 7*(1), 1–12.

Twigg, R. (2006). *Withstanding the test of time: What we know about the treatment foster care*. Hackensack, NJ: Foster Family-Based Treatment Association.

Twigg, R. (2009). Passion for those who care: What foster carers need. In S. McKay, D. Fuchs, & I. Brown (Eds.), *Passion for action in child and family services: Voices from the prairies* (pp. 165–84). Regina, SK: Canadian Plains Research Center.

Twigg, R., & Swan, T. (2007). Inside the foster family: What research tells us about the experience of foster carers' children. *Adoption and Fostering, 31*(4), 49–61.

Tyrer, P., Chase, E., Warwick, I., & Angleton, P. (2005). "Dealing with it": Experiences of young fathers in and leaving care. *British Journal of Social Work, 35*(7), 1107–21.

UNAIDS. (n.d.). *Questions and answers about the AIDS epidemic and its impact*. Retrieved September 30, 2008, from <http://www.unaids.org/epi/2005/doc/resources.asp>.

UNAIDS, UNICEF, et al. (2004). *The framework for the protection, care and support of orphans and vulnerable children living a world with HIV and AIDS*. New York: United Nations. Accessible at <http://www.unicef.org/aids/files/Framework_English.pdf>.

Ungar, M. (2004). *Nurturing hidden resilience in troubled youth.* Toronto: University of Toronto Press.

UNICEF. (n.d.). *Child protection from violence, exploitation and abuse: Child labor.* Retrieved September 17, 2008, from <http://www.unicef.org/protection/index_childlabour.html>.

UNICEF. (2002, February 12). Bellamy and Otunnu hail entry into force of Optional Protocol on Child Soldiers. New York: UNICEF Press Centre. Retrieved September 15, 2008, from <http://www.unicef.org/newsline/02pr04op.htm>.

United Nations Millennium Project. (2005). *The Millennium development goals report 2005.* New York: United Nations.

United Nations Office of the High Commissioner for Human Rights. (1989). *Convention on the Rights of the Child.* Originally retrieved March 26, 2009; accessible at <http://www2.ohchr.org/english/law/crc.htm>.

United Nations Permanent Forum on Indigenous Issues. (2007). Who are Indigenous peoples? (Indigenous peoples, Indigenous voices factsheet.) Retrieved June 1, 2009, from <http://www.wipce2008.com/enews/pdf/wipce_fact_sheet_21-10-07.pdf>.

United States Department of Health and Human Services. (2008). *The AFCARS Report: Preliminary FY 2006 estimates as of January 2008.* Retrieved October 16, 2008, from <http://www.acf.hhs.gov/programs/cb/stats_research/afcars/tar/report14.pdf>.

United States Department of Health and Human Services, Administration for Children and Families/Children's Bureau and Office of the Assistant Secretary for Planning and Evaluation. (2003). *National study of child protective services systems and reform efforts: Findings on local CPS practices.* Washington, DC: US Government Printing Office.

United States Department of Health and Human Services, Administration on Children, Youth and Families. (2006). *Child maltreatment 2004.* Washington, DC: U.S. Government Printing Office.

United States Department of Health and Human Services, Children's Bureau. (2006). *Child welfare outcomes 2002–2005.* Washington, DC: Author.

United States Department of State. (2007). *Trafficking in persons report 2007.* Washington, DC: Author.

Unrau, Y. A., Seita, J. R., & Putney, K. S. (2008). Former foster youth remember multiple placement moves: A journey of loss and hope. *Children and Youth Services Review, 30*(11), 1256–66.

Usher, C. L., & Wildfire, J. B. (2003). Evidence-based practice in community-based child welfare systems. *Child Welfare, 82*(5), 597–614.

Vachon, J. (1997). Prévention du placement, réunification familiale et maintien des liens. In M. Simard (Ed.), *Maintien des liens familiaux et placement d'enfants* (pp. 23–32). Actes du colloque de recherche. Québec: Centre de recherche sur les services communautaires, Université Laval.

Vail, D. J. (1966). *Dehumanization and the institutional career*. Springfield, IL: Charles C. Thomas.

Van Riper, M. (1999). Maternal perceptions of family-provider relationships and well-being in families of children with Down syndrome. *Research in Nursing & Health*, *22*(5), 357–68.

Vig, S., Chinitz, S., & Shulman, L. (2005). Young children in foster care: Multiple vulnerabilities and complex service needs. *Infants and Young Children*, *18*(2), 147–60.

Virginia Department of Social Services. (2008). *Evaluation of the differential response system*. Richmond, VA: Author.

Vondra, J. I. (1990). Social and ecological factors. In R. T. Ammerman & M. Hersen (Eds.), *Children at risk: An evaluation of the factors contributing to child abuse and neglect* (pp. 149–70). New York: Plenum Press.

Vungkhanching, M., Sher, K., Jackson, K. & Parra, G. (2004). Relation of attachment style to family history of alcoholism and alcohol use disorders in early adulthood. *Drug and Alcohol Dependence*, *75*(1), 47–53.

Waites, C., Macgowan, M. J., Pennell, J., Carlton-LaNey, I., & Weil, M. (2004). Increasing the cultural responsiveness of family group conferencing. *Social Work*, *49*(2), 291–300.

Walberg, R., & Mrozek, A. (2009). *Private choices, public costs: How failing families cost us all*. Institute of Marriage and Family Canada. Accessible via <http://www.imfcanada.org/Default.aspx?go=article&aid=1277&tid=8>.

Wald, M., & Woolverton, M. (1990). Risk assessment: The emperor's new clothes? *Child Welfare*, *69*(6), 483–511.

Waldegrave, S., & Coy, F. (2005). A differential response model for child protection in New Zealand: Supporting more timely and effective responses to notifications. *Social Policy Journal of New Zealand*, *25*, 32–48.

Waldfogel, J. (1998). Rethinking the paradigm for child protection. *The Future of Children*, *8*(1), 104–19.

Waldfogel, J. (2001). Differential response: A new paradigm for child protective services. In J. Waldfogel (Ed.), *The future of child protection: How to break the cycle of child abuse and neglect* (pp. 137–60). Cambridge, MA: Harvard University Press.

Walker, P. J. (1990). *Kin group care in the Department of Social Welfare: An historical perspective*. Unpublished master's thesis, Victoria University, Wellington, New Zealand.

Walker, T. G. (1994). Educating children in the public care: A strategic approach. *Oxford Review of Education*, *20*(3), 339–47.

Walmsley, C. (2005). *Protecting Aboriginal children*. Vancouver: University of British Columbia Press.

Walmsley, C., Strega, S., Brown, L., Dominelli, L. & Callahan, M. (2009). More than a playmate, less than a co-parent: Fathers in the Canadian BSW curriculum. *Canadian Social Work Review*, *26*(1), 73–96.

Walsh, F. (2003a). Family resilience: Strengths forged through adversity. In F. Walsh (Ed.), *Normal family processes: Growing diversity and complexity* (3rd ed.) (pp. 399–423). New York: Guilford Press.

Walsh, F. (2003b). *Normal family processes: Growing diversity and complexity* (3rd ed.). New York: Guilford Press.

Walter, I., Nutley, S. M., & Davies, H.T.O. (2003). *Developing a taxonomy of interventions used to increase the impact of research: Discussion paper 3*. St. Andrews, Scotland: University of St. Andrews, Research Unit for Research Utilisation.

Ward, H. (2000). Translating messages from research on child development into social work training and practice. *Social Work Education, 19*(6), 543–51.

Ward, H. (Ed.). (1995). *Looking after children: Research into practice*. London: Her Majesty's Stationery Office.

Ward, H., Holmes, L., & Soper, J. (2008). *Costs and consequences of placing children in care*. London: Jessica Kingsley Publishers.

Ward, H., & Rose, W. (Eds.). (2002). *Approaches to needs assessment in children's services*. London: Jessica Kingsley Publishers.

Ward, H., & Skuse, T. (2002). *Transforming data into management information, 1996–2001*. Loughborough, UK: Centre for Child and Family Research.

Washington State Department of Social and Health Services. (2005). *Alternative response systems program progress report July 1, 2003—June 30, 2004*. Retrieved October 15, 2009, from <http://www.dshs.wa.gov/pdf/ca/ARS_FY04.pdf>.

Washington State Department of Social and Health Services. (2006). *2006 Children's administration performance report*. Olympia, WA: Author.

Washington State Department of Social and Health Services. (2008). Native American breakdown data supplied March 6, 2008.

Watson, A., & Jones, D. (2002). The impact of fostering on foster carers' own children. *Adoption and Fostering, 26*(1), 49–55.

Weaver, M. (2008, May 22). China earthquake deaths top 50,000. *The Guardian*. Retrieved September 2, 2008, from <http://www.guardian.co.uk/world/2008/may/22/chinaearthquake.china1>.

Webber, M. (1998). *As if kids mattered: What's wrong in the world of child protection and adoption*. Toronto: Key Porter Books.

Webster, D., Barth, R. P., & Needell, B. (2000). Placement stability for children in out-of-home care: A longitudinal analysis. *Child Welfare, 79*(5), 614–32.

Weil, R. H. (1984). International adoptions: The quiet migration. *International Migration Review, 18*(2), 276–93.

Welch, M. A. (2009, December 5). Awasis director forced aside. *Winnipeg Free Press*, p. A4.

Welch, M. A. (2010, February 12). Chiefs ruled CFS agency, review finds. *Winnipeg Free Press*, p. A8.

Wells, K., & Guo, S. (1999). Reunification and reentry of foster children. *Children and Youth Services Review, 21*(4), 273–94.

Wells, K., & Guo, S. (2004). Reunification of foster children before and after welfare reform. *Social Service Review, 78*(1), 74–95.

Welsh Assembly Government. (2006). *The Wales Accord for the sharing of personal information.* Cardiff: Welsh Assembly Government.

Werner, E. E. (1989). High-risk children in young adulthood: A longitudinal study from birth to 32 years. *American Journal of Orthopsychiatry, 59*(1), 72–81.

Wharf, B. (2002). *Community work approaches to child welfare.* Peterborough, ON: Broadview Press.

Wheelaghan, S., Hill, M., Lambert, L. Borland, M., & Triseliotis, J. (1999). *Looking After Children in Scotland.* Edinburgh: Scottish Office Central Research Unit.

Whitelaw Downs, S., Moore, E., McFadden, E. J., & Costin, L. B. (2004). *Child welfare and family policies.* New York: Pearson.

Whitford-Numan, R. L. (1994). *Reflections on special needs adoption: An exploratory descriptive study of parental perceptions.* Unpublished master's thesis, University of Calgary.

Williams, L. (2000). Urban Aboriginal education: The Vancouver experience. In M. B. Castellano, L. Davis, & L. Lahache (Eds.), *Aboriginal education: Fulfilling the promise* (pp. 129–46). Vancouver: University of British Columbia Press.

Williams, R. L. (2002). A note on robust variance estimation for cluster-correlated data. *Biometrics, 56,* 645–6.

Wilson, D., & Horner, W. (2005). Chronic child neglect: Needed developments in theory and practice. *Families in Society: The Journal of Contemporary Social Services, 86*(4), 471–81.

Wilson, K., Sinclair, I., & Gibbs, I. (2000). The trouble with foster care: The impact of stressful "events" on foster carers. *British Journal of Social Work, 30*(2), 193–209.

Wilson, S. (2008). *Research is ceremony: Indigenous research methods.* Halifax: Fernwood.

Windsor, J., Glaze, L., Koga, S., & Bucharest Early Intervention Project Core Group. (2007). Language acquisition with limited input: Romanian institution and foster care. *Journal of Speech, Language, and Hearing Research, 50*(5), 1365–81.

Winefield, H., & Bradley, P. (1992). Substantiation of reported Child Abuse and Neglect, Predictors and implications. *Child Abuse and Neglect, 16,* 661–71.

Winokur, M. A., Crawford, G. A., Longobardi, R. C., & Valentine, D. P. (2008). Matched comparison of children in kinship care and foster care on child welfare outcomes. *Families in Society: The Journal of Contemporary Social Services, 89*(3), 338–46.

Winokur, M., Holtan, A., & Valentine, D. (2009). *Kinship care for the safety, permanency, and well-being of children removed from the home for maltreatment.* Philadelphia: Campbell Collaboration Social Welfare Group.

Wise, S. (1999). *The UK Looking After Children approach in Australia.* Melbourne: Australian Institute of Family Studies.

Wise, S. (2003a). Using *Looking After Children* to create an Australian out-of-home care database. *Children Australia, 28*(2), 38–44.

Wise, S. (2003b). An evaluation of a trial of *Looking After Children* in the state of Victoria, Australia. *Children and Society, 17*(1), 3–17.

Wise, S. (2007). *Attachment and wellbeing in foster care children.* Unpublished doctoral thesis. University of Melbourne, Melbourne, Australia.

Wise, S., & Egger, S. (2008). *The Looking After Children Outcomes Data Project: Final Report prepared for the Department of Human Services by the Australian Institute of Family Studies: DHS Children, Youth and Families.* Melbourne: Department of Human Services.

Witkin, S. L., & Harrison, W. D. (2001). Whose evidence and for what purpose? *Social Work, 46*(4), 293–6.

Woldeguiorguis, I. M. (2003). Racism and sexism in child welfare: Effects on women of color as mothers and practitioners. *Child Welfare, 82*(2), 273–88.

Wolock, I. (1982). Community characteristics in child abuse and neglect cases. *Social Work Research and Abstracts, 18*(2), 9–15.

Wolock, I., & Horowitz, B. (1979). Child maltreatment and material deprivation among AFDC-recipient families. *Social Service Review, 53*(2), 175–94.

Wolock, I., & Horowitz, B. (1989). *Child maltreatment as a social problem: The neglect of neglect.* Ottawa: National Clearinghouse on Family Violence.

Wolock, I., Sherman, P., Feldman, L. H., & Metzger, B. (2001). Child abuse and neglect referral patterns: A longitudinal study. *Children and Youth Services Review, 23*(1), 21–47.

World Bank. (2008). New data show 1.4 billion live on less than US$1.25 a day, but progress against poverty remains strong. Accessible via <http://www.world bank.org/>.

World Food Programme. (2008). Cash roll-out to help hunger hot spots. *World Food Programme News.* Originally retrieved September 30, 2009; accessible at <http://www.wfp.org/node/157>.

World Health Organization. (2008). *Food security.* Retrieved September 30, 2008, from <http://www.who.int/entity/trade/glossary/story028/en>.

Woronoff, R., & Estrada, R. (2006). Regional listening forums: An examination of the methodology used by the Child Welfare League of America and Lambda Legal to highlight the experiences of LGBTQ youth in care. *Child Welfare, 85*(2), 341–60.

Worrall, J. (1996). *Because we're family: A study of kinship care of children in New Zealand.* Unpublished master's thesis, Massey University, Palmerston North, New Zealand.

Worrall, J. (2001). Kinship care of the abused child: The New Zealand experience. *Child Welfare, 80*(5), 497–512.

Worrall, J. (2005). *Grandparents and other relatives raising kin children in Aotearoa/New Zealand.* Auckland, NZ: Grandparents Raising Grandchildren Charitable Trust.

Worrall, J. (2007). Parenting second time around: Achieving work-life-family balance for custodial grandparents. In M. Waring & C. Fouche (Eds.), *Managing mayhem: Work-life balance in New Zealand* (pp. 157–74). Wellington, NZ: Dunmore Publishing.

Worrall, J. (2008). Kin care—Understanding the dynamics. *Social Work Now: The Practice Journal of Child Youth and Family, 41*, 4–11.

Wright, A., Hiebert-Murphy, D., Mirwaldt, J., & Muswaggon, G. (2008). *Final report: Factors that contribute to positive outcomes in the Awasis Pimicikamak Cree Nation kinship care program*. Ottawa: Centre of Excellence for Child Welfare and Health Canada.

Wulczyn, F. (1996). A statistical and methodological framework for analyzing the foster care experiences of children. *Social Service Review, 70*(2), 318–29.

Wulczyn, F. (2003). Closing the gap: Are changing exit patterns reducing the time African American children spend in foster care relative to Caucasian children? *Children and Youth Services Review, 25*(5/6), 431–62.

Wulczyn, F. (2004). Family reunification. *The Future of Children, 14*(1), 95–113.

Wulczyn, F., Hislop, K. B., & Harden, B. J. (2002). The placement of infants in foster care. *Infant Mental Health Journal, 23*(5), 454–75.

Wyatt, D. T., Simms, M. D., & Horwitz, S. (1997). Widespread growth retardation and variable growth recovery in foster children in the first year after initial placement. *Archives of Pediatrics and Adolescent Medicine, 151*(8), 813–16.

Yeatman, A., & Penglase, J. (2004). Looking after children: A case of individualised service delivery. *Australian Journal of Social Issues, 39*, 233–47.

Yoo, J. (2002). The relationship between organizational variables and client outcomes: A case study in child welfare. *Administration in Social Work, 26*(2), 39–61.

Youll, P. J., & McCourt-Perring, C. (1993). *Raising voices: Ensuring quality in residential care*. London: Her Majesty's Stationery Office.

Younes, M. N., & Harp, M. (2007). Addressing the impact of foster care on biological children in their families. *Child Welfare, 86*(4), 21–40.

Yuan, Y-Y. T. (2005). Potential policy implications of alternative response. *Protecting Children, 20*(2 & 3), 22–31.

Zlotnik, J. L., Strand, V. C., & Anderson, G. R. (2009). Introduction: Achieving positive outcomes for children and families: Recruiting and retraining a competent child welfare workforce. *Child Welfare, 88*(5), 7–21.

Zuravin, S., Orme, J., & Hegar, R. (1995). Disposition of child physical abuse reports: Review of the literature and test of a predictive model. *Children and Youth Services Review, 17*(4), 547–66.

LIST OF CONTRIBUTORS

James Anglin is a professor in the School of Child and Youth Care, University of Victoria.

Dorothy Badry is an assistant professor in the Faculty of Social Work, University of Calgary, where her research focuses on child welfare and Fetal Alcohol Spectrum Disorder.

Nicholas Bala is a professor at the Faculty of Law, Queen's University, and an expert in issues related to children, families, and the justice system.

Madeleine Beaudry is a professor, now retired, from the School of Social Work, Laval University, in Quebec City.

Cindy Blackstock is Executive Director of the First Nations Child and Family Caring Society of Canada.

Michèle Brousseau is an adjunct professor at the School of Social Work, Laval University, in Quebec City, and former researcher at the Centre Jeunesse de Québec – Institut universitaire, also in Quebec City.

Leslie Brown is the Associate Dean of Research of the Faculty of Human and Social Development, University of Victoria.

Marilyn Callahan is Professor Emeritus at the School of Social Work, University of Victoria.

Gary Cameron is a professor and Lyle S. Hallman Chair in Child and Family Welfare in the Faculty of Social Work, Wilfrid Laurier University.

Ruth Champion is Senior Policy and Program Advisor with the Children, Youth and Families Division of the Department of Human Services in Melbourne, Australia.

Cécile Charbonneau is a researcher from Quebec City.

Deirdre Cheers is Executive Director Centacare Broken Bay, a Catholic agency providing a range of family services, including residential and foster care, in New South Wales, Australia. In a previous role with Barnardos Australia, she was responsible for the implementation of the *Looking After Children* system within this agency.

Jan Christianson-Wood is a Senior Manager at the General Child and Family Services Authority of Manitoba.

Lorry Coughlin is the manager of clinical information systems for the Division of Professional Services at Batshaw Youth and Family Centres in Montreal.

Béatrice Decaluwe is a doctoral candidate at the School of Psychology, Laval University, in Quebec City.

Katharine Dill is Executive Director of Practice and Research Together (PART) in Ontario.

Lena Dominelli is a professor in the Department of Applied Social Sciences, Durham University, Durham, England.

Tyrone Donnon is an associate professor in the Department of Community Health Sciences at the Faculty of Medicine, University of Calgary.

Tonino Esposito is a doctoral candidate at McGill University, and the researcher and data coordinator of the Royal Bank Children Services Data Laboratory at McGill University's Centre for Research on Children and Families.

Barbara Fallon is an assistant professor in the Factor-Inwentash Faculty of Social Work, University of Toronto.

Elizabeth Fernandez is an associate professor in the School of Social Sciences and International Studies, University of New South Wales, in Sydney, Australia, and coordinator of the postgraduate research degree program.

Nancy Freymond is an assistant professor in the Faculty of Social Work, Wilfrid Laurier University.

Don Fuchs is a professor in the Faculty of Social Work, University of Manitoba, and a founding member of the Prairie Child Welfare Consortium.

Jordan Gail is a social worker in Nanaimo, British Columbia.

Carolyn Golden is a family services worker at the Catholic Children's Aid Society of Toronto.

Wayne Hammond is the Executive Director, Resiliency Canada, and an adjunct assistant professor in the Department of Community Health Sciences, University of Calgary.

Lirondel Cheyne-Hazineh is currently Research Coordinator at Pathways to Education in Kitchener, Ontario, and a past researcher with the Partnerships for Children and Families Project at Wilfrid Laurier University.

Diane Hiebert-Murphy is a professor in the Faculty of Social Work at the University of Manitoba.

Carol Hubberstey is a principal of Nota Bene Consulting Group, based in Victoria, British Columbia.

Shelly Johnson (Mukwa Musayett) is an assistant professor in the School of Social Work and Human Service, Thompson Rivers University, in Kamloops, British Columbia. She is Saulteaux from Keeseekoose First Nation.

Kathleen Kufeldt is an adjunct professor at the University of New Brunswick and former Chair in Child Protection at Memorial University of Newfoundland.

Bruce MacLaurin is an assistant professor in the Faculty of Social Work, University of Calgary.

Varda Mann-Feder is an associate professor of Applied Human Sciences at Concordia University in Montreal.

Brad McKenzie is a professor in the Faculty of Social Work at the University of Manitoba.

Myrna McNitt is a lecturer in social work at Dominican University Graduate School of Social Work in River Forest, Illinois, with research and practice interests in child welfare and juvenile justice.

Jude Morwitzer is Senior Manager of the Practice Development Centre with Barnardos Australia, a major Australian non-governmental provider of family support and child placement services, including foster care, adolescent community placement, and adoption.

Meghan Mulcahy is a mental health social worker in Nova Scotia.

Véronique Noel is a researcher with the Commission des droits de la personne et des droits de la jeunesse in Quebec.

Marie-Andrée Poirier is a professor at the School of Social Work, Université de Montréal, and co-director of the Groupe de recherche et d'action sur la victimisation des enfants (GRAVE).

Deborah Rutman is an adjunct associate professor and senior research associate with the School of Social Work, University of Victoria, and a principal of Nota Bene Consulting Group, based in Victoria, B.C.

Kate Schumaker is a doctoral student at the Factor-Inwentash Faculty of Social Work, University of Toronto.

Jane Scott is a consultant who has managed many complex research and development projects in the United Kingdom.

Corbin Shangreaux is the administrator of Southeast Child and Family Services, and has held a number of senior administrative and consulting positions in First Nations child and family services.

Aron Shlonsky is an associate professor of social work at the University of Toronto, where he holds the Factor-Inwentash Chair in Child Welfare and directs the Bell Canada Child Welfare Research Unit and the Ontario Child Abuse and Neglect Data System.

Marie Simard is Professor Emeritus at the School of Social Work, Laval University, in Quebec City.

Marie-Claude Simard is a social worker and researcher at the *Centre jeunesse de Québec-Institut universitaire* and an associate professor at the School of Social Work, Laval University, in Quebec City.

Vandna Sinha is an associate professor at the Centre for Research on Children and Families at McGill University.

Susan Strega is an associate professor in the School of Social Work, University of Victoria.

Tracy Swan is an assistant professor at the School of Social Work, Memorial University of Newfoundland/Labrador.

June Thoburn is Emeritus Professor of Social Work at the University of East Anglia, Norwich, England.

Clare Tilbury is an associate professor at the School of Human Services and Social Work, Griffith University, in Brisbane, Australia.

Sue Tregeagle is Senior Manager, Program Services and Research, with Barnardos Australia, a major non-government provider of family support and child placement services, including foster care, adolescent community placement, and adoption.

Nico Trocmé is a professor of social work at McGill University, where he holds the Philip Fisher Chair in Social Work and directs the Centre for Research on Children and Families.

Robert Twigg recently retired from the Faculty of Social Work, University of Regina.

Christopher Walmsley is an associate professor, School of Social Work and Human Service, Thompson Rivers University in Kamloops, British Columbia.

Sarah Wise is the General Manager Policy, Research and Innovation at Anglicare Victoria, based in Melbourne, Australia.

Jill Worrall has retired from the position of Senior Lecturer in Social Work and is now an Honorary Research Associate at Massey University in New Zealand.

Alexandra Wright is an associate professor in the Faculty of Social Work at the University of Manitoba.